Time Out

London

timeout.com/london

Time Out Guides Ltd
Universal House
251 Tottenham Court Road
London W1T 7AB
United Kingdom
Tel: +44 (0)20 7813 3000
Fax: +44 (0)20 7813 6001
Email: guides@timeout.com
www.timeout.com

Published by Time Out Guides Ltd, a wholly owned subsidiary of Time Out Group Ltd.
Time Out and the Time Out logo are trademarks of Time Out Group Ltd.

© Time Out Group Ltd 2013
Previous editions 1989, 1990, 1992 and annually from 1994 to 2012.

10 9 8 7 6 5 4 3 2 1

This edition first published in Great Britain in 2012 by Ebury Publishing
A Random House Group Company
20 Vauxhall Bridge Road, London SW1V 2SA

Random House Australia Pty Ltd 20 Alfred Street, Milsons Point, Sydney, New South Wales 2061, Australia

Random House New Zealand Ltd 18 Poland Road, Glenfield, Auckland 10, New Zealand

Random House South Africa (Pty) Ltd Isle of Houghton, Corner Boundary Road & Carse O'Gowrie,
Houghton 2198, South Africa

Random House UK Limited Reg. No. 954009

Distributed in the US and Latin America by Publishers Group West (1-510-809-3700)

For further distribution details, see www.timeout.com.

ISBN: 978-1-84670-380-5

A CIP catalogue record for this book is available from the British Library.

Printed and bound in Great Britain by Butler Tanner & Dennis, Frome, Somerset.

The Random House Group Limited supports The Forest Stewardship Council (FSC®), the leading international forest certification organisation. Our books carrying the FSC label are printed on FSC® certified paper. FSC is the only forest certification scheme endorsed by the leading environmental organisations, including Greenpeace. Our paper procurement policy can be found at www.randomhouse.co.uk/environment

Time Out carbon-offsets its flights with Trees for Cities (www.treesforcities.org).

MIX
Paper from
responsible sources
FSC® C023561

Contents

EXPERIENCE IT
DISNEY PRESENTS
THE LION KING
THE AWARD-WINNING MUSICAL
Visit www.thelionking.co.uk or call 0844 871 3000
LYCEUM THEATRE
21 Wellington Street, London Covent Garden
Photos of London Company by Simon Turtle and Catherine Ashmore. Andile Gumbi as 'Simba'. ©Disney.

Introduction

Never shy of grabbing publicity from other people's labours, London's City Hall came up with quite a slogan for 2012: 'A summer like no other', the adverts crowed. And even in this town of dyed-in-the-wool cynics, most of us were won over. Olympic triumphs, cultural festivals, whole new areas of the city opening up – what wasn't to like? But in another sense, the slogan is empty: every London summer is a summer like no other.

There's a very strong argument for 2013, not 2012, being the year to visit London. Surprised? Consider a few salient points. Dozens of spiffy new hotels have been built. Lots of familiar attractions have been buffed up, expanded or reopened (the *Cutty Sark* and Kensington Palace are just two examples), and they've been joined by plenty of brand-new thrills – a cable car over the Thames, for instance. There are new restaurants and bars, new clubs, revivified arty institutions right across town – especially to the east, where the 2012 Games were based, and where the Olympic Park is now being made over for public use.

Even that unattractive essential of city life – the creaking transport infrastructure – has seen major improvements, although anyone who expected the extremely smooth-running public transport of the Games to continue beyond the closing ceremony of the Paralympics has had a rude awakening. You can anticipate weekend engineering closures and delays.

Nonetheless, the truth is that London is in boom times, even as life for many, even most, residents gets harder, trapped between stagnant wages and rising living costs. This is one of the rare world cities that manages to balance up-to-the-minute vitality – in fashion, music, art – with its proud history – red double-decker buses, Beefeaters, princes and palaces.

We each spent many happy hours researching this guide: while one hunted for the remaining stubs of 2,000-year-old Roman wall, the other tested touchscreen tablet controls in a swish hotel. Some pleasures in the Big Smoke a free, some – we admit – are costly, but has there ever been a time when London offered so many pleasures and so varied?

We don't think so. Pay our city a visit and find out for yourself.

Simon Coppock and Ros Sales, Editors

★★★★★

'THE SUNNIEST OF ALL MUSICALS,
IT PROVIDES NEW PLEASURES
EVERY TIME'
SUNDAY EXPRESS

BENNY ANDERSSON & BJÖRN ULVAEUS'

MAMMA MIA!®

THE SMASH HIT MUSICAL BASED ON THE SONGS OF ABBA®

NOW
PLAYING
THURS
3PM

www.mamma-mia.com

NOVELLO THEATRE
ALDWYCH I WC2B I ⊖ COVENT GARDEN
A DELFONT MACKINTOSH THEATRE

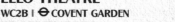

About the Guide

GETTING AROUND

The back of the book contains street maps of London, as well as overview maps of the city and its surroundings. The maps start on page 392; on them are marked the locations of hotels (❶), restaurants and cafés (❶), and pubs and bars (❶). The majority of businesses listed in this guide are located in the areas we've mapped; the grid-square references in the listings refer to these maps.

THE ESSENTIALS

For practical information, including visas, disabled access, emergency numbers, lost property, useful websites and local transport, please see the Essential Information Section. It begins on page 360.

THE LISTINGS

Addresses, phone numbers, websites, transport information, hours and prices are all included in our listings, as are selected other facilities. All were all checked and correct at press time. However, business owners may alter their arrangements at any time, and fluctuating economic conditions can cause prices to change rapidly.

The very best venues in the city, the must-sees and must-dos in every category, have been marked with a red star (★). In the Sights chapters, we've also marked venues with free admission with a FREE symbol.

PHONE NUMBERS

The area code for London is 020, but within the city, dialling from a landline, you only need the eight-digit number as listed.

From outside the UK, dial your country's international access code (011 from the US) or a plus symbol, followed by the UK country code (44), 20 for London (dropping the initial zero) and the eight-digit number as listed in the guide. So, to reach the British Museum, dial +44 20 7323 8000. For more on phones, including information on calling abroad from the UK and details of local mobile phone access, *see pp373-374*.

FEEDBACK

We welcome feedback on this guide, both on the venues we've included and on any other locations you'd like to see featured in future editions. Please email us at guides@timeout.com.

Time Out Guides

Founded in 1968, Time Out has grown from humble beginnings into the leading resource for anyone wanting to know what's happening in the world's greatest cities. Alongside our influential weeklies in London, New York, Chicago and Dubai, we publish more than 20 magazines in cities as varied as Beijing and Beirut; a range of travel books, with City Guides now joined by the pocket-sized Shortlist series; and an information-packed website. The company remains proudly independent, still owned by Tony Elliott four decades after he launched *Time Out London*.

Written by local experts, and illustrated with original photography, our books also

retain their independence. No business has been featured because it has advertised, and all restaurants and bars are visited and reviewed anonymously.

ABOUT THE EDITORS

Simon Coppock and **Ros Sales** have lived in London for a combined total of 43 years, and have edited Time Out guides to London, Washington, Istanbul and San Francisco, among other titles. They have also written travel features and reviews for such publications as the *Sunday Times* and the *Sunday Telegraph*.

A full list of the book's contributors can be found on page 13.

SOHO

The pervy nightlife has mostly moved on, leaving Soho with a staggering density of cafés and restaurants – scoff noodles, ceviche, tacos, haute cuisine or just sip a coffee. *See pp165-171.*

SOUTH KENSINGTON

A cultural must-visit: three world-class collections – the Natural History Museum, the Science Museum and the V&A – with Kensington Gardens nearby. *See pp112-114.*

WESTMINSTER

Westminster Abbey, 'Big Ben' and the Houses of Parliament (*see pp99-103*), with Buckingham Palace up the road – no wonder this is a UNESCO World Heritage site.

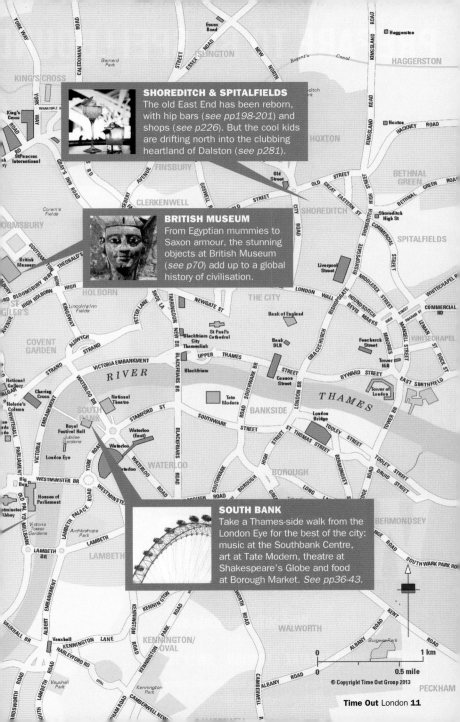

SHOREDITCH & SPITALFIELDS
The old East End has been reborn, with hip bars (*see pp198-201*) and shops (*see p226*). But the cool kids are drifting north into the clubbing heartland of Dalston (*see p281*).

BRITISH MUSEUM
From Egyptian mummies to Saxon armour, the stunning objects at British Museum (*see p70*) add up to a global history of civilisation.

SOUTH BANK
Take a Thames-side walk from the London Eye for the best of the city: music at the Southbank Centre, art at Tate Modern, theatre at Shakespeare's Globe and food at Borough Market. *See pp36-43*.

© Copyright Time Out Group 2013

0   1 km

0   0.5 mile

Time Out London

Editorial
Editor Simon Coppock, Ros Sales
Listings Editors William Crow, Matthew Bremner
Proofreader Tamsin Shelton
Indexer Holly Pick

Editorial Director Sarah Guy
Management Accountant Margaret Wright

Design
Senior Designer Kei Ishimaru
Designer Darryl Bell
Guides Commercial Senior Designer Jason Tansley

Picture Desk
Picture Editor Jael Marschner
Picture Researcher Ben Rowe
Freelance Picture Researcher Isidora O'Neill

Advertising
Sales Director St John Betteridge
Account Managers Deborah Maclaren, Bobbie Kelsall-Freeman @ The Media Sales House

Marketing
Senior Publishing Brand Manager Luthfa Begum
Group Commercial Art Director Anthony Huggins
Head of Circulation Dan Collins

Production
Group Production Manager Brendan McKeown
Production Controller Katie Mulhern-Bhudia

Time Out Group
Chairman & Founder Tony Elliott
Chief Executive Officer Aksel Van der Wal
Editor-in-Chief Tim Arthur
Group Financial Director Paul Rakkar
Time Out Communications Ltd MD David Pepper
Time Out International Ltd MD Cathy Runciman
Group Marketing Director Carolyn Sims

Contributors

Introduction Simon Coppock. **London Today** Peter Watts. **After the Games** Simon Coppock. **Diary** William Crow, Loren Harway. **Sights** Simon Coppock (*The Shard of Glass, Behind the Palace Door* Ros Sales; *Walk: The Sidestreet Shuffle* Helen Walasek). **Restaurants & Cafés** Sarah Guy, contributors to *Time Out London Eating & Drinking*. **Pubs & Bars** contributors to *Time Out London Eating & Drinking* (*Shaken & Perhaps Stirred* Ros Sales). **Shops & Services** Anna Norman, Dan Jones (*Roboshop* Maggie Davis, Dan Jones). **Hotels** Simon Coppock, Ros Sales (*Going Dutch, Straight to the Top* Simon Coppock). **Children** Emma Perry. **Film** Dave Calhoun, John Watson. **Gay & Lesbian** Patrick Welch. **Nightlife** Jonny Ensall, Eddy Lawrence, Kate Hutchinson, Chris Parkin, Patrick Welch, Ben Williams. **Performing Arts** Simon Coppock, Caroline McGinn, Ros Sales, Lyndsey Winship (*Bars, Beer & Bach* Simon Coppock; *Mormons, Chocolate & Computer Geeks* Ros Sales). **Sport & Fitness** Rob Greig, Ros Sales. **Escapes & Excursions** Holly Pick, Anna Norman & contributors to *Time Out Great Days Out*. **History** Simon Coppock, Ros Sales (*Time Machine* Museum of London curators; *Another London* Ros Sales). **Architecture** Simon Coppock. **Essential Information** William Crow.

The editors would like to thank contributors to previous editions of *Time Out London* and *Time Out* magazine, whose work forms the basis for parts of this book.

Maps john@jsgraphics.co.uk

Cover photography The Shard and Tower Bridge by Charles Bowman
Back cover photography Britta Jaschinski
Photography page 3 Burns and Nice; 4 (top left), 5 (top), 11 (top and middle), 38 (bottom), 56 (bottom), 72, 94, 110, 118 (bottom), 120, 122, 140, 152, 157, 170 (top), 199, 189, 201, 203, 215, 216, 219, 222, 226, 322, 256, 331 Britta Jaschinski; 4 (top right), 7, 34/35, 98, 320/321, 328, 329, 335 (left), 352, 353, 355, 356, 388/389 Shutterstock; 4 (bottom left) Cutty Sark Trust; 4 (bottom right), 5 (bottom right), 144, 149, 161 Olivia Rutherford; 5 (bottom left), 10 (top), 156, 165, 169, 176, 184, 196, 199 Michael Franke; 10 (middle), 43, 63, 79, 314 Tove K Breitstein; 10 (bottom) Boguslaw Bafia/Shutterstock.com; 11 (bottom), 31, 78, 142, 146, 168 (bottom), 191 Scott Wishart; 14/15 WH Chow/Shutterstock.com; 16, 21, 343, 349 Getty Images; 20 (bottom) Padmayogini/Shutterstock.com; 24 Benjamin Eagle; 25 (top and middle) Martyn J Brooks; 25 (bottom), 273, 277, 278, 318 Heloise Bergman; 26 Ascot Racecourse; 27, 32, 66 (bottom), 91 (top), 205 Elisabeth Blanchet; 37, 41, 51, 66 (top), 86, 91 (bottom), 93, 95, 124, 145, 279 (top), 283, 289, 317, 336/337, 360/361 Jonathan Perugia; 38 (top), 73, 125, 134, 260/261, 279 (bottom), 281, 286, 301, 308 Michelle Grant; 39, 60 www.simonleigh.com; 42 (top) Duncan McKenzie; 42 (left), 45, 105, 262, 264, 268, 292 Andrew Brackenbury; 44 (top), 59, 183 208 Alys Tomlinson; 19, 44 (bottom), 46, 55, 58 (left), 81, 87, 121, 129, 141, 168 (top), 170 (bottom), 186, 187, 192, 200, 204, 265, 270, 274 (bottom), 327 (top), 357 Rob Greig; 50 Will Pryce; 56 (top), 116, 123, 138, 188 Ed Marshall; 57 Derek Hammond; 67, 139, 309 Nick Ballon; 68 (top) Matt Carr; 68 (bottom) Nigel Tradewell; 76 Heike Bohnstengel; 77 Susie Rea; 82 (top) Gordon Rainsford; 82 (bottom), 83, 99, 113, 126, 148, 151 Ben Rowe; 84 Stuart Monk/Shutterstock.com; 102 Bikeworldtravel/Shutterstock.com; 106 Sverlova Mariya/Shutterstock.com; 109 Emma Wood; 112, 118 (top), 135 Anthony Webb; 115 Zaha Hadid Architects; 117, 319 Haris Artemis; 131 Oliver Dixon/Imagewise; 133 Andrew Baker, Newham Council; 136 National Maritime Museum; 143, 153, 164, 181 (left) Tricia de Courcy Ling; 154/155, 197 Marc de Groot; 181 (right) Louise Haywood-Scheiffer; 195 Hayley Harrison; 207, 220, 229 Ming Tang-Evans; 221 Gemma Day; 263 Thomas Skovsende; 266 Susannah Stone; 274 (top) Paul Mattsson; 275 Stephen Finn/Shutterstock.com; 284 Sin Bozkurt; 285 Dave Swindells; 276 Sam Kestevan; 298, 310 Belinda Lawley; 299 Joe Plommer; 306 Alastair Muir; 313 ODA; 324 © 2011 Warner Bros. Ent; 327 (bottom) Richard Rowland; 334, 335 (right) Nerida Howard; 338 Getty Images/Gallo Images; 339, 340, 342, 346, 347 Museum of London; 245 Tate Photography; 253 Amy Murrell; 359 Clive Little.

The following images were supplied by the featured establishments: pages 20 (top), 33, 42 (right), 58 (top and right), 71, 114, 127, 137, 159, 173, 178, 209, 217, 225, 231, 233, 234, 235, 239, 242, 243, 245, 246, 255, 271, 280, 297, 303, 307, 309.

London Today

Peter Watts tells us what to expect after the 2012 party is over.

In retrospect, 2012 was always going to be a good year for London. The twin jamborees of the Royal Jubilee and the Olympics ensured the world was eyeballing the capital pretty much endlessly from June to September. And it held up well. Sure, the Royal festivities amounted to little more than a bunch of old people in boats getting rained on for two hours, but it allowed commentators to eulogise endlessly about how wonderfully British it all was.

The Olympics were a different story. Understandable fears that the spectacle would be ruined by public transport and heavy-handed sponsorship arrangements were largely forgotten the second Danny Boyle's wittily brilliant opening ceremony got under way. London didn't just embrace the Games, it absorbed them into its DNA in a way this usually dispassionate and often cynical city rarely allows. It was love before the Olympic Flame was even alight.

Peter Watts is a freelance journalist who writes for Prospect, *the* New Statesman *and his blog* The Great Wen.

AFTER THE PARTY'S OVER

And now what? London has been concentrating on 2012 for so long that it was always going to be a hard act to follow. The danger is that investment and attention could now move elsewhere, making life a lot tougher – and duller – for spotlight-hoarding mayor Boris Johnson to maintain his shadowy challenge on Prime Minister and fellow Conservative David Cameron. Johnson, though, has a ham actor's ability to upstage the people around him, whether that's somehow managing to take much of the credit for the Olympics or riding the wave of a mini-boom that's fuelled in part by property investors abroad taking advantage of the weak pound.

Johnson, a dynamic personality with haystack hair and the timing of a stand-up comedian, also retains a quite extraordinary gift for shrugging off the sort of controversies that blight other politicians, whether that's defending national pariahs such as the banks and Rupert Murdoch's News International or any of his more personal peccadillos ('I wouldn't trust Boris with my wife nor – from painful experience – my wallet,' was the damning assessment of Conservative journalist Max Hastings). His record as London mayor remains, at best, mixed. Transport is a perennial concern for Londoners, but Johnson favours headline-grabbing initiatives such as the much-discussed Boris Bikes which cost a lot of money without really solving any pressing transport problem. The bikes reaped considerable publicity for Johnson and sponsors Barclays but despite a promise that they wouldn't cost taxpayers, the scheme is heavily subsidised by Londoners, who barely use them but pay via local councils and Transport for London. This is a typical pattern for Johnson's pet projects – public money subsidising heavily branded, whimsical, transport schemes. He introduced two in 2012: the expensive but attractive 'Borismaster' New Bus for London (*see p102* **The New Old Bus**) and the bizarre Emirates-sponsored cable car (*see p130*) across the Thames (rechristened the ArabFly Dangleway by unimpressed London bloggers) in Greenwich, which has amazing views but doesn't go anywhere useful and costs users quite a lot of money. It is believed to be running well shy of capacity.

As these projects suggest, the mayor is desperate to put a Johnson-sized stamp on London. His primary concern for his second term appears to be the construction of a new airport – something London needs if the City is to maintain its position as Europe's financial centre, but which is proving problematic as nobody can decide on a location. A new airport would be a real legacy for London, and Johnson clearly believes he has the political capital to pull it off. Whether he has the will is another matter and pundits are still half-anticipating Johnson will stand down before the end of his term to return to Parliament for the 2015 general election.

If he does that, presumably with an eye on taking a shot at Downing Street, it will at least have confirmed the London mayoralty as a position for genuine heavy-hitters rather than just – or as well as – a high-profile pulpit for outspoken egomaniacs. Until then, London has to deal with the more mundane realities of 2013. There's no Olympics, but there is, er, the 150th anniversary of the world's first underground railway journey. Something to celebrate certainly, but it's hardly Mo Farah and Usain Bolt.

IT'S THE ECONOMY, STUPID

The partial reopening of the Olympic Park – now the Queen Elizabeth Olympic Park (*see pp21-23* **After the Games**) – in August for a new annual cycling festival will raise a cheer and a thousand Olympic retrospectives in the media, but otherwise for London it's back to normal. For most Londoners, that means finding a rewarding balance between rising rents and transport costs and the myriad small and large pleasures London has to offer, whether that's parks, arts, restaurants or being a place to earn a decent salary (although 20 per cent of Londoners can't even get that, earning below the mayor's recommended London Living Wage). Helping to bring the expense of London down just a little is the welcome

IN FOCUS

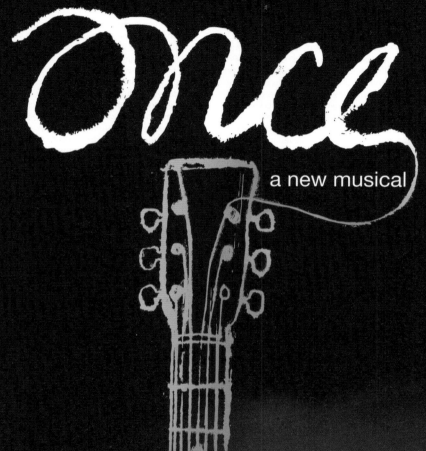

WINNER OF 8 TONY AWARDS INCLUDING
BEST MUSICAL 2012

once

a new musical

His music needed
one thing. Her.

phoenix theatre
charing cross road | london WC2H 0JP
oncemusical.co.uk

phenomenon of free media. The *Evening Standard*, London's only evening newspaper, went free several years ago and is now turning a profit. It was followed in September 2012 by our own weekly entertainment guide, *Time Out London*, which almost instantly saw its circulation rocket from 50,000 to 300,000. On a smaller scale, south London's *Brixton Bugle* and the east London *Hackney Citizen* are hyperlocal independent newspapers edited by local bloggers and distributed free – a workable model for local journalism that others may imitate.

The various London publications offer some insight into the occasionally schizophrenic nature of the city, which at times seems to feature two distinct groups – the über-wealthy and everybody else – whose paths rarely cross. London's skyline is increasingly filled with gigantic towers of luxury apartments – the Shard (*see p46*) is only the most prominent – while expensive restaurants, schools, boutiques and hotels appear to be prospering. Demand for butlers is, apparently, soaring. While this is good for London's economy, it's questionable how it helps the city's sense of community. One leading property figure has commented privately that despite the huge influx of foreign money into areas like Belgravia, Kensington and Chelsea, local shops struggle because these new residents only actually live in their swanky London townhouses for a few weeks each year.

WINNING WESTFIELD

For the most part, London's retail economy is holding up, but that's thanks to a few big hitters. While nobody is entirely sure what effect the Olympics had on London's economy, one definite winner was Westfield Stratford City (*see p209*), the terrifyingly huge shopping centre near the Olympic Park, which recorded large visitor numbers. Westfield's original site in White City is also doing well, and the company has now set its sights on Croydon for a third outlet. Although it had a poor Olympics, the West End remains the key retail destination but rival districts have taken full advantage of the extensive

disruption caused along Oxford Street by tunnelling for Crossrail, a high-speed train link that appears to be being built by sloths and isn't due to open until 2018. The West End's old dominance is long over, as everything shifts eastwards.

The story in many of the outer suburbs is not so pretty, which is what makes Croydon such an interesting and welcome destination for Westfield. Like many of London's outer suburbs, this heavily populated south London town is still feeling the cost of the 2008 recession and 2011 riots – in 2012, key employer Nestlé left town and flagship department store Allders closed down – and the high street is spotted by charity shops and empty units. The decline is magnified by local councils, who have been forced to take an axe to services, often in the face of strong opposition. In Barnet, for instance, residents unilaterally occupied and restocked their local library after the council tried to close up and flog the premises. It's a version of the Olympic can-do spirit, but one thing is for sure: 2013 will be nothing like 2012.

IN FOCUS

New Bus for London. *See p17.*

Building on the Buzz

We look past London 2012 with the city's boss of tourism.

In September 2012 we talked to Martine Ainsworth-Wells, at that time Director of Marketing & Communications at London & Partners, the organisation responsible for promoting London tourism. She explained the London & Partners strategy for making the most of the warm glow that enveloped London after the 2012 Games.

Our job is to promote London as a tourist destination, as a business destination, and as a destination for foreign students. Our post-Olympic campaign is called London, Now Come and See It For Yourself. It's essentially playing back all the coverage we got from the Games. There's a very positive image now etched on people's minds for those who have seen this amazing city, but what normally happens for host cities is that the image fades very quickly. If you don't act on it, you don't get the benefit. The window of opportunity is small. You have between three and six months, a year at most, before attention moves elsewhere.

Selling London is about what you can get from us. Our tone is very invitational: this is our canvas, but you can draw on it too. We want people to know they can get whatever they want from this crackling energy and potential. People can come here and see world-class performing arts and historic attractions, but that's a given, our audience knows that those things will always be here, so we don't reinforce those images. We don't need to promote the icons like Buckingham Palace. People these days want a little bit more of the exotic, a bit more off the beaten track. It's an old-fashioned tourist who will come and just tick off the key sights. People are happy to go off-piste.

In 2013, we're going to push the fact that it's the 150th anniversary of the tube, and the reopening of the Olympic Park. Anniversaries are a good way of reminding people of our history and culture, which we know are huge drivers for tourism. Our role is to keep Londoners in jobs by keeping the city vibrant, so we ask our partners what they are doing and then we tell the world.

After the Games

A cool £8.92 billion was spent – and what did we get?

We weren't alone. It was the last weekend of the London 2012 Paralympic Games. We'd taken a nephew to see the Japanese go down 59-45 to the Aussies in wheelchair rugby, amazed at Daisuke Ikezaki ghosting past defenders to score, gliding through invisible gaps in a solid wall of wheelchairs. Our nephew had been much more excited by a photo-op with Games mascot Mandeville in the Great British Garden. It was a hot, sunny day. Beer had been drunk. The Olympic Park had proved a huge chunk of land to traipse across. Exhausted, we flopped down on the grass by the river, looked at the blue sky, and realised with a jolt that it was over: we would never walk the Olympic Park again.

Next time the public use some of the facilities that cost the taxpayers £8.92bn – sports minister Hugh Robertson, not slow to claim credit for the £377m 'underspend' that figure represents, has been less keen to remind us that the 2005 Games bid was accepted with a budget roughly a quarter as big – will be in July 2013. By then this will be the Queen Elizabeth Olympic Park, the temporary venues – the Basketball, the Riverbank and Water Polo Arenas – will be gone. The indefatigably cheerful volunteer Games Makers will no longer be high-fiving visitors through the main gate. There will be no roar of crowds to quicken your step towards the remaining venues. So what will be here?

Simon Coppock is resident in east London and has edited more than a dozen London travel guides for Time Out.

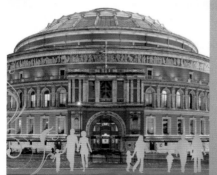

A PARK FIT FOR A QUEEN

In autumn 2010, we had a fascinating conversation with John Hopkins, Project Sponsor for Parklands and Public Realm for the Olympic Delivery Authority. 'It will be very different to any park that anyone's seen before,' he said. Few of the 12 million ticketholders who saw it during the Games would disagree. Hopkins was justifiably proud of the UK's largest urban river and wetland planting – some 300,000 plants and 2,000 British trees, including ash, hazel and London plane – and the extraordinarily complex work that had gone into the parklands, with years of planning that first became visible in July 2010 when the 'golden meadow' bloomed into the headlines. That meadow was ready right on cue for the opening of the Olympics in July 2012, still delightful when the Paralympics closed after 27 days of sport.

The North Park will be the first section to reopen in July 2013. Through it runs a single river, which Hopkins said had been almost lost under 'factories, warehouses and dereliction – a huge Victorian tip site', the leftovers from 100 years of the Industrial Revolution. It is now 110 acres of intricate marshland, flood modelled to cope with 'a 100-year storm' (a water-level rise of 13 feet), a new habitat that will protect new buildings from extreme weather by returning the area to an earlier natural state. 'It's really ironic: we ran flood models and the only places that didn't flood were the marshes.'

This northern area will eventually have three of the remaining five venues: the curvy wood-clad Velodrome, centrepiece of a VeloPark that combines it with a BMX track and cycling trail; the Lee Valley Tennis Centre and Hockey Centre (what was Eton Manor, enhanced with the hockey pitch from the dismantled Riverside Arena); and a Multi-Use Arena (previously the Copper Box), due to open in July, but with its future otherwise not yet certain as we go to press. The Lee Valley VeloPark is to open in December 2013, although the inaugural RideLondon cycling festival is due to take place in the park in August; the Lee Valley Tennis Centre and Hockey Centre will probably follow in early 2014.

HOMES AND MUDDY WATER

By then, the Athletes' Village will have been made over into housing – as the East Village it should be 'ready for living' by summer 2013, joined from 2014 by around 8,000 homes in five new districts: Chobham Manor, East Wick, Sweetwater, Marshgate Wharf, Pudding Mill Lane. The new London Legacy Development Corporation, in charge of the transition, will need to make good the brave words of the Olympic Park Legacy Company, which talked up 'traditional family neighbourhoods of terraced and mews houses, set within tree-lined avenues'.

No doubt these new homes will be snapped up, but whether their vaunted 'affordability' will be cheap enough for inhabitants of Newham next door, one of Britain's poorest boroughs, is not clear. And boring issues of civil governance – tartly raised in the 2012 update to Anna Minton's *Ground Control* – are murky: a mess of quangos and private investors have roles, but perhaps not obligations.

AND IN CONCLUSION...

In spring 2014, the South Park should open. Here, the headline sporting venues – the Aquatics Centre and the Olympic Stadium, neither with confirmed operators or tenants – were set on islands between the Waterworks River, City Mill River and the River Lee. This created massive structural challenges, with vast bridges having to be built over railtracks and rivers, and ground levelled and sloped to make it wheelchair-accessible. You'd barely notice this work now: rivers flow serenely beneath broad walkways, lorded over by the the 374-foot tower of red spaghetti that is the ArcelorMittal Orbit, which it is hoped will become a major tourist attraction in its own right. Under the Orbit, the British Olympic Association has announced, an £10m Olympic Museum will built.

Keep track of official progress at http://noordinarypark.co.uk. For enthusiastic and knowledgeable Blue Badge guided walks around the Park's perimeter, call 7936 2568 or visit www.toursof2012sites.com.

IN FOCUS

Diary

Your guide to what's happening when.

Forget about British reserve. Lots of Londoners like nothing more than finding a crowd and making fools of themselves. Festivals and events play ever more elaborate variations on the age-old themes of parading and dancing, nowadays with ever-larger sprinklings of often-innovative arts and culture. Weather plays a part in the timing, with a concentration of things to do in the hotter months, but the city's calendar is busy for most of the year.

The free weekly *Time Out* magazine has salient highlights of festivals and events. Check the website, www.timeout.com, for full comprehensive listings.

INFORMATION

The main cultural festivals in all genres are included in this chapter; a series of boxes throughout the Arts & Entertainment section (*pp260-319*) details more specialist events. London's sporting calendar can be found on pp313-314.

Always confirm details of any event well in advance – events can be cancelled and dates may change with little notice.

ALL YEAR ROUND

For the **Changing of the Guard**, *see p27* **Standing on Ceremony**.

Ceremony of the Keys

Tower of London, Tower Hill, the City, EC3N 4AB (3166 6278, www.hrp.org.uk). Tower Hill tube or Tower Gateway DLR. **Date** 9.30pm daily (advance bookings only). **Map** p403 R7.
Join the Yeoman Warders after-hours at the Tower of London as they ritually lock the fortress's

---

INSIDE TRACK STAY OUT LATE

Most of the city's blockbuster museums and galleries combine late opening with a monthly one-off evening event (usually with films, DJs or live music, and always a cash bar). For details of the current programme, see www.timeout.com.

---

entrances in this 700-year-old ceremony. You enter the Tower at 9.30pm and it's all over just after 10pm, but places are hotly sought after – apply at least two months in advance; full details can be found on the website.

Gun Salutes

Green Park, Mayfair & St James's, W1, & Tower of London, the City, EC3. **Dates** 6 Feb (Accession Day); 21 Apr & 15 June (Queen's birthdays); 2 June (Coronation Day); 10 June (Duke of Edinburgh's birthday); 15 June (Trooping the Colour); State Opening of Parliament (*see p33*); 9 Nov (Lord Mayor's Show); 10 Nov (Remembrance Sunday); also for state visits. **Map** p398 H8.
There are gun salutes on many state occasions – see the list of dates given above for a complete breakdown of when the cannons roar out. A cavalry charge features in the 41-gun salutes mounted by the King's Troop Royal Horse Artillery in Hyde Park at noon (it takes place opposite the Dorchester Hotel; *see p248*), whereas, on the other side of town, the Honourable Artillery Company ditches the ponies and piles on the firepower with its 62-gun salutes (1pm at the Tower of London). If the dates happen to fall on a Sunday, the salute is held on the following Monday.

JANUARY-MARCH

This is a good time of year for dance events, among them **Resolution!** at the Place; *see p311* **Festivals**. For the **London Lesbian & Gay Film Festival**, *see p311*.

★ Chinese New Year Festival

Around Gerrard Street, Chinatown, W1, Leicester Square, WC2, & Trafalgar Square, WC2 (7851 6686, www.lccauk.com). Leicester Square or Piccadilly Circus tube. **Date** 29 Jan. **Map** p416 W3.
Launch the Year of the, er, Dragon in style at celebrations that engulf Chinatown and Leicester Square. Dragon dancers writhe alongside a host of acts in the grand parade to Trafalgar Square, while the restaurants of Chinatown get even more packed than usual.

Joseph Grimaldi Memorial Service

Clowns Church, Beechwood Road, Dalston. E8 3DY (www.clowns-international.co.uk). King's Cross tube/rail. **Date** 3 Feb.
Join hundreds of motley-clad 'Joeys' for their annual service commemorating the legendary British clown, Joseph Grimaldi (1778-1837).

Pancake Day Races

Great Spitalfields *Dray Walk, off Brick Lane, E1 6QL (7375 0441, www.alternativearts.co.uk). Liverpool Street tube/rail.*
Poulters Annual *Guildhall Yard, the City, EC2P 2EJ (www.poulters.org.uk). Bank tube/DLR or Moorgate tube/rail.*
Both Date 12 Feb.
Shrove Tuesday brings out charity pancake racers. Don a silly costume and join the Great Spitalfields Pancake Race (register in advance) or watch City livery companies race in full regalia at the event organised by the Worshipful Company of Poulters.

Who Do You Think You Are? Live

Olympia, Hammersmith Road, Kensington, W14 8UX (www.whodoyouthinkyouarelive.co.uk). Kensington Olympia tube/rail. **Date** 22-24 Feb 2013.
A spin-off from the hugely successful BBC TV series that keeps Brits glued to the box watching weepy celebs uncover their ancestry, this enormous family history event could help you trace yours.

★ Kew Spring Festival

For listings, *see p145* **Royal Botanic Gardens**.
Date early Feb-Mar.
Kew Gardens is at its most beautiful in spring, with five million flowers carpeting the grounds.

National Science & Engineering Week

7019 4937, www.britishscience association.org. **Date** 15-25 Mar.
From the weirdly wacky to the profound, this annual series of events engages the public in celebrating science, engineering and technology.

St Patrick's Day Parade & Festival

7983 4000, www.london.gov.uk. **Date** 17 Mar.
Join the London Irish out in force for this huge annual parade through central London followed by toe-tapping tunes in Trafalgar Square.

Chinese New Year Festival.

IN FOCUS

Royal Ascot.

IN FOCUS

Oxford & Cambridge Boat Race
*River Thames, from Putney to Mortlake
(www.theboatrace.org). Putney Bridge tube,
or Barnes Bridge, Mortlake or Putney rail.*
Date 31 Mar.
Blue-clad Oxbridge students race each other in a
pair of rowing eights, watched by tens of millions
worldwide. Experience the excitement from the
riverbank (along with 250,000 other fans) for the
158th instalment of the historic race.

APRIL-JUNE

Early summer is a terrific time for outdoor
events. There's excellent alfresco theatre
at the **Greenwich & Docklands
International Festival** and, on the South
Bank, **Watch This Space** (for both, *see
p305* **Festivals**). Fans of sport can go racing
(**Royal Ascot**, the **Epsom Derby**), queue
for **Wimbledon** tickets or watch a football
playoff; for all, *see p313*. For classical music
at the **City of London Festival** and the
Hampton Court Palace Festival, *see*

p299 **Festivals**; for rockier fare at the
Camden Crawl, the **Wireless Festival**
and the **Somerset House Summer Series**,
see p287 **Festivals**.

★ Virgin London Marathon
*Greenwich Park to the Mall via the Isle of
Dogs, Victoria Embankment & St James's Park
(7902 0200, www.virginlondonmarathon.com).
Blackheath & Maze Hill rail (start), or Charing
Cross tube/rail (end).* **Date** 21 Apr.
One of the world's elite long-distance races, the
London Marathon is also one of the world's largest
fundraising events – nearly 80% of participants run
for charity, so zany costumes abound among the
35,000 starters. If you haven't already applied to run,
you're too late: just go along to watch.

Shakespeare's Birthday
For listings, *see p42* **Shakespeare's Globe**.
Date wknd closest to 23 Apr.
To celebrate the Bard's birthday, the Globe Theatre
throws open its doors for a series of events.

Sundance London 2013
*O2 Arena, Millennium Way, North Greenwich,
SE10 0BB (www.sundance-london.com).*
Date 26-29 Apr.
Robert Redford's mini-version of the Sundance Film
Festival, his annual celebration of independent film.

Covent Garden May Fayre & Puppet Festival
*Garden of St Paul's Covent Garden, Bedford
Street, Covent Garden, WC2E 9ED (7375 0441,
www.punchandjudy.com/coventgarden.htm).
Covent Garden tube.* **Date** 12 May.
Map p416 Y4.
All-day puppet mayhem (10.30am-5.30pm) devoted
to celebrating Mr Punch at the scene of his first
recorded sighting in England in 1662. Mr P takes to
the church's pulpit at 11.30am.

Art Car Boot Fair
www.artcarbootfair.com. **Date** mid May.
Cheaper and certainly more fun than your average
art fair, this afternoon event is an opportunity to
purchase specially made, usually humorous pieces
by the likes of Gavin Turk, Peter Blake, Bob and
Roberta Smith, and Pam Hogg.

Chelsea Flower Show
*Royal Hospital, Royal Hospital Road, Chelsea,
SW3 4SR (www.rhs.org.uk). Sloane Square tube.*
Date 21-25 May. **Map** p395 F12.
Elbow past the huge crowds to admire perfect
blooms, or get ideas for your own plot. The first two
days are reserved for Royal Horticultural Society
members and tickets for the open days can be hard
to come by. The show closes at 5.30pm on the final
day, with display plants sold off from around 4.30pm.

Coin Street Festival
Bernie Spain Gardens (next to Oxo Tower Wharf), South Bank, SE1 9PH (7021 1600, www.coinstreet.org). Southwark tube or Waterloo tube/rail. **Date** June-Aug. **Map** p402 N8.
Celebrating London's cultural diversity, this free, summer-long Thames-side festival features a series of music-focused events, usually involving guest musicians or theatre groups from across the world alongside local talent – last year, the London-based Elysian Quartet performed with Syrian qanun-player Maya Youssef. There are food stalls, too.

Open Garden Squares Weekend
www.opensquares.org. **Date** 8-9 June.
Secret – and merely exclusive – gardens are thrown open to the public for this horticultural shindig. You can visit roof gardens, prison gardens and children-only gardens, as well as a changing selection of those tempting oases railed off in the middle of the city's finest squares. Some charge an entrance fee.

World Naked Bike Ride
www.worldnakedbikeride.org. **Date** mid June.
Help expose the problem of pollution caused by motor vehicles by exposing yourself in honour of the World Naked Bike Ride. Cyclists across the globe strip off and saddle up to mark the occasion.

Marylebone Summer Fayre
http://marylebonesummerfayre.com. **Date** mid June.
Streets in the Marylebone Village neighbourhood are closed to traffic and filled with market stalls and entertainment, including a farmers' market and a fairground, in aid of the Teenage Cancer Trust.

Standing on Ceremony

London is a past master when it comes to parades and ceremonials.

On alternate days from 10.45am (www. royal.gov.uk/RoyalEventsandCeremonies/ ChangingtheGuard/Overview.aspx has the details), one of the five Foot Guards regiments lines up in scarlet coats and tall bearskin hats in the forecourt of Wellington Barracks; at exactly 11.27am, the soldiers start to march to **Buckingham Palace** (*see p106*), joined by their regimental band, to relieve the sentries there in a 45-minute ceremony for the **Changing of the Guard**.

Not far away, at **Horse Guards Parade** in Whitehall, the Household Cavalry mounts the guard daily at 11am (10am on Sunday). Although this ceremony isn't as famous as the one at Buckingham Palace, it's more visitor-friendly: the crowds aren't as thick as they are at the palace, and spectators aren't held far back from the action by railings. After the old and new guard have stared each other out in the centre of the parade ground, you can nip through to the Whitehall side to catch the departing old guard perform their hilarious dismount choreography, a synchronised, firm slap of approbation to the neck of each horse before the gloved troopers all swing off.

As well as these near-daily ceremonies, London sees other, less frequent parades on a far grander scale. The most famous is **Trooping the Colour**, staged to mark the Queen's official birthday on 13 June (her real one's in April). At 10.45am, the Queen rides in a carriage from Buckingham Palace to Horse Guards Parade to watch the soldiers, before heading back to Buckingham Palace for a midday RAF flypast and the impressive gun salute from Green Park.

Also at Horse Guards, on 3-4 June, a pageant of military music and precision marching begins at 7pm when the Queen (or another royal) takes the salute of the 300-strong drummers, pipers and musicians of the Massed Bands of the Household Division. This is known as **Beating the Retreat** (7414 2271, tickets 7839 5323).

Horse Guards Parade.

IN FOCUS

Exhibition Road Music Day

*Exhibition Road, South Kensington, SW7
(www.exhibitionroad.com). South Kensington
tube.* **Date** mid June. **Map** p395 D9.
London's counterpart to France's midsummer Fête
de la Musique ranges through institutions that border Exhibition Road and spills into Hyde Park. With
Imperial College and the Ismaili Centre among the
participants, you can expect anything from experimental, electronic music to Sufi chants.

Greenwich & Docklands International Festival

Various venues (www.festival.org). **Date** 20-29 June.
This annual festival of outdoor arts, theatre, dance
and family entertainment is consistently spectacular. Events take place at the Old Royal Naval College
and other sites in Greenwich including St Alfege
Park, also Canary Wharf, the Isle of Dogs, Woolwich
and Mile End Park.

JULY-SEPTEMBER

In addition to the events listed below,
summer sees some of the most important
music festivals of the year – namely, the **BBC
Sir Henry Wood Promenade Concerts**
(more commonly, the Proms), the **Lovebox
Weekender**, the **English Heritage Picnic
Concerts** at Kenwood House and the teenager-
friendly **Underage** festival (for all, *see p287
and p300* **Festivals**) – as well as the city's
major gay event, **Pride London** (*see p311*
Festivals). There are also two cutting-edge
dance events, the **Place Prize** and **Dance
Umbrella** (for both, *see p311* **Festivals**).

London Literature Festival

*Southbank Centre, Belvedere Road, South Bank,
SE1 8XX (0844 847 9939, www.londonlitfest.
com). Waterloo tube/rail.* **Date** 1st 2wks of July.
Map p399 M8.
The London Literature Festival combines superstar
writers with stars from other fields: architects, comedians, sculptors and cultural theorists examining
anything from queer literature to migration.

Shoreditch Festival

www.shoreditchfestival.org.uk. **Date** 14-22 July.
Last year's event saw screenings, music, dance, art
commissions, fashion, spoken word, walks and food
markets on tow paths, green spaces, basins, bridges
and other venues adjacent to Regent's Canal between
Shoreditch Park, N1, and Victoria Park, E3.

★ Chap Olympiad

www.thechapolympiad.com. **Date** mid July.
English eccentrics are in full cry at this annual event
mounted by the *Chap* magazine, which starts with
the lighting of the Olympic Pipe. 'Sports' include
cucumber sandwich discus and hop, skip and G&T.

Check the venue closer to the time: it has been held
in Bloomsbury for the last few years.

Great British Beer Festival

*Olympia, Hammersmith Road, Kensington,
W14 8UX (01727 867201, www.camra.org.uk).
Kensington Olympia tube/rail.* **Date** 13-17 Aug.
Real ale is the star at this huge event devoted to the
finest in British brews, including cider and perry
(that's a pear cider for the uninitiated). Foreign beers
and lagers get a look-in at what's been called 'the
biggest pub in the world'.

Carnival del Pueblo

*Various locations from City Hall to Burgess Park
(www.carnavaldelpueblo.co.uk). Elephant & Castle
tube/rail.* **Date** 18 Aug.
This vibrant outdoor parade and festival is more
than just a loud-and-proud day out for South
American Londoners: it attracts people from all
walks of life (as many as 60,000, most years) looking
to inject a little Latin spirit into the weekend.

London Mela

*Gunnersbury Park, Ealing, W3 (7387 1203,
www.londonmela.org). Acton Town or South
Ealing tube.* **Date** mid Aug.
Thousands flock to west London for this exuberant
celebration of Asian culture, dubbed the Asian
Glastonbury. You'll find urban, classical and experimental music, circus, dance, visual arts, comedy,
children's events, and great food.

★ Notting Hill Carnival

*Notting Hill, W10, W11 (7727 0072, www.
thenottinghillcarnival.com). Ladbroke Grove,
Notting Hill Gate or Westbourne Park tube.*
Date 25-26 Aug. **Map** p404 Z4.
Two million people stream in to Notting Hill to
Europe's largest street party, full of the smells, colours
and music of the Caribbean. Massive mobile sound
systems dominate the streets with whatever bass-
heavy party music is currently hip, but there's plenty
of tradition from the West Indies too: calypso music
and a spectacular costumed parade. *Photos p31.*
► *For sightseeing in Notting Hill, see p90-91.*

► *For sightseeing in Notting Hill, see p90-91.*

INSIDE TRACK
TRAFALGAR SQUARE

Among ex-mayor Ken Livingstone's most
popular initiatives was pedestrianising the
north side of Trafalgar Square, and then
programming almost weekly events in it.
Even under budget-slashing Boris, various
entertainments happen here – music,
film, theatre, dance – and usually for free.
For details, check www.london.gov.uk/
trafalgarsquare.

IN FOCUS

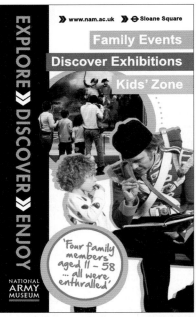

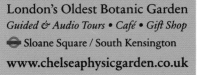

Great River Race

River Thames, from Millwall Docks, Docklands, E14, to Ham House, Richmond, Surrey TW10 (8398 8141, www.greatriverrace.co.uk). **Date** tbc. The alternative Boat Race (*see p26*) is much more fun, with an exotic array of around 300 traditional rowing boats from across the globe racing the 22 miles from Richmond to Greenwich. Hungerford Bridge, the Millennium Bridge and Tower Bridge all provide good viewpoints.

Mayor of London's Skyride

www.goskyride.com. **Date** early Sept. Each year since 2007, this cycling festival has encouraged around 50,000 people to don branded fluorescent vests and ride a traffic-free route from Buckingham Palace to the Tower of London, as well as any number of subsidiary routes. Enjoy music, car-less roads and the chance to meet sports stars on the way.

Mayor's Thames Festival

Between Westminster Bridge & Tower Bridge (7928 8998, www.thamesfestival.org). Waterloo tube/rail or Blackfriars rail. **Date** 14-15 Sept. **Map** p402 N7. A giant party along the Thames, this is the largest free arts festival in London. It's a spectacular and family-friendly mix of carnival, pyrotechnics, art installations, river events and live music alongside craft and food stalls. The highlight is the last-night lantern procession and firework finale.

London Fashion Week

Somerset House, the Strand, WC2R 1LA (7759 1999, www.londonfashionweek.co.uk). Charing Cross tube/rail or Embankment tube. **Date** mid Sept. The biannual showcase embellishes London's reputation for cutting-edge street style and sartorial innovation. Until recently, it was considered the least significant of the big four trade shows, behind New York, Milan and Paris. Not any more. *Photos p32.*

★ Open-City London

3006 7008, www.open-city.org.uk. **Date** 21-22 Sept. Londoners' favourite opportunity to snoop round other people's property: more than 500 palaces, private homes, corporate skyscrapers, pumping stations and bomb-proof bunkers, many of which are normally closed to the public. Along with the building openings, there's a programme of debates on architecture, plus the 20-mile London Night Hike.

Great Gorilla Run

Mincing Lane, the City, EC3 (7916 4974, www. greatgorillas.org/london). Monument or Tower Hill tube, or Fenchurch Street rail. **Date** 21 Sept. **Map** p403 R7. Go ape with a 600-strong pack of gorilla-suited runners, who take on a 7km course through the City in aid of gorilla conservation. *Photo p33.*

Notting Hill Carnival. *See p29.*

IN FOCUS

London Fashion Week. *See p31.*

Pearly Kings & Queens Harvest Festival

St Martin-in-the-Fields, Trafalgar Square, Westminster, WC2N 4JJ (7766 1100, www. pearlysociety.co.uk). Leicester Square tube or Charing Cross tube/rail. **Date** late Sept/early Oct. **Map** p416 Y4.

London's Pearly Kings and Queens assemble for their annual thanksgiving service dressed in spangly (and colossally heavy) Smother Suits covered in hundreds of pearl buttons. These sensational outfits evolved from Victorian costermongers' love of decorating their clothes with buttons, and remain a cherished Cockney tradition.

OCTOBER-DECEMBER

Along with the launch of the Turner Prize, the **Frieze Art Fair** and **Zoo** are huge art events. The **London Film Festival** (*see p269* **Festivals**) takes place in October, and this is also the season for the **London Jazz Festival** (*see p294* **Festivals**) and the winter instalment of the **Spitalfields Festival** (*see p300* **Festivals**).

Big Draw

8351 1719, www.campaignfordrawing.org. **Date** 1-31 Oct.

Engage with your inner artist at the Big Draw, a nationwide frenzy of drawing using anything from pencils to vapour trails. The British Library's Big Picture Party brings out heavy art hitters.

Bloomsbury Festival

www.bloomsburyfestival.org.uk. **Date** late Oct. Around 150 events for art-lovers, music fans, shopaholics, literature buffs, young people and families in venues across Bloomsbury. Last year's event included a lantern-lit procession in Russell Square Gardens and a lively street party on Lamb's Conduit Street.

Diwali

Trafalgar Square, Westminster, WC2 (7983 4100, www.london.gov.uk). Charing Cross tube/rail. **Date** 28 Oct. **Map** p416 X5.

A vibrant celebration of the annual Festival of Light by London's Hindu, Jain and Sikh communities. All ages get together for fireworks, food, music and dancing.

London to Brighton Veteran Car Run

Serpentine Road, Hyde Park, W2 2UH (01483 524433, www.veterancarrun.com). Hyde Park Corner tube. **Date** 1st Sun of Nov. **Map** p393 E8.
The London to Brighton is not so much a race as a sedate procession southwards by around 500 pre-1905 cars. The first pair trundles off at sunrise (7-8.30am), but you can catch them a little later crossing Westminster Bridge or view them in lovingly polished repose on a closed-off Regent's Street the day before the event (11am-3pm).

Bonfire Night

Date 5 Nov & around.
Diwali pyrotechnics segue seamlessly into Britain's best-loved excuse for setting off fireworks: the celebration of Guy Fawkes's failure to blow up the Houses of Parliament in 1605. Try Battersea Park, or Alexandra Palace for fireworks, or pre-book a late ride on the London Eye (*see p37*).

★ Lord Mayor's Show

Through the City (7332 3456, www. lordmayorsshow.org). **Date** 9 Nov.
This big show marks the traditional presentation of the new Lord Mayor for approval by the monarch's justices. The Lord Mayor leaves Mansion House in a fabulous gold coach at 11am, along with a colourful procession of floats and marchers, heading to the Royal Courts of Justice (*see p49*). There he makes his vows, and is back home easily in time for afternoon tea. At 5pm, there's a fireworks display launched from a Thames barge.
▶ *The Lord Mayor is a City officer, elected each year by the livery companies and with no real power outside the City of London; don't confuse him with the Mayor of London, Boris Johnson.*

Remembrance Sunday Ceremony

Cenotaph, Whitehall, Westminster, SW1. Charing Cross tube/rail. **Date** 10 Nov. **Map** p399 L8.
Held on the Sunday nearest to 11 November – the day World War I ended – this solemn commemoration honours those who died fighting in the World Wars and later conflicts. The Queen, the prime minister and other dignitaries lay poppy wreaths at the Cenotaph (*see p99*). A two-minute silence at 11am is followed by a service of remembrance.

State Opening of Parliament

Palace of Westminster, Westminster, SW1A 0PW (7219 4272, www.parliament.uk). Westminster tube. **Date** Nov. **Map** p399 L9.
Pomp and ceremony attend the Queen's official reopening of Parliament after its summer recess. She arrives and departs in the state coach, accompanied by troopers of the Household Cavalry.

Christmas Celebrations

Covent Garden (0870 780 5001, www. coventgardenlondonuk.com); Bond Street (www.bondstreetassociation.com); St Christopher's Place (www.stchristophersplace.com); Marylebone High Street (7580 3163, www.marylebone village.com); Trafalgar Square (7983 4100, www.london.gov.uk). **Date** Nov-Dec.
Of the big stores, Fortnum & Mason (*see p203*) still creates enchantingly old-fashioned Christmas windows, and Harvey Nichols usually produces showstopping displays. Otherwise, though, skip the commercialised lights on Oxford and Regent's streets and head, instead, for smaller shopping areas such as St Christopher's Place, Bond Street, Marylebone High Street and Covent Garden. It's traditional to sing carols beneath a giant Christmas tree in Trafalgar Square (*see p97*) – an annual gift from Norway in gratitude for Britain's support during World War II – but you can also join in a mammoth singalong at the Royal Albert Hall (*see p300*) or an evocative carol service at one of London's historic churches. London's major cathedrals all, naturally, celebrate Christmas with splendid liturgies and music.

New Year's Eve Celebrations

Date 31 Dec.
The focus of London's public celebrations has officially moved from overcrowded Trafalgar Square (though it's still sure to be packed) to the full-on fireworks display launched from the London Eye and rafts on the Thames. The best view is from nearby bridges, but you'll have to get there early. Those with stamina can take in the New Year's Day Parade in central London the following day (www.londonparade.co.uk).

Great Gorilla Run. *See p31.*

IN FOCUS

Explore

The South Bank & Bankside

Capital views, cultural clout and appreciative crowds.

An estimated 14 million people come this way each year, and it's easy to see why. Between the **London Eye** and **Tower Bridge**, the south bank of the Thames offers a two-mile procession of diverting, largely state-funded arts and entertainment venues and events, while also affording breezy, traffic-free views of the succession of landmarks ('Big Ben', St Paul's, the Tower of London) on the other side of the water.

The area's modern-day life began in 1951 with the Festival of Britain, staged in a bid to boost morale in the wake of World War II. The **Royal Festival Hall** stands testament to the inclusive spirit of the project; it was later expanded into the Southbank Centre, alongside **BFI Southbank** and the concrete ziggurat of the **National Theatre**. However, it wasn't until the new millennium that the riverside really took off, with the arrival of the **London Eye**, **Tate Modern**, the **Millennium Bridge** and the expansion of **Borough Market**. Ever since, the area has been top of most tourists' itineraries and pulses with life.

| Map p399 & pp402-403 | Restaurants & cafés pp157-158 |
| Hotels p232 | Pubs & bars pp187-188 |

THE SOUTH BANK
Lambeth Bridge to Hungerford Bridge

Embankment or Westminster tube, or Waterloo tube/rail.

Thanks to the sharp turn the Thames makes around Waterloo, **Lambeth Bridge** lands you east of the river, not south, opposite the Tudor gatehouse of **Lambeth Palace**. Since the 12th century, it's been the official residence of the Archbishops of Canterbury. The palace is not normally open to the public, except on holidays. The church next door, St Mary at Lambeth, is now the **Garden Museum** (*see p37*).

The benches along the river here are great for viewing the Houses of Parliament opposite, before things get crowded after **Westminster Bridge**, where London's major riverside tourist zone begins. Next to the bridge is **County Hall**, once the seat of London government, currently home to the **London Film Museum** (*see p37*), the **Sea Life London Aquarium** (*see p38*) and, from spring 2013, the **London Dungeon** (*see p38*). In front of all three attractions, in full view of the lovely new **Jubilee Gardens**, the wheel of the **London Eye** (*see p37*) rotates serenely.

Florence Nightingale Museum
St Thomas's Hospital, 2 Lambeth Palace Road, SE1 7EW (7620 0374, www.florence-nightingale.co.uk). Westminster tube or Waterloo tube/rail. **Open** 10am-5pm daily. **Admission** £5.80; £4.80 reductions; £16 family; free under-5s. **Credit** AmEx, MC, V. **Map** p399 M9.
The nursing skills and campaigning zeal that made Nightingale a Victorian legend are honoured here. Reopened after refurbishment for the centenary of

her death in 2010, the museum is a chronological tour through a remarkable life under three key themes: family life, the Crimean War, health reformer. Among the period mementoes – clothing, furniture, books, letters and portraits – are Nightingale's lantern and stuffed pet owl, Athena.

Garden Museum
Lambeth Palace Road, SE1 7LB (7401 8865, www.gardenmuseum.org.uk). Lambeth North tube or Waterloo tube/rail. **Open** 10.30am-5pm Mon-Fri; 10.30am-4pm Sat; closed 1st Mon of mth. **Admission** £7.50; £3-£6.50 reductions; free under-16s. **Credit** AmEx, MC, V. **Map** p399 L10.
The world's first horticulture museum fits neatly into the old church of St Mary's. A 'belvedere' gallery (built from eco-friendly Eurban wood sheeting) contains the permanent collection of artworks, antique gardening tools and horticultural memorabilia, while the ground floor is used for interesting temporary exhibitions. In the small back garden, the replica of a 17th-century knot garden was created in honour of John Tradescant, intrepid plant hunter and gardener to Charles I; Tradescant is buried here. A stone sarcophagus contains the remains of William Bligh, the captain of the mutinous HMS *Bounty*.

★ London Eye
Jubilee Gardens, SE1 7PB (0870 500 0600, www.londoneye.com). Westminster tube or Waterloo tube/rail. **Open** times vary; check website for details. **Admission** £18.90; £11.10-£15 reductions; free under-4s. **Credit** AmEx, MC, V. **Map** p399 M8.
Here only since 2000, the Eye is already up there with Tower Bridge and 'Big Ben' as one of the capital's most postcard-friendly tourist assets.

Assuming you choose a clear day, a 30-minute circuit on the Eye affords predictably great views of the city. Take a few snaps from the comfort of your pod and your sightseeing's done.

The London Eye was the vision of husband-and-wife architect team Julia Barfield and David Marks, who entered a 1992 competition to design a structure for the millennium. The Marks' giant wheel idea came second in the contest; the winning entry is conspicuous by its absence. The Eye was planned as a temporary structure but its removal now seems unthinkable. Indeed, the wheel's popularity is such that owner Merlin Entertainments has seen fit to future-proof its investment with a three-year, £12.5m renovation programme. Much of the work concerned reducing the Eye's carbon footprint, but each of the wheel's 32 pods (one for every London borough) now has a touchscreen to guide you around the vista.

London Film Museum
County Hall, Riverside Building, SE1 7PB (7202 7040, www.londonfilmmuseum.com). Westminster tube or Waterloo tube/rail. **Open** 10am-5pm Mon-Fri; 10am-6pm Sat; 11am-6pm Sun. **Admission** £13.50; £9.50-£11.50 reductions; free under-5s. **Credit** MC, V. **Map** p399 M8.
Dedicated to British film since the 1950s (the brief is for films that were *made* in Britain, which allows unexpected blockbusters such as *Star Wars* and the Indiana Jones movies to be sneaked in alongside the more obvious *Kind Hearts and Coronets* and *Brief Encounter*), the London Film Museum is at the heart of the former home of London's metropolitan government, County Hall. The interactive displays tell the stories of great studios such as Pinewood and Ealing, discussing major directors, and detail different types of movie that have come from these islands. The box-like offices lining the corridors contain sets and props – among thousands of original artefacts, you can see the Rank gong.
► *A new branch of the London Film Museum opened in Covent Garden in 2012: 45 Wellington Street, WC2E 7BN (3617 3010).*

London Film Museum.

EXPLORE

Sea Life London Aquarium.

London Dungeon
County Hall, Westminster Bridge Road, SE1 7PB (0871 423 2240, www.thedungeons.com). Westminster tube or Waterloo tube/rail. **Open** times vary; check website for details. **Admission** £15-£24; £8-£18 reductions. **Credit** AmEx, MC, V. **Map** p399 M8.

This jokey and rather expensive celebration of torture, death and disease (book your tickets online to keep the prices down) should reopen near the London Eye for spring 2013, having moved west along the river from Tooley Street. The attraction itself will remain much the same, with visitors led through a dry-ice fog past gravestones and hideously rotting corpses to experience nastiest sides of the last 1,000 years of London history. Expect an actor-led medley of boils, projectile vomiting, worm-filled skulls and scuttling rats for the Black Death, gory skulduggery from the likes of Guy Fawkes and Jack the Ripper, and any number of unspeakable royals doing unspeakable things – Henry VIII prominent among them.

Sea Life London Aquarium
County Hall, Westminster Bridge Road, SE1 7PB (0871 663 1678, tours 7967 8007, www.sealife. co.uk). Westminster tube or Waterloo tube/rail. **Open** *July, Aug* 10am-8pm daily. *Sept-June* 10am-6pm Mon-Thur, Sun; 10am-7pm Fri, Sat. **Admission** £19.80; £14.40 reductions; £68.40 family; free under-3s. **Credit** MC, V. **Map** p399 M8.

This is one of Europe's largest aquariums and a huge hit with kids. The inhabitants are grouped by geographical origin, beginning with the Atlantic, where blacktail bream swim alongside the Thames Embankment. The 'Rainforests of the World'

exhibit has introduced poison arrow frogs, crocodiles and piranhas. The Ray Lagoon is still popular, though touching the friendly flatfish is no longer allowed (it's bad for their health). Starfish, crabs and anenomes can be handled in special open rock pools instead, and the clown fish still draw crowds. There's a mesmerising Seahorse Temple, a tank full of turtles and enchanting Gentoo peguins. The centrepieces, though, are the massive Pacific and Indian Ocean tanks, with menacing sharks quietly circling fallen Easter Island statues and dinosaur bones.

Hungerford Bridge to Blackfriars Bridge

Embankment tube or Waterloo tube/rail.

When the **Southbank Centre** (*see p301*) was built in the 1950s, the big concrete boxes that together contain the Royal Festival Hall (RFH), the Queen Elizabeth Hall (QEH) and the Purcell Room were hailed as a daring statement of modern architecture. Along with the Royal National Theatre and the Hayward, they comprise one of the largest and most popular arts centres in the world.

The centrepiece is Sir Leslie Martin's **Royal Festival Hall** (1951), given a £75m overhaul in 2007. The main auditorium has had its acoustics

BFI Southbank.

enhanced and seating refurbished; the upper floors include an improved Poetry Library, and event rooms in which readings are delivered against the backdrop of the Eye and, on the far side of the river, Big Ben. Behind the hall on Belvedere Road, **Festival Square** now hosts off-beat but crowd-pulling events, markets and exhibitions, and there are busy cafés and chain restaurants all around. Underneath the arches towards Waterloo Station is a real curiosity: **Topolski Century** (150-152 Hungerford Arches, SE1 8XU, 7928 5433, www.topolski century.org.uk), an extensive mural depicting an extraordinary procession of 20th-century events and faces, from Bob Dylan to Winston Churchill via Malcolm X. The work of Feliks Topolski, a Polish-born artist who travelled the world from 1933 until his death in 1989, it can now only be visited on pre-arranged tours.

Next door to the Royal Festival Hall, just across from the building housing the QEH and the Purcell Room, the **Hayward** (*see below*) is a landmark of Brutalist architecture – all three venues are set to benefit from a £3.3m Arts Council grant for refurbishments. Tucked under Waterloo Bridge is **BFI Southbank** (*see p272*); the UK's premier arthouse cinema, it's run by the British Film Institute. At the front is a second-hand book market – fun, but not brilliant for real finds. Due to its relative height and location just where the Thames bends from north–south to east–west, **Waterloo Bridge** provides some of the finest views of London, especially at dusk. It was designed by Sir Giles Gilbert Scott, the man behind Tate Modern (*see p43*), in 1942.

East of the bridge is Denys Lasdun's terraced **National Theatre** (*see p305*), another Brutalist concrete structure, and one that still divides opinion like few other London buildings. There are popular free performances outside in the summer and free chamber music within during winter. Shaded by trees dotted with blue LEDs, the river path leads past a rare sandy patch of riverbed, busy with sand sculptors in warm weather, to **Gabriel's Wharf**, a collection of small independent shops that range from stylish to kitsch.

Next door, the deco tower of **Oxo Tower Wharf** was designed to circumvent advertising regulations for the stock-cube company that used to own the building. Saved by local action group Coin Street Community Builders, it now provides affordable housing, interesting designer shops and galleries, and restaurants (including a rooftop restaurant and bistro with more wonderful views). Behind, **Bernie Spain Gardens** is great for a break from the crowds.

Hayward

Southbank Centre, Belvedere Road, SE1 8XX, (0844 875 0073, www.southbankcentre.co.uk).

Hayward Gallery.

Embankment tube or Waterloo tube/rail. **Open** 10am-6pm Mon-Wed, Sat, Sun; 10am-8pm Thur, Fri. **Admission** varies; check website for details. **Credit** AmEx, MC, V. **Map** p399 M8.
This versatile gallery has no permanent collection, but runs a good programme of temporary exhibitions, with a particular taste for participatory installations: Antony Gormley's fog-filled chamber for 'Blind Light', a rooftop rowing boat for group show 'Psycho Buildings', a kind of informal university for the arts at the 'Wide Open School', even an exhibition that contained no art. Visitors can hang out in the industrial-look café downstairs (it's a bar at night), before visiting free contemporary exhibitions at the inspired Hayward Project Space; take the stairs to the first floor from the glass foyer extension, an elliptical pavilion designed in collaboration with light artist Dan Graham.

Around Waterloo

Waterloo tube/rail.

Surprisingly, perhaps, there's plenty of interest around the stone-meets-glass rail terminus of London Waterloo. The most obvious attraction is the massive **BFI IMAX** (*see p272*), located in the middle of a roundabout at the southern end of Waterloo Bridge. The £20m cinema makes imaginative use of a desolate space that, in the 1990s, was notorious for its 'Cardboard City' population of homeless residents.

South, on the corner of Waterloo Road and the Cut, is the restored Victorian façade of the **Old Vic** theatre (*see p305*), now overseen by Kevin Spacey. Further down the Cut is the renovated home of the **Young Vic** (*see p311*), a hotbed

LONDON DUCK TOURS
AMAZING AMPHIBIOUS
ADVENTURE

A QUIRKY & UNIQUE WAY TO SEE LONDON!

THE CLASSIC TOUR
Travel in style by road and river on an incredible journey to remember! Our lively, entertaining and informative tours are suitable for the whole family. Let our professional character tour guides bring the sights and sounds of London to life in a completely new way, before splashing down into the Thames.
(Available daily)

THEMED TOURS!
Selected dates

THE JAMES BOND TOUR
Experience a tour packed with intrigue, espionage and the excitement of James Bond's London before entering the water Bond style.

THE D-DAY DUCK TOUR
We'll take you on an exhilarating journey back to the blitz, before heading to the river for the D-Day landings.

Visit us at: www.londonducktours.co.uk
Call us on: 0207 928 3132

LONDON DUCK TOURS

of theatrical talent with a stylish balcony bar. Both bring a touch of West End glamour across the river. To the north of the Cut, off Cornwall Road, are a number of atmospheric terraces made up of mid 19th-century artisans' houses.

BANKSIDE

Borough or Southwark tube, or Blackfriars or London Bridge tube/rail.
In Shakespeare's day, the area known as Bankside was the centre of bawdy Southwark, neatly located just beyond the jurisdiction of the City fathers. As well as playhouses such as the Globe and the Rose, there were the famous 'stewes' (brothels) presided over by the Bishops of Winchester, who made a tidy income from the fines they levied on the area's 'Winchester Geese' (or, in common parlance, prostitutes). There's less drinking, carousing and mischief-making here these days, but the area's cultural heritage remains alive thanks to the reconstructed **Shakespeare's Globe** (*see p42*) and, pretty much next door to it, **Tate Modern** (*see p43*), a former power station that's now a gallery.

Spanning the river in front of the Tate, the **Millennium Bridge** opened in 2000, when it became the first new Thames crossing in London since Tower Bridge (1894). Its early days were fraught with troubles; after just two days, the bridge was closed because of a pronounced wobble, and didn't reopen until 2002. Its troubles long behind it, the bridge is an elegant structure; a 'ribbon of steel' in the words of its conceptualists, architect Lord Foster and sculptor Anthony Caro. Cross it and you're at the foot of the stairs leading up to St Paul's Cathedral (*see p53*); to its left, the massively refurbished Blackfriars rail station not only has a brand-new entrance on the south bank of the river, but runs train platforms right across the river on the podiums of an earlier, incomplete version of **Blackfriars Bridge** (*see p49* **Inside Track**).

Continue east past the Globe and Southwark Bridge and you'll reach the **Anchor Bankside** pub (34 Park Street, 7407 1577). Built in 1775 on the site of an even older inn, the Anchor has, at various points, been a brothel, a chapel and a ship's chandlers. The outside terrace, across the pathway, offers fine river views – a fact lost on no one each summer, when it's invariably crammed with people.

All that's left of the Palace of Winchester, home of successive bishops, is the ruined rose window of the Great Hall on Clink Street. It stands next to the site of the bishops' former Clink prison, where thieves, prostitutes and debtors all served their sentences; it's now the **Clink Prison Museum** (1 Clink Street, SE1 9DG, 7403 0900, www.clink.co.uk). Around the

corner is the entrance to the wine showcase **Vinopolis** (*see p43*). At the other end of Clink Street, St Mary Overie's dock contains a terrific full-scale replica of Sir Francis Drake's ship, the **Golden Hinde** (*see below*).

🆓 Bankside Gallery
48 Hopton Street, SE1 9JH (7928 7521, www. banksidegallery.com). Blackfriars tube/rail or Southwark tube. **Open** 11am-6pm daily. **Admission** free; donations appreciated. **Credit** MC, V. **Map** p402 O7.
In the shadow of Tate Modern, this tiny gallery is the home of the Royal Watercolour Society and the Royal Society of Painter-Printmakers. The gallery runs a frequently changing programme of delightful print and watercolour exhibitions throughout the year; many of the works on show are for sale. Both societies hold frequent events here, including talks and demonstrations.

Golden Hinde
Pickfords Wharf, Clink Street, SE1 9DG (7403 0123, www.goldenhinde.com). London Bridge tube/rail. **Open** 11am-6pm daily. **Admission** £6; £4.50 reductions; £18 family; free under-4s. **Credit** AmEx, MC, V. **Map** p402 P8.
This meticulous replica of Sir Francis Drake's 16th-century flagship is thoroughly seaworthy: the ship has even reprised the privateer's circumnavigatory voyage. You can visit by means of a self-guided tour,

Shakespeare's Globe. *See p42.*

EXPLORE

Tate Modern.

but if you've got kids it's much more fun to join in on a 'living history' experience (some overnight): participants to dress in period clothes, eat Tudor fare and learn the skills of the Elizabethan seafarer; book well in advance. On weekends, the ship swarms with children dressed up as pirates for birthday dos.

★ Shakespeare's Globe
21 New Globe Walk, SE1 9DT (7401 9919, www.shakespeares-globe.org). Blackfriars tube/ rail or Southwark tube. **Open** *Exhibition* 9am-5pm daily. *Globe Theatre tours* Oct-Apr 10am-5pm daily. May-Sept 9.30am-5pm Mon; 9.30am-12.30pm Tue-Sat; 9.30-11.30am Sun. *Rose Theatre tours* May-Sept 1.30-5pm Tue-Fri. *Tours* every 30mins. **Admission** £13.50; £8-£12 reductions; £35 family; free under-5s. **Credit** AmEx, MC, V. **Map** p402 O7.

The original Globe Theatre, where many of William Shakespeare's plays were first staged and which he co-owned, burned to the ground in 1613 during a performance of *Henry VIII*. Nearly 400 years later, it was rebuilt not far from its original site, using construction methods and materials as close to the originals as possible, and is now open to the public for tours throughout the year (allow 90 minutes for the visit). During matinées, the tours go to the site of the Rose (21 New Globe Walk, SE1 9DT, 7261 9565, www.rosetheatre. org.uk), built by Philip Henslowe in 1587 as the first theatre on Bankside; red lights show the position of the original theatre. Funds are being sought to continue excavations and preserve the site.

Under the adventurous artistic directorship of Dominic Dromgoole, the Globe is also a fully operational theatre. From 23 April, conventionally regarded as the bard's birthday, into early October,

Shakespeare's plays and the odd new drama are performed. For more on the theatre, *see p307. Photo p41.*

★ FREE **Tate Modern**
Bankside, SE1 9TG (7887 8888, www.tate. org.uk). Blackfriars tube/rail or Southwark tube.
Open 10am-6pm Mon-Thur, Sun; 10am-10pm Fri, Sat. *Tours* 11am, noon, 2pm, 3pm daily.
Admission free. *Temporary exhibitions* vary.
Credit AmEx, MC, V. **Map** p402 O7.
Thanks to its industrial architecture, this powerhouse of modern art is awe-inspiring even before you enter. Built after World War II as Bankside Power Station, it was designed by Sir Giles Gilbert Scott, architect of Battersea Power Station (*see p143*). The power station shut in 1981; nearly 20 years later, it opened as an art museum, and has enjoyed spectacular popularity ever since. The gallery attracts five million visitors a year to a building intended for half that number; the first fruits of work on the immensely ambitious, £215m TM2 extension opened in 2012: the Tanks, so-called because they occupy vast, subterranean former oil tanks, will stage performance and film art. As for the rest of the extension, a huge new origami structure, designed by Herzog & de Meuron (who were behind the original conversion), will gradually unfold above the Tanks until perhaps 2016, but the work won't interrupt normal service in the main galleries.

In the main galleries themselves, the original cavernous turbine hall is still used to jaw-dropping effect as the home of large-scale, temporary installations. Beyond, the permanent collection draws from the Tate's collections of modern art (international works from 1900) and features heavy hitters such as Matisse, Rothko and Beuys – a genuinely world-class collection, expertly curated. There are vertiginous views down inside the building from outside the galleries, which group artworks according to movement (Surrealism, Minimalism, Post-war abstraction) rather than by theme.
▶ *The polka-dotted Tate-to-Tate boat zooms to Tate Britain (see p104) every 40 minutes, with a stop-off at the London Eye (see p37). Tickets are available at both Tates, on board, online or by phone (7887 8888; £5, £1.65-£3.75 reductions).*

Vinopolis
1 Bank End, SE1 9BU (7940 8300, www. vinopolis.co.uk). London Bridge tube/rail. **Open** 2-10pm Thur, Fri; noon-10pm Sat; noon-6pm Sun.
Admission £22.50-£40. **Credit** AmEx, MC, V.
Map p402 P8.
Glossy Vinopolis is more of an introduction to wine-tasting than a resource for cognoscenti, but you do need to have some prior interest to get a kick out of it. Participants are introduced to systematic wine tasting and then given a wine glass. Exhibits are set out by country, with opportunities to taste wine or champagne from different regions. Gin crashes the party courtesy of a Bombay Sapphire cocktail, and you can also sample Caribbean rum, whisky and beer.

BOROUGH

Borough or Southwark tube, or London Bridge tube/rail.

At Clink Street, the route cuts inland, skirting the edge of the district of Borough. The landmark here is the Anglican **Southwark Cathedral** (*see p44*), formerly St Saviour's and before that the monastic church of St Mary Overie. Shakespeare's brother Edmund was buried in the graveyard; there's a monument to the playwright inside.

Just south of the cathedral you'll find the roof of **Borough Market**, a busy food market dating from the 13th century, although with its new glass-fronted premises you'd hardly think so. There's still plenty of Victorian ironwork to enjoy. The market is wholesale only for most of the week, but hosts London's foodiest public food market (*see p223*) on Thursdays, Fridays and Saturdays (when it gets very crowded). It's surrounded by good places to eat and drink. Not far away, the quaint **George** (77 Borough High Street, 7407 2056) is London's last surviving galleried coaching inn.

With the **London Dungeon** due to close on Tooley Street in early 2013 prior to its move to County Hall (*see pX38*), fans of gore should head to the far more interesting and no less grisly **Old Operating Theatre, Museum & Herb Garret** (*see p44*), with its body parts

Old Operating Theatre, Museum & Herb Garret. *See p44.*

EXPLORE

and surgical implements. By contrast, you'll hear the dulcet tones of Vera Lynn wafting from **Winston Churchill's Britain at War Experience** (*see below*). But nothing can compete with the monstrous, 1,016-foot **Shard** development at London Bridge station (*see p46* **The Shard of Glass**).

★ Old Operating Theatre, Museum & Herb Garret

9A St Thomas's Street, SE1 9RY (7188 2679, www.thegarret.org.uk). London Bridge tube/rail. **Open** 10.30am-5pm daily. **Admission** £6; £3.40-£5 reductions; £13.90 family; free under-6s. **No credit cards**. **Map** p403 Q8.

The tower that houses this reminder of the surgical practices of the past used to be part of the chapel of St Thomas's Hospital. Before moving there, operations took place in the wards. Visitors enter via a vertiginous spiral staircase to inspect a pre-anaesthetic operating theatre dating from 1822, with tiered viewing seats for students. The operating tools look more like torture implements. *Photo p43.*

FREE Southwark Cathedral

London Bridge, SE1 9DA (7367 6700, www. southwark.anglican.org). London Bridge tube/rail. **Open** 9am-5pm daily (closing times vary on religious holidays). *Services* 8am, 8.15am, 12.30pm, 12.45pm, 5.30pm Mon-Fri; 9am, 9.15am, 4pm Sat; 8.45am, 9am, 11am, 3pm, 6.30pm Sun. *Choral Evensong* 5.30pm Mon, Thur (girls); 5.30pm Tue (boys & men); 5.30pm Fri (men only). **Admission** free; suggested donation £4. **Credit** MC, V. **Map** p402 P8.

The oldest bits of this building date back more than 800 years. The retro-choir was the setting for several Protestant martyr trials during the reign of Mary Tudor. Inside, there are memorials to Shakespeare, John Harvard (benefactor of the American university) and Sam Wanamaker (the force behind the reconstruction of the Globe); Chaucer features in the stained glass. There are displays throughout the cathedral explaining its history. The courtyard is one of the area's prettiest places for a rest.

Winston Churchill's Britain at War Experience

64-66 Tooley Street, SE1 2TF (7403 3171, www.britainatwar.co.uk). London Bridge tube/ rail. **Open** *Apr-Oct* 10am-5pm daily. *Nov-Mar* 10am-4.30pm daily. **Admission** £14.50; £5.50-£7.50 reductions; £35 family; free under-5s. **Credit** AmEx, MC, V. **Map** p403 Q8.

This old-fashioned exhibition recalls the privations endured by the British during World War II. Visitors descend from street level in an ancient lift to a reconstructed tube station shelter. The experience continues with displays about London during the Blitz, including bombs, rare documents, photos and reconstructed shopfronts. The displays on rationing, food

Borough Market. *See p43.*

EXPLORE

production and Land Girls are fascinating, and the set-piece walk-through bombsite is quite disturbing.

LONDON BRIDGE TO TOWER BRIDGE

Bermondsey tube/London Bridge tube/rail.

Across the street from the Dungeon is **Hay's Galleria**. Once an enclosed dock, it's now dominated by a peculiar kinetic sculpture called *The Navigators*. Exiting on the riverside, you can walk east past the great grey hulk of **HMS Belfast** (*see p46*) to Tower Bridge.

Beyond the battleship you pass the pristine environs of **City Hall**, home of London's current government. There's a pleasant outside area called the Scoop, used for outdoor events.

South of here, many of the historic houses on Bermondsey Street now host hip design studios or funky shops. This is also where you'll find the **Fashion & Textile Museum** (*see right*), as well as the newest of the city's three pioneering **White Cube** galleries (nos.144-152, 7930 5373, http://whitecube.com; closed Mon). At the street's furthest end, the redevelopment of Bermondsey Square created an arthouse cinema and the Bermondsey Square Hotel, alongside a charming cemetery park, but old-timers linger on: the classic eel and pie shop **M Manze** and a Friday antique market (6am-2pm) – great for browsing, but get there early if you want to find a bargain.

If the Borough Market (*see p43*) crowds are too much on a Saturday, there is a winning cluster of food stalls on **Maltby Street**, at Spa

Terminus and on the redeveloped **Ropewalk**, not far west of Bermondsey Street.

Back on the riverfront, a board announces when **Tower Bridge** is next due to be raised. The bridge is one of the lowest to span the Thames, hence its twin lifting sections or bascules. The original steam-driven machinery can be seen at the **Tower Bridge Exhibition** (*see p64*). Further east, the former warehouses of **Butler's Wharf** are now mainly given over to expensive riverside dining; one of them currently houses the **Design Museum** (*see below*).

Design Museum

Shad Thames, SE1 2YD (7403 6933, www. designmuseum.org). Tower Hill tube or London Bridge tube/rail. **Open** 10am-5.45pm daily. **Admission** £11; £7-£10 reductions; free under-12s. **Credit** AmEx, MC, V. **Map** p403 S9. Exhibitions in this former banana warehouse focus on modern and contemporary design. The temporary shows run from major installations to design artefacts, from architects' travel photographs to retrospectives of key theorists of the built environment. The Blueprint Café has a balcony overlooking the Thames, and you can buy designer books and items relating to the current show in the museum shop.

▶ *Terence Conran – whose idea it was to have a museum of design – made a major donation in 2011 to enable the museum to move west to the former Commonwealth Institute by 2014.*

Fashion & Textile Museum

83 Bermondsey Street, SE1 3XF (7407 8664, www. ftmlondon.org). London Bridge tube/rail. **Open**

HMS Belfast. *See p46.*

11am-6pm Tue-Sat. **Admission** £7; £4 reductions; free under-12s. **Credit** MC, V. **Map** p403 Q9.

As flamboyant as its founder, fashion designer Zandra Rhodes, this pink and orange museum holds 3,000 of Rhodes's garments and her archive of paper designs, sketchbooks, silk screens and show videos. Temporary shows explore the work of trend-setters or themes such as the development of underwear. A quirky shop sells ware by new designers.

HMS Belfast

Morgan's Lane, Tooley Street, SE1 2JH (7940 6300, www.iwm.org.uk). London Bridge tube/rail. **Open** *Mar-Oct* 10am-6pm daily. *Nov-Feb* 10am-5pm daily. **Admission** £14; £11.20 reductions; free under-16s (must be accompanied by an adult). **Credit** MC, V. **Map** p403 R8.

This 11,500-ton 'Edinburgh' class large light cruiser is the last surviving big gun World War II warship in Europe. A floating branch of the Imperial War Museum, it makes an unlikely playground for children, who tear around its complex of gun turrets, bridge, decks and engine room. The *Belfast* was built in 1938, ran convoys to Russia, supported the Normandy Landings and helped UN forces in Korea before being decommissioned in 1965. *Photo p45.*

Shard

32 London Bridge Street, SE1 9SS (www.the viewfromtheshard.com). London Bridge tube/rail. **Open** 10am-6pm daily. **Admission** £24.95; £18.95 reductions; free under-3s. **Credit** AmEx, MC, V. **Map** p403 Q8.
See below **The Shard of Glass**.

The Shard of Glass

London's boldest landmark is unmissable in more ways than one.

You can't miss the **Shard** (*see above*) – which is, after all, the point of the structure. It shoots into the sky 'like a shard of glass' – to use the words of its architect, Renzo Piano, who envisaged his enigmatic, glass-covered, spire-like tower as 'a vertical city', combining private and public spaces. Apparently he scribbled the initial idea for the building on the back of a restaurant menu.

The Shard.

Since 2009, Londoners have watched as first a concrete and steel core grew skywards, and then the plates of its glass shell began to grow upon it. Already by 2010, when it was still a skeleton, the Shard had overtaken **One Canada Square** ('Canary Wharf', *see p129*) as London's tallest building. And it kept going: in December 2011, it became the tallest building in the EU, but even then it had still to reach its full height. Finally, in March 2012, when its 217-foot, 500-tonne spire was winched into place, it topped out at 1,016 feet.

As is the fate of skyscrapers, the Shard's claims to be the tallest are relative: Moscow's 1,089ft-tall Mercury City Tower is scheduled to have overtaken it by the end of 2012, and that's before we consider the Arab Emirates or South-east Asia. But the Shard's slim, slightly irregular pyramid will remain visible from right across London – except, ironically, from those Victorian alleys that remain at its foot, where the monstrous building seems to play peek-a-boo with visitors as they scurry around looking for a good vantage point for a snapshot.

From February 2013, high-speed lifts will whisk visitors up to see what – weather permitting – will be stunning 360-degree, 40-mile views of London and its surrounds. This year also promises the arrival of the 200-room, five-star Shangri-La – premises for which the term 'landmark hotel' will be no empty cliché – as well as restaurants on floors 31-33, which feature a spectacular glass atrium as a centrepiece.

EXPLORE

The City

Where London began – and where much of its wealth is made.

The City's current fame merely as the financial heart of London does no justice to its 2,000-year history. Here Romans founded the city they called Londinium, building a bridge to the west of today's **London Bridge**. Here were a forum-basilica, an amphitheatre, public baths and the defensive wall that still defines what we now call the Square Mile (an area, in fact, of 1.21 square miles).

Although the City has just over 9,000 residents, 330,000 people arrive each weekday to work as bankers, lawyers and traders, taking over 85 million square feet of office space. Tourists come, too, to see **St Paul's Cathedral** and the **Tower of London**, but there's much else besides. No area of London offers quite so much in so small a space. Roman ruins? Medieval? Iconic 21st-century offices? You're in the right place.

To understand the City properly, visit on a weekday when the great economic machine is running at full tilt and the commuter is king. Despite efforts by the City authorities to improve the district's prospects as a weekend leisure destination, many of the streets still fall eerily quiet. If you do visit at the weekend, try the Cheapside shops and the street's anchor mall, the rather antiseptic **One New Change**; drop in on the always wonderful **Museum of London**; or just do as a discerning minority of locals do – potter about enjoying the place's odd nooks and crannies in relative tranquillity.

Map pp400-403	**Pubs & bars**
Restaurants &	pp188-189
cafés pp158-159	**Hotels** pp232-235

EXPLORE

TEMPLE & THE INNS OF COURT

Temple tube.

At its western end, the arterial Strand (*see p77*) becomes Fleet Street at **Temple Bar**, the City's ancient western boundary and once the site of Wren's great gateway (now in Paternoster Square beside St Paul's; *see p53*). A newer, narrower, but still impressive wyvern-topped monument marks the original spot. The area has long been linked to the law, and here stands the splendid neo-Gothic **Royal Courts of Justice** (*see p49*). On the other side of the road, stretching almost to the Thames, are the several courtyards that make up **Middle Temple** (7427 4800, www.middletemple. org.uk) and **Inner Temple** (7797 8250,

www.innertemple.org.uk), two of the Inns of Court that provided training and lodging for London's medieval lawyers. Anybody may visit the grounds, but access to the grand, collegiate buildings is for lawyers and barristers only.

INSIDE TRACK **IN THE KNOW**

Perfectly located on the river side of St Paul's Cathedral (*see p53*), the spiky-roofed **City of London Information Centre** (7332 1456, www.cityoflondon.gov.uk) opens 9.30am-5.30pm Mon-Sat and 10am-4pm Sun. It has information and brochures on sights, events, walks and talks, as well as offering tours with specialist guides.

THE WORLD CAN BE AN UNJUST AND TREACHEROUS PLACE, BUT THERE ARE THOSE WHO STRIVE TO MAKE IT SAFE FOR EVERYONE.

Operating in some of the world's most dangerous and oppressed countries, **Human Rights Watch** conducts rigorous investigations to bring those who have been targets of abuse to the world's attention. We use strategic advocacy to push people in power to end their repressive practices. And we work for as long as it takes to see that oppressors are held accountable for their crimes.

KNOWLEDGE IS POWER. LEARN ABOUT LIFE-CHANGING EVENTS IN YOUR WORLD THAT DON'T ALWAYS MAKE THE HEADLINES AND HOW YOU CAN HELP EFFECT POSITIVE CHANGE.

Stay informed, visit HRW.org

HUMA
RIGHTS
WATCH

The site was formerly the headquarters of the Knights Templar, an order of warrior monks founded in the 12th century to protect pilgrims to the Holy Land. The Templars built the original **Temple Church** (*see below*) in 1185, but fell foul of Catholic orthodoxy during the Crusades and their order was disbanded.

Almost due south of Temple Bar, right alongside Middle Temple, is the virtually unknown and thoroughly fabulous **Two Temple Place** (*see below*).

FREE Royal Courts of Justice

Strand, WC2A 2LL (7947 6000, tours 7947 7684, www.hmcourts-service.gov.uk). Temple tube. **Open** 9am-4.30pm Mon-Fri. **Admission** free. *Tours* £10. **Credit** MC, V. **Map** p397 M6.
Two of the highest civil courts in the land sit in these imposing buildings: the High Court and the Appeals Court, justice at its most bewigged and ermine-robed. Visitors are welcome to observe the process of law in any of the 88 courtrooms, but very little happens in August and September. There are also two-hour tours on the first and third Tuesday of the month (11am or 2pm; pre-book on 7947 7684 or rcj-tours@talktalk.net). Cameras and children under 14 are not allowed on the premises.

Temple Church

Fleet Street, EC4Y 7HL (7353 8559, www.templechurch.com). Chancery Lane or Temple tube. **Open** times vary; check website for details. **Admission** £4; free reductions. **Map** p402 N6.
Inspired by Jerusalem's Church of the Holy Sepulchre, the Temple Church was the chapel of the Knights Templar. The rounded apse contains the worn grave-stones of several Crusader knights, but the church was refurbished by Wren and the Victorians, and was damaged in the Blitz. Not that it puts off the wild speculations of fans of Dan Brown's *Da Vinci Code*. There are organ recitals most Wednesdays.

FREE Two Temple Place

2 Temple Place, WC2R 3BD (7836 3715, www.twotempleplace.org). Temple tube. **Open** *Late Jan-mid Apr* 10am-4.30pm Mon, Wed-Sat; 11am-4.30pm Sun. **Admission** free. **Map** p399 M7.
See p50 **A Temple to... Well, What Exactly?**

FLEET STREET

Temple tube or Blackfriars rail.

Without Fleet Street, the daily newspaper might never have been invented. Named after the vanished River Fleet, Fleet Street was a major artery for the delivery of goods into the City, including the first printing press, which was installed behind **St Bride's Church** (*see p50*) in 1500 by William Caxton's assistant, Wynkyn de Worde, who also set up a bookstall in the churchyard of St Paul's. London's first daily newspaper, the *Daily Courant*, rolled off the presses in 1702; in 1712, Fleet Street saw the first of innumerable libel cases when the *Courant* leaked the details of a private parliamentary debate.

By the end of World War II, half a dozen offices were churning out scoops and scandals between the Strand and Farringdon Road. Most of the newspapers moved away after Rupert Murdoch won his war with the print unions in the 1980s; the last of the news agencies, Reuters, finally followed suit in 2005. Until recently, the only periodical published on Fleet Street was a comic, the much-loved *Beano*. However, in 2009, left-wing weekly the *New Statesman* moved into offices around the corner from Fleet Street on Carmelite Street. Relics from the media days remain: the Portland-stone **Reuters building** (no.85), the Egyptian-influenced **Daily Telegraph building** (no.135) and the sleek, black **Daily Express building** (nos.121-128), designed by Owen Williams in the 1930s and arguably the finest art deco building in London. Tucked away on an alley behind St Bride's Church is the **St Bride Foundation Institute**, its library (7353 4660, www.stbride.org; open 11am-6pm Wed) dedicated to printing and typography. The library mounts temporary exhibitions showing off its collections, which include rare works by Eric Gill and maquettes for Kinnear and Calvert's distinctive road signs.

At the top of Fleet Street itself is the church of **St Dunstan-in-the-West** (7405 1929, www.stdunstaninthewest.org; closed Sat & Sun,

EXPLORE

INSIDE TRACK
RIVER CROSSING

Blackfriars Bridge is certainly worth exploring, and not just for its splendid red-and-white painted Victorian ironwork. It also offers a great vantage point on a rather interesting initiative: London's first cross-river railway station. The new Blackfriars Station makes use of pillars left over from an 1864 rail bridge, but has incorporated environmentally friendly features into its design: notably a roof that supports the capital's largest array of photovoltaic solar panels, which will supply half of the station's energy. At the time of writing, the station itself still has hoardings blocking views from within – but when the work is complete, they should be impressive too. To have a look, just turn south from the St Paul's end of Fleet Street.

EXPLORE

A Temple to… Well, What Exactly?

One of the loveliest houses in the City is also one of the most mysterious.

Set back from the Thames beside Middle Temple, the pale Portland stone exterior and oriel windows of **Two Temple Place** (for listing, *see p49*) are handsome enough – but the interior is extraordinary.

You get a hint about what's to come before you open the door: look right and there's a cherub holding an old-fashioned telephone to his ear. Ring the bell and you'll be warmly welcomed by volunteers

into a house with decor that combines sublime, extravagant craftsmanship with a total lack of interest in coherence. Above porphyry tiles, the Three Musketeers adorn the banisters of a fine wood staircase. A host of intricately carved literary characters crowd the first floor, mixing Shakespeare with Hawthorne and Fenimore Cooper. Then there's the Great Hall: medieval in style, but for the stunning rising and setting sun stained glass to east and west, and above you 54 apparently random busts: Voltaire and Marlborough, Anne Boleyn enjoying the company of Mary Queen of Scots.

Built as an estate office in 1895 to the close specifications of William Waldorf Astor, Two Temple Place now opens to the public three months a year with exhibitions of 'publicly-owned art from around the UK', displayed by an up-and-coming curator. This year 'Amongst Heroes: the artist in working Cornwall' will see an oyster boat dragged into the downstairs room. The Bulldog Trust is as crazy as the house it now owns, but it's the good kind of crazy.

except for services), where the poet John Donne was rector in the 17th century. The church was rebuilt in the 1830s, but the eye-catching clock dates to 1671. The clock's chimes are beaten by clockwork giants who are said to represent Gog and Magog, tutelary spirits of the City. Next door, no.186 is the house where Sweeney Todd, the 'demon barber of Fleet Street', reputedly murdered his customers before selling their bodies to a local pie shop. The legend, sadly, is a porky pie: Todd was invented by the editors of a Victorian penny dreadful in 1846 and propelled to fame rather later by a stage play.

Fleet Street was always known for its pubs; half the newspaper editorials in London were composed over liquid lunches, but there were also more literary imbibers. If you walk down Fleet Street, you'll see **Ye Olde Cheshire Cheese** (no.145, 7353 6170), a favourite of Dickens and Yeats. In its heyday, it hosted the bibulous literary salons of Dr Samuel Johnson, who lived nearby at 17 Gough Square (*see right* **Dr Johnson's House**). It also had a famous drinking parrot, the death of which prompted hundreds of newspaper obituaries. At no.66, the **Tipperary** (7583 6470) is the oldest Irish pub outside Ireland: it sold the first pint of Guinness on the British mainland in the 1700s.

Dr Johnson's House

17 Gough Square, off Fleet Street, EC4A 3DE (7353 3745, www.drjohnsonshouse.org). Chancery Lane tube or Blackfriars tube/rail. **Open** *May-Sept* 11am-5.30pm Mon-Sat. *Oct-Apr* 11am-5pm Mon-Sat. *Tours* by arrangement, groups of 10 or more only. **Admission** £4.50; £1.50-£3.50 reductions; £10 family; free under-5s. *Tours* free. **No credit cards. Map** p402 N6.
Famed as the author of one of the first – as well as the most significant and unquestionably the wittiest – dictionaries of the English language, Dr Samuel Johnson (1709-84) also wrote poems, a novel and one of the earliest travelogues, an acerbic account of a tour of the Western Isles with his biographer James Boswell. You can tour the stately Georgian town-house off Fleet Street where Johnson came up with his inspired definitions – 'to make dictionaries is dull work,' was his definition of the word 'dull'. The house has been open to the public since 1911.
▶ *A neat statue of Johnson's cat Hodge sits contentedly in the square outside.*

FREE St Bride's Church

Fleet Street, EC4Y 8AU (7427 0133, www.st brides.com). Temple tube. **Open** 8am-6pm Mon-Fri; 11am-3pm Sat; 10am-6.30pm Sun. Times vary Mon-Sat, so phone ahead to check. **Admission** free. **No credit cards. Map** p402 N6.

Hidden down an alley south of Fleet Street, St Bride's is known as the journalists' church: in the north aisle, a shrine is dedicated to hacks killed in action. Down in the crypt a surprisingly interesting little museum displays fragments of the churches that have existed on this site since the sixth century.

▶ *An 18th-century Fleet Street pâtissier, William Rich, was famous for tiered bride cakes modelled on the church's lovely Wren-designed spire.*

ST PAUL'S & AROUND

St Paul's tube.

The towering dome of **St Paul's Cathedral** (*see p53*) is, excluding the 'Big Ben' clocktower, probably the definitive symbol of traditional London. It was also an architectural two fingers to the Great Fire and, later, the Nazi bombers that pounded the city in 1940 and 1941. North of the cathedral is the redeveloped **Paternoster Square**, a modern plaza incorporating a sundial that rarely tells the time. The name harks to the days when priests from St Paul's walked the streets chanting the Lord's Prayer (*Pater noster*, Latin for 'Our Father').

Also of interest is Wren's statue-covered **Temple Bar**. It once stood at the intersection of Fleet Street and the Strand (*see p77*), marking the boundary between the City of London and neighbouring Westminster; during the Middle Ages, the monarch was only allowed to pass through the Temple Bar into the City with the approval of the Lord Mayor of London. The archway was dismantled as part of a Victorian road-widening programme in 1878 and became a garden ornament for a country estate in Hertfordshire, before being installed in its current location, as the gateway between St Paul's and Paternoster Square, in 2004. The gold-topped pillar in the centre of the square looks as if it commemorates something important, but's just an air vent for the Underground.

South of St Paul's, steps cascade down to the **Millennium Bridge**, which spans the river to Tate Modern (*see p43*) and now offers the main gateway to the City for tourists. The grand **St Lawrence Jewry Memorial Fountain** is another peripatetic monument: kept in storage since the 1970s after it was removed from the

St Paul's Cathedral. *See p53.*

EXPLORE

church (*see p59*), it was placed here in 2011. The structure dates to 1866. The stairs take you close to the 17th-century **College of Arms** (*see p53*), official seat of British heraldry.

East of the cathedral is the huge **One New Change** shopping mall and office development (*see p207*). Designed by French starchitect Jean Nouvel, its most interesting aspects are a gash that gives views straight through the building to St Paul's and, for a fine roof-level panorama, the sixth-floor public terrace and bar-restaurant. Meekly hidden among the alleys behind it, you'll find narrow Bow Lane. At one end sits **St Mary-le-Bow** (7248 5139, www.stmarylebow.co.uk; open 7.30am-6pm Mon-Wed; 7.30am-6.30pm Thur; 7am-4pm Fri), built by Wren between 1671 and 1680. The church bell's peals once defined anyone born within earshot as a true Cockney. At the other end of Bow Lane is **St Mary Aldermary** (7248 9902, www.stmary aldermary.co.uk; open 11am-3pm Mon-Fri). With a pin-straight spire designed by Wren's office, this was the only Gothic church by him to survive World War II. Inside, there's a fabulous moulded plaster ceiling and original wooden sword rest (London parishioners carried arms until the late 19th century). Roman coins are sold here to fund renovation work.

There are more Wren creations south of St Paul's. On Garlick Hill, named for the medieval garlic market, is **St James Garlickhythe** (7236 1719, www.stjamesgarlickhythe.org.uk; open 10.30am-4pm Thur). The official church of London's vintners and joiners, it was built by Wren in 1682. Hidden in the tower are the naturally mummified remains of a young man, nicknamed Jimmy Garlick, discovered in the vaults in 1855. The church was hit by bombs in both World Wars, and partly ruined by a falling crane in 1991, but the interior has been convincingly restored. Off Victoria Street, **St Nicholas Cole Abbey** was the first church rebuilt after the Great Fire.

Built on the site of the infamous Newgate prison to the north-west of the cathedral is the **Old Bailey** (*see below*). A remnant of the prison's east wall can be seen in Amen Corner.

FREE College of Arms

130 Queen Victoria Street, EC4V 4BT (7248 2762, www.college-of-arms.gov.uk). St Paul's tube or Blackfriars tube/rail. **Open** *10am-4pm Mon-Fri. Tours by arrangement.* **Admission** *free.* **No credit cards.** **Map** p402 O7.

Originally created to identify competing knights at medieval jousting tournaments, coats of arms soon became an integral part of family identity for the landed gentry of Britain. Scriveners still work here to create beautiful heraldic certificates. Only the Earl Marshal's Court is open to the general public, but visitors can book for evening tours (Mon-Fri) around the historic interior, led by a herald who will usually be able to show you documents from the archive.

FREE Old Bailey (Central Criminal Court)

Corner of Newgate Street & Old Bailey, EC4M 7EH (7248 3277, www.cityoflondon.gov.uk). St Paul's tube. **Open** *Public gallery 9.45am-12.45pm, 2-4.30pm Mon-Fri.* **Admission** *free. No under-14s; 14-16s only if accompanied by adults.* **No credit cards.** **Map** p402 O6.

A gilded statue of blind (meaning impartial) justice stands atop London's most famous criminal court. The current building was completed in 1907; the site itself has hosted some of the most famous trials in British history, including that of Oscar Wilde. Anyone is welcome to attend a trial, but bags, cameras, dictaphones, mobile phones and food are banned (and no storage facilities are provided).

▶ *A blocked-up door in St Sepulchre Without is the visible remains of a priest tunnel into the court; the Newgate Execution Bell is also there.*

★ St Paul's Cathedral

Ludgate Hill, EC4M 8AD (7236 4128, www.st pauls.co.uk). St Paul's tube. **Open** *8.30am-4pm Mon-Sat. Galleries, crypt & ambulatory 9.30am-4.15pm Mon-Sat. Special events may cause* closure; check before visiting. *Tours of cathedral & crypt 10.45am, 11.15am, 1.30pm, 2pm Mon-Sat.* **Admission** *Cathedral, crypt & gallery (incl tour) £15; £6-£14 reductions; £36 family; free under-6s.* **Credit** AmEx, MC, V. **Map** p402 O6.

The first cathedral to St Paul was built on this site in 604, but fell to Viking marauders. Its Norman replacement, a magnificent Gothic structure with a 490ft spire (taller than any London building until the 1960s), burned in the Great Fire. The current church was commissioned in 1673 from Sir Christopher Wren as the centrepiece of London's resurgence from the ashes. Modern buildings now encroach on the cathedral from all sides, but the passing of three centuries has done nothing to diminish the appeal of London's most famous cathedral.

Start with the exterior. Over the last decade, a £40m restoration project has painstakingly removed most of the Victorian grime from the walls and the extravagant main façade looks as brilliant today as it must have when the last stone was placed in 1708. On the south side of the cathedral, an austere park has been laid out, tracing the outline of the medieval chapter house whose remains lie 4ft under it.

The vast open spaces of the interior contain memorials to national heroes such as Wellington and Lawrence of Arabia. The statue of John Donne, metaphysical poet and former Dean of St Paul's, is often overlooked, but it's the only monument to have been saved from Old St Paul's. There are also more modern works, including a Henry Moore sculpture and temporary Arts Project displays of major contemporary art. The Whispering Gallery, inside the dome, is reached by 259 steps from the main hall; the acoustics here are so good that a whisper can be bounced clearly to the other side of the dome. Steps continue up to first the Stone Gallery (119 tighter, steeper steps), with its high external balustrades, then outside to the Golden Gallery (152 steps), with its giddying views.

Before leaving St Paul's, head down to the maze-like crypt (through a door whose frame is decorated with skull and crossbones), which contains a shop and café and memorials to such dignitaries as Alexander Fleming, William Blake and Admiral Lord Nelson, whose grand tomb (purloined from Wolsey by Henry VIII but never used by him) is right beneath the centre of the dome. To one side is the small, plain tombstone of Christopher Wren himself, inscribed by his son with the epitaph, 'Reader, if you seek a monument, look around you'; at their request, Millais and Turner were buried near him.

As well as tours of the main cathedral and self-guided audio tours (which are free), you can join special tours of the Triforium, visiting the library and Wren's 'Great Model', at 11.30am and 2pm Monday and Tuesday and at 2pm on Friday (pre-book on 7246 8357, £19.50 incl admission). *Photo p51.*

▶ *The crypt now also houses Oculus – a 270° film that tells the cathedral's history and flies you up the dome, past the Whispering Gallery, to look out over the City from the Golden Gallery.*

EXPLORE

NORTH TO SMITHFIELD

Barbican or St Paul's tube.

North of St Paul's Cathedral on Foster Lane is **St Vedast-alias-Foster** (7606 3998; open 8am-5.30pm Mon-Fri; 11am-4pm Sat), another finely proportioned Wren church, restored after World War II using spare trim from other churches in the area. Off nearby Aldersgate Street, peaceful **Postman's Park** contains the Watts Memorial to Heroic Sacrifice: a wall of ceramic plaques, each of which commemorates a heroic but doomed act of bravery. Most date to Victorian times – pantomime artiste Sarah Smith, for example, who received 'terrible injuries when attempting in her inflammable dress to extinguish the flames which had engulfed her companion (1863)' – but the first new plaque for 70 years was added in 2009. It was dedicated to 30-year-old Leigh Pitt, who died while saving a child from drowning.

Further west on Little Britain (named after the Duke of Brittany) is **St Bartholomew-the-Great** (*see below*), founded along with **St Bartholomew's Hospital** in the 12th century. Popularly known as St Bart's, the hospital treated air-raid casualties throughout World War II; shrapnel damage from German bombs is still visible on the exterior walls. Scottish nationalists now come here to lay flowers at the monument to William Wallace, executed in front of the church on the orders of Edward I in 1305. Just beyond St Bart's is the fine ironwork of Smithfield Market (*see p68*).

FREE Museum of St Bartholomew's Hospital

St Bartholomew's Hospital, North Wing, West Smithfield, EC1A 7BE (3465 5798, www.barts andthelondon.nhs.uk/museums). Barbican tube or Farringdon tube/rail. **Open** 10am-4pm Tue-Fri. **Admission** free; donations welcome. **No credit cards. Map** p400 O5.
Be glad you're living in the 21st century. Many of the displays in this small museum inside St Bart's Hospital relate to the days before anaesthetics, when surgery and carpentry were kindred occupations.

Every Friday at 2pm, visitors can take a guided tour of the museum that takes in the Hogarth paintings in the Great Hall, the little church of St Bartholomew-the-Less, neighbouring St Bartholomew-the-Great and Smithfield.

St Bartholomew-the-Great

West Smithfield, EC1A 9DS (7606 5171, www. greatstbarts.com). Barbican tube or Farringdon tube/rail. **Open** 8.30am-5pm Mon-Fri (until 4pm Nov-Feb); 10.30am-4pm Sat; 8.30am-8pm Sun. **Admission** £4; £3 reductions; £10 family; free under-7s. **Credit** AmEx, MC, V. **Map** p400 O5.
This atmospheric medieval church was built over the remains of the 12th-century priory hospital of St Bartholomew, founded by Prior Rahere, a former courtier of Henry I. The church was chopped about during Henry VIII's reign and the interior is now firmly Elizabethan, although it also contains donated works of modern art. You may recognise the main hall from *Shakespeare in Love* or *Four Weddings and a Funeral*.
▶ *If you need refreshment, the church has a bar-café in the 15th-century cloister, serving coffee, monastery beers and home-made weekday lunches.*

NORTH OF LONDON WALL

Barbican tube or Moorgate tube/rail.

From St Bart's, the road known as London Wall runs east to Bishopsgate, following the approximate route of the old Roman walls. Tower blocks have sprung up here like daisies, but the odd lump of weathered stonework can still be seen poking up between the office blocks, marking the path of the old City wall. You can patrol the remaining stretches of the wall, with panels (some barely legible) pointing out highlights on a route of two miles. The walk starts near the brilliant **Museum of London** (*see right*) and runs to the Tower of London.

The area north of London Wall was reduced to rubble by German bombs in World War II. In 1958, the City of London and London County Council clubbed together to buy the land for the construction of 'a genuine residential neighbourhood, with schools, shops, open spaces and amenities'. What Londoners got was the **Barbican**, a vast concrete estate of 2,000 flats that feels a bit like a university campus after the students have gone home. Casual visitors may get the eerie feeling they have been miniaturised and transported into a giant architect's model, but design enthusiasts will recognise the Barbican – with its landmark saw-toothed towers – as a prime example of 1970s Brutalism, softened a little by time and rectangular ponds of friendly resident ducks. Learn to love the place by taking one of the regular, 90-minute architectural tours of the

Barbican.

complex (www.barbican.org.uk/education) – which will also help you navigate its famously confusing layout.

The main attraction here is the Barbican arts complex, with its library, cinema, theatre and concert hall – each reviewed in the appropriate chapters – plus an art gallery (*see below*) and the **Barbican Conservatory** (open noon-5pm Sun), a steamy greenhouse full of tropical plants, exotic fish and twittering birds. Marooned amid the towers is the only pre-war building in the vicinity: the restored 16th-century church of **St Giles Cripplegate** (7638 1997, www.stgilescripplegate.com; open 11am-4pm Mon-Fri), where Oliver Cromwell was married and John Milton buried.

North-east of the Barbican on City Road are **John Wesley's House** (*see below*) and **Bunhill Fields**, the nonconformist cemetery where William Blake, the preacher John Bunyan and novelist Daniel Defoe are buried.

Barbican Art Gallery

Barbican Centre, Silk Street, EC2Y 8DS (7638 8891, www.barbican.org.uk). Barbican tube or Moorgate tube/rail. **Open** 11am-8pm Mon, Fri-Sun; 11am-6pm Tue, Wed; 11am-10pm Thur. **Admission** varies; check website for details. **Credit** AmEx, MC, V. **Map** p400 P5.
The art gallery at the Barbican Centre on the third floor isn't quite as 'out there' as it would like you to think, but the exhibitions on architecture, fashion, design and pop culture are usually pretty diverting, and accompanied by interesting events.

► *On the ground floor, the Curve is a long, thin gallery (yes, it's curved) that commissions free large-scale installations. They're often superb.*

John Wesley's House & the Museum of Methodism

Wesley's Chapel, 49 City Road, EC1Y 1AU (7253 2262, www.wesleyschapel.org.uk). Moorgate or Old Street tube/rail. **Open** 10am-4pm Mon-Sat; after the service until 1.45pm Sun. *Tours* arrangements on arrival; groups of 10 or more phone ahead. **Admission** free; donations welcome. **Credit** AmEx, MC, V. **Map** p401 Q4.
John Wesley (1703-91), the founder of Methodism, was a man of legendary self-discipline. You can see the minister's nightcap, preaching gown and personal experimental electric-shock machine on a tour of his austere home on City Road. The adjacent chapel has a small museum on the history of Methodism and fine memorials of dour, sideburn-sporting preachers. Downstairs (to the right) are some of the finest public toilets in London, built in 1899 with original fittings by Sir Thomas Crapper.

★ Museum of London

150 London Wall, EC2Y 5HN (7001 9844, www.museumoflondon.org.uk). Barbican or St Paul's tube. **Open** 10am-6pm daily. **Admission** free; suggested donation £3. **Credit** MC, V. **Map** p400 P5.
A five-year, £20m refurbishment came to completion in 2010 with the unveiling of a thrilling lower-ground-floor gallery that covers the city from 1666 to the present day. The new space features everything from an unexploded World War II bomb, suspended in a room where the understated and very moving testimony of ordinary Blitz survivors is screened, to clothes by the late Alexander McQueen. There are displays and brilliant interactives on poverty (an actual debtor's cell has been reconstructed, complete with graffiti), finance, shopping and 20th-century fashion, including a recreated Georgian pleasure garden, with mannequins that sport Philip Treacy masks and hats. Some displays are grand flourishes – the suspended installation that chatters London-related web trivia in the Sackler Hall, a printing press gushing changing newsheets – others ingeniously solve problems: games to engage the kids, glass cases in the floors to maximise display space.

EXPLORE

Clockmakers' Museum. *See p60.*

The museum's biggest obstacle had always been its location: the entrance is two floors above street level, hidden behind a dark and rather featureless brick wall. To solve this, a new space was created on the ground floor, allowing one key exhibit – the Lord Mayor's gold coach – to be seen from outside.

Upstairs, the chronological displays begin with 'London Before London', where artefacts include flint axes from 300,000 BC, found near Piccadilly, and the bones of an aurochs. 'Roman London' includes an impressive reconstructed dining room complete with mosaic floor. Windows overlook a sizeable fragment of the City wall, whose Roman foundations have clearly been built upon many times over the centuries. Sound effects and audiovisual displays illustrate the medieval, Elizabethan and Jacobean city, with particular focus on the plague and the Great Fire. *Photos p58.*
▶ *The museum has issued two excellent free apps: Streetmuseum and Streetmuseum Londinium. They offer archive images and information about historic sites near your current location.*

BANK & AROUND

Mansion House tube or Bank tube/DLR.

Above Bank station, seven streets come together to mark the symbolic heart of the Square Mile, ringed by some of the most important buildings in the City. Constructed from steely Portland stone, the Bank of England, the Royal Exchange and Mansion House form a stirring monument to the power of money: most decisions about the British economy are still made within this small precinct. Few places in London have quite the same sense of pomp and circumstance.

Easily the most dramatic building is the **Bank of England**, founded in 1694 to fund William III's war against the French. It's a fortress, with no accessible windows and just one public entrance (leading to the **Bank of England Museum**; *see p59*). The outer walls were designed in 1788 by Sir John Soane, whose own museum can be seen in Holborn (*see p66* **Sir John Soane's Museum**). Millions have been stolen from its depots elsewhere in London, but the bank itself has never been robbed. Today, it's responsible for printing the nation's banknotes and setting the base interest rate. On the south side of the junction is the Lord Mayor of London's official residence, **Mansion House** (7626 2500, www.cityoflondon.gov.uk, group visits by written application to Diary Office, Mansion House, Walbrook, EC4N 8BH, or by phone), an imposing neoclassical building constructed by George Dance in 1753. It's the only private residence in the country to have its own court and prison cells for unruly guests. Just behind Mansion House is the superbly elegant church of **St Stephen Walbrook**

(7626 9000, www.ststephenwalbrook.net; open 10am-4pm Mon-Fri), built by Wren in 1672. Its gleaming domed, coffered ceiling was borrowed from Wren's original design for St Paul's; other features include an incongruous modernist altar, sculpted by Sir Henry Moore and cruelly dubbed 'the camembert'. The Samaritans were founded here in the 1950s.

To the east of Mansion House is the **Royal Exchange**. It's the Parthenon-like former home of the London Stock Exchange, founded back in 1565 to facilitate the newly invented trade in stocks and shares with Antwerp. In 1972, the exchange shifted to offices on Threadneedle Street, thence to Paternoster Square in 2004; today, the Royal Exchange houses a posh champagne bar and some expensive fashion and gift shops. Flanking the Royal Exchange are statues of James Henry Greathead, who invented the machine that cut the tunnels for the London Underground, and Paul Reuter, who founded the Reuters news agency here in 1851.

The period grandeur is undermined by the monstrosity on the west side of the square, **No.1 Poultry**. The name fits: it's a turkey. A short walk down Queen Victoria Street is the most recent site of the Roman **Temple of Mithras**; further south, turn left on to Cannon

The Stones that Rolled

A pair of Roman monuments are on the move – again.

At the beginning of 2012, controversy erupted over a lump of limestone that property company Minerva wanted to move from its location at 111 Cannon Street. The snag was that this is the **London Stone**, possibly a Roman milestone, cited by Shakespeare and Blake, and first written of in 1188. One of its many legends insists that, should it be moved, the City will founder. In fact, it has already moved twice (1742, 1798), and was in 1962 put back in place when the current office replaced Blitz-damaged St Swithin's church. For now, it can still be touched through its grille.

By coincidence, a second development will end up moving the Roman **Temple of Mithras** back to where it was found, in a blaze of publicity, back in 1954. Builders had stumbled across the head of a young Roman god; archaeologists then uncovered a temple, dating from the AD 240s, to the bull cult of Mithras. What was left of that temple was plonked, in public view, on top of a car park. Now the Museum of London is re-investigating the remains, prior to them being reconstructed in the basement of a new office – exactly where they were first discovered.

EXPLORE

Museum of London. *See p55.*

Street, where you can see the **London Stone**. Surprisingly, there are plans afoot to move both of these unremarkable-looking ancient memorials; for more details, *see p57* **The Stones that Rolled**. Near Cannon Street Station, roughly opposite the London Stone, is the late Wren church of **St Michael Paternoster Royal** (7248 5202; open 9am-5pm Mon-Fri), the final resting place of Richard 'Dick' Whittington. Later transformed into a rags-to-riches pantomime hero, the real Dick Whittington was a wealthy merchant elected Lord Mayor of London four times between 1397 and 1420. The role of Dick Whittington's cat is less clear – many now believe that 'cat' was actually slang for a ship – but an excavation to find Whittington's tomb in 1949 did uncover a mummified medieval moggy. The happy pair are shown in the stained-glass windows.

Returning to Bank, stroll north along Prince's Street, beside the Bank of England's blind wall. Look right along Lothbury to find **St Margaret Lothbury** (7726 4878, www.stml.org.uk; open 7am-5.15pm Mon-Fri). The grand screen dividing the choir from the nave was designed by Wren himself; other works here by his favourite woodcarver, Grinling Gibbons, were recovered from various churches damaged in World War II. Lothbury also features a beautiful neo-Venetian building, now apartments, built by 19th-century architect Augustus Pugin, who worked with Charles Barry on the Houses of Parliament.

South-east of Bank on Lombard Street is Hawksmoor's striking, twin-spired church of **St Mary Woolnoth** (7626 9701; open 9.30am-4.30pm Mon-Fri), squeezed in between what were 17th-century banking houses. Only their gilded signboards now remain, a hanging heritage artfully maintained by the City's planners. The gilded grasshopper at 68 Lombard Street is the heraldic emblem of Sir Thomas Gresham, who founded the Royal Exchange and **Gresham College**.

Further east on Lombard Street is Wren's **St Edmund the King** (7621 1391, www.spiritualitycentre.org; open 10am-6pm Mon-Fri), which now houses a centre for modern spirituality. Other significant churches in the area include Wren's handsome red-brick **St Mary Abchurch**, off Abchurch Lane, and **St Clement**, on Clement's Lane, immortalised in the nursery rhyme 'Oranges and Lemons'. Over on Cornhill are two more Wren churches: **St Peter-upon-Cornhill**, mentioned by Dickens in *Our Mutual Friend*, and **St Michael Cornhill**, which contains a bizarre statue of a pelican feeding its young with pieces of its own body – a medieval symbol for the Eucharist, it was sculpted by someone who had plainly never seen a pelican.

North-west of the Bank of England is the **Guildhall**, the City of London headquarters. 'Guildhall' can either describe the original banqueting hall or the cluster of buildings around it, of which the **Guildhall Art Gallery**, the **Clockmakers' Museum & Library** (for all three, *see p60*) and the church of **St Lawrence Jewry** (7600 9478, www.stlawrencejewry.org.uk; open 8am-5pm Mon-Fri), opposite the hall, are also open to the public. St Lawrence is another restored Wren, with an impressive gilt ceiling. Within, you can hear the renowned Klais organ at lunchtime organ recitals (usually from 1pm Tue).

Glance north along Wood Street to see the isolated tower of **St Alban**, built by Wren in 1685 but ruined in World War II and now an eccentric private home. At the end of the street is **St Anne & St Agnes** (7606 4986; open 10.30am-5pm Mon-Fri, Sun), laid out in the form of a Greek cross. Recitals take place here on weekday lunchtimes.

FREE Bank of England Museum

Entrance on Bartholomew Lane, EC2R 8AH (7601 5545, www.bankofengland.co.uk/museum). Bank tube/DLR. **Open** 10am-5pm Mon-Fri. **Admission** free. **No credit cards**. **Map** p403 Q6. Housed inside the former Stock Offices of the Bank of England, this engaging and surprisingly lively museum explores the history of the national bank. As well as ancient coins and original artwork for British banknotes, the museum offers a rare chance to lift nearly 30lbs of gold bar (you reach into a secure box, closely monitored by CCTV). One exhibit looks at the life of Kenneth Grahame, author of *The Wind in the Willows* and a long-term employee of the bank. Child-friendly exhibitions take place in the museum lobby.

Guildhall.

EXPLORE

Tower Bridge. *See p64.*

FREE Clockmakers' Museum & Guildhall Library

Aldermanbury, EC2V 7HH (Guildhall Library 7332 1868, www.clockmakers.org). St Paul's tube or Bank tube/DLR. **Open** 9.30am-4.45pm Mon-Sat. **Admission** free. **No credit cards. Map** p402 P6.

Hundreds of clocks and watches are displayed in this single-room museum, from the egg-sized Elizabethan pocket watches to marine chronometers via a 'fuse for a nuclear device'. Highlights include Marine Chronometer H5, built by John Harrison (1693-1776) to solve the problem of longitude, and the plain Smith's Imperial wristwatch worn by Sir Edmund Hillary on the first (Rolex-sponsored) ascent of Everest. Just down the corridor, the library has books, manuscripts and prints relating to the history of London – original historic works can be requested for browsing (bring ID), but much of the archive is now at the London Metropolitan Archives in Clerkenwell (www.cityoflondon.gov.uk/lma). *Photo p56.*

FREE Guildhall

Gresham Street, EC2P 2EJ (7606 3030, www.guildhall.cityoflondon.gov.uk). St Paul's tube or Bank tube/DLR. **Open** *May-Sept* 10am-5pm daily. *Oct-Apr* 10am-4.30pm Mon-Sat. Closes for functions; phone ahead. **Admission** free. **No credit cards. Map** p402 P6.

The City of London and its progenitors have been holding grand ceremonial dinners in this hall for eight centuries. Memorials to national heroes line the walls, shields of the 100 livery companies grace the ceiling, and every Lord Mayor since 1189 gets a namecheck on the windows. Many famous trials have taken place here, including the treason trial of 16-year-old Lady Jane Grey, 'the nine days' queen', in 1553. Above the entrance to the Guildhall are statues of Gog and Magog. Born of the union of demons and exiled Roman princesses, these two mythical giants are said to protect the City of London. The current statues replaced 18th-century forebears that were destroyed during the Blitz.

★ Guildhall Art Gallery

Guildhall Yard, off Gresham Street, EC2P 2EJ (7332 3700, www.guildhall-art-gallery.org.uk). St Paul's tube or Bank tube/DLR. **Open** 10am-5pm Mon-Sat; noon-4pm Sun. **Admission** free. *Temporary exhibitions £5; £3 reductions; free under-16s.* **Credit** MC, V. **Map** p402 P6.

The City of London's gallery contains numerous dull or unimpressive portraits of royalty and long-gone mayors, but also some wonderful surprises, including a brilliant Constable, some superbly camp Pre-Raphaelite works (Clytemnestra looks mighty riled) and a number of absorbing paintings of London, from moving depictions of war and melancholy working streets to the likes of the grandiloquent (and never-enacted) George Dance plan for a new London Bridge. The collection's centrepiece is the massive *Siege of Gibraltar* by John Copley, which spans two entire storeys of the purpose-built gallery. A sub-basement contains the scant remains of London's 6,000-seater Roman amphitheatre, built around AD 70; *Tron*-like figures and crowd sound effects give a quaint inkling of scale.

MONUMENT & THE TOWER OF LONDON

Aldgate, Monument or Tower Hill tube, Liverpool Street tube/rail, or Tower Gateway DLR.

From Bank, King William Street runs south-east towards London Bridge, passing the small square containing the **Monument** (*see p63*). South on Lower Thames Street is the moody-looking church of **St Magnus the Martyr** (*see p64*); nearby are several relics from the days when this area was a busy port, including the old Customs House and **Billingsgate Market**, London's main fish market until 1982 (when it was relocated to east London).

North of the Monument along Gracechurch Street is the atmospheric **Leadenhall Market,** constructed in 1881 by Horace Jones (who also built the market at Smithfield; *see p68*). The vaulted roof was restored to its original Victorian finery in 1991 and City workers come here in droves to lunch at the pubs, cafés and restaurants, including the historic Lamb Tavern. Fantasy fans may recognise the market as Diagon Alley in *Harry Potter & the Philosopher's Stone*.

Behind the market is Lord Rogers's high-tech **Lloyd's of London** building, constructed in 1986, with all its ducts, vents, stairwells and lift shafts on the outside, like an oil rig dumped in the heart of the City. Rogers has a new building – 122 Leadenhall (the **Cheesegrater**) – taking shape directly opposite, perhaps reaching completion in 2014. The original Lloyd's Register of Shipping, decorated with evocative bas-reliefs of sea monsters and nautical scenes, is on Fenchurch Street, where the next in the sequence of distinctive new City skyscrapers is emerging: Rafael Viñoly's 20 Fenchurch Street (www.20fenchurchstreet.co.uk), nicknamed the **Walkie Talkie** due to its distinctive top-heavy shape, already very visible despite only coming due for completion in 2014. South of Fenchurch Street, on Eastcheap (derived from the Old English *ceap* meaning 'barter'), is Wren's **St Margaret Pattens**, with an original 17th-century interior.

Several more of the City's tallest buildings are nearby. To the north, the ugly and rather dated **Tower 42** (25 Old Broad Street) was the tallest building in Britain until the construction of One Canada Square (*see p129*) in Docklands in 1990. And topped out at 755 feet (including a radio mast), **Heron Tower** (110 Bishopsgate, www.herontower.com) became the City's tallest building at the end of 2009. Its 46 storeys include Sushisamba restaurant and bar, a bit under 600 feet up on the 38th and 39th floors – complete with outdoor terraces, and reached by an external, glass-sided lift. A rival, 945-foot monster called the **Pinnacle** has been begun on Bishopsgate – currently stalled, work may start on it again in early 2013. Also on Bishopsgate, behind Tower 42, is **Gibson Hall**, ostentatious former offices of the National Provincial Bank of England.

A block south, St Mary Axe is an insignificant street named after a vanished church that is said to have contained an axe used by Attila the Hun to behead English virgins. It is now known for Lord Foster's **30 St Mary Axe**, arguably London's finest modern building. The building is known as 'the Gherkin' (and, occasionally, more suggestive nicknames) for reasons that are obvious. On curved stone benches either side of 30 St Mary Axe are inscribed the 20 lines of Scottish poet Ian Hamilton Finlay's 'Arcadian Dream

Garden', a curious counterpart to Lord Foster's building. Nearby are two medieval churches that survived the Great Fire: **St Helen's Bishopsgate** (*see p64*) and **St Andrew Undershaft** (*see below* **Inside Track**).

The north end of St Mary Axe intersects with two interesting streets. The more northerly, Houndsditch, is where Londoners threw dead dogs and other rubbish in medieval times – the ditch ran outside the London Wall (*see p54*), dividing the City from the East End. The southerly one is Bevis Marks, home to the superbly preserved **Bevis Marks Synagogue** (7626 1274; open 10.30am-2pm Mon, Wed, Thur; 10.30am-1pm Tue, Fri; 10.30am-12.30pm Sun), founded in 1701 by Sephardic Jews fleeing the Spanish Inquisition. Services are still held in Portuguese as well as Hebrew. On neighbouring Heneage Lane is the classy kosher **Bevis Marks Restaurant** (no.4, 7247 5474, www.bevismarkstherestaurant.com).

South along Bevis Marks are **St Botolph's-without-Aldgate** (*see p63*) and the tiny stone church of **St Katharine Cree** (7283 5733; open 9.30am-4pm Mon-Fri) on Leadenhall Street, one of only eight churches to survive the Great Fire. Inside is a memorial to Sir Nicholas Throckmorton, Queen Elizabeth I's ambassador to France, who was imprisoned for treason on numerous occasions, despite – or perhaps because of – his friendship with the temperamental queen. Just north of St Katharine is Mitre Square, site of the fourth Jack the Ripper murder.

Further south, towards the Tower of London, streets and alleys have evocative names: Crutched Friars, Savage Gardens, Pepys Street and the like. The famous diarist lived in nearby Seething Lane and observed the Great Fire of London from **All Hallows by the Tower** (*see below*). Pepys is buried in the church of **St Olave** (www.sanctuaryinthecity.net) on Hart Street, nicknamed 'St Ghastly Grim' by Dickens due to the skulls above the entrance.

Marking the eastern edge of the City, the **Tower of London** (*see p64*) was the palace of the medieval kings and queens of England.

INSIDE TRACK
THE WRITE STUFF

In the shadow of the Gherkin, **St Andrew Undershaft** has a statue of John Stow, who wrote London's first guidebook, the *Survey of London* in 1598. In a ceremony every 5 April, the Lord Mayor places a new quill in the statue's hand; the old quill is given to the child who has written the best essay on London.

EXPLORE

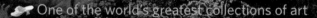

Home to the Crown Jewels and the Royal Armoury, it's one of Britain's best-loved tourist attractions and, accordingly, is mobbed by visitors seven days a week. Overlooking the Tower from the north, beside the tube station, **Trinity Square Gardens** are a humbling memorial to the tens of thousands of merchant seamen killed in the two World Wars, and across the road is a small square in which London's druids celebrate each spring equinox with an elaborate ceremony. Just beyond is one of the City's finest Edwardian buildings: the former **Port of London HQ** at 10 Trinity Square, with a huge neoclassical façade and gigantic statues symbolising Commerce, Navigation, Export, Produce and Father Thames. Plans are afoot to make this into a superluxury hotel, although not in the immediate future. Next door is **Trinity House**, the home of the General Lighthouse Authority, founded by Henry VIII for the upkeep of shipping beacons along the river.

At the south-east corner of the Tower is **Tower Bridge** (*see p64*), built in 1894 and still London's most distinctive bridge. Used as a navigation aid by German bombers, it escaped the firestorm of the Blitz. East across Bridge Approach is **St Katharine Docks**, the first London docks to be formally closed. The restaurants around the marina, slightly hidden behind modern office blocks, offer more dignified dining than those around the Tower.

Tower of London. *See p64.*

FREE **All Hallows by the Tower**
Byward Street, EC3R 5BJ (7481 2928, www. ahbtt.org.uk). Tower Hill tube or Tower Gateway DLR. **Open** 8am-5pm Mon-Fri; 10am-5pm Sat, Sun. *Tours* phone for details; donation requested. **Admission** free; donations appreciated. **No credit cards. Map** p403 R7.
Often described as London's oldest church, All Hallows is built on the foundations of a seventh-century Saxon church. Much of what survives today was reconstructed after World War II, but several Saxon details can be seen in the main hall, where the Knights Templar were tried by Edward II in 1314. The undercroft contains a museum with Roman and Saxon relics and a Crusader altar. William Penn, founder of Pennsylvania, was baptised here in 1644.

★ **Monument**
Monument Street, EC3R 8AH (7626 2717, www.themonument.info). Monument tube. **Open** 9.30am-5pm daily. **Admission** £3; £1.50-£2 reductions; free under-5s. **No credit cards. Map** p403 Q7.
One of 17th-century London's most important landmarks, the Monument is a magnificent Portland stone column, topped by a landmark golden orb with more than 30,000 fiery leaves of gold – it looks decidedly like the head of a thistle. The Monument was designed by Sir Christopher Wren and his (often overlooked) associate Robert Hooke as a memorial to the Great Fire. The world's tallest free-standing stone column, it measures 202ft from the ground to the tip of its golden flames, exactly the distance east to Farriner's bakery in Pudding Lane, where the fire is supposed to have begun on 2 September 1666. The viewing platform is surrounded by a lightweight mesh cage, but the views are great – you have to walk 311 steps up the internal spiral staircase to enjoy them, though. At least everyone who makes it to the top gets a certificate.

FREE **St Botolph's-without-Aldgate**
Aldgate High Street, EC3N 1AB (7283 1670, www.stbotolphs.org.uk). Aldgate tube. **Open** 10am-2pm Mon, Wed; 10am-3pm Tue, Thur, Fri; 10am-12.30pm Sun. *Eucharist* 1.05pm Tue, Thur; 10.30am Sun. **Admission** free; donations appreciated. **No credit cards. Map** p403 R6.
The oldest of three churches of St Botolph in the City, this handsome monument was built at the gates of Roman London as a homage to the patron saint of travellers. The building was reconstructed by George Dance in 1744 and a beautiful ornamental ceiling was added in the 19th century by John Francis Bentley, who also created Westminster Cathedral.

FREE **St Ethelburga Centre for Reconciliation & Peace**
78 Bishopsgate, EC2N 4AG (7496 1610, www. stethelburgas.org). Bank tube/DLR or Liverpool Street tube/rail. **Open** 11am-3pm Fri. **Admission** free; donations appreciated. **No credit cards. Map** p403 R6.
Built around 1390, the tiny church of St Ethelburga was reduced to rubble by an IRA bomb in 1993 and

rebuilt as a centre for peace and reconciliation. Behind the chapel is a Bedouin tent where events are held to promote dialogue between the faiths (phone or check the website for details), an increasingly heated issue in modern Britain. Lunchtime meditation classes are held here on Thursdays.

FREE St Helen's Bishopsgate

Great St Helen's, off Bishopsgate, EC3A 6AT (7283 2231, www.st-helens.org.uk). Liverpool Street tube/rail or Bank tube/DLR. **Open** 9.30am-12.30pm Mon-Fri, afternoons by appointment only. **Admission** free.
No credit cards. Map p403 R6.

Founded in 1210, St Helen's Bishopsgate is actually two churches knocked into one, which explains its unusual shape. The church survived the Great Fire and the Blitz, but was partly wrecked by IRA bombs in 1992 and 1993. The hugely impressive 16th- and 17th-century memorials inside include the grave of Thomas Gresham, founder of the Royal Exchange (*see p57*).

FREE St Magnus the Martyr

Lower Thames Street, EC3R 6DN (7626 4481, www.stmagnusmartyr.org.uk). Monument tube. **Open** 10am-4pm Tue-Fri; 10am-1pm Sun. *Mass* 12.30pm Tue, Thur, Fri; 11am Sun. **Admission** free; donations appreciated. **No credit cards. Map** p403 Q7.

Downhill from the Monument, this looming Wren church marked the entrance to the original London Bridge. There's a scale model of the old bridge inside the church, and the porch has a timber from the original version. There's also a statue of axe-wielding St Magnus, the 12th-century Earl of Orkney. The church is mentioned at one of the climaxes of TS Eliot's *The Waste Land*: 'Where the walls/Of Magnus Martyr hold/Inexplicable splendour of Ionian white and gold.' ▶ *St Mary Woolnoth (see p59) is another star of* The Waste Land: *keeping 'the hours/With a dead sound on the final stroke of nine'.*

Tower Bridge Exhibition

Tower Bridge, SE1 2UP (7403 3761, www.tower bridge.org.uk). Tower Hill tube or Tower Gateway DLR. **Open** Apr-Sept 10am-6.30pm daily. Oct-Mar 9.30am-6pm daily. **Admission** £8; £3.40-£5.60 reductions; £12.50-£18 family; free under-5s.
Credit AmEx, MC, V. **Map** p403 R8.

Opened in 1894, this is the 'London Bridge' that wasn't sold to America. Originally powered by steam, the drawbridge is now opened by electric rams when big ships need to venture upstream (check when the bridge is next due to be raised on the bridge's website or follow the feed on Twitter). The bridge is looking resplendent after a three-year restoration, completed in 2011. An entertaining exhibition on its history is displayed in the old steam-rooms and the west walkway, which provides a crow's-nest view along the Thames. *Photo p60.*

★ Tower of London

Tower Hill, EC3N 4AB (0844 482 7777, www. hrp.org.uk). Tower Hill tube or Tower Gateway DLR. **Open** Mar-Oct 10am-5.30pm Mon, Sun; 9am-5.30pm Tue-Sat. Nov-Feb 10am-4.30pm Mon, Sun; 9am-4.30pm Tue-Sat. **Admission** £20.90; £10.45-£17.60; £55 family; free under-5s. **Credit** AmEx, MC, V. **Map** p403 R8.

If you haven't been to the Tower of London before, you should go now. Despite the exhausting crowds and long climbs up barely accessible, narrow stairways, this is one of Britain's finest historical attractions. Who would not be fascinated by a close-up look at the crown of Queen Victoria or the armour (and prodigious codpiece) of King Henry VIII? The buildings of the Tower span 900 years of – mostly violent – history, and the bastions and battlements house a series of interactive displays on the lives of British monarchs, and the often excruciatingly painful deaths of traitors. There's easily enough to do here to fill a whole day, which makes the steep entry price pretty good value, and it's worth joining one of the highly recommended and entertaining free tours led by the Yeoman Warders (or Beefeaters).

Make the Crown Jewels your first stop, and as early in the day as you possibly can: if you wait until you've pottered around a few other things the queues are usually immense. Beyond satisfyingly solid vault doors, you get to glide along a set of travelators (each branded with the Queen's official 'EIIR' badge) past such treasures of state as the Monarch's Sceptre, mounted with the Cullinan I diamond, and the Imperial State Crown, which is worn by the Queen each year for the opening of Parliament.

The other big draw is the Royal Armoury in the central White Tower, with its swords, armour, pole-axes, halberds, morning stars (spiky maces) and other gruesome tools for separating human beings from their body parts. Kids are entertained by swordsmanship games, coin-minting activities and even a child-sized longbow. The garderobes (medieval toilets) also seem to appeal.

Back outside, Tower Green – where executions of prisoners of noble birth were carried out, continuing until 1941 – is marked by a poem and a stiff glass pillow, sculpted by poet and artist Brian Catling. Overlooking the green, Beauchamp Tower, dating to 1280, has an upper floor full of intriguing graffiti by the prisoners who were held here (including Anne Boleyn, Rudolf Hess and the Krays).

Towards the entrance, the 13th-century Bloody Tower is another must-see that gets overwhelmed by numbers later in the day. The ground floor is a reconstruction of Sir Walter Raleigh's study, the upper floor details the fate of the Princes in the Tower. In the riverside wall is the unexpectedly beautiful Medieval Palace, with its reconstructed bedroom and throne room, and spectacularly complex stained glass in the private chapel. The whole palace is deliciously cool if you've been struggling round on a hot summer's day. *Photo p63.*

EXPLORE

Holborn & Clerkenwell

Home to 18th-century scholar-eccentrics and medieval friars.

Along Fleet Street and Holborn, the West End dives into the City of London and heads for St Paul's Cathedral. The newspapers that once called **Fleet Street** home have long since jumped ship for Docklands and Kensington, but some of their grand old offices remain, flanked by the collegiate quiet of the barristers' ancient **Inns of Court**.

Meanwhile, across Farringdon Road, the boom years have transmogrified **Clerkenwell** from an earnest and shabby suburb of Grub Street into a playground for afterwork City boys, bambi-eyed clubbers and design-led media businesses. And in one of London's typically startling juxtapositions, the butchers of **Smithfield Market** still ply their bleeding trade in the thick of the party.

Map p397 & p400   **Hotels** pp235-236
Pubs & bars   **Restaurants &**
pp189-190   **cafés** pp159-161

HOLBORN

Holborn tube.

A sharp left turn out of Holborn tube and then another left leads into the unexpectedly lovely **Lincoln's Inn Fields**. Surely London's largest square (indeed, it's more of a park), it's blessed with gnarled oaks casting dappled shade over a tired bandstand. On the south side of the square, the neoclassical façade of the Royal College of Surgeons hides the **Hunterian Museum**; facing it from the north is the magical **Sir John Soane's Museum** (for both, *see p66*).

East of the square lies **Lincoln's Inn** (7405 1393, www.lincolnsinn.org.uk), one of the city's four Inns of Court. Its grounds are open to the public, ogling an odd mix of Gothic, Tudor and Palladian buildings. On nearby Portsmouth Street lies the **Old Curiosity Shop** (nos.13-14, WC2A 2ES, 7405 9891, www.curiosityuk.com), its timbers apparently known to Charles Dickens, but now selling Daita Kimura's decidedly modern shoes. Nearby, Gray's Inn Road runs north alongside the second Inn of Court.

The sculpted gardens at **Gray's Inn** (7458 7800, www.graysinn.org.uk), dating to 1606, are open on weekdays, noon-2.30pm.

Opened in 1876 on Chancery Lane as a series of strongrooms in which the upper classes could secure their valuables, the **London Silver Vaults** (7242 3844, www.thesilvervaults.com) are now a hive of dealers buying, selling and repairing silverware. There are also glittering displays on **Hatton Garden**, the city's jewellery and diamond centre. It's no distance to walk but a million miles in nature from the Cockney fruit stalls and sock merchants of the market on **Leather Lane** (10am-2.30pm Mon-Fri).

Further on is **Ely Place**, its postcode absent from the street sign as a result of it technically falling under the jurisdiction of Cambridgeshire. The church garden of ancient **St Etheldreda** (*see p66*) produced strawberries so delicious that they made the pages of Shakespeare's *Richard III*; a celebratory Strawberrie Fayre is still held on the street each June. The 16th-century **Ye Olde Mitre** (1 Ely Court, EC1N 6SJ, 7405 4751, http:// yeoldemitreholburn.co.uk) remains an atmospheric pub, hidden down a barely marked alley.

EXPLORE

Exmouth Market.

FREE Hunterian Museum

Royal College of Surgeons, 35-43 Lincoln's Inn Fields, WC2A 3PE (7869 6560, www.rcseng. ac.uk/museums). Holborn tube. **Open** 10am-5pm Tue-Sat. **Admission** free. **No credit cards. Map** p397 M6.

The collection of medical specimens once held by John Hunter (1728-93), physician to King George III, can be viewed in this museum. The sparkling glass cabinets of the main room offset the goriness of the exhibits, which include Charles Babbage's brain and Winston Churchill's dentures, as well as shelf after shelf of diligently classified pickled body parts. The upper floor holds a brutal account of surgical techniques. Notably interesting kids' activities have included demonstrations by a 'barber surgeon'.

FREE St Etheldreda

14 Ely Place, EC1N 6RY (7405 1061, www. stetheldreda.com). Chancery Lane tube. **Open** 8am-5pm Mon-Sat; 8am-12.30pm Sun. **Admission** free; donations appreciated. **No credit cards. Map** p400 N5.

Dedicated to the saintly seventh-century Queen of Northumbria, this is Britain's oldest Catholic church and London's only surviving example of 13th-century Gothic architecture; it was saved from the Great Fire by a change in the wind. The crypt is darkly atmospheric, untouched by traffic noise, and the stained glass (actually from the 1960s) is stunning.

★ FREE Sir John Soane's Museum

13 Lincoln's Inn Fields, WC2A 3BP (7405 2107, www.soane.org). Holborn tube. **Open** 10am-5pm Tue-Sat; 10am-5pm, 6-9pm 1st Tue of mth. *Tours* 11am Sat. **Admission** free; donations appreciated. *Tours* £5; free reductions. **Credit** (shop) MC, V. **Map** p397 M5.

When he wasn't designing notable buildings (among them the original Bank of England), Sir John Soane (1753-1837) obsessively collected art, furniture and architectural ornamentation. In the 19th century, he turned his house into a museum to which, he said, 'amateurs and students' should have access. The result is this perfectly amazing place.

Much of the museum's appeal derives from the domestic setting. The modest rooms were modified by Soane with ingenious devices to channel and direct daylight, and to expand space, including walls that open out like cabinets to display some of his many paintings (Canaletto, Turner, Hogarth). The Breakfast Room has a beautiful domed ceiling, inset with convex mirrors. The extraordinary Monument Court contains a sarcophagus of alabaster, so fine that it's almost translucent, that was carved for the pharaoh Seti I (1291-78 BC) and discovered in his tomb in Egypt's Valley of the Kings. There are also numerous examples of Soane's eccentricity, not least the cell for his imaginary monk 'Padre Giovanni'. *See p67* **Happy Birthday, Sir John's House!**

CLERKENWELL & FARRINGDON

Farringdon tube/rail.

Few places encapsulate London's capacity for reinvention quite like Clerkenwell, an erstwhile religious centre that takes its name from the parish clerks who once performed Biblical mystery plays on its streets. The most lasting holy legacy is that of the 11th-century knights of the **Order of St John**; the remains of their priory can still be seen at St John's Gate, a crenellated gatehouse that dates from 1504 and is home to the **Museum & Library of the Order of St John** (*see p68*).

By the 17th century, this was a fashionable locale, but the Industrial Revolution soon buried it under warehouses and factories. Printing houses were established, and the district gained a reputation as a safe haven for radicals, from 16th-century Lollards to 19th-century Chartists. In 1903, Lenin is believed to have met Stalin for a drink in what is now the **Crown Tavern** (43 Clerkenwell Green, 7253 4973, www.the crowntavernec1.co.uk), one year after moving the publication of *Iskra* to neighbouring 37A (now the **Marx Memorial Library**; 7253 1485, www.marx-memorial-library.org).

Industrial dereliction and decay were the theme until property development in the 1980s and '90s turned Clerkenwell into a desirable area. The process was aided by a slew of artfully distressed gastropubs (following the lead of the **Eagle**; *see p160*), and the food stalls, fashion boutiques, restaurants and bars along the colourful strip of **Exmouth Market**.

Happy Birthday, Sir John's House!

The wonderful Sir John Soane's Museum gets a 200th anniversary makeover.

A favourite of many locals, the little **Sir John Soane's Museum** (*see p66*) has changed status over the years from a treasured secret to something approaching a must-visit. These days you can expect queues at the front door of this eccentric house of curiosities – more than 93,000 people visit each year.

In July 2012, the 200th anniversary of the building of the house was marked by the completion of the first phase of an ambitious £7m restoration. A former staff lavatory had returned to its original function as the Tivoli Recess – the city's first gallery of contemporary sculpture, with a stained-glass window and skylights with plaster sunbursts. Further stained glass illuminates the Shakespeare Recess, with William's likeness from his Stratford-upon-Avon tomb set there.

Less exciting, but arguably as important, is the use to which the next-door building (no.12) is being put. The old entrance to the house – a narrow corridor where all those visitors had to sign in, buy their guides and postcards, and leave coats and bags with the volunteers – was far too cramped. Now you leave your clutter at no.12, before strolling into the main house untrammelled, ready to be enthralled.

Once you've toured the treasures, seen the ingenious fold-out walls of paintings and admired the clever lighting effects and archaeological oddments, you exit through no.12, past a new shop and an Exhibition Room that gives details on Soane and the objects you've just seen. (Soane wasn't much given to labelling and the museum is obliged, by the 1833 Act of Parliament that set up the museum, to follow his lead.)

Over the years up to 2014, the entire second floor will open to the public – for the first time since his death in 1837. Working from watercolour paintings done in around 1825, the museum will recreate his bedroom, Model Room (containing 80 fine architectural models), the Oratory (a memorial to his dead wife, using what was already at the time antiquarian stained glass) and the mirrored bookshelves of the Book Passage. Most typical of all will be one small feature of the Ante-Room: once restored, this space full of sculptures and plastercasts will also have a hole in the floor, through which Soane's modern-day guests will be able to peer into a catacomb full of funerary urns from ancient Rome.

EXPLORE

Smithfield Market.

CLOTH
COURT
EC1

FREE Islington Museum

245 St John Street, Finsbury, EC1V 4NB (7527 3235, www.islington.gov.uk). Angel tube. **Open** 10am-5pm Mon, Tue, Thur-Sat. **Admission** free. **No credit cards. Map** p400 O3.

The Islington Museum covers local history and the political and ethical credentials of the borough, exemplified by local residents such as reformist preacher John Wesley, playwright Joe Orton and eminent feminist Mary Wollstonecraft.

FREE Museum of the Order of St John

St John's Gate, St John's Lane, Clerkenwell, EC1M 4DA (7324 4005, www.museumstjohn. org.uk). Farringdon tube/rail. **Open** 10am-5pm Mon-Sat. *Tours* 11am, 2.30pm Tue, Fri, Sat. **Admission** free. *Tours* free. Suggested donation £5; £4 reductions. **Credit** MC, V. **Map** p400 O4.

Now best known for its ambulance service, the Order of St John's roots lie in Christian medical practices from the Crusades of the 11th to 13th centuries. Artefacts related to the Order of Hospitaller Knights, from Jerusalem, Malta and the Ottoman Empire, are displayed; there's a separate collection relating to the ambulance service. A major refurbishment has reorganised the galleries in the Tudor gatehouse and, across St John's Square, opened the Priory Church (11am-4pm Mon-Sat), its secluded garden, and the pleasingly gloomy 12th-century crypt to the public.

SMITHFIELD

Farringdon tube/rail.

Smithfield Market provides a colourful, not to say visceral, link to an age when the quality of British beef was a symbol of national virility and good humour. Meat has been traded here for a millennium; the current market, which was designed by Horace Jones, opened in 1868, though it's since been altered (in part out of necessity, thanks to World War II bombs) and seems under almost constant threat of redevelopment, usually with associated promises to maintain historic façades. The meat trucks start arriving around 11pm; early risers will find traders setting up stalls at first light.

The meat traders are joined at night these days by revellers settling in for dinner at vast **Smiths of Smithfield** (67-77 Charterhouse Street, EC1M 6HJ, 7251 7950, www.smiths ofsmithfield.co.uk) or nearby **St John** (*see p161*), tucking into a glass or two at **Vinoteca** (*see p190*) or taking to the dancefloor at superclub **Fabric** (*see p281*). For a little peace and quiet, stroll by the **Charterhouse**. This Carthusian monastery, founded in 1370, is now Anglican almshouses that retain the original 14th-century chapel and a 17th-century library. It's right beside the **Malmaison** (*see p235*).

Bloomsbury & King's Cross

Culture – global, intellectual and literary bohemian – is celebrated here.

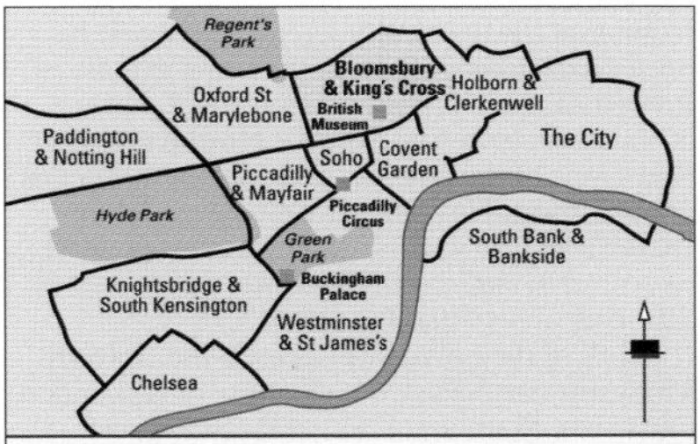

London's neighbourhoods north of Oxford Street are bookish and bohemian. **Bloomsbury** is best known as the home of the **British Museum** (*see p70*), but the presence of University College London (UCL) also helps lend the area a youthful, if studious, tone. The unofficial heart of the area is the redeveloped **Brunswick Centre** and the buzzing network of surrounding streets.

Next door to the west, **Fitzrovia** is a favourite source of stories for London nostalgists, but those days of postwar spivs and never-knowingly-sober poets have almost vanished beneath a tide of new media offices. At least they keep the pubs lively and the quality of the restaurants high. A recent influx of private galleries suggest that the area's artistic DNA might yet run into a new generation.

To the north of Bloomsbury, the legendarily seedy **King's Cross** may be going the way of formerly raffish Fitzrovia. The arrival of the **British Library** (*see p73*) and the rebirth of **St Pancras Station** (*see p73*) as an international rail hub led the redevelopment of an area formerly notorious for drugs and fleshpots into a destination and des-res. As **King's Cross Central** (*see p71* **Hip to Be a Square**) nears completion, the reality behind the developers' dream of a new residential neighbourhood, throbbing with students and tourists, can begin to be tested.

| Map pp396-397 | Hotels pp237-239 |
| Pubs & bars pp190-192 | Restaurants & cafés pp161-162 |

EXPLORE

BLOOMSBURY

Euston Square, Holborn, Russell Square or Tottenham Court Road tube.

Bloomsbury's florid name is, prosaically, taken from 'Blemondisberi' – the manor ('bury') of William Blemond, who acquired the area in the 13th century. It remained rural until the 1660s, when the fourth Earl of Southampton built Bloomsbury Square around his house. The Southamptons intermarried with the Russells, the Dukes of Bedford; together, they developed the area as one of London's first planned suburbs.

Over the next two centuries, the group built a series of grand squares. **Bedford Square** (1775-80) is London's only complete Georgian square (regrettably, its central garden is usually closed to the public); huge **Russell Square** has been restored as a public park with a popular café. To the east, the cantilevered postwar **Brunswick Centre** is full of shops, flats, restaurants and a cinema. The nearby streets, particularly **Marchmont Street**, are some of the more characterful in the West End.

Bloomsbury's charm is the sum of its parts, best experienced on a meander through its bookshops (many on **Great Russell Street**)

EXPLORE

and pubs. The blue plaques are a *Who's Who* of literary modernists – TS Eliot, Virginia Woolf, WB Yeats – with a few interlopers from more distant history: Edgar Allan Poe (83 Southampton Row), Anthony Trollope (6 Store Street) and, of course, Dickens (48 Doughty Street; *see p71* **Charles Dickens Museum**).

On Bloomsbury's western border, Malet Street, Gordon Street and Gower Street are dominated by the **University of London**. The most notable building is Gower Street's University College, founded in 1826. Inside is the 'autoicon' of utilitarian philosopher and founder of the university Jeremy Bentham: his preserved cadaver, fully clothed, sits in a glass-fronted cabinet. The university's main library is housed in towering **Senate House** on Malet Street, one of the city's most imposing examples of monumental art deco. It was the model for Orwell's Ministry of Truth in *1984* – but don't be scared to step inside: the lower floors and little café are open to the public.

South of the university sprawls the **British Museum** (*see below*), the must-see of all London must-sees. Running off Great Russell Street, where you'll find the museum's main entrance, are three attractive parallel streets (Coptic, Museum and Bury) and, nearby, the **Cartoon Museum** (*see below*); also close by, Bloomsbury Way is home to Hawksmoor's restored **St George's Bloomsbury** (*see p72*). Across from here, **Sicilian Avenue** is a fancy-pants, Italianate, pedestrian precinct of colonnaded shops – take it in over a fine ale and beer fodder at the Holborn Whippet (3137 9937, www.holbornwhippet.com).

North-east of the British Museum, **Lamb's Conduit Street** is a convivial neighbourhood lined with interesting shops. At the north end of the street is **Coram's Fields** (*see p267*), a delightful children's park on the grounds of the former Thomas Coram's Foundling Hospital. Coram's legacy is commemorated in the beautiful **Foundling Museum** (*see p71*).

★ FREE British Museum

Great Russell Street, WC1B 3DG (7323 8299, www.britishmuseum.org). Russell Square or Tottenham Court Road tube. **Open** *Galleries* 10am-5.30pm Mon-Thur, Sat, Sun; 10am-8.30pm Fri. *Great Court* 9am-6pm Mon-Thur, Sat, Sun; 9am-8.30pm Fri. *Multimedia guides* 10am-4.30pm Thur, Sat, Sun; 10am-7.30pm Fri. *Eye Opener tours* (40mins) phone for details. **Admission** free; donations appreciated. *Temporary exhibitions* prices vary. *Multimedia guides* £5; £3.50-£4.50 reductions. *Eye Opener tours* free. **Credit** (shop) AmEx, DC, MC, V. **Map** p397 K5.

Officially the country's most popular tourist attraction, the British Museum opened to the public in 1759 in Montagu House, which then occupied this site. The current building is a neoclassical marvel built in 1847 by Robert Smirke, one of the pioneers of the Greek Revival style. The most high-profile addition since then was Lord Foster's popular if rather murky glass-roofed Great Court, open since 2000 and now claimed to be 'the largest covered public square in Europe'. This £100m landmark surrounds the domed Reading Room (used by the British Library until its move to King's Cross; *see p73*), where Marx, Lenin, Dickens, Darwin, Hardy and Yeats once worked.

Star exhibits include ancient Egyptian artefacts – the Rosetta Stone on the ground floor (with a barely noticed, perfect replica in the King's Library), mummies upstairs – and Greek antiquities, including the marble friezes from the Parthenon known as the Elgin Marbles. The Celts gallery upstairs has Lindow Man, killed in 300 BC and so well preserved in peat you can see his beard, while the Wellcome Gallery of Ethnography holds an Easter Island statue and regalia collected during Captain Cook's travels. The King's Library provides a calming home to a permanent exhibition that is entitled 'Enlightenment: Discovering the World in the 18th Century', a 5,000-piece collection devoted to the extraordinary formative period of the museum. The remit covers archaeology, science and the natural world; the objects displayed range from Indonesian puppets to a beautiful orrery.

You won't be able to see everything in one day, so buy a souvenir guide and pick out the showstoppers, or plan several visits. Highlights tours focus on specific aspects of the huge collection; Eye Opener tours offer specific introductions to world cultures. There are also regular blockbuster exhibitions, for which it may be necessary to book.

▶ *A fine range of cask beer makes historic Museum Tavern (49 Great Russell Street, 7242 8987), by the front gate, no mere tourist trap.*

Cartoon Museum

35 Little Russell Street, WC1A 2HH (7580 8155, www.cartoonmuseum.org). Tottenham Court Road tube. **Open** 10.30am-5.30pm Tue-Sat; noon-5.30pm Sun. **Admission** £5.50; free-£4 reductions. **Credit** (shop) MC, V. **Map** p416 Y1.

The best of British cartoon art is displayed on the ground floor of this former dairy. The displays start in the early 18th century, when high-society types back from the Grand Tour introduced the Italian practice of *caricatura* to polite company. From Hogarth, it moves through Britain's cartooning 'golden age' (1770-1830) to examples of wartime cartoons, ending up with modern satirists such as Gerald Scarfe and the wonderfully loopy Ralph Steadman. Upstairs is a celebration of UK comic art, with original 1921 *Rupert the Bear* artwork by Mary Tourtel, Frank Hampson's Dan Dare, Leo Baxendale's Bash Street Kids and a painted *Asterix* cover by that well-known Briton, Albert Uderzo.

Charles Dickens Museum

48 Doughty Street, WC1N 2LX (7405 2127, www.dickensmuseum.com). Chancery Lane or Russell Square tube. **Open** 10am-5pm daily. *Tours* by arrangement. **Admission** £8; £4-£6 reductions; free under-11s. **Credit** AmEx, DC, MC, V. **Map** p397 M4.

London is scattered with plaques marking addresses where Dickens lived, but this is the only building still standing. He lived here from 1837 to 1840, writing *Nicholas Nickleby* and *Oliver Twist* while in residence. Ring the doorbell to gain access to four floors of Dickensiana, collected over the years from various former residences. Some rooms are arranged as they might have been when he lived here; others deal with different aspects of his life, from struggling hack to famous performer.

Foundling Museum

40 Brunswick Square, WC1N 1AZ (7841 3600, www.foundlingmuseum.org.uk). Russell Square tube. **Open** 10am-5pm Tue-Sat; 11am-5pm Sun. **Admission** £7.50; £5 reductions; free under-16s. **Credit** MC, V. **Map** p397 L4.

Hip to Be a Square

Granary Square is the first, impressive conclusion of a huge redevelopment.

Granary Square.

What's the new fashion in London? Having your own postcode. That chunk of real estate out east, the Olympic something-or-other, is now E20, and here – north of the station – is King's Cross Central, N1C to the postman. To earn such an accolade, you're looking at serious redevelopment. The stats alone for King's Cross Central are impressive: 67 acres, 20 'historic structures' being refurbed, 'up to 2,000 homes and serviced apartments', 'up to 500,000 sq ft of retail space', 20 new streets, three new bridges, ten new parks and squares, and 400 trees planted.

The concept behind the numbers is interesting. The developers are trying to create from scratch a 'mixed-use' development – one with the virtues of multiplicity and resilience normally found with communities that have grown up over time. To this end, they are paying careful attention to the area's industrial heritage, to attracting the right mix of residents, and to the kind of events that might draw in visitors. No doubt the Olympic Park's London Legacy Develoment Corporation is paying close attention.

How's it shaping up? Nicely, in fact. Heading north-east from the station, **King's Boulevard** – a rather lively changing collection of street-food stalls organised by Petra Barran's KERB (www.kerbfood.com; 10am-2.30pm Tue-Fri) – leads directly to the superb **Granary Square**. Filled with choreographed fountains (1,080 water spouts, operating 8am-8pm daily), the square's terracing down to the canal is already populated most sunny days. No wonder: there's a ready supply of students from St Martins College of Art, which last year moved into the building behind – a sensitively and impressively converted, Grade II-listed 1850s industrial building. This is also home to the **King's Cross Visitor Centre** (3479 1795, www.kings crosscentral.com; open 10am-6pm Mon-Thur; 10am-5pm Fri). A little further along the canal, the Filling Station houses **Shrimpy's** restaurant (8880 6111, www. shrimpys.co.uk) until it's knocked down in 2014. From there, as you look one way to once-stranded **Kings Place** (*see p300*), another to the station and the square, you might think it's all starting to make sense.

EXPLORE

The Foundling Museum recalls the social history of the Foundling Hospital, set up in 1739 by shipwright and sailor Thomas Coram. Returning to England from America in 1720, Coram was appalled by the number of abandoned children he saw. Securing royal patronage, he persuaded Hogarth and Handel to become governors; it was Hogarth who made the building Britain's first public art gallery; works by artists as notable as Gainsborough and Reynolds are on display. The most heart-rending display is a tiny case of mementoes that were all mothers could leave the children they abandoned here.

★ FREE Grant Museum

Rockefeller Building, 21 University Street, WC1E 6JJ (3108 2052, www.ucl.ac.uk/museums/zoology). Goodge Street tube. **Open** 1-5pm Mon-Sat. **Admission** free. **No credit cards. Map** p397 K4.
Now re-housed in a former Edwardian library in the University College complex, the Grant Museum retains the air of an avid Victorian collector's house. Its 67,000 specimens include the remains of many rare and extinct creatures, including skeletons of the dodo and the zebra-like quagga, which was hunted out of existence in the 1880s. Visitors are engaged in dialogue about the distant evolutionary past via the most modern means available, including iPads and smartphones.
▶ *If the grisliness of body parts in jars appeals, check out the Hunterian as well; see p66.*

FREE Petrie Museum of Egyptian Archaeology

University College London, Malet Place, WC1E 6BT (7679 2884, www.petrie.ucl.ac.uk). Goodge Street or Warren Street tube. **Open** 1-5pm Tue-Sat. **Admission** free; donations appreciated. **No credit cards. Map** p397 K4.
Set up in 1892 by eccentric traveller and diarist Amelia Edwards, the refurbished (and now much easier to find) museum is named after Flinders Petrie, tireless excavator of ancient Egypt. Where the British Museum's Egyptology collection is strong on the big stuff, the Petrie is dim case after dim case of minutiae: pottery shards, grooming accessories, beads. Highlights include artefacts from the heretic pharaoh Akhenaten's capital Tell el Amarna. Wind-up torches illuminate gloomy corners and computers offer 3D views of select objects.

FREE St George's Bloomsbury

Bloomsbury Way, WC1A 2HR (7242 1979, www.stgeorgesbloomsbury.org.uk). Holborn or Tottenham Court Road tube. **Open** times vary; phone for details. *Services* 9am Tue-Fri; 1.10pm Wed, Fri; 10.30am Sun. **Admission** free. **No credit cards. Map** p397 L5.
Consecrated in 1730, St George's is a grand and disturbing Nicholas Hawksmoor church, with an offset, stepped spire that was inspired by Pliny the Elder's account of the Mausoleum at Halicarnassus.

Highlights of its renovation include the mahogany reredos and the sculptures of lions and unicorns clawing at the base of the steeple. The hours are erratic, but on Sundays, the church always remains open for visitors after the regular service. Check online for details of concerts.

★ FREE Wellcome Collection

183 Euston Road, NW1 2BE (7611 2222, www.wellcomecollection.org). Euston Square tube or Euston tube/rail. **Open** 10am-6pm Tue, Wed, Fri, Sat; 10am-10pm Thur; 11am-6pm Sun. *Library* 10am-6pm Mon-Wed, Fri; 10am-8pm Thur; 10am-4pm Sat. **Admission** free. **Credit** MC, V. **Map** p397 K4.
Sir Henry Wellcome, a pioneering 19th-century pharmacist, amassed a vast and idiosyncratic collection of implements and curios relating to the medical trade, now displayed here. In addition to these fascinating and often grisly items – ivory carvings of pregnant women, used guillotine blades, Napoleon's toothbrush – there are several serious works of modern art, most on display in a smaller room to one side of the main chamber of curiosities. The temporary exhibitions – usually a single word: Brains, Superhuman and, most recently, Death – are often brilliant and come with all manner of associated events, from talks and walks to experimental food.

Wellcome Collection.

EXPLORE

KING'S CROSS & ST PANCRAS

King's Cross tube/rail.

North-east of Bloomsbury, King's Cross is becoming a major European transport hub, thanks to a £500m makeover of the area. The renovated and restored **St Pancras International** (*see below*) was the key arrival, but neighbouring King's Cross station has now benefitted with an expanded station concourse, a rather snazzy new cascading roof and much-improved restaurants and cafés; 2013 should see the completion, in front of the original 1851 façade, of a new public square. What were once gaping badlands to the north have been transformed into a mixed-use nucleus called **King's Cross Central**, with the University of the Arts London the key new resident (*see p71* **Hip to Be a Square**) and a significance registered by it being granted its own postcode: N1C. There were, however, already several places to explore: the **London Canal Museum** (*see below*), north of King's Cross Station by the **Kings Place** arts complex (*see p300*), and **St Pancras Old Church** (*see p74*).

★ FREE British Library
96 Euston Road, NW1 2DB (0843 208 1114, www.bl.uk). Euston or King's Cross tube/rail. **Open** 9.30am-6pm Mon, Wed-Fri; 9.30am-8pm Tue; 9.30am-5pm Sat; 11am-5pm Sun. **Admission** free; donations appreciated. **Credit** (shop) AmEx, MC, V. **Map** p397 K3.
'One of the ugliest buildings in the world,' opined a Parliamentary committee on the opening of the new British Library in 1997. But don't judge a book by its cover: the interior is a model of cool, spacious functionality, the collection is unmatched (150 million items and counting), and the reading rooms (open only to cardholders) are so popular that regular users are now complaining that they can't find a seat. The focal point of the building is the King's Library, a six-storey glass-walled tower housing George III's collection, but the library's main treasures are on permanent display in the John Ritblat Gallery: Magna Carta, the Lindisfarne Gospels, original Beatles lyrics. There is also a great programme of temporary exhibitions and associated events: the Foyle Gallery (upstairs from the foyer) is free and hosts focused little shows based around key artefacts (such as Kerouac's *On the Road* scroll manuscript), while the engaging blockbuster shows are ticketed but cover meaty themes such as sci-fi, the Mughal Empire and the English language itself.

London Canal Museum
12-13 New Wharf Road, off Wharfdale Road, N1 9RT (7713 0836, www.canalmuseum.org.uk). King's Cross tube/rail. **Open** 10am-4.30pm Tue-Sun; 10am-7.30pm 1st Thur of mth. **Admission** £4; £2-£3 reductions; free under-5s. **Credit** AmEx, MC, V. **Map** p397 M2.

St Pancras International.

Housed on two floors of a former 19th-century ice warehouse, the London Canal Museum has a barge cabin to sit in and models of boats, but the displays (photos and videos about ice-importer Carlo Gatti) on the history of the ice trade are perhaps the most interesting. The installation of new, low-energy lighting should help make the most of the collections. The canalside walk (for which you can download a free MP3 audio tour from the museum website) from Camden Town to the museum is lovely.
► *In summer, don't miss the dank exploration of the Islington Tunnel, organised by the museum.*

FREE St Pancras International
Pancras Road, N1C 4QP (7843 7688, www. stpancras.com). King's Cross tube/rail. **Open** 24hrs daily. **Admission** free. **No credit cards**. **Map** p397 L3.
The redeveloped St Pancras station has become a destination in more ways than the obvious, now containing large sculptures, the self-proclaimed 'longest champagne bar in Europe', high-end boutiques – even a gastropub and farmers' market. But the new additions are mere window-dressing for the stunning original structures: famously George Gilbert Scott's grandiloquent red-brick exterior (much of which is now the St Pancras Renaissance hotel, *see*

INSIDE TRACK HAWK EYES

If a distant movement from above catches your eye in **St Pancras International** (*see above*), you might just have spotted Comet or Electra, the two Harris hawks employed, with their handler, to ensure the great shed stays pigeon-free.

EXPLORE

EXPLORE

p237), but perhaps more impressively William Barlow's gorgeous Victorian glass-and-iron roof to the train shed, a single span that is airy and light like some kind of cathedral to 19th-century industry.
► *Can't afford a night in the St Pancras Renaissance hotel? Sip something special at the hotel's Booking Hall café-bar (see p191) instead.*

FREE St Pancras Old Church & St Pancras Gardens
St Pancras Road, NW1 1UL (7387 4193, http://oldstpancrasteam.wordpress.com). Mornington Crescent tube or King's Cross tube/rail. **Open** *Gardens 7am-dusk daily. Services times vary; check website for details.* **Admission** free. **No credit cards. Map** p397 K2.
St Pancras Old Church has been ruined and rebuilt many times. The current structure is handsome, but it's the churchyard that delights. Among those buried here are writer William Godwin and his wife, Mary Wollstonecraft; over their grave, their daughter Mary Godwin (author of *Frankenstein*) declared her love for poet Percy Bysshe Shelley. Also here is the last resting place of Sir John Soane, one of only two Grade I-listed tombs (the other is Karl Marx's, in Highgate Cemetery; *see p121*). Designed for his wife, the tomb's dome influenced Gilbert Scott's design for the red British phone box.

FITZROVIA

Goodge Street or Tottenham Court Road tube.

Squeezed in between Tottenham Court Road, Oxford Street, Great Portland Street and Euston Road, Fitzrovia isn't as famous as Bloomsbury, but its history is just as rich. The origins of the name are hazy: some believe it comes from **Fitzroy Square**, named after Henry Fitzroy (son of Charles II); others insist it's due to the famous **Fitzroy Tavern** (16 Charlotte Street, 7580 3714), focal venue for London bohemia of the 1930s and '40s and a favourite with the likes of Dylan Thomas and George Orwell. Fitzrovia also had its share of artists: James McNeill Whistler lived at 8 Fitzroy Square, later taken over by British Impressionist Walter Sickert, while Roger

Fry's Omega Workshops, blurring the distinction between fine and decorative arts, had its studio at no.33. Fitzrovia's raffish image is largely a thing of the past – media offices are in the ascendance these days – but the steady arrival of new galleries – notably **Pilar Corrias** (*see below*) – have given the district back some of its artiness, even if local rents means it will never again be home to the dissolute.
The district's icon is the **BT Tower**, completed in 1964 as the Post Office Tower.Its revolving restaurant and observation deck featured in any film that wanted to prove how much London was swinging (*Bedazzled* is just one example). The restaurant is now reserved for corporate functions, but **Charlotte Street** and neighbouring byways have plenty of good options for food and drink.

FREE All Saints
7 Margaret Street, W1W 8JG (7636 1788, www.allsaintsmargaretstreet.org.uk). Oxford Circus tube. **Open** *7am-7pm daily. Services 7.30am, 8am, 1.10pm, 6pm, 6.30pm Mon-Fri; 7.30am, 8am, 6pm, 6.30pm Sat; 8am, 10.20am, 11am, 5.15pm, 6pm Sun.* **Admission** free. **No credit cards. Map** p416 U1.
Respite from the tumult of Oxford Street, this 1850s church was designed by William Butterfield, one of the great Gothic Revivalists. The church looks as if it has been lowered into its tiny site, so tight is the fit; its lofty spire is the second-highest in London. Behind the polychromatic brick façade, the lavish interior is one of the capital's finest ecclesiastical triumphs, with luxurious marble, flamboyant tile work and glittering stones built into its pillars.

Pilar Corrias
54 Eastcastle Street, W1W 8EF (7323 7000, www.pilarcorrias.com). Oxford Circus tube. **Open** *10am-6pm Mon-Fri; 11am-6pm Sat.* **No credit cards. Map** p416 V1.
Formerly a director at the pioneering Lisson and Haunch of Venison galleries, Corrias opened this 3,800sq ft, Rem Koolhaas-designed gallery in 2008 with a giant aluminium Christmas tree by Philippe Parreno. It was one of the first of an influx of private galleries to the area – several from the art-infested East End. *See also left* **Inside Track**.

Pollock's Toy Museum
1 Scala Street, W1T 2HL (7636 3452, www. pollockstoymuseum.com). Goodge Street tube. **Open** *10am-5pm Mon-Sat.* **Admission** £6; £3-£5 reductions; free under-3s. **Credit** AmEx, MC, V. **Map** p396 J5.
Named after Victorian toy theatre printer Benjamin Pollock, this place is in turns beguiling and creepy, a nostalgia-fest of old board games, tin trains, porcelain dolls and gollies – fascinating for adults but less so for children; describing a pile of painted woodblocks in a cardboard box as a 'Build a skyscraper' kit may make them feel lucky to be going home to their Wii.

Covent Garden & the Strand

An eminently strollable area of markets, boutiques and theatres.

From the capital's wholesale fruit and veg market, decades-since relocated to Vauxhall, to the Royal Opera House, still regal overlord of the market's north-east corner, **Covent Garden** has always been an index of the extremes of London life. At which end of the slippery scale you think it sits will depend on your tolerance for crowds. The masses descend daily on the restored 19th-century market and its cobbled 'piazza' to peruse the increasingly high-end shops and gawp at the street entertainment. Yet even the most crowd-averse Londoner finds plenty that's irresistible:

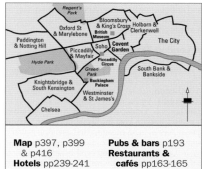

| **Map** p397, p399 & p416 | **Pubs & bars** p193 |
| **Hotels** pp239-241 | **Restaurants & cafés** pp163-165 |

the **London Transport Museum** (*see p76*); the **Royal Opera House** (*see p76*), eager nowadays to draw in all kinds of visitor; and, down towards the river on the grubbily historic **Strand**, the **Courtauld Gallery** just off the vast courtyard of **Somerset House** (for both, *see p79*).

COVENT GARDEN

Covent Garden or Leicester Square tube.

Covent Garden was once the property of the medieval Abbey ('convent') of Westminster. When Henry VIII dissolved the monasteries, it passed to John Russell, first Earl of Bedford, in 1552; his family still owns land hereabouts. During the 16th and 17th centuries, they developed the area: the fourth Earl employed Inigo Jones to create the Italianate open square that remains the area's centrepiece.

A market was first documented here in 1640 and grew into London's pre-eminent fruit and vegetable wholesaler, employing over 1,000 porters; its success led to the opening of coffee-houses, theatres, gambling dens and brothels. A flower market was added (where the London Transport Museum now stands).

In the second half of the 20th century, it became obvious that the congested streets of central London were unsuitable for such market traffic

and the decision was taken to move the traders out. In 1974, with the market gone, the threat of property development loomed for the empty stalls and offices. It was only through demonstrations that the area was saved. It's now a pleasant place for a stroll, especially if you catch it early on a fine morning before the crowds descend.

Covent Garden Piazza

Centred on Covent Garden Piazza, the area now offers a combination of gentrified shops, restaurants and cafés, supplemented by street artists and busking musicians in the lower courtyard. The majority of the entertainment takes place under the portico of **St Paul's Covent Garden** (*see p76*).

Tourists favour the 180-year-old **covered market**, which combines upmarket chain stores with a collection of small, sometimes quirky but often rather twee independent shops. Its handsome architecture is best viewed from the Amphitheatre Café Bar's terrace loggia at the

EXPLORE

Royal Opera House. The whole area has benefited from a major, ongoing revamp, with much classier shops being drawn in (*see p78* **Market Makeover**). There's also been an improvement in the sightseeing, with the always excellent **London Transport Museum** (*see below*) joined by a new outpost of the South Bank's **London Film Museum** (*see p37*), in the building opposite the Opera House that used to be the Theatre Museum.

Change is barely evident elsewhere. The **Apple Market**, in the North Hall, still has arts and crafts stalls from Tuesday to Sunday, and antiques on Monday. Across the road, the tackier **Jubilee Market** deals mostly in novelty T-shirts and other tat.

★ London Transport Museum

Covent Garden Piazza, WC2E 7BB (7379 6344, www.ltmuseum.co.uk). Covent Garden tube. **Open** 10am-6pm Mon-Thur, Sat, Sun; 11am-6pm Fri. **Admission** £13.50; £10 reductions; free under-16s. **Credit** AmEx, MC, V. **Map** p416 Z3.

The London Transport Museum traces the city's transport history from the horse age to the present day. It does so in an engaging and inspiring fashion, with a focus on social history and design, illustrated by a superb array of preserved buses, trams and trains, and backed up by some brilliant temporary exhibitions. The collections are in broadly chronological order, beginning with the Victorian gallery, where a replica of Shillibeer's first horse-drawn bus service in 1829 takes pride of place. Another gallery is dedicated to the museum's truly impressive collection of poster art. Under the leadership of Frank Pick, in the early 20th century London Transport developed one of the most coherent brand identities in the world. The new museum also raises some interesting and impor-

tant questions about the future of public transport in the city, with a display on ideas that are 'coming soon'.

Royal Opera House

Bow Street, WC2E 9DD (7304 4000, www.roh.org.uk). Covent Garden tube. **Open** 10am-3.30pm Mon-Sat. **Admission** free. *Stage tours* £12; £8.50-£11 reductions. **Credit** AmEx, DC, MC, V. **Map** p416 Y3.

The Royal Opera House was founded in 1732 by John Rich on the profits of his production of John Gay's *Beggar's Opera*; the current building, constructed roughly 150 years ago but extensively remodelled since, is the third on the site. Visitors can explore the massive eight-floor building as part of an organised tour, including the main auditorium, the costume workshops and sometimes even a rehearsal. Certain parts of the building are also open to the general public, including the glass-roofed Paul Hamlyn Hall, the Crush Bar (so named because in Victorian times the only thing served during intermissions was orange and lemon crush) and the Amphitheatre Café Bar.

▶ *For music at the Opera House, see p302.*

FREE St Paul's Covent Garden

Bedford Street, WC2E 9ED (7836 5221, www.actorschurch.org). Covent Garden or Leicester Square tube. **Open** 8.30am-5pm Mon-Fri; 9am-1pm Sun. Times vary Sat; phone for details. *Services* 1.10pm Tue, Wed; 6pm Thur; 11am Sun. *Choral Evensong* 4pm 2nd Sun of mth. **Admission** free; donations appreciated. **No credit cards. Map** p416 Y3.

Known as the Actors' Church for its long association with Covent Garden's theatres, this pleasingly spare building was designed by Inigo Jones in 1631. A lovely limewood wreath by the 17th-century master

London Transport Museum.

carver Grinling Gibbons hangs inside the front door as a reminder that he and his wife are interred in the crypt. But most visitors come to see the memorial plaques: many thespians are commemorated here, among them Vivien Leigh, Charlie Chaplin and Hattie Jacques of *Carry On…* fame.

Elsewhere in Covent Garden

Outside Covent Garden Piazza, the area offers a mixed bag of entertainment, eateries and shops. Nearest the markets, most of the more unusual shops have been superseded by a homogeneous mass of cafés, while big fashion chains – and the **St Martin's Courtyard** mall (www.stmartins courtyard.co.uk) – have all but domesticated Long Acre. There are more interesting stores north of here on Neal Street and Monmouth Street; Earlham Street is also home to the **Donmar Warehouse** (*see p310*), a former banana-ripening depot that's now an intimate and groundbreaking theatre. On tiny Shorts Gardens next door is the **Neal's Yard Dairy** (*see p224*), purveyor of exceptional UK cheeses; down a passageway one door along is **Neal's Yard** itself, known for its co-operative cafés, herbalists and head shops.

South of Long Acre and east of the Piazza, historical depravity is called to account at the former **Bow Street Magistrates Court**. Once home to the Bow Street Runners, the precursors of the Metropolitan Police, this was also where Oscar Wilde entered his plea when arrested for 'indecent acts' in 1895. Plans to convert it into a hotel have not yet come to fruition. To the south, Wellington and Catherine streets mix restaurants and theatres, including the grand **Theatre Royal**. Other diversions in and around Covent Garden include the museum at **Freemasons' Hall** (7395 9257, www.freemasonry.london.museum; call for details of tours), the eye-catchingly bombastic white stone building where Long Acre becomes Great Queen Street; and, at opposite ends both of St Martin's Lane and the cultural spectrum, lap-dancing club **Stringfellows** (16-19 Upper St Martin's Lane, 7240 5534, www.stringfellows. co.uk) and the **Coliseum** (*see p302*), home of the English National Opera.

THE STRAND & EMBANKMENT

Embankment tube or Charing Cross tube/rail.

Until as recently as the 1860s, the Strand ran beside the Thames; indeed, it was originally the river's bridlepath. In the 14th century, it was lined with grand residences with gardens that ran down to the water. It wasn't until the 1870s that the Thames was pushed back with the creation of the Embankment and its adjacent gardens. By the time George Newnes's famed

Royal Opera House.

EXPLORE

Strand magazine was introducing its readership to Sherlock Holmes (1891), the street boasted the Cecil Hotel (long since demolished), **Simpson's**, **King's College** and **Somerset House** (*see p79*). Prime Minister Benjamin Disraeli described it as 'perhaps the finest street in Europe'. Nobody would make such a claim today – there are too many overbearing office blocks and underwhelming restaurants – but there's still plenty to interest visitors.

In 1292, the body of Eleanor of Castile, consort to King Edward I, completed its funerary procession from Lincoln in the small hamlet of Charing, at the western end of what is now the Strand. The occasion was marked by the erection of the last of 12 elaborate crosses. A replica of the Eleanor Cross (originally set just south of nearby Trafalgar Square; *see pp97-98*) was placed in 1865 on the forecourt of **Charing Cross Station**; it remains there today, looking like the spire of a sunken cathedral. Across the road, behind **St Martin-in-the-Fields** (*see p98*), is Maggie Hambling's weird memorial to a more recent queen, *A Conversation with Oscar Wilde*.

The Embankment itself can be reached down Villiers Street. Pass through the tube station to the point at which boat tours with on-board entertainment depart. Just to the east stands **Cleopatra's Needle**, an obelisk presented to the British nation by the viceroy of Egypt, Mohammed Ali, in 1820 but not set in place by the river for a further 59 years. The obelisk was originally erected around 1500 BC by the pharaoh Tuthmosis III at a site near modern-day Cairo, before being moved to Alexandria,

Cleopatra's capital, in 10 BC. By this time, however, the great queen was 20 years dead.

Back on the Strand, the majestic **Savoy** hotel (*see p241*) is back to its august best after a tortuously long and thorough refurbishment. The hotel first opened in 1889, financed by profits from Richard D'Oyly Carte's productions of Gilbert and Sullivan's light operas at the neighbouring **Savoy Theatre**. The theatre, which pre-dates the hotel by eight years, was the first to use electric lights.

Benjamin Franklin House

36 Craven Street, the Strand, WC2N 5NF (7925 1405, www.benjaminfranklinhouse.org). Charing Cross tube/rail. **Open** noon-5pm Wed-Sun. *Tours* noon, 1pm, 2pm, 3.15pm, 4.15pm Wed-Sun. **Admission** £7; £5 reductions; free under-16s. **Credit** AmEx, MC, V. **Map** p416 Y5.

This is the house where Franklin – scientist, diplomat, philosopher, inventor and Founding Father of the US – lived between 1757 and 1775. It isn't a museum in the conventional sense, but can be enjoyed on 'experiences' lasting 45 minutes (noon, 1pm, 2pm, 3.15pm and 4.15pm Wed-Sun; booking advised). The tours are led by an actress playing Franklin's landlady's daughter Polly Stevenson, using projections and sound to conjure up the world in which Franklin lived. From noon on Mondays, more straightforward, 20-minute tours are given by house interns (£3.50).

Market Makeover

Covent Garden is undergoing a transformation.

The Covent Garden area was always a huge hit with tourists – to a large extent for the same reasons it wasn't much more than tolerated by locals. There were always crowds gathered round the buskers and living statues, but the selection of shops was easily bettered elsewhere. So why bother? Over the last few years, this unloved cobbled square has begun giving some pretty compelling answers to that question.

Since 2006, property investor Capco has consumed great chunks of prime real estate in Covent Garden, scooping up property on the Piazza, King Street, James Street, Long Acre and beyond – £780m of it, to be exact. And Capco's marketing and communications director, Bev Churchill, has been carefully re-editing the place. As a former marketing director of Selfridges, she knows a thing or two about retail. And knows how to think big. A slew of ho-hum shops have been replaced by high-street heavyweights and luxury brands. Fred Perry, Whistles, L'Artisan Parfumier, Kurt Geiger, Ralph Lauren's Rugby brand and Burberry Brit have all appeared. The world's largest **Apple Store** (*see p213*) set up shop, and with a cool buzz about the place, events started happening: a giant inflatable Jeff Koons bunny was hung in the Market Building, and there have been pop-ups from the likes of Chanel and NYC cult store and label Opening Ceremony. Perhaps most tellingly, the West Cornwall Pasty Co has become a Ladurée café, with waistcoated staff dispensing dainty orange-blossom macaroons where once they trowelled out steak and stilton pastries.

'We've seen so many changes in the last couple of years,' says Jane Shepherdson, CEO of Whistles. 'We've started to see a serious fashion customer come back to the area.' Restaurateurs popular with the style set have also been lured back: **Polpo Covent Garden** (7836 8448, www.polpo.co.uk) on Maiden Lane, **Terroirs** (*see p193*) on King William IV Street and **Delauney** (*see p163*) on the Aldwych are all near.

But what of Covent Garden's bawdy personality? To Bev, it's all about plonking niche, indie shops, bars and restaurants up against luxury retailers and contemporary art, and also about uncovering what's already there. The Rugby store, a late-1600s townhouse with library-like rooms and grand façade, is a case in point. 'Covent Garden has great bone structure,' explains Bev. 'It just needed a little facelift.'

Apple Store.

Courtauld Gallery.

THE ALDWYCH

Temple tube.

At the eastern end of the Strand is the Aldwych, guarded by two grand hotels: **One Aldwych** and, directly opposite, the hip new **ME by Meliá London** (for both, *see p241*). This grand crescent dates only from 1905, but the name 'ald wic' (old settlement or market) has its origins in the 14th century. To the south is **Somerset House**; even if you're not interested in the galleries, it's worth visiting the regal fountain courtyard. Almost in front of it is **St Mary-le-Strand** (7836 3126, www.stmarylestrand.org, open 11am-4pm Tue-Sat, 10am-3pm Sun), James Gibbs's first public building, completed in 1717. On Strand Lane, reached via Surrey Street, is the so-called **'Roman' bath** where Dickens took the waters – you have to peer through a dusty window.

On a traffic island just east of the Aldwych is **St Clement Danes** (7242 2380, www.raf.mod.uk/stclementdanes). It's believed that a church was first built here by the Danish in the ninth century, but the current building is mainly Wren's handiwork. It's the principal church of the RAF. Just beyond the church are the Royal Courts of Justice (*see p49*) and the original site of Temple Bar (*see p47*).

★ Courtauld Gallery

The Strand, WC2R 1LA (7848 2526, www. courtauld.ac.uk/gallery). Temple tube or Charing Cross tube/rail. **Open** 10am-6pm daily. *Tours* phone for details. **Admission** £6; £4.50 reductions. Free 10am-2pm Mon; students & under-18s daily. **Credit** MC, V. **Map** p399 M7.
Located for the last two decades in the north wing of Somerset House (*see below*), the Courtauld has one of Britain's greatest collections of paintings, and contains several works of world importance. Although there are some outstanding early works (Cranach's *Adam & Eve*, for one), the collection's strongest suit is in Impressionist and Post-Impressionist paintings. Popular masterpieces include Manet's *A Bar at the Folies-Bergère*, alongside plenty of superb Monets and Cézannes, important Gauguins, and some Van Goghs and Seurats. On the top floor, there's a selection of gorgeous Fauvist works, a lovely room of Kandinskys and plenty more besides. Hidden downstairs, the sweet little gallery café is delightful.
▶ *Bulky backpacks must be carried, not worn, through the gallery, but there are coin-operated lockers downstairs.*

FREE Somerset House & the Embankment Galleries

The Strand, WC2R 1LA (7845 4600, www. somersethouse.org.uk). Temple tube or Charing Cross tube/rail. **Open** 10am-6pm (last entry 5.15pm) daily. *Tours* phone for details. **Admission** *Courtyard & terrace* free. *Embankment Galleries* prices vary; check website for details. *Tours* phone for details. **Credit** MC, V. **Map** p399 M7.
The original Somerset House was a Tudor palace commissioned by the Duke of Somerset. In 1775, it was demolished to make way for the first purpose-built office block in the world. Architect Sir William Chambers spent the last 20 years of his life working on the neoclassical edifice overlooking the Thames, built to accommodate learned societies such as the Royal Academy and government departments.

The taxmen are still here, but the rest of the building is open to the public. Attractions include the Courtauld (*see above*), the handsome fountain court, and a terraced café and a classy restaurant. The Embankment Galleries explore connections between art, architecture and design in temporary exhibitions, and at Christmas usually host a market. In summer, children never tire of running through the choreographed fountains while parents watch from café tables; in winter, an ice rink takes over the courtyard.

Soho & Leicester Square

Soho has character all its own – and Leicester Square is finding some.

For more than two centuries, poseurs, spivs, tarts, whores, toffs, drunks and divas have gathered in **Soho** to ply their trades. Many of the area's music, film and advertising businesses have moved on, but the gay scene still thrives, and contributes to a non-stop party atmosphere.

Hemmed in by Oxford Street to the north, Charing Cross Road to the east, Shaftesbury Avenue to the south and Regent Street to the west, Soho is packed with a huge range of restaurants, shops, clubs and bars, sharing the streets with a sizeable residential community. There are a few more chains than there used to be, but independent businesses – and an independent frame of mind – still dominate.

Just to the south of Soho, beyond London's bustling little **Chinatown**, **Leicester Square** – mainly known for cinemas and, for many years, drunk and disappointed out-of-towners – is beginning to build a classier reputation.

| Map p416 | Hotels pp242-244 |
| Pubs & bars pp193-195 | Restaurants & cafés pp165-171 |

SOHO SQUARE

Tottenham Court Road tube.

Forming the area's northern gateway, **Soho Square** was laid out in 1681. It was initially called King's Square; a weather-beaten statue of Charles II stands just north of the centre. On warmer days, the grassy spaces are filled with courting couples as snacking workers occupy its benches; one of these benches is dedicated to singer Kirsty MacColl, in honour of her song named after the square. The denominations of the two churches on the square testify to the area's long-standing European credentials: as well as the French Protestant church, you'll find St Patrick's, one of the first Catholic churches built in England after the Reformation.

Two classic Soho streets run south from the square. **Greek Street**, its name a nod to a church that once stood here, is lined with restaurants and bars, among them 50-year-old Hungarian eaterie the **Gay Hussar** (no.2, 7437 0973, http://gayhussar.co.uk) and the nearby **Pillars of Hercules** pub (no.7, 7437 1179), where the literati once enjoyed long liquid lunches. Just by the Pillars, an arch leads to Manette Street and Charing Cross Road, where you'll find **Foyles** (*see p261*). Back on Greek Street, no.49 was once Les Cousins, a folk venue (note the heldover mosaic featuring a musical note); Casanova lived briefly at no.46.

INSIDE TRACK SO LONG, SOHO

With so much of Soho lost to history, it's pleasing to see someone is trying to keep track of the ephemera: **www.the museumofsoho.org.uk** has the stories of the Colony Room, Windmill Girls, the Pierpoint Monument and all sorts of interesting odds and ends.

Parallel to Greek Street is **Frith Street**, once home to Mozart (1764-65, no.20) and painter John Constable (1810-11, no.49). Humanist essayist William Hazlitt died in 1830 at no.6, now a discreet hotel named in his memory (*see p243* **Hazlitt's**). Further down the street are **Ronnie Scott's** (*see p294*), Britain's best-known jazz club, and, across from Ronnie's, the similarly mythologised **Bar Italia** (no.22, 7437 4520). A large portrait of Rocky Marciano dominates Italia's narrow, chrome bar, but it's the place's 24-hour opening that makes it likely you'll have to fight for a seat.

This area has been suffering from major disruption caused by works on the Crossrail link. It's tedious and unsightly, but you can usually find your way around it down one of the area's characteristic backstreets or alleys.

OLD COMPTON STREET & AROUND

Leicester Square or Tottenham Court Road tube.

Linking Charing Cross Road to Wardour Street and crossed by Greek, Frith and Dean streets, **Old Compton Street** is London's gay catwalk. Tight T-shirts congregate around **Balans** (*see p310*), **Compton's** (nos.51-53) and the **Admiral Duncan** (no.54). However, the street has an interesting history that dates back long before rainbow flags were hung above its doors: no.59 was formerly the 2i's Coffee Bar, the skiffle venue where stars and svengalis mingled in the late 1950s and early '60s.

Visit Old Compton Street in the morning for a sense of the mostly vanished immigrant Soho of old. Cheeses and cooked meats from **Camisa** (no.61, 7437 7610, www.icamisa.co.uk) and roasting beans from the **Algerian Coffee Stores** (*see p222*) scent the air, as **Pâtisserie Valerie** (no.44, 7437 3466, www.patisserie-valerie.co.uk), first of a now significant national chain, does a brisk trade in croissants and cakes.

Valerie's traditional rival is the older **Maison Bertaux** (7437 6007, www.maisonbertaux.com), an atmospheric holdover from the 19th century that sits near the southern end of Greek Street. At the corner of Greek and Romilly streets the **Coach & Horses** (no.29, 7437 5920, www.coachandhorsessoho.co.uk), where irascible Soho flâneur Jeffrey Bernard held court for decades. It's almost opposite the members' club **Soho House** (no.40, 7734 5188), where media types and wannabes hope to channel the same vibe. Two streets along, Dean Street holds the **French House** (*see p194*); formerly the York Minster pub, it was de Gaulle's London base for French resistance in World War II and in later years became a favourite of painters Francis Bacon and Lucian Freud. Upstairs is Polpetto,

one of Russell Norman's clutch of fashionable wine-bar restaurants, which are spreading across Soho and Covent Garden.

North of Old Compton Street on Dean Street sits the **Groucho Club** (no.45), a members-only media hangout that was founded in the mid 1980s and named in honour of the familiar Groucho Marx quote about not wanting to join any club that would have him as a member. A few doors along, at no.28, the other famous Marx lived in a garret from 1850 to 1856; he would probably not have approved of the high-class, high-cost dinners served there now – at **Quo Vadis** (nos.26-29). To the north is the **Soho Theatre** (*see p311*), which programmes comedy shows and new plays.

WARDOUR STREET & AROUND

Leicester Square or Tottenham Court Road tube.

Parallel to Dean Street, **Wardour Street** provides offices for film and TV production companies, but is also known for its rock history. No.100 was, for nearly three decades, the Marquee, where Led Zeppelin played their first London gig and Hendrix appeared four times. The latter's favourite Soho haunt was the nearby **Ship** pub (no.116), still with a sprinkling of music-themed knick-knacks. There's more music history at Trident Studios on nearby **St Anne's Court**: Lou Reed recorded *Transformer* here, and David Bowie cut both *Hunky Dory* and *The Rise and Fall of Ziggy Stardust* on the site.

Soho Square.

EXPLORE

Old Compton Street. *See p81.*

Back when he was still known as David Jones, Bowie played a gig at the Jack of Clubs on Brewer Street, now **Madame JoJo's** (*see p295*). But this corner of Soho is most famous not for music but for its position at the heart of Soho's dwindling but still notorious sex trade. The Raymond Revuebar opened on the neon alleyway of Walker's Court in 1958, swiftly becoming London's most famous strip club. It closed in 2004, became a series of short-lived gay nightclubs, then reopened as edgy, celebrity-loved, exclusive alt-cabaret club the **Box** (www. theboxsoho.com), the London branch of a New York original. A handful of small, seedy establishments continue to tout for business close by on Brewer Street and Tisbury Court.

North of here, **Berwick Street** is a lovely mix of old-school London raffishness and new-Soho style. The former comes courtesy of the amiable fruit and veg market (support it: more custom needed), and the egalitarian, old-fashioned and unceasingly popular **Blue Posts** pub (no.22, 7437 5008), where builders, post-production editors, restaurateurs and market traders gabble and glug as one beneath a portrait of Berwick Street-born star of stage and radio Jessie Matthews (1907-81). It's quite a contrast with the **Endurance** (no.90, 7437 2944, www.theendurance.co.uk), the street's gastropub, and **Flat White** (no.17, 7734 0370, www.flatwhitecafe.com) coffee bar.

WEST SOHO

Piccadilly Circus tube.

The area west of Berwick Street was rebranded 'West Soho' in a misplaced bid to give it some kind of upmarket identity. **Brewer Street** does have some interesting places; among them is the **Vintage Magazine Store** (nos.39-43, 7439 8525), offering everything from retro robots to pre-war issues of *Vogue*. Star restaurant **Hix** with its hip downstairs bar (*see p170*) is also here. On Great Windmill Street is the **Windmill Theatre** (nos.17-19), which gained fame in the 1930s and '40s for its 'revuedeville' shows with erotic 'tableaux' – naked girls who remained stationary in order to stay within the law. The place is now a lap-dancing joint. North of Brewer Street is **Golden Square**. Developed in the 1670s, it became the political and ambassadorial district of the late 17th and early 18th centuries, and remains home to some of the area's grandest buildings (many now bases for media firms) and a purveyor of excellent cinnamon buns: the **Nordic Bakery** (no.14A, 3230 1077, www.nordicbakery.com).

Just north of Golden Square is **Carnaby Street**, which became a fashion mecca shortly after John Stephen opened His Clothes here in

1956; Stephen, who went on to own more than a dozen fashion shops on the street, is now commemorated with a plaque at the corner with Beak Street. After thriving during the Swinging Sixties, Carnaby Street became a rather seamy commercialised backwater. However, along with nearby **Newburgh Street** and **Kingly Court** (*see p205*), it's undergone a revival, with the tourist traps and chain stores joined by a wealth of independent stores.

A little further north, near Oxford Street, is the new **Photographers' Gallery**.

Photographers' Gallery

16-18 Ramillies Street, W1F 7LW (0845 262 1618, http://thephotographersgallery.org.uk). Oxford Circus tube. **Open** 11am-6pm Mon-Wed, Fri, Sat; 11am-8pm Thur; 11.30am-6pm Sun. **Admission** free. *Temporary exhibitions vary.* **Map** p416 U2.

Given a handsome refit by Irish architects O'Donnell+Tuomey, this old brick corner building reopened in 2012 as the new home for London's only gallery dedicated solely to the photographic arts. The upper floors have two airy new exhibition

Leicester Square Gets All Dressed Up

Central London's least appealing space has really pulled up its socks.

Leicester Square.

Locals have for many years scorned the low-grade steak restaurants and horrid cocktail bars of **Leicester Square**, visiting reluctantly to part with heavy money for a blockbuster movie that demands the big-screen treatment, but otherwise leaving the place to the tourists and drunk suburban kids.

Not any more. Where once the **tkts** booth, selling cut-price theatre tickets, and a pair of unlikely neighbours just to the north of the square on Leicester Place – the excellent **Prince Charles** rep cinema (*see p272*) and the French Catholic church of **Notre Dame de France** (no.5, 7437 9363, www.ndfchurch.org), with its Jean Cocteau murals – were the only reasons to recommend a visit, now discerning visitors might even find themselves staying here. Both the **W** and **St John** hotels (for both, *see pp243-244*) are high-class establishments that opened in 2011. Then in 2012 the castle-like red-brick **Hippodrome** (www.hippodromecasino.com), on the corner of Cranbourn Street and Charing Cross Road beside the tube station, reopened as a casino.

Now you may not be a high-rolling gambler yourself, but this is one impressive edifice. Designed by the prolific theatre architect

Frank Matcham, it became famous as the 'Talk of the Town' cabaret venue in the 1960s, featuring the likes of Shirley Bassey and Judy Garland, before suffering the indignities of life as a Peter Stringfellow nightclub. Now it has painstakingly restored interiors, grown-up restaurants and a cabaret venue – albeit one where the programming tends more to the midbrow chanteuse than the more experimental fare that can be found elsewhere in London.

Most importantly, Westminster Council spent £15.5m and four years on the square itself, simplifying the layout of the centre of the square, improving lighting and ringing the garden with modish white 'ribbon' seating – handsome enough, although perhaps designed with the thought in mind that it might prevent drunks and the homeless getting a good kip.

The simplification temporarily banished 19th-century busts of the artists Hogarth and Reynolds, scientist Newton and surgeon John Hunter, but they are due to return at the beginning of 2013. The Grade II-listed Shakespeare, at the top of a marble fountain in the centre of the garden, is still being spruced up until the spring. The fate of the rather popular but pretty silly 1981 statue of Charlie Chaplin ('The comic genius who gave pleasure to so many') remains uncertain, but fate of the square seems promising: iPad-wielders seem more in evidence now than the footpads and ne'er-do-wells of the past.

Still, not all memories of the square's cheerfully tacky phase have gone: the Swiss Glockenspiel, a clock that used to draw crowds outside the Swiss Centre, has returned. With its 27 bells and mechanical mountain farmers, it still chimes out the time on behalf of Switzerland Tourism.

EXPLORE

spaces, while a bookshop, print sales room and café (open the same hours as the gallery) are tucked into the ground floor and basement. The exhibitions are varied, and enhanced by quirky details such as the camera obscura in the third floor Eranda Studio and a projection wall in the café.

CHINATOWN & LEICESTER SQUARE

Leicester Square tube.

Shaftesbury Avenue is the very heart of Theatreland. The Victorians built seven grand theatres here, six of which still stand. The most impressive is the gorgeous **Palace Theatre** on Cambridge Circus, which opened in 1891 as the Royal English Opera House; when grand opera flopped, the theatre reopened as a music hall two years later. Appropriately, it's most famous for the musicals it has staged: *The Sound of Music* (1961) and *Jesus Christ Superstar* (1972) had their London premières here, and *Les Misérables* racked up 7,602 performances between 1985 and 2004. The current resident is *Singin' in the Rain*.

Just opposite the Palace Theatre, Marks & Co, the shop that was made famous by Helene Hanff's *84 Charing Cross Road*, used to stand. A few (and, sadly, getting fewer) second-hand bookshops line **Charing Cross Road** to the south, heading towards Leicester Square, where **Cecil Court** (*see p205*) is a better bet for bibliophiles. West of Charing Cross Road and south of Shaftesbury Avenue, and officially just outside Soho, is the city's **Chinatown**.

The Chinese are relative latecomers to this part of town. London's original Chinatown was set around Limehouse in east London, but hysteria about Chinese opium dens and criminality led to 'slum clearances' in 1934 (interestingly, the surrounding slums were deemed to be in less urgent need of clearance). It wasn't until the 1950s that the Chinese put down roots here, attracted by the cheap rents along Gerrard and Lisle streets.

The ersatz oriental gates, stone lions and pagoda-topped phone boxes around Gerrard Street suggest a Chinese theme park, but this remains a close-knit residential and working enclave, a genuine focal point for London's Chinese community. The area is crammed with restaurants, Asian grocery stores, great bakeries and a host of small shops selling iced-grass jelly, speciality teas and cheap air tickets to Beijing.

South of Chinatown, **Leicester Square** was one of London's most exclusive addresses in the 17th century; in the 18th, it became home to the royal court of Prince George (later George II). Satirical painter William Hogarth had a studio here (1733-64), as did 18th-century artist Sir Joshua Reynolds – busts of both once resided in the small gardens at the heart of the square, along with a now vanished statue of Charlie Chaplin. They've been swept away in the fine refurbishment of the square (*see p83* **Leicester Square Gets All Dressed Up**). Film premières are still regularly held in the monolithic **Odeon Leicester Square** (*see p270*), which once boasted the UK's largest screen and probably still has the UK's highest ticket prices; this is where the **London Film Festival** (*see p269*) kicks off every year.

Chinatown.

Oxford Street & Marylebone

The main(stream) shopping drag, and its more interesting environs.

Oxford Street is working hard to stay top of London's shopping destinations, with a revamped roundabout at **Marble Arch** (*see p86*), wider pavements, the innovative pedestrian crossings at Oxford Circus, and an all-new 'eastern gateway' development – where the new flagship **Primark** (*see p216*) distracts most visitors from ugly duckling redevelopment at the foot of the landmark **Centre Point** skyscraper, due to be born as the fabulous new Tottenham Court Road superstore for Crossrail some time before 2018. But the changes and improvements are unlikely to draw crowd-phobic locals from the luxury cafés and boutiques of **Marylebone** or flowering green acres of **Regent's Park** (*see p89*) for quite a while yet.

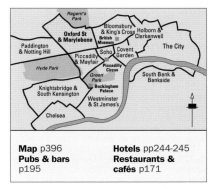

| **Map** p396 | **Hotels** pp244-245 |
| **Pubs & bars** p195 | **Restaurants & cafés** p171 |

OXFORD STREET

Bond Street, Marble Arch, Oxford Circus or Tottenham Court Road tube.

Official estimates put the annual footfall at somewhere near 200 million people per year, but few Londoners love **Oxford Street**. A shopping district since the 19th century, it's unmanageably busy on weekends and in the run-up to Christmas. Even outside these times, it's never pretty, lined with over-familiar chain stores and choked with bus traffic. The New West End Company (www.newwestend.com) has been charged with changing all that, and Oxford Circus, Marble Arch and Regent Street are beginning to feel the benefits.

The street gets smarter as you walk from east to west. The eastern end around Tottenham Court Road station is under major redevelopment for Crossrail, but its lack of destination shops was solved at a stroke in 2012 by the opening of bargain-basement fashion flagship **Primark** (*see p215*). The string of classy department stores – **John Lewis** (nos.278-306, 7629 7711),

Debenhams (nos.334-348, 0844 561 6161) and **Selfridges** (no.400; *see p207*) – begins west of chaotic **Oxford Circus**, where there are more Crossrail works at Bond Street station. Apart from the art deco splendour of Selfridges, architectural interest along Oxford Street is largely limited to Oxford Circus's four identical convex corners, constructed between 1913 and 1928. The crowds and rush of traffic hamper investigations, a problem the council attempted to address a couple of years ago by widening pavements, removing street clutter and creating Tokyo Shibuya-style diagonal crossings, which actually work rather well.

Oxford Street gained notoriety as the route by which condemned men were conveyed from Newgate Prison to the old Tyburn gallows, stopping only for a last pint at the **Angel** (61-62 St Giles High Street, 7240 2876), in the shadow of Centre Point. For over six centuries, crowds would gather to watch executions at the west end of the street, at Tyburn; held in 1783, the final execution to be carried out here is marked by an X on a traffic island at the junction of the Edgware and Bayswater roads.

Close by, also at the western end of Oxford Street, stands **Marble Arch**, with its Carrara marble cladding and sculptures celebrating Nelson and Wellington. It was designed by John Nash in 1827 as the entrance to a rebuilt Buckingham Palace, but the arch was moved here in 1851, after – it is said – a fuming Queen Victoria found it to be too narrow for her coach. Now given a £2m revamp, it's been joined by renovated water fountains and gardens that contain an ongoing series of large-scale public sculpture commissions.

North of Oxford Circus

Great Portland Street, Oxford Circus or Regent's Park tube.

North of Oxford Circus runs **Langham Place**, notable for the Bath stone façade of John Nash's **All Souls Church** (Langham Place, 2 All Souls Place, 7580 3522, www.allsouls.org). Its bold combination of a Gothic spire and classical rotunda wasn't popular: in 1824, a year after it opened, the church was condemned in the House of Commons as 'deplorable and horrible'.

Tucked to one side of the church you'll find the BBC's **Broadcasting House**, an oddly asymmetrical art deco building that's shipshape in more ways than one. Prominent among the carvings is a statue of Shakespeare's Prospero and Ariel, his spirit of the air – or, in this case,

Oxford Street. *See p85.*

INSIDE TRACK
SCRAMBLED EGGS

A young Paul McCartney woke up one morning in 1965 at **57 Wimpole Street**, the house of then-girlfriend Jane Asher's parents. He dashed to the piano to transcribe a tune that had been playing in his dreams: only the lyrics didn't quite work. Until, that is, he decided to change 'Scrambled Eggs' into 'Yesterday'.

the airwaves. The statue caused controversy when it was unveiled due to the flattering size of the airy sprite's manhood; artist Eric Gill was recalled and asked to make it more modest. It contains the Radio Theatre, where the public can join the audience for shows, and now has a flashy new set of studios for BBC News right next door. For tours (£11.75, free-£10.75 reductions) and tickets for shows, visit www.bbc.co.uk/showsandtours/tours/. Over the road is the **Langham Hotel** (7636 1000, http://london.langhamhotels.co.uk), which opened in 1865 as Britain's first grand hotel and has been home at various points to Mark Twain, Napoleon III and Oscar Wilde.

North, Langham Place turns into **Portland Place**, designed by Robert and James Adam as the glory of 18th-century London. Its Georgian terraced houses are now mostly occupied by embassies and swanky offices. At no.66 is the **Royal Institute of British Architects** (RIBA; *see p358*). Parallel to Portland Place are **Harley Street**, famous for its high-cost dentists and doctors, and **Wimpole Street**, erstwhile home to the poet Elizabeth Barrett Browning (no.50), Sir Arthur Conan Doyle (2 Upper Wimpole Street) and Sir Paul McCartney (*see above* **Inside Track**).

MARYLEBONE

Baker Street, Bond Street, Marble Arch, Oxford Circus or Regent's Park tube.

North of Oxford Street, the fashionable district known to its boosters as 'Marylebone Village' has become a magnet for moneyed Londoners. Many visitors to the area head directly for the waxworks of **Madame Tussauds** (*see p87*); there's also a small and oft-overlooked museum at the neighbouring **Royal Academy of Music** (7873 7300, www.ram.ac.uk). However, the area's beating heart is **Marylebone High Street**, teeming with interesting shops.

St Marylebone Church stands in its fourth incarnation at the northern end of the street. The name of the neighbourhood is a contraction

EXPLORE

Wallace Collection. *See p88.*

Madame Tussaud brought her show to London in 1802, 32 years after it was founded in Paris, and it's been expanding ever since, on these very premises since 1884. There are now some 300 figures in the collection: current movie A-listers who require no more than a first name (Brad, Keira, Arnie), as well as their illustrious forebears for whom the surname seems more fitting (Monroe, Chaplin); a bevy of Royals (not least Wills and Kate), and sundry sportsmen and -women – not just Nadal, Tendulkar, Muhammad Ali and Messi, but an Athletes' Village of 2012 Olympians, among them Jessica Ennis and Usain Bolt. Rihanna can be found hanging out among the Music Megastars, while Dickens and Einstein kick back together in the Culture section, and even French president François Hollande has sat for the modellers. If you're not already overheating, your palms will be sweating by the time you descend to the Chamber of Horrors in 'Scream', where only teens claim to enjoy the floor drops and scary special effects. Much more pleasant is the kitsch 'Spirit of London' ride, whisking you through 400 years of London life in a taxi pod.

Tussauds also hosts Marvel Super Heroes 4D. Interactives and waxworks of Iron Man, Spiderman and an 18ft Hulk provide further photo ops, but the highlight is the nine-minute film in '4D' (as well as 3D projections, there are 'real' effects such as a shaking floor and smoke in the auditorium).
▶ *Get here before 10am to avoid the enormous queues, and book online in advance to make the steep admission price more palatable.*

of the church's earlier name, St Mary by the Bourne; the 'bourne' in question, Tyburn stream, still filters into the Thames near Pimlico, but its entire length is now covered. The church's lovely garden hosts designer clothing and artisan food stalls at the **Cabbages & Frocks** market on Saturdays (www.cabbagesandfrocks.co.uk).

More lovely boutiques can be found on winding **Marylebone Lane**, along with the **Golden Eagle** (no.59, 7935 3228), which hosts regular singalongs around its piano. There's fine food here, too, with smart, often upmarket eateries snuggling alongside delicatessens such as **La Fromagerie** (2-6 Moxon Street, 7935 0341, www.lafromagerie.co.uk) and century-old lunchroom **Paul Rothe & Son** (35 Marylebone Lane, 7935 6783). **Marylebone Farmers' Market** takes place in the Cramer Street car park every Sunday.

Further south, the soaring neo-Gothic interior of the 19th-century **St James's Roman Catholic Church** (22 George Street, 7935 0943) is lit dramatically by stained-glass windows; Vivien Leigh (née Hartley) married barrister Herbert Leigh Hunt here in 1932. Other cultural diversions include the **Wallace Collection** (*see p88*) and the **Wigmore Hall** (*see p301*).

Madame Tussauds

Marylebone Road, NW1 5LR (0870 400 3000, www.madametussauds.com/london). Baker Street tube. **Open** times vary; check website for details. **Admission** £30; £25.80 reductions; £108 family; free under-4s. **Credit** MC, V. **Map** p396 G4.
Streams of humanity jostle excitedly here for the chance to take pictures of each other planting a smacker on the waxen visage of fame and fortune.

EXPLORE

ZSL London Zoo. *See p88.*

★ FREE Wallace Collection

Hertford House, Manchester Square, W1U 3BN (7935 0687, www.wallacecollection.org). Bond Street tube. **Open** 10am-5pm daily. **Admission** free. **Credit** (shop) MC, V. **Map** p396 G5.

Built in 1776, this handsome house contains an exceptional collection of 18th-century French furniture, painting and objets d'art, as well as an amazing array of medieval armour and weaponry. It all belonged to Sir Richard Wallace, who, as the illegitimate offspring of the fourth Marquess of Hertford, inherited in 1870 the treasures his father had amassed in the last 30 years of his life. Room after grand room contains Louis XIV and XV furnishings and Sèvres porcelain; the galleries are hung with paintings by Titian, Gainsborough, Velázquez, Fragonard and Reynolds; Franz Hals's *Laughing Cavalier* (neither laughing nor a cavalier) is one of the best known, along with Fragonard's *The Swing*. The refurbished West Galleries display 19th-century and Venetian works, including paintings by Canaletto, and the collections of miniatures and gold boxes are on show in the Boudoir Cabinet. New East Galleries, dedicated to Dutch paintings, opened in 2012. *Photo p87.*

Walk The Sidestreet Shuffle

Avoid Oxford Street's clogged pavements with a trail through the backstreets.

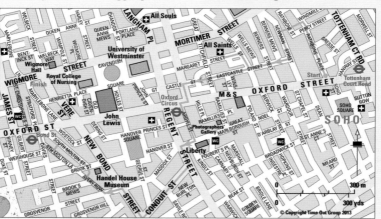

This hour-long walk follows the hinterlands of Oxford Street, which offer not only useful routes parallel to the main drag but a backstreet take on retail and London life.

Rathbone Place marks the lower reaches of Fitzrovia, where the worlds of media and design collide with the rag trade. The fun begins at **Hobgoblin** (no.24, 7323 9040), a folk music store where musicians test-drive zithers, banjos and ukuleles. Close by on Percy Street, **Contemporary Applied Arts** (*see p224*) sells outstanding British crafts, from jewellery to furniture.

Keep north up restaurant-lined Charlotte Street, buzzing with media types, then turn left beside the suave **Charlotte Street Hotel** (*see p237*) through Percy Passage. Cross the dog-leg of Rathbone Street, and head on via Dickensian Newman Passage to emerge in Newman Street. Pause for a snap of the **BT Tower**, then go left and right on to Eastcastle Street. Detour up Margaret Street to **All Saints** church (*see p74*).

Back on Eastcastle Street sits cutting-edge gallery **Stuart Shave/Modern Art** (nos.23-25, 7299 7950). Over the road, **Fever** (no.52, 7636 6326) mixes cute retro-inspired clothing and accessories with vintage, while the **Getty Images Gallery** (no.46, 7291 5380) holds great photography exhibitions. Market Place opens ahead, a mellow collection of sidewalk cafés yards from the frenzy of Oxford Street. Stop for refreshment and then head across Oxford Street down Argyll Street, aiming for the half-timbered **Liberty** building (*see p204*).

Next, cross Regent Street towards Conduit Street, where a visit to **Vivienne Westwood**'s flamboyant flagship store (no.44, 7439 1109, www.vivienne westwood.com) provides a taste of punky

▶ *The museum restaurant is beautifully set in a glass-roofed courtyard and makes a good – if pricey – choice for a shopping-day lunch.*

REGENT'S PARK

Baker Street or Regent's Park tube.

Regent's Park (open 5am-dusk daily) is one of London's most delightful open spaces. Originally a hunting ground for Henry VIII, it remained a royals-only retreat long after it was formally

London couture. Continue to New Bond Street into Grosvenor Street, then right up Avery Row. This is the land of Victorian London's great aristocratic estates, where narrow service alleys brought tradesmen to the rear entrances of the grand residences. The alleys still offer services to the gentry, but they're now exclusive little boutiques and restaurants that are hidden from the dazed tourists wandering nearby. On Avery Row, check out the **Paul Smith Sale Shop** (*see p216*).

Adjoining Lancashire Court is home to restaurants and the **Handel House Museum** (*see p94*), which faces Brook Street and, close by, Italian design legend **Alessi** (no.22, 7518 9090). Move on to pedestrianised South Molton Street and its strong mix of chain stores, cafés and independents, among them glittery **Butler & Wilson** (no.20, 7409 2955). Take the passage to the left of fashion queen **Browns** (*see p213*) and pop out by the imposing terracotta structure of **Grays Antique Market** (*see p228*).

Cross Oxford Street again, battling your way to the freestanding clock signposting the narrow entrance to St Christopher's Place. This warren of little streets houses a traffic-free complex of cafés and shops, including Finnish designer **Marimekko** (nos.16-17, 7486 6454). There's also a fountain and a flower-decked Victorian WC.

Need a rest? Head north to Wigmore Street for one last stop at **Robert Clergerie Shoes** (no.67, 7935 3601), before heading a couple of doors down to **Comptoir Libanais** (no.65, 7935 1110, www.lecomptoir.co.uk). This colourful and inviting Lebanese eaterie is the perfect place to mull over your purchases with a rosewater macaroon and a mint tea.

designed by John Nash in 1811; only in 1845 did it open to the public. Attractions run from the animal noises and odours of **ZSL London Zoo** (*see below*) to the enchanting **Open Air Theatre** (*see p306*); rowing boat hire, beautiful rose gardens, ice-cream stands and the **Garden Café** (7935 5729, www.companyofcooks.com) complete the postcard-pretty picture.

West of Regent's Park rises the golden dome of the **London Central Mosque** (www.iccuk. org), while the northern end of **Baker Street** is unsurprisingly heavy on nods of respect to the world's favourite freelance detective. At the **Sherlock Holmes Museum** (no.221B, 7935 8866, www.sherlock-holmes.co.uk), Holmes stories are earnestly re-enacted using mannequins, but studious fans may find more of interest among the books and photos of the **Sherlock Holmes Collection** at Marylebone Library (7641 1206, by appointment only).

The Beatles painted 94 Baker Street with a psychedelic mural before opening it in December 1967 as the Apple Boutique, a clothing store run on such whimsical hippie principles that it had to close within six months due to financial losses. Fab Four pilgrims head to the **London Beatles Store** (no.231, 7935 4464, www.beatles-storelondon.co.uk), where the ground-floor shop offers a predictable array of Beatles-branded accessories alongside genuine collectibles.

★ ZSL London Zoo
Regent's Park, NW1 4RY (7722 3333, www.zsl. org/london-zoo). Baker Street or Camden Town tube then bus 274, C2. **Open** times vary; check website for details. **Admission** £21.50-£23; £16-£21 reductions; free under-3s. **Credit** AmEx, MC, V. **Map** p396 G2.
London Zoo has been open in one form or another since 1826. Spread over 36 acres and containing more than 600 species, it cares for many of the endangered variety – part of the entry price (pretty steep at £23 in peak season) goes towards the ZSL's projects around the world. Regular events include 'animals in action' and keeper talks. Exhibits are entertaining: look out, for example, for the re-creation of a kitchen overrun with large cockroaches. The big new attraction (due for spring 2013) will be Tiger Territory, where Sumatran tigers can be watched through floor-to-ceiling windows. The relaunched 'Rainforest Life' biodome and the 'Meet the Monkeys' attractions allow visitors to walk through enclosures that re-create the natural habitat of, respectively, tree anteaters and sloths, and black-capped Bolivian squirrel monkeys, while personal encounters of the avian kind can be had in the Victorian Blackburn Pavilion – as well as at Penguin Beach, where you can watch the black-and-white favourites swim underwater. 'Gorilla Kingdom' is another highlight, as are the snakes and crocs in the reptile house. Bring a picnic and you could easily spend the day here. *Photo p87.*

EXPLORE

Paddington & Notting Hill

Chic shops, Middle Eastern émigrés and a very famous market.

Sprawled beneath the Westway flyover, with its railway terminus and branch of the Grand Union Canal, **Paddington** is where central London meets the west of England. It's not an attractive area, but it holds appeal thanks to the Arab influence around the Edgware Road and the goodies hidden away in Alfie's Antique Market. There's nothing hidden away about **Notting Hill**, where **Portobello Market** is surrounded by some of the most desirable addresses in west London, one of which houses the inimitable **Museum of Brands, Packaging & Advertising**.

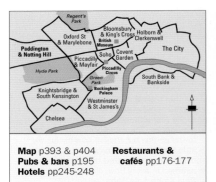

Map p393 & p404	Restaurants &
Pubs & bars p195	cafés pp176-177
Hotels pp245-248	

Map p393 & p404
Pubs & bars p195
Hotels pp245-248
Restaurants & cafés pp176-177

EDGWARE ROAD & PADDINGTON

Edgware Road, Lancaster Gate or Marble Arch tube, or Paddington tube/rail.

Part of the Romans' Watling Street from Dover to Wales, **Edgware Road** rules a definite north–south line marking where the West End stops and central west London begins. It's now the heart of the city's Middle East end: if you want to pick up your copy of *Al Hayat*, cash a cheque at the Bank of Kuwait or catch Egyptian football, head here. North of the Marylebone Road, **Church Street** is home to the wondrous **Alfie's Antique Market** (*see p228*).

INSIDE TRACK MARKET FINDS

Portobello Green Market has the area's best vintage fashion stalls. Look out for the excellent second-hand boot and shoe stall and brilliant vintage handbag stall (usually outside Falafel King), along with vintage clothing stall Sage Femme, often outside the Antique Clothing Shop.

The fact that the name Paddington has been immortalised by a certain small, ursine Peruvian émigré is appropriate, given that the area has long been home to refugees and immigrants. It was a country village until an arm of the Grand Union Canal arrived in 1801, linking London to the Midlands, followed in the 1830s by the railway. **Paddington Station**, with its fine triple roof of iron and glass, was built in 1851 to the specifications of the great engineer Isambard Kingdom Brunel.

Paddington's proximity to central London eventually drew in developers. To the east of the station, gleaming **Paddington Central** now provides a million square feet of office space, canalside apartments and restaurants. In St Mary's Hospital, the old-fashioned **Alexander Fleming Laboratory Museum** gives a sense of what the district used to be like.

Alexander Fleming Laboratory Museum
St Mary's Hospital, Praed Street, W2 1NY (7886 6528, www.imperial.nhs.uk/aboutus/museums andarchives/index.htm). Paddington tube/rail. **Open** 10am-1pm Mon-Thur. *By appointment* 2-5pm Mon-Thur; 10am-5pm Fri. **Admission** £4; £2 reductions; free under-5s. **No credit cards**. **Map** p393 D5.

EXPLORE

Portobello Road Market.

Buzz in at the entrance on your left as you enter the hospital and head up the stairs to find this tiny, dusty, instrument-cluttered lab. Enthusiastic guides conjure up the professor who, in 1928, noticed that mould contamination had destroyed some staphylococcus bacteria on a set-aside culture plate: he had discovered penicillin. The keen entrepreneurs across the street immediately began to advertise their pub's healthful properties, claiming the miracle fungus had blown into the lab from them. The video room has a documentary on Fleming's life and discovery.

NOTTING HILL

Notting Hill Gate, Ladbroke Grove or Westbourne Park tube.

Head north up Queensway from Kensington Gardens and turn west along **Westbourne Grove**. The road starts humble but gets posher the further west you go; cross Chepstow Road and you're in upmarket **Notting Hill**. A host of fashionable restaurants and bars exploit the lingering street cred of the fast-disappearing black and working-class communities; posh shops are a better reflection of the area's current character. **Notting Hill Gate** isn't a pretty street, but the leafy avenues to the south are; so is **Pembridge Road**, to the north, leading to the boutique-filled streets of Westbourne Grove and Ledbury Road, and to **Portobello Road** and its renowned market (*see p209*).

Halfway down, **Blenheim Crescent** boasts a couple of independent booksellers, but the **Travel Bookshop** (nos.13-15), the store on which Hugh Grant's bookshop was based in the movie *Notting Hill*, has now closed down. Under the Westway, that elevated section of the M40 motorway linking London with Oxford, is the small but busy **Portobello Green Market** (*see left* **Inside Track**).

North of the Westway, Portobello's vitality fizzles out. It sparks back to life at **Golborne Road**, the heartland of London's North African community. Here, too, is a fine Portuguese café-deli, the **Lisboa Pâtisserie** (no.57, 8968 5242). At the north-eastern end of the road stands **Trellick Tower**, an architecturally significant, like-it-or-loathe-it piece of Ernö Goldfinger modernism. At its western end, Golborne Road connects with Ladbroke Grove, which can be followed north to **Kensal Green Cemetery**.

FREE Kensal Green Cemetery
Harrow Road, Kensal Green, W10 4RA (8969 0152, www.kensalgreen.co.uk). Kensal Green tube. **Open** *Apr-Sept* 9am-6pm Mon-Sat; 10am-6pm Sun. *Oct-Mar* 9am-5pm Mon-Sat; 10am-5pm Sun. **Tours** *Mar-Oct* 2pm Sun. *Nov-Feb* 2pm 1st & 3rd Sun of mth. **Admission** free. *Tours* £5 (£4 reductions) donation. **No credit cards**.
Behind a neoclassical gate is a green oasis of the dead. It's the resting place of both the Duke of Sussex, sixth son of George III, and his sister, Princess Sophia; also buried here are Wilkie Collins, Anthony Trollope and William Makepeace Thackeray.

Museum of Brands, Packaging & Advertising
Colville Mews, Lonsdale Road, W11 2AR (7908 0880, www.museumofbrands.com). Notting Hill Gate tube. **Open** 10am-6pm Tue-Sat; 11am-5pm Sun. **Admission** £6.50; £2.25-£4 reductions; £15 family; free under-7s. **Credit** MC, V. **Map** p404 Y4.
Robert Opie began collecting the things others throw away when he was 16. His collection now includes anything from milk bottles to vacuum cleaners and cereal packets. The emphasis is on the last century of British consumerism, design and domestic life, but there are older items, such as an ancient Egyptian doll.

Kensal Green Cemetery.

Piccadilly Circus & Mayfair

Beyond the neon frenzy of Piccadilly lies the deep calm of old money.

EXPLORE

Top dog since the 1930s, when it was a playground for London's aristocracy, **Mayfair** oozes wealth. The area is now the haunt of hedge funders, who defy the lingering effects of recession as they flash cash in restaurants and hotel bars, but there are vestiges of old Mayfair: the tailors of Savile Row, marginally destuffed, blue-chip galleries, and the bijou shopping rookery of Shepherd Market. To the south-east, the neon-lit frenzy of **Piccadilly Circus** remains the one part of town that every Londoner does their best to avoid.

Map p396, p398 p416	**Pubs & bars** p196
Hotels pp248-250	**Restaurants & cafés** pp171-172

PICCADILLY CIRCUS & REGENT STREET

Oxford Circus or Piccadilly Circus tube.

Frantic **Piccadilly Circus** is an uneasy mix of the tawdry and the grand, a mix with little to do with the vision of its architect. John Nash's 1820s design for the intersection of Regent Street and Piccadilly, two of the West End's most elegant streets, was a harmonious circle of curved frontages. But 60 years later, Shaftesbury Avenue muscled in, creating the lopsided and usually pandemonious traffic junction still in place today. A revamp by the same design consultants who successfully remodelled Oxford Circus is nearing completion, with a mile of ugly, pedestrian-funnelling and cyclist-shredding railings ripped out.

Alfred Gilbert's memorial fountain in honour of child-labour abolitionist Earl Shaftesbury was erected in 1893. It's properly known as the **Shaftesbury Memorial**, with the statue on top intended to show the Angel of Christian Charity, but critics and public alike recognised the likeness of **Eros** and their judgement has stuck. The illuminated advertising panels around the intersection appeared late in the 19th century and have been present ever since: a Coca-Cola ad

has been here since 1955, making it the world's longest-running advertisement. Running Sky News broadcasts indicate the likely media-saturated future for the illuminations.

Opposite the memorial, the **Trocadero Centre** (www.londontrocadero.com) has seen several ventures come and go, driven out by high rents and low footfall in a prime but tired location, although **Ripley's Believe It or Not!** (*see p93*) seems already to be well established. Planning permission was granted (for the third time) in 2012 for a massive revamp of the site, including a huge new hotel – perhaps, at last, the boost the area needs.

Connecting Piccadilly Circus to Oxford Circus to the north and Pall Mall to the south, the broad curve of **Regent Street** was designed by Nash in the early 1800s with the aims of improving access to Regent's Park and bumping up

---

INSIDE TRACK DEEP WATER

The water feature in the basement of **Grays Antique Market** (*see p228* is formed from the Tyburn Brook. One of London's buried rivers, it runs underground from Hampstead to Westminster.

property values in Haymarket and Pall Mall. Much of Nash's architecture was destroyed in the early 20th century, but the grandeur of the street remains impressive. Among the highlights are the mammoth children's emporium **Hamleys** (nos.188-196, 0871 704 1977, www. hamleys.com), landmark department store **Liberty** (*see p204*) and, first of a new Regent Street breed, **Anthropologie** (*see p214*).

Ripley's Believe It or Not!

1 Piccadilly Circus, W1J 0DA (3238 0022, www. ripleyslondon.com). Piccadilly Circus tube.
Open 10am-midnight daily (last entry 10.30pm).
Admission £25.95; £19.95-£23.95 reductions; £81.95 family; free under-4s. **Credit** MC, V.
Map p416 W4.
This 'odditorium' follows a formula more or less unchanged since Robert Ripley opened his first display at the Chicago World Fair in 1933: an assortment of 800 curiosities is displayed, ranging from the world's smallest road-safe car to da Vinci's *Last Supper* painted on a grain of rice – via the company's signature shrunken heads.

MAYFAIR

Bond Street or Green Park tube.

The gaiety suggested by the name of Mayfair, derived from a long-gone spring celebration, isn't matched by its latter-day atmosphere today. Even on Mayfair's busy shopping streets, you may feel out of place without the reassuring heft of a platinum card. Nonetheless, there are many pleasures to enjoy if you fancy a stroll, not least the rapidly changing roster of blue-chip commercial art galleries.

The Grosvenor and Berkeley families bought the rolling green fields that would become Mayfair in the middle of the 17th century. In the 1700s, they developed the pastures into a posh new neighbourhood, focused on a series of landmark squares. The most famous of these, **Grosvenor Square** (1725-31), is dominated by the supremely inelegant US Embassy, due to close in 2017 for its move to supremely inelegant Vauxhall. The embassy's only decorative touches are a fierce eagle and a mass of post-9/11 protective barricades. Out front, pride of place is taken by a statue of President Dwight Eisenhower, who stayed in nearby **Claridge's** (*see p248*) when in London; Roosevelt is in the park nearby.

Brook Street has impressive musical credentials: GF Handel lived and died at no.25, and Jimi Hendrix roomed briefly next door at no.23, adjacent buildings that have been combined into the **Handel House Museum** (*see p94*). For most visitors, however, this part of town is all about shopping. Connecting Brook

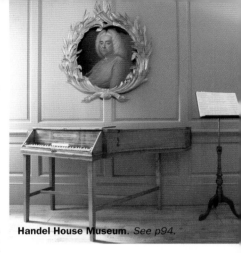
Handel House Museum. *See p94.*

Street with Oxford Street to the north, **South Molton Street** is home to the fabulous boutique-emporium **Browns** (*see p213*) and the excellent **Grays Antique Market** (*see p228*), while **New Bond Street** is an A-Z of top-end, mainstream fashion houses.

Beyond New Bond Street, **Hanover Square** is another of the area's big squares, now a busy traffic chicane. Just to the south is **St George's Church**, built in the 1720s and once everyone's favourite place to be seen and to get married. Handel, who married nobody, attended services here. South of St George's, salubrious **Conduit Street** is where fashion shocker Vivienne Westwood (no.44) faces staid Rigby & Peller (no.22A), corsetière to the Queen.

Running south off Conduit Street is the most famous Mayfair shopping street of all, **Savile Row**. Gieves & Hawkes (no.1) is a must-visit for anyone interested in the history of British menswear; at no.15, the estimable Henry Poole & Co has cut suits for clients including Napoleon III, Charles Dickens and 'Buffalo' Bill Cody. No.3 was the home of the Beatles' Apple Records and their rooftop farewell concert.

Two streets west, **Cork Street** was long the heart of the West End art scene, but nearly a dozen of the long-established street-front galleries are under threat from two new developments. Instead, major US art dealers seem to be driving the Mayfair art scene: notably David Zwirner's 10,000sq ft space at 24 Grafton Street (3538 3165, www.davidzwirner.com), but other new galleries include Michael Werner (22 Upper Brook Street, 7495 6855, www. michaelwerner.com) and Skarstedt (23 Old Bond Street, 7499 5200, www.skarstedt.com), while Pace (www.pacegallery.com) is sharing the Royal Academy's premises at 6 Burlington Gardens (*see p95* **Inside Track**). A couple of streets over is Albemarle Street, where you'll

Dignity in Death

London begins to remember those killed in peacetime and in war.

On 7 July 2005, 52 people were killed by suicide bombers as they made their way to work. London has suffered numerous terrorist attacks over the last 150 years, with waves of bombings by Fenians, three different generations of the IRA, as well as leftist militants the Angry Brigade, pro-Palestinians and a racist homophobe, but death toll on 7 July was unprecedented. Nonetheless, the city's memorial to the victims is calm and unrhetorical. Located in the south-east corner of **Hyde Park** (*see p114*), between the Lovers' Walk and busy Park Lane, it consists of 52 10ft-tall, square steel columns, one for each fatality. Each is marked with the date, time and location of that person's death; they're arranged in four groups, according to which of the four explosions killed the person in question. It is an austerely beautiful, quietly modern and human-scale tribute.

Despite widespread commemoration events for the 70th anniversary of the Blitz (57 consecutive nights of German bombing which began on 7 September 1940), there is no unified memorial to the perhaps 20,000 London civilians killed in their homes, right across the capital, during World War II. But there is a growing concentration of fine war memorials at Hyde Park Corner, surrounding **Wellington Arch** (*see p96*). The newest, the result of a long campaign, is the Bomber Command Memorial. Unveiled in 2012, the memorial recognises the sacrifice of the 55,573 men of Bomber Command, killed between 1939 and 1945 as they

pulverised Nazi-held Europe into submission. Between grand, but rather stiff, walls of Doric columns stands a group of seven aircrew, in sombre mood, accompanied by quotes from Churchill and Pericles.

While you're here, spare a moment for a rather older memorial: Charles Sargeant Jagger's moving tribute to the 49,076 men of the Royal Regiment of Artillery slain between 1914 and 1919. It's both vast – a massive Portland stone slab with giant gunners on three sides – and strangely muted, with a dead soldier lying on the monument's north side. Thoughtful and deeply moving.

Wellington Arch.

---

find the handsomely rejuvenated **Royal Institution**, home to the **Faraday Museum**.

★ Handel House Museum

25 Brook Street (entrance in Lancashire Court), W1K 4HB (7399 1953, www.handelhouse.org). Bond Street tube. **Open** 10am-6pm Tue, Wed, Fri, Sat; 10am-8pm Thur; noon-6pm Sun. **Admission** £6; £2-£5 reductions; free under-5s. **Credit** MC, V. **Map** p396 H6.

Handel moved to Britain from his native Germany aged 25 and settled in this house 12 years later, remaining here until his death in 1759. It has been beautifully restored with original and re-created furnishings, paintings and a welter of the composer's scores (in the same room as photos of Jimi Hendrix, who lived in the attic). The programme of events includes Thursday recitals. *Photo p93.*

★ FREE Royal Institution & Faraday Museum

21 Albemarle Street, W1S 4BS (7409 2992, www.rigb.org). Green Park tube. **Open** 9am-6pm Mon-Fri. Closes for events; phone ahead. **Admission** free. *Multimedia tours* £3. **Credit** MC, V. **Map** p416 U4.

The Royal Institution was founded in 1799 for 'diffusing the knowledge… and application of science to the common purposes of life'; from behind its neo-classical façade, it's been at the forefront of London's scientific achievements ever since. In 2008, Sir Terry Farrell completed a £22m rebuild, improving accessibility and luring people in with more open frontage and a licensed café.

The Michael Faraday Laboratory, a complete replica of Faraday's former workspace, is in the basement, alongside a working laboratory in which

Royal Institution & Faraday Museum.

RI scientists can be observed researching their current projects. Some 1,000 of the RI's 7,000-odd scientific objects are on display, including the world's first electric transformer, a prototype Davy lamp and, from 1858, a print of the first transatlantic telegraph signal. The RI also holds a terrific rolling programme of talks and demonstrations in its lecture theatre, most famously at Christmas.

Shepherd Market

Just west of Albemarle Street, **44 Berkeley Square** is one of the original houses in this grand square. Built in the 1740s, it was described by architectural historian Nikolaus Pevsner as 'the finest terrace house of London'. Curzon Street, which runs off the south-west corner of Berkeley Square, was home to MI5, Britain's secret service, from 1945 until the '90s. It's also the northern boundary of **Shepherd Market**, named after a food market set up here by architect Edward Shepherd in the early 18th century and now a curious little enclave in the heart of this exclusive area.

From 1686, this was where the raucous May Fair was held, until it was shut down in the late 18th century due to 'drunkenness, fornication, gaming and lewdness'. You'll still manage the drunkenness easily enough at a couple of good pubs (such as **Ye Grapes**, at 16 Shepherd Market). The cobbler on adjoining White Horse Street ('Don't throw away old shoes, they can be restored!') and the ironmongers on Shepherd Street keep things from becoming too genteel.

PICCADILLY & GREEN PARK

Green Park, Hyde Park Corner or Piccadilly Circus tube.

Piccadilly's name is derived from the 'picadil', a type of suit collar that was in vogue during the 18th century. The first of the area's main buildings was built by tailor Robert Baker and, indicating the source of his wealth, nicknamed 'Piccadilly Hall'. A stroll through the handful of Regency shopping arcades confirms that the rag trade is still flourishing mere minutes away from Savile Row and Jermyn Street. At the renovated **Burlington Arcade** (*see p207*), the oldest and most famous of these arcades, top-hatted security staff known as 'beadles' ensure there's no singing, whistling or hurrying in the arcade: such uncouth behaviour is prohibited by archaic bylaws. Formerly Burlington House (1665), the **Royal Academy of Arts** (*see p96*) is next door to the arcade's entrance. It hosts several lavish, crowd-pleasing exhibitions each year and has a pleasant courtyard café.

On Piccadilly are further representatives of high-end retail. **Fortnum & Mason** (*see p203*), London's most prestigious food store, was founded in 1707 by a former footman to Queen Anne. Look for the fine clock: a 1964 articulated

INSIDE TRACK
NEW WINE IN OLD SKINS

In October 2012, the Royal Academy (*see p96*) expanded into another 19th-century building: **6 Burlington Gardens**. Coveniently located directly behind the RA's main location, its debut exhibition made a fierce contrast with the handsome Grade II-listed surrounds: 'RA Now' showcased the likes of Tracey Emin, David Hockney, Zaha Hadid and Cindy Sherman. That show is now over, but until 17 Feb you can catch the ethereally glowing installations of Mariko Mori's 'Rebirth' – or during the day make use of the 42º Raw café and Studio Shop.

EXPLORE

effort, it features 18th-century effigies of Mr Fortnum and Mr Mason, who bow to each other on the hour. The plain church at no.197 is **St James's Piccadilly** (*see below*), where William Blake was baptised.

To the west along Piccadilly, smartly uniformed doormen mark the **Wolseley** (*see p172*), a former car showroom that is now a fine (if tiresomely frequently lauded) restaurant, and the expensive, exclusive **Ritz** (*see p249*). The flat green expanse just beyond the Ritz is **Green Park**; it's rather dull in itself, but makes a very pleasant middle section of walk through three Royal Parks, connecting St James's Park (*see p105*) to Hyde Park (*see p114*). Work your way along Piccadilly, following the northern edge of Green Park past the queue outside the Hard Rock Café (where the Vault's displays of memorabilia are free to visit and open every day; www.hardrock.com) to the Duke of Wellington's old home, **Apsley House**, opposite **Wellington Arch**. This is hectic **Hyde Park Corner**; Buckingham Palace (*see p106*) is just a short walk south-east, while Hyde Park and the upper-crust enclave of Belgravia are to the west, but it also has a collection of memorials that are worth lingering over in themselves (*see p94* **Death and Dignity**).

Apsley House

149 Piccadilly, W1J 7NT (7499 5676, www. english-heritage.org.uk). Hyde Park Corner tube. **Open** *Nov-Mar* 11am-4pm Sat, Sun. *Apr-Oct* 11am-5pm Wed-Sun. *Tours* by arrangement. **Admission** £6.30; £4.90-£5.90 reductions; free under-5s. *Tours* phone in advance. *Joint ticket with Wellington Arch* £8.20; £4.70-£7.40 reductions; £20.50 family. **Credit** MC, V. **Map** p398 G8.
Called No.1 London because it was the first London building encountered on the road to the city from the village of Kensington, Apsley House was built by Robert Adam in the 1770s. The Duke of Wellington kept it as his London home for 35 years. Although his descendants still live here, several rooms are open to the public, providing a superb feel for the man and his era. Admire the extravagant porcelain dinnerware and plates or ask for a demonstration of the crafty mirrors in the scarlet and gilt picture gallery, where a fine Velázquez and a Correggio hang near Goya's portrait of the Iron Duke after he defeated the French in 1812. This was a last-minute edit: X-rays have revealed that Wellington's head was painted over that of Joseph Bonaparte, Napoleon's brother.
▶ *Come here for the atmospheric twilight tours in winter to appreciate the dazzling floor- and ceiling-mounted chandeliers.*

ᴵᴿᴱᴱ Royal Academy of Arts

Burlington House, W1J 0BD (7300 8000, www. royalacademy.org.uk). Green Park or Piccadilly Circus tube. **Open** 10am-6pm Mon-Thur, Sat,
Sun; 10am-10pm Fri. **Admission** free. *Exhibitions* vary. **Credit** AmEx, MC, V. **Map** p416 U4.
Britain's first art school was founded in 1768 and moved to the extravagantly Palladian Burlington House a century later, but it's now best known not for education but exhibitions. Ticketed blockbusters are generally held in the Sackler Wing or the main galleries; shows in the John Madejski Fine Rooms are drawn from the RA's holdings, which range from Constable to Hockney, and are free. The Academy's biggest event is the Summer Exhibition, which for more than two centuries has drawn from works entered by the public. For the Royal Academy's new-old extension, *see p95* **Inside Track**.
▶ *Several attractions have, like the RA, installed user-friendly courtyard fountains, where children can splash while parents admire the surroundings, among them Somerset House (see p79), the V&A (see p113) and the new Granary Square (see p71* **Hip to be a Square***).*

ᴵᴿᴱᴱ St James's Piccadilly

197 Piccadilly, W1J 9LL (7734 4511, www. st-james-piccadilly.org). Piccadilly Circus tube. **Open** 8am-6.30pm daily. *Evening events* times vary. **Admission** free. **Credit** (concerts only) AmEx, DC, MC, V. **Map** p416 U4.
Consecrated in 1684, St James's is the only church Sir Christopher Wren built on an entirely new site. A calming building with few architectural airs or graces, it was almost destroyed in World War II, but painstakingly reconstructed. Grinling Gibbons's delicate limewood garlanding around the sanctuary survived and is one of the few real frills. Beneath a new tiled roof, the church stages regular classical concerts, provides a home for the William Blake Society and hosts markets in the churchyard: food on Monday, antiques on Tuesday, and arts and crafts from Wednesday to Saturday. There's also a handy café in the basement with plenty of tables.

Wellington Arch

Hyde Park Corner, W1J 7JZ (7930 2726, www. english-heritage.org.uk). Hyde Park Corner tube. **Open** *Apr-Oct* 10am-5pm Wed-Sun. *Nov-Mar* 10am-4pm Sat, Sun. **Admission** £4; £2.40-£3.60 reductions; free under-5s. *Joint ticket with Apsley House* £8.20; £4.90-£7.40 reductions; £20.50 family. **Credit** AmEx, MC, V. **Map** p398 G8.
Built in the late 1820s to mark Britain's triumph over Napoleonic France, Decimus Burton's Wellington Arch was initially topped by an out-of-proportion equestrian statue of Wellington. However, Captain Adrian Jones's 38-ton bronze *Peace Descending on the Quadriga of War* has finished it with a flourish since 1912. The Arch has three floors, with a bookshop and various displays, covering the history of the arch and the Blue Plaques scheme, and in the Quadriga Gallery providing space for temporary exhibtions. There are great views from the balcony in winter (leafy trees rather obscure the sightlines in spring and summer).

EXPLORE

Westminster & St James's

For members' clubs and members of Parliament.

England is ruled from **Westminster**. The monarchy has been in residence here since the 11th century, when Edward the Confessor moved west from the City, and the government of the day also calls it home. It's a key destination for visitors as well, with the most significant area designated a UNESCO World Heritage Site back in 1987.

For such an important part of London, it's surprisingly spacious. **St James's Park** is one of London's finest green spaces, **Trafalgar Square** (overlooked by the **National Gallery**) is a tourist hotspot, and the **Mall** offers a properly regal route to Buckingham Palace.

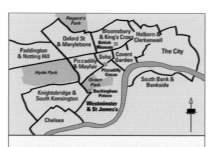

Map pp398-399 & p416	**Pubs & bars** pp196-197
Restaurants & cafés pp172-173	**Hotels** pp250-251

TRAFALGAR SQUARE

Leicester Square tube or Charing Cross tube/rail.

Laid out in the 1820s by John Nash, Trafalgar Square is the heart of modern London. Tourists come in their thousands to pose for photographs in front of **Nelson's Column**. It was erected in 1840 to honour Vice Admiral Horatio Nelson, who died at the point of victory at the Battle of Trafalgar in 1805. The statue atop the 150-foot Corinthian column is foreshortened to appear in perfect proportion from the ground. The granite fountains were added in 1845; Sir Edwin Landseer's bronze lions joined them in 1867.

Once surrounded on all sides by busy roads, the square was improved markedly by pedestrianisation in 2003 of the North Terrace, right in front of the **National Gallery**. A ban on feeding pigeons was another positive step. The square feels more like public space now, and is a focus for performance and celebration.

Around the perimeter are three plinths bearing statues of George IV and two Victorian military heroes, Henry Havelock and Sir Charles James Napier. The long-empty fourth plinth, which never received its planned martial statue, has been used since 1998 to display temporary, contemporary art. Until April 2013, Elmgreen and Dragset's *Powerless Structures, Fig.101* – the bronze cast of a boy on a rocking horse, playing on the militarism of the other statues – will be in place, after which Katharina Fritsch's *Hahn/Cock*, a larger-than-life cockerel in ultramarine blue, will stand in its stead. Other points of interest around the square include an equestrian statue of Charles I, dating

INSIDE TRACK
STAY OFF THE LIONS!

A scholarly report found that nearly 150 years of people climbing on their backs is wearing away the lions in **Trafalgar Square** (*see above*). Bronze on the beasts' flanks and backs, which was originally 15mm thick, is now down to just 3mm in some areas. To make matters worse, deep gashes have been made by people gouging the statues with coins and keys.

from the 1630s, with a plaque behind it that marks the original site of Edward I's Eleanor Cross, the official centre of London. (A recently renovated Victorian replica of the cross stands outside Charing Cross Station; *see p77*.) At the square's north-east corner is the refurbished **St Martin-in-the-Fields** (*see below*).

★ FREE National Gallery

Trafalgar Square, WC2N 5DN (7747 2885, www.nationalgallery.org.uk). Leicester Square tube or Charing Cross tube/rail. **Open** 10am-6pm Mon-Thur, Sat, Sun; 10am-9pm Fri. *Tours* 11.30am, 2.30pm daily. **Admission** free. *Special exhibitions* vary. **Credit** (shop) MC, V. **Map** p416 X5.

Founded in 1824 to display 36 paintings, the National Gallery is now one of the world's great repositories for art. There are masterpieces from virtually every European school of art, from austere 13th-century religious paintings to the sensual delights of Caravaggio and Van Gogh.

Furthest to the left of the main entrance, the modern Sainsbury Wing extension contains the gallery's earliest works: Italian paintings by masters such as Giotto and Piero della Francesca, as well as the *Wilton Diptych*, the finest medieval English picture in the collection, showing Richard II with the Virgin and Child. The basement of the Sainsbury Wing is the setting for important temporary exhibitions.

In the West Wing (left of the main entrance) are Italian Renaissance masterpieces by Correggio, Titian and Raphael. Straight ahead on entry, in the North Wing, are 17th-century Dutch, Flemish, Italian and Spanish Old Masters, including works such as Rembrandt's *A Woman Bathing in a Stream* and Caravaggio's *Supper at Emmaus*. Velázquez's *Rokeby Venus* is one of the artist's most famous paintings, a reclining nude asking herself – and us – 'How do we look?' Also in this wing are works by the great landscape artists Claude and Poussin. Turner insisted that his *Dido Building Carthage* and *Sun Rising through Vapour* should hang alongside two Claudes here that particularly inspired him.

In the East Wing (to the right of the main entrance, and most easily reached via the new street-level entrance on Trafalgar Square) are some of the gallery's most popular paintings: works by the French Impressionists and Post-Impressionists, including Monet's *Water-Lilies*, one of Van Gogh's *Sunflowers* and Seurat's *Bathers at Asnières*. Don't miss Renoir's astonishingly lovely *Les Parapluies*. You shouldn't plan to see everything in one visit, but free guided tours, audio guides and the superb Art Start computer (which allows you to tailor and map your own itinerary of must-sees) help you make the best of your time.

★ FREE National Portrait Gallery

St Martin's Place, WC2H 0HE (7306 0055, www.npg.org.uk). Leicester Square tube or Charing Cross tube/rail. **Open** 10am-6pm Mon-Wed, Sat, Sun; 10am-9pm Thur, Fri. **Admission** free. *Special exhibitions* vary. **Credit** AmEx, MC, V. **Map** p416 X4.

Portraits don't have to be stuffy. The excellent National Portrait Gallery has everything from oil paintings of stiff-backed royals to photographs of soccer stars and gloriously unflattering political caricatures. The portraits of musicians, scientists, artists, philanthropists and celebrities are arranged in chronological order from the top to the bottom of the building, with the oldest at the top.

At the top of the escalator up from the main foyer, on the second floor, are the earliest works, portraits of Tudor and Stuart royals and notables, including Holbein's 'cartoon' of Henry VIII and the 'Ditchley Portrait' of his daughter, Elizabeth I, her pearly slippers placed firmly on a colourful map of England. On the same floor, the 18th-century collection features Georgian writers and artists, with one room devoted to the influential Kit-Cat Club of bewigged Whig (leftish) intellectuals, Congreve and Dryden among them. More famous names include Wren and Swift. The second floor also shows Regency greats, military men such as Wellington and Nelson, plus Byron, Wordsworth and other Romantics. The first floor is devoted to the Victorians (Dickens, Brunel, Darwin) and to 20th-century luminaries, such as TS Eliot and Ian McKellen.

FREE St Martin-in-the-Fields

Trafalgar Square, WC2N 4JJ (7766 1100, www.smitf.org). Leicester Square tube or Charing Cross tube/rail. **Open** 8am-6pm Mon-Fri; 9am-6pm

Trafalgar Square.

National Gallery.

Sat; 8am-7.30pm Sun. *Services* 8am, 1.15pm, 6pm
Mon, Tue, Thur, Fri; 8am, 1pm, 5pm, 6.15pm Wed;
8am, 10am, 5pm, 6.30pm Sun. *Brass Rubbing
Centre* 10am-6pm Mon-Wed; 10am-8pm Thur-Sat;
11.30am-5pm Sun. **Admission** free. *Brass rubbing*
£4.50. **Credit** MC, V. **Map** p416 X4.

There's been a church 'in the fields' between
Westminster and the City since the 13th century, but
the current one was built in 1726 by James Gibbs,
using a fusion of neoclassical and Baroque styles.
The parish church for Buckingham Palace (note the
royal box to the left of the gallery), St Martin's bright
interior was fully restored a few years back, with
Victorian furbelows removed and the addition of a
brilliant altar window that shows the Cross, stylised
as if rippling on water. Downstairs in the crypt are
a fine café and the London Brass Rubbing Centre.
▶ *For lunchtime and evening concerts, see p301.*

WHITEHALL TO
PARLIAMENT SQUARE

Westminster tube or Charing Cross tube/rail.

The offices of the British government are lined
along **Whitehall**, itself named after Henry VIII's
magnificent palace, which burned to the ground
in 1698. Walking south from Trafalgar Square,
you pass the old **Admiralty Offices** and **War
Office**, the **Ministry of Defence**, the **Foreign
Office** and the **Treasury**, as well as the
Banqueting House (*see p101*), one of the few

buildings to survive the blaze. Also here is **Horse
Guards**, headquarters of the Household Cavalry,
the elite army unit that protects the Queen.

Either side of **Downing Street** – home
to the prime minister (no.10) and chancellor
(no.11), but closed to the public after IRA
attacks in the 1980s – are significant war
memorials. The millions who died in the
service of the nation in World Wars I and II are
commemorated by Sir Edwin Lutyens's dignified
Cenotaph, focal point of Remembrance Day
(*see p33*), while a separate memorial to the
women of World War II, by sculptor John Mills,
recalls the seven million women who contributed
to the war effort. Just past the Cenotaph and
hidden beneath government offices at the St
James's Park end of King Charles Street, the
claustrophobic **Churchill War Rooms** (*see
p101*) are where Britain's wartime PM planned
his campaigns and delivered his fiery speeches.

The broad sweep of Whitehall is an apt
introduction to the monuments of **Parliament
Square**. Laid out in 1868, this tiny green space
is flanked by the extravagant **Houses of
Parliament** (*see p101*), the neo-Gothic
Middlesex Guildhall (now the **Supreme
Court**; *see p103*) and the twin, square spires
of **Westminster Abbey** (*see p103*). Like a
pre-pedestrianised Trafalgar Square, Parliament
Square can seem little more than a glorified
traffic island, despite all the statues of British
politicians (Disraeli, Churchill) and foreign

dignitaries (Lincoln, Mandela), but its symbolic value has been brought back into focus in recent years through court battles over its suitability as a site for different kinds of political protest.

Parliament itself simply dazzles. An outrageous neo-Gothic fantasy, the seat of the British government is still formally known as the Palace of Westminster, though the only remaining parts of the medieval palace are **Westminster Hall** and the **Jewel Tower** (*see below*). At the north end of the palace is the clocktower housing the huge **'Big Ben'** bell that gives the clocktower its popular name; more than seven feet tall, the bell (itself formally known as the 'Great Bell') weighs over 13 tons. The tower was, in fact, renamed in 2012: rather than bowing to common usage, it became the Elizabeth Tower – in honour of the Queen's Diamond Jubilee.

Banqueting House

Whitehall, SW1A 2ER (0844 482 7777, www.hrp.org.uk). Westminster tube or Charing Cross tube/rail. **Open** 10am-5pm Mon-Sat. **Admission** £5; £4 reductions; free under-16s. **Credit** MC, V. **Map** p399 L8.

This handsome Italianate mansion, which was designed by Inigo Jones and constructed in 1620, was the first true Renaissance building in London. The sole surviving part of the Tudor and Stuart kings' Whitehall Palace, the Banqueting House features a lavish painted ceiling by Rubens, glorifying James I, 'the wisest fool in Christendom'. Regrettably, James's successor, Charles I, did not rule so wisely. After losing the English Civil War to Cromwell's Roundheads, he was executed in front of Banqueting House in 1649 (the event is marked by a curious bunch of royalists every 31 January). Lunchtime concerts are held on the first Monday of every month except August.

▶ *Call before you visit: the Banqueting House is sometimes closed for corporate functions.*

Churchill War Rooms

Clive Steps, King Charles Street, SW1A 2AQ (7930 6961, www.iwm.org.uk). St James's Park or Westminster tube. **Open** 9.30am-6pm daily. **Admission** £16.50; £13.20 reductions; free under-16s. **Credit** MC, V. **Map** p399 K9.

Out of harm's way beneath Whitehall, this cramped and spartan bunker was where Winston Churchill planned the Allied victory in World War II. Open to the public since 1984, the rooms powerfully bring to life the reality of a nation at war. The cabinet rooms were sealed on 16 August 1945, keeping the complex in a state of suspended animation: every pin stuck into the vast charts was placed there in the final days of the conflict. The humble quarters occupied by Churchill and his deputies give a tangible sense of wartime hardship, an effect reinforced by the wailing sirens and wartime speeches on the audio guide (free with admission).

Houses of Parliament

Parliament Square, SW1A 0AA (Commons information 7219 4272, Lords information 7219 3107, www.parliament.uk). Westminster tube. **Open** (when in session) *House of Commons Visitors' Gallery* 2.30-10.30pm Mon, Tue; 11.30am-7.30pm Wed; 10.30am-6.30pm Thur; 9.30am-3pm Fri. *House of Lords Visitors' Gallery* 2.30-10.30pm Mon, Tue; 3-10pm Wed; 11am-7.30pm Thur; from 10am Fri. *Tours* 9.15am-4.30pm Sat & summer recess; check website for details. **Admission** *Visitors' Gallery* free. *Tours* £15; £6-£10 reductions; £37 family; free under-5s. **Credit** MC, V. **Map** p399 L9.

The British parliament has an extremely long history, with the first parliamentary session held in St Stephen's Chapel in 1275. The Palace of Westminster, however, only became the permanent seat of Parliament in 1532, when Henry VIII moved to a new des-res in Whitehall. The current Palace is a wonderful mish-mash of styles, dominated by Gothic buttresses, towers and arches. It looks much older than it is: the Parliament buildings were designed in 1860 by Charles Barry (ably assisted by Augustus Welby Northmore Pugin) to replace the original building, which had been destroyed by fire in 1834. Now the compound contains 1,000 rooms, 11 courtyards, eight bars and six restaurants, plus a small cafeteria for visitors. Of the original palace, only the Jewel Tower (*see below*) and the ancient Westminster Hall remain.

Visitors are welcome (subject to stringent security checks at St Stephen's Gate, the only public access point into Parliament) to observe the political debates in the House of Lords and House of Commons, but tickets must be arranged in advance through your embassy or MP, who can also arrange tours – even free trips up the 334 spiral steps of the Elizabeth Tower to hear 'Big Ben'. The experience of listening in on the Houses of Parliament in session is often soporific, but Prime Minister's Question Time at noon on Wednesday is usually fun: the PM has alternately to rebuff a barrage of hostile questions from the opposition (and occasionally their own rebellious backbenchers) and massage value out of present soft questions from loyal backbenchers eager to present the government in a good light.

▶ *The best way to see these historic buildings is to book on one of the revealing 75min guided tours (0844 847 1672, www.ticketmaster.co.uk) on Saturday or during summer recess. Tours take in both Houses, Westminster Hall, the Queen's Robing Room and the Royal Gallery.*

Jewel Tower

Abingdon Street, SW1P 3JY (7222 2219, www. english-heritage.org.uk). Westminster tube. **Open** *Apr-Oct* 10am-5pm daily. *Nov-Mar* 10am-4pm Sat, Sun. **Admission** £3.20; £1.90-£2.90 reductions; free under-5s. **Credit** AmEx, MC, V. **Map** p399 L9.

This easy-to-overlook little stone tower opposite Parliament was built in 1365 to house Edward III's

EXPLORE

The New Old Bus

The Routemaster returns, sort of.

The Routemaster, London's original, hop-on, hop-off bus, was finally sent to the great garage in the sky in 2005 by then-mayor Ken Livingstone. Noting the bus's perennial popularity, his successor, Boris Johnson, promised to bring a new generation of Routemasters to London's streets. A design was unveiled by Transport for London in 2010 – not looking all that much like the old Routemasters, of course, but designer Thomas Heatherwick (who also designed the Olympic Cauldron for the 2012 Games) managed to retain the savour of the Routemaster's curves without looking dated, and kept that open back as well. The New Bus for London was a clever piece of kit too: the hybrid diesel-electric engines would make each bus '15 per cent more fuel efficient than existing hybrid buses, 40 per cent more efficient than conventional diesel double decks and much quieter on the streets'. Other innovations included a battery that is recharged using energy generated by braking.

Then came the news that – contrary to early reports – the rest of the public transport world was not crying out for expensive new buses. It was understood that the £11.3m cost of developing the New Bus would be met, not by the public through fares, but by sales of the bus to transport companies. Instead of which, Transport for London announced in September 2012 that it had placed 'the biggest order of hybrid

buses ever placed in Europe' – some 600 vehicles by 2016. TfL also provided some complex economics that proved that doing so, then renting the vehicles out to the franchises that would run them, was a long-term win for hard-pressed London commuters who are already wondering how much higher their fares will go. It will all prove an interesting test case for Boris-nomics – especially as the actual costs of the new Emirates Air Line cable car (*see p130*) become clearer with time.

Not to worry. The operating buses have been appreciated by those who have tried them. Eight have been plying the no.38 route between Hackney and Victoria, but not in the evening or at weekends. By April 2013, the next 30 will be gliding through town: 'enough to convert a full route', says TfL. At which point you'll be able to enjoy our investment for the price of a single fare.

Alternatively, experience the joy of the old on two 'heritage routes'. Refurbished buses from the 1960-64 Routemaster fleet run on routes nos.9 (from Aldwych via the Strand, Trafalgar Square and Piccadilly Circus to the Royal Albert Hall) and 15 (from Trafalgar Square to Tower Hill, with glimpses of the Strand, Fleet Street and St Paul's Cathedral); head to stops B or S in the south-west corner of Trafalgar Square. Buses run every 15 minutes from 9.30am; fares match ordinary buses, but you must buy a ticket before boarding (*see p364*).

treasure. It is, with Westminster Hall, all that remains of the medieval Palace of Westminster. It contains a small exhibition on Parliament's history.
▶ *Nowadays, the Crown Jewels are on display in the Tower of London; see p64.*

FREE St Margaret's Church

Parliament Square, SW1P 3PA (7654 4840, www.westminster-abbey.org). St James's Park or Westminster tube. **Open** 9.30am-3.30pm Mon-Fri; 9.30am-1.30pm Sat; 2-5pm Sun (times vary due to services). *Services* 11am Sun. **Admission** free. **No credit cards**. **Map** p399 L9.

Tucked in under the grandeur of Westminster Abbey, this little church was founded in the 12th century; since 1614, it's served as the official church of the House of Commons. The interior features some of the most impressive pre-Reformation stained glass in London. The east window (1509) commemorates the marriage of Henry VIII and Catherine of Aragon; others celebrate Britain's first printer, William Caxton (buried here in 1491), explorer Sir Walter Raleigh (executed in Old Palace Yard in 1618), and writer John Milton (1608-74) who married his second wife here in 1656.

FREE Supreme Court

Parliament Square, SW1P 3BD (7960 1900, www.supremecourt.gov.uk). St James's Park or Westminster tube. **Open** 9.30am-4.30pm Mon-Fri. *Tours* 10am, 11.30am, 1.30pm, 3pm Fri. **Admission** free. *Tours* £5; £3.50 reductions. **Credit** AmEx, MC, V. **Map** p399 K9.

In 2005, Parliament made a momentous decision – not that anyone noticed. The right to adjudicate final appeals was taken from the House of Lords and given to a new, independent Supreme Court, which was duly opened by the Queen in 2009, directly opposite Parliament. Part of the notion was to open up higher processes of law to the public – in plain English, you can visit any time you like (through airport-style security gates) to see lawyers debate 'points of law of general public importance' in front of the country's most senior judges. Recent cases have included whether an MP can be tried in a magistrate's court for alleged criminal misconduct within Parliament, and how binding a pre-nuptial agreement should be. You can also look around the lovely Grade II*-listed, neo-Gothic premises, built for Middlesex County Council in 1913. There's even a café and souvenirs on sale.
▶ *Although you're welcome to visit on a Friday, the Supreme Court doesn't sit that day.*

★ Westminster Abbey

20 Dean's Yard, SW1P 3PA (7222 5152 information, 7654 4834 tours, www.westminster-abbey.org). St James's Park or Westminster tube. **Open** 9.30am-4.30pm Mon, Tue, Thur, Fri; 9.30am-7pm Wed; 9.30am-2.30pm Sat. *Abbey Museum, Chapter House & College Gardens* 10am-

4pm daily. *Tours* phone for details. **Admission** £16; £6-£13 reductions; £32 family; free under-10s with adult. *Tours* £3. **Credit** AmEx, MC, V. **Map** p399 K9.

The cultural, historic and religious significance of Westminster Abbey is impossible to overstate, but also hard to remember as you're shepherded around, forced to elbow fellow tourists out of the way to read a plaque or see a tomb – even more so after the 2012 Royal Wedding 'twixt Prince William and Kate Middleton, which resulted in a mighty impressive 36% boost in visitor numbers. The best plan is to get here as early in the day as you can. Edward the Confessor commissioned a church to St Peter on the site of a seventh-century version, but it was only consecrated on 28 December 1065, eight days before he died. William the Conqueror subsequently had himself crowned here on Christmas Day 1066 and, with just two exceptions, every English coronation since has taken place in the abbey.

Many royal, military and cultural notables are interred here. The most haunting memorial is the Grave of the Unknown Warrior, in the nave. Elaborate resting places in side chapels are taken up by the tombs of Elizabeth I and Mary Queen of Scots. In Innocents Corner lie the remains of two lads believed to be Edward V and his brother Richard (their bodies were found at the Tower of London), as well as two of James I's children. Poets' Corner is the final resting place of Chaucer, the first to be buried here. Few of the other writers who have stones here are buried in the abbey, but the remains of Dryden, Johnson, Browning and Tennyson are all present. Henry James, TS Eliot and Dylan Thomas have dedications – on the floor, fittingly for Thomas.

In the vaulted area under the former monks' dormitory, one of the abbey's oldest parts, the Abbey Museum celebrated its centenary in 2008. You'll find effigies and waxworks of British monarchs, among them Edward II and Henry VII, wearing the robes they donned in life. The 900-year-old College Garden (pictured on p105) is one of the oldest cultivated spaces in Britain and a useful place to escape the crowds. For snacks, a new refectory-style restaurant – the Cellarium Café & Terrace (www.cellariumcafe.com) – opened in autumn 2012. *Photo p105.*

MILLBANK

Pimlico or Westminster tube.

Running south from Parliament along the river, Millbank leads eventually to **Tate Britain** (*see p104*), built on the site of an extraordinary pentagonal prison that held criminals destined for transportation to Botany Bay. If you're walking south from the Palace of Westminster, look out on the left for **Victoria Tower Gardens**, which contain a statue of suffragette leader Emmeline Pankhurst and the rather colourful Buxton Drinking Fountain, which

EXPLORE

commemorates the emancipation of slaves.
There's also a version of Rodin's sombre
Burghers of Calais.

On the other side of the road, Dean Stanley
Street leads to Smith Square, home to the
architecturally striking **St John's Smith
Square** (see p301), built as a church in grand
Baroque style and now a popular venue for
classical music. **Lord North Street**, the elegant
row of Georgian terraces running north from
the square, has long been a favourite address
of politicians; note, too, the directions on the
wall for wartime bomb shelters.

Across the river from Millbank is **Vauxhall
Cross**, the oddly conspicuous HQ of the Secret
Intelligence Service (SIS), commonly referred to
by its old name MI6. In case any enemies of the
state were unaware of its location, the cream and
green block appeared as itself in the 1999 James
Bond film *The World is Not Enough* – reprising
the role (and suffering serious bomb damage
along the way) in 2012's *Skyfall*.

★ **FREE** **Tate Britain**
*Millbank, SW1P 4RG (7887 8888, www.tate.
org.uk). Pimlico tube.* **Open** 10am-6pm daily;
10am-10pm 1st Fri of mth. *Tours* 11am, noon,
2pm, 3pm Mon-Fri; noon, 3pm Sat, Sun.
Admission free. *Special exhibitions* vary.
Credit MC, V. **Map** p399 K11.
Tate Modern (see p43) gets the attention, but the
original Tate Gallery, founded by sugar magnate Sir
Henry Tate, has a broader brief. Housed in a stately
building on the riverside, Tate Britain is second only
to the National Gallery (see p98) when it comes to
British art. It's also looking to steal back a bit of the
limelight from its starrier sibling with a 20-year redevelopment plan called the Millbank Project: conserv-
ing the building's original features, upgrading the
galleries, opening new spaces to the public and
adding a new café in two phases, with the first due

to be completed in 2013. Despite the work, the art
here is exceptional. The historical collection includes
work by Hogarth, Gainsborough, Reynolds,
Constable (who gets three rooms) and Turner (in the
superb Clore Gallery). Many contemporary works
were shifted to the other Tate when it opened, but
Stanley Spencer, Lucian Freud and Francis Bacon
are well represented, and Art Now installations
showcase up-and-coming Britsh artists. Temporary
exhibitions include headline-hungry blockbusters
and the annual controversy-courting Turner Prize
exhibition (Oct-Jan). The gallery has a good restaurant and an exemplary gift shop.
▶ *The handy Tate-to-Tate boat (see p43) zips
along the river to Tate Modern every 40mins.*

VICTORIA

Pimlico tube or Victoria tube/rail.

As you might expect from London's main
backpacker hangout, Victoria is colourful and
chaotic. Victoria rail station is a major hub for
trains to southern seaside resorts and ferry
terminals, while the nearby coach station is
served by buses from all over Europe. Catering
to new arrivals, Belgrave Road provides an
almost unbroken line of cheap and often shabby
B&Bs, hotels and hostels, most set in fading
townhouses. The theatres dotted around Victoria
form a western outpost of the West End's
Theatreland, with a similar programme of
star-vehicle dramas and musicals.

Not to be confused with Westminster Abbey
(see p103), **Westminster Cathedral** is the
headquarters of the Roman Catholic Church
in England. South and east of Victoria Station
are the Georgian terraces of **Pimlico** and
Belgravia. Antique stores and restaurants
line Pimlico Road; the intriguing independent
shops of Tachbrook Street are worth a look.

North of Victoria Street towards Parliament
Square is **Christchurch Gardens**, burial site
of Thomas ('Colonel') Blood, who stole the Crown
Jewels in 1671. He was apprehended making his
getaway but, amazingly, managed to talk his
way into a full pardon. Also in the area are **New
Scotland Yard**, with its famous revolving
sign, and the art deco headquarters of **London
Underground** at 55 Broadway. Public outrage
about Jacob Epstein's graphic nudes on the
façade almost led to the resignation of the
managing director in 1929.

FREE **Westminster Cathedral**
*42 Francis Street, SW1P 1QW (7798 9055,
www.westminstercathedral.org.uk). Victoria
tube/rail.* **Open** 7am-6pm Mon-Fri; 8am-6.30pm
Sat; 8am-7pm Sun. *Exhibition* 10am-5pm Mon-Fri;
10am-6pm Sat, Sun. *Bell tower* 9.30am-4.30pm daily.
Admission free; donations appreciated. *Exhibition*

£5; free-£2.50 reductions; £11 family. *Bell tower & exhibition* £8; free-£4 reductions; £17.50 family. **Credit** MC, V. **Map** p398 J10.

With its domes, arches and soaring tower, the most important Catholic church in England looks surprisingly Byzantine. There's a reason: architect John Francis Bentley, who built it between 1895 and 1903, was heavily influenced by Hagia Sophia in Istanbul. Compared to the candy-cane exterior, the interior is surprisingly restrained (in fact, it's unfinished), but there are still some impressive marble columns and mosaics. Eric Gill's sculptures of the Stations of the Cross (1914-18) were dismissed as 'Babylonian' when they were first installed, but worshippers have come to love them. An upper gallery holds the 'Treasures of the Cathedral' exhibition, where you can see an impressive Arts and Crafts coronet, a Tudor chalice, holy relics and Bentley's amazing architectural model of his cathedral, complete with tiny hawks.

▶ *There are great views from the bell tower's viewing gallery – as well as a lift to help you climb the 210 feet to get up there.*

AROUND ST JAMES'S PARK

St James's Park tube.

Handsome **St James's Park** was founded as a deer park for the royal occupants of St James's Palace, and remodelled by John Nash on the orders of George IV. The central lake is home to various species of wildfowl; pelicans have been kept here since the 17th century, when the Russian ambassador donated several of the bag-jawed birds to Charles II. The pelicans are fed between 2.30pm and 3pm daily, though they supplement their diet at other times of the day with the occasional pigeon. Lots of humans picnic here, too, notably around the bandstand during the summer weekend concerts. The bridge over the lake offers good views of Buckingham Palace. Head that way and you'll see Green Park, the beginning of a relaxing stroll that will take you under trees as far as Hyde Park Corner (for both, see p96).

Along the north side of the park, the Mall connects Buckingham Palace with Trafalgar Square (*see p97*). It looks like a classic processional route, but the Mall was actually laid out as a pitch for Charles II to play 'pallemaille' (an early version of croquet imported from France) after the pitch at Pall Mall became too crowded. On the south side of the park, Wellington Barracks contains the **Guards Museum** (*see p106*); to the east, Horse Guards contains the **Household Cavalry Museum** (*see p106*).

Carlton House Terrace, on the north flank of the Mall, was the last project completed by John Nash before his death in 1835. Part of the terrace now houses the **ICA** (*see p107*). Just

Westminster Abbey. *See p103.*

EXPLORE

Buckingham Palace.

EXPLORE

behind is the **Duke of York column**, commemorating Prince Frederick, Duke of York, who led the British Army against the French. He's the nursery rhyme's 'Grand old Duke of York', who marched his 10,000 men neither up nor down Cassel hill in Flanders.

Buckingham Palace & Royal Mews

The Mall, SW1A 1AA (Palace 7766 7300, Royal Mews 7766 7302, Queen's Gallery 7766 7301, www.royalcollection.org.uk). Green Park tube or Victoria tube/rail. **Open** times vary; check website for details. **Admission** prices vary; check website for details. **Credit** AmEx, MC, V. **Map** p398 H9.
Although nearby St James's Palace (*see opposite*) remains the official seat of the British court, every monarch since Victoria has used Buckingham Palace as their primary home. Originally known as Buckingham House, the present home of the British royals was constructed as a private house for the Duke of Buckingham in 1703, but George III liked it so much he purchased it for his German bride Charlotte in 1761. George IV decided to occupy the mansion himself after taking the throne in 1820 and John Nash was hired to convert it into a palace befitting a king. Construction was beset with problems, and Nash – whose expensive plans had always been disliked by Parliament – was dismissed in 1830. When Victoria came to the throne in 1837, the building was barely habitable. The job of finishing the palace fell to the reliable but unimaginative Edward Blore ('Blore the Bore'). The neoclassical frontage now in place was the work of Aston Webb in 1913.
As the home of the Queen, the palace is usually closed to visitors, but you can view the interior for a brief period each year while the Windsors are away on their holidays; you'll be able to see the State Rooms, still used to entertain dignitaries and guests of state, and part of the garden. There's even a café – paper

cups, sadly, but coloured a pretty blue-green and clearly marked with the palace crest for souvenir-hunters. At any time of year, you can visit the Queen's Gallery to see her personal collection of treasures, including paintings by Rubens and Rembrandt, Sèvres porcelain and the Diamond Diadem crown. Further along Buckingham Palace Road, the Royal Mews is a grand garage for the royal fleet of Rolls-Royces and home to the splendid royal carriages and the horses, individually named by the Queen, that pull them.

Guards Museum

Wellington Barracks, Birdcage Walk, SW1E 6HQ (7414 3428, www.theguardsmuseum.com). St James's Park tube. **Open** 10am-4pm daily. **Admission** £5; £2.50 reductions; free under-16s. **Credit** (shop) AmEx, MC, V. **Map** p398 J9.
Just down the road from Horse Guards, this small museum tells the 350-year story of the Foot Guards, using flamboyant uniforms, period paintings, medals and intriguing memorabilia, such as the stuffed body of Jacob the Goose, the Guard's Victorian mascot, who was regrettably run over by a van in barracks. Appropriately, the shop is well stocked with toy soldiers of the British regiments.
▶ *The Guards assemble on the parade ground here before marching to the palace for the Changing of the Guard; see p27* **Standing on Ceremony**.

Household Cavalry Museum

Horse Guards, Whitehall, SW1A 2AX (7930 3070, www.householdcavalrymuseum.co.uk). Westminster tube or Charing Cross tube/rail. **Open** *Mar-Sept* 10am-6pm daily. *Oct-Feb* 10am-5pm daily. **Admission** £6; £4 reductions; £15 family ticket; free under-5s. **Credit** MC, V. **Map** p399 K8.
Household Cavalry is a fairly workaday name for the military peacocks who make up the Queen's official

guard. They get to tell their stories through video diaries at this small but entertaining museum, which also offers the chance to see medals, uniforms and shiny cuirasses (breastplates) up close. You'll also get a peek – and sniff – of the magnificent horses that parade just outside every day: the stables are separated from the main museum by no more than a screen of glass. Interactive displays on the horses have recently been added.

FREE ICA (Institute of Contemporary Arts)

The Mall, SW1Y 5AH (7930 0493 information, 7930 3647 tickets, www.ica.org.uk). Piccadilly Circus tube or Charing Cross tube/rail. **Open** Galleries (during exhibitions) 11am-6pm Tue, Wed, Fri-Sun; 11am-9pm Thur. **Admission** free. **Credit** AmEx, MC, V. **Map** p399 K8.
Founded in 1947 by a collective of poets, artists and critics, the ICA has recently found itself somewhat adrift. The institute moved to the Mall in 1968 and set itself up as a venue for arthouse cinema, performance art, philosophical debates, exhibitions, art-themed club nights and anything else that might challenge convention – but 'convention' is much harder to challenge now, when everyone's doing it. New director Gregor Muir has some interesting ideas, including a redesigned interior and Friday lunchtime talks from top contemporary artists.

ST JAMES'S

Green Park or Piccadilly Circus tube.

One of London's most refined residential areas, St James's was laid out in the 1660s for royal and aristocratic families, some of whom still live here. It's a rewarding district, a sedate bustle of intriguing mews and grand squares. Bordered by Piccadilly, Haymarket, the Mall and Green Park, the district is centred on **St James's Square**. Just south of the square, **Pall Mall** is lined with exclusive, members-only gentlemen's clubs (in the old-fashioned sense of the word). Polished nameplates reveal such prestigious establishments as the **Institute of Directors** (no.116) and the **Reform Club** (nos.104-105), site of Phileas Fogg's famous bet in *Around the World in Eighty Days*. Around the corner on St James's Street, the **Carlton Club** (no.69) is the official club of the Conservative Party; Lady Thatcher remains the only woman to be granted full membership. Nearby on King Street is **Christie's** (7839 9060, www.christies.com), the world's oldest fine art auctioneers.

At the south end of St James's Street, **St James's Palace** was built for Henry VIII in the 1530s. Extensively remodelled over the centuries, the red-brick palace is still the official address of the Royal Court, even though every monarch since 1837 has lived at Buckingham Palace. From here, Mary Tudor surrendered Calais and Elizabeth I led the campaign against the Spanish Armada; this is also where Charles I was confined before his 1649 execution. The palace is home to the Princess Royal (the title given to the monarch's eldest daughter, currently Princess Anne); it's closed to the public, but you can attend Sunday services at its historic **Chapel Royal** (1st Sun of mth, Oct-Easter Sunday; 8.30am, 11.15am).

Adjacent to St James's Palace is **Clarence House**, former residence of the Queen Mother; a few streets north, delightful **Spencer House** (for both, *see below*) is the ancestral home of the family of the late Princess Diana. Across Marlborough Road lies the pocket-sized **Queen's Chapel**, designed by Inigo Jones in the 1620s for Charles I's Catholic queen Henrietta Maria, at a time when Catholic places of worship were officially banned. The Queen's Chapel can only be visited for Sunday services (Easter-July; 8.30am, 11.15am).

Clarence House

The Mall, SW1A 1AA (7766 7303, www.royal collection.org.uk). Green Park tube. **Open** *Aug-early Sept* 10am-4pm Mon-Fri; 10am-5.30pm Sat, Sun. Advance bookings only. **Admission** £8.50; £4.50 reductions; free under-5s. *Tours* pre-booked tickets only. **Credit** AmEx, MC, V. **Map** p398 J8.
Currently the official residence of Prince Charles and the Duchess of Cornwall, this austere royal mansion was built between 1825 and 1827 for Prince William Henry, Duke of Clarence, who stayed on in the house after his coronation as King William IV. Designed by John Nash, the house has been much altered by its many inhabitants, among them the late Queen Mother. Five receiving rooms and the Queen Mother's British art collection usually open to the public in summer, but for advance bookings only.

Spencer House

27 St James's Place, SW1A 1NR (7499 8620, www.spencerhouse.co.uk). Green Park tube. **Open** *Feb-July, Sept-Dec* 10.30am-5.45pm Sun. Last tour 4.45pm. *Gardens* phone or see website for details. **Admission** £12; £10 reductions. Under-10s not allowed. **Credit** MC, V. **Map** p398 J8.
One of the last surviving private residences in St James's, this handsome mansion was designed for John Spencer by John Vardy, but was completed in 1766 by Hellenophile architect James Stuart, which explains the mock Greek flourishes. Lady Georgiana, the 18th-century socialite and beauty – glamorous enough to be played by Keira Knightley in the 2008 bodice-ripper *The Duchess* – lived here, but the Spencers left generations before their most famous scion, Diana, married into the Windsor family. The palatial building has painstakingly restored interiors, now mainly used for corporate entertaining, and a simply wonderful garden.

EXPLORE

Chelsea

Blue blood, red coats and an exquisite green space.

Chelsea is where London's wealthy classes play in cultural and geographical isolation. Originally a fishing hamlet, the area was a 'village of palaces' by the 16th century, home to the likes of Henry VIII's ill-fated advisor Sir Thomas More. Artists and poets (Whistler, Carlyle, Wilde) followed from the 1880s, before the fashionistas arrived with the opening of Mary Quant's Bazaar in 1955. Soon after, Chelsea had acquired a raffish reputation and was at the forefront of successive youth culture revolutions. Those days are long gone. Now there are smart shops and street after sleepy street of immaculate terraced housing, but – with the notable exceptions of the **Saatchi Gallery** (*see p109*) and the exquisite **Chelsea Physic Garden** (*see p110*) – cultural pleasures are few.

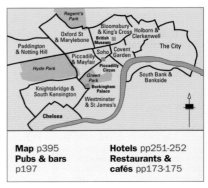

Map p395

Pubs & bars p197

Hotels pp251-252

Restaurants & cafés pp173-175

EXPLORE

SLOANE SQUARE & THE KING'S ROAD

Sloane Square tube then various buses.

Synonymous with the Swinging Sixties and immortalised by punk, the dissipated phase of the King's Road is now a matter for historians as the street teems with pricey fashion houses and air-conditioned poodle parlours. Yet on a sunny day, it does make a vivid stroll. For one thing, you don't have to take yourself as seriously as the locals. And for another, the area is figuratively rich with historical associations, and literally so with the expensive red-brick houses that slumber down leafy mews and charming, cobbled sidestreets.

INSIDE TRACK ESPIONAGE

Chelsea has long been a popular haunt for spies, real and fictional. KGB agent Kim Philby held meetings at the Markham Arms at 138 King's Road, now a branch of the Santander bank, and both James Bond and George Smiley were given homes in the area by their respective creators.

At the top (east end) of the King's Road is **Sloane Square**. It's named after Sir Hans Sloane, who provided the land for the Chelsea Physic Garden (*see p110*), invented milk chocolate in the early 18th century and was instrumental in the founding of the British Museum (which was set up to hold his collections when he died). In the middle of the square sits a fountain erected in 1953, a gift to the borough from the Royal Academy of Arts. The shaded benches in the middle of the square provide a lovely counterpoint to the looming façades of Tiffany & Co and the enormous Peter Jones department store, in a 1930s building with excellent views from its top-floor café. A certain edginess is lent to proceedings by the **Royal Court Theatre** (*see p306*), which shocked the nation with its 1956 première of John Osborne's *Look Back in Anger*.

To escape the bustle and fumes, head to the **Duke of York Square**, a pedestrianised enclave of boutiques and restaurants presided over by a statue of Sir Hans. In the summer, the cooling fountains attract hordes of children, their parents sitting to watch from the outdoor café tables or taking advantage of the Saturday food market. The square is also home to the mercilessly modern art of the **Saatchi Gallery** (*see p109*), housed in former military barracks.

The once-adventurous shops on the King's Road are now a mix of trendier-than-thou fashion houses and high-street chains, but there are still a few gems around: **Shop at Bluebird** (*see p215*) and London's second branch of **Anthropologie** (*see p214*) suggest future directions. Wander Cale Street for some pleasing boutiques, or head for the **Chelsea Farmers' Market** on adjoining Sydney Street to find a clutter of artfully distressed rustic sheds housing restaurants and shops selling everything from cigars to garden products. Sydney Street leads to **St Luke's Church**, where Charles Dickens married Catherine Hogarth in 1836.

Towards the western end of the King's Road is **Bluebird**, a dramatic art deco former motor garage housing a café, a restaurant and the hip shop mentioned above. A little further up the road, the **World's End** store (no.430) occupies what was once Vivienne Westwood's notorious leather- and fetishwear boutique Sex; a green-haired Johnny Rotten auditioned for the Sex Pistols here in 1975 by singing along to an Alice Cooper record on the shop's jukebox.

FREE Saatchi Gallery

Duke of York's HQ, King's Road, SW3 4SQ (7811 3070, www.saatchi-gallery.co.uk). Sloane Square tube. **Open** 10am-6pm daily. **Admission** free. **Credit** (shop) AmEx, MC, V. **Map** p395 F11. Charles Saatchi's gallery offers 50,000sq ft of space for temporary exhibitions. Given his fame as a promoter in the 1990s of what became known as the Young British Artists – Damien Hirst, Tracey Emin, Gavin Turk, Sarah Lucas et al – it will surprise many that the opening exhibition a few years back was devoted to new Chinese art. More recent shows have continued the international feel.

CHEYNE WALK & CHELSEA EMBANKMENT

Sloane Square tube then various buses.

Chelsea's riverside has long been noted for its nurseries and gardens. The borough's horticultural curiosity is still alive, lending a village air that befits a place of retirement for the former British soldiers living in the **Royal Hospital Chelsea** (*see p110*). In summer, the Chelsea Pensioners, as they're known, regularly don red coats and tricorn hats when venturing beyond the gates. The Royal Hospital's lovely gardens host the **Chelsea Flower Show** (*see p26*) in May each year. Next door is the **National Army Museum** (*see p110*).

West from the river end of Royal Hospital Road is **Cheyne Walk**, less peaceful than it once was due to Embankment traffic. Its riverview benches remain good spots for a sit-down, but the tranquillity of the **Chelsea Physic Garden** (*see p110*) is the real treat.

Further west on Cheyne Walk, the park benches of **Chelsea Embankment Gardens** face Albert Bridge, where signs still order troops to 'Break step when marching over this bridge'. In the small gardens, you'll find a statue of the great historian Thomas Carlyle – the 'sage of Chelsea', whose home is preserved (*see p110* **Carlyle's House**). Nearby, a gold-faced statue of Sir Thomas More looks out over the river from the garden of **Chelsea Old Church** (*see p110*), where he once sang in the choir and may well be (partially) buried. Follow Old Church Street north and you'll find the **Chelsea Arts Club** (no.143), founded in 1871 by Whistler and now host to occasional public events, including classical recitals.

EXPLORE

Saatchi Gallery.

North of the western extremity of Cheyne Walk are **Brompton Cemetery** (*see p149*) and the home ground of Chelsea FC, **Stamford Bridge** (*see p315*). The excellent **Chelsea Centenary Museum** (www.chelseafc.com, 10.30am-4.30pm daily, £10, £8-£9 reductions) may be the only museum in England to display a photograph of Raquel Welch wearing football kit – oh, and for much of 2013 the small matter of the Champions League trophy.

Carlyle's House
24 Cheyne Row, SW3 5HL (7352 7087, www. nationaltrust.org.uk). Sloane Square tube or bus 11, 19, 22, 49, 170, 211, 319. **Open** *Mar-Oct* 11am-5pm Wed-Sun. **Admission** £5.10; £2.60 children; £12.80 family. **No credit cards.** **Map** p395 E12.

Thomas Carlyle and his wife Jane moved to this four-storey, Queen Anne house in 1834. The house was inaugurated as a museum in 1896, 15 years after Carlyle's death, offering an intriguing snapshot of Victorian life. The writer's quest for quiet (details of his valiant attempts to soundproof the attic) strikes a chord today: he was plagued by the sound of revelry from Cremorne Pleasure Gardens.

FREE Chelsea Old Church
Old Church Street, SW3 5DQ (7795 1019, www. chelseaoldchurch.org.uk). Sloane Square tube or bus 11, 19, 22, 49, 319. **Open** 2-4pm Tue-Thur; 1.30-5pm Sun. *Services* 8am, 10am, 11am, 12.15pm Sun. *Evensong* 6pm Sun. **Admission** free; donations appreciated. **No credit cards. Map** p395 E12.

Chelsea Physic Garden

Legend has it that the Thomas More Chapel, which remains on the south side, contains More's headless body buried somewhere under the walls (his head, after being spiked on London Bridge, was 'rescued' and buried in a family vault in St Dunstan's church, Canterbury). There's a striking statue of More outside the church. Guides are on hand on Sundays.

★ Chelsea Physic Garden
66 Royal Hospital Road, SW3 4HS (7352 5646, www.chelseaphysicgarden.co.uk). Sloane Square tube or bus 11, 19, 22. **Open** *Apr-Oct* noon-5pm Tue-Fri; noon-6pm Sun. *Tours* times vary; phone to check. **Admission** £9; £6 reductions; free under-5s. *Tours* free. **Credit** MC, V. **Map** p395 F12.

The capacious grounds of this gorgeous botanic garden are filled with healing herbs and vegetables, rare trees and dye plants. The garden was founded in 1673 by Sir Hans Sloane with the purpose of cultivating and studying plants for medical purposes. The first plant specimens were brought to England and planted here in 1676, with the famous Cedars of Lebanon (the first to be grown in England) arriving a little later. The garden opened to the public in 1893.

FREE National Army Museum
Royal Hospital Road, SW3 4HT (7730 0717, www.nam.ac.uk). Sloane Square tube or bus 11, 137, 170. **Open** 10am-5.30pm daily. **Admission** free. **Credit** (shop) AmEx, MC, V. **Map** p395 F12.

More entertaining than its modern exterior might suggest, this museum dedicated to the history of the British Army runs chronologically, running from the wars of Empire ('Changing the World, 1784-1904'), through the two World Wars and into contemporary conflicts including the Falklands, Northern Ireland and Afghanistan ('Conflicts of Interest, 1969-present'). Key artefacts include a French eagle standard from the Napoleonic Wars and a model of Waterloo with 70,000 soldiers. There's also a gallery of military art since the early 17th century, including paintings of boozing soldiers and bloody battles, a bust of Florence Nightingale, and such items of furniture as a brigadier's chest from the Indian Mutiny.

FREE Royal Hospital Chelsea
Royal Hospital Road, SW3 4SR (7881 5200, www.chelsea-pensioners.org.uk). Sloane Square tube or bus 11, 19, 22, 137, 170. **Open** 10am-noon, 2-4pm Mon-Sat. **Admission** free. **Credit** MC, V. **Map** p395 F12.

Roughly 350 Chelsea Pensioners (retired soldiers) live at the Royal Hospital, founded in 1682 by Charles II and designed by Sir Christopher Wren (with adjustments by Robert Adam and Sir John Soane). Retired soldiers are still eligible to apply for a final posting here if they're over 65 and in receipt of an Army or War Disability Pension for Army Service. The pensioners have their own club room, bowling green and gardens, and get tickets to Chelsea FC home games. The museum (same times) has more about their lives.

EXPLORE

Knightsbridge & South Kensington

Shop 'til you... pop into a museum.

A certain type of Londoner goes to **Knightsbridge** to spend, spend, spend. Or, at least, to hang around people who are spend, spend, spending. Many of the key designer labels have major shops in the area, which gets plenty of foot traffic thanks to its world-famous department stores and high-end restaurants. Nearby, **South Kensington**'s footprint is cultural rather than commercial: you'll find three of the world's greatest museums, some extraordinary colleges, a concert hall and a cutting-edge contemporary art gallery.

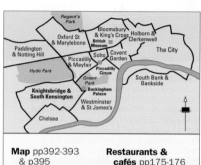

Map pp392-393 & p395	**Restaurants & cafés** pp175-176
Hotels pp252-254	**Pubs & bars** p197

KNIGHTSBRIDGE

Knightsbridge tube.

Knightsbridge in the 11th century was a village celebrated for its taverns, highwaymen and the legend that two knights once fought to the death on the bridge spanning the Westbourne River (later dammed to form Hyde Park's Serpentine lake). In modern Knightsbridge, urban princesses would be too busy unsheathing the credit card to notice such a farrago. Voguish **Harvey Nichols** holds court at the top of **Sloane Street**, which leads down to Sloane Square. Expensive brands – Gucci, Prada, Chanel – dominate. East of Sloane Street is **Belgravia**, characterised by a cluster of embassies around **Belgrave Square**. Hidden behind the stucco-clad parades fronting the square are numerous mews, worth exploring for the pubs they conceal, notably the **Nag's Head** (53 Kinnerton Street, 7235 1135).

For many tourists, Knightsbridge means one thing: **Harrods** (*see p204*). From its tan bricks and olive green awning to its green-coated doormen, it's an instantly recognisable retail legend. Further along is the imposing **Brompton Oratory**.

FREE Brompton Oratory

Thurloe Place, Brompton Road, SW7 2RP (7808 0900, www.bromptonoratory.com). South Kensington tube. **Open** 6.30am-8pm daily. **Admission** free; donations appreciated. **No credit cards. Map** p395 E10.

The second-biggest Catholic church in the country (after Westminster Cathedral; *see p104*) is formally the Church of the Immaculate Heart of Mary, but almost universally known as the Brompton Oratory. Completed in 1884, it feels older, partly because of the Baroque Italianate style but also because much of the decoration pre-dates the structure: Mazzuoli's 17th-century apostle statues, for example, are from Siena cathedral. The 11am Solemn Mass sung in Latin on Sundays is enchanting, as are Vespers, at 3.30pm; the website has details. *Photo p112.*

▶ *During the Cold War, KGB agents used the church as a dead-letter box.*

SOUTH KENSINGTON

Gloucester Road or South Kensington tube.

As far as cultural and academic institutions are concerned, this is the land of plenty. It was Prince Albert who oversaw the inception of its world-class museums, colleges and concert hall, using the profits of the 1851 Great Exhibition;

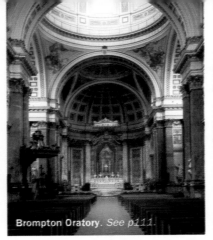

Brompton Oratory. *See p111.*

the area was nicknamed 'Albertopolis' in his honour. You'll find the **Natural History Museum**, the **Science Museum**) and the **Victoria & Albert Museum**, **Imperial College**, the **Royal College of Art** and the **Royal College of Music** (Prince Consort Road, 7589 3643; call for details of the musical instrument museum), which forms a unity with the **Royal Albert Hall** (*see p200*), open since 1871 and variously used for boxing, motor shows, marathons, table tennis tournaments, fascist rallies and rock concerts. Opposite is the **Albert Memorial**.

FREE Albert Memorial
Kensington Gardens (7936 2568). South Kensington tube. **Tours** *Mar-Dec* 2pm, 3pm 1st Sun of mth. **Admission** *Tours* £6; £5 reductions. **No credit cards**. **Map** p393 D8.
'I would rather not be made the prominent feature of such a monument,' was Prince Albert's reported response when the subject of his commemoration arose. Hard, then, to imagine what he would have made of this extraordinary thing, unveiled 15 years after his death. Created by Sir George Gilbert Scott, it centres around a gilded Albert holding a catalogue of the 1851 Great Exhibition, guarded on four corners by the continents of Africa, America, Asia and Europe. The pillars are crowned with bronze statues of the sciences, and the frieze at the base depicts major artists, architects and musicians. It's one of London's most dramatic monuments.

★ FREE Natural History Museum
Cromwell Road, SW7 5BD (7942 5000, www.nhm.ac.uk). South Kensington tube. **Open** 10am-5.50pm daily. **Admission** free; charges apply for special exhibitions. *Tours* free. **Credit** MC, V. **Map** p395 D10.
Both a research institution and a fabulous museum, the NHM opened in Alfred Waterhouse's purpose-built, Romanesque palazzo on the Cromwell Road in

1881. Now joined by the splendid Darwin Centre extension, the original building still looks quite magnificent. The pale blue and terracotta façade just about prepares you for the natural wonders within.

Taking up the full length of the vast entrance hall is the cast of a *Diplodocus* skeleton. A left turn leads into the west wing or Blue Zone, where long queues form to see animatronic dinosaurs – especially the endlessly popular *T rex*. A display on biology features an illuminated, man-sized model of a foetus in the womb along with graphic diagrams of how it might have got there.

A right turn from the central hall leads past the 'Creepy Crawlies' exhibition to the Green Zone. Stars include a cross-section through a Giant Sequoia tree and an amazing array of stuffed birds, including the chance to compare the egg of a hummingbird, smaller than a little finger nail, with that of an elephant bird (now extinct), almost football-sized. Beyond is the Red Zone. 'Earth's Treasury' is a mine of information on a variety of precious metals, gems and crystals; 'From the Beginning' is a brave attempt to give the expanse of geological time a human perspective. Outside, the delightful Wildlife Garden (Apr-Oct only) showcases a range of British lowland habitats, including a 'Bee Tree', a hollow tree trunk that opens to reveal a busy hive.

Many of the museum's 22 million insect and plant specimens are housed in the new Darwin Centre, where they take up nearly 17 miles of shelving. With its eight-storey Cocoon, this is also home to the museum's research scientists, who can be watched at work. But a great deal of this amazing institution is hidden from public view, given over to labs and specialised storage.

★ FREE Science Museum
Exhibition Road, SW7 2DD (switchboard 7942 4000, information 0870 870 4868, www.sciencemuseum.org.uk). South Kensington tube. **Open** 10am-6pm daily. **Admission** free; charges apply for special exhibitions. **Credit** MC, V. **Map** p395 D9.
The Science Museum is a celebration of the wonders of technology in the service of our daily lives. On the ground floor, the shop – selling brilliant toys, not least because you can pretend they're educational – is part of the 'Energy Hall', which introduces the museum's collections with impressive 18th-century steam engines. In 'Exploring Space', rocket science and the lunar landings are illustrated by dramatically lit mock-ups and models, before the museum gears up for its core collection in 'Making the Modern World'. Introduced by Puffing Billy, the world's oldest steam locomotive (built in 1815), the gallery also contains Stephenson's Rocket. Also here are the Apollo 10 command module, classic cars and an absorbing collection of everyday technological marvels from 1750 right up to the present.

In the main body of the museum, the second floor holds displays on computing, marine engineering

and mathematics; the third floor is dedicated to flight, among other things, including the hands-on Launchpad gallery, which has levers, pulleys, explosions and all manner of experiments for children (and their associated grown-ups). On the fifth floor, you'll find an old-fashioned but intriguing display on the science and art of medicine.

Beyond 'Making the Modern World', bathed in an eerie blue light, the three floors of the Wellcome Wing are where the museum makes sure it stays on the cutting edge of science. On the ground floor, 'Antenna' is a web-savvy look at breaking science stories, displaying video interviews and Q&As with real research scientists alongside the weird new objects they've been working on. Upstairs is the enjoyable and troubling 'Who Am I?' gallery. A dozen silver pods surround brightly lit cases of objects with engaging interactive displays – from a cartoon of ethical dilemmas that introduces you to your dorsolateral prefrontal cortex to a chance to find out what gender your brain is. Compelling objects include a jellyfish that's 'technically immortal', the statistically average British man (he's called Jose) and a pound of human fat, displayed alongside a gastric band. There's also contemporary art, including installations and Stephen Wiltshire's amazingly detailed drawing, from memory, of the Houses of Parliament.

▶ *There are plenty of other scientific and medical museums in London: the Wellcome Collection (see p72), the Hunterian (see p66) and the Royal Observatory (see p141) are all also recommended.*

★ FREE Victoria & Albert Museum

Cromwell Road, SW7 2RL (7942 2000, www.vam. ac.uk). South Kensington tube. **Open** 10am-5.45pm Mon-Thur, Sat, Sun; 10am-10pm Fri. *Tours* hourly, 10.30am-3.30pm daily. **Admission** free; charges for special exhibitions. **Credit** MC, V. **Map** p395 E10.
The V&A is one of the world's most magnificent museums, its foundation stone laid on this site by Queen Victoria in her last official public engagement in 1899. It is a superb showcase for applied arts from around the world, appreciably calmer than its tearaway cousins on the other side of Exhibition Road. Some 150 grand galleries on seven floors contain countless pieces of furniture, ceramics, sculpture, paintings, posters, jewellery, metalwork, glass, textiles and dress, spanning several centuries. Items are grouped by theme, origin or age, but any attempt to comprehend the whole collection in a single visit is doomed. For advice, tap the patient staff, who field a formidable combination of leaflets, floorplans, general knowledge and polite concern.

Highlights include the seven Raphael Cartoons painted in 1515 as tapestry designs for the Sistine Chapel; the finest collection of Italian Renaissance sculpture outside Italy; the Ardabil carpet, the world's oldest and arguably most splendid floor covering, in the Jameel Gallery of Islamic Art; and the Luck of Edenhall, a 13th-century glass beaker from Syria. The Fashion galleries run from 18th-century court dress right up to contemporary chiffon numbers; the Architecture gallery has videos, models, plans and descriptions of various styles; and the famous Photography collection holds over 500,000 images.

The V&A's ongoing FuturePlan transformation has been a revelation. The completely refurbished Medieval & Renaissance Galleries are stunning, but there are many other eye-catching new or redisplayed exhibits: the Gilbert Collection of silver, gold and gemmed ornaments has arrived from Somerset House; the Ceramics Galleries have been renovated and supplemented with an eye-catching bridge; there's lovely Buddhist sculpture in the Robert HN Ho Family Foundation Galleries; and the new Theatre & Performance Galleries take over where Covent Garden's defunct Theatre Museum left off. The restored mosaic floors and beautiful stained glass of the 14th- to 17th-century sculpture rooms, just off the central John Madejski Garden, enhance the already striking statuary, and we can't wait for the new Furniture Gallery (which should be open by

---

**INSIDE TRACK
STREET RADICAL**

Exhibition Road has been refurbished with much broader pavements, no kerbs and a 20mph speed limit for vehicles. Why? The notion – somewhat controversial – is to force road-users to actively share the space: rather than policing cars, bikes and pedestrians with hectoring road signs and traffic lights, the slight confusion caused by having no obvious boundaries has been shown by some research to encourage more considerate behaviour on all sides. Though don't expect the same lack of rules to apply to that queue for ice-cream in the **Natural History Museum** or **Science Museum** (for both, *see left*).

---

the time you read this) or to see what's been done with the magnificent Cast Courts – the public should be allowed back in among the 18ft-high plaster *David*, Trajan's Column and monumental cathedral doors at some point in 2013.

HYDE PARK & KENSINGTON GARDENS

Hyde Park Corner, Knightsbridge, Lancaster Gate or Queensway tube.

At one and a half miles long and about a mile wide, **Hyde Park** (7298 2000, www.royalparks. gov.uk) is one of the largest of London's Royal Parks. The land was appropriated in 1536 from the monks of Westminster Abbey by Henry VIII for hunting deer. Although opened to the public in the early 1600s, the parks were favoured only by the upper echelons of society.

At the end of the 17th century, William III, averse to the dank air of Whitehall Palace, relocated to **Kensington Palace** (*see p115*). A corner of Hyde Park was sectioned off to make grounds for the palace and closed to the public, until King George II opened it on Sundays to those wearing formal dress. Nowadays, **Kensington Gardens** is delineated from Hyde Park only by the line of the Serpentine and the Long Water. Beside the Long Water is a bronze

Behind the Palace Door

Hear tales of the generations of royals who have called Kensington Palace home.

Newly restored, **Kensington Palace** (*see p115*) is open again to the public. This is not just another grand house with old furniture and paintings. Here, visitors follow a whimsical trail focused on four 'stories' of former residents, unearthing facts about them and their times through 'newspapers' – really handily placed crib sheets, relating the news of the day. There are whispering in the galleries and poignant reminiscences.

The first, and briefest, story is that of Princess Diana: stylised 'Diana' wallpaper lines a narrow corridor leading to a room containing some of her dresses.

The Queen's State Apartments are modest, liveable rooms. The lives featured here, we learn, are those of William and Mary, and Mary's sister, Queen Anne. Suitcases and sounds of the sea allude to William and Mary's arrival from the Netherlands to depose James II in the Glorious Revolution of 1688. William and Mary were childless and eventually

succeeded by Anne. She had 17 pregnancies, but only one child, the sickly Prince William, survived beyond infancy; doted on by his mother, he was the hope for the continuation of the Stuart line. But he took ill at his tenth birthday party, where it is said he overheated while dancing, leading to a fever and his death. The place settings for that doomed party are re-created here, along with dreamlike installations reflecting a childhood curtailed.

The King's State Apartments were created for George I and George II. George arrived from Hanover to take the throne following the death of Queen Anne without an heir. In contrast with the home-loving Queen's rooms, the grandeur of these semi-public spaces is palpable: the Presence Chamber, with its throne; the Privy Chamber for more intimate meetings; and the Gallery, with paintings by the likes of Tintoretto, used for chats with confidantes (you can still hear them today if you stand by the windows).

The fourth 'story', 'Victoria Revealed', traces the life of Queen Victoria through objects and extracts from her writings. Among the artefacts is her (tiny) wedding dress, jewellery and other gifts from Prince Albert, photographs of her children and dolls.

Much of the exhibition covers her private life: her love for Albert, their cosy domesticity, her devastation at his death and prolonged mourning. But major events of the period feature, too, with a section devoted to the Great Exhibition and another to the Diamond Jubilee.

Serpentine Sackler Gallery.

statue of **Peter Pan**, erected in 1912: it was in Kensington Gardens beside the Round Pond eight years earlier that playwright JM Barrie met Jack Llewelyn Davies, the boy who was the inspiration for Peter. The **Diana, Princess of Wales Memorial Playground** (*see p267*) is a kids' favourite, as is Kathryn Gustafson's ring-shaped **Princess Diana Memorial Fountain**. Near the fountain, Simon Gudgeon's giant bird *Isis* was in 2009 the first sculpture added to the park for half a century. There are changing exhibitions of contemporary art at the **Serpentine Gallery**, which have a brand-new gallery due to open in the park in 2013.

The **Serpentine** itself is London's oldest boating lake, home to ducks, coots, swans, tufty-headed grebes and, every summer, gently perspiring blokes rowing their children or lovers about. The lake is at the bottom of **Hyde Park**, which isn't a beautiful park, but is of historic interest. The legalisation of public assembly in the park led to the establishment of **Speakers' Corner** in 1872 (close to Marble Arch tube), where political and religious ranters – sane and otherwise – still have the floor. Marx, Lenin, Orwell and the Pankhursts all spoke here. It has made the park a traditional destination for protest marches: notably the million opponents of the Iraq War in 2003, more recently trades union protests against government austerity measures in 2012.

The park perimeter is popular with skaters, as well as with bike- and horse-riders. If you're exploring on foot and the vast expanses defeat you, look out for the **Liberty Drives** (May-Oct). Driven by volunteers, these electric buggies, each with space for a wheelchair, pick up groups

of sightseers and ferry them around; there's no fare, but offer a donation if you can.

Kensington Palace
Kensington Gardens, W8 4PX (information 0844 482 7777, reservations 0844 482 7799, www.hrp.org.uk). High Street Kensington or Queensway tube. **Open** *Mar-Oct* 10am-6pm daily. *Nov-Feb* 10am-5pm daily. **Admission** £14.50; £12 reductions; £43 family; free under-5s. **Credit** AmEx, MC, V. **Map** p392 B8.
Sir Christopher Wren extended this Jacobean mansion to palatial proportions on the instructions of William III, initiating the palace's long love affair with royalty – which culminated with the floral memorials for one particular resident, Princess Diana, at the palace's gate after her fatal accident in 1997. For more on the refurbished palace and its stories, *see p114* **Behind the Palace Door**.

★ FREE Serpentine & Serpentine Sackler Galleries
Kensington Gardens, nr Albert Memorial, W2 3XA (7402 6075, www.serpentinegallery.org). Lancaster Gate or South Kensington tube. **Open** 10am-6pm daily. **Admission** free; donations appreciated. **Credit** (shop) AmEx, MC, V. **Map** p393 D8 & E7.
The secluded location south-west of the Long Water and Serpentine makes this small 1930s tea house an attractive destination for lovers of contemporary art. The rolling two-monthly programme of exhibitions features a mix of up-to-the-minute artists and edgy career retrospectives. Every spring, a renowned architect, who's never before built in the UK, is commissioned to build a new pavilion. It then opens to the public, with cultural events from June to September.

In 2013, the gallery will undergo a massive expansion, opening the Serpentine Sackler Gallery just across the Serpentine. Devoted to emerging art in all forms, the new gallery will be in a Grade II-listed, 1815 building whose Palladian styling belies its original function as a gunpowder store. Starchitect Zaha Hadid is supervising the transformation.
▶ *Zaha Hadid designed the first Serpentine Pavilion back in 2000, but now has the Olympic Aquatics Centre (see p23) as a London representative of her singular architectural vision.*

EXPLORE

INSIDE TRACK GIDDY-UP!

Watch members of the Household Cavalry emerge from their South Carriage Drive barracks in **Hyde Park** at 10.30am daily (9.30am Sunday). They then ride to Horse Guards Parade for the **Changing of the Guard** (*see p27* **Standing on Ceremony**).

North London

Birthplace of Britpop and leafy retreat of great thinkers.

The list of famous residents gives an idea of the scope of north London: rich popstrel Amy Winehouse, émigré psychoanalyst Sigmund Freud, brainy leftie Karl Marx and frilly shirted young poet John Keats have all been drawn here, whether for the area's pretty, sleepy retreats or its buzzing, creative party zones. First stop for most is **Camden Town**, with its markets, indie pubs and alternative vibe, but there's fun to be found in the squares of **Islington** and among the grown-up bohemians of **Stoke Newington** and fashionable **Dalston**. To the north, **Hampstead** and **Highgate** offer genteel village life.

Map p404	**Restaurants &**
Pubs & bars p198	**cafés** pp177-179
Hotels pp254-255	

CAMDEN

Camden Town or Chalk Farm tube.

Despite the pressures of gentrification, Camden refuses to leave behind its grungy history as the cradle of British rock music. Against a backdrop of social deprivation in Thatcher's Britain, venues such as the Electric Ballroom and Dingwalls provided a platform for musical rebels. By the 1990s, the Creation label was based in nearby Primrose Hill (*see p118*), unleashing My Bloody Valentine and the Jesus & Mary Chain on the world, before making it big with Oasis. The Gallaghers were often seen trading insults with Blur at the **Good Mixer** (30 Inverness Street, 7916 7929). The music still plays at Camden icon the **Roundhouse** (*see p288*) in the north, **Koko** (*see p286*) to the south, and any number of pubs and clubs between.

Before the Victorian expansion of London, Camden was a watering stop on the highway to Hampstead (*see p119*), with two notorious taverns – the Mother Black Cap and Mother Red Cap (now the **World's End** pub, opposite Camden Town tube) – frequented by highwaymen and brigands. After the gaps were filled in with terraced houses, the borough became a magnet for Irish and Greek railway workers, many of them working in the engine turning-house that is now the Roundhouse. The squalor of the area had a powerful negative influence on the young Charles Dickens, who lived briefly on Bayham Street; a blue plaque commemorates his stay. From the 1960s, things started to pick up for Camden, helped by an influx of students, lured by low rents and the growing arts scene that nurtured punk, then indie, then Britpop – and now any number of short-lived indie-electro and alt-folk hybrids.

Parts of Camden still have a rough quality, but the hardcore rebellion of the rock 'n' roll years has been replaced by a more laid-back carnival vibe, as young shoppers join the international parade of counterculture costumes. Tourists travel here in their thousands for the sprawling mayhem of **Camden Market** (*see p117*), which stretches north from the tube along boutique-lined Camden High Street and Chalk Farm Road.

There are unmistakeable signs of a move upmarket: **Shaka Zulu** (Stables Market, Chalk Farm Road, 3376 9911, www.shaka-zulu.com), a hugely over-the-top Zulu-themed bar-restaurant, right beneath **Gilgamesh** (7428 4922, www. gilgameshbar.com), a hugely over-the-top Sumerian-themed bar-restaurant, may point to the future. Drop in to **Proud** (*see p282*) if you want to reset your cultural compass.

Cutting through the market is **Regent's Canal**, which opened in 1820 to provide a link between east and west London for horse-drawn narrowboats loaded with coal. Today, the canal is used by the jolly tour boats of the London Waterbus Company (7482 2550, www.london waterbus.com) and Walker's Quay (7485 4433, www.walkersquay.com), which run between Camden Lock and **Little Venice** in summer and on winter weekends. Locals use the canal towpath as a convenient walking route west to Regent's Park and **ZSL London Zoo** (*see p89*), or east to Islington (*see p121*).

Camden's one avowed 'sight' is west of Camden Town – the excellent **Jewish Museum** (*see right*) – but it's still a good bit of town for gigs. As well as Koko and the Roundhouse, there are plenty of pub stages where this year's hopefuls try to get spotted: try the **Barfly** (*see p288*), **Underworld** (*see p291*) and the **Dublin Castle** (94 Parkway, 7485 1773), where Madness and, later, Blur were launched. The **Jazz Café** (*see p291*) and the **Blues Kitchen** (*see p289*) offer a different vibe.

Camden Market

Camden Lock *Camden Lock Place, off Chalk Farm Road, NW1 8AF (7485 7963, www.camden lockmarket.com).* **Open** 10am-6pm Mon-Thur, Sun; 10am-6.30pm Fri, Sat. Note: there are fewer stalls Mon-Fri.
Camden Lock Village *east of Chalk Farm Road, NW1 (www.camdenlock.net).* **Open** 10am-6pm daily.
Camden Market *Camden High Street, at Buck Street, NW1 (www.camdenmarkets.org).* **Open** 10am-5.30pm Thur-Sun.

Inverness Street Market *Inverness Street, NW1 (www.camdenlock.net).* **Open** 8.30am-5pm daily.
Stables Market *off Chalk Farm Road, opposite Hartland Road, NW1 8AH (7485 5511, www. stablesmarket.com).* **Open** 10.30am-6pm Mon-Fri (reduced stalls); 10am-6pm Sat, Sun.
All *Camden Town or Chalk Farm tube.*
Map p404 Y2.
Camden Market actually refers to the microcosm of markets that make up the northern Camden Town area – more than 700 shops and stalls in all. The Camden Market is the place for neon sunglasses and pseudo-witty slogan garments. Almost next door, and perennially threatened by proposed tube station expansions, is the listed building the Electric Ballroom, which sells vinyl and CDs on weekends and is also a music venue. The Inverness Street Market opposite sells similar garb to the Camden Market as well as a diminishing supply of fruit and veg. North, next to the railway bridge, is Camden Lock, with stalls selling crafts, home furnishings, jewellery, toys and gifts – head into the West Yard for global food. There are further crafty doodads, fashion and nibbles in the Camden Lock Village, which runs along the towpath. ► *From Camden Lock Village, it's a very pleasant half-hour walk east then south on the Regent's Canal to Granary Square (see p71), passing the sweet little Camley Street Natural Park (www.wildlondon. org.uk) on the opposite bank.*

Jewish Museum

Raymond Burton House, 129-131 Albert Street, NW1 7NB (7284 7384, www.jewishmuseum.

EXPLORE

Camden.

org.uk). Camden Town tube. **Open** 10am-5pm
Mon-Thur, Sat, Sun; 10am-2pm Fri. **Admission**
£7.50; £3.50-£6.50 reductions; free under-5s.
Credit MC, V. **Map** p404 Y3.
This museum is a brilliant exploration of Jewish life
in Britain since 1066, combining fun interactives –
you can wield the iron in a tailor's sweatshop, sniff
chicken soup, pose for a wedding photo or take part
in some Yiddish theatre – with serious history.
There's a powerful Holocaust section, using the testimony of a single survivor, Leon Greenman, to
bring tight focus to the unimaginable horror of it all.
Opposite, a beautiful room of religious artefacts,
including a 17th-century synagogue ark and centrepiece chandelier of Hanukkah lamps, does an elegant
job of introducing Jewish ritual. Access is free to the
downstairs café, located beside an ancient ritual
bath, and to the shop you enter past.

Around Camden

Primrose Hill, to the west of Camden, is just
as attractive as the celebrities who frequent the
gastropubs and quaint cafés along **Regent's
Park Road** and **Gloucester Avenue**. On
sunny Sunday mornings, there's no better spot to
read the papers than the pavement tables in front
of Ukrainian café **Trojka** (101 Regent's Park
Road, 7483 3765). Other favourite hangouts on
Regent's Park Road include the long-established
Primrose Pâtisserie (no.136, 7722 7848) and
upmarket Greek bistro **Lemonia** (no.89, 7586
7454). For a gastropub feed, head to Gloucester
Avenue: both the **Engineer** (no.65, 7483 1890)
and **Lansdowne** (no.90, 7483 0409) are here. On
a clear day, the walk up the hill is a delight; on
a dull one, try one of the excellent art galleries.

Museum of Everything
*Corner of Regent's Park Road & Sharpleshall
Street, NW1 (www.museumofeverything.com).
Chalk Farm tube.* **Map** p404 W2.
Not so much a gallery as an itinerant series of superb
exhibitions (here, Tate Modern, Turin, Moscow…
you know, all the local venues), this quirky former
dairy in Primrose Hill opens periodically with changing displays of naïve, outsider and folk art. Check
the website for the latest show.

Zabludowicz Collection
*176 Prince of Wales Road, Chalk Farm, NW5
3PT (7428 8940, www.zabludowiczcollection.com).
Chalk Farm tube or Kentish Town West rail.*
Open noon-6pm Thur-Sun. **Credit** MC, V.
Map p404 W1.
This former Methodist chapel – a remarkable neoclassical building that makes a superb setting for art
exhibitions – holds three shows a year, enabling
artists to create experimental new work and curators
to build exhibitions around the Collection's global
emerging art in all media.

Hampstead Heath.

ST JOHN'S WOOD
St John's Wood or Swiss Cottage tube.

The woodland that gives St John's Wood its
name was part of the great Middlesex Forest,
before the land was claimed by the Knights of St
John of Jerusalem. Areas of forest were cleared
for private villas in the mid 19th century, and
uncharacteristically sensitive redevelopment
during the 1950s left the area smart and
eminently desirable: even a modest semi can cost
£2m. The expensive tastes of locals are reflected
in the posh boutiques along the High Street. The
main tourist attraction is **Lord's** cricket ground
(*see p315*), but a steady stream of music fans pay
tribute to the Beatles by walking over the zebra

crossing in front of **Abbey Road Studios** (3 Abbey Road). The studio, founded in 1931 by Sir Edward Elgar, is still used to record albums and film scores, including *The Lord of the Rings*.

Lord's Tour & MCC Museum

St John's Wood Road, NW8 8QN (7616 8595, www.lords.org). St John's Wood tube. **Open** *Tours* phone or check website for details. **Admission** £15; £9 reductions; free under-5s; £40 family. **Credit** AmEx, MC, V.

Lord's is more than just a famous cricket ground. As the headquarters of the Marylebone Cricket Club (MCC), it is official guardian of the rules – and self-appointed guardian of the elusive 'spirit' – of cricket. As well as staging Test matches and internationals, the ground is home to the Middlesex County Cricket Club (MCCC). Visitors can take an organised tour round the futuristic, pod-like JP Morgan Media Centre and the august, portrait-bedecked Long Room. Highlights of the museum include the tiny urn containing the Ashes (this coveted trophy never leaves Lord's, even if the Australians do manage to win it back in summer 2013) and memorabilia celebrating the achievements of such legends of the game as WG Grace.

HAMPSTEAD

Hampstead tube, or Gospel Oak or Hampstead Heath rail.

It may have been absorbed into London during the city's great Victorian expansion, but hilltop Hampstead still feels like a Home Counties' village. It has long been a favoured roost for literary and artistic types: Keats and Constable lived here in the 19th century, and sculptors Barbara Hepworth and Henry Moore took up residence in the 1930s. However, the area is now popular with City workers, who are among the only people able to afford what is some of London's priciest property.

The undisputed highlight of the district is **Hampstead Heath**, the vast and in places wonderfully overgrown tract of countryside between Hampstead village and Highgate that is said to have inspired CS Lewis's Narnia. The heath covers 791 acres of woodland, playing fields, swimming ponds and meadows of tall grass that attract picnickers and couples in search of privacy. It will feel even more delightfully rural if the City of London Corporation's 'aspiration' to graze sheep on the heath as a flock of organic lawnmowers comes to fruition.

The south end of the heath is where you'll find dinky Hampstead village, all genteel shops and cafés, restaurants and lovely pubs such as the **Holly Bush** (*see p198*). While you're there, tour the gorgeous sunken gardens and antique collection at **Fenton House** (*see right*) or gaze

at the stars from the **Hampstead Scientific Society Observatory** (Lower Terrace, www.hampsteadscience.ac.uk/astro), open on clear Friday and Saturday evenings and Sunday lunchtimes from mid September to mid April. A stroll along nearby Judges Walk reveals a line of horse chestnuts and limes virtually unchanged since they appeared in a Constable painting in 1820. Constable was buried nearby at **St John-at-Hampstead Church** (7794 5808, www.hampsteadparishchurch.org.uk), as was the comedian Peter Cook. At the top of Hampstead, North End Way divides the main heath from the wooded West Heath, one of London's oldest gay cruising areas (but perfectly family-friendly by day). Just off North End Way is Hampstead's best-kept secret, the secluded and charmingly overgrown **Hill Garden & Pergola** (open 8.30am-dusk daily), which was built by Lord Leverhulme using soil from the excavation of the Northern line's tunnels.

East of Hampstead tube, a maze of postcard-pretty residential streets shelters **Burgh House** (New End Square, 7431 0144, www.burgh house.org.uk), a Queen Anne house with a small local history museum and gallery. Also in the area are **2 Willow Road** (*see p120*), architect Ernö Goldfinger's self-designed 1930s residence, and **40 Well Walk**, Constable's home for the last ten years of his life. Downhill towards Hampstead Heath Overground station is **Keats House** (*see p120*). Further west, and marginally closer to Finchley Road tube, is the **Freud Museum** (*see p120*), while the innovative contemporary art exhibitions of **Camden Arts Centre** (*see below*) are almost opposite Finchley Road & Frognal Overground station.

Camden Arts Centre

Arkwright Road, NW3 6DG (7472 5500, www.camdenartscentre.org). Finchley Road tube or Finchley Road & Frognal rail. **Open** 10am-6pm Tue, Thur-Sun; 10am-9pm Wed. **Credit** MC, V.
Under the directorship of Jenni Lomax, Camden Arts Centre has eclipsed larger venues. The annual artist-curated shows – sculpture, automata, film works – have been among the most memorable in recent history. The Centre also hosts a comprehensive programme of talks, events and workshops and boasts a good bookshop and a great café, which opens on to a surprisingly tranquil garden.

Fenton House

3 Hampstead Grove, NW3 6RT (7435 3471, www.nationaltrust.org.uk). Hampstead tube. **Open** *Mar-Oct* times vary; check website for details. **Admission** *House & gardens* £6.50; £3 reductions; £16 family; free under-5s. *Gardens* £2. *Joint ticket with 2 Willow Road* £9. **Credit** MC, V.
Set in a gorgeous garden, with a 300-year-old apple orchard, this manor house is notable for its 17th- and

EXPLORE

INSIDE TRACK
CROWD CONTROL

Camden Market's crowds can be awful at the weekends – which means it's also the best time to visit. So recuperate after the madness by slipping out of the markets sideways on to the canal, then strolling five minutes west into sedate **Primrose Hill** (*see p118*), the perfect place to reassess your purchases.

18th-century harpsichords, virginals and spinets, which are still played at lunchtime and evening concerts (phone for details). Also on display are European and Chinese porcelain, Chippendale furniture and some artful 17th-century needlework.

Freud Museum

20 Maresfield Gardens, NW3 5SX (7435 2002, www.freud.org.uk). Finchley Road tube. **Open** noon-5pm Wed-Sun. **Admission** £6; £3-£4.50 reductions; free under-12s. **Credit** AmEx, MC, V. Driven from Vienna by the Nazis, Sigmund Freud lived in this quiet suburban house in north London with his wife Martha and daughter Anna until his death in 1939. Now a museum with imaginative temporary exhibitions, the house displays Freud's antiques, art and therapy tools, including his famous couch. Unusually, the building has two blue plaques, one for Sigmund and another for Anna, a pioneer in child psychiatry.

Keats House

Keats Grove, NW3 2RR (7332 3868, www. cityoflondon.gov.uk/keatshousehampstead). Hampstead tube, Hampstead Heath rail or bus 24, 46, 168. **Open** *Apr-Oct* 1-5pm Tue-Sun. *Nov-Mar* 1-5pm Fri-Sun. **Admission** £5; £3 reductions; free under-16s. **Credit** MC, V. Keats House was the Romantic poet's last British home before tuberculosis forced him to Italy and death at the age of only 25. A leaflet guides you through each room, starting from the rear, as well as providing context for Keats's life and that of his less famous friend and patron, Charles Brown. Painstaking renovation has ensured the decorative scheme is entirely accurate, down to pale pink walls in Keats's humble bedroom. The garden, in which he wrote 'Ode to a Nightingale', is particularly pleasant.

FREE Kenwood House/Iveagh Bequest

Hampstead Lane, NW3 7JR (8348 1286, www. english-heritage.org.uk). Hampstead tube, or Golders Green tube then bus 210. **Open** 11.30am-4pm daily. **Admission** free. *Tours* (for groups by appointment only) £5-£7. **Credit** AmEx, MC, V. Set in lovely grounds at the top of Hampstead Heath, Kenwood House is every inch the country manor house. Built in 1616, the mansion was remodelled in the 18th century for William Murray, who made the pivotal court ruling in 1772 that made it illegal to own slaves in England. The house was purchased by brewing magnate Edward Guinness, who was kind enough to donate his art collection to the nation in 1927. It has been closed for renovations, but is due to open in autumn 2013, when such highlights as Vermeer's *The Guitar Player*, Gainsborough's *Countess Howe*, and one of Rembrandt's finest self-portraits (dating to c1663) will again be on display.

2 Willow Road

2 Willow Road, NW3 1TH (7435 6166, www.nationaltrust.org.uk). Hampstead tube or Hampstead Heath rail. **Open** *Mar-Oct* 11am-5pm Wed-Sun. *Tours* 11am, noon, 1pm, 2pm Wed-Sun. **Admission** £6; £3 children; free under-5s; £15 family. *Joint ticket with Fenton House* £9. **No credit cards.**
A surprising addition to the National Trust's collection of historic houses, this small modernist building was designed by Hungarian-born architect Ernö Goldfinger. The house was made to be flexible, with ingenious movable partitions and folding doors. Home to the architect and his wife until their deaths, it contains a fine, idiosyncratic collection of art by the likes of Max Ernst and Henry Moore. Goldfinger also designed Notting Hill's Trellick Tower (*see p91*).

Kenwood House.

HIGHGATE

Archway or Highgate tube.

Taking its name from the tollgate that once stood on the High Street, Highgate is inexorably linked with London's medieval mayor, Richard 'Dick' Whittington. As the story goes, the disheartened Whittington, having failed to make his fortune, fled the City as far as Highgate Hill, but turned back when he heard the Bow Bells peal out 'Turn again, Whittington, thrice Mayor of London'. Today, the area is best known for the atmospheric grounds of **Highgate Cemetery** (*see below*). Adjoining the cemetery is pretty **Waterlow Park**, created by low-cost housing pioneer Sir Sydney Waterlow in 1889, with ponds, a mini-aviary, tennis courts and a cute garden café in 16th-century **Lauderdale House** (8348 8716, www.lauderdalehouse.co.uk), former home of Charles II's mistress, Nell Gwynn. North of Highgate tube, shady **Highgate Woods** are preserved as a conservation area, with a nature trail, adventure playground and a café that hosts live jazz during the summer.

★ Highgate Cemetery
Swains Lane, N6 6PJ (8340 1834, www.highgate-cemetery.org). Archway tube. **Open** *East Cemetery* Mar-Oct 10am-5pm Mon-Fri; 11am-5pm Sat, Sun. Nov-Mar 10am-4pm Mon-Fri; 11am-4pm Sat, Sun. *West Cemetery* by tour only. **Admission** £3; £2 reductions. *Tours* £7; £5 reductions. **No credit cards.**
The final resting place of some very famous Londoners, Highgate Cemetery is a wonderfully overgrown maze of ivy-cloaked Victorian tombs and time-shattered urns. Visitors can wander at their own pace through the East Cemetery, with its memorials to Karl Marx, George Eliot and Douglas Adams, but the most atmospheric part of the cemetery is the foliage-shrouded West Cemetery, laid out in 1839. Only accessible on an organised tour (book ahead, dress respectfully and arrive 30mins early), the shady paths wind past gloomy catacombs, grand Victorian pharaonic tombs, and the graves of notables such as poet Christina Rossetti, scientist Michael Faraday and poisoned Russian dissident Alexander Litvinenko.
▶ *The cemetery closes during burials, so call ahead before you visit. Note that children under eight are not allowed in the West Cemetery.*

ISLINGTON

Angel tube or Highbury & Islington tube/rail.

Islington started life as a country village beside one of Henry VIII's expansive hunting reserves. It soon became an important livestock market supplying the Smithfield meat yards, before being enveloped into Greater London. The 19th century

Highgate Cemetery.

brought industrial development along the Regent's Canal and later industrial decay, but locals kept up their spirits at the area's music halls, launchpads for such working-class heroes as Marie Lloyd, George Formby and Norman Wisdom. From the 1960s, there was an influx of arts and media types, who gentrified the Georgian squares and Victorian terraces and opened cafés, restaurants and boutiques around Upper Street and Essex Road. It is now a suburban bower of the *Guardian*-reading middle classes.

Close to the station on Upper Street, the **Camden Passage** antique market (*see p228*) bustles with browsing activity on Wednesdays and Saturdays. The music halls have long gone, but locals still take advantage of the celluloid offerings at the **Screen on the Green** (*see p270* **Everyman & Screen Cinemas**) and the stage productions at the **Almeida** theatre (*see p309*).

East of Angel, Regency-era **Canonbury Square** was once home to George Orwell (no.27) and Evelyn Waugh (no.17A). One of the handsome townhouses now contains the **Estorick Collection of Modern Italian Art** (*see p122*). Just beyond the end of Upper Street is **Highbury Fields**, where 200,000 Londoners fled in 1666 to escape the Great Fire. The surrounding district is best known as the home of Arsenal Football Club, who abandoned the charming Highbury Stadium in 2006 for the gleaming

60,000-seater behemoth that is the **Emirates Stadium** (*see p315*). Fans can either take a fine self-guided audio tour of the stadium or check out the memorabilia at the **Arsenal Museum** (7619 5000, www.arsenal.com). Dedicated football fans will enjoy walking a couple of blocks east to Avenell Road, where Archibald Leitch's palatial East Stand has been preserved as offices; on parallel Highbury Hill, a single painted house marks the entrance to the vanished West Stand.

★ Estorick Collection of Modern Italian Art

39A Canonbury Square, N1 2AN (7704 9522, www.estorickcollection.com). Highbury & Islington tube/rail or bus 271. **Open** 11am-6pm Wed-Sat; noon-5pm Sun. **Admission** £5; £3.50 reductions; free under-16s, students. **Credit** AmEx, MC, V. Originally owned by American political scientist and writer Eric Estorick, this is a wonderful depository of early 20th-century Italian art. It is one of the world's foremost collections of futurism, Italy's brash and confrontational contribution to international modernism. The four galleries are full of movement, machines and colour, while the temporary exhibits meet the futurist commitment to fascism full on. There is also a shop and café.

DALSTON & STOKE NEWINGTON

Dalston Kingsland, Dalston Junction, Rectory Road, Stamford Hill or Stoke Newington rail.

Occupying the area around the junction of Balls Pond Road and Kingsland Road, scruffy Dalston may be summed up these days by African-flavoured Ridley Road market: routinely praised by hipsters for its authentic cultural mix, it's still 'real' enough that some stallholders were caught selling 'illicit' meat in 2012. Safer to head to one of the delicious Turkish *ocakbaşı* (grill restaurants) along Stoke Newington Road, including excellent **Mangal II** (no.4, 7254 7888), although the throng of hipsters wowing at the sharing plates of 'travelling food and drink collaboration' **Rita's** (nos.33-35, www.ritasbaranddining. com) might be a more accurate sign of things to come. Studenty nightowls are already being replaced by wealthier branding types, but they all play together happily enough at the appealingly urban **Dalston Jazz Bar** (4 Bradbury Street, 7254 9728), the brilliant **Vortex Jazz Club** (*see p294*) and **Café Oto** (*see p292*), and dynamic **Arcola** theatre (*see p303*).

Neighbouring **Stoke Newington** is the richer cousin of Dalston and poorer cousin of Islington. At weekends, pretty **Clissold Park** (www.clissoldpark.com) is overrun with picnickers and mums pushing prams.

Most visitors head to Stoke Newington for bijou **Church Street**. This curvy road is lined with second-hand bookshops, cute boutiques and kids' stores, and superior cafés and restaurants – Keralan vegetarian restaurant **Rasa** (no.55, 7249 0344) is probably the best of them. Another local highlight is **Abney Park Cemetery** (www.abney-park.org.uk), a wonderfully wild, overgrown Victorian boneyard and nature reserve.

Screen on the Green.

East London

The 2012 Games have gone – the clubs, boutiques and galleries remain.

The planners of London 2012 chose well. For years, east London has been on the cultural cutting edge. Read the style mags, and it's hard to believe how recently the East End was notorious for its slums, petty gangsters and urban blight. It was also cursed with the smelliest and most unpleasant of London's dock-side industries.

How things change. East London now has some of London's most vital areas. Alongside the City, **Spitalfields** and **Brick Lane** are tourist must-visits, with markets, boutiques, restaurants and – as they shade beyond increasingly upmarket **Shoreditch** into **Hackney** – art-student trendy nightlife. To the north, **London Fields** drives the arts and fashion zeitgeist; eastwards, **Docklands** rivals the City for blue-chip institutions. And, beyond it all, eyes are repeatedly drawn to the **Queen Elizabeth Olympic Park** (*see pp21-23*): can those heady promises of a 'legacy' for east London be delivered?

Map p401 & p403	**Pubs & bars**
Restaurants &	pp198-201
cafés pp179-182	**Hotels** pp255-257

EXPLORE

SPITALFIELDS

Aldgate East tube/Liverpool Street tube/rail.

Approach this area from Liverpool Street Station, up Brushfield Street, and you'll know you're on the right track when the magnificent spiky spire of **Christ Church Spitalfields** (*see p124*) comes into sight. The area's other signature sight, **Spitalfields Market**, has emerged from redevelopment and the market stalls have moved back underneath the vaulted Victorian roof of the original building.

Outside, along Brushfield Street, the shops might look as if they're from Dickens's day, but most are recent inventions: the charming grocery shop **A Gold** (no.42, 7247 2487) was lovingly restored in the noughties; the owners of the **English Restaurant** (nos.50-52, 7247 4110) put reclaimed wood panelling and creaky furniture into an empty shell; and the deli **Verde & Co** (no.40, 7247 1924) was opened by its owner, author Jeanette Winterson, inspired by the local food shops she found in – whisper it – France. This tendency will, after Mayor Boris Johnson overruled the council's objections, be made literal

by the redevelopment of the **Fruit & Wool Exchange**, built in 1920 – only the façade will remain of a building that sheltered as many as 10,000 East Enders from the Blitz, and still bears graffiti from those days. Settle any anxieties about gentrification by heading a few streets south: on Sundays, the salt-of-the-earth **Petticoat Lane Market** hawks knickers and cheap electronics around Middlesex Street, while, at the foot of Goulston Street, **Tubby Isaacs** seafood stall has been selling whelks and cockles since 1919.

A block north of Spitalfields Market is **Dennis Severs' House** (*see p124*), while across from the market, on the east side of Commercial Street and in the shadow of Christ Church, the **Ten Bells** (84 Commercial Street, 7366 1721) is where one of Jack the Ripper's prostitute victims drank her last gin. On the next corner, Sandra Esqulant's **Golden Heart** pub (no.110, 7247 2158) has hosted every Young British Artist of note, ever since the day Gilbert & George decided to pop in on their new local. The streets between here and Brick Lane to the east are dourly impressive, lined with tall, shuttered Huguenot houses; **19 Princelet**

Time Out London **123**

Spitalfields Market.

Street (www.19princeletstreet.org.uk) is open to the public a few times a year. This unrestored 18th-century house was home first to French silk merchants and later Polish Jews who built a synagogue in the garden.

FREE Christ Church Spitalfields

Commercial Street, E1 6QE (7859 3035, www.christchurchspitalfields.org). Liverpool Street tube/rail or Shoreditch High Street rail. **Open** 11am-4pm Tue; 1-4pm Sun. **Admission** free. **No credit cards. Map** p401 S5.

Built in 1729 by architect Nicholas Hawksmoor, this splendid church has in recent years been restored to its original state (tasteless alterations had been made to the building following a lightning strike in the 19th century). Most tourists get no further than cowering before the wonderfully overbearing spire, but the revived interior is impressive too, its pristine whiteness in marked contrast to its architect's dark reputation. The formidable 1735 Richard Bridge organ is almost as old as the church. Regular concerts are held here, notably during the two annual Spitalfields festivals (*see p300* **Festivals**).

★ Dennis Severs' House

18 Folgate Street, E1 6BX (7247 4013, www.dennissevershouse.co.uk). Liverpool Street tube/rail or Shoreditch High Street rail. **Open** noon-4pm Sun; noon-2pm Mon following 1st & 3rd Sun of mth; times vary Mon evenings.

Admission £10 Sun; £7 noon-2pm Mon; £14 Mon evenings. **Credit** MC, V. **Map** p401 R5.

The ten rooms of this original Huguenot house have been decked out to recreate vivid snapshots of daily life in Spitalfields between 1724 and 1914. A tour through the compelling 'still-life drama', as American creator Dennis Severs dubbed it, takes you through the cellar, kitchen, dining room, smoking room and upstairs to the bedrooms. With hearth and candles burning, smells lingering and objects scattered apparently haphazardly, it feels as though the inhabitants have deserted the building only moments before you arrived.

BRICK LANE

Aldgate East tube.

Join the crowds flowing east from Spitalfields Market along Hanbury Street during the weekend, and the direction you turn at the end determines which Brick Lane you see. Turn right and you'll know you're in 'Banglatown', the name adopted by the ward back in 2002: until you hit the bland modern offices beside the kitsch Banglatown arch, it's almost all Bangladeshi cafés, curry houses, grocery stores, money transfer services and sari shops – plus the **Pride of Spitalfields** (3 Heneage Street, 7247 8933), an old-style East End boozer serving ale to all-comers.

Despite the street's global reputation for Indian food (there's even a Brick Lane restaurant in Manhattan), most of the food on offer in the street is disappointing, but nearby there are some good restaurants: try **Tayyabs** (*see p182*) or **Needoo Grill** (*see p180*). Alternatively, opt for Bengali sweets from the **Madhubon Sweet Centre** at no.42.

Between Fournier Street and Princelet Street, **Jamme Masjid Mosque** is a key symbol of Brick Lane's hybridity. It began as a Huguenot chapel, became a synagogue and was converted, in 1976, into a mosque – in other words, immigrant communities have been layering their experiences on this street at least since 1572, when the St Bartholomew's Day Massacre forced many French Huguenots into exile.

The newest layer is boho gentrification. On Sunday, there's the lively street market, complemented by the trendier UpMarket – superior, clothes-wise, to Spitalfields Market – and Backyard Market (for arts and crafts), both held in the **Old Truman Brewery** (nos.91-95). Pedestrianised Dray Walk, full of hip independent businesses, is crowded every day. Heading north on Brick Lane, you'll find bars, cafés and vintage fashion shops – with the cavernous **Beyond Retro** (*see p218*) frequently making a detour east on Cheshire Street worth its weight in clobber.

WHITECHAPEL

Aldgate East or Whitechapel tube.

Not one of the prettier thoroughfares to be found in London, busy but anonymous Whitechapel Road sets the tone for this area. One bright spot is **Whitechapel Gallery** (*see below*), west from the foot of Brick Lane, while a little to the east, the **Whitechapel Bell Foundry** (nos.32 & 34, 7247 2599, www.whitechapelbellfoundry.co.uk) continues to manufacture bells, as it has since 1570. It famously produced Philadelphia's Liberty Bell and 'Big Ben'. To join one of the fascinating Saturday tours you'll have to reserve a place (usually well in advance).

At Whitechapel's foremost place of worship, it isn't bells but a muezzin that summons the faithful each Friday: the **East London Mosque**, founded elsewhere in 1910 and now the focal point for the largest Muslim community in Britain, can accommodate 10,000 worshippers. Behind is Fieldgate Street and the dark mass of **Tower House**, a former doss house whose 700 rooms have, inevitably, been redeveloped into flats. This 'sought after converted warehouse building' was a dismal – but decidedly cheaper – proposition when Joseph Stalin and George Orwell (researching his book *Down and Out in Paris and London*) kipped here for pennies. The

Whitechapel Gallery.

red-brick alleys give a flavour of what Victorian Whitechapel must have been like.

East again is the Royal London Hospital and, in a small crypt on Newark Street, the **Royal London Hospital Archives & Museum** (7377 7608, closed Mon, Sat & Sun). Inside are reproduction letters from Jack the Ripper (including the notorious missive 'From Hell', delivered with an enclosed portion of human kidney) and information on Joseph Merrick, the 'Elephant Man'. Rescued by surgeon Sir Frederick Treves, Merrick was given his own room in the Royal London Hospital. Behind the hospital is the high-tech **Centre of the Cell** (4 Newark Street, 7882 2562, www.centreofthecell.org), which gives visitors a lively, interactive insight into cell biology in a purpose-built pod, suspended over labs investigating cancer and tuberculosis.

★ FREE Whitechapel Gallery
77-82 Whitechapel High Street, E1 7QX (7522 7888, www.whitechapelgallery.org). Aldgate East tube. **Open** 11am-6pm Tue, Wed, Fri-Sun; 11am-9pm Thur. **Admission** free. *Temporary exhibitions vary.* **Credit** MC, V. **Map** p403 S6.
This East End stalwart reopened in 2009, following a major redesign that saw the Grade II-listed building expand into the similarly historic former library next door – rather brilliantly, the architects left the two buildings stylistically distinct rather than trying to smooth out their differences. As well as nearly

EXPLORE

tripling its exhibition space, the Whitechapel gave itself a research centre and archives, plus a proper restaurant (see p182) and café. It looks set to improve a stellar reputation as a contemporary art pioneer built on shows of Picasso – *Guernica* was shown here in 1939 – Jackson Pollock, Mark Rothko and Frida Kahlo. With no permanent collection, there's a rolling programme of temporary shows, but an increasing number of artists have contributed permanently to the fabric of the building: most recently Rachel Whiteread added a lovely frieze with gold vine leaves to a space on the front of the gallery.

SHOREDITCH & HOXTON

Old Street tube/rail.

The story is familiar: in the 1980s, impecunious artists moved into the derelict warehouses in the triangle formed by Old Street, Shoreditch High Street and Great Eastern Street, and quickly turned it into the place to be. Rising rents have since driven many of the artists further east, but they've been replaced by the tech-hip denizens of 'silicon roundabout'. The area around Old Street roundabout has become a focus for digital start-ups, the beginning of Prime Minister David Cameron's **East London Tech City** (www.eastlondontechcity.com), a vision of digital entrepreneurs stretching all the way from here to the Queen Elizabeth Olympic Park (*see pp21-23* **After the Games**). The dream may be made more real when Joanna Shields, former European boss for Facebook, takes over at the start of 2013.

Nightlife permeates the area (linking conveniently to Brick Lane), with centres on Curtain Road, the lower end of Kingsland Road and around Hoxton Square. But the nature of the scene has changed dramatically: growing up in some people's eyes, losing its edge for others. The closure of the long-standing 333 club and the final eviction in 2010 of squatters from scuzzy club the Foundry (84-86 Great Eastern Street) to make way for a luxury hotel may be a sign of things to come. The independent boutiques of **Redchurch Street** are a more hopeful emblem of the new East End (*see p226* **Style Street**). Commercial culture of a different type was uncovered in 2011 behind a pub on Plough Yard, south of Great Eastern Street, where Museum of London archaeologists found the remains of the Curtain Theatre. The Curtain, which opened in 1577, is intimately connected to Shakespeare's early career, probably hosting the première of *Romeo & Juliet*.

Apart from seemingly countless galleries – White Cube was due to leave focal Hoxton Square in December 2012, but the Wharf Road neighbours (**Parasol Unit**, no.14, N1 7RW, 7490 7373, www.parasol-unit.org; **Victoria Miro**, no.16, N1 7RW, 7336 8109, www.victoria-miro.com) and not-for-profit pioneer **Raven Row** (56 Artillery Lane, E1 7LS, 7377 4300, www.ravenrow.org) are notable – the area's sole bona fide tourist attraction is the exquisite **Geffrye Museum** (*see below*), a short walk north up Kingsland Road. The surrounding area is dense with good, cheap Vietnamese restaurants (try **Sông Quê**; *see p181*).

★ FREE Geffrye Museum
136 Kingsland Road, E2 8EA (7739 9893, www.geffrye-museum.org.uk). Hoxton rail.
Open 10am-5pm Tue-Sat; noon-5pm Sun. *Almshouse tours* 1st Sat, 1st & 3rd Tue, Wed of mth. **Admission** free; donations appreciated. *Almshouse tours* £2.50; free under-16s. **Credit** (shop) MC, V. **Map** p401 R3.
Housed in a set of 18th-century almshouses, the Geffrye Museum offers a vivid physical history of the English interior. Displaying original furniture, paintings, textiles and decorative arts, the museum recreates a sequence of typical middle-class living rooms from 1600 to the present. It's an oddly interesting way to take in domestic history, with any number of intriguing details to catch your eye – from a bell jar of stuffed birds to a particular decorative flourish on a chair. There's an airy restaurant overlooking the lovely gardens, which include a walled plot for herbs and a chronological series in different historical styles.

Geffrye Museum.

EXPLORE

If You Build It, Will They Come?

The bleak Royal Docks suddenly have a host of new attractions.

When film-maker Derek Jarman chose to set his post-apocalyptic *Last of England* on Royal Victoria Dock in 1987, no one thought it unsuitable. When Bob Hoskins strolled dodgy US investors along a pier imagining a future Olympics in *The Long Good Friday* (1980), the notion appeared absurd. It seems we got it all upside down.

Following an Olympics where the ExCeL conference centre on Royal Victoria Dock was one of busiest venues, the docks are being put vigorously on the tourist map. Next door to the **Emirates Air Line** (*see p130*) is a black, pointy building. Sponsored by Siemens, the **Crystal** (for listings, *see p129*) attempts to explain in an engaging fashion how cities work, and how they might meet the challenges of population growth, global warming, ageing and the shortage of key resources, especially water. The two floors of interactives are slick and fun: try to beat the computer at face recognition, say, or plan the transport mix for different cities. Cynics might ask whether, for example, 'No city will survive unless it is economically competitive against global peers' is a key message for 'A Sustainable Cities Initiative' to deliver – or even true – but at least there's a good café in which to debate such matters.

Even more unlikely is the outbreak of beach culture: a licensed beach hut, which rents out gear for people who want to treat a surfboard like a canoe (paddleboarding) or clip themselves on a motor-driven zipwire to hurtle over jumps (wakeboarding), is run

Royal Docks.

by watersports initiative **Wake Up Docklands** (www.wakeupdocklands.com).

You can also cross the slightly hair-raising, high white bridge from ExCeL to find two historic ships: a red lightship and, floating on a raft to preserve it, **SS Robin** (www.ssrobin.org), a steamship so rare it is included (with the *Cutty Sark* and HMS *Belfast*) in the National Historic Fleet. It's due to reopen to the public in 2013. Not even Hoskins would adam-and-eve it.

EXPLORE

The Crystal.

BETHNAL GREEN

Bethnal Green tube/rail/Cambridge Heath rail/Mile End tube.

Once a gracious suburb of spacious townhouses, by the mid 19th century Bethnal Green was one of the city's poorest neighbourhoods. As in neighbouring Hoxton, a recent upturn in fortunes has in part been occasioned by Bethnal Green's adoption as home by a new generation of artists, attracted by the low rents resulting from the area's long-standing misfortunes. The **Maureen Paley** gallery (no.21) in Herald Street remains the key venue, but the new Bethnal Green is typified by places such as **Herald Street** (no.2), just down the road, and the arrival of the ambitious **Town Hall Hotel** (*see p256*) and **Viajante** restaurant (*see p182*). Take a seat at **E Pellicci** (*see p180*), the exemplary traditional London caff, for a taste of the old Bethnal Green.

The **V&A Museum of Childhood** (*see below*) is close to Bethnal Green tube station, but the area's other main attraction is a bit of a walk away. Nonetheless, a visit to the weekly **Columbia Road flower market** (*see p209*) is a lovely way to fritter away a Sunday morning. A microcosmic retail community has grown up around the market: **Treacle** (nos.110-112, 7729 0538) for groovy crockery and cup cakes; **Angela Flanders** (no.96, 7739 7555) for perfume; **Marcos & Trump** (no.146, 7739 9008) for vintage fashion.

FREE **Ragged School Museum**

46-50 Copperfield Road, E3 4RR (8980 6405, www.raggedschoolmuseum.org.uk). Mile End tube. **Open** 10am-5pm Wed, Thur; 2-5pm 1st Sun of mth. *Tours* by arrangement; phone for details. **Admission** free; donations appreciated. **No credit cards.**

Ragged schools were an early experiment in public education: they provided tuition, food and clothes for destitute children. This one was the largest in London, and Dr Barnardo himself taught here. It's now a sweet local museum that contains complete mock-ups of a ragged classroom and Edwardian kitchen, with displays on vanished local history. The events programme is increasingly lively.

★ FREE **V&A Museum of Childhood**

Cambridge Heath Road, E2 9PA (8983 5235, www.museumofchildhood.org.uk). Bethnal Green tube/rail or Cambridge Heath rail. **Open** 10am-5.45pm daily. **Admission** free; donations appreciated. **Credit** MC, V.

Home to one of the world's finest collections of children's toys, dolls' houses, games and costumes, the Museum of Childhood shines brighter than ever after extensive refurbishment, which has given it an impressive entrance. Part of the Victoria & Albert

Museum (*see p113*), the museum has been amassing childhood-related objects since 1872 and continues to do so, with *Incredibles* figures complementing bonkers 1970s puppets, Barbie Dolls and Victorian praxinoscopes. The museum has lots of hands-on stuff for kids dotted about the many cases of historic artefacts. Regular exhibitions are held upstairs, while the café in the centre of the main hall helps to revive flagging grown-ups.

DOCKLANDS

London's docks were fundamental to the prosperity of the British Empire. Between 1802 and 1921, ten separate docks were built between Tower Bridge in the west and Woolwich in the east. These employed tens of thousands of people. Yet by the 1960s, the shipping industry was changing irrevocably. The new 'container' system of cargo demanded larger, deep-draught ships, as a result of which the work moved out to Tilbury, from where lorries would ship the containers into the city. By 1980, the London docks had closed.

The London Docklands Development Corporation (LDDC), founded in 1981, spent £790m of public money on redevelopment during the following decade, only for a country-wide property slump in the early 1990s to leave the shiny new high-rise offices and luxury flats unoccupied. Nowadays, though, as a financial hub, Docklands is a booming rival to the City, with an estimated 90,000 workers commuting to the area each day, on improved transport links. For visitors, regular **Thames Clippers** (0870 781 5049, www.thames clippers.com) boat connections with central London and the **Docklands Light Railway** (DLR) make the area easily accessible.

Just a few stops from where the DLR starts at Bank station is Shadwell, south of which is **Wapping**. In 1598, John Stowe described Wapping High Street as 'a filthy strait passage, with alleys of small tenements or cottages, inhabited by sailors' 'victuallers'. This can still just about be imagined as you walk along it now, flanked by tall Victorian warehouses. The historic **Town of Ramsgate** pub (no.62, 7481 8000), dating to 1545, helps. Here 'hanging judge' George Jeffreys was captured in 1688, trying to escape to Europe in disguise as a woman. Privateer Captain William Kidd was executed in 1701 at Execution Dock, near Wapping New Stairs; the bodies of pirates were hanged from a gibbet until seven tides had washed over them. Further east, the more touristy **Prospect of Whitby** (57 Wapping Wall, 7481 1095) dates from 1520 and has counted Samuel Pepys and Charles Dickens among its regulars. It has good riverside terraces and a fine pewter bar counter. Opposite sits a rather more

Emirates Air Line. *See p130.*

modern 'victualler': **Wapping Food** (7680 2080, www.thewappingproject.com) occupies an ivy-clad Victorian hydraulic power station.

East of here are the **Isle of Dogs** and Canary Wharf. The origin of the name 'Isle of Dogs' remains uncertain, but the first recorded use is on a map of 1588; one theory claims Henry VIII kept his hunting dogs here. In the 19th century, a huge system of docks and locks transformed what had been just drained marshland; in fact, the West India Docks cut right across the peninsula, so the Isle of Dogs did eventually become true to its name.

Almost all the interest for visitors is to be found in the vicinity of Cesar Pelli's dramatic **One Canada Square**, which was the country's tallest habitable building between 1991 and 2012, when it was topped by the Shard (*see p46* **The Shard of Glass**). The only slightly shorter HSBC and Citigroup towers joined it in the noughties, and clones are springing up thick and fast. Shopping options are limited to the mall beneath the towers (www.mycanarywharf.com), but you'll find a calm but crisp Japanese garden beside Canary Wharf tube station. Across a floating bridge over the dock to the north, there's the brilliant **Museum of London Docklands** (*see p130*).

It's also well worth hopping on the DLR and heading south to **Island Gardens** station at the tip of the Isle of Dogs. From narrow Island Gardens park, there's a famous Greenwich view – and the entrance to the Victorian pedestrian tunnel. Nearby to the north, at **Mudchute Park & Farm** (Pier Street, 7515 5901, www.mudchute.org), a complete farmyard of animals ruminate in front of the skyscrapers.

Further east (get off at East India DLR), the Lea River empties into the Thames at **Bow Creek**, almost directly opposite the white,

deflated balloon of the O2 Arena (*see p287*). Here, **Trinity Buoy Wharf** (64 Orchard Place, E14 0JW, www.trinitybuoywharf.com) is pure incongruity. Built in the early 1800s, it was a depot and repair yard for shipping buoys, and it was here, in the 1860s, that James Douglass – later designer of the fourth Eddystone Lighthouse – built London's only lighthouse. Open to the public every weekend from 11am to 4pm (5pm in summer), the lighthouse is the perfect setting for the haunting *Longplayer* sound installation (http://longplayer.org).

A couple more stops east give you access to the **Royal Docks** – get off at Royal Victoria or Royal Albert – as well as the ExCeL conference centre, a docked steamship and a new attraction, the Crystal (*see p127* **If You Build It, Will They Come?**). But most visitors will come here for one reason only: a ride across the Thames on the **Emirates Air Line cable car** (*see p130*). A footbridge from ExCeL, high above Royal Victoria Dock, takes you to the beautiful **Thames Barrier Park**. Opened in 2001, this was London's first new park in half a century. It has a lush sunken garden of waggly hedges and offers perhaps the best views from land of the Thames Barrier (*see p141*). If you don't fancy walking, enter the park from Pontoon Dock DLR.

Unless you're checking in at **London City Airport** (*see p362*), keep on the DLR as far as King George V to get a free ferry (every 15mins daily, 8853 9400) that chugs pedestrians and cars across the river, or stay in your carriage as the DLR passes under the river all the way to its final stop at Woolwich Arsenal (*see p141*).

FREE Crystal
Royal Victoria Dock, 1 Siemens Brothers Way, E16 1GB (7055 6400, http://thecrystal.org). Royal

Victoria DLR. **Open** 10am-5pm Tue-Sat. *Café* 10am-5pm daily. **Admission** free. **Credit** AmEx, MC, V.
See p127 **If You Build It, Will They Come?**

★ Emirates Air Line

North terminal *27 Western Gateway, E16 4FA. Royal Victoria DLR.*
South terminal *Edmund Halley Way, SE10 0FR. North Greenwich tube.*
Both Open 7am-9pm Mon-Fri; 8am-9pm Sat; 9am-9pm Sun. **Tickets** £4.30 single; £2.20 5-15s, free under-5s. **Credit** AmEx, MC, V.

Arguments for a cable car across the Thames as a solution to any of London's many transport problems are, at best, moot, but its value as a tourist thrill is huge. The comfy pods zoom 295 feet up elegant stanchions at a gratifying pace. Suddenly there are brilliant views of the expanses of water that make up the Royal Docks, the ships on the Thames, Docklands and the Thames Barrier. Good fun and good value – but note that the cable car may not run in high winds. *Photo p129.*
▶ *Tickets are cheaper if you use an Oyster card, and you'll avoid any ticket desk queues.*

★ Museum of London Docklands

No.1 Warehouse, West India Quay, Hertsmere Road, E14 4AL (7001 9844, www.museumin docklands.org.uk). Canary Wharf tube or West India Quay DLR. **Open** 10am-6pm daily. **Admission** free. *Temporary exhibitions* vary; check website for details. **Credit** MC, V.

Housed in a 19th-century warehouse (itself a Grade I-listed building), this huge museum explores the complex history of London's docklands and the river over two millennia. Displays spreading over three storeys take you from the arrival of the Romans all the way to the docks' 1980s closure and the area's subsequent redevelopment. The Docklands at War section is very moving, while a haunting new permanent exhibition sheds light on the dark side of London's rise as a cen-

---

IINSIDE TRACK
HEARING HISTORY

Much loved by weekending locals, **Victoria Park** (*see right*) has an extraordinary history. Did you know, for instance, that there are chunks of the medieval London Bridge lying about in the park? All is revealed on a free audio tour, which can be downloaded from www.memoryscape. org.uk. The tour was put together by oral historian and University of East London lecturer Toby Butler, in collaboration with composer Lewis Gibson.

Other Memoryscape tours by Butler cover the **Royal Docks** (*see p129*), **Greenwich** (*see pp138-141*) and **Hampton Court Palace** (*see p146*).

---

tre for finance and commerce, exploring its involvement in the slave trade. You can also walk through full-scale mock-ups of a quayside and a dingy riverfront alley. Temporary exhibitions are set up on the ground floor, where you'll also find a café and a docks-themed play area for kids. Just like its elder brother, the Museum of London (*see p55*), the MoLD has a great programme of screenings and special events.

HACKNEY & AROUND

London Fields or Hackney Central rail.

The opening of the East London line in 2010 leaves even bus-averse visitors few excuses to ignore this part of town. Hackney has few blockbuster sights, but is one of London's fastest changing areas, a large borough with energetic, creative locals. Its admistrative centre is Town Hall Square on Mare Street, where you'll find a century-old music hall, the **Hackney Empire** (291 Mare Street, 8985 2424, www. hackneyempire.co.uk); an art deco town hall; a multiscreen cinema in the old Victorian library; and the fine little **Hackney Museum** (1 Reading Lane, 8356 3500, www.hackney. gov.uk/cm-museum.htm), in the 21st-century library. Opposite an ambitious failed music venue has become a successful cinema (**Hackney Picturehouse**; *see p270*). Within walking distance to the east is the historic **Sutton House**.

The area of London Fields, to the west of central Hackney, demonstrates the borough's changing demographics. Once a failing fruit and veg market, **Broadway Market** is now brimming – sometimes choking – with young urbanites and trendy families. The food and vintage garb market on Saturdays has been joined by two eclectic food and collectibles markets on Westgate Street; the street is lined with browsable boutiques, curiosity shops and modish boho eating and drinking venues. The old days are respectably represented by **F Cooke** (no.9, 7254 6458), a pie and mash place that's been here since the early 1900s.

Further west, Dalston (*see p122*) is clinging on to its reputation as London's hipster quarter, even as the brand managers descend.

From the south end of Broadway Market, you can walk east along the Regent's Canal to **Victoria Park**. Opened in 1845 to give the impoverished working classes access to green space, this sprawling, 290-acre oasis was designed by Sir James Pennethorne, a pupil of John Nash; its elegant landscaping (complete with rose garden and waterfowl lake) is reminiscent of Nash's Regent's Park (*see p89*). There's also a cool waterfront café and an occasional summer musical festival. For a new way to enjoy the park, *see left* **Inside Track**. At the eastern end of the park, across a nasty dual carriageway, is the mish-mash of artist-colonised post-industrial buildings that makes up Hackney Wick (*see p132*).

Sutton House

2-4 Homerton High Street, E9 6JQ (8986 2264, www.nationaltrust.org.uk). Bethnal Green tube then bus 254, 106, D6, or Hackney Central rail. **Open** times vary; check website for details. **Admission** £3; £1 reductions; £6.90 family; free under-5s, National Trust members. **Credit** MC, V. Built in 1535 for Henry VIII's first secretary of state, Sir Ralph Sadleir, this red-brick Tudor mansion is east London's oldest home. Now beautifully restored in authentic original decor, with a real Tudor kitchen to boot, it makes no secret of its history of neglect: even some 1980s squatter graffiti has been preserved. The house closes for January each year.

LEA VALLEY

Bromley-by-Bow tube or Stratford tube/DLR/rail.

The Lea River (also known as the Lee at points along its length) wriggles south-east for 50 miles from its source near Luton, Bedfordshire to join the River Thames. Through history, it has been a working river used for transport, irrigation, infrastructure and industry: the latter turned its lower reaches into neglected industrial land that was taken over as the focal Olympic Park for the London 2012 Games.

The atmospheric **Lea Valley Walk** (www.leavalleywalk.org.uk) is 50 miles of waterside path following the length of the river. It is a magical glimpse of hidden London and its suburbs; a mixture of bucolic greenery, bleak forgotten warehouses, moody marshland, wildlife sanctuaries, posh new-build flats – and what will reopen in two phases as the **Queen Elizabeth Olympic Park**. Many of the riverside paths were improved for the 2012 Games, and when the Park re-emerges for public use it will offer beautifully landscaped routes along and over the river's several channels. The northern area of the park – around the Velodrome – is due to open in July 2013, joined by the southern part in spring 2014. For the low-down on what's happening to the site, *see pp21-23* **After the Games**.

William Morris Gallery. *See p132.*

Unless you fancy walking all the way up from the Thames, get off the tube at Bromley-by-Bow and follow the signs past the thundering roads to **Three Mills Island** (*see below*), with its film and TV studio. The **Greenway** should have reopened by the time you read this, providing a pleasant route (apart from the point where you have to cross the A11) north from Abbey Mills Pumping Station right past the Park. The best vantage point over the Park is the **View Tube** (*see below*) – easily accessible from Pudding Mill DLR, if you don't fancy a longer walk. A little further up the river, at pretty **Old Ford Lock**, the river splits again into the straighter, artificial Lee Navigation and the windier river proper.

If you turn left (west) off the Lea Navigation, by crossing the bridge just past the Olympic Stadium, you can get on to the towpath of the mile-long Hertford Union Canal. A pedestrian bridge, still in sight of the stadium, takes you on to **Fish Island**, an industrial park with the terrific two-floor Counter Café (Stour Space, 7 Roach Road, E3 2PA, 07834 275920, www.thecountercafe.co.uk) and Forman's salmon smokery, restaurant and art gallery (Stour Road, E3 2NT, http://smokehousegallery.org). Keep on the towpath and you'll cut past graffiti artists, a garden centre and a houseboat colony, eventually running alongside leafy Victoria Park (*see p130*) before joining up with Regent's Canal, which can take you through Hackney (including an exit at funky, fashionable Broadway Market), Islington and Little Venice (about eight miles in total).

North of the Hertford Union, **Hackney Wick** combines edgy gallery-studio spaces – www.timeout.com lists new exhibitions and openings – and the Hackney Pearl restaurant (*see p180*). The White Building (Unit 7, Queen's Yard, 43 White Post Lane, E9 5EN, http://the whitebuilding.org.uk), facing on to the Lea Navigation, contains the fine Crate microbrewery, which serves good pizza. If you stay on the Lea Navigation north, the path heads along **Hackney Marshes**, with its famous amateur football pitches, passing what was for the Games called the Copper Box – and is now referred to as the 'Multi-use Arena' – and the former International Broadcast Centre/Main Press Centre.

As the path meanders north, it alternates between urban grit (soap factories), natural beauty (Tottenham Marshes is dotted with wild flowers), nature reserve/pitch and putt (WaterWorks Nature Reserve, Lammas Road, 8988 7566, open 8am-8pm or dusk daily) and, far to the north, historical splendour (Waltham Abbey, a fine Norman church). A few miles north of the abbey, the sluices of the **Lee Valley White Water Centre** (*see p319*) – built for the 2012 Games – are already open for adventurous paddlers.

Three Mills Island

Three Mill Lane, E3 3DU (8980 4626, www.housemill.org.uk). Bromley-by-Bow tube. **Tours** *May-Oct* 11am-4pm Sun. **Admission** £3; £1.50 reductions; free under-16s. **No credit cards.**
This pretty island in the River Lea takes its name from the mills that, until the 18th century, ground flour and gunpowder here. The House Mill, built in 1776, is the oldest and largest tidal mill in Britain and, though out of service, it is occasionally opened to the public; it contains a café. The island has pleasant walks that can feel quite rural, as well as much improved waterside walkways. To puncture the idyll, one of the mills is a film and TV studio.

View Tube

The Greenway, Marshgate Lane, E15 2PJ (www.theviewtube.co.uk). Pudding Mill Lane DLR. **Open** 9am-5pm daily. **Admission** free.
Made out of recycled shipping containers painted a vivid yellow-green, the View Tube feels like it's in touching distance of the Olympic Stadium. Information boards help you figure out what's where and give interesting information about the site, and there's good coffee at the Container Café (*see p180*).

WALTHAMSTOW

Walthamstow Central tube/rail.

Quaint **Walthamstow Village**, a few minutes' walk east of the tube station, is centred on ancient St Mary's Church and the neat little **Vestry House Museum** (Vestry Road, 8496 4391, www.walthamforest.gov.uk; closed Mon, Tue), which contains one of the first motor cars and has a fine garden for picnics. Further north, near the junction of Hoe Street and Forest Road, is peaceful Lloyd Park; the grand Georgian house at its entrance is home to the **William Morris Gallery** (*see below*) – the Arts and Crafts pioneer was a Walthamstow boy. A major refurbishment of both was completed in September 2012.

FREE William Morris Gallery

Lloyd Park, Forest Road, E17 4PP (8496 4390, www.wmgallery.org.uk). Walthamstow Central tube/rail or bus 34, 97, 215, 275. **Open** 10am-5pm Wed-Sun. *Tours* phone for details. **Admission** free; donations appreciated. **Credit** (shop) MC, V.
Artist, socialist and source of flowery wallpaper, William Morris lived here between 1848 and 1856. There are plenty of designs in fabric, stained glass and ceramic on show, produced by Morris and his acolytes. Improved displays feature such interesting artefacts as the medieval-style helmet and sword the designer used as props for murals, the satchel from which he distributed political tracts, and humble domestic objects such as his coffee cup. The refurbishments also created a tea room. *Photos p131.*

South-east London

A World Heritage Site and several unjustly overlooked attractions.

Beyond the world-famous sights of Greenwich, south-east London used to be ignored by many tourists – largely because the absence of the Underground in this part of the city made it seem remote from the centre. Then the London Overground made the journey from trendy east London to Rotherhithe, Forest Hill and Crystal Palace simple. The wonderful **Horniman Museum** (*see p137*) and the sweet little **Brunel** (*see p137*) and **Crystal Palace** (*see p135*) museums are key beneficiaries of this new transport link.

Map p393 & p404	Restaurants &
Pubs & bars p202	cafés pp182-185
Hotels pp257	

In any case, the area's transport difficulties are relative. The most visited neighbourhood is still, deservedly, **Greenwich** (*see p138*), an area that rivals even South Kensington for historic cultural destinations. It's easily reached on the DLR from Bank tube. The superb **Imperial War Museum** (*see below*) always had a tube station nearby. And, in fact, the rest of south-east London benefits from an extensive bus and rail network: if you're prepared to use it, such delights as the **Dulwich Picture Gallery** (*see p135*) are yours to enjoy.

KENNINGTON & THE ELEPHANT

Kennington tube or Elephant & Castle tube/rail.

Even back in the 17th century, the **Elephant & Castle** (named, perhaps, after the ivory-dealing Cutlers Company, or maybe after Charles I's once-intended, the Infanta of Castille) was a busy place. In the early 20th century, it was a tram terminus and south London's West End, before losing its looks to World War II bombs and a grisly 1960s makeover. Regeneration of this ugly corner of town has been promised for nearly a decade without ever looking like it might happen, but then the most visible part of a £1.5bn, 170-acre redevelopment project appeared: the new Strata residential skyscraper (www.strata london.com) isn't much loved, but it is instantly recognisable – look for a black-and-white building shaped like a beard-trimmer, with three giant wind turbines set into the roof. Much more modest, and as much more interesting, is the **Cinema Museum** (The Master's House, 2 Dugard Way, off Renfrew Road, 7840 2200,

www.cinemamuseum.org.uk), a collection of artefacts, memorabilia and equipment telling the history of cinema from the 1890s; it is currently open only by appointment.

Behind the **Imperial War Museum**, Kennington Road leads through an area once blighted by factory stink; the smell was young resident Charlie Chaplin's abiding memory of the place. Today, the area's smarter houses are favoured by second-home politicians and lawyers requiring easy access to the city. For many, Kennington means cricket, especially in the beery atmosphere of a Test match at the **Kia Oval** (*see p135*).

★ FREE Imperial War Museum
Lambeth Road, Elephant & Castle, SE1 6HZ (7416 5320, www.iwm.org.uk). Lambeth North tube or Elephant & Castle tube/rail. **Open** 10am-6pm daily. **Admission** free. *Special exhibitions* prices vary. **Credit** MC, V. **Map** p402 N10.
Another of London's great museums, IWM London has decided on a major refit – by Foster & Partners architects – in time for the 2014 centenary of World

Imperial War Museum.

CAMBERWELL & PECKHAM

Denmark Hill or Peckham Rye rail.

At first glance, Camberwell's blend of run-down Georgian buildings, ugly tower blocks and traffic-choked roads appears less than artful, but its been a fertile ground for culture since Victorian times. The **South London Gallery** (has been an artistic highlight for more than a century, while the neighbouring **Camberwell College of Arts** (45-65 Peckham Road, 7514 6302, www.camberwell.arts.ac.uk) educated the likes of Pink Floyd's Syd Barrett and film director Mike Leigh. Outside the college, its students continue to colonise Camberwell bars such as the **Sun & Doves** (61-63 Coldharbour Lane, 7733 1525, www.sunanddoves.co.uk) and the **Bear** (296A Camberwell New Road, 7274 7037, www.thebear-freehouse.co.uk).

East of here, **Peckham** is still unfairly associated with teenage gangs and dodgy traders, but regeneration schemes continue to spruce up the streets. Rye Lane looks like old Peckham; the new might be Peckham Square, where Will Alsop's award-winning and frankly odd-looking **Peckham Library** (122 Peckham Hill Street, 7525 2000) was joined in 2010 by Camberwell College's **Peckham Space** (7358 9645, www.peckhamspace.com), a new contemporary art venue that has added to the good programme of free public exhibitions and events already staged at the college's Camberwell Space. Due south on Rye Lane is **Peckham Rye**, where poet-visionary William Blake saw his angels; it's now a prettily laid-out park with well-kept gardens – the 1908 Japanese Garden, restored in 2005, is lovely. Keep walking south from Peckham Rye (or take a P4 or P12 bus) to enjoy views over London and Kent from **Honor Oak** and **One Tree Hill**, where Elizabeth I picnicked with Richard Bukeley of Beaumaris in 1602.

South London Gallery

65 Peckham Road, Peckham, SE5 8UH (7703 6120, www.southlondongallery.org). Oval tube then bus 436, or Elephant & Castle tube/rail then bus 12, 171. **Open** 11am-6pm Tue, Thur-Sun; 11am-9pm Sun. **Credit** MC, V.

In 1891, William Rossiter opened the pioneering South London Fine Art Gallery. A century later, renamed the South London Gallery, it found new renown as first exhibitor of *Everyone I Have Ever Slept With 1963-1995*, Tracey Emin's infamous tent. A Brit Art beacon during the 1990s, the gallery remains one of London's leading contemporary art venues. A £1.8m extension, swallowing up the three-storey Victorian townhouse next door in order to add a café, two exhibition spaces and a resident artist's flat, is helping keep it on the cutting edge.

War I, which means it will be closed from January to June 2013. When it reopens, the Central Hall will still be the attention-grabbing repository of major artefacts: guns, tanks and aircraft hung from the ceiling (not least a Harrier GR9 that saw action in Afghanistan). Terraced galleries will allow this section of the museum also to show a Snatch Land Rover from Iraq and an Argentine operating table from the Falklands. The already extensive World War I gallery will be expanded, then you head into the original displays for World War II.

The museum's tone darkens as you ascend. On the third floor, the Holocaust Exhibition (not recommended for under-14s) traces the history of European anti-Semitism and its nadir in the concentration camps. Upstairs, Crimes Against Humanity (unsuitable for under-16s) is a minimalist space in which a film exploring contemporary genocide and ethnic violence rolls relentlessly. At the top will be a new gallery exploring contemporary conflicts.

The imposing premises were built in 1814 as a lunatic asylum (the Bethlehem Royal Hospital, aka Bedlam). After the inmates were moved out in 1930, the central block became the war museum, only to be damaged by World War II air raids. Today, the museum provides a compelling, frequently hard-hitting history of armed conflict since World War I, as well as many excellent, long-running temporary exhibitions that are suitable for children.

DULWICH & CRYSTAL PALACE

Crystal Palace, East Dulwich, Herne Hill, North Dulwich or West Dulwich rail.

Dulwich is a little piece of rural England that fiercely guards its bucolic prosperity. Tasteful fingerposts offer directions: perhaps towards the attractive park (once a duelling spot), the historic boys' public school or the **Dulwich Picture Gallery**. It's a pleasant, brisk half-hour's walk from the gallery across Dulwich Park and up Lordship Lane to the **Horniman Museum** in Forest Hill.

East and west of Dulwich sit **East Dulwich** and **Herne Hill**, the latter home to an exquisite art deco lido in Brockwell Park. The two areas are the middle(-class) way: not as expensive or charismatic as Dulwich, less challenging than the relentless pace of Brixton. **Crystal Palace** is named in honour of Joseph Paxton's famous structure, built for the Great Exhibition in Hyde Park in 1851, moved here three years later and destroyed by fire in 1936. **Crystal Palace Park** contains arches and the sphinx from the Exhibition's Egyptian-themed display; the Dinosaur Park, a lake ringed by Benjamin Waterhouse-Hawkins's life-sized (and decidedly inaccurate) dinosaur statues; and the **National Sports Centre** (*see p314*). The **Crystal Palace Museum** (Anerley Hill, SE19 2BA, 8676 0700, www.crystalpalacemuseum.org.uk), staffed by volunteers, has an 'exhibition of the Exhibition'.

INSIDE TRACK FANS OF TEA

As well as its fan collection, the **Fan Museum** (*see p140*) has a small tearoom, and serves classic English cream teas on Tuesdays and Sundays after 3pm. The orangery overlooks a pretty garden, replete with Japanese themed plantings and fan-shaped flowerbeds.

★ Dulwich Picture Gallery

Gallery Road, Dulwich, SE21 7AD (8693 5254, www.dulwichpicturegallery.org.uk). North Dulwich or West Dulwich rail. **Open** 10am-5pm Tue-Fri; 11am-5pm Sat, Sun. **Admission** £5; free-£4 reductions. *Special exhibitions* £13; free-£12 reductions. **Credit** MC, V.
Lending weight to the idea that the best things come in small packages, this bijou attraction was designed by Sir John Soane in 1811 as the first purpose-built gallery in the UK. It's a beautiful space that shows off Soane's ingenuity with lighting effects, especially in the quiet mausoleum at the heart of the building where the gallery's founders rest. The gallery displays a small but outstanding collection of work by Old Masters, offering a fine introduction to the Baroque era through works by Rembrandt, Rubens, Poussin and Gainsborough. It also has some brilliant temporary exhibitions.
► *For our listing of the superb Sir John Soane's Museum, see p66.*

EXPLORE

Dulwich Picture Gallery.

A Ship that Floats on Air

Historic tea clipper the Cutty Sark has been restored to her former glory.

When the **Cutty Sark** (*see p139*) went up in flames in May 2007, it looked like the end of an adventurous life for one of London's best-loved landmarks. Permanently berthed in a purpose-built dry dock beside the Thames, she'd been enjoying a useful retirement as a popular tourist attraction after a working life that began in 1870, crossing the world's oceans with cargos of tea, wine, spirits, beer, coal, jute, wool and castor oil. The tea trade in particular involved reckless races from China to London, with the captain of the swiftest vessel in line for a substantial additional payout for delivering the first tea of the year. Sailing clippers were gradually put out of business by the arrival of steamships, but the *Cutty Sark* hung on until 1922, the last of her breed to ply the waves.

The damage resulting from the 2007 fire (caused by an industrial vacuum cleaner that overheated) was extensive, but could have been much worse. The vessel was closed for conservation when the disaster occurred, so many parts had already been removed for storage – the ship was not after all, sunk. Now, five years on, she's splendidly restored and open to visitors.

In fact, the fire had its compensations: the £50m restoration (by Grimshaw Architects, the firm behind the Eden Project) has been far more extensive and innovative

than was originally planned. As well as preserving a substantial portion of the ship's original fabric, the scheme has raised the *Cutty Sark* three metres off the ground and surrounded her with a dramatic glass 'skirt'. Critics have complaints that the glazed canopy obscures the elegant go-faster lines of her hull – as well as raising fears about the stresses this might place on the elderly ship – but it does allow visitors to admire the hull from underneath for the first time.

The space beneath the ship has also made it possible to display a collection of more than 80 merchant navy figureheads in its entirety for the first time. The carved wooden figures – representing Florence Nightingale, William Wilberforce, Hiawatha and Sir Lancelot, among others – were positioned on the prow of sailing ships for decoration and to aid identification. Sailors, famously superstitious, took loving care of each figure, believing they represented the spirit of the vessel and protected her crew.

They were donated to the Cutty Sark Preservation Society in 1953 by a London businessman, Sydney Cumbers. Known as 'Captain Long John Silver' on account of his eye-patch, Cumbers liked to refer to his wife as 'the mate'. He kept the figureheads at his second home in Gravesend, which was fitted out like a ship – they must feel comfortable in their new location.

Cutty Sark

★ FREE Horniman Museum

100 London Road, Forest Hill, SE23 3PQ (8699 1872, www.horniman.ac.uk). Forest Hill rail or bus 122, 176, 185, 363, P4, P13. **Open** 10.30am-5.30pm daily. **Admission** free; donations appreciated. *Temporary exhibitions prices vary. Aquarium* £2.50; £1 reductions; £6 family; free under-3s. **Credit** MC, V.

South-east London's premier free family attraction, the Horniman was once the home of tea trader Frederick J Horniman. It's an eccentric-looking art nouveau building (check out the clocktower, which starts as a circle and ends as a square), with a main entrance that gives out on to extensive gardens.

The oldest section is the Natural History gallery, dominated by an ancient walrus (mistakenly over-stuffed by Victorian taxidermists, who thought they ought to get the winkles out of the animal's skin) and now ringed by glass cabinets containing pickled animals, stuffed birds and insect models. Other galleries include the Nature Base, African Worlds and the Centenary Gallery, which focuses on world cultures. Downstairs, the Music Gallery contains hundreds of instruments: their sounds can be unleashed via touch-screen tables, while hardier instruments (flip-flop drums, thumb pianos) can be bashed with impunity.

The most popular part of the museum is its show-piece Aquarium, where a series of tanks and rock-pools cover seven distinct aquatic ecosystems. There are mesmerising moon jellyfish, strangely large British seahorses, starfish, tropical fish and creatures from the mangroves. It forms a key part of the Evolution 2010 project, which brought together the natural history collection, aquarium and gardens to explore biodiversity and the story of how life has evolved on earth.

ROTHERHITHE

Rotherhithe tube.

Once a shipbuilding village and, in the 17th and 18th centuries, a centre for London's whaling trade, the ghostly locale of Rotherhithe has long since seen its docks filled in. Go back in time at the **Brunel Museum** or the mariners' church of **St Mary's Rotherhithe** (St Mary Church Street, SE16 4JE, www.stmaryrotherhithe.org), which contains maritime oddities; among them is a communion table and bishop's chair made from timber salvaged from the HMS *Temeraire*, immortalised by Turner (the painting is in the National Gallery; *see p98*). Captain Christopher Jones was buried here in 1622; his ship, the *Mayflower*, set sail from Rotherhithe in 1620. A waterside pub of the same name marks the spot from which the pilgrims are said to have embarked on their journey.

Rotherhithe's road tunnel takes cars across to Limehouse. At the mouth of the tunnel stands

Brunel Museum.

the **Norwegian Church & Seaman's Mission**, one of a number of Scandinavian churches in the area. There's also a Finnish church – with a sauna – at 33 Albion Street (7237 1261). Across Jamaica Road, **Southwark Park** has a gallery (7237 1230, www.cafe galleryprojects.com), an old bandstand, a lake and playgrounds.

Brunel Museum

Brunel Engine House, Railway Avenue, SE16 4LF (7231 3840, www.brunel-museum.org.uk). Rotherhithe rail. **Open** 10am-5pm Mon, Wed-Sun; 10am-9pm Tue. *Tours* by appointment only. **Admission** £2; £1.50 reductions; free under-16s. **No credit cards**.

This little museum occupies the engine house where the father-and-son team of Sir Marc and Isambard Kingdom Brunel worked to create the world's first tunnel beneath a navigable river. The story of their achievement is told most entertainingly during guided tours, which can either start at the museum or include a walk along the river before descending into the Grand Entrance Hall at the start of the Thames Tunnel; see the website for details. There's a decent little shop, a café and outdoor space should you wish to picnic.

▶ *If you visit the museum using the Overground line from north of the river, you'll actually travel under the Thames through the master engineers' tunnel, still in perfect working order.*

EXPLORE

GREENWICH

Cutty Sark for Maritime Greenwich DLR.

Riverside Greenwich is an irresistible mixture of maritime, royal and horological history, a combination that earned it recognition as a UNESCO World Heritage Site, but the summer of 2012 was memorable even for such a distinguished part of London. It was elevated to the status of a Royal Borough as part of the Queen's Jubilee celebrations. The beautiful tea clipper **Cutty Sark** opened again to the public after years of restoration. And, from July to September, it hosted Equestrian events for the 2012 Olympic and Paralympic Games. A number of local attractions, the *Cutty Sark* included, are now proudly clustered as the Royal Museums Greenwich.

In truth, royalty has stalked the area since 1300, when Edward I stayed here. Henry VIII was born in Greenwich Palace; the palace was built on land that later contained Wren's Royal Naval Hospital, now the **Old Royal Naval College**. The College is now a very handy first port-of-call. Its Pepys Building not only contains the **Greenwich Tourist Information Centre** (0870 608 2000, www.greenwich.gov.uk), but is also the home of a new exhibition that provides a great overview of Greenwich's numerous attractions. Just opposite, shoppers swarm to **Greenwich Market**, which is subject to controversial redevelopment – a new boutique hotel is scheduled for 2015.

Near the DLR stop is Greenwich Pier; every 15 minutes (peak times), the popular and speedy **Thames Clipper** boats (0870 781 5049, www.thamesclippers.com) shuttle passengers to and from central London. This is where you'll find the *Cutty Sark*, as well as a domed structure that is the entrance to a Victorian **pedestrian tunnel** that emerges on the far side of the Thames in Island Gardens. The tunnel is rather dingy, due to incomplete repair work, but it's still fun to walk beneath the river.

To the north, at the bottom of Greenwich Park, are the **Queen's House** and steadily improving **National Maritime Museum**,

beyond which it's a ten-minute walk (or shorter shuttle-bus trip) up the steep slopes of Greenwich Park to the **Royal Observatory**. The building looks even more stunning at night, when the bright green Meridian Line Laser illuminates the path of the Prime Meridian across the London sky.

The riverside Thames Path leads past rusting piers and boarded-up factories to the **Greenwich Peninsula**, dominated by the **O2 Arena**. Designed by the Richard Rogers Partnership as the Millennium Dome, this once-maligned structure's fortunes have improved considerably since its change of use. Alongside the concerts and sporting events in the huge arena (*see p287*) and movies in the cineplex, attractions include restaurants, big temporary exhibitions and the glossy, permanent **British Music Experience** – you can now even book **Up at the O2** tickets (www.theo2.co.uk/upattheo2) to walk right over the top of the Dome, safely attached to a security line. A rather elegant (but, for public transport purposes, almost entirely useless) cable car, the **Emirates Air Line** (*see p263* **Inside Track**), runs from the east flank of the peninsula right across the Thames to the ExCeL conference centre on the far side.

The Dome and its environs are all something of a contrast with the **Greenwich Peninsula Ecology Park** (www.urbanecology.co.uk), and with the nearby riverside walks that afford broad, flat, bracing views and works of art; you could hardly miss *Slice of Reality*, a rusting ship cut in half by Richard Wilson, and Antony Gormley's 100-foot *Quantum Cloud*, which consists of a seemingly random cloud of steel sections, but look into it from a

Greenwich Market.

Old Royal Navy College.

distance and you'll see a denser area at the centre in the shape of a human body.

To the south of Greenwich is grassy, upmarket **Blackheath**. Smart Georgian homes and a few stately pubs surround a heath on which some of the world's earliest sports clubs started; among them is the Royal Blackheath Golf Club, said to be the oldest golf club in the world. Blackheath also has a long history of radical protest that runs back to the Peasants' Revolt in 1381, consciously echoed by a week-long Climate Camp of 3,000 anti-capitalist and environmental protesters here in 2009.

British Music Experience

O2 Bubble, Millennium Way, SE10 0BB (8463 2000, www.britishmusicexperience.com). North Greenwich tube. **Open** 11am-7.30pm daily. **Admission** £12; £6-£8 reductions; free under-5s. **Credit** AmEx, MC, V.

The memorabilia on show on the top floor of the O2 Arena (*see p287*) includes David Bowie's Ziggy Stardust costume and Noel Gallagher's Union Jack guitar. The main focus here, though, is on interactive exhibits: downloading archive music, trying your hand at guitar tutorials and similar activities. Workshops, lectures and concerts are also part of the experience.

Cutty Sark

King William Walk, SE10 9HT (8858 2698, www.cuttysark.org.uk). Cutty Sark DLR. **Open** 11am-7.30pm daily. **Admission** £12; £6.50-£8.50 reductions; £20-£29 family; free under-5s. **Credit** MC, V. **Map** p405 X2.

Built in Scotland in 1869, this tea clipper was the quickest in the business when it was launched in 1870 – renovation was rather slower, but is now complete, with visitors able to buy timed tickets. *See p136* **A Ship that Floats in Air**.

★ **FREE** **Discover Greenwich & the Old Royal Naval College**

2 Cutty Sark Gardens, SE10 9LW (8269 4799, www.oldroyalnavalcollege.org.uk). Cutty Sark DLR or Greenwich DLR/rail. **Open** 10am-5pm daily. *Tours* 2pm daily; other times by arrangement. **Admission** free. **Credit** (shop) MC, V. **Map** p405 X1.

The block of the Old Royal Naval College nearest to the *Cutty Sark*, the pier and Cutty Sark DLR is now the excellent Discover Greenwich. It's full of focused, informative exhibits on architecture and building techniques of the surrounding buildings, the life of Greenwich pensioners, Tudor royalty and so forth, delivered with a real sense of fun: while grown-ups read about coade stone or scagliola (popular fake stone building materials), for example, the nippers can build their own chapel with soft bricks or try on a knight's helmet. There's also a well-stocked shop and a Tourist Information Centre.

It's a perfect introduction to the superb collection of buildings that make up the Naval College. Designed by Wren in 1694, with Hawksmoor and Vanbrugh helping to complete the project, it was originally a hospital for the relief and support of seamen and their dependants, with pensioners living here from 1705 to 1869, when the complex became the Royal Naval College. The Navy left in 1998, and the neoclassical buildings now house part of the University of Greenwich and Trinity College of Music. The public are allowed into the impressive rococo chapel, where there are free organ recitals, and Painted Hall, a tribute to William and Mary that took Sir James Thornhill 19 years to complete. Nelson lay in state in the Painted Hall for three days in 1806, before being taken to St Paul's Cathedral for his funeral.

There's a lively events programme in the grounds, ranging from comedy shows and early music to weekend appearances from historic figures – cos-

EXPLORE

National Maritime Museum.

Ground-level galleries include Explorers, which covers great sea expeditions back to medieval times, and Maritime London, which concentrates on the city as a port. Here, too, you'll find Nelson's Trafalgar uniform, blood-stained and with fatal bullet-hole, as well as a 3D reconstruction of him, as if laid in a coffin. Upstairs is the Environment Gallery, which reveals our dependence on the health of the world's oceans. Level two holds the interactives: the Bridge has a ship simulator, and All Hands lets children load cargo, and you can even try your hand as a ship's gunner. The Ship of War is the museum's superb collection of models, dating from 1660 to 1815, and the Atlantic: Slavery, Trade, Empires gallery looks at the transport of goods between Britain, Africa and the Americas during the 17th to 19th centuries.

New for 2013 will be the Great Map, a floor installation for the Upper Deck that should be in place by March, and a brand-new Nelson, Navy, Nation gallery, which should open in October.

costumed actors – ranging from Pepys and Sir James to the 'pirate queen' Grace O'Malley and Joe Brown, veteran of the Battle of Trafalgar.

▶ Attached to Discover Greenwich, the Old Brewery is an ace bar-restaurant that serves own-brewed beers; see p182.

Fan Museum
12 Crooms Hill, SE10 8ER (8305 1441, www. fan-museum.org). Cutty Sark DLR or Greenwich DLR/rail. **Open** 11am-5pm Tue-Sat; noon-5pm Sun. **Admission** £4; £3 reductions; £10 family; free under-7s. **Credit** MC, V. **Map** p405 X2.
The world's most important collection of hand-held fans is displayed in a pair of restored Georgian townhouses. There are about 3,500 fans, including some beauties in the Hélène Alexander collection, but not all are on display at any one time. For details of the regular fan-making workshops and temporary exhibitions, check the website.

★ FREE National Maritime Museum
Romney Road, SE10 9NF (8858 4422, information 8312 6565, www.nmm.ac.uk). Cutty Sark DLR or Greenwich DLR/rail. **Open** 10am-5pm daily. *Tours* phone for details. **Admission** free; donations appreciated. *Temporary exhibitions* vary; check website for details. **Credit** MC, V. **Map** p405 X2.
The world's largest maritime museum contains a huge store of creatively organised maritime art, cartography, models, interactives and regalia – and its even bigger since the impressive expansion in 2011 into the new Sammy Ofer Wing. Centred on Voyagers: Britons and the Sea – a collection of 200 artefacts, accompanied by an impressive audiovisual installation called the Wave – this extension also has the Compass Lounge (with free Wi-Fi), where you can explore the collection using computers, and a brasserie, café and shop.

FREE Queen's House
Romney Road, SE10 9NF (8312 6565, www.nmm.ac.uk). Cutty Sark DLR or Greenwich DLR/rail. **Open** 10am-5pm daily. *Tours* phone for details. **Admission** free. *Tours* free. **No credit cards. Map** p405 X2.
The art collection of the National Maritime Museum (*see left*) is displayed in what was formerly the summer villa of Charles I's queen, Henrietta Maria. Completed in 1638 by Inigo Jones, the house has an interior as impressive as the paintings on the walls. As well as the stunning 1635 marble floor, look for Britain's first centrally unsupported spiral stair, fine painted woodwork and ceilings, and the Great Hall, which is a perfect cube. The collection includes portraits of famous maritime figures and works by Hogarth and Gainsborough, as well as some wartime art from the 20th century and exotic pictures from Captain Cook's explorations.

Ranger's House
Chesterfield Walk, SE10 8QX (8853 0035, www.english-heritage.org.uk). Blackheath rail, Cutty Sark DLR or bus 53. **Open** Apr-Sept 11am-5pm Sun. *Tours* 11.30am, 2.30pm Mon-Wed. *Oct* group bookings only. **Admission** £6; £3.90-£5.90 reductions; free under-5s. **Credit** MC, V. **Map** p405 Y4.
The house of the 'Ranger of Greenwich Park' (a post that was held by George III's niece, Princess Sophia Matilda, from 1815) now contains the collection of treasure – medieval and Renaissance art, jewellery, bronzes, tapestries, furniture, porcelain, paintings – amassed by Julius Wernher, a German who made his considerable fortune trading in South African diamonds. His booty is displayed through a dozen lovely rooms in this red-brick Georgian villa, the back garden of which is the fragrant Greenwich Park rose collection.

★ FREE Royal Observatory & Planetarium

Greenwich Park, SE10 9NF (8312 6565, www. rog.nmm.ac.uk). Cutty Sark DLR or Greenwich DLR/rail. **Open** 10am-5pm daily. *Tours* phone for details. **Admission** prices vary; check website for details. **Credit** MC, V. **Map** p405 Y3.

The northern section of this two-halved attraction chronicles Greenwich's horological connection. Flamsteed House, the observatory built in 1675 on the orders of Charles II, containing the apartments of Sir John Flamsteed and other Astronomers Royal, as well as the instruments used in timekeeping since the 14th century. John Harrison's four timekeepers, used to crack the problem of longitude, are here, while the onion dome houses the country's largest (28-inch) refracting telescope – it was completed in 1893.

The south site houses the Astronomy Centre, home to the Peter Harrison Planetarium and Weller Astronomy Galleries. The 120-seater planetarium's architecture cleverly reflects its astrological position: the semi-submerged cone tilts at 51.5 degrees, the latitude of Greenwich, pointing to the north star, and its reflective disc is aligned with the celestial equator. Dail and weekend shows include 'Sky Tonight Live' and 'The Universe Exposed'.

▶ *In the Flamsteed House courtyard lies the Prime Meridian Line, featured in many a visitor photo.*

WOOLWICH ARSENAL & THE THAMES BARRIER

Woolwich Arsenal DLR/rail or Woolwich Dockyard rail.

Established by the Tudors as the country's main source of munitions, **Woolwich Arsenal** stretched 32 miles along the river by World War I, with its own internal railway system. Much of the land was sold off during the 1960s, but the main section has been preserved and is now home to **Firepower**. To the south, the **Royal Artillery Barracks** has the longest Georgian façade in the country. The river is spanned by an architectural triumph that is the Barracks' modern equal: the **Thames Barrier**.

This is a grim bit of London, but regeneration has begun to arrive in the form of an extension of the DLR from King George V station under the river to Woolwich Arsenal. More charismatic, though, is the ramshackle **Woolwich Ferry** (8853 9400), diesel-driven boats that take pedestrians (for free) and cars across the river every ten minutes daily. Refurbishment of the **Woolwich Foot Tunnel** is still incomplete, after various commercial wranglings, but the tunnel is at least open to the public.

Firepower

Royal Arsenal, Woolwich, SE18 6ST (8855 7755, www.firepower.org.uk). Woolwich Arsenal DLR/rail.

Open 10.30am-6pm Wed-Sun. **Admission** £5.30; £2.50-£4.60 reductions; £12.50 family; free under-5s. **Credit** MC, V.

In a series of converted arsenal buildings beside the river, Firepower bristles with preserved artillery pieces, some of them centuries old. 'Field of Fire' has four screens relaying archive film and documentary footage of desert and jungle warfare. Smoke fills the air, searchlights pick out the ordnance that surrounds you and exploding bombs shake the floor. Across the courtyard, another building contains a huge collection of trophy guns and the Cold War gallery, focused on the 'monster bits' (tanks and guns used from 1945 to the present). Army-obsessed kids can get shouted at by real soldiers when they take part in drill call.

Thames Barrier Information & Learning Centre

1 Unity Way, Woolwich, SE18 5NJ (8305 4188, www.environment-agency.gov.uk/thamesbarrier). Woolwich Dockyard rail, or North Greenwich tube then bus 472. **Open** 10.30am-5pm daily. **Admission** £3.50; £2-£3 reductions; free under-5s. **Credit** MC, V.

This adjustable dam has been variously called a triumph of modern engineering and the eighth wonder of the world. The shiny silver fins, lined up across Woolwich Reach, are indeed an impressive sight. Built in 1982 at a cost of £535m, they've already saved London from flooding some 80 times. The barrier is regularly in action for maintenance purposes; check the website for a current timetable.

To learn more, pay £3.50 for a look around the recently refurbished learning centre, where you'll find an account of the 1953 flood that led to the barrier's construction, as well as displays on wildlife in the Thames and how a flood would affect London. There's a pleasant café with picnic benches.

Woolwich Ferry.

EXPLORE

South-west London

Between deprivation and the posh, south-west London is gentrifying too.

Towards the Surrey border, south-west London starts to feel like a collection of villages rather than a single sprawling metropolis. In **Richmond**, **Barnes** and **Wimbledon**, pretty Georgian houses overlook quaint greens and expansive commons where the blessed clichés of Englishness – tea-drinking, cricket – still hold sway. The rich and royal took advantage of the area's leafy proximity to the central city a long time ago, with visitors able to enjoy their legacy as world-class tourist attractions: **Kew Gardens** (*see p145*), **Hampton Court Palace** (*see p146*); and the huge Royal Park in **Richmond** (*see p144*).

Map p388	Restaurants &
Pubs & bars p202	cafés pp183-186
Hotels pp257-258	

Industrialisation and urban creep soon took over the fields. **Stockwell** and **Brixton** are now just like their south-east London neighbours: diverse, busy and vibrant, despite creeping gentrification. Between them and the posh suburbs, **Wandsworth** and **Clapham** are a vision of the gentrified future: herds of young professionals picnic on the fine commons at weekends, fill the bars and restaurants, and fall asleep on Egyptian cotton sheets dreaming of an apartment beside the river in **Battersea**.

VAUXHALL, STOCKWELL & BRIXTON

Stockwell tube, or Brixton or Vauxhall tube/rail.

The area now known as Vauxhall was, in the 13th century, home to a house owned by one Falkes de Bréauté, a soldier rewarded for carrying out King John's dirtier military deeds. Over time, Falkes' Hall became Fox Hall and finally Vauxhall. Vauxhall's heyday was in the 18th century when the infamous Pleasure Gardens, built back in 1661, reached the height of their popularity, a mingling of wealthy and not-so-wealthy, with everyone getting into trouble on 'lovers' walks'. When the Gardens closed in 1859, the area became reasonably respectable – all that remains is Spring Garden, behind popular gay haunt the Royal Vauxhall Tavern (aka **RVT**; *see p312*). For a glimpse of old Vauxhall head to **Bonnington Square**. Down on the river is the cream and emerald ziggurat designed by Terry Farrell for the Secret Intelligence Service (formerly MI6).

At the top end of the South Lambeth Road, **Little Portugal** – a cluster of Portuguese cafés, shops and tapas bars – is an enticing oasis. At the other end, **Stockwell** is prime commuter territory, with little to lure visitors except some charming Victorian streets: Albert Square, Durand Gardens and Stockwell Park Crescent; van Gogh was briefly resident at 87 Hackford Road.

South of Stockwell is **Brixton**, a lively hub of clubs and music. The town centre has been enjoying significant redevelopment, with Windrush Square completed at the end of Coldharbour Lane in 2010 (*see also p143* **Inside Track**). The square's name is significant: HMS *Windrush* was the boat that brought West Indian immigrants from Jamaica in 1948. They were hardly welcomed, but managed to make Brixton a thriving community. As late as the 1980s, tensions were still strong, as the Clash song 'Guns of Brixton' famously illustrates. The rage of the persecuted black community, still finding themselves isolated and under

Brixton.

suspicion decades after arriving, is better expressed by dub poet Linton Kwesi Johnson – try 'Sonny's Lettah (Anti-Sus Poem)' for starters. The riots of 1981 and 1985 around Railton Road and Coldharbour Lane left the district scarred for years.

Now, most visitors come to Brixton for Brixton Village Market (*see p208* **The World in a Village**). The two covered arcades date to the 1920s and '30s and have been – with Market Row – Grade II-listed. The district's main roads are modern and filled with chain stores, but there's also some attractive architecture – check out the **Ritzy Cinema** (Brixton Oval, Coldharbour Lane, 0871 902 5739, www.picturehouses.co.uk), dating to 1911. Brixton's best-known street, **Electric Avenue**, got its name when, in 1880, it became one of the first shopping streets to get electric lights.

Minutes south of Brixton's hectic centre, flanked by Tulse Hill and Dulwich Road, **Brockwell Park** (www.brockwellpark.com) is one of London's most underrated green spaces. Landscaped in the early 19th century for a wealthy glass-maker, the park contains his Georgian country house – now a café – an open-air swimming pool, bowling green, walled rose garden and miniature railway. Each July, there's an enjoyable traditional country fair. If that doesn't seem bucolic enough, visit **Brixton Windmill** (*see below*) just off Brixton Hill a little further west.

FREE Brixton Windmill
Windmill Gardens, off Blenheim Gardens, SW2 5BZ (www.brixtonwindmill.org). Brixton tube.
Open pre-booked tours Apr-Oct; see website for details. **Admission** free.
Built in 1816 and in service until 1934, Brixton Windmill reopened to the public in 2011, and had already won several tourism and heritage awards in 2012. There are about 20 open days a year, during which you can visit without booking (but may have to queue: there isn't much room in the windmill), but the 30-45min pre-booked guided tours give access to the upper floors – and are a fascinating glimpse into a lost London industry.

**INSIDE TRACK
BLACK AND PROUD**

Gathered over a quarter of a century, the **Black Cultural Archives** (www.bca heritage.org.uk) are getting a permanent new home. They will be in Britain's first black cultural centre, due to open – after recession-led troubles – later this year in the Grade II-listed Raleigh Hall on Windrush Square in Brixton (*see p142*).

BATTERSEA
Battersea Park or Clapham Junction rail.

Battersea started life as an island in the Thames, but it was reclaimed when the surrounding marshes were drained. Huguenots settled here from the 16th century and, prior to the Industrial Revolution, the area was mostly farmland. The river is dominated by Sir Giles Gilbert Scott's magnificent four-chimneyed **Battersea Power Station** (www.batterseapowerstation.org.uk), which can be seen close up from all trains leaving Victoria Station. Images of this iconic building have graced album covers (notably Pink Floyd's *Animals*) and films (among them Ian McKellen's *Richard III* and Michael Radford's *1984*), and its instantly recognisable silhouette pops up repeatedly as you move around the capital. Work started on what was to become the largest brick-built structure in Europe in 1929, and the power station was in operation through to the early 1980s. Too impressive to be destroyed, its future continues to be the subject of intense public debate – meanwhile, it's carved out a niche as a venue for circus spectaculars and extreme sports festivals.

Overlooking the river a little further west, **Battersea Park** (www.batterseapark.org) has beautiful lakes (one with a fine Barbara Hepworth sculpture) and gardens. Much of the park was relandscaped in 2004 according to the original 19th-century plans, albeit with some modern additions left in place: the Russell Page Garden, designed for the 1951 Festival of Britain; a Peace Pagoda, built by a Buddhist sect in 1985 to commemorate Hiroshima Day; a petting zoo; and an art gallery (the Pumphouse, 8871 7572, http://pumphousegallery.org.uk). The park extends to the Thames; from the wide and lovely riverside walk you can see both the elaborate **Albert Bridge** and the

EXPLORE

simpler **Battersea Bridge**, rebuilt between 1886 and 1890 by visionary sewer engineer Joseph Bazalgette.

West of the bridges, you'll find the beautiful church of **St Mary's Battersea** (Battersea Church Road); this was where poet William Blake was married and Benedict Arnold, who contrived to fight on both sides during the American War of Independence, is buried. From here, JMW Turner used to paint the river.

CLAPHAM & WANDSWORTH

Clapham Common tube, or Wandsworth Common or Wandsworth Town rail.

In the 18th and 19th centuries, **Clapham** was colonised by the wealthy upper classes and social reformers, notably abolitionist William Wilberforce's Clapham Sect. But the coming of the railways meant that the posh folk upped sticks, and from 1900 the area fell into decline. Nowadays, it is once again one of the capital's more desirable addresses. **Clapham Common** provides an oasis of peace amid busy traffic, with Holy Trinity Church, which dates from 1776, at its perimeter. From Clapham Common station, turn north into the **Pavement** – it leads to the pubs and shops of Clapham Old Town. Alternatively, head south to the smart shops and cafés of **Abbeville Road**. The area to the west of the common is known as 'Nappy Valley', because of the many young middle-class families who reside there. If you can fight your way between baby carriages, head for **Northcote Road** – especially on weekends, when a lovely little market sets up.

PUTNEY & BARNES

East Putney or Putney Bridge tube, or Barnes or Putney rail.

If you want proof of an area's well-to-do credentials, count the rowing clubs: **Putney** has a couple of dozen. **Putney Bridge** is partly responsible, as its buttresses made it difficult for large boats to continue upstream, creating a stretch of water conducive to rowing. The **Oxford & Cambridge Boat Race** (*see p26*) has started in Putney since 1845. The river has good paths in either direction; heading west along the Putney side of the river will take you past the **WWT Wetland Centre** (*see right*), which lies alongside Barnes Common. The main road across the expanse, Queen's Ride, humpbacks over the railway line below. It was here, on 16 September 1977, that singer Gloria Jones's Mini drove off the road, killing her passenger (and boyfriend) T-Rex singer Marc Bolan. The slim trunk of the sycamore

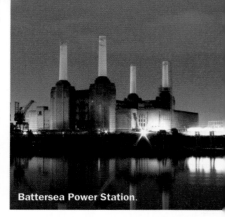

Battersea Power Station.

hit by the car is covered with notes, poems and declarations of love; steps lead to a bronze bust.

★ WWT Wetland Centre

Queen Elizabeth's Walk, Barnes, SW13 9WT (8409 4400, www.wwt.org.uk). Hammersmith tube then bus 283, Barnes rail or bus 33, 72, 209. **Open** *Mar-Oct* 9.30am-6pm daily. *Nov-Feb* 9.30am-5pm daily. **Admission** £9.99; £5.55-£7.45 reductions; £27.82 family; free under-4s. **Credit** MC, V.
Reclaimed from industrial reservoirs a decade ago, the 43-acre Wildfowl & Wetlands Trust Wetland Centre is four miles from central London, but feels a world away. Quiet ponds, rushes, rustling reeds and wildflower gardens all teem with bird life – some 150 species – as well as the now very rare water vole. Naturalists ponder its 27,000 trees and 300,000 aquatic plants and swoon over 300 varieties of butterfly, 20 types of dragonfly and four species of bat (now sleeping in a stylish house designed by Turner Prize-winning artist Jeremy Deller). You can explore water-recycling initiatives in the RBC Rain Garden or check out the interactive section: pilot a submerged camera around a pond, learn about the life-cycle of a dragonfly or make waves in a digital pool. Traditionalists needn't be scared – plain old pairs of binoculars can be hired.

KEW & RICHMOND

Kew Gardens or Richmond tube/rail, or Kew Bridge rail.

Much of Kew has a rarified air, with leafy streets that lead you into a quaint world of teashops, tiny bookstores and gift shops, a sweet village green, ancient pubs and pleasant riverparks. Kew's big appeal is its vast and glorious **Royal Botanic Gardens** (*see p145*), but the **National Archives** – formerly the Public Records Office – are housed here too, a repository for everything from the Domesday Book to recently released government documents. The place is always full of people researching their family trees. Overlooking the gardens, **Watermans Arts Centre** (40 High Street, 8232 1010, www.watermans.org.uk) contains a gallery, cinema and theatre focusing on Brit-Asian and South Asian arts.

Originally known as the Shene, the wealthy area of **Richmond**, about 15 minutes' walk west down Kew Road, has been linked with royalty for centuries: Edward III had a palace here in the 1300s and Henry VII loved the area so much that in 1501 he built another (naming it Richmond after his favourite earldom); this was where Elizabeth I spent her last summers. Ultimately, the whole neighbourhood took the palace's name, although the building itself is long gone – pretty much all that's left is a small gateway on **Richmond Green**. On the east side of the green, medieval alleys (such as Brewer's Lane) replete with ancient pubs lead to the traffic-choked high street. The **Church of St Mary Magdalene**, on Paradise Road, blends architectural styles from 1507 to 1904.

A short walk away in Richmond's Old Town Hall, you'll find the small **Museum of Richmond** (Whittaker Avenue, 8332 1141, www.museumofrichmond.com, closed Mon & Sun). Nearby, the riverside promenade is eminently strollable and dotted with pubs; the **White Cross** (Water Lane, 8940 6844), which has been here since 1835, has a special 'entrance at high tide' – the river floods regularly. The 13 arches of **Richmond Bridge** date from 1774 – this is the oldest surviving crossing over the Thames and offers fine sweeping views.

Richmond Park is the largest of the Royal Parks, occupying some 2,500 acres. There are hundreds of red and fallow deer roaming free across it – presumably much happier without having to listen out for the 'View halloo!' of one of Henry VIII's hunting parties. Within

the park's bounds is the Palladian splendour of White Lodge and Pembroke Lodge, childhood home to philosopher Bertrand Russell – and now a café.

★ Royal Botanic Gardens (Kew Gardens)

Kew, Richmond, Surrey TW9 3AB (8332 5655, www.kew.org). Kew Gardens tube/rail, Kew Bridge rail or riverboat to Kew Pier. **Open** times vary; check website for details. **Admission** £16; £14 reductions; free under-17s. **Credit** AmEx, MC, V. Kew's lush, landscaped beauty represents the pinnacle of our national gardening obsession. From the early 1700s until 1840, when the gardens were given to the nation, these were the grounds for two fine royal residences – the White House and Richmond Lodge. Early resident Queen Caroline, who was wife of George II, was very fond of exotic plants brought back by botanists voyaging to far-flung parts of the world. In 1759, the renowned 'Capability' Brown was employed by George III to improve on the work of his predecessors here, William Kent and Charles Bridgeman. Thus began the shape of the extraordinary garden that today attracts hundreds of thousands of visitors each year.

Covering half a square mile, Kew feels surprisingly big – pick up a map at the ticket office and follow the handy signs. Head straight for the 19th-century greenhouses, filled to the roof with plants – some of which have been here as long as the enormous glass structures themselves. The sultry Palm House holds tropical plants: palms, bamboo, tamarind, mango and fig trees, not to mention fragrant hibiscus and frangipani. The Temperate House features *Pendiculata sanderina*, the Holy Grail for orchid hunters, with petals some 3ft long.

Also worth seeking out are the Princess of Wales Conservatory, divided into ten climate zones; the Marine Display, downstairs from the Palm House (it isn't always open, but when it is you can see the delightful seahorses); the lovely, quiet indoor pond of the Waterlily House (closed in winter); and the exquisite Victorian botanical drawings found in the fabulous Marianne North Gallery. The Xstrata Treetop Walkway has been a hugely popular addition to the gardens, allowing you a completely different woodland walk 60ft up in the leaf canopy. *Photo p146.*

► *Britain's smallest royal palace is also within the gardens: Kew Palace (www.hrp.org.uk/KewPalace; closed Oct-Mar; £6, free-£4.50 reductions) dates all the way back to the 18th century.*

WIMBLEDON

Wimbledon tube/rail.

Beyond the world-famous tennis tournament, **Wimbledon** is little but a wealthy and genteel suburb. Turn left out of the station on to the

WWT Wetland Centre.

EXPLORE

Royal Botanic Gardens (Kew Gardens). *See p145.*

uninspiring Broadway, and you'll wonder why you bothered. So turn right instead, climbing a steep hill lined with palatial houses. At the top is **Wimbledon Village**, a trendy little enclave of posh shops, eateries and some decent pubs.

From here you can hardly miss **Wimbledon Common**, a huge, wild, partly wooded park that is criss-crossed by paths and horse tracks. The windmill (Windmill Road, 8947 2825, www.wimbledonwindmill.org.uk; closed Nov-Mar) provides an eccentric touch: Robert Baden-Powell wrote *Scouting for Boys* (1910) here; it's now home to a tearoom and a hands-on milling museum.

East of the common lies **Wimbledon Park**, with its boating lake, and the **All England Lawn Tennis Club** and **Wimbledon Lawn Tennis Museum** (*see below*). Two other attractions are worth seeking out – Grade II-listed **Cannizaro Park** (www.cannizaropark.com) is lovely, as is the **Buddhapadipa Temple** (14 Calonne Road, Wimbledon Parkside, 8946 1357, www.buddhapadipa.org). When it was built in the early 1980s, this was the only Thai temple in Europe. The Shrine Room contains a golden statue of the Buddha, a copy of the Buddhasihing that is on show in Bangkok's National Museum.

Wimbledon Lawn Tennis Museum

Museum Building, All England Lawn Tennis Club, Church Road, SW19 5AE (www.wimbledon.org/museum). Southfields tube or bus 493. **Open** 10am-5pm daily; ticket holders only during championships. **Admission** (incl tour) £20; £12.50-£17 reductions; free under-5s. **Credit** MC, V.

Highlights at this popular museum on the history of tennis include a 200° cinema screen that allows you to find out what it's like to play on Centre Court and a re-creation of a 1980s men's dressing room, complete with a 'ghost' of John McEnroe. Visitors can also enjoy a behind-the-scenes tour.

FURTHER SOUTH-WEST

Richmond tube/rail, or Hampton Court or St Margaret's rail.

If the water level allows, follow the river from Richmond west. You could stop at **Petersham**, home to the **Petersham Nurseries** with its café (Church Lane, off Petersham Road, 8940 5230, www.petershamnurseries.com), or take in a grand country mansion, perhaps **Ham House** (*see below*) or **Marble Hill House**, with the **Orleans House Gallery** (for both, *see p147*) next door.

The river runs on past **Twickenham**, home to rugby's **Twickenham Stadium**, to the curious Gothic 'castle' **Strawberry Hill** (for both, *see p147*). Several miles further along the Thames, the river passes beside **Hampton Court Palace** (*see below*). Few visitors will want to walk this far, of course – instead take a train from Waterloo or, for that extra fillip of adventure, a boat.

Ham House

Ham Street, Richmond, Surrey TW10 7RS (8940 1950, www.nationaltrust.org.uk/hamhouse). Richmond tube/rail then bus 371. **Open** times vary; check website for details. **Admission** prices vary; check website for details. **Credit** MC, V.

Built in 1610 for one of James I's courtiers, Thomas Vavasour, this lavish red-brick mansion is full of period furnishings, rococo mirrors and ornate tapestries. Detailing is exquisite, down to a table in the dairy with sculpted cows' legs. The restored formal grounds also attract attention: there's a lovely trellised Cherry Garden and some lavender parterres. The tearoom turns out historic dishes (lavender syllabub, for instance) using ingredients from the Kitchen Gardens.
▶ *Between February and October (weekends only for the winter months), a ferry crosses the river to Marble Hill House; see p147.*

★ Hampton Court Palace

East Molesey, Surrey KT8 9AU (0844 482 7777, www.hrp.org.uk). Hampton Court rail, or riverboat from Westminster or Richmond to Hampton Court Pier (Apr-Oct). **Open** *Palace Apr-Oct 10am-6pm daily; Nov-Mar 10am-4.30pm daily. Park dawn-dusk daily.* **Admission** *Palace, courtyard, cloister & maze* £16.95; £8.50-£14.30 reductions; £43.46 family; free under-5s. *Maze only* £3.85; £2.75 reductions. *Gardens only* Apr-Oct £5.50; free-£4.70 reductions; Nov-Mar free. **Credit** AmEx, MC, V.

It may be a half-hour train ride from central London, but this spectacular palace, once owned by Henry VIII, is well worth the trek. It was built in 1514 by Cardinal Wolsey, the high-flying Lord Chancellor, but Henry liked it so much he seized it for himself in 1528. For the next 200 years it was a focal point of English history: Elizabeth I was imprisoned in a tower by her jealous and fearful elder sister Mary I; Shakespeare gave his first performance to James I in 1604; and, after the Civil War, Oliver Cromwell was so besotted by the building he ditched his puritanical principles and moved in to enjoy its luxuries.

Centuries later, the rosy walls of the palace still dazzle. Its vast size can be daunting, so it's a good idea to take advantage of the guided tours. If you do decide to go it alone, start with Henry VIII's State Apartments, which include the Great Hall, noted for its beautiful stained-glass windows and elaborate religious tapestries; in the Haunted Gallery, the ghost of Catherine Howard – Henry's fifth wife, executed for adultery in 1542 – can reputedly be heard shrieking. The King's Apartments, added in 1689 by Wren, are notable for a splendid mural of Alexander the Great, painted by Antonio Verrio. The Queen's Apartments and Georgian Rooms feature similarly elaborate paintings, chandeliers and tapestries. The Tudor Kitchens are great fun, with their giant cauldrons, fake pies and blood-spattered walls.

More extraordinary sights await outside, where the exquisitely landscaped gardens contain topiary, Thames views, a reconstruction of a 16th-century heraldic garden and the famous Hampton Court maze.

Marble Hill House

Richmond Road, Twickenham, Middx TW1 2NL (8892 5115, www.english-heritage.org.uk). St Margaret's rail or bus 33, 490, H22, R70. **Open** *times vary; check website for details.* **Admission** £5.50; £3.30-£5 reductions; £14.30 family; free under-5s. **Credit** MC, V.

King George II spared no expense to win the favour of his mistress, Henrietta Howard. Not only did he

build this perfect Palladian house (1724) for his lover, he almost dragged Britain into a war while doing so: by using Honduran mahogany to construct the grand staircase, he managed to spark off a major diplomatic row with Spain. Frankly, it was worth it. Picnickers are welcome to the grounds.

▶ *A programme of concerts runs in summer, and ferries cross the river to Ham House; see p146.*

FREE Orleans House Gallery

Riverside, Twickenham, Middx TW1 3DJ (8831 6000, www.richmond.gov.uk/orleans_house_gallery). Richmond tube then bus 33, 490, H22, R68, R70, or St Margaret's or Twickenham rail. **Open** *Apr-Sept 1-5.30pm Tue-Sat; 2-5.30pm Sun. Oct-Mar 1-4.30pm Tue-Sat; 2-4.30pm Sun.* **Admission** *free.* **Credit** MC, V.

Secluded in pretty gardens, this Grade I-listed riverside house was constructed in 1710 for James Johnson, Secretary of State for Scotland. It was later named after the Duke of Orleans, Louis-Philippe, who lived in exile here from 1800 until 1817. Though partially demolished in 1926, the building retains James Gibbs's neoclassical Octagon Room. There are also regularly changing temporary exhibitions here.

▶ *The café (Karmarama, open Wed-Sun) is a welcome addition, offering good coffee and snacks.*

Strawberry Hill

268 Waldegrave Road, Twickenham, Middx TW1 4ST (8744 1241, www.strawberryhillhouse.org.uk). Richmond tube then bus R68, or Strawberry Hill rail. **Open** *Apr-Oct 2-4.30pm Mon-Wed; noon-4.30pm Sat, Sun.* **Admission** £8; £7 reductions; £20 family; free under-5s. **Credit** MC, V.

Antiquarian and novelist Horace Walpole, who created the Gothic novel with his book *The Castle of Otranto*, laid the groundwork for the Gothic Revival of Victorian times as early as the 1700s. Pre-booked tickets, timed at 20min intervals, will allow you to explore the crepuscular nooks and crannies of his 'play-thing house', this 'little Gothic castle'.

World Rugby Museum/ Twickenham Stadium

Twickenham Rugby Stadium, Rugby Road, Twickenham, Middx TW1 1DZ (8892 8877, www.rfu.com). Hounslow East tube then bus 281, or Twickenham rail. **Open** *Museum 10am-5pm Tue-Sat; 11am-5pm Sun. Tours 10.30am, noon, 1.30pm, 3pm Tue-Sat; 1pm, 3pm Sun.* **Admission** £15; £9 reductions; £45 family; free under-5s. **Credit** AmEx, MC, V.

Twickenham Stadium is the home of English rugby union. Tickets for international matches are hard to come by, but the Museum of Rugby is on the site to provide some compensation. Guided tours take in the England dressing room, the players' tunnel and the Royal Box. Memorabilia (a jersey from 1871, the Calcutta Cup) charts the game's development from the late 19th century, and there's a scrum machine.

INSIDE TRACK CREEPY CASTLE

Chiming with the vogue for all things vampiric, the twilight and moonlight tours of **Strawberry Hill** (*see right*), 18th-century home of proto-Goth Horace Walpole, show this folly of a house at its most theatrical, spooky best.

EXPLORE

West London

Grand houses and old money meet the curry capital of London.

It's fitting that west London still has a distinct air of aristocash. This was, after all, the first of the city's frontiers to be developed, outside the political hub of the City of Westminster and out of the way of the westerly smog-carrying winds. Even today, the elegant Georgian townhouses of **Holland Park** and **Kensington** retain their high status.

Unlike London's north, east and south, where the posher neighbourhoods are tucked away in more remote, leafier suburbs, the smartest parts of the west – chiefly Fulham, Kensington and Notting Hill – are conveniently central, while the working-class districts of **Southall** and **Wembley**, now the first stop for those who've arrived in the country via Heathrow, are further out.

| **Map** p394 | **Hotels** pp258-259 |
| **Pubs & bars** p202 | **Restaurants & cafés** p186 |

Map p394   Hotels pp258-259   Pubs & bars p202   Restaurants & cafés p186

KENSINGTON & HOLLAND PARK

High Street Kensington or Holland Park tube.

There are more millionaires per square mile in this corner of London than in any other part of Europe, a hangover from the days when Kensington was a semi-rural retreat for aristocrats. Just off **Kensington High Street**, a smart but rarely intoxicating shopping drag, an array of handsome squares are lined with grand 19th-century houses, many of which still serve as single-family homes. The houses here are not as ostentatiously grand as they are in, say, Belgravia, but nor is the wealth worn as lightly as it is in many corners of Mayfair. You're always aware that you're around money.

Linking with Notting Hill (*see p90*) to the north, **Kensington Church Street** has many antique shops selling furniture so fine you would probably never dare use it. **St Mary Abbots** (7937 6032/5136, http://smanews.weebly.com), at the junction of Church Street and High Street, is a Victorian neo-Gothic church, built on the site of the 12th-century original by Sir George Gilbert Scott between 1869 and 1872. Past worshippers have included Isaac Newton and William Wilberforce. As well as beautiful stained-glass windows, it has London's tallest spire (278 feet).

Across the road is a striking art deco building, once the department store Barkers but now taken over by Texan organic food giant **Whole Foods Market** (nos.63-97, 7368 4500, www.wholefoodsmarket.co.uk). South down Derry Street, past the entrance to the **Roof Gardens** – a restaurant and private members' club, which boasts flamingos and a stream, 100 feet above central London – is Kensington Square, which has a mighty concentration of blue plaques. The writer William Thackeray lived at no.16 and the painter Edward Burne-Jones at no.41; at no.18, John Stuart Mill's maid made her bid for 'man from Porlock' status by using Carlyle's sole manuscript of *The French Revolution* to start the fire. The houses, though much altered, date from the development of the square in 1685, and – hard to believe now – were surrounded by fields until 1840.

Further to the west is one of London's finest green spaces: **Holland Park**. Along its eastern edge, Holland Walk is one of the most pleasant paths in central London, but the heart of the park is the Jacobean **Holland House**. Left derelict after World War II, it was bought by the London County Council in 1952; the east wing now houses the city's best-sited youth hostel (*see p259*). In summer, open-air theatre and opera are staged on the front terrace. Three lovely formal gardens are laid out near the house. A little further west, the

Japanese-style Kyoto Garden has huge koi carp and a bridge at the foot of a waterfall. Elsewhere, rabbits hop about and peacocks stroll around with the confidence due to such supremely beautiful creatures. To the south of the park are another two historic houses: **Linley Sambourne House** and, extensively refurbished, **Leighton House** (for both, *see below*).

★ Leighton House

12 Holland Park Road, W14 8LZ (7602 3316, www.rbkc.gov.uk). High Street Kensington tube. **Open** 10am-5.30pm Mon, Wed-Sun. *Tours* 3pm Wed (other times by appointment only). **Admission** £5; £3 reductions. **Credit** MC, V. **Map** p394 A9.

In the 1860s, artist Frederic Leighton commissioned a showpiece house. Behind the sternly Victorian red-brick façade, he made sure it was full of treasures from all over the world, as well as his own works and those of his contemporaries. Every inch of the house is decorated in high style: magnificent downstairs reception rooms designed for lavish entertaining; a dramatic staircase leading to a light-filled studio that takes up most of the first floor; and, above all, the 'Arab Hall', which showcases Leighton's huge collection of 16th-century Middle Eastern tiles. The only private space in the whole house is a tiny single bedroom. *Photos p151.*

Linley Sambourne House

18 Stafford Terrace, W8 7BH (tours 7602 3316, www.rbkc.gov.uk/linleysambournehouse). High Street Kensington tube. **Open** (pre-booked tours only) *Mid Sept-mid June* 11.15am, 2.15pm Wed; 11.15am, 1pm, 2.15pm, 3.30pm Sat, Sun. **Tours** £8; £3-£6 reductions. **Credit** MC, V. **Map** p394 A9.

The home of cartoonist Edward Linley Sambourne was built in the 1870s and has almost all of its original fittings and furniture. Tours last 90mins, with the weekend tours (except at 11.15am) led by an actor in period costume.

▶ *If you enjoy the costume tours here, try those at Benjamin Franklin House; see p78.*

EARL'S COURT & FULHAM

Earl's Court, Fulham Broadway or West Brompton tube.

Earl's Court sells itself short, grammatically speaking, since it was once the site of the courthouse of two earls: the Earls of Warwick and of Holland. The 1860s saw Earl's Court move from rural hamlet to investment opportunity as the Metropolitan Railway arrived. Some 20 years later it was already much as we see it today, bar the fast food joints. The terraces of grand old houses are mostly subdivided into bedsits and cheap hotels; today, the transient population tends to be eastern European or South American.

In 1937, the **Earls Court Exhibition Centre** was built, and in its day it was the largest reinforced concrete building in Europe. It has hosted innumerable trade shows, Olympic events (for both the 1948 and 2012 Games) and pop concerts – Pink Floyd built and tore down *The Wall* here, which may prove prophetic if bitterly contested plans to redevelop the centre and nearby social housing go ahead. The Exhibition Centre is close to the diverting little **Metropolitan Police Museum** (ground floor, Empress State Building, Empress Approach, Lillie Road, SW6 1TR, 7161 1234; open 10am-4pm Mon-Fri). Two minutes south down Warwick Road is a tiny venue, with an impressive pedigree: the **Troubadour** (263-267 Old Brompton Road, 7370 1434, www.troubadour.co.uk), a 1950s coffeehouse with a downstairs club that hosted Jimi Hendrix, Joni Mitchell, Bob Dylan and Paul Simon in the 1960s. While it's no longer at the cutting edge, it still delivers a crunchy programme of music, comedy and especially poetry.

Heading west along Warwick Road you come to the gates of **Brompton Cemetery**. It's full of magnificent monuments to the famous and infamous, including suffragette Emmeline Pankhurst and, his grave marked by a lion, boxer 'Gentleman' John Jackson – 'Gentleman' John taught Lord Byron to box. The peace and

Kensington.

EXPLORE

quiet of the cemetery are regularly disturbed at its southern end by neighbouring **Stamford Bridge**, home of Chelsea FC (for the stadium museum, *see p110*).

Further west, **Craven Cottage** (*see p315*), the smaller home ground of Fulham FC, has a lovely historic red-brick stand designed by Archibald Leitch in 1905. The walk to the ground from Putney Bridge tube is a pleasant one, along the Thames and through the grounds of **Fulham Palace** (*see below*).

FREE Fulham Palace & Museum

Bishop's Avenue, off Fulham Palace Road, SW6 6EA (7736 3233, www.fulhampalace.org). Putney Bridge tube or bus 14, 74, 220, 414, 430. **Open** *Museum & gallery* 1-4pm Mon-Wed, Sat, Sun. Gallery closes for functions; phone in advance. *Gardens* dawn-dusk daily. *Tours* 2pm 3rd Tue, 2nd & 4th Sun of mth. **Admission** free; under-16s must be accompanied by an adult. *Tours* £5; free under-16s. **No credit cards**.

Fulham Palace was the episcopal retreat of the Bishops of London. The present building was built in Tudor times, with later significant Georgian and Victorian additions. It would be more accurate to call it a manor house than a palace, but it gives a fine glimpse into the changing lifestyles and architecture of nearly 500 years, from the Tudor hall to the splendid Victorian chapel; try out the echo in the courtyard. There's also access to a fine stretch of riverside walk, and the restored vineries and walled garden.

SHEPHERD'S BUSH

Goldhawk Road, Shepherd's Bush Market or White City tube, or Shepherd's Bush tube/rail.

Shepherd's Bush was once west London's impoverished backwater, the setting for the BBC's junkyard sitcom *Steptoe & Son*. Now, a couple of decades after house prices started going through the roof, there's visible evidence of gentrification. The third west London Premiership side, **Queens Park Rangers** (*see p315*), continues to underperform despite a huge cash injection from some of the world's richest businessmen, and while Shepherd's Bush got a big boost from the opening of the gargantuan **Westfield London** shopping mall a few years back, it remains to be seen what the departure of hundreds of BBC News employees from the unlovely **Television Centre** on Wood Lane – or the probable sale of the property once empty – will do for the area's fortunes. The **Bush** theatre (*see p310*) stages excellent leftfield drama, while **Bush Hall** (*see p289*), a beautifully restored former snooker hall, and the **O2 Shepherd's Bush Empire** (*see p287*), an old BBC theatre, have become essential destinations on the music scene.

HAMMERSMITH

Hammersmith tube.

Dominated by the grey concrete of its flyover, the centre of Hammersmith, **Hammersmith Broadway**, was once a grotty bus garage. It's now a shiny new shopping mall. Make it over the road and you'll find the **HMV Hammersmith Apollo** (*see p286*. Opened in 1932 as the Gaumont Palace, it entered rock legend as the Hammersmith Odeon, hosting gigs by such bands as the Beatles, Motörhead and Public Enemy.

Hammersmith Bridge, the city's oldest suspension bridge, is a green and gold hymn to the strength of Victorian ironwork, and there's a lovely walk west along the Thames Path from there that takes in a clutch of historic pubs including the **Blue Anchor** (13 Lower Mall, W6 9DJ, 8748 5774); head in the opposite direction for cultural happenings at the **Riverside Studios** (*see p272*).

CHISWICK

Turnham Green tube or Chiswick rail.

Once a sleepy, semi-rural suburb, Chiswick is now one of London's swankiest postcodes, its residents including broadcasters, directors, actors, advertising bods and a smattering of rock 'n' roll royalty. In recent years, **Chiswick High Road**, its main thoroughfare, has developed something of a gastronomic reputation, too, with several high-end eateries.

The area also has a surprising number of sightseeing attractions. **Chiswick Mall** is a beautiful residential path that runs alongside the river from Hammersmith, and includes **Kelmscott House** (26 Upper Mall, 8741 3735, www.morrissociety.org.uk), once home to pioneering socialist William Morris but now a private house that opens to the public 2-5pm on Thursdays and Saturdays. From here, it's a short walk to **Fuller's Brewery** (*see p151*) and

---

INSIDE TRACK
BEAUTY ON THE INSIDE

Printer Emery Walker was a friend and colleague of William Morris, the founder of the Arts and Crafts Movement, and his house at 7 Hammersmith Terrace is an immaculately preserved time capsule of a perfectly realised Arts and Crafts home. Tours take place every Saturday from April to September and by prior arrangement. See www.emerywalker. org.uk for further details.

Hogarth's House (*see below*), while the **Kew Bridge Steam Museum** (*see below*) and the **Musical Museum** (*see p152*) are only a bus ride away. It's possible to return to the river path after visiting **Chiswick House** (*see below*), and the wonderful Royal Botanic Gardens at Kew (*see p145*) are just over the bridge. Further upstream is **Syon House** (*see p152*).

Chiswick House

Burlington Lane, W4 2RP (8995 0508, www. chgt.org.uk). Hammersmith tube then bus 190, or Chiswick rail. **Open** *Apr-Oct* 10am-5pm Mon-Wed, Sun. **Admission** £5.70; £3.40-£5.10 reductions; free under-5s. **Credit** MC, V.

Richard Boyle, third Earl of Burlington, designed this Palladian villa in 1725 as a place to entertain the artistic and philosophical luminaries of his day. The Chiswick House & Gardens Trust has restored the gardens to the original design. The restoration was helped by details from the newly acquired painting *A View of Chiswick House from the South-west* by Dutch landscape artist Pieter Andreas Rysbrack (c1685-1748).
▶ *There's an impressive café (8995 6356, www.chiswickhousecafe.co.uk) in the grounds, designed in a startlingly effective modern style.*

Fuller's Brewery

Griffin Brewery, Chiswick Lane South, W4 2QB (8996 2000, www.fullers.co.uk). Turnham Green tube. **Open** *Tours* hourly 11am-3pm Mon-Fri, by appointment only. *Shop* 10am-8pm Mon-Fri; 10am-6pm Sat. **Admission** (incl tasting session) £10; £8 reductions. **Credit** MC, V.

Fuller Smith & Turner PLC is London's last family-run brewery. Most of this current building dates back to 1845 but there's been a brewery on this site since Elizabethan times. The two-hour tours need to be booked in advance, but – surprise – there is a pub next door if you can't get on a tour.
▶ *London Pride and ESB are the most popular Fuller's brews in London pubs.*

FREE Hogarth's House

Hogarth Lane, Great West Road, W4 2QN (8994 6757). Turnham Green tube or Chiswick rail. **Open** noon-5pm Tue-Sun. **Admission** free; donations appreciated. **No credit cards**.

Recently reopened – fittingly, by comedian, satirist and Chiswick resident Dara O'Brien – after refurbishment, this was the country retreat of the 18th-century artist and social commentator William Hogarth. On display are some famous engravings, including *Gin Lane, Marriage à la Mode* and a copy of *Rake's Progress*, and plenty biographical information. Despite the setting on a horrid main road, the garden is a charming – and amazingly tranquil – retreat.

★ Kew Bridge Steam Museum

Green Dragon Lane, Brentford, Middx TW8 0EN (8568 4757, www.kbsm.org). Gunnersbury

Leighton House. See p149.

Syon House

tube/rail or Kew Bridge rail. **Open** 11am-4pm Tue-Sun. **Admission** £10; £4-£9 reductions; free under-5s. **Credit** AmEx, MC, V.

One of London's most engaging small museums, this old Victorian pumping station is a reminder that steam wasn't just used for powering trains but also for supplying enough water to the citizens of an expanding London. It's now home to an extraordinary collection of different engines. There are lots of hands-on exhibits for kids, a great dressing-up box and even a miniature steam train. The engines crank into action at weekends and Bank Holidays.

★ Musical Museum

399 High Street, Brentford, Middx TW8 0DU (8560 8108, www.musicalmuseum.co.uk). Kew Bridge rail or bus 65, 237, 267. **Open** 11am-5.30pm (last admission 4.30pm) Tue-Sun. **Admission** £8; £6.50 reductions; free accompanied under-16s. **Credit** MC, V.

Housed in a converted church, this museum contains one of the world's foremost collections of automatic instruments. From tiny Swiss musical boxes to the self-playing Mighty Wurlitzer, the collection has an impressive array of sophisticated pianolas, cranky barrel organs, spooky orchestrions, residence organs and violin players, as well as over 30,000 piano rolls.

Syon House

Syon Park, Brentford, Middx TW8 8JF (8560 0882, www.syonpark.co.uk). Gunnersbury tube/rail then bus 237, 267. **Open** *House (mid Mar-Oct only)* 11am-5pm Wed, Thur, Sun. *Gardens (all year)* 10.30am-dusk daily. *Tours* by arrangement. **Admission** *House & gardens* £10.50; £4-£8 reductions; £22 family; free under-5s. *Gardens only* £5.50; £2.50-£3.50 reductions; £11 family; free under-5s. *Tours* free. **Credit** MC, V.

The Percys, Dukes of Northumberland, were once known as 'the Kings of the North' such was their power in the land. Their old house is on the site of a Bridgettine convent, suppressed by Henry VIII in 1534. The building was converted into a house in 1547 for the Duke of Northumberland, its neoclassical interior created by Robert Adam in 1761; there's an outstanding range of Regency portraits by the likes of Gainsborough. The gardens, which were designed by 'Capability' Brown, are enhanced by the splendid Great Conservatory and in winter you can take an evening walk through illuminated woodland; the grounds are also now home to a Waldorf Astoria luxury hotel (www.londonsyonpark.com).

SOUTHALL & WEMBLEY

Southall rail.

Immigrants used to enter London via the docks and settle in the East End. Now, though, they come via Heathrow and settle in the area around the airport: thus a huge arc of suburban west London – Hounslow, Hayes, Southall, Harrow, Wembley, Neasden – has become home to Europe's biggest South Asian population. **Southall** is Britain's best-established immigrant community. From the 1950s onwards, Punjabi Sikhs flocked to the area to work at the Wolf Rubber Factory and in London Transport; the area soon developed a thriving Asian infrastructure of restaurants, shops and wholesalers that attracted Hindus, Muslims, Tamils, Indian Christians and, more recently, Somalis and Afghans. Take a 607 bus from Shepherd's Bush or a Great Western train from Paddington and, on arrival in Southall, you'll think you're in downtown Delhi – all pounding Bollywood hits, sari fabrics, pungent spices and freshly fried samosas.

Southall Broadway is well worth a visit if only to gawp at **Southall Market**, a unique mix of rural India and Cockney London, which until 2007 sold squawking poultry and horses. It still does a brisk trade in general bric-a-brac on Friday and, on Saturday, pretty much everything else. Equally worthy of diversion is the programme of movies at the three-screen **Himalaya Palace** (14 South Road, www.himalayapalacecinema. co.uk), a restored old movie house dedicated to Bollywood epics. But it's the food that makes Southall really special; fans of South-east Asian food can hardly go wrong eating here.

A short walk south of Southall railway station, the **Gurdwara Sri Guru Singh Sabha Southall** (Havelock Road, 8574 4311, www. sgsss.org) is the largest Sikh place of worship outside India. Its golden dome is visible from the London Eye in the east and Windsor Castle to the west; it also provides vegetarian food free to all visitors from the *langar*, or communal kitchen. Non-Sikh visitors are welcome but must take off their shoes before entering, and women must wear a headscarf (they're provided, should you not have one to hand). Enthroned within is the Guru Granth Sahib, the Sikh scripture and supreme spiritual authority of Sikhism.

To the north, **Wembley** is home to a secular religion: British football has its home and heart at **Wembley Stadium** (*see p314*), stunningly

INSIDE TRACK ALL ABOARD!

Transport boffins and fans of design classics: the **London Transport Museum** (*see p76*) opens its Acton depot to visitors on a few weekends a year. The warehouse contains over 370,000 objects that wouldn't fit into the Covent Garden premises, including vehicles – a 1950s Routemaster bus prototype among them – and vintage posters and uniforms. See www.ltmuseum.co.uk for details.

redeveloped by Lord Foster. The distinctive arch has become a welcome sign of home-coming for Londoners driving back to the city from the West Country. Less visually impressive is the adjoining **Wembley Arena** (*see p288*), one of London's key stadium-scale concert venues.

The neighbouring suburb of Neasden has its own claim to British Asian fame: the **Shri Swaminarayan Mandir** (105-119 Brentfield Road, 8965 2651, www.mandir.org), which is the largest Hindu temple outside India to have been built using traditional methods. Nearly 5,000 tons of stone and marble were shipped out to India, where craftsmen carved it into the intricate designs that make up the temple. Then the temple was shipped, piece by piece, to England, where it was assembled on site.

EXPLORE

Gurdwara Sri Guru Singh Sabha Southall.

Consume

Restaurants & Cafés

London's dining scene just keeps getting more interesting.

CONSUME

Whether it's an haute cuisine extravaganza or a barbecue blow-out, the capital's multi-faceted dining scene can provide a quality restaurant to match your needs, including any number of excellent British options, from **St John** (responsible for rebooting British dining in 1995, *see p161*) to **Poppies** (new wave fish and chips, *see p181*). Gastropubs continue to be a big factor, with some – **Harwood Arms** (*see p186*), say, or the **Bull & Last** (*see p177*) – offering stellar food; for more of a drinking experience, try **Pubs & Bars** (*see pp187-202*). Along with the sheer

diversity of places to eat, one of the best things about dining out in London is the choice of independent restaurants. They thrive alongside big names (and the ever-present chains), so as well as landmark openings such as the **Delaunay** (*see p163*) and **Sushisamba** (*see p159*), one-offs like **10 Greek Street** (*see p171*) and **Dabbous** (*see p161*) are also gaining plaudits, and customers.

In the last year it seems we've fallen in love all over again with the Americas: Peru in particular is having a moment, with recently opened **Lima London** (*see p163*) and **Ceviche** (*see p168*) both excellent ambassadors for the cuisine. Imports include **Bar Boulud** (*see p175*) and **La Bodega Negra** (*see p167*), while home-grown siblings **Spuntino** (*see p171*) and **Mishkins** (*see p165*) pay homage to an ideal of Stateside fast food; in addition, the barbecue craze continues to rage.

Simple is good too: restaurants offering limited choice are set to be a major trend in 2013; fine examples are the self-explanatory **Burger & Lobster** (*see p167*) and the chicken-and-steak focused **Tramshed** (*see p182*).

While you're here, make sure you sample the culinary riches London's many immigrants have brought here. Fine Indian, Moroccan, Korean, Turkish and Vietnamese restaurants are listed in this chapter, as are top-notch exponents of the cuisines of France, Italy, Japan, Spain, China and Thailand. And also welcome the coffee revolution (*see p185*): finally, some genuine conoisseurship is going into selecting and serving the bean – and, this being England, the cake alongside.

ESSENTIAL INFORMATION

Try to book a table in advance. At many establishments, booking is vital; at a select few restaurants, you may need to book far in advance. Smoking is banned in all restaurants and cafés. Tipping is standard practice: ten to 15 per cent is usual. Many restaurants add this charge as standard to bills; some do so but still present the credit card slip as 'open', cheekily encouraging the customer to tip twice. Always check the bill.

We've included a range of meal prices for each establishment that we've listed. However, restaurants often change their menus, so treat these prices only as guidelines. Budget venues are marked **£**. For good places to eat with children, *see pp264-265*.

About the reviews

This chapter is compiled from Time Out's annual London Eating & Drinking guide (£11.99), available from www.timeout.com. Time Out reviews anonymously and pays for all meals.

THE SOUTH BANK & BANKSIDE

Borough Market (*see p223*), full of stalls selling all kinds of wonderful food, is a superb forage for gourmet snackers. **Tate Modern Café: Level 2** (*see p264*) is great for those with children, as are the neighbouring outposts of chains **Wagamama** and **Giraffe** under the Royal Festival Hall.

Anchor & Hope

36 The Cut, SE1 8LP (7928 9898). Southwark tube or Waterloo tube/rail. **Open** 5-11pm Mon; 11am-11pm Tue-Sat; 12.30-5pm Sun. **Main courses** £12-£20. **Credit** MC, V. **Map** p402 N8 ❶ **Gastropub**

The most common complaint about this relaxed Waterloo gastropub is the no-booking policy. Those who end up having to wait at the bar can salivate over the seasonal British menu on the blackboard: thinly sliced ox tongue with lentils, green sauce and mustard fruits, say, or braised suckling kid with bacon, fennel, chickpeas and aïoli. There's a single sitting on Sundays.

Baltic

74 Blackfriars Road, SE1 8HA (7928 1111, www.balticrestaurant.co.uk). Southwark tube. **Open** noon-3pm, 5.30-11.15pm Mon-Sat; noon-10.30pm Sun. **Main courses** £10.50-£17.50. **Credit** AmEx, MC, V. **Map** p402 N8 ❷ **Eastern European**

This stylish spot remains the brightest star on London's east European restaurant scene. The menu combines the best of east European cuisine – from Georgian-style lamb with aubergines to Romanian sour cream *mamaliga* (polenta) – with a light, modern European twist. Great cocktails, a wide choice of vodkas, an eclectic wine list and friendly service add to the appeal. In the high-ceilinged restaurant, gaze up at hundreds of shards of golden amber in the stunning chandelier.

Canteen

Royal Festival Hall, Belvedere Road, SE1 8XX (0845 686 1122, www.canteen.co.uk). Embankment tube or Waterloo tube/rail. **Open** 8am-11pm Mon-Fri; 9am-11pm Sat, Sun. **Main courses** £7.50-£18.50. **Credit** AmEx, MC, V. **Map** p399 M8 ❸ **British**

Furnished with utilitarian tables and booths, this branch of Canteen is tucked into the back of the Royal Festival Hall. No surprise, then, that it's often busy. Dishes range from a bacon sandwich and afternoon jam scones to full roast dinners. Classic breakfasts (eggs benedict, welsh rarebit) are served throughout the day, joined by the likes of macaroni cheese or sausage and mash from lunchtime. Quality can be variable, but it's a useful spot. **Other locations** 2 Crispin Place, off Brushfield Street, Spitalfields, E1 6DW; Park Pavilion, 40 Canada Square, Docklands, E14 5FW; 55 Baker Street, Marylebone, W1U 8EW. 21 Wellington Street, Covent Garden, WC2E 7DN.

> ❶ Blue numbers given here correspond to the location of each restaurant and café on the street maps. *See pp392-416.*

CONSUME

Roast. *See p158.*

CONSUME

INSIDE TRACK BARBECUE

Bodean's (see p158) led the way, but now there are hipper places in which to chow down on that most American of pig-outs, barbecued meat. **Pitt Cue Co** (1 Newburgh Street, W1F 7RB, 7287 5578) made the transition from street van to small restaurant in 2011, and now serves unparalleled meaty ribs. **Duke's Brew & Que** (33 Downham Road, N1 5AA, 3006 0795) is a little bit of the Deep South in Haggerston, while just up the road in Islington, **North Pole** (188-190 New North Road, N1 7BJ, 7354 5400) also serves sweet, smoky US barbecue cooking. Both have a great range of drinks too, with Duke's even brewing its own beer.

£ Gelateria 3bis
4 Park Street, SE1 9AB (no phone). London Bridge tube/rail. **Open** 8am-10pm Mon-Sat; 10am-6pm Sun. **Credit** MC, V. **Map** p402 P8 ➍ Ice-cream

Tucked between Neal's Yard Dairy and Monmouth Coffee at Borough Market, 3bis is an Italian gelateria; step inside and watch the gelato machines churning out new flavours. There's an emphasis on creamy, milky ones, from fior di panna ('cream' ice-cream) to panna cotta. While the classics (such as chocolate or pistachio) are not neglected, the team likes to experiment – gooseberry gelato was a big hit.

£ M Manze
87 Tower Bridge Road, SE1 4TW (7407 2985, www.manze.co.uk). Bus 1, 42, 188. **Open** 11am-2pm Mon; 10.30am-2pm Tue-Thur; 10am-2.30pm Fri; 10am-2.45pm Sat. **Main courses** £2.75-£5.20. **No credit cards. Map** p403 Q10 ➎ Pie & mash

Manze's is the finest remaining purveyor of the dirt-cheap traditional foodstuff of London's working classes. It's the oldest pie shop in town, established in 1902, with tiles, marble-topped tables and worn wood benches. Orders are simple: minced beef pies or, for braver souls, stewed eels with mashed potato and liquor (a thin parsley sauce).

Roast
Floral Hall, Borough Market, Stoney Street, SE1 1TL (7940 1300, www.roast-restaurant.com). London Bridge tube/rail. **Open** 7-10.45am, noon-2.45pm, 5.30-10.30pm Mon, Tue; 7-10.45am, noon-3.45pm, 5.30-10.30pm Wed-Fri; 8-11.30am, noon-3.45pm, 6-10.30pm Sat; 11.30am-8.45pm Sun. **Main courses** £16.50-£35. **Set meal** (Sun) £32 3 courses. **Credit** AmEx, MC, V. **Map** p402 P8 ➏ British

A big airy restaurant by Borough Market, Roast gets crammed on market days, but staff cope admirably. The same, bracingly pricey but extensive carte is served at lunch and dinner; set price menus aren't much of a bargain either. Portions, though, are hearty. Meltingly tender pork belly with apple sauce is typical, with Neal's Yard cheeses and trad desserts for afters. Add to this an impressive drinks list, including a fine roster of teas, and you have a great all-rounder. *Photo p157.*

Tapas Brindisa
18-20 Southwark Street, SE1 1TJ (7357 8880, www.brindisa.com). London Bridge tube/rail. **Open** 9am-11pm Mon-Sat; 11am-10pm Sun. **Tapas** £3.75-£21.50. **Credit** AmEx, MC, V. **Map** p402 P8 ➐ Spanish

Top-quality ingredients have always been the key at Brindisa, but its genius lies in the ability to assemble them into eminently tempting tapas. The set-up is equally simple: a bar area at one end dotted with high tables, and a close-packed, concrete-floored dining room at the other. Both are generally thronged with eager customers. Behind the bar is a hatch into the kitchen, which produces a succession of deceptively simple dishes. **Other locations** 7-9 Exhibition Road, South Kensington, SW7 2HE (7590 0008); 46 Broadwick Street, Soho, W1F 7AF (7534 1690); 152 Curtain Road, Shoreditch, EC2A 3AT.

Zucca
184 Bermondsey Street, SE1 3TQ (7378 6809, www.zuccalondon.com). Bermondsey tube or London Bridge tube/rail. **Open** noon-3pm, 6-10pm Tue-Fri; noon-3.30pm, 6-10pm Sat; noon-3.30pm Sun. **Main courses** £14-£16. **Credit** MC, V. **Map** p403 Q9 ➑ Italian

The formula is simple and impeccably executed: modern Italian food based on top-notch ingredients at competitive prices, served by clued-up staff in contemporary surroundings. Wraparound windows offer great people-watching opportunities, as does the open kitchen running half the length of the room. A forte at Zucca is the fresh pasta; for example, intensely golden-yellow taglierini with fresh peas, lemon and ricotta.

THE CITY

In several parts, the City remains a working-hours kind of place, with venues shut in the evenings and at weekends. Pretty much everywhere is busiest for weekday lunches.

Bodean's
16 Byward Street, EC3R 5BA (7488 3883, www.bodeansbbq.com). Tower Hill tube. **Open** noon-11pm Mon-Sat; noon-10.30pm Sun. **Main courses** £6.75-£19.95. **Credit** AmEx, MC, V. **Map** p403 R7 ➒ American

Sushisamba.

Bodean's now has several branches across town, but this one is very handy for the Tower of London. The schtick remains unchanged at each of them: Kansas City barbecue, plus burgers, hotdogs and steaks, with a small informal upstairs and bigger, smarter downstairs with US sport on TV. The food is decent, generous and very, very meaty – bring an appetite. **Other locations** throughout the city.

£ Fish Central
149-155 Central Street, EC1V 8AP (7253 4970, www.fishcentral.co.uk). Old Street tube/rail or bus 55. **Open** 11am-2.30pm Mon-Sat; 5-11pm Mon-Thur; 5-11pm Fri, Sat. **Main courses** £5.95-£19.95. **Credit** MC, V. **Map** p400 P3 ⑩ **Fish & chips**
A smart restaurant and takeaway in a nondescript shopping precinct in the no-man's land between Barbican and Islington, Fish Central defies all expectations. It's a treat to eat in the white-painted dining room, whether you're having lobster (a perfectly cooked beast, with plenty of juicy flesh) or hake and chips (one of many blackboard specials).

Sushisamba
Floors 38 & 39, Heron Tower, 110 Bishopsgate, EC2N 4AY (3640 7330, www.sushisamba.com). Liverpool Street tube/rail. **Open** 11.30am-2.30pm, 5.30-11pm daily. **Main courses** £4-£24. **Credit** AmEx, MC, V. **Map** p402 R6 ⑪ **Japanese/ Brazilian/Peruvian**
A Japanese-Brazilian-Peruvian restaurant may seem like a fusion too far, but there's logic to the Latin American mash-up, as Peru and Brazil have large Japanese immigrant populations. As well as sushi and sashimi there are South American ceviches

(fresh, light and tongue-zappingly zingy). Elsewhere the menu is peppered with Peruvian ingredients (quinoa salad and large-kernelled Peruvian corn); Brazilian dishes get a look-in with churrasco, a big beefy barbecue. A great glass elevator whisks diners from the ground floor to the 38th with stomach-churning speed, and the views across London are breathtaking. Note that prices are sky-high.

Sweetings
39 Queen Victoria Street, EC4N 4SA (7248 3062, www.sweetingsrestaurant.com). Mansion House tube. **Open** 11.30am-3pm Mon-Fri. **Main courses** £13.50-£32. **Credit** AmEx, MC, V. **Map** p402 P6 ⑫ **Fish & seafood**
No-nonsense British food served in a quintessentially English setting. Diners at the communal tables at the rear can survey walls hung with old cartoons, photos and cricket mementos. Specials might include gull's eggs and smoked salmon pâté while the 'bill of fare' proffers traditional dishes. Sweetings opens only for lunch, takes no bookings, and is full soon after noon, so order a silver pewter mug of Guinness and enjoy the wait. A City classic.

HOLBORN & CLERKENWELL

Home to pioneers of the two huge trends in contemporary London food – modern British at **St John**, the gastropub at the **Eagle** – this is where you'll find a surprising proportion of London's best eating options.

★ Bistrot Bruno Loubet
St John's Square, 86-88 Clerkenwell Road, EC1M 5RJ (7324 4455, www.bistrotbrunoloubet.com).

Farringdon tube/rail. **Open** 7-10.30am, noon-2.30pm, 6-10.30pm Mon-Fri; 7.30-11am, noon-3pm, 6-10.30pm Sat; 7.30-11am, noon-3pm, 6-10pm Sun. **Main courses** £13.50-£21.50. **Credit** AmEx, MC, V. **Map** p400 O4 ⓱ **French**

Bruno Loubet has completely reinvigorated the restaurant at the Zetter hotel (*see p235*) with his classy reimagining of French staples. The menu changes regularly but beetroot ravioli, fried breadcrumbs and sage with rocket salad has become a much-loved standard. The dining room is fairly plain, with quirky touches (including a waiters' station made from refashioned furniture, along with retro lamps). Huge windows look straight out on to St John's Square.

▶ *Bruno Loubet is opening a bar-restaurant, Granary Square Kitchen, at King's Cross in January 2013.*

★ Caravan

11-13 Exmouth Market, EC1R 4QD (7833 8115, www.caravanonexmouth.co.uk). Farringdon tube/rail. **Open** 8-11.30am, noon-10.30pm Mon-Fri; 10am-4pm, 5-10.30pm Sat; 10am-4pm Sun. **Main courses** £4.50-£16. **Credit** AmEx, MC, V. **Map** p400 N4 ⓮ **International**

Caravan has a deceptively casual vibe and industrial-funky design – rough wooden tables, white pipework, light fittings made from old-fashioned cow-milking bottles – plus excellent, inventive food. Expect a parade of unusual, international tastes: peanut butter and blue cheese wontons, salt beef fritters with green beans.

▶ *New branch, Caravan King's Cross (1 Granary Square, N1C 4AA, 7101 7661), has opened in a handsome Grade II-listed granary conversion and has plenty of outdoor tables.*

Le Comptoir Gascon

61-63 Charterhouse Street, EC1M 6HJ (7608 0851, www.comptoirgascon.com). Farringdon tube/rail. **Open** noon-2pm, 7-10pm Mon, Tue, Sat; noon-2pm, 7-11pm Thur, Fri. **Main courses** £8.50-£14. **Credit** AmEx, MC, V. **Map** p400 O5 ⓯ **French**

This small and convivial brick-lined bistro is a deservedly popular offshoot of Club Gascon. Beef onglet, cassoulet and duck rillettes are typical dishes, and well priced; the french fries cooked in duck fat are a must-try. Booking is essential.

▶ *The smarter, similarly excellent Club Gascon (57 West Smithfield, EC1A 9DS, 7796 0600, www.clubgascon.com) is across the meat market.*

Eagle

159 Farringdon Road, EC1R 3AL (7837 1353). Farringdon tube/rail. **Open** noon-11pm Mon-Sat; noon-5pm Sun. *Meals served* 12.30-3pm, 6.30-10.30pm Mon-Fri; 12.30-3.30pm, 6.30-10.30pm Sat; 12.30-3.30pm Sun. **Main courses** £5-£15. **Credit** MC, V. **Map** p400 N4 ⓰ **Gastropub**

Widely credited with being the first gastropub (it opened in 1991), the Eagle is still recognisably a pub with quality food: noisy, often crowded (you'll usually be sharing a table), with no-frills service. The room is dominated by a giant open range at which T-shirted cooks toss earthy grills in theatrical bursts of flame. The kitchen takes up one half of the long bar, with the hearty Med-influenced menu chalked up above it. A short wine list is available by glass or bottle; there are also real ales on tap.

Hix Oyster & Chop House

36-37 Greenhill Rents, off Cowcross Street, EC1M 6BN (7017 1930, www.hixoysterandchophouse.co.uk). Farringdon tube/rail. **Open** noon-3pm, 5.30-11pm Mon-Fri; 5.30-11pm Sat; noon-9pm Sun. **Main courses** £16.50-£36.50. **Set meal** (noon-6.30pm, 10-11pm Mon-Fri; 5-6.30pm, 10-11pm Sat) £17.50 2 courses, £22.50 3 courses. **Credit** AmEx, MC, V. **Map** p400 O5 ⓱ **British**

Although the name tells diners what to expect, there's more to Mark Hix's place than chops and oysters: free-range Goosnargh chicken with wild garlic sauce (for two), for example. But oysters (such as Helford natives or Colchester rocks), chops and steaks feature prominently; accordingly, most diners are male. Puddings are nicely retro, but usually with an imaginative modern twist.

▶ *Mark Hix now has several Hix restaurants to his name in London, plus the meat-centred Tramshed (see p182).*

Modern Pantry

47-48 St John's Square, EC1V 4JJ (7250 0833, www.themodernpantry.co.uk). Farringdon tube/rail. **Open** *Café* 8-11am, noon-10pm Mon; 8-11am, noon-11pm Tue-Fri; 9am-4pm, 6-11pm Sat; 10am-4pm, 6-10pm Sun. *Restaurant* noon-3pm, 6-11pm Tue-Fri; 6-11pm Sat; 10am-4pm Sun. **Main courses** £15.50-£22. **Credit** (both) AmEx, MC, V. **Map** p400 O4 ⓲ **International**

The on-plate magic at the Modern Pantry – fabulous ingredients conjured into inventive combinations by Anna Hansen's very capable kitchen – is beautifully balanced by the calm setting. Spread over two floors, plus some attractive outdoor tables, it's all lovely clean lines in a gentle colour palette of white and grey, and works equally well for brunch or dinner. Pleasant, engaged staff add to the feel-good vibe.

★ Moro

34-36 Exmouth Market, EC1R 4QE (7833 8336, www.moro.co.uk). Farringdon tube/rail or bus 19, 38, 341. **Open** 12.30-10.30pm Mon-Sat. **Main courses** £16.50-£21. **Tapas** £3.50-£14.50. **Credit** AmEx, DC, MC, V. **Map** p400 N4 ⓳ **North African/Spanish**

A meal that excites the senses is a rarity, but Sam and Sam Clark's Moro often manages to produce just that. For a restaurant with a big reputation, its decor is unpretentious, the centrepiece being a simple view

Lima London. See p163.

of the kitchen's big wood-fired oven. You can enjoy tapas at the bar or dine at leisure on the likes of char-grilled sea bass with spiced rice and fried okra in yoghurt with pomegranate from the regularly changing Moorish menu. The drinks list is a point of pride: almost all the wines, sherries and cava come from the Iberian peninsula.

▶ *Next door, Morito (no.32, EC1R 4QE, 7278 7007, closed Sun) is a fine no-booking tapas bar offshoot.*

★ St John

26 St John Street, EC1M 4AY (7251 0848, www.stjohnrestaurant.com). Barbican tube or Farringdon tube/rail. **Open** noon-3pm, 6-11pm Mon-Fri; 6-11pm Sat; 1-3pm Sun. **Main courses** £13.80-£24.50. **Credit** AmEx, DC, MC, V. **Map** p400 O5 ❷⓿ **British**

Fergus Henderson opened the daddy of new-wave British restaurants in the shell of a Smithfield smoke-house in 1995, and hasn't looked back since. 'Black cuttlefish & onions' is a typically terse dish description – but everything you'll eat here will be near-perfect, unfussy celebrations of good food, with emphasis on the underused and the overlooked. Interesting wines are available by the glass at uncynical prices. Although it's a world-famous restaurant, it's completely unstuffy: staff are approachable as well as highly competent. While prices aren't low, they're not excessive for the quality; if you are a bit strapped for cash, having a snack in the airy bar is even cheaper.

▶ *St John has a hotel too; see p244.*

BLOOMSBURY & FITZROVIA

★ Dabbous

39 Whitfield Street, W1T 2SF (7323 1544, www.dabbous.co.uk). Goodge Street or Warren Street tube. **Open** noon-3pm, 5.30-11.30pm Tue-Sat. **Main courses** £11-£16. **Set lunch** (noon-2pm Tue-Sat) £22 3 courses, £26 4 courses. **Set meal** (noon-2pm, 6.30-9pm Tue-Sat) £54 tasting menu. **Credit** AmEx, MC, V. **Map** p396 J5 ❷❶ **International**

Every so often a chef and restaurant pop up, seemingly from nowhere, and cause a sensation. In early 2012, that chef was Ollie Dabbous. His restaurant (pronounced 'Dabbou – the 's' is silent) first wowed the critics, then wowed the public; it's now nigh-on impossible to book a dinner table here (try at lunch). The kitchen offers gossamer-light cooking of the haute school; it's served in a modernist and hard-edged semi-industrial concrete space.

Giaconda Dining Room

9 Denmark Street, WC2H 8LS (7240 3334, www.giacondadining.com). Tottenham Court Road tube. **Open** noon-2.15pm, 6-9.15pm Tue-Fri; 6-9.15pm Sat. **Main courses** £13.50-£19.50. **Cover** £1.50. **Credit** AmEx, MC, V. **Map** p416 X2 ❷❷ **Modern European**

CONSUME

Rainforest Cafe

A WILD PLACE TO SHOP AND EAT ®

HOW ABOUT A WILD DAY OUT?

Located in Piccadilly Circus, Rainforest Cafe is a unique and vibrant restaurant and bar bringing together the sights and sounds of the jungle.

15% DISCOUNT
off your final food bill*

**PERFECT FOR KIDS & BIG KIDS
GREAT FOR GROUPS &
BIRTHDAY CELEBRATIONS**

Book online: www.therainforestcafe.co.uk
Tel: 020 7434 3111
Email: sales@therainforestcafe.co.uk

*Offer valid seven days a week. Maximum party size of 6. Please present to your safari guide when seated. Cannot be used in conjunction with any other offer.

Giaconda is an unpretentious, tiny, dining room – revamped in summer 2012 – serving serious, French-based food. Dishes run from poached ox tongue with parsley, bread and lentil salad to risotto of the day with saffron and squash. Staff are as friendly and unstuffy as the surroundings.

Hakkasan
8 Hanway Place, W1T 1HD (7927 7000, www.hakkasan.com). Tottenham Court Road tube. **Open** *Restaurant* noon-3pm, 6-11pm Mon-Wed; noon-3pm, 6pm-midnight Thur, Fri; noon-4pm, 6pm-midnight Sat; noon-4pm, 6-11pm Sun. *Bar* noon-12.30am Mon-Wed; noon-1.30am Thur-Sat; noon-midnight Sun. **Main courses** £9.50-£58. *Dim sum* £3-£20. **Credit** AmEx, MC, V. **Map** p416 W1 ❷❸ Chinese

Hakkasan's capacious basement marks the spot where Chinese dining in London became hip. The beautiful bar serves classy cocktails; food highlights include the 'classics with a twist' dim sum, while the main menu carries the innovative likes of black truffle roast duck. To drink, only high-rollers should venture on to the designed-to-impress wine list; we recommend the specialist teas. And for celeb-spotting, try the newer Mayfair branch.
Other location 17 Bruton Street, Mayfair, W1J 6QB (7907 1888).

Koba
11 Rathbone Street, W1T 1NA (7580 8825). Goodge Street or Tottenham Court Road tube. **Lunch served** noon-2.15pm, 6-10.30pm Mon-Sat; 6-10.30pm Sun. **Main courses** £8-£11. **Set lunch** £6.50-£11.50. **Set meal** £25-£35. **Credit** AmEx, MC, V. **Map** p396 J5 ❷❹ Korean

From the minimalist decor, to friendly service and meticulously prepared food, Koba is a slick operation. It makes a great spot for anything from a business lunch or special-occasion feast to a casual dinner. The tender barbecued meat, crispy p'ajeon pancakes, attractively stacked Korean-style beef tartare or black sesame ice-cream are all good, especially washed down with a Hite beer.

£ Lantana
13 Charlotte Place, W1T 1SN (7637 3347, www.lantanacafe.co.uk). Goodge Street tube. **Open** 8am-6pm Mon-Fri; 9am-5pm Sat, Sun. **Main courses** £6-£12. **Credit** MC, V. **Map** p396 J5 ❷❺ Café

This cheerful but busy Aussie café is open for breakfast through to lunch (dinner at the end of the week). Sweetcorn fritters with crispy bacon or smoked salmon with lime aïoli is one highlight, the delicious banana bread another. The combination of Monmouth beans and a La Marzocco espresso machine ensures flawless coffee every time.
Other location Salvation Jane, 1 Oliver's Yard, 55 City Road, Shoreditch, EC1Y 1HQ (7253 5273).

★ Lima London
31 Rathbone Place, W1T 1JH (3002 2640, www.limalondon.com). Tottenham Court Road tube. **Main courses** £16-£22. **Set lunch** (Mon-Fri) £20 3 courses. **Credit** AmEx, DC, MC, V. **Map** p397 K5 **Peruvian** ❷❻

The space is understated and becalmed, but the menu reads like a collection of food haikus, and the dishes crafted by chef Virgilio Martinez look like Modernist works of art. Sweet, sharp and hot are the defining tastes here, and they work as brilliant counterpoints to the soft texture and bland flavour of avocado, corn – and potatoes. *Photo p161.*
▶ *The 2012 winner of Time Out's Best New Latin American Restaurant Award.*

Paramount
32nd floor, Centre Point, 101-103 New Oxford Street, WC1A 1DD (7420 2900, www.paramount. uk.net). Tottenham Court Road tube. **Open** 8-10.30am, noon-3pm, 6-11pm Mon-Fri; 11.30am-3pm, 6-11pm Sat; noon-3pm Sun. **Main courses** £15.50-£26. **Credit** AmEx, MC, V. **Map** p416 X1 ❷❼ Modern European

The 360-degree viewing gallery and cocktail bar on the 33rd floor is dramatic, and the restaurant (plus additional bar space) one floor below buzzes with chatter and a sense of occasion. Cooking is ambitious – seared scallop with crab tortellini, curry oil, green apple salad, carrot and coriander purée is a typical starter – but doesn't always succeed. Still, it's not every night you get to eat with a panorama of London before you.
▶ *If dinner prices are too vertiginous, check out the surprisingly reasonable breakfast menu.*

COVENT GARDEN

Delaunay
55 Aldwych, WC2B 4BB (7499 8558, www.the delaunay.com). Covent Garden or Temple tube, or Charing Cross tube/rail. **Open** 7am-midnight Mon-Fri; 8am-midnigh Sat; 11am-11pm Sun. **Main courses** £6.50-£27.50. **Cover** £2. **Credit** AmEx, MC, V. **Map** p397 M6 ❷❽ Brasserie

As you might expect from the younger sibling of the Wolseley (*see p172*), there's glam-factor aplenty here. Its interior echoes European grand brasserie design and the menu celebrates the heritage dishes of Mitteleuropa, particularly Austria, Germany and France, including what might well be London's best sachertorte. The adjacent café (called the Counter) is open throughout the day, supplying snacks such as chicken soup with dumplings. A real treat of a place.
▶ *Winner of Best New Restaurant 2012 in the Time Out Eating Awards.*

£ Dishoom
12 Upper St Martin's Lane, WC2H 9FB (7420 9320, www.dishoom.com). Covent Garden or

CONSUME

Mishkin's.

Leicester Square tube. **Open** 8am-11pm Mon-Thur; 11am-midnight Fri; 10am-midnight Sat; 10am-10pm Sun. **Main courses** £6.50-£11.50. **Credit** AmEx, MC, V. **Map** p416 X3 ㉙ **Pan-Indian**
Dishoom describes itself as 'a Bombay café in London' and is fashioned after that city's 'Irani' caffs, where a cup of spicy masala chai and small eats are always on offer. The place is undoubtedly a crowd-puller, open from breakfast (for egg, bacon or sausage naan rolls with chilli jam), straight through to lunch and dinner, with soups, salads, grills and curries.

£ Food for Thought
31 Neal Street, WC2H 9PR (7836 9072, www.foodforthought-london.co.uk). Covent Garden tube. **Open** noon-8.30pm Mon-Sat; noon-5.30pm Sun. **Main courses** £4.90-£8. **No credit cards**. **Map** p416 Y2 ㉚ **Vegetarian café**
Taking the stairs to this old basement café, where sharing tables is the norm, is like making a steady descent to the 1970s. The menu changes daily, with soup, quiche, three hot mains – perhaps stir-fried veg with rice, or zingy cauliflower, spinach and pea curry – assorted salads, desserts and cakes. Vegan, wheat-free and gluten-free options are marked.

Great Queen Street
32 Great Queen Street, WC2B 5AA (7242 0622). Covent Garden or Holborn tube. **Open** *Restaurant* noon-2.30pm, 6-10.30pm Mon-Sat. *Bar* 5-11.30pm Tue-Sat. **Main courses** £10.80-£22. **Credit** MC, V. **Map** p416 Z2 ㉛ **British**
The staff at this casual eaterie are a helpful young bunch. The ex-pub premises have been tarted up, but not too much, and the food is direct and robust;

expect the likes of Old Spot pork chop with lemon, caper and sage butter. Other plus points: desserts are taken seriously, and wines come in glass, carafe and bottle sizes. In the basement, drinks and snacks are served. As you'd expect, booking is essential here – but later drop-ins can sometimes be accommodated.

★ Hawksmoor Seven Dials
11 Langley Street, WC2H 9JJ (7856 2154, www.thehawksmoor.co.uk). Covent Garden tube. **Open** noon-3pm, 5-10.30pm Mon-Thur; noon-3pm, 5-11pm Fri, Sat; noon-4.30pm Sun. **Main courses** £28-£49.50. **Credit** AmEx, MC, V. **Map** p416 Y3 ㉜ **Steakhouse**
This former fruit warehouse is now carnivore central in Will Beckett and Huw Gott's confidently expanding empire, and the bar a place of pilgrimage in its own right for cocktail geeks. It's expensive, but the good news is the express menu (ideal pre-theatre when tables are easy to snare) offers two courses for £22 and three courses for £25 – and still allows enjoyment of fine Ginger Pig Longhorn ribeye (a more-than-strictly-needed 250g), and bone marrow with onions.
Other locations 157 Commercial Street, Shoreditch, E1 6BJ, 7247 7392; 10 Basinghall Street, City, EC2V 5BQ (7397 8120).

Kopapa
32-34 Monmouth Street, WC2H 9HA (7240 6076, www.kopapa.co.uk). Covent Garden or Leicester Square tube. **Open** 8.30-11am, noon-10.45pm Mon-Fri; 10am-3pm, 3.30-10.45pm Sat; 10am-3pm, 3.30-9.30pm Sun. **Main courses** £10.50-£20. **Credit** AmEx, DC, MC, V. **Map** p416 X2 ㉝ **Fusion**

CONSUME

Co-owner Peter Gordon, Britain's best exponent of fusion cooking, oversees a menu that reassures with fry-ups, burgers and steak sandwiches, while dazzling with combinations such as burrata, mint, black vinegar and medjool dates. You can order small plates to share, or traditional courses. A gloriously handy place you'll want to return to.

£ Mishkin's
25 Catherine Street, WC2B 5JS (7240 2078, www.mishkins.co.uk). Covent Garden tube. **Open** 11am-11.30 Mon-Sat; noon-10.30pm Sun. **Main courses** £3-£12. **Credit** AmEx, DC, MC, V. **Map** p416 Z3 ❸ **American**
Another hot destination from restaurateurs Richard Beatty and Russell Norman (of Spuntino acclaim), this 1950s-themed New York diner has a weathered-retro look. The menu is divided into sandwiches, meatballs, all-day brunch and supper choices, salads, sides and extras. The fat pork hot dog comes with a tumble of sauerkraut and vinegary jalapeños.

★ Opera Tavern
23 Catherine Street, WC2B 5JS (7836 3680, www.operatavern.co.uk). Covent Garden tube. **Open** noon-3pm, 5-11.30pm Mon-Sat; noon-3pm Sun. **Tapas** £2.55-£14.95. **Credit** AmEx, DC, MC, V. **Map** p416 Z3 ❸ **Spanish/Italian tapas**
Perfect for pre- or post-theatre suppers, this former pub now has a ground-floor bar and a first-floor restaurant serving a winning mix of Spanish- and Italian-inspired tapas (similar to highly regarded siblings Dehesa and Salt Yard). However, sustainable British produce plays an increasing role in the repertoire. There's an appealing choice of sherries, with all ten available by the glass, starting at £4.50.

J Sheekey
28-34 St Martin's Court, Leicester Square, WC2N 4AL (7240 2565, www.j-sheekey.co.uk). Leicester Square tube. **Open** noon-3pm, 5.30pm-midnight Mon-Sat; noon-3.30pm, 6-11pm Sun. **Main courses** £13.50-£39.50. **Credit** AmEx, DC, MC, V. **Map** p416 X4 ❸ **Fish & seafood**
Sheekey's – now owned by the Caprice group – remains a theatreland institution. Dishes aren't cheap, but the range, freshness and presentation are impressive; Sheekey's fish pie is a renowned favourite. Waiting staff are smartly suited and courteous, but not especially personable.
▶ *Next door, the J Sheekey Oyster Bar (nos.33-34, WC2N 4AL) serves a similar menu to customers sitting casually at the counter, and with an expanded choice of oysters.*

£ Wahaca
66 Chandos Place, WC2N 4HG (7240 1883, www.wahaca.co.uk). Covent Garden or Leicester Square tube. **Open** noon-11pm Mon-Sat; noon-10.30pm Sun. **Main courses** £3.60-£9.95. **Credit** AmEx, MC, V. **Map** p416 Y4 ❸ **Mexican**

This steadily expanding chain made its debut in 2005. Neither pork pibil tacos nor black bean and cheese quesadilla tend to last long, and the Michelada (a hangover-trouncing beer concoction with lime and spicy tomato juice) verges on the addictive. The decor is cheerfully ad hoc, creating a relaxed feel.
Other locations throughout the city.

SOHO & CHINATOWN

Chinatown stalwarts such as **Mr Kong** (21 Lisle Street, 7437 7341) and **Wong Kei** (41-43 Wardour Street, 7437 8408) still ply their reliable Anglo-Cantonese trade, but there's more gastronomic excitement offered by the newer likes of **Barshu** (*see p167*) or, on Ganton Street a little to the west, **Cha Cha Moon** (*see p168*).

Opera Tavern.

CONSUME

The HACHÉ Experience

TimeOut London

★ ★ ★ ★ ★

CAMDEN · CHELSEA · CLAPHAM · SHOREDITCH

★ Arbutus

63-64 Frith Street, W1D 3JW (7734 4545, www.arbutusrestaurant.co.uk). Tottenham Court Road tube. **Open** noon-2.30pm, 5-11pm Mon-Thur; noon-2.30pm, 5-11.30pm Fri, Sat; noon-3pm, 5.30-10.30pm Sun. **Main courses** £17-£18. **Credit** AmEx, MC, V. **Map** p416 W2 **❸ Modern European**

A cool (and sometimes noisy) space, serving a menu of seasonal dishes that hit the spot every time. Cod with crisp chicken wings and pink grapefruit, ginger and honey preserve is a favourite, belly pork with lentils is another popular dish, and the set lunch menu is great value for money. Every bottle on the carefully selected wine list is available by 250ml carafe, a much-praised move that offers a real chance to experiment. *Photo p168.*

▶ *Sister restaurant to Arbutus, Wild Honey (12 St George Street, W1S 2FB, 7758 9160, www.wildhoneyrestaurant.co.uk), is also great value for lunch.*

Barrafina

54 Frith Street, W1D 4SL (no phone, www.barrafina.co.uk). Leicester Square or Tottenham Court Road tube. **Open** noon-3pm, 5-11pm Mon-Sat; 1-3.30pm, 5.30-10.30pm Sun. **Tapas** £2-£18.50. **Credit** AmEx, MC, V. **Map** p416 W2 **❸ Spanish tapas**

Barrafina is very much a bar, the only seating being stools around an L-shaped bar in gleaming steel, behind which chefs display their skills in grilling seafood and assembling complex salads with stunning panache. The tapas, supplemented by larger specials, are exceptional. No bookings are taken, but staff deal with the constant flow in a friendly and efficient manner.

▶ *For a more formal – and bookable – Spanish experience, try sibling restaurant Fino (33 Charlotte Street, entrance on Rathbone Street, W1T 1RR, 7813 8010).*

Barshu

28 Frith Street, W1D 5LF (7287 6688, www.bar-shu.co.uk). Leicester Square or Tottenham Court Road tube. **Open** noon-11pm Mon-Thur, Sun; noon-11.30pm Fri, Sat. **Main courses** £8.90-£28.90. **Credit** AmEx, MC, V. **Map** p416 W3 **❹ Chinese**

When it comes to Sichuan cooking, the gang of three – Barshu, Ba Shan and Baozi Inn – lead the London pack. Barshu, the original restaurant, is spread over three floors, adorned with intricate wooden carvings. Offal plays a big role, from pig's intestines to chicken gizzards, with all arriving bathed in searingly hot chilli.

▶ *For more unusual (and cheap) Chinese food in Soho, try Barshu's siblings Ba Shan (24 Romilly Street, W1D 5AH, 7287 3266) and Baozi Inn (25 Newport Court, WC2H 7JS, 7287 6877).*

La Bodega Negra

16 Moor Street, W1D 5NH (7758 4100, www.labodeganegra.com). Leicester Square tube. **Open** *Café* noon-midnight Mon-Sat; noon-11pm Sun. *Restaurant* 6pm-midnight Mon-Sat; 6-10.30pm Sun. Main courses £8-£16. **Credit** AmEx, MC, V. **Map** p416 X2 **❹ Mexican**

This new transatlantic import is the London outpost of the NYC-based La Esquina, an ultra-trendy downtown café-taqueria. It's an upstairs-downstairs affair; with a ground-level café (entrance on Moor Street) and a downstairs restaurant and bar (entrance in Old Compton Street), where the main action happens. The underground space is like a Hammer Horror interpretation of a Mexican Day of the Dead fiesta. Foodwise, think tacos, tostaditas, steaks and grills. *Photo p169.*

Bocca di Lupo

12 Archer Street, W1D 7BB (7734 2223, www.boccadilupo.com). Piccadilly Circus tube. **Open** 12.30-3pm, 5.30-11pm Mon-Sat; noon-4pm Sun. **Main courses** £5-£25.50. **Credit** AmEx, MC, V. **Map** p416 W3 **❹ Italian**

This busy, informal Italian restaurant has a lively open kitchen and tapas-style menu of regional specialities. Select one small dish from several different categories on the menu (raw and cured, fried, pastas and risottos, soups and stews, roasts, and so on) and you'll enjoy a balanced meal. If you're feeling adventurous, try the Calabrian sanguinaccio dessert – a bit like a chocolate and black pudding spread.

▶ *The same team runs the fine gelateria Gelupo, down the road at no.7 (7287 5555, www.gelupo.com).*

Burger & Lobster

36 Dean Street, W1D 4PS (7432 4800, www.burgerandlobster.com). Leicester Square tube. **Open** noon-10.30pm Mon-Sat; noon-10pm Sun. **Main courses** £20. **Credit** AmEx, MC, V. **Map** p416 W3 **❹ American**

Proof that less can be more, the late 2011 launch of Burger & Lobster, with its no-nonsense, three-item menu of burger, lobster, or lobster roll, was a runaway hit. This second branch – a large Soho diner tricked out with lobster-red banquettes – is no less popular. Food costs £20, an all-in price that includes

---

INSIDE TRACK CHINATOWN

For atmosphere, drop in for a 'bubble tea' (sweet, icy, full of balls of jelly and slurped up with a straw) at late-night fave **HK Diner** (22 Wardour Street, 7434 9544). If you need to eat especially late, Cantonese old-stager the **New Mayflower** (68-70 Shaftesbury Avenue, 7734 9207) is open nightly until 4am.

Arbutus. *See p167.*

CONSUME

a huge carton of thin-cut fries and a side salad: you won't go hungry here. The burger is good, but for ultimate value, choose the lobster. The Snickers-in-a-tub pud is rich chocolate mousse layered on to a devilish peanut-studded salt caramel. Cheery staff smooth the ride along.

£ Cha Cha Moon
15-21 Ganton Street, W1F 9BN (7297 9800, www.chachamoon.com). Oxford Circus or Piccadilly Circus tube. **Open** 11.30am-11pm Mon-Thur; 11.30am-11.30pm Fri, Sat; noon-10.30pm Sun. **Main courses** £6-£8. **Set meal** £15 2 courses, £18 3 courses. **Credit** AmEx, MC, V. **Map** p416 U3 ❹❹ **Chinese**
Business is still brisk and service has improved at Cha Cha Moon, but standards can be inconsistent. Taiwan noodles with brisket of beef and mustard greens was delicious, though slightly overcooked. We also liked sichuan wun tun, filled with prawns and chicken, which was pepped up by a garlicky chilli sauce. But it was the Wen Wen cocktail, a mix of peach and raspberry with a dash of vodka, that stole the limelight.

Ceviche
17 Frith Street, W1D 4RG (7292 2040, www.cevicheuk.com). Leicester Square tube. **Open** noon-11.30pm Mon-Sat; noon-10.30pm Sun. **Tapas** £6.75-£13.50. **Credit** AmEx, MC, V. **Map** p416 W2 ❹❺ **Peruvian**
Peruvian food may be terra incognita for many Londoners, but the country's indigenous ingredients provide common ground. Corn, potatoes and the signature dish of ceviche – raw citrus-marinated fish (or veg), served here in seven versions – are the stars of the menu. Anticuchos (barbecued skewers of fish, chicken or beef), typical street food, are a good option too. Ceviche is a good-time place with a colourful interior and a buzzing pisco bar at the front.

★ £ Hummus Bros
88 Wardour Street, W1F 0TH (7734 1311, www.hbros.co.uk). Oxford Circus or Tottenham Court Road tube. **Open** noon-10pm Mon-Wed, Sun; noon-11pm Thur-Sat. **Main courses** £6.65-£8.45. **Credit** AmEx, MC, V. **Map** p416 W3 ❹❻ **Café**
'Give peas a chance' is the cheeky slogan for this laid-back snack bar devoted to houmous. This Soho shop has shiny red communal tables, bench seating and large windows. You'll get a bowl of silky-smooth houmous, with a dollop of tahini, a sprinkling of paprika and two warm wholemeal pittas (regular size – just one pitta with the small), plus a topping of your choice. Chunky slow-cooked beef, perhaps, or juicy guacamole.
Other locations 37-63 Southampton Row, Bloomsbury, WC1B 4DA (7404 7079); 128 Cheapside, the City, EC2V 6BT (7726 8011).

La Bodega Negra. *See p167.*

£ Koya

*49 Frith Street, W1D 4SG (7434 4463,
www.koya.co.uk). Tottenham Court Road tube.*
Open noon-3pm, 5.30-10.30pm Mon-Sat; noon-
3pm, 5.30-10pm Sun. **Main courses** £6.70-£14.70.
Credit AmEx, MC, V. **Map** p416 W3 ❹
Japanese

You can easily spot London's favourite Japanese
noodle bar by the queue regularly winding from its
entrance (bookings not accepted). Fear not – there's
a fairly rapid turnover at the shared wooden tables,
and the food is well worth the wait. The menu stars
udon noodles in all their glorious possibilities: hot in
soup, cold and served with hot soup, or cold served
with cold sauce. There are also rice dishes and an
impressive list of salads and sides.

Manchurian Legends

*16 Lisle Street, WC2H 7BE (7287 6606,
www.manchurianlegends.com). Leicester Square or
Piccadilly Circus tube.* **Open** 11am-11pm Mon-Wed,
Sun; 11am-11.30pm Thur-Sat. **Main courses**
£7.50-£12.80. **Set lunch** £5.50-£11 2 courses. **Set
dinner** £18.80-£23.80 2 courses. **Credit** MC, V.
Map p416 W3 ❹ Chinese

Manchurian Legends offers faithful renditions of
the hearty rib-sticking cuisine of China's frosty
north. Robust stews are a highlight, and the yang
rou chuan (the classic Muslim lamb kebabs that are
popular street food throughout the People's
Republic) are the best we've had in London. In July
2012, Manchurian Legends moved to this Lisle
Street address, and now occupies a pleasant if cosy
tented dining room.

Pollen Street Social

*8 Pollen Street, W1S 1NQ (7290 7600, www.
pollenstreetsocial.com). Oxford Circus tube.* **Open**
noon-midnight Mon-Sat. **Main courses** £25.50-
£34. **Credit** AmEx, MC, V. **Map** p416 U2 ❹
Modern European

Behind the narrow street frontage of Pollen Street
Social lies an Alice in Wonderland complex of
restaurant rooms showcasing the well-honed skills
of Jason Atherton. Much has been written in praise
of Atherton's food, and his creations continue to surprise and delight – sorbet of beetroot and strawberry
with wild fruit and wafers of basil ash meringue is
a typical treat.

★ £ Princi

*135 Wardour Street, W1F 0UF (7478 8888,
www.princi.co.uk). Leicester Square or Tottenham
Court Road tube.* **Open** 8-11am, noon-11.30pm
Mon-Fri; 8am-4.30pm, 5-11.30pm Sat; 8.30am-
4.30pm, 5-10pm Sun. **Main courses** £6.50-
£12.50. **Credit** AmEx, MC, V. **Map** p416 W3
❺ Bakery-café

The southern reaches of Wardour Street are home
to several bakers these days, giving the super-glam-
orous Princi a run for its money, but this Italian
panetteria has upped its game accordingly and still
reigns supreme. Presentation is classy. Wide glass
cases are filled with pretty Italian pâtisserie and
desserts. Further down the long counter, a great
selection of focaccia, pizza and hearty salads features perfect Italian ingredients. Note that it can be
a nightmare finding a seat once you've done the self-
service shuffle.

CONSUME

Chef's Table

Where London's best cooks go to eat.

John Torode is well known for *MasterChef*, and also runs the **Luxe** (109 Commercial Street, E1 6BG, 7101 1751). 'My favourite restaurant is the **River Café** (*see p186*),' he says. 'I think it's an extraordinary institution. The food changes depending on what's in season: whenever you walk in the door, you know you're going to eat very good food.' And after a day in the kitchen, Torode says he's taken by the tapas approach to dining. 'When you work in the sort of environment we do, you don't want heavy meals. You want to go somewhere and eat something very tasty, but not very much of it. I love **Bocca di Lupo** (*see p167*). The sort of place you can go late at night, get a lovely glass of wine – perfect. I'm certainly not going out for seven-course degustation menus.'

Hereford Road.

Thomasina Miers, executive chef and co-founder of the **Wahaca** (*see p165*) chain of restaurants and writer on Mexican cooking, recommends the welsh rarebit at the Soho **Hix** (66-70 Brewer Street, W1F 9UP, 020 7292 351), and in keeping with the 'grazing and sharing' trend, a visit to nearby **Spuntino** (*see right*) for deep-fried olives and sliders. 'It only has 26 covers, and serves delicious New York-style food. It's perfect for an early supper or late lunch: the atmosphere is great and so are the cocktails. I also love the laid-back cooking at **Hereford Road** (*see p177*), the luxury of the River Café and the great, seasonal food at **Corrigan's** (*see p172*).'

It's the lucky Londoner who doesn't have to travel far to a favourite restaurant, and

Marcus Wareing, chef patron of the Gilbert Scott in the St Pancras Hotel, is among them. 'I love **Chez Bruce** (2 Bellevue Road, Wandsworth, SW17 7EG, 8672 0114, www.chezbruce.com) – I can walk there, it's got a Michelin star but is very relaxed, and the quality of food is always high.'

Yotam Ottolenghi's London restaurant/takeaways are acclaimed, and he's recently opened **NOPI** (21 Warwick Street, W1B 5NE, 7494 9584, www.nopi-restaurant.com) in Soho. But he's another chef who prefers the down-to-earth over the starry when eating out. 'One place I really like going to is **Mangal Ocakbaşı** (*see p177* **Inside Track**), a Turkish place in Dalston. I love the grilled lamb chops and the mixed salad with tomato and cucumber.'

Mangal Ocakbaşı.

CONSUME

£ Spuntino

61 Rupert Street, W1D 7PW (no phone, www.spuntino.co.uk). Piccadilly Circus tube. **Open** 11am-midnight Mon-Sat; noon-11pm Sun. **Main courses** £5.50-£10. **Credit** AmEx, MC, V. **Map** p416 W3 ❹ **North American**

At lunchtime at least, the long queues that used to discourage visits to this no-phone, no-bookings and not-exactly-large retro American joint have dissipated. It's a carefully constructed London take on a New York take on road-food and Italian classics. Sliders amp up the flavour; pulled pork inauthentically but deliciously packs in crackling and pickled apple.

► *Owner Russell Norman also runs the excellent Polpo mini-chain (www.polpo.co.uk).*

★ 10 Greek Street

10 Greek Street, W1D 4DH (7734 4677, www. 10greekstreet.com). Tottenham Court Road tube. **Open** noon-10.45pm Mon-Sat. *Lunch served* noon-2.30pm, *tapas served* 2.30-5.30pm, *dinner served* 5.30-10.45pm. **Main courses** £12-£19. **Tapas** £3-£7. Credit AmEx, DC, MC, V. **Map** p416 W2 ❷ **Modern European**

There's no flashy name, no flashy decor. Yet this small Soho newcomer punches well above its weight, delivering exceptional cooking in relaxed, buzzy surroundings. At face value, the menu – Modern Brit via the Med – seems fairly straightforward, but the results are impressive, from steamed clams and mussels in a fragrant parsley and leek broth, flecked with chilli and slivers of garlic to berry-packed champagne jelly with creamy, heavily perfumed lavender ice-cream over a crunchy, biscuity base. You can book for lunch, but not for dinner.

► *Winner of the 2012 Time Out Best New No Bookings Restaurant award.*

OXFORD STREET & MARYLEBONE

★ £ Busaba Eathai

8-13 Bird Street, W1U 1BU (7518 8080, www. busaba.com). Bond Street tube. **Open** noon-11pm Mon-Thur; noon-11.30pm Fri, Sat; noon-10pm Sun. **Main courses** £6.20-£10.90. **Credit** AmEx, MC, V. **Map** p396 G6 ❸ **Thai**

All the branches of this handsome Thai fast food canteen are excellent and busy, but this one is superbly located for Oxford Street shoppers. The interior combines shared tables and bench seats with a touch of oriental mystique, and the dishes are always intriguing and reliably good.

Other locations throughout the city.

Fairuz

3 Blandford Street, W1U 3DA (7486 8108, www.fairuz.uk.com). Baker Street or Bond Street tube. **Open** noon-11pm Mon-Sat; noon-10.30pm Sun. **Main courses** £12.95-£22. *Set meze* £19.95. *Cover* £1.50. **Credit** AmEx, MC, V. **Map** p396 G5 ❺ **Middle Eastern**

The combination of Lebanese food, neighbourhood-taverna surroundings and West End location has proved enduringly popular for this long-standing Marylebone favourite. Its collection of meze – smooth houmous, zingy fuul moukala (broad beans with olive oil, lemon and coriander), tabouleh, spinach fatayer – is well executed.

£ La Fromagerie

2-6 Moxon Street, W1U 4EW (7935 0341, www.lafromagerie.co.uk). Baker Street or Bond Street tube. **Open** 8am-7.30pm Mon-Fri; 9am-7pm Sat; 10am-6pm Sun. **Main courses** £6-£15. **Credit** AmEx, MC, V. **Map** p396 G5 ❺ **Café**

Patricia Michelson's high-end deli-café has always ploughed its own, very stylish, culinary furrow, and its communal tables are often packed with devotees. The basic menu, which includes a classy ploughman's lunch, is supplemented by a separate breakfast offer (own-made baked beans, granola with posh French yoghurt) and a 'kitchen menu' from 12.30pm.

Other locations 30 Highbury Park, Highbury, N5 2AA (7359 7440).

£ Roti Chai

3-4 Portman Mews South, W1H 6HS (7408 0101, www.rotichai.com). Marble Arch tube. **Meals served** noon-10.30pm Mon-Sat; 12.30-9pm Sun. **Main courses** £4.50-£8.50. **Credit** AmEx, MC, V. **Map** p396 G6 ❺ **Pan-Indian**

The name provides the clue: Roti Chai (bread, tea) is dedicated to serving inexpensive, café-style Indian food. It does so with some panache, in a stylish, contemporary setting. The menu offers street snacks from across India: from the crisp bhel pooris of Mumbai beaches, to Gujarati steamed dokhla (a savoury sponge well matched with coconut chutney). Railway lamb curry was a light, punchy dish incorporating chunks of potatoes, while a Bengali fish curry had been pungently flavoured with mustard seeds. Service can be a bit distracted.

PICCADILLY CIRCUS & MAYFAIR

Bentley's Oyster Bar & Grill

11-15 Swallow Street, W1B 4DG (7734 4756, www.bentleys.org). Piccadilly Circus tube. **Open** *Oyster Bar* 7.30-11am, noon-midnight Mon-Fri; noon-midnight Sat; noon-10pm Sun. *Restaurant* noon-3pm, 5.30-11pm Mon-Fri; 5.30-11pm Sat. **Main courses** *Oyster Bar* £9-£26.50. *Restaurant* £19-£29. **Credit** AmEx, MC, V. **Map** p416 V4 ❼ **Fish & seafood**

A deep reverence for heritage, combined with unsurpassed culinary credentials, has meant that chef-patron Richard Corrigan's 2005 overhaul of this 1916

CONSUME

grande dame has been an indisputable success. Upstairs is the formal Grill restaurant, but we prefer the more relaxed ground-floor oyster bar. As well as oysters, there's a tempting range of dishes – from scallop ceviche to classic fish pie.

► *Corrigan also runs the estimable Corrigan's Mayfair (28 Upper Grosvenor Street, W1K 7EH, 7499 9943), which serves high-class British food.*

Momo

25 Heddon Street, W1B 4BH (7434 4040, www.momoresto.com). Piccadilly Circus tube. **Open** noon-5.30pm, 6.30-11.30pm Mon-Sat; 6.30-11pm Sun. **Main courses** £17-£28. **Credit** AmEx, DC, MC, V. **Map** p416 U3 ⑤⑧ **North African**
Still London's most glamorous Moroccan restaurant, Momo's soundtrack of classic Maghrebi beats and attractive young francophone waiting staff create a seductive buzz. Order the near-perfect couscous: silky fine grains served with vegetables in a light cumin-scented broth, with tender, juicy chicken, plump golden raisins, chickpeas and harissa – all served separately so you can mix them as you please.

Parlour

1st floor, Fortnum & Mason, 181 Piccadilly, W1A 1ER (7734 8040, www.fortnumandmason.co.uk). Green Park or Piccadilly Circus tube. **Open** 10am-8pm Mon-Sat; noon-5.30pm Sun. **Ice-cream** £8-£15. **Credit** AmEx, MC, V. **Map** p416 V5 ⑤⑨ **Ice-cream**
David Collins's quirky design for this café is all ice-cream and chocolate tones, with retro kitchenette seating. It's a great place to meet friends, though prices are high. The best option is an ice-cream 'flight': you'll get three scoops of your choice, served with wonderfully silky Amedei dark- or milk-chocolate sauce for £10. The range of Viennese cakes is another crowd-pleaser.

Sketch: The Parlour

9 Conduit Street, W1S 2XJ (0870 777 4488, www.sketch.uk.com). Oxford Circus tube. **Open** 10am-9pm Mon-Sat. *Tea served* 1-6.30pm Mon-Sat. **Main courses** £4-£8.50. Set tea £10.50-£32. **Credit** AmEx, MC, V. **Map** p416 U3 ⑥⓪ **Café**
Of the three parts of Pierre Gagnaire's legendarily expensive Sketch, which also includes destination dining at the Gallery and the Lecture Room's haute-beyond-haute cuisine, Parlour appeals the most for its tongue-in-cheek sexiness. Gagnaire's menu runs from cooked breakfasts to amazing cake creations.

★ Theo Randall at the InterContinental

1 Hamilton Place, Park Lane, W1J 7QY (7409 3131, www.theorandall.com). Hyde Park Corner tube. **Open** noon-3pm, 5.45-11pm Mon-Fri; 5.45-11pm Sat. **Main courses** £28-£38. **Credit** AmEx, DC, MC, V. **Map** p398 G8 ⑥① **Italian.**

Since 2007, following a long stint as head chef at the renowned River Café, Theo Randall has been turning out peerless Italian cuisine in this Mayfair hotel restaurant. Outstanding-value set lunches and early/late suppers allow diners to sample a sublime experience at unusually democratic pricing(£27 two courses, £33 three courses). The unfussy, smiling staff make the experience a relaxing one.

★ Wolseley

160 Piccadilly, W1J 9EB (7499 6996, www.thewolseley.com). Green Park tube. **Open** 7am-midnight Mon-Fri; 8am-midnight Sat, Sun. *Tea served* 3-6.30pm Mon-Fri; 3.30-5.30pm Sat; 3.30-6.30pm Sun. **Main courses** £6.75-£32.75. Set tea £9.75-£32.50. **Cover** £2. **Credit** AmEx, DC, MC, V. **Map** p416 U5 ⑥② **Brasserie**
Self-described 'café-restaurant in the grand European tradition', the Wolseley is one of London's premier destination restaurants, as popular for power breakfasts as it is for birthday celebrations. The high-ceilinged room is a handsome homage to Viennese coffeehouses. The main menu has Mittel european leanings (excellent chopped liver and glorious, generous boiled salt beef with light herb dumplings) along with many brasserie classics (note-perfect soufflé suisse, steak frites, crustacea).

► *Owners Chris Corbin and Jeremy King have in 2012 also opened the Delaunay (see p163) and Brasserie Zédel (20 Sherwood Street, W1F 7ED, 7734 4888) and have more ventures in the pipeline.*

WESTMINSTER & ST JAMES'S

Cinnamon Club

Old Westminster Library, 30-32 Great Smith Street, SW1P 3BU (7222 2555, www.cinnamonclub.com). St James's Park or Westminster tube. **Open** 7.30-9.30am, noon-2.45pm, 6-10.45pm Mon-Fri; noon-2.45pm, 6-10.45pm Sat. **Main courses** £15-£35. **Credit** AmEx, DC, MC, V. **Map** p399 K9 ⑥③ **Indian**
The former Westminster Library, a glorious Grade II-listed red-brick building, holds one of London's top Indian restaurants. Executive chef Vivek Singh creates elegant, innovative dishes such as venison and prune kofta (meatballs), served over creamy black lentils and wilted spinach. It's a pity that the dining room itself is bland, and the lighting overly bright.
Other locations Cinnamon Kitchen, 9 Devonshire Square, the City, EC2M 4WY (7626 5000); Cinnamon Soho, 5 Kingly Street, Soho, W1B 5PF (7437 1664).

Inn the Park

St James's Park, SW1A 2BJ (7451 9999, www.innthepark.com). St James's Park tube. **Open** 8am-11pm Mon-Fri; 9am-11pm Sat, Sun. *Tea served* 3-4.30pm daily **Main courses** £14.50-£22.50. **Credit** MC, V. **Map** p399 K8 ⑥④ **British**

It's all about the location at this beautifully appointed and designed café-restaurant. The seasonal British cooking isn't always up to expectations, especially given the prices, but there is plenty on the plus side: staff are lovely, and the setting (overlooking the duck lake, with trees all around and the London Eye in the distance) is really wonderful.

National Dining Rooms

Sainsbury Wing, National Gallery, Trafalgar Square, WC2N 5DN (7747 2525, www.peyton andbyrne.co.uk). Charing Cross tube/rail. **Open** 10am-5.30pm Mon-Thur, Sat, Sun; 10am-8.30pm Fri. **Main courses** *Bakery* £6.50-£15.50. *Restaurant* £14.50-£21.50. **Credit** AmEx, MC, V. **Map** p416 X4 ⊕ **British**
Oliver Peyton's restaurant in the Sainsbury Wing of the National Gallery (*see p98*) offers far better food than run-of-the-mill museum fare – lemon sole with clams, summer greens and samphire, perhaps – albeit at a price. The few window seats have prized views over Trafalgar Square, and the bakery side of the operation ably fulfils the cakes-and-a-cuppa role of the traditional museum café.
▶ *The National Café, on the east side of the Gallery (entrance on St Martin's Place), has a continental brasserie atmosphere and similarly good food.*

Sake No Hana

23 St James's Street, SW1A 1HA (7925 8988, www.sakenohana.com). Green Park tube. **Open** noon-3pm, 6-11pm Mon-Thur; noon-3pm, 6-11.30pm Fri; noon-4pm, 6-11.30pm Sat.

Main courses £6.50-£28.50. **Credit** AmEx, MC, V. **Map** p398 J8 ⊕ **Japanese**
Japanese architect Kengo Kuma has created an interior at Sake No Hana that MC Escher would be proud of. The menu is lengthy, but staff are happy to guide you through it. Food is far from cheap and can be a little inconsistent, but dining here is definitely an experience. If you're out for a special occasion, stop off at the futuristic ground-floor bar beforehand for a decadent saké cocktail.

CHELSEA

Gallery Mess

Saatchi Gallery, Duke of York's HQ, King's Road, SW3 4LY (7730 8135, www.saatchi-gallery.co.uk). Sloane Square tube. **Open** 10am-11.30pm Mon-Sat; 10am-7pm Sun. **Main courses** £13-£18.50. **Credit** AmEx, MC, V. **Map** p395 F11 ⊕ **Brasserie**
Attached to the Saatchi Gallery (*see p109*), Gallery Mess is one of the best pitstops in Chelsea. You can sit inside surrounded by modern art, but the grounds outside – littered with portable tables until 6pm, if the weather's fair – can be a better option in summer. There's a simple breakfast menu of pastries, eggs and toast or fry-up served until 11.30am, then lunch and dinner take over, with the expected salads, pastas and burgers joined by more ambitious daily specials.

Medlar

438 King's Road, SW10 0LJ (7349 1900, www. medlarrestaurant.co.uk). Fulham Broadway tube or bus 11, 22. **Open** noon-3pm, 6.30-10.30pm

Mazi. *See p177.*

CONSUME

daily. **Set lunch** (Mon-Fri) £26 3 courses; (Sat, Sun) £30 3 courses. **Set dinner** £39.50 3 courses. **Credit** AmEx, MC, V. **Map** p395 D12
⑥⑧ Modern European
Medlar's seasonal menu and wine list are close to perfection. Roast hake with summer bean ragoût and palourde clams followed by raspberry and frangipane tart are typical of the dishes relished by Chelsea's lunching ladies. Staff are exemplary and the experience very civilised.

Tom's Kitchen
27 Cale Street, SW3 3QP (7349 0202, www. tomskitchen.co.uk). Sloane Square or South Kensington tube. **Open** 8-11.30am, noon-2.30pm, 6-10.30pm Mon-Fri; 10am-12.15pm, 12.30-3.30pm, 6-9.30pm Sat, Sun. **Main courses** £9-£29.50. **Credit** AmEx, MC, V. **Map** p395 E11
Brasserie ⑦⓪
White-tiled walls, vast expanses of marble and a busy open kitchen ensure Tom Aikens' place sounds full even when it isn't – for weekend lunches it can often be packed. The big draw here is the pancake: well over an inch thick and almost as big as the serving plate, it's one of London's best, filled with blueberries and drizzled with maple syrup. Lunch and dinner menus make the most of the wood-smoked oven, spit-roast and grill. Expect hearty, big-tasting comfort food.
▶ *For similar food and prices that match the superb river views, try Tom's Kitchen & Terrace at Somerset House.*

KNIGHTSBRIDGE & SOUTH KENSINGTON

★ Bar Boulud
Mandarin Oriental Hyde Park, 66 Knightsbridge, SW1X 7LA (7201 3899, http://danielnyc.com/ barboulud_hub.html). Knightsbridge tube. **Open** noon-11pm Mon-Sat; noon-10pm Sun. **Main courses** £8.25-£29. **Credit** AmEx, MC, V. **Map** p393 F8 **⑦⓪ Brasserie**
Bar Boulud may be within the luxurious Mandarin Oriental Hotel (like Dinner by Heston Blumenthal, *see below*), but you don't have to be minted to eat at this superb bistro. A winning informality emanates from the room, which is always busy. Burgers here are among the best in town, and new this year is the 'BB', where the patty is topped by a layer of short-ribs (braised in red wine), a slice of foie gras and a truffle garnish; it's one hell of a burger and not to be missed.

Dinner by Heston Blumenthal
Mandarin Oriental Hyde Park, 66 Knightsbridge, SW1X 7LA (7201 3833, www.dinnerbyheston. com). Knightsbridge tube. **Open** noon-2.30pm, 6.30-10.30pm daily. **Main courses** £26-£38. Set lunch (Mon-Fri) £36 3 courses. **Credit** AmEx, DC, MC, V. **Map** p393 F8 **⑦⓵ British**

INSIDE TRACK
ICE-CREAM EXPERTISE

The last couple of years have seen a boom in proper ice-cream parlours of all persuasions, filling what had been a sad gap in London's culinary landscape. The most experimental ice-cream makers are **Chin Chin Laboratorists** (49 Camden Lock Place, NW1 8AF, 07885 604284; truffle popcorn ice-cream) who make their ices to order using liquid nitrogen, but we're also big fans of **La Gelatiera** (27 New Row, WC2N 4LA 7836 9559; chocolate and chilli); **Gelupo** (7 Archer Street, W1 7AU, 7287 5555; ewe's milk ricotta with sour cherry), **Dri Dri Gelato** (189 Portobello Road, W11 2ED, 3490 5027; pink grapefruit sorbet); **Oddono's** (14 Bute Street, SW7 3EX, 7052 0732; salted caramel) and newcomer **Gelateria 3bis** (*see p158*).

Housed on the ground floor of the Mandarin Oriental hotel, Dinner is a little corporate in appearance. The menu, devised by Heston Blumenthal and his right-hand man Ashley Palmer-Watts (who heads the kitchen), takes its essence from historical British dishes. With a bit of innovation, these are transformed into something befitting a fine-dining establishment. *Photo p176.*

£ Lido Café
South side of the Serpentine, Hyde Park, W2 2UH (7706 7098, www.companyofcooks.com). Hyde Park Corner or Marble Arch tube. **Open** 8am-5.30pm daily (times may vary). **Main courses** £4.60-£12.80. **Credit** MC, V. **Map** p393 E8 **⑦② Café**
The Lido Café is a year-round haven with a menu ranging from cooked breakfasts, to soups and salads to cheeseburger and chips – and plenty of outdoor seating. Children's plates include pizzettas and fish fingers. Ice-cream sundaes cost £5.15, and there's a good range of drinks too.
▶ *At the eastern end of the lake, the Serpentine Bar & Kitchen (7706 8114, www.serpentine barandkitchen.com) also has great lakeside tables.*

Nahm
Halkin, Halkin Street, SW1X 7DJ (7333 1234, www.nahm.como.bz). Hyde Park Corner tube. **Open** noon-2.30pm, 7-11pm Mon-Fri; 7-11pm Sat; 7-10pm Sun. **Main courses** £14.50-£23.50. **Credit** AmEx, MC, V. **Map** p398 G9 **⑦③ Thai**
David Thompson's restaurant in the Halkin hotel (*see p252*) is wood-panelled and quietly stylish – if somewhat corporate – and lightened by a wall of windows overlooking a leafy garden. Service combines total professionalism with warmth. Dishes

CONSUME

such as scallop salad with Asian celery, thai basil and peanut nahm jim sauce show why this is so much more than just a hotel restaurant.

Racine

239 Brompton Road, SW3 2EP (7584 4477, www.racine-restaurant.com). Knightsbridge or South Kensington tube. **Open** noon-3pm, 6-10.30pm Mon-Fri; noon-3.30pm, 6-10.30pm Sat; noon-3.30pm, 6-10pm Sun. **Main courses** £16.50-£28.50. **Credit** AmEx, MC, V. **Map** p395 E10 **74** **French**

Handily placed between the Knightsbridge shops and the South Kensington museums, Racine comes close to the French bistro ideal. The mirrors, leather banquettes, white linen and gleaming glassware are as familiar and comforting as the sight of 'daube de boeuf à la bourguignonne, pomme mousseline' on the carte. Charming staff ensure the place runs like clockwork.

Yashin

1A Argyll Road, W8 7DB (7938 1536, www.yashinsushi.com). High Street Kensington tube. **Open** noon-3pm, 6-11pm daily. **Set meals** £6.20-£24.50. **Credit** AmEx, MC, V. **Map** p394 B9 **75** **Sushi**

In a discreet location just off Kensington High Street, Yashin has a modern eclectic look and superior sushi. Behind the green-tiled sushi counter, a neon sign states 'without soy sauce – but if you want to', as the chefs disapprove of the salty sauce masking their sushi. Instead, the industrious throng

of itamae (sushi chefs) finish their nigiri with a drizzle of truffle oil, a quick blast from a blowtorch or some other carefully considered garnish.

★ Zuma

5 Raphael Street, SW7 1DL (7584 1010, www.zumarestaurant.com). Knightsbridge tube. **Open** *Restaurant* noon-2.30pm, 6-11pm Mon-Thur; noon-3pm, 6-11pm Fri; 12.30-3.30pm, 6-11pm Sat; 12.30-3.30pm, 6-10.30pm Sun. *Bar* noon-11pm Mon-Fri; 12.30-11pm Sat; 12.30-10.30pm Sun. **Main courses** £14.80-£70. **Credit** AmEx, DC, MC, V. **Map** p395 F9 **76** **Japanese**

It's hard to believe there is a recession when you enter Zuma. The bar and dining room of this ultra-chic destination buzzes with well-heeled diners. The interior design is earthy, with stone flooring and cedar-wood furniture. Sushi and sashimi are of premier league quality, the raw tuna belly and sea urchin being notable gems. Presentation is eye-catching. An impressively diverse saké and wine list tops it all off.

PADDINGTON & NOTTING HILL

Assaggi

1st floor, 39 Chepstow Place, W2 4TS (7792 5501). Bayswater, Notting Hill Gate or Queensway tube. **Open** 12.30-2.30pm, 7.30-11pm Mon-Fri; 1-2.20pm, 7.30-11pm Sat. **Main courses** £19.80-£29.50. **Credit** MC, V. **Map** p404 Z5 **77** **Italian**

Dinner by Heston. See p175.

It's some years since Assaggi was the hottest restaurant in London but dining here remains a deservedly popular treat. It has an off-duty Notting Hill vibe and above-a-pub setting; decor is simple, with white walls and an old wooden floor. The menu is much as it always has been, varying a little with the seasons but including perennials such as tagliatelle with herbs and walnuts, and grilled veal chop.

★ Le Café Anglais
8 Porchester Gardens, W2 4DB (7221 1415, www.lecafeanglais.co.uk). Bayswater tube. **Open** noon-3.30pm, 6.30-10.30pm Mon-Thur; noon-3.30pm, 6.30-11pm Fri, Sat; noon-3.30pm, 6.30-10pm Sun. **Main courses** £10.50-£26.50. *Cover* £1.85. **Credit** AmEx, MC, V. **Map** p392 B6 ❼⓼
Modern European
Rowley Leigh's brasserie-restaurant has been around since 2008, but feels much more established. In a lovely art deco-influenced room in stately old Whiteley's, Café Anglais is very assured. Delicious unfaddy food, charming service and a sense of occasion make this a model restaurant.

Hereford Road
3 Hereford Road, W2 4AB (7727 1144, www.herefordroad.org). Bayswater tube. **Open** noon-3pm, 6-10.30pm Mon-Fri; noon-3.30pm, 6-10.30pm Sat; noon-4pm, 6-10pm Sun. **Main courses** £10-£21. **Credit** AmEx, MC, V. **Map** p404 Z5 ❼⓽ **British**
Hereford Road has the assurance of somewhere that's been around much longer than it actually has. It's an easy place in which to relax, with a mixed crowd and a happy buzz. The menu changes on a daily basis, but dishes such as braised rabbit leg with fennel and bacon are sure-fire treats.

★ Ledbury
127 Ledbury Road, W11 2AQ (7792 9090, www.theledbury.com). Westbourne Park tube. **Open** 6.30-10.15pm Mon; noon-2pm, 6.30-10.15pm Tue-Sat; noon-2.30pm, 7-10pm Sun. **Set meals** £30-£32.50. **Credit** AmEx, MC, V. **Map** p404 Y4 ❽⓪ **French**
On a busy weeknight, the Ledbury has all the relaxed bustle and hum of a hit brasserie, yet as the international crowd and full reservations book show, this edge-of-Notting-Hill spot has become a place of pilgrimage for lovers of fine dining. Chef Brett Graham is arguably Australia's most successful culinary export, and his dishes have thrillingly layered flavours: witness a pre-dessert of olive oil panna cotta with hibiscus-poached peach and sweet cicely granita.

Mazi
12-14 Hillgate Street, W8 7SR (7229 3794, www.mazi.co.uk). Notting Hill tube. **Open** noon-3.30pm, 6.30-11pm Mon-Fri; noon-11pm Sat; noon-10pm Sun. **Main courses** £6-£25. **Credit** AmEx, MC, V. **Map** p392 A7 ❽⓵ **Greek**

INSIDE TRACK EAT TURKISH

From Dalston Kingsland station north to Stoke Newington Church Street is the Turkish and Kurdish heart of Hackney: both **19 Numara Bos Cirrik** (34 Stoke Newington Road, N16 7XJ, 7249 0400) and **Mangal Ocakbaşı** (10 Arcola Street, E8 2DJ, 7275 8981, www.mangal1.com) serve superb grilled meats, marinated and cooked to perfection.

As properly Greek as you'll find in London, this Notting Hill newcomer showcases both traditional dishes and progressive cooking. The wine list is entirely Greek, sourced from new-wave producers as well as classic appellations. Even Mazi's retsina is in the modern style: only lightly resinated and very palatable. Benchmark dishes such as Greek salad (horiátiki) were near-perfect; matsata – rabbit stew with fresh pasta – also had correctly rustic flavours. It's a simply but attractively furnished place, with eager, attentive service. *Photo p173.*

£ Taqueria
139-143 Westbourne Grove, W11 2RS (7229 4734, www.taqueria.co.uk). Notting Hill Gate tube. **Open** noon-11pm Mon-Thur; noon-11.30pm Fri, Sat; noon-10.30pm Sun. **Main courses** £4.10-£6.60. **Credit** MC, V. **Map** p404 Z4 ❽⓶ **Mexican**
Mexican food is on the ascendancy in London, and this cheerful café serving hearty, classic (if rather plebeian) dishes, is among the city's best. The use of authentic ingredients is the key; Mexican comfort food is its métier. Old Mexican film posters adorn the walls.

NORTH LONDON

The new area behind King's Cross station is shaping up to be a gastro-destination, with an excellent set of restaurants and a healthy street food scene (*see p71* **Hip to be a Square**).

★ Bull & Last
168 Highgate Road, Kentish Town, NW5 1QS (7267 3641, www.thebullandlast.co.uk). Kentish Town tube/rail then bus 214, C2, or Gospel Oak rail then bus C11. **Open** noon-11pm Mon-Thur; 9am-midnight Fri, Sat; 9am-10.30pm Sun. **Main courses** £14-£28. **Credit** AmEx, MC, V.
Gastropub
It may seem as though a country pub complete with abundant hanging baskets has been plopped on to busy Highgate Road, but inside lies an edgy kitchen working sustainable practices into culinary magic. The kitchen cures its own meats and fish, churns a dazzling range of ices and even the oatcakes on the cheeseboard are made on site. A brief, punchy

CONSUME

Shrimpy's.

CONSUME

international wine list starts at £16 a bottle, while a pleasing choice of hand-pumped ales changes frequently and is strong on London breweries.

£ Haché

24 Inverness Street, Camden, NW1 7HJ (7485 9100, www.hacheburgers.com). Camden Town tube. **Open** noon-10.30pm Mon-Wed; 10.30am-11pm Thur-Sat; noon-10pm Sun. **Main courses** £6.95-£17.95. **Credit** AmEx, MC, V. **Map** p404 Y2 ⑬ **Burgers**

A smart burger joint with a distinctly continental approach, Haché even offers the option of brioche buns, or French cheeses to match the meat. The menu is much more creative than most, with chicken, duck and good vegetarian alternatives. Frites are thin and properly crisp, and all the other details are correct. Service is cheery and the atmosphere jolly.
Other locations 329 Fulham Road, Chelsea, SW10 9QL (7823 3515); 153 Clapham High Street, Clapham, SW4 7SS (7738 8760).

Manna

4 Erskine Road, Chalk Farm, NW3 3AJ (7722 8028, www.mannav.com). Chalk Farm tube or bus 31, 168. **Open** 6.30-10.30pm Tue-Fri; noon-3pm, 6.30-10.30pm Sat, Sun. **Main courses** £8-£20. **Credit** AmEx, MC, V. **Map** p404 W2 ⑭ **Vegetarian**

Few customers are confirmed vegetarians, which is a tribute to the quality and heartiness of the cooking here. Portions are large, and help compensate for the steep pricing. Dishes range from veggie caff staples

to creative concoctions such as tempeh-filled cabbage rolls with Thai-style dipping sauce. The dining space consists of a tiny conservatory and a cosy, curtained snug for more intimate encounters.

Made in Camden

Roundhouse, Chalk Farm Road, Camden NW1 8EH (7424 8495, www.madeincamden.com). Chalk Farm tube. **Open** noon-2.30pm, 6-10.30pm Mon-Fri; 10.30am-3pm, 6-10.30pm Sat; 10.30am-3pm, 6-10pm Sun. **Main courses** £4.40-£16. Set lunch £10 2 courses. **Credit** AmEx, MC, V. **Map** p404 W1 ⑮ **Brasserie**

A note-perfect mix of concert posters, panoramic windows, dark wood and red seating is the setting for the confident fusion dishes of Camden Town boy Josh Katz (ex-Ottolenghi). Small plates – sumac and lemon-pepper calamares with pumpkin jam and sriracha chilli aïoli, or grilled chicken with miso carrot purée, pickled cucumber, shiitake and coconut – are consistently good. The weekend brunch menu features a global mix of eggy and cheesy things.

Market

43 Parkway, Camden, NW1 7PN (7267 9700, www.marketrestaurant.co.uk). Camden Town tube. **Open** noon-2.30pm, 6-10.30pm Mon-Sat; 1-3.30pm Sun. **Main courses** £13-£16. **Credit** AmEx, DC, MC, V. **Map** p404 Y2 ⑯ **British**

With old school chairs, open brickwork and blackboard specials, this slim Parkway unit doffs its cap to the gastropub while sporting a more formal look. Daily changing menus start with British traditions and ingredients and veer to the Mediterranean on occasions. Market's signature single-crusted pies, such as steak and ale, are great, but need to be served with a spoon. Service is brisk, but comes with a smile.

£ Ottolenghi

287 Upper Street, Islington, N1 2TZ (7288 1454, www.ottolenghi.co.uk). Angel tube or Highbury & Islington tube/rail. **Open** 8am-11pm Mon-Sat; 9am-7pm Sun. **Main courses** £8-£12. **Credit** AmEx, MC, V. **Map** p400 O1 ⑰ **Bakery-café**
Ottolenghi is more than an inviting bakery. Behind the pastries piled in the window is a comparatively prim deli counter with lush salads, available day and evening, eat-in or take away. This is a brilliant and stylish daytime café, but people book well in advance for dinner too – the inventive fusion menu (currently only available at this branch) is fabulous. **Other locations** 1 Holland Street, Kensington, W8 4NA (7937 0003); 63 Ledbury Road, Notting Hill, W11 2AD (7727 1121); 13 Motcomb Street, Belgravia, SW1X 8LB (7823 2707).
▶ *For more Yotam Ottolenghi food in a restaurant setting, try Nopi (21-22 Warwick Street, W1B 5NE, 7494 9584).*

Shrimpy's

The King's Cross Filling Station, Goods Way, King's Cross, N1C 4UR (8880 6111, www. shrimpys.co.uk). King's Cross or St Pancras tube/rail. **Open** 11am-10.30pm daily. **Main courses** £15-£20. **Credit** AmEx, MC, V. **Map** p397 L2 ⑱ **North American**
Shrimpy's occupies an ex-filling station destined for demolition in 2014 – until then it's a strikingly designed, hip destination in the newly revitalised area behind King's Cross station. The menu pays homage to down-home American food: glazed burger bun filled with deep-fried soft-shell crab is typical.

★ Trullo

300-302 St Paul's Road, Islington, N1 2LH (7226 2733, www.trullorestaurant.com). Highbury & Islington tube/rail. **Open** *Bar* 6-10.30pm Thur-Sat. *Restaurant* 6.30-10.15pm Mon-Thur; 12.30-2.45pm, 6.30-10.15pm Fri, Sat; 12.30-3pm Sun. **Main courses** £14-£20. **Tapas** £2.50-£10. *Both* **Credit** MC, V. **Italian**
A super-popular local serving some of the best food in Islington. The menu packs a lot of interest into a short space, and changes daily: a sprightly salad of broad bean, pecorino, little gem lettuce and mint, say, followed by pappardelle with beef shin ragù. Desserts run from melon granita to caprese chocolate torte.

EAST LONDON

Spitalfields, Shoreditch and Hoxton are key nightlife districts and well furnished with bars; *see pp200-202.* The curry restaurants of Brick Lane rarely live up to their reputation.

Brawn. *See p180.*

CONSUME

CONSUME

£ Albion

2-4 Boundary Street, Shoreditch, E2 7DD (7729 1051, www.albioncaff.co.uk). Shoreditch High Street rail. **Open** 8am-11pm daily. **Main courses** £8.75-£12.50. **Credit** AmEx, MC, V. **Map** p401 R4 ➒
British
Almost every new London restaurant seems to be mining the vein of nostalgia for traditional British cuisine these days, but few have pulled it off as well as Terence Conran's stand-out 'caff'. The menu mixes up a bit of gastropub, a bit of café and a bit of hotel (breakfast served all day and a late-night menu featuring welsh rarebit and hot chocolate with shortbread). From the beef-dripping chips to the old-school puddings, it's reliably good.
▶ *For the hotel upstairs, see p255* **Boundary**.

★ Brawn

49 Columbia Road, Bethnal Green, E2 7RG (7729 5692, www.brawn.co). Hoxton rail or bus 48, 55. **Open** 6-11pm Mon; noon-3pm, 6-11pm Tue-Sat; noon-4pm Sun. **Main courses** £6-£17. **Credit** MC, V. **Map** p401 S3 ➓ **Modern European**
Brawn is nicely pitched to appeal to a hip east London crowd without alienating other diners. The decor is unfussy, as is the terse menu: 'Cod's roe £4', for example, doesn't do justice to the deluxe taramasalata that appears. Unmissable crêpes with salted caramel butter are among the puddings. 'Natural' wine is showcased on the drinks list. *Photo p179*.

★ £ Brick Lane Beigel Bake

159 Brick Lane, Spitalfields, E1 6SB (7729 0616). Liverpool Street tube/rail or bus 8. **Open** 24hrs daily. **Main courses** £1.95-£5.95. **No credit cards. Map** p401 S4 ➒ **Jewish**
This little East End institution rolls out perfect bagels (egg, cream cheese, salt beef, at seriously low prices), good bread and moreish cakes. Even at 3am, fresh-baked goods are pulled from the ovens at the back; no wonder the queue for bagels trails out the door when the local bars and clubs close.

£ Container Café

View Tube, the Greenway, Marshgate Lane, Stratford, E15 2PJ (07702 125081, www.the viewtube.co.uk). Pudding Mill Lane DLR. **Open** 9am-5pm Mon-Fri; 10am-6pm Sat, Sun. **Main courses** £4-£7. **Credit** AmEx, MC, V. **Café**
Right opposite the Olympic Stadium, and on the Greenway walking and cycling route, this is a perfect location from which to view the Queen Elizabeth Olympic Park. It's also no slouch on the refreshments front, offering toothsome cakes, snacks and sandwiches and properly made coffees in an attractive wood-furnished room.

Eyre Brothers

70 Leonard Street, Shoreditch, EC2A 4QX (7613 5346, www.eyrebrothers.co.uk). Old Street tube/rail. **Open** noon-2.45pm, 6.30-10.45pm Mon-Fri; 7-10.45pm Sat. **Main courses** £12-£21. **Credit** AmEx, DC, MC, V. **Map** p401 Q4 ➒
Portuguese/Spanish
David and Robert Eyre's restaurant is dedicated to the sterling ingredients and punchy flavours of the Iberian peninsula, and successfully manages to appeal to both sides of the Shoreditch/City demographic. The signature dish remains the acorn-fed Ibérico pork fillet, marinated in smoked paprika, thyme and garlic, then grilled medium rare. At the back is a long wooden bar: perch here for tapas or to sample the all-Iberian drinks list.

Hackney Pearl

11 Prince Edward Road, Hackney Wick, E9 5LX (8510 3605, www.thehackneypearl.com). Hackney Wick rail. **Open** 8am-11pm Tue-Fri; 10am-11pm Sat, Sun. **Main courses** £10-£14. **Credit** MC, V. **Café-bar**
This affable all-day café is hidden among the artists' studios and semi-industrial sprawl of Hackney Wick. There's an airy main room with an open kitchen, and a sunny terrace spilling on to the street. Pitched as an all-purpose neighbourhood hangout, it's a welcoming spot for coffee and own-made cake, drinks, or a proper meal from the short, weekly-changing menu.

Jamie's Italian

Unit 17, 2 Churchill Place, Canary Wharf, E14 5RB (3002 5252, www.jamieoliver.com). Canary Wharf tube/DLR. **Open** 11.30am-11pm Mon-Fri; noon-11pm Sat; noon-10.30pm Sun. **Main courses** £6.25-£17.50. **Credit** AmEx, DC, MC, V. **Italian**
Jamie Oliver's likeable chain of mid-price restaurants serves crowd-pleasing dishes such as grilled free-range chicken on tomato sauce with olives, black squid-ink angel hair pasta with scallops, capers, garlic and chilli, and burger Italiano. All are punchily flavoured, thoughtfully sourced and served with panache. The acoustics conspire against but don't spoil the enjoyment.
Other locations throughout the city.

£ Needoo Grill

87 New Road, Whitechapel, E1 1HH (7247 0648, www.needoogrill.co.uk). Whitechapel tube. **Open** 11.30am-11.30pm daily. **Main courses** £6-£6.50. **Credit** AmEx, MC, V. **Pakistani**
Just round the corner from the perennially heaving, ever-popular Tayyabs, Needoo Grill is a civilised provider of Punjabi grills, curries and snacks. The relative lack of queues also means it's a useful and speedy spot for takeaway. Everything is good value, and there's no corkage on BYO.

★ £ E Pellicci

332 Bethnal Green Road, Bethnal Green, E2 0AG (7739 4873). Bethnal Green tube/rail or bus 8. **Open** 7am-4pm Mon-Sat. **Main courses** £6.40-£8.20. **No credit cards. Café**

Poppies.

You go to Pellicci's as much for the atmosphere as the food. Opened in 1900, and still in the hands of the same family, this Bethnal Green landmark has chrome and Vitrolite outside, wood panelling with deco marquetry, Formica tabletops and stained glass within – it earned the café a Grade II listing in 2005. Recommended are the fry-ups, spaghetti 'Toscana', Friday fish and chips, and desserts.

Pizza East
56 Shoreditch High Street, Shoreditch, E1 6JJ (7729 1888, www.pizzaeast.com). Shoreditch High Street rail. **Open** noon-11pm Mon-Wed; noon-midnight Thur; noon-1am Fri; 10am-1am Sat; 10am-11pm Sun. **Main courses** £8-£16. **Credit** AmEx, MC, V. **Map** p401 R4 ❸ **Pizza**
The huge room, filled with big tables of noisy diners, and hard, industrial decor, serves amazing pizzas; bases are perfectly crusty around the outside, thin and gorgeously saturated in the middle, and toppings employ fresh, quality ingredients. Antipasti and salads are also good.
Other locations 310 Portobello Road, Ladbroke Grove, W10 5TA (8969 4500); 53-79 Highgate Road, Kentish Town, NW5 1TL (3310 2000).
► *Downstairs in the lower basement, Concrete serves up food, booze and varied club nights until midnight (1am or 2am at weekends).*

★ Poppies
6-8 Hanbury Street, Spitalfields, E1 6QR (7247 0892, www.poppiesfishandchips.co.uk). Aldgate East tube or Liverpool Street tube/rail. **Open** 11am-11.30pm Mon-Sat; 11am-10.30pm Sun. **Main courses** £9.90-£15.90. **Credit** AmEx, MC, V. **Map** p401 S5 ❸ **Fish & chips**

Poppies serves fish and chips as they were meant to be, but probably never were. Fine fillets of haddock, plaice, rock and the rest arrive in crisp batter, flesh firm to the fork, chips soft but never limp. The premises follow a bright, retro theme, with a 1950s jukebox kicking out doo-wop hits. The takeaway counter at the door even serves your tucker in a traditional twist of newspaper.

Princess of Shoreditch
76-79 Paul Street, Shoreditch, EC2A 4NE (7729 9270, www.theprincessofshoreditch.com). Old Street tube/rail or bus 55. **Open** noon-11pm Mon-Sat; noon-10pm Sun. **Main courses** £11.50-£19. **Credit** AmEx, MC, V. **Map** p401 Q4 ❸ **Gastropub**
Indeed a princess among gastropubs, somewhere you'll feel equally comfortable scoffing (Cornish brill with pea purée and black pudding) or quaffing (local cask ales, a respectable list of wines by the glass, bottle and carafe, bloody marys). The no-nonsense ground floor is geared towards drinkers; there's a smart dining room up a spiral staircase.
► *The same owners also run the Lady Ottoline in Bloomsbury and the Pig & Butcher in Islington.*

£ Song Que
134 Kingsland Road, Shoreditch, E2 8DY (7613 3222, www.songque.co.uk). Hoxton rail. **Open** noon-3pm, 5.30-11pm Mon-Sat; 12.30-11pm Sun. **Main courses** £4.80-£14.80. **Credit** MC, V. **Map** p401 R3 ❸ **Vietnamese**
There are several restaurants of note in the Vietnamese hotspot on Kingsland Road, but the stalwart Song Que is somewhere that stands out over repeat visits. The menu is a formidably extensive

list of dishes from the north and south of Vietnam, but classics are brilliantly executed. The beef pho – warming, subtly spiced, generous with the meat – is one of the best bowlfuls in London.

£ Tayyabs
83 Fieldgate Street, Whitechapel, E1 1JU (7247 9543, www.tayyabs.co.uk). Aldgate East or Whitechapel tube. **Open** noon-11.30pm daily. **Main courses** £6.50-£25.80. **Credit** AmEx, MC, V. **Pakistani**

Every year this Punjabi grill seems to be bigger and busier – as of 2012, the cellar and first floor of the former pub have been renovated and pressed into service to accommodate the endless stream of diners. Tayyabs serves some of the best and cheapest Indian food in London: to start try juicy seekh kebabs or hot, charred, gingery grilled lamb chops; for mains, full-flavoured curries accompanied by tandoor-fresh breads. An unmissable London dining experience, despite the crush and queues.

Tramshed
32 Rivington Street, Shoreditch, EC2A 3LX (7749 0478, www.chickenandsteak.co.uk). Old Street tube/rail. **Open** noon-10pm Mon-Wed; noon-11pm Thur, Fri; noon-10.30pm Sat; noon-9.30pm Sun. **Main courses** £13.50-£20. **Credit** AmEx, MC, V. **Map** p401 R4 ㊲ **British**

Chef Mark Hix has always had a thing for meat, and his latest venture takes things to extremes. To be precise, you can have roast chicken for one or to share, steak, chicken salad, or steak salad. (A few 'bar snax' include ox cheek croquettes and – the sole veggie option – radishes with celery salt.) All this happens in a turn-of-the-century Grade II-listed industrial building, a vast room with a soaring ceiling. In pride of place is a work by Damien Hirst: a formaldehyde-filled tank containing a preserved bullock and rooster. Winner of Time Out's Best New Meat Restaurant award 2012.

★ Viajante
Town Hall Hotel, Patriot Square, Bethnal Green, E2 9NF (7871 0461, www.viajante.co.uk). Bethnal Green tube/rail or Cambridge Heath rail. **Open** 6-9.30pm Mon-Thur; noon-2pm, 6-9.30pm Fri-Sun. **Set lunch** £35-£80. **Set dinner** £70-£95. **Credit** AmEx, MC, V. **Pan-Asian & fusion**

Globetrotting culinary adventurer Nuno Mendez is chef-patron at Viajante, still a must-visit destination for style-conscious gastronauts following its stellar debut in 2010. A meal here doesn't come cheap, but it's a fun ride through extraordinary combinations of flavour and texture, no doubt influenced by Mendez's spell at El Bullí. His newer Corner Room, in the same hotel, is a no-booking, lower-price exponent of the same inquiring spirit, whose quietly arty, first-floor corner space belies its provocative flavours.

Whitechapel Gallery Dining Room
Whitechapel Gallery, 77-82 Whitechapel High Street, E1 7QX (7522 7888, www.whitechapelgallery.org/dining-room). Aldgate East tube. **Open** noon-3pm Tue; noon-3pm, 6-9.30pm Wed-Sat; noon-3.45pm Sun. **Main courses** £5-£15. **Credit** AmEx, MC, V. **Map** p403 S6 ㊳ **Modern European**

The warm, intimate Dining Room is a welcome contrast to the urban grit of Whitechapel High Street. The menu, overseen by star chef Angela Hartnett, makes a lively read. Dishes run from canapé-size bites of whipped goat's curd with roast garlic to sea trout with caponata. Ice-creams and sorbets are wonderful, especially the salted caramel – and they're only £1.65 a scoop.

Yi-Ban
London Regatta Centre, Dockside Road, Docklands, E16 2QT (7473 6699, www.yi-ban.co.uk). Royal Albert DLR. **Open** noon-11pm Mon-Sat; 11am-10.30pm Sun. **Main courses** £4-£30. **Credit** AmEx, MC, V. **Chinese**

Yi-Ban's exterior is little more than a large concrete rectangle with a glass door. But inside is a bustling space with a spectacular view of planes taking off and landing across the dock at City Airport. The regular menu has all the standards you'd expect, from ma po bean curd to lemon chicken, but ask about the one with a fine range of hotpots, as well as frogs' legs, intestines, bitter melon and tripe. There's an extensive dim sum menu, too. Note that the restaurant gets very busy at weekends, so do book.

SOUTH-EAST LONDON

No 67
South London Gallery, 67 Peckham Road, Peckham, SE5 8UH (7252 7649, www.southlondongallery.org). Bus 12, 36 or 171. **Open** 9-11.30am, noon-3.30pm Tue; 9-11.30am, noon-3.30pm, 6.30-10pm Wed-Fri; 10am-3.30pm, 6.30-10pm Sat; 10am-3.30pm Sun. **Main courses** £9.80-£13.80. **Credit** AmEx, MC, V. **Café**

Hip as it is, this area isn't blessed with smart restaurants serving innovative food, which makes No 67 such a revelation. Housed in the refurbished South London Gallery, by day it's a delightful café serving tarts, salads, nice cakes and good coffee (and weekend brunches). In the evenings (Wed-Sat), it becomes an intimate dining room serving dishes such as morcilla-stuffed pork belly and plaice with samphire.

Old Brewery
Pepys Building, Old Royal Naval College, Greenwich, SE10 9LW (3327 1280, www.oldbrewerygreenwich.com). Cutty Sark DLR. **Open** 11am-11pm daily. **Main courses** £8.50-£24.50. **Credit** MC, V. **Map** p405 X1 ㊳ **British**

By day, the Old Brewery is a café; by night, a restaurant. There's a small bar, with tables outside in a large walled courtyard – a lovely spot in which to test the 50-strong beer list – but most of the action is in the vast, high-ceilinged main space, beneath a wave-like structure of empty bottles and a wall of shiny copper vats. The short menu highlights provenance and seasonality (blue cheese salad with Kentish cobnuts), with matching beers suggested for each dish.

Buenos Aires Café

17 Royal Parade, Blackheath, SE3 0TL (8318 5333, www.buenosairesltd.com). Blackheath rail. **Open** noon-3pm, 6-10.30pm Mon-Fri; noon-4pm, 6-10.30pm Sat, Sun. **Main courses** £9-£22. **Credit** MC, V. Argentinian

This relaxed restaurant is the perfect place to while away an afternoon gazing across the heath – aim for a table outside or on the ground floor rather than in the tiny basement bar area. High ceilings and white-washed walls are countered by reassuring clutter; every inch of the walls is covered in framed prints and wine racks well stocked with Argentinian reds.

Flavoursome steaks from grass-fed Argentinian cattle dominate the menu, backed up by a number of vegetarian dishes and a pizza list.

SOUTH-WEST LONDON

For a rich mix of cheap eats and fun atmosphere, check out Brixton Village (*see p208*), where the choice includes a Pakistani café and a burger joint, as well as **Franco Manca**.

Brunswick House Café

30 Wandsworth Road, Vauxhall Cross, Vauxhall SW8 2LG (7720 2926, www.brunswickhouse cafe.co.uk). Vauxhall tube/rail. **Open** 8.30am-5pm Mon; 8.30am-5pm, 6.30-10.30pm Tue-Fri; 10am-5pm, 6.30-10.30pm Sat; 10am-5pm Sun. **Main courses** £4-£16. **Credit** MC, V. Café

A lone Georgian mansion, marooned amid a tangle of A-roads near Vauxhall station – but handy for Tate Britain. It shares its premises with architectural

Tramshed.

salvage company Lassco, whose finds furnish the bar and dining room. A daily changing one-page menu has a focus on seasonal ingredients: a feather-light soufflé of new season asparagus, sprinkled with pea shoots and chives, perhaps. Come the week-end, the emphasis shifts to sturdy brunches.

Bistro Délicat

124 Northcote Road, SW11 6QU (7924 3566, www.bistrodelicat.com). Clapham Junction rail then bus 319. **Open** 9.30am-3pm, 6-10.30pm Tue-Fri; 9.30am-4pm, 6-10.30pm Sat; 9.30am-4pm Sun. **Main courses** £11-£18. Set meal (11.30am-3pm Tue-Fri) £13.50 2 courses, £17.50 3 courses. **Credit** AmEx, MC, V. **Austrian**

Resembling the best sort of new-wave Viennese *beisl* (neighbourhood brasserie), Bistro Délicat has styl-ish, simple decor (white tiled walls at the front, black at the rear) and a welcoming vibe. The Austro-French menu runs from breakfast to dinner (steak frites, nürnberger sausages with own-made sauer-kraut, first-class bouillabaisse, a superior beef goulash, served with spätzle and pickled gherkin. Coffee is taken seriously and carefully made.

Earl Spencer

260-262 Merton Road, Southfields, SW18 5JL (8870 9244, www.theearlspencer.co.uk). Southfields tube. **Open** 4-11pm Mon-Fri; 11am-midnight Sat; 11am-10.30pm Sun. **Main courses** £9.50-£16. **Credit** AmEx, MC, V. **Gastropub**

Every neighbourhood should have an Earl Spencer – somewhere that appeals to anyone who appreciates inviting food and audible conversation; it's so devoid of faddishness, and focused on decent grub, that the epithet 'gastropub' – with its increasing connotations of the assembly line – doesn't quite do it justice. Justin Aubrey's menu changes daily and is posted online like clockwork. Such care extends to the dishes (mor-eish duck salad, delicious eton mess) themselves.

★ £ Franco Manca

4 Market Row, Electric Lane, Brixton, SW9 8LD (7738 3021, www.francomanca.co.uk). Brixton tube/rail. **Open** noon-5pm Mon-Wed; noon-10pm Thur-Fri; 11.30am-10pm Sat; noon-5pm Sun. **Main courses** £5-£7.50. **Credit** MC, V. **Pizza**

One of the originators of Brixton's über-cool market scene, Franco Manca keeps it simple. The restau-rant's Italian owner, Giuseppe Mascoli, pays homage to Neapolitan pizzerias, serving delicious slow-rise sourdough-crust pizzas (the best – and the most rea-sonably priced – in London). There are frequent queues, and the tables have a fairly rapid turnover. **Other locations** 144 Chiswick High Road, W4 1PU (8747 4822); Unit 2003, The Balcony, Westfield Stratford City, E20 1ES (8522 6669).

Lawn Bistro

67 High Street, Wimbledon, SW19 5EE (8947 8278, www.thelawnbistro.co.uk). Wimbledon tube/rail/tram. **Open** noon-2.30pm, 6.30-10.30pm Mon-Sat; noon-3pm Sun. **Set lunch** £14.95-£19.50 2 courses, £18.95-£22.50 3 courses. **Set dinner** £32.50 2 courses, £33.50 3 courses. **Credit** MC, V. **French**

CONSUME

Bistro Délicat.

Chef Ollie Couillaud runs this modern French restaurant in the heart of Wimbledon Village. The cooking, grounded in France, but with forays into Britain, Spain and North Africa, is very accomplished. Menus are fixed-price and lunch is a particular bargain, as it offers many of the same dishes that are available in the evening, alongside more casual fare such as croque monsieur with big chips and salad.

WEST LONDON

Clarke's
124 Kensington Church Street, Kensington, W8 4BH (7221 9225, www.sallyclarke.com). Notting Hill Gate tube. **Open** 12.30-2pm, 6.30-10pm Mon-Fri; noon-2pm, 6.30-10pm Sat; noon-2pm Sun. **Main courses** £22.50-£24. **Set dinner** £40.50 3 courses. **Credit** AmEx, DC, MC, V. **Map** p404 Z6 ⑩ **Modern European**
Chef-proprietor Sally Clarke has been espousing the 'seasonal and local' ethic since the mid 1980s. The food at this stylishly low-key restaurant shows influences from western Europe, executed with a deft hand, and the wine list has some very good bottles. Don't miss the breads, for which the deli next door (& Clarke's) is justly famed.

★ Harwood Arms
Corner of Walham Grove & Farm Lane, Fulham, SW6 1QP (7386 1847, www.harwoodarms.com). Fulham Broadway tube. **Open** 5.30-11pm Mon; noon-11pm Tue-Fri; noon-midnight Sat; noon-10pm Sun. **Credit** AmEx, MC, V. **Map** p394 A13 ⑩ **Gastropub**
Set in what used to be an corner pub, the Harwood Arms is now firmly at the restaurant end of the gastropub spectrum, although there are stools for perching at the bar so customers can enjoy a pint The atmosphere and young staff are laid-back, but the artfully arranged food takes things to a different level. Game is a speciality and the Sunday lunches are knockout.

£ Masala Zone
147 Earl's Court Road, Earl's Court, SW5 9RQ (7373 0220, www.masalazone.com). Earl's Court tube. **Open** 12.30-3pm, 5.30-11pm Mon-Fri; 12.30-11pm Sat; 12.30-10.30pm Sun. **Main courses** £7.75-£13. **Credit** MC, V. **Map** p394 B10 ⑩ **Indian**
This low-priced, canteen-like chain now has seven branches across town. The pan-Indian menu features popular street snacks (hot and cold), meat grills, thalis and regional curries, from Goan prawn curry to Gujarati undhiyu and lentil khichadi, a hearty medley of sweet potato, purple yam, aubergine and dahl. You can eat well for surprisingly little money, especially if you choose the set menus, lunch deals or online offers.
Other locations throughout the city.

Mesopotamia
115 Wembley Park Drive, Wembley, Middx HA9 8HG (8453 5555, www.mesopotamia.ltd.uk). Wembley Park tube. **Open** 6-11.30pm Mon-Thur; 6pm-midnight Fri, Sat. **Main courses** £6.95-£11.45. **Credit** AmEx, DC, MC, V. **Iraqi**
Outside is traffic-clogged Wembley; inside is Middle Eastern romance. Under a ceiling of billowing silk, Mesopotamia's long, dimly lit interior is an enchanting spot, helped along by kindly service. Food is a cut above, and special set dinners are served before events at Wembley Stadium.

Mohsen
152 Warwick Road, Earl's Court, W14 8PS (7602 9888). Earl's Court tube or Kensington (Olympia) tube/rail. **Open** noon-midnight daily. **Main courses** £15-£20. Unlicensed. Corkage no charge. **No credit cards. Map** p394 A10 ⑩ **Iranian**
We've long been fans of Mohsen, where little has changed over the years: the blink-and-miss-it façade; the tightly packed, functional tables; the laminated menus and the walls decorated with dog-eared Iranian tourist posters. The warm welcome remains equally undiminished. And the food is still very good. There's always a list of expertly marinated kebabs, but try the daily-changing specials, such as zereshk polo ba morgh – a quarter of a chicken served with bittersweet barberry-spiked rice.

River Café
Thames Wharf, Rainville Road, Hammersmith, W6 9HA (7386 4200, www.rivercafe.co.uk). Hammersmith tube. **Open** noon-2.15pm, 7-9pm Mon-Thur; noon-2.15pm, 7-9.15pm Sat; noon-3pm Sun. **Main courses** £30-£37. **Credit** AmEx, DC, MC, V. **Italian**
Seemingly impervious to fashion or recession, the River Café is one of London's most name-checked restaurants, even after 25 years. And although the food is very good (and sourced with the utmost care), it's also eye-wateringly expensive – which makes the longevity even more noteworthy. Chargrilled marinated leg of lamb with carrots 'dada', roast red and golden beetroot, Italian spinach and salsa bagnet is typical of the robust, satisfying food. Casually dressed young staff help keep the atmosphere informal.

£ Sakonis
129 Ealing Road, Wembley, Middx HA0 4BP (8903 9601, www.sakonis.co.uk). Alperton tube. **Open** noon-9.30pm daily. **Main courses** £3.50-£6.99. **Credit** MC, V. **Gujarati vegetarian**
A mainstay of the Ealing Road Indian dining scene, Sakonis attracts hordes of shoppers at the weekend. It's a sizeable, utilitarian café with tiled walls, melamine tableware and easy-wipe tables. There's a broad menu of Gujarati, South Indian and Indo-Chinese food. At the front is a snack counter, a well-liked source of takeaways, while to the rear is a buffet popular with South Asian families.

CONSUME

Hot Coffee

Where dedicated followers of the bean go.

In the last couple of years, London has got serious about its coffee, with local roasteries springing up (the best known is Square Mile) and a new wave of passionate and knowledgeable barista-proprietors trading in carefully sourced beans and sophisticated production methods. On the side: wireless, large slices of cake and a distinctly non-chain atmosphere.

Birdhouse
123 St John's Hill, SW11 1SZ (7228 6663).
A contemporary looking spot where staff take a quiet, unflashy pride in making first-rate coffee. All beans come from Climpson & Sons.

Brill
27 Exmouth Market, EC1R 4QL (7833 9757). **Map** p400 N4 ⓲
Superior coffees – Union Hand Roasted's Revelation espresso blend – plus CDs and Brick Lane bagels.

Climpson & Sons
67 Broadway Market, E8 4PH (7812 9829, www.climpsonandsons.com).
Macchiato, piccolo, zola, gibraltar... you can have it all in this charming coffee-geek haven.

Espresso Room
31-35 Great Ormond Street, WC1N 3HZ (07760 714883, www.theespresso room.com). **Map** p397 L4 ⓴
A tiny space opposite the famous hospital, in which carefully brewed coffee comes from a La Marzocco machine.

Federation Coffee
Unit 46, Brixton Village Market, Coldharbour Lane, SW9 8PS (no phone, www.federationcoffee.com).
A groovy little coffee shop serving a range of coffees from Nude Espresso.

Fernandez & Wells
16A St Anne's Court, W1F 0BG (7494 4242, www.fernandezandwells.com). **Map** p416 W2 ⓵

Invigorating triple ristretto shots are served at the 'espresso bar' branch of F&W.

Flat White
17 Berwick Street, W1F 0PT (7734 0370, www.flatwhitecafe.com). **Map** p416 V2 ⓵
Flat White's shabby chic resembles cafés found on the central New South Wales coast; its namesake coffee is good and strong.

Leila's Shop
15-17 Calvert Avenue, E2 7JP (7729 9789). **Map** p401 R4 ⓵
Leila McAlister's eclectic deli-café is a long-time favourite for consistently excellent coffee.

Monmouth Coffee
2 Park Street, SE1 9AB (7940 9960, www.monmouth coffee.co.uk). **Map** p402 P8 ⓵
Well-made espresso and derivatives are served here, but brewed coffees are the stars: take your pick from Monmouth's peerless single-origin selection, or choose its suggestion of the day.

Prufrock
23-25 Leather Lane, EC1N 7TE (07852 243470, www.prufrockcoffee.com). **Map** p400 N5 ⓵
Gwilym Davies is a demi-god among those who take their cup of joe seriously; test his wares at this large airy space with plenty of comfortable seating.

Scootercaffè
132 Lower Marsh, SE1 7AE (7620 1421). **Map** p399 M9 ⓵
A coffee shop in a former Vespa repair garage, employing a vintage Faema espresso machine.

Tapped & Packed
26 Rathbone Place, W1T 1JD (7580 2163, www.tappedandpacked.co.uk). **Map** p416 W1 ⓵
Choose your method – siphon, Aeropress, cafetière – as well as your bean. Coffee comes from Has Bean roasters.

Pubs & Bars

Traditional boozers, swanky cocktail lounges, stylish beer bars.

The drinking map of London has changed radically over the last few years. The bad news is that the traditional British pub has been in decline for a while, and nowhere more so than in the capital. But the good news is that pubs have adapted to survive – 'wet' pubs, where food is limited to crisps and peanuts, are few and far between these days – and the best ones continue to do a roaring trade. In addition, the recent surge of interest in craft beers has led to the opening of 'beer bars' that look like pubs, feel like pubs and are often on the premises of old boozers. Pubs, in fact, by another name. For four of the best, *see p199* **Here for the Beer**.

Meanwhile, the capital's bar scene remains as dynamic as ever. The trend over the last couple of years has been to ape the speakeasies of the Prohibition era in the US, and pastiches of these establishments have sprung up all over town, among them the **Mayor of Scaredy Cat Town** (*see p189*). But while this trend may wear itself out, good cocktails have a more timeless appeal, and London has these in spades, at venues as diverse as the splendid Victorian **Booking Office** (*see p191*) in the St Pancras Renaissance hotel and the industrial-look **Dabbous** (*see p191*). The other side of today's cocktail scene is the experimentation of bartenders using 'scientific' methods, unusual ingredients and lab equipment, resulting in intricate concoctions such as those found at **Purl** (*see p195*).

Wine bars, too, continue to flourish. For the past few years, 'natural' wines have been in vogue: fermented grape juice with little added or taken away. **Terroirs** (*see p193*) was a pioneer in this sector. Some others, such as **28°-50°**, also offer wine flights: groups of taster samples built around a theme, giving an excellent opportunity for getting to know a region or collection of vintages.

CONSUME

THE SOUTH BANK & BANKSIDE

If top-quality beer is your priority when choosing a pub, then you could do much worse than the superb ranges at the tiny **Rake** (14A Winchester Walk, SE1 9AG, 7407 0557), in Borough Market, and at a branch of **Draft House** (206-208 Tower Bridge Road, SE1 2UP, 7924 1814, www.drafthouse.co.uk), at the south side of Tower Bridge.

★ **Gladstone Arms**
64 Lant Street, SE1 1QN (7407 3962, www.thegladpub.com). Borough tube.
Open noon-11pm Mon-Thur; noon-midnight Fri, Sat; noon-10.30pm Sun. *Food served* noon-10pm daily. **Credit** MC, V. **Map** p402 P9 ❶ **Pub**
While the Victorian prime minister still glares from the massive mural on the outer wall, inside is now funky, freaky and candlelit. Gigs (blues, folk, acoustic, five nights a week) take place at one end of a cosy space; opposite is the bar. Pies provide sustenance. Retro touches include an old-fashioned 'On Air' studio sign and a communist-style railway clock.

> ❶ Green numbers given in this chapter correspond to the location of each pub or bar on the street maps. *See pp392-416.*

CONSUME

Hawksmoor.

Skylon
Royal Festival Hall, Belvedere Road, SE1 8XX (7654 7800, www.danddlondon.com). Waterloo tube/rail. **Open** 11am-midnight daily. *Food served* noon-11pm daily. **Credit** AmEx, MC, V. **Map** p399 M8 ❷ Bar

There can't be many better views than this in town. Sit at the cocktail bar (between the two restaurant areas), and gaze at trains trundling out of Charing Cross, cars and buses whizzing across Waterloo Bridge, and boats and cruisers pootling along the Thames. Drinks include ten bellinis, a large range of liqueurs and a list of classics (manhattans, sidecars, negronis), all at a price.

Wine Wharf
Stoney Street, SE1 9AD (7940 8335, www. winewharf.co.uk). London Bridge tube/rail. **Open** 4-11.30pm Mon, Tue; noon-11.30pm Wed-Sat. *Food served* 5.30-9.45pm Mon-Wed; noon-2.45pm, 5.30-9.45pm Thur, Fri; noon-11pm Sat. **Credit** AmEx, DC, MC, V. **Map** p402 P8 ❸ Wine bar

Part of the Vinopolis complex, Wine Wharf inhabits two storeys of a reclaimed Victorian warehouse, all exposed brickwork and high-ceilinged industrial chic. You could drink very well indeed here: the 250-bin list stretches to 1953 d'Yquem and some very serious prestige cuvée champagnes. But with nearly half the wines available by the glass, there's a great opportunity to experiment.
Other locations Brew Wharf, Stoney Street, Bankside, SE1 9AD (7378 6601, www.brew wharf.com).

THE CITY

Artillery Arms
102 Bunhill Row, EC1Y 8ND (7253 4683, www.artillery-arms.co.uk). Moorgate or Old Street tube/rail. **Open** noon-11pm Mon-Sat; noon-10.30pm Sun. *Food served* noon-3pm, 5-9pm Mon-Thur; noon-7pm Sat, Sun. **Credit** AmEx, MC, V. **Map** p400 P4 ❹ Pub

Close to the Barbican and opposite Bunhill Fields, this small tucked-away pub has an agreeably local feel, as post-work City folk mix easily with neighbourhood stalwarts at the sturdy, immovable bar. It has a slightly austere feel, but is an easy place to lose track of an evening, aided by the local vibe and the predictably fine Fuller's beers: easygoing Chiswick, toothsome London Pride and potent ESB.

Hawksmoor
157 Commercial Street, E1 6BJ (7426 4856, www.thehawksmoor.com). Shoreditch High Street rail. **Open** noon-midnight Mon-Fri; 11am-midnight Sat; 11am-8.45pm Sun. **Credit** AmEx, MC, V. **Map** p401 R5 ❺ Cocktail bar

All three of Hawksmoor's bars would be worthy of inclusion here, but this year's refurbishment of the Spitalfields branch's basement has created a separate arena to indulge in the exquisite cocktails. A small but focused list includes one of our favourite cocktails ever – Shaky Pete's Ginger Brew, with gin, ginger, lemon and London Pride beer. A monthly changing 'specials' section is curated by one of the personable staff – you might find the powerful-sounding

Gangster Grappa, which involves the Italian firewater, cognac, Campari, plum sherbet and lemon. All mixes are priced fairly – usually less than a tenner. **Other locations** 10 Baskinghall Street, City, EC2V 5BQ (7397 8120); 11 Langley Street, Covent Garden, WC2H 9JG (7420 9390).

Mayor of Scaredy Cat Town
12-16 Artillery Lane, E1 7LS (7078 9639, www.themayorofscaredycattown.com). Liverpool Street tube/rail or Shoreditch High Street rail. **Open** 5-11pm Mon-Thur; noon-11.30pm Fri, Sat; noon-10.30pm Sun. **Credit** AmEx, MC, V. **Map** p403 R5 ❻ **Cocktail bar**
One of several new 'secret' speakeasies, this one is a basement bar beneath Breakfast Club in Spitalfields. The entrance is the one that looks like a big Smeg fridge door, located in the BC's dining area. Venture inside and you'll find a quirky, dimly lit cocktail bar clad in exposed brick and wood: it's all a bit like a cabin from *Twin Peaks*. The drinks menu makes an amusing mockery of more self-conscious 'underground' venues. The cocktails, consisting of classics and house specials, are well crafted on the whole – we liked the chilli and lemongrass margarita.

Vertigo 42
Tower 42, 25 Old Broad Street, EC2N 1HQ (7877 7842, www.vertigo42.co.uk). Bank tube/DLR or Liverpool Street tube/rail. **Open** noon-4.30pm, 5-11pm Mon-Fri; 5-11pm Sat. *Food served* noon-2.15pm, 5-9.30pm Mon-Fri; 5-9.30pm Sat. **Credit** AmEx, DC, MC, V. **Map** p403 Q6 ❼ **Bar**
Stretching out across the City, the views from this 42nd-floor bar are breathtaking. So, too, are the prices (house wine, £9 a glass). Food is more down to earth: options include wild mushroom tart with artichoke salad, and seared peppered tuna steak. Seating is arranged so everyone can enjoy the 360° panorama; for the privilege, you must book ahead, promise a minimum £10 spend and then undergo airport-style security.
▶ *Vertigo has some competition for the high-life: nearby Heron Tower, the City's newest tallest building, opened Sushi Samba restaurant and bar in 2012.*

★ Worship Street Whistling Shop
63 Worship Street, EC2A 2DU (7247 0015, www.whistlingshop.com). Old Street tube/rail. **Open** 5pm-midnight Tue, Wed; 5pm-1am Thur; 4pm-2am Fri, Sat. **Credit** MC, V. **Map** p401 Q4 ❽ **Cocktail bar**
A semi-secret location, Victoriana, reinterpretations of classic British drinks: it's all here at the Worship Street Whistling Shop. The cellar room is darkly Dickensian, full of cosy corners and leather armchairs. In the back is a windowed laboratory crammed with equipment modern and antiquated, used to create the wondrously described ingredients

that constitute the cocktails. You may find 'chip pan bitters', 'Hereford soil distillate', or 'high pressure hydrosol' used as ingredients for the original and stimulating drinks, priced around the £10 mark (although the 'Living Cocktail', with Penicilium roquefortii, from blue stilton cheese), 'biologically aged', costs £20).

HOLBORN & CLERKENWELL

Clerkenwell has a compelling claim to being the birthplace of the now ubiquitous gastropub: the **Eagle** (*see p160*) kicked things off. Other food pioneers that provide great drinking are **St John** (*see p160*), **Le Comptoir Gascon** (*see p161*) and **Caravan** (*see p160*).

Café Kick
43 Exmouth Market, EC1R 4QL (7837 8077, www.cafekick.co.uk). Angel tube or Farringdon tube/rail. **Open** 11am-11pm Mon-Thur; 11am-midnight Fri, Sat; noon-10.30pm Sun. *Food served* noon-3pm, 6-10pm Mon-Thur; noon-3pm, 6-10.30pm Fri, Sat; 1-10pm Sun. **Credit** AmEx, MC, V. **Map** p400 N4 ❾ **Bar**
Clerkenwell's most likeable bar is this table-football themed gem. The soccer paraphernalia is authentic, retro-cool and mainly Latin (you'll find a Zenit St Petersburg scarf amid the St Etienne and Lusitanian gear); bar staff, beers and bites give the impression you could be in Lisbon. A modest open kitchen ('we don't microwave or deep-fry') dishes out tapas, sandwiches and charcuterie platters.
Other locations Bar Kick, 127 Shoreditch High Street, Shoreditch, E1 6JE (7739 8700).

CONSUME

Mayor of Scaredy Cat Town.

★ Fox & Anchor

115 Charterhouse Street, EC1M 6AA (7250 1300, www.foxandanchor.com). Barbican tube or Farringdon tube/rail. **Open** 7am-11pm Mon-Thur; 7am-1am Fri; 8.30am-1am Sat; 8.30am-10pm Sun. *Food served* 7am-11am, noon-9.45pm Mon-Fri; 8.30am-11am, noon-9.45pm Sat; 8.30am-11am, noon-4pm, 6-9pm Sun. **Credit** AmEx, MC, V. **Map** p400 O5 ⑩ **Pub**

Pristine mosaic tiling and etched glass paired together indicate 'sensitive refurbishment' at this Smithfield treasure. The dark wood bar is lined with pewter tankards; to the back is the Fox's Den, a series of intimate rooms used for both drinking and dining. Local sourcing is a priority and a pleasure: in addition to the own-label ale, cask beers might include Red Poll and Old Growler from Suffolk's fine Nethergate brewery. There are plenty more delights among the bottles.

Three Kings of Clerkenwell

7 Clerkenwell Close, EC1R 0DY (7253 0483). Farringdon tube/rail. **Open** noon-11pm Mon-Fri; 5.30-11pm Sat. *Food served* noon-3pm, 6.30-10pm Mon-Fri. **Credit** MC, V. **Map** p400 N4 ⑪ **Pub**

Rhinoceros heads, Egyptian felines and photos of Dennis Bergkamp provide the decorative backdrop against which a regular bunch of discerning bohos glug Scrumpy Jack, Beck's Vier, Old Speckled Hen or London Pride, and tap the well-worn tables to the Cramps and other gems from an outstanding jukebox that is crammed with fabulous old platters.

28°-50° Wine Workshop & Kitchen

140 Fetter Lane, EC4A 1BT (7242 8877, www.2850.co.uk). Farringdon tube/rail. **Open** 11am-11pm Mon-Fri. *Food served* noon-2.30pm, 6-9.30pm Mon-Fri. **Credit** AmEx, MC, V. **Map** p402 N6 ⑫ **Wine bar**

This venture, named after the latitudes between which wine is produced, is at once serious and relaxed. Serious, in that the wines – a changing roster available by the glass and a distinctive collector's list – are assembled with specialist knowledge; relaxed in that the staff are great communicators

---

INSIDE TRACK PISCO

The Peruvian bar and restaurant **Ceviche** (*see p168*) is the place to pay homage to the Peruvian spirit and national drink, pisco. Pisco is a type of colourless brandy diluted from grapes that mixes well into cocktails, such as the classic pisco sour, which is made with egg white; the version here is the best in London. Other pisco cocktails include the chica sour, which has an unusual clove aroma, plus there are shots of pisco flavoured with various infusions.

---

and not at all wine-snobby. They offer flights (minimum glass size is a sensible 75ml) to sample a particular style or theme, and ensure that the seasonal menu complements the wines nicely – though the food isn't just second fiddle: there's a good palate at work here, too, ensuring distinctive tastes in the French-influenced menu. It's a pleasant basement space with a modern-rustic feel.

Other location 15-17 Marylebone Lane, Marylebone, W1U 2NE (7486 7922).

Vinoteca

7 St John Street, EC1M 4AA (7253 8786, www.vinoteca.co.uk). Barbican tube or Farringdon tube/rail. **Open** noon-11pm Mon-Sat. *Food served* noon-2.45pm, 5.45-10pm Mon-Fri; noon-4pm, 5.45-10pm Sat. **Credit** MC, V. **Map** p400 O5 ⑬ **Wine bar**

Inspired in name and approach by the Italian *enoteca* (a blend of off-licence and wine bar, with snacks thrown in), Vinoteca is more of a serious gastropub in spirit. But even if you're not in the mood for much more than a plate of bread and olive oil, it's worth heading here for the impressive 200-bottle wine list, of which 25 are available by the glass. Bonus: all wines are available to take away at retail price.

Other locations 15 Seymour Place, Marylebone, W1H 5BD (7724 7288); 55 Beak Street, Soho, W1F 9SH (3544 7411).

★ Zetter Townhouse

49-50 St John's Square, EC1V 4JJ (7324 4545, www.thezettertownhouse.com). Farringdon tube/rail. **Open** 10am-midnight Mon-Wed, Sun; 10am-1am Thur-Sat. *Food served* noon-5pm, 6-10.30pm daily. **Credit** AmEx, MC, V. **Map** p400 O4 ⑭ **Cocktail bar**

If conversation is more important to you than general hubbub, and you love cocktails, you may well regard this place as one of the best bars in London. The decor looks something like a country-house hotel run by a compulsive antique collector: every surface is packed with artefacts. Seating, often on ultra-comfortable sofas, has been artfully planned to give maximum privacy to each table. Serving staff are eager, friendly and well informed about their drinks. The list was created by Tony Conigliaro of 69 Colebrooke Row (*see p198*), who loves tweaking classics with his own minerals, bitters and infusions, and here they're used subtly and unobtrusively, as in a lemon balm gimlet featuring own-made lemon balm cordial with Beefeater gin.

BLOOMSBURY, FITZROVIA & KING'S CROSS

For sheer style, try the bar at **Hakkasan** (*see p163*). In King's Cross, **Camino** (3 Varnishers Yard, N1 9FD, 7841 7331, http://www.camino.uk.com) added a dedicated sherry bar called Pepito, while the **Big Chill House** (*see p281*) is a great place for boozy music fans to stop at.

Dabbous.

All Star Lanes

Victoria House, Bloomsbury Place, WC1B 4DA (7025 2676, www.allstarlanes.co.uk). Holborn tube. **Open** 4-11.30pm Mon-Wed; 4pm-midnight Thur; noon-2am Fri; 11am-2am Sat; 11am-11pm Sun. *Food served* 5-10pm Mon-Thur; noon-10pm Fri-Sun. *Bowling £7.75-£8.75/person per game.* **Credit** AmEx, MC, V. **Map** p397 L5 **Bar**

Of Bloomsbury's two subterranean bowling dens, this is the one with aspirations. Walk past the lanes and smart, diner-style seating, and you'll find yourself in a comfortable, subdued side bar with chilled glasses, classy red furnishings, an unusual mix of bottled lagers (try Anchor Steam) and some impressive cocktails. There's an American menu and, at weekends, a range of DJs.

Other locations Whiteleys, 6 Porchester Gardens, Bayswater, W2 4DB (7313 8363); Old Truman Brewery, 91 Brick Lane, Spitalfields, E1 6QL (7426 9200). Westfield Stratford City, Stratford, E20 1ET (3167 2434).

▶ *Nearby, Bloomsbury Bowling Lanes (Bedford Way, 7183 1979, WC1H 9EU, www.bloomsbury bowling.com) offers a pints-and-worn-carpets take on the game – and private karaoke booths.*

Booking Office

St Pancras Renaissance London Hotel, NW1 2AR (7841 3540, www.bookingofficerestaurant.com). King's Cross or St Pancras tube/rail. **Open** 6.30am-2.45am daily. **Credit** AmEx, DC, MC. **Map** p397 L3 **Cocktail bar**

Superlatives come easily when describing the Booking Office: epic, soaring, magnificent. As part of the architect George Gilbert Scott's 1873 Midland Grand Hotel at St Pancras station, this former railway booking office was designed to instil in passengers a sense of awe at the wonder of the railways. These days, it serves as an equally awe-inspiring bar, and its refit has made the most of the Victorian splendour. The drinks demonstrate equal attention to detail, with a cocktail list, created by great London

mixers Nick Strangeway and Henry Besant, that shows a deep respect for the history of British drinking. Sours, fizzes and cobblers are represented, but perhaps most exciting are the punches, served with dash from handmade copper mugs.

Bradley's Spanish Bar

42-44 Hanway Street, W1T 1UT (7636 0359, www.bradleysspanishbar.co.uk). Tottenham Court Road tube. **Open** noon-11pm Mon-Sat; 3-10.30pm Sun. **Credit** MC, V. **Map** p416 W1 **Bar**

There's something of the Barcelona dive bar about the place, and San Miguel or Cruzcampo on draught, but Bradley's isn't really very Spanish. A hotchpotch of local workers, shoppers and foreign exchange students fill the cramped two-floor space, or enrage taxi drivers by spilling on to the narrow street, unperturbed by the routinely unpleasant toilets. After all, there's a good jukebox and good atmosphere – what more could anyone want?

★ Dabbous

39 Whitfield Street, W1T 2SF (7323 1544, www.dabbous.co.uk). Goodge Street tube. **Open** noon-3pm, 5.30-11.30pm Tue-Sat. **Credit** AmEx, MC, V. **Map** p396 J5 **Cocktail bar**

Dabbous astonishes with its cutting-edge cooking (*see p161*), and its downstairs cocktail bar sets out to do the same. There are plenty of unorthodox ingredients, and at times the combinations look forbidding: the Giddy Up contains tequila, bramley and gage slider (traditional sloe-infused cider from Devon), elderflower cordial, lemon juice and camomile-infused acacia honey topped with Sierra Nevada IPA. But other drinks stay closer to classicism, and you can always order off-menu if you're feeling timid. We loved the 2091210 (gin, Aperol and citrus juices topped with cream soda). The bar has the same stripped-back industrial decor as the restaurant, with bare walls that do a great but unwelcome job of bouncing noise all over the shop. Service is sweet and solicitous, and bar snacks a cut above.

Shaken and Possibly Stirred

Cocktail bars in every mode, for every mood.

CLASSIC

For smooth service, sophisticated surroundings and a sense of things being just right, it's hard to beat some of London's hotel bars. The **Coburg Bar** (*see p196*) in the Connaught Hotel, for instance, not only serves complimentary nibbles along with its drinks, but a little skewer of iced fruit comes as a palate cleanser between cocktails, all faultlesssly delivered. At the **Booking Office** (*see p191*), drinkers can take in the Victorian splendour of this former railway booking office while embibing cocktails like sours, fizzes and cobblers, inspired by the bar's palpable sense of history. Or, for a totally classic martini, try **Dukes** hotel (*see p197*). Sipping a drink here, with nuts and olives, in glamorous surroundings with fellow sophisticates, has to be one of London's most elegant experiences.

SCENE

For clubby, on-trend bars, head east. At the **Book Club** (*see p199*) in Shoreditch, cocktails are scrawled up in black felt tip, most just £7 and have in-joke names like Shoreditch Twat and Don't Go to Dalston. There's music and events too. Nearby, **Callooh Callay** (*see p200*) is a stalwart of the bar Shoreditch scene. There's wackiness in the some of the drinks (like the marmite-flavoured Marmageddon), but not all (thank goodness). DJs spin at weekends.

SPEAKASY

Go back to those heady days of Prohibiton at – well, any number of places. For one of the best, the **Mayor of Scaredy Cat Town** (*see p189*), head through a door that resembles a big SMEG fridge, and down into a hidden basement that's like a brick and log cabin. Or, find the small brass plaque with a picture of a nightjar on City Road, head inside and downstairs to the gorgeous basement hangout (guess what, it's called **Nightjar**, *see p201*), table service only so no standing, just sumptuous, textbook drinks. And for the speakeasy theme done lightl, with a short drinks list that is faithful to the golden age of the cocktail served in opulent surroundings, there's **Bar Américain** (*see p196*) at Brasserie Zédel.

SCIENCE

The molecular approach to cocktail making is best observed at venues such as **Purl** (*see p195*), where laboratory inventiveness leads to presentations complete with smoke and sleight of hand, as well as well-rendered classics. Over at the **Worship Street Whistling Shop** (*see p189*, from the same stable as Purl), there's a windowed laboratory, crammed with equipment ancient and modern, used to create some fantastically described ingredients. Tony Conigliaro at **69 Colebrooke Row** (*see p198*), meanwhile, uses unusual ingredients and serious attention to detail to come up with exciting combinations.

Bar Américain.

Lamb

94 Lamb's Conduit Street, WC1N 3LZ (7405 0713, www.youngs.co.uk). Holborn or Russell Square tube. **Open** *noon-11pm Mon-Wed; noon-midnight Thur-Fri; noon-10.30pm Sun. Food served noon-9pm daily.* **Credit** AmEx, MC, V. **Map** p397 M4 ⑲ **Pub**

The standard range of Young's beers is dispensed from a central horseshoe bar in this 280-year-old pub, around which are ringed original etched-glass snob screens, used to prevent Victorian gentlemen from being seen when liaising with 'women of dubious distinction'. A sunken back area gives access to a convenient square of summer patio.

Shochu Lounge

Basement, Roka, 37 Charlotte Street, W1T 1RR (7580 9666, www.shochulounge.com). Goodge Street or Tottenham Court Road tube. **Open** *noon-midnight Mon-Fri; 5.30pm-midnight Sat; 5.30-10.30pm Sun. Food served noon-2.30pm, 5.30-11.15pm Mon-Fri; 5.30-10.15pm Sun.* **Credit** AmEx, DC, MC, V. **Map** p396 J5 ⑳ **Cocktail bar**

Beneath landmark Japanese restaurant Roka, the chic Shochu Lounge offers drinks based on the vodka-like distilled spirit of the same name. Shochu is often overlooked for its better-known and more widespread counterpart, saké, but it's here used in healthy tonics, in cocktails, and sold by the 50ml measure. With a 13.5% service charge, drinks run to around £10. The full Roka menu is available if you're hungry.

VOC

2 Varnishers Yard, Regents Quarter, N1 9AWN1 9AW (7713 8229, www.voc-london.co.uk). King's Cross tube/rail. **Open** *5pm-1am Mon-Thur; 5pm-2am Fri, Sat.* **Credit** AmEx, MC, V. **Map** p397 L3 ㉑ **Cocktail bar**

This small bar in the busy Regents Quarter of King's Cross is yet another by the chaps behind Purl (*see p195*) and Worship Street Whistling Shop (*see p189*). It looks like Phileas Fogg's front room, with cartography adorning the brick walls, telescopes and cosy candlelight. It takes its name and 17th-century maritime theme from the Vereenigde Oost-Indische Compagnie, otherwise known as the Dutch East India Company, and is big on punches. Some are individually bottled; others are aged in new and ex-sherry casks and dangle in mini barrels from the ceiling. There's an array of bottle-matured cocktails decanted into apothecary-style vessels. Each bottled is wax-sealed, then individually labelled with the date of creation and priced accordingly – the older, the dearer.

COVENT GARDEN & THE STRAND

★ Gordon's Wine Bar

47 Villiers Street, Strand, WC2N 6NE (7930 1408, www.gordonswinebar.com). Embankment tube or Charing Cross tube/rail. **Open** *11am-11pm Mon-Sat; noon-10pm Sun. Food served noon-10pm Mon-Sat; noon-9pm Sun.* **Credit** AmEx, MC, V. **Map** p416 Y5 ㉒ **Wine bar**

Gordon's Wine Bar was established in its present form as long ago as 1890, but the atmospheric exposed brickwork and flickering candlelight make this basement feel older still. Although this is the definitive old-school wine bar, it gets packed with a young and lively crowd, half of whom seem to be on first dates. The wine list is surprisingly modern; still, in such surroundings, it seems a shame not to drink the fortified wines, which are drawn directly from casks behind the bar.

Lamb & Flag

33 Rose Street, WC2E 9EB (7497 9504, www.lambandflagcoventgarden.co.uk). Covent Garden tube. **Open** *11am-11pm Mon-Sat; noon-10.30pm Sun. Food served noon-7.30pm Mon-Sat; noon-6pm Sun.* **Credit** MC, V. **Map** p416 Y3 ㉓ **Pub**

This dog-leg alleyway used to be a pit of prostitution and bare-knuckle bashes, the latter hosted at this historic, low-ceilinged Covent Garden tavern back when it was called the Bucket of Blood; poet John Dryden was beaten up here in 1679. The place is popular and space is always at a premium, hence the pavement cluster on summer evenings. Two centuries of mounted cuttings and caricatures amplify the sense of character.

► *If it's too busy, try the Benelux-themed beer-café Lowlander (36 Drury Lane, WC2B 5RR, 7379 7446, www.lowlander.com).*

★ Terroirs

5 William IV Street, WC2N 4DW (7036 0660, www.terroirswinebar.com). Charing Cross tube/rail. **Open/food served** *noon-11pm Mon-Sat.* **Credit** AmEx, MC, V. **Map** p416 Y4 ㉔ **Wine bar**

Now extending over two floors, Terroirs is a superb and very popular wine bar that specialises in the new generation of organic and biodynamic, sulphur-, sugar- or acid-free wines. The list of wines is only slightly shorter than the Bible and almost as profound, with tasting notes that are honest to a fault – a wine like a hedgehog? All in all, a place for oenophiliac adventure. The line-up of Calvados and Armagnac bottles is impressive and the food terrific: a tapas-style selection of French bar snacks, charcuterie and seafood.

SOHO & LEICESTER SQUARE

Dog & Duck

18 Bateman Street, W1D 3AJ (7494 0697, www.nicholsonspubs.co.uk). Tottenham Court Road tube. **Open** *10am-11pm daily. Food served 10am-10pm daily.* **Credit** AmEx, MC, V. **Map** p416 W2 ㉕ **Pub**

CONSUME

Pubs & Bars

This Soho landmark is known for its literary heritage, vintage interior (etched mirrors, carved mahogany) and ever-changing selection of good ales, ranging from the familiar likes of London Pride to an altogether rarer range of beers from the Newman Brewery. Sausages are another feature. The George Orwell room upstairs, where the writer sometimes drank, offers more space; downstairs, punters spill out on to the pavement.

★ Experimental Cocktail Club
13A Gerrard Street, W1D 5PS (7434 3559, www.chinatownecc.com). Leicester Square tube. **Open** 6pm-3am Mon-Sat; 6pm-midnight Sun. **Map** p416 W3 ㉖ **Cocktail bar**
This bar has a central London location, a great cocktail list, and attempts an air of exclusivity. To get in, the only sure way is to email in advance, Tuesday to Saturday before 5pm (reservation@chinatownecc.com). You can't book by phone, and reservations aren't accepted for more than four people. Next you'll have to limbo-dance your way past the door bouncers (entrance) and schmooze the reservations staff (top of the first stairs), to arrive at the small, tasteful bar, a blend of fin-de-siècle opulence and antique shop chic. But why the popularity? Mainly because the drinks are sensational. A gang of clearly fanatical barmen work in front of a display of top-end spirits. The concise list shows great creativity; current favourites include an infusion of tawny port, sage, thyme and cachaca.

French House
49 Dean Street, W1D 5BG (7437 2799, www.frenchhousesoho.com). Leicester Square or Piccadilly Circus tube. **Open** noon-11pm Mon-Sat; noon-10.30pm Sun. *Food served* noon-3pm, 5.30-11pm Mon-Sat. **Credit** AmEx, DC, MC, V. **Map** p416 W3 ㉗ **Pub**
Through the door of this venerable Gallic establishment have passed many titanic drinkers of the pre- and post-war era, the Bacons and the Behans. The venue's French heritage also enticed de Gaulle to run a Resistance operation from upstairs – it's now, incongruously, a tiny Venetian-style restaurant. De Gaulle's image survives behind the bar, where beer is served in half-pints and litre bottles of Breton cider are still plonked on the famed back alcove table.
▶ *The little upstairs restaurant, Polpetto (7734 1969, www.polpetto.co.uk), is the first offshoot of the popular Polpo – and every bit as crammed.*

★ LAB
12 Old Compton Street, W1D 4TQ (7437 7820, www.labbaruk.com). Leicester Square or Tottenham Court Road tube. **Open** 4pm-midnight daily. *Food served* 4-10pm daily. **Credit** MC, V. **Map** p416 X2 ㉘ **Cocktail bar**
Newer spots have overtaken the '70s-meets-'90s decor, but few can match the sheer enthusiasm and knowledge of the staff at the London Academy of

Bartending. Cocktails are king here, and many original combinations are mixed using LAB's own infusions and syrups (chorizo tequila, anyone?). Pull up a chair and let one of the ultra-helpful mixologists guide you through the menu. The unashamed party vibe means this place fills up early.

Lucky Voice
52 Poland Street, W1F 7LR (7439 3660, www.luckyvoice.co.uk). Oxford Circus tube. **Open/food served** 5.30pm-1am Mon-Thur; 3pm-1am Fri, Sat; 3-10.30pm Sun. **Credit** AmEx, MC, V. **Map** p416 V2 ㉙ **Karaoke bar**
There are nine rooms at this karaoke venue, each of them with space for between four and 12 singers; some come with props such as hats, wigs and inflatable electric guitars. A drinks menu includes cocktails (£7), saké and spirits, brought to your room when you press the 'thirsty' button; food is limited to pizzas and snacks. The perfect place to discover your inner Susan Boyle.
Other location 173-174 Upper Street, Islington, N1 1RG (7354 6280).

★ Mark's Bar
66-70 Brewer Street, W1F 9UP (7292 3518, www.marksbar.co.uk). Piccadilly Circus tube. **Open/food served** 11am-1am Mon-Sat; 11.30am-midnight Sun. **Credit** AmEx, MC, V. **Map** p416 V3 ㉚ **Cocktail bar**
It's impossible to recommend Mark's Bar without first pointing out that this basement space is still one of the hardest places in London to get a seat. Bookings are not taken, but arrive at the right time, sweet-talk the receptionist, and you might be lucky. This initiation only makes you want to linger longer once esconced in a padded leather sofa in the rakishly dim room. The cocktail list has a similar emphasis on ingredient provenance than that preached by restaurateur Mark Hix in his restaurant upstairs (*see p170*): you might see drinks made with the likes of Kentish redcurrants, sea buckthorn and rhubarb. Historically revived mixed drinks also feature heavily: step back to the golden age of bartending with a Criterion Milk Punch, a Scoff Law Cocktail or a Pegu Club.

★ Milk & Honey
61 Poland Street, W1F 7NU (7065 6841, www.mlkhny.com). Oxford Circus tube. **Open** *Non-members* 6-11pm Mon-Sat (2hrs max, last admission 9pm). *Members* 6pm-3am Mon-Sat. **Credit** AmEx, DC, MC, V. **Map** p416 V2 ㉛ **Cocktail bar**
This, the popular myth has it, has always been one of the best cocktail bars in London. It might well be so, but it's hard to tell unless you have night vision like an owl – the lighting is turned down so low you'll need to borrow a candle to read the drinks list, let alone see your drink. And then there's the difficulty of getting in. It's a members'

CONSUME

club most of the time, although the rest of us can book a table in the early evening for up to two hours – as long as you reserve at least a day in advance, and arrive before 9pm. However, if you're prepared to put up with all that ballyhoo, this is a great place for perfectly executed classic cocktails. We were impressed with our negroni, not least by our bartender inquiring about our preferences of gin and vermouth combinations.

OXFORD STREET & MARYLEBONE

The bar at **Paramount** (*see p163*) in Centre Point (main bar on floor 32, viewing gallery on floor 33) has amazing views over London.

Artesian

Langham Hotel, 1C Portland Place, W1B 1JA (7636 1000, www.artesian-bar.co.uk). Oxford Circus tube. **Open** noon-2am Mon-Sat; noon-midnight Sun. **Credit** AmEx, DC, MC, V. **Map** p396 H5 ㉜ **Cocktail bar**

It's worth getting your best togs on and heading to the Langham just to admire David Collins's handsome bar design. The result blends grand Victorian decadence (marble bar, soaring inset mirrors) with modern details (purple snakeskin-effect leather seats, carved pagoda-style back bar). As if that's not enough, world-renowned bartender Alex Kratena has won more awards for his mixology skills than Michael Phelps has gold medals. Service is faultless, and the drinks list is divided into categories such as 'rum de luxe', 'tonic and gin', 'heritage' and 'Artesian classics'. The only catch is that such opulence and perfection doesn't come cheap, with most cocktails starting at around £15, excluding service.

Artesian.

★ Purl

50 Blandford Street, W1U 7HX (7935 0835, www.purl-london.com). Bond Street tube. **Open** 5-11.30pm Mon-Thur; 5pm-midnight Fri, Sat. **Credit** AmEx, MC, V. **Map** p396 G5 ㉝ **Cocktail bar**

The first bar from the people who went on to create the Worship Street Whistling Shop (*see p189*) and VOC (*see p193*), Purl was a clear taste of things to come. It uses the speakeasy feel and look that is now de rigueur everywhere, but pairs this with some excellent bar skills. The list of cocktail creations is divided between molecular mixology and a confident mastery of the classics. The former often have spectacular presentation, with smoke, unusual glassware, balloon popping and clever sleight of hand. Drinks change frequently, but options might include a Backward Bellini – a lavender-soaked sugarcube topped with prosecco, finished with pomegranate foam; or a marmalade vodka with Aperol and bitters, with a 'juniper oil burner'.

PADDINGTON & NOTTING HILL

★ Lonsdale

48 Lonsdale Road, W11 2DE (7727 4080, www.thelonsdale.co.uk). Ladbroke Grove or Notting Hill Gate tube. **Open** 6pm-midnight Mon-Thur; 6pm-1am Fri, Sat. **Food served** 6-11pm Mon-Sat. **Credit** AmEx, MC, V. **Map** p404 Y4 ㉞ **Cocktail bar**

This well-established bar has been an unwavering champion of well-made cocktails as other Notting Hill bars have come and gone. The 'London contemporary classics' offer the best in British mixes from recent times, such as the elderflower martini (Zubrowka bisongrass vodka stirred with apple juice and elderflower cordial for £8.75), though there is also a page devoted to modern classics created by legendary bartender Dick Bradsell, which includes the Wibble, the Bramble and a rose petal martini. Mixing and service are fittingly old-school, and the setting – a sun-catching front terrace, a long bar counter and wide, candlelit main seating area at the back – remains a very attractive proposition.

Portobello Star

171 Portobello Road, W11 2DY (7229 8016, www.portobellostarbar.co.uk). Ladbroke Grove or Notting Hill Gate tube. **Open** 11am-11.30pm Mon-Thur, Sun; 11am-12.30am Fri, Sat. **Credit** MC, V. **Map** p404 X4 ㉟ **Cocktail bar/pub**

This 'cocktail tavern' deftly blends discerning bar and traditional boozer. The bountifully stocked bar is manned by friendly staff thoroughly educated in the art of adult refreshment; 'Drink less but better' is the mantra of leading mixologist Jake Burger. His impeccable, approachable directory of discerning drinks is the last word on sophisticated intoxication. If you want to mix drinking with music, there are DJs on Friday and Saturday nights.

CONSUME

CONSUME

PICCADILLY CIRCUS & MAYFAIR

Bar Américain

Brasserie Zédel, 20 Sherwood Street, W1F 7ED (7734 4888, www.brasseriezedel.com). Piccadilly Circus tube. **Open** 4.30pm-midnight daily. **Credit** AmEx, MC, V. **Map** p416 V2 ❸ **Cocktail bar**
A message to all aspiring bartenders considering a leap on to the already overcrowded Prohibition/1930s-theme bandwagon: this is how you do it properly. Brasserie Zédel is housed in what used to be the Atlantic Bar & Grill. A short list of mixed drinks ('classic' and 'house') are faithful to the golden age of cocktails. There's a martini, a manhattan and a mint julep, as well as a fabulous sazerac; fancier creations include a beautifully balanced Belle Zédel (with vodka, crème de myrtille, rose liqueur and rhubarb bitters among its constituents), or a spiky Spritz Américain, with champagne, grapefruit liqueur and bitters. They all cost £9.75 – even those charged with bubbly – and come with trays of olives and cashews. This, coupled with the attentive service and the fact you'll be drinking in one of the most truly opulent bars in London, is excellent value.

★ Coburg Bar

The Connaught, Carlos Place, W1K 2AL (7499 7070, www.the-connaught.co.uk). Bond Street or Green Park tube. **Open** 11am-11pm Mon, Sun; 11am-1am Tue-Sat. **Credit** AmEx, MC, V. **Map** p398 H7 ❼ **Cocktail bar**

There's no velvet rope barring your way to the Connaught hotel's destination bar, and no strict door policy: you can just walk straight on in. What's more, once you've done so, the service will be faultless. The room oozes sophistication, with modern touches (grey velvet wingback chairs, black glass tables) that enhance the historic character of the space.The drinks list charts the evolution of the cocktail, with each drink – the greatest hits of the last two centuries, more or less – well worth the considerable expense. Tip-top nibbles are free of charge; better, a tiny skewer of iced fruit on a silver dish appears with each cocktail as a palate-cleanser. Luxurious, elegant and discreet, the Coburg Bar is everything a good hotel bar should be.
▶ *If the Coburg isn't 'scene' enough for you, the hotel's other, noisier and busier bar (the Connaught) is just a stroll away down the corridor.*

Galvin at Windows

London Hilton, Park Lane, W1K 1BE (7208 4021, www.galvinatwindows.com). Hyde Park Corner tube. **Open** 11am-1am Mon-Wed; 11am-3am Thur, Fri; 3pm-3am Sat; 11am-10.30pm Sun. *Food served* noon-midnight Mon-Wed; noon-1am Thur, Fri; 6pm-1am Sat. **Credit** AmEx, DC, MC, V. **Map** p398 G8 ❸ **Cocktail bar**
There's suddenly no shortage of rooftop venues in London, but the location of Windows is still superb. It offers remarkable panoramic views from the 28th floor of the Park Lane Hilton. Add a sleek interior that mixes art deco glamour with a hint of 1970s petrodollar kitsch, and you can't go wrong. The wine and cocktails don't come cheap, but the drinks are assembled with care, and the service is attentive without being obsequious.

WESTMINSTER & ST JAMES'S

Albannach

66 Trafalgar Square, WC2N 5DS (7930 0066, www.albannach.co.uk). Charing Cross tube/rail. **Open** noon-1am Mon-Sat; noon-7pm Sun. *Food served* noon-11pm Mon-Sat; noon-5pm Sun. **Credit** AmEx, DC, MC, V. **Map** p416 X5 ❸ **Bar**
Right on Trafalgar Square, Albannach (as opposed to 'sassanach') specialises in Scotch whiskies and cocktails thereof. A map in the menu details the origins of these Highland and Island malts, the pages brimming with 17-year-old Glengoynes, 12-year-old Cragganmore and 29-year-old Auchentoshan. That said, kilted staff, illuminated reindeer and too many loud office groups detract from the quality on offer.

Boisdale

13-15 Eccleston Street, SW1W 9LX (7730 6922, www.boisdale.co.uk). Victoria tube/rail. **Open/food served** noon-1am Mon-Fri; 6pm-1am Sat. **Admission** free before 10pm, then £12. **Credit** AmEx, DC, MC, V. **Map** p398 H10 ❹ **Bar**

Coburg Bar.

The Book Club. *See p198*.

There's nowhere quite like this posh, Scottish-themed enterprise, and that includes its sister branch in the City. If you're here to drink, you'll be drinking single malts from a terrific range. That said, the outstanding wine list is surprisingly affordable, with house selections starting at under £20. Additional appeal comes from live jazz (six nights a week) and a heated cigar terrace.

Other locations Boisdale of Bishopsgate, Swedeland Court, 202 Bishopsgate, the City, EC2M 4NR (7283 1763); Cabot Place, Canary Wharf, E14 4QT (7715 5818).

★ Dukes Bar

35 St James's Place, SW1A 1NY (7491 4840, www.campbellgrayhotels.com). Green Park tube. **Open** 2pm-midnight Mon-Thur; noon-midnight Fri, Sat; 4pm-midnight Sun. **Credit** AmEx, DC, MC, V. **Map** p398 J8 ⑪ **Cocktail bar**

This is *the* hotel bar to visit for a martini. Well-mannered waiters flick dry vermouth into an iced glass, fill it with gin or vodka (various premium options, all priced accordingly) and then drop in a sliver of lemon peel. Simple, but wonderful. Sipping a drink amid the murmur of the very adult clientele , while munching nuts and Puglian olives, is one of the most elegant drinking experiences in London. If you're looking for a hipster bar, look elsewhere; with its engravings and fringed chairs, this tiny but comfortable space resembles a Georgian railway carriage, and the atmosphere is surprisingly sober.

St Stephen's Tavern

10 Bridge Street, SW1A 2JR (7925 2286, www.hall-woodhouse.co.uk). Westminster tube. **Open** 10am-11.45pm Mon-Sat; 10.30am-10.45pm Sun. *Food served* 10am-10pm Mon-Sat; 10.30am-10pm Sun. **Credit** MC, V. **Map** p399 L9 ⑫ **Pub**

Done out with dark woods, etched mirrors and Arts and Crafts-style wallpaper, this is a lovely old pub. The food is reasonably priced and the ales are excellent, but drinks can be expensive. Opposite Big Ben,

its location is terrific, yet it's neither too touristy nor too busy. If the downstairs bars are full, head upstairs and look for a seat on the mezzanine.

▶ *St Stephen's nearest rival is the Red Lion (48 Parliament Street, SW1A 2NH, 7930 5826), by tradition the politicians' favourite.*

CHELSEA

★ Cadogan Arms

298 King's Road, SW3 5UG (7352 6500, www.thecadoganarmschelsea.com). Sloane Square tube then bus 19, 22, 319. **Open** 11am-11pm Mon-Sat; 11am-10.30pm Sun. *Food served* noon-3.30pm, 6-10.30pm Mon-Fri; noon-10.30pm Sat; noon-9pm Sun. **Credit** AmEx, DC, MC, V. **Map** p395 E12 ⑬ **Pub**

In 2009, this 19th-century Chelsea pub was given a major rebuild by its new owners, the Martin brothers. It now has a countrified look, complete with stuffed animals and fly-fishing displays, and remains a proper boozer, with top-quality real ales, notwithstanding the snug and smoothly run dining area, where great food is on offer.

▶ *On Sloane Square, the Martin brothers' Botanist (no.7, 7730 0077) provides a similar mix of fine booze and hearty food.*

KNIGHTSBRIDGE & SOUTH KENSINGTON

Anglesea Arms

15 Selwood Terrace, SW7 3QG (7373 7960, www.capitalpubcompany.com). South Kensington tube. **Open** 11am-11pm Mon-Sat; noon-10.30pm Sun. *Food served* noon-3pm, 6-10pm Mon-Fri; noon-5pm, 6-10pm Sat; noon-5pm, 6-9.30pm Sun. **Credit** AmEx, MC, V. **Map** p395 D11 ⑭ **Pub**

Formerly the local of both Charles Dickens and DH Lawrence, this old boozer is packed tight on summer evenings, the front terrace and main bar filled with professional blokes chugging ale, and their female equivalents putting bottles of Sancerre on

CONSUME

expenses. But the Anglesea has always had more aura than the average South Kensington hostelry; perhaps it's the link with the Great Train Robbery, reputedly planned here.

Blue Bar

Berkeley, Wilton Place, SW1X 7RL (7235 6000, www.the-berkeley.co.uk). Hyde Park Corner tube. **Open** 9am-1am Mon-Sat; 9am-11pm Sun. **Credit** AmEx, MC, V. **Map** p398 G9 ⑮ **Cocktail bar**

It isn't just a caprice: this David Collins-designed bar really lives up to its name. The sky-blue bespoke armchairs, the deep-blue ornate plasterwork and the navy-blue leather-bound menus combine with discreet lighting to striking effect. It's more a see-and-be-seen place than somewhere to kick back, but don't let the celeb-heavy reputation put you off: staff treat everyone like royalty, and the cocktails are a masterclass in sophistication.

NORTH LONDON

The **Lock Tavern** and **Proud** (for both, *see p282*) are excellent Camden DJ bars, while the **Blues Kitchen** (*see p289*) and scuzzy indie-den the **Dublin Castle** (94 Parkway, NW1 7AN, 7485 1773) supply live music. In Islington, the **Old Queen's Head** (*see p282*) is a boisterous and lively pub. The **Horseshoe** (28 Heath Street, NW3 6TE, 020 7431 7206) in Hampstead is an excellent gastropub which doesn't disappoint on the own-brewed ale front.

★ 69 Colebrooke Row

69 Colebrooke Row, Islington, N1 8AA (07540 528593, www.69colebrookerow.com). Angel tube. **Open** 5pm-midnight Mon-Wed, Sun; 5pm-1am Thur; 5pm-2am Fri, Sat. **Credit** AmEx, MC, V. **Map** p400 O2 ⑯ **Cocktail bar**

This tiny bar opened in mid 2009, and is overseen by Tony Conigliaro, widely considered to be one of London's top bartenders and cocktail experts. With just a handful of seats, the understated, intimate space proves a fine environment in which to enjoy the pristine cocktails (peach and figleaf bellini, martinis made with 'woodland bitters', rhubarb gimlet), mixed with quiet ceremony. The attention to detail includes impeccably attired staff, handwritten bills and tall glasses of water poured from a cocktail shaker, which add to the sense of occasion. At £9 for most house cocktails, the prices are very fair. Note that the small room is rammed at peak times.

Brewdog

113 Bayham Street, Camden, NW1 0AG (7284 4626, www.brewdog.com). Camden Town tube or Camden Road rail. **Open** noon-11.30pm Mon-Thur; noon-midnight Fri, Sat; noon-10.30pm Sun. **Credit** MC, V. **Map** p404 Y3. ⑰ **Beer bar** *See right* **Here for the Beer.**

Bull

13 North Hill, Highgate, N6 4AB (8341 0510, www.thebullhighgate.co.uk). Highgate tube. **Open** noon-11pm Mon-Wed, Sun; noon-midnight Thur-Sat, Sun. **Credit** AmEx, MC, V. **Beer bar** *See right* **Here for the Beer.**

Driver

2-4 Wharfdale Road, King's Cross, N1 9RY (7278 8827, www.driverlondon.co.uk). King's Cross tube/rail. **Open** 10am-midnight Mon-Thur; 10am-3am Fri; 6pm-4am Sat. *Food served* noon-3pm, 6-10pm Mon-Sat. **No credit cards**. **Map** p397 M2 ⑱ **Bar**

Spread over five floors, with decor alternating from urban to intricate, this soaring yet svelte Swiss army knife of a venue encompasses a pub-style restaurant, a small roof terrace, a members' bar, a lounge and a dining room that, later, transforms *Bugsy Malone*-style into a dancefloor with decks. There's a living plant wall on the outside.

★ Holly Bush

22 Holly Mount, Hampstead, NW3 6SG (7435 2892, www.hollybushhampstead.co.uk). Hampstead tube or Hampstead Heath rail. **Open** noon-11pm Mon-Sat; noon-10.30pm Sun. *Food served* noon-3pm, 6-10pm Mon-Fri; noon-4pm, 6-10pm Sat; noon-5pm, 6-9pm Sun. **Credit** (over £10) MC, V. **Pub**

As the trend for gutting old pubs claims yet more Hampstead boozers, this place's cachet increases. Located on a quiet hilltop backstreet, it was built as a house in the 1790s and used as the Assembly Rooms in the 1800s, before becoming a pub in 1928. A higgledy-piggledy air remains, with three low-ceilinged bar areas and one bar counter at which are poured decent pints. Sound food and a good choice of wines by the glass are further draws.

Railway Tavern

2 St Jude Street, N16 8JT (020 0011 1195). Dalston Kingsland rail. **Open** noon-11pm Mon-Sat; noon-10.30pm Sun. **Credit** MC, V. **Beer bar** *See left* **Here for the Beer.**

EAST LONDON

Late-night **Charlie Wright's International Bar** (*see p294*) is as much about drinking as it is about music; there's music, food and booze at Concrete, beneath **Pizza East** (*see p181*).

Book Club

100-106 Leonard Street, EC2A 4RH (7684 8618, www.wearetbc.com). Old Street tube/rail or Shoreditch High Street rail. **Open** 8am-midnight Mon-Wed; 8am-2am Thur, Fri; 10am-2am Sat; noon-midnight Sun. **Admission** Club free-£10. **Credit** MC, V. **Map** p401 R4 ⑲ **Cocktail bar**

Here for the Beer

Beer bars are giving the brew a new lease of life.

Relief for Londoners from generic lagers and boring bitters began arriving from craft breweries a few years ago. The new creative way with beer has also fuelled a trend for beer bars, where the drink is taken seriously and served in many varieties. We like the fact that many of the new bars springing up around town are really pubs by any other name, compensating in a small way for the decline of the traditional local. What follows is a survey of some of London's best – the runners-up and winner of *Time Out Eating & Drinking Guide*'s award for best new beer bar.

The London outpost of the Scottish craft brewery **Brewdog** (*see left*) offers a great initiation into the world of craft beer, but never feels intimidating. Admit to bar staff you've no idea where to start and they'll gladly guide you through the list, offering tasters. And what a list it is – every one of Brewdog's beers on keg draught (with occasional guests) and bottle, from the smooth, amber 5am Saint to the quadruple IPA Sink the Bismarck at 41 per cent abv. Fridges hold a selection from other microbreweries, mainly from the US (the likes of Stone, Evil Twin and Anchor, although there's plenty from the Scandic Mikkeller and Nøgne Ø too). English beer producers barely get a look-in – almost certainly a typical Brewdog provocation.

Further up the Northern line, the **Bull** (*see left*) in Highgate may look like just another suburban gastropub, but look closer and you'll spot much enamelled beer memorabilia on the walls, and garlands of hop flowers on the beams. You might also catch a glimpse of the steampunk tubing and brass vats of the brewing equipment. The beer taps are almost unrecognisable from the average high-street chain pub. Five of the pumps dispense the fine products of the London Brewing Company, made on the premises – a zesty raspberry wheat beer, say, or Beer Street best bitter. And keg fonts advertise the likes of Sierra Nevada Torpedo and Veltins Pilsener. Among the bottles, you'll find several unusual imports from Great Divide and Odell in the US, as well as cans from Kona.

The **Railway Tavern** (*see left*), on a residential street in Dalston, has been given a thoughtful, mid-century-style makeover, with a few bits of artful railway ephemera here and there. Food is Thai; musicians frequently play. But the beer selection is something special. There are six regularly changing real ales on tap, and they're often made in London – from Redemption, Brodie's or the East London Brewing Company, for instance. On the keg taps are Meantime London Lager, König Pilsner, Black Isle Porter and Brewdog's 5am Saint. The bottles pay homage to the microbrewing nous of the Americans, with the likes of Brooklyn, Anchor and Sierra Nevada, although there are a good few Europeans too. This is also a place to sample the latest hop explosions from Bermondsey's cult Kernel Brewery. No mainstream sops for the unadventurous sipper in sight, and brews are served in handled, dimpled pint mugs: magic.

Coming out on top with the Time Out judges was the **Crown & Anchor** (*see p202*) in Brixton. A no-frills restoration has stripped things back to bare brick and given the wraparound windows smart gunmetal-grey frames; the most exciting feature, though, is the lengthy bar and its endless fonts (or so it seems – there are seven real ales from the cask, and 14 keg beers and ciders). The breweries you'll see represented regularly are Redemption, Dark Star, Magic Rock, Camden Town, Brewdog, Brooklyn and Kernel; bottles take a more global approach and include a fair few Belgians. Clued-up staff are keen to recommend and offer tasting notes and samples. What makes this pub really stand out is the way it bridges the apparent divide between Camra-endorsed real ale and its hip young cousin, craft beer. The Crown & Anchor is friendly, unpretentious and devoted to the cause.

Crown & Anchor

CONSUME

Happiness Forgets.

This busy bar-club comprises one expansive room – divided by a wall with an oval hole in the middle, giving the illusion that half of Hoxton is here – and a small pool room downstairs. Cocktails are scrawled up in black felt-tip on white tiles by the bar, most in the £7 range and with in-joke names; perennial favourites include the Shoreditch Twat (Jägermeister, tequila and chartreuse shaken with an egg) and the Don't Go to Dalston (vodka, raspberry and cherry). And if you can't be bovvered with that, there are jugs of cocktails such as Pimm's, iced teas or Hoxton Triomphe, flavoured with elderflower. Come here for the scene, if nothing else. *See also p282. Photo p197.*

Callooh Callay

65 Rivington Street, Shoreditch, EC2A 3AY (7739 4781, www.calloohcallaybar.com). Old Street tube/rail or Shoreditch High Street rail. **Open/food served** 6pm-midnight Mon-Wed, Sun; 6pm-1am Thur-Sat. **Credit** MC, V. **Map** p401 R4 ⑤⓪ **Cocktail bar**

This landmark of the Shoreditch bar scene tends to divide visitors. Many simply adore it; others find it pretentious. We're not sure that the silly names of the cocktails, the Marmite-tinged number (the Marmageddon) or another flavoured like a black forest gateau will be for everyone, but mostly, the drinks meet with approval, and the list has won international awards. In the main bar room, with its low, purple seating, said drinks are served from a long bar counter by savvy staff featured in the childhood photos pinned to the wall. This being Shoreditch, DJs spin at weekends.

Carpenter's Arms

73 Cheshire Street, Brick Lane, E2 6EG (7739 6342, www.carpentersarmsfreehouse.com). Liverpool Street tube/rail. **Open** 4-11.30pm Mon-Wed; noon-11.30pm Thur-Sun. *Food served* 5-10pm Mon-Wed; 4-10pm Thur-Sun. **Credit** MC, V. **Map** p401 S4 ⑤① **Pub**

At one time, this cosy boozer took centre stage in East End gangsterland. It was bought by the Kray twins in 1967 for their dear old mum, and it was here that Ronnie tanked up on dutch courage before murdering Jack 'the Hat' McVitie in Stoke Newington. Today, Hoxtonites, fashionistas, the odd ironic moustache and a few ambitious hats fill the snug space. The drinks selection is great, and the cut-above food (boards of cheese, Sunday roasts) isn't sold at stupid prices.

Commercial Tavern

142 Commercial Street, Spitalfields, E1 6NU (7247 1888). Liverpool Street tube/rail or Shoreditch High Street rail. **Open** 5-11pm Mon-Fri; noon-11pm Sat; noon-10.30pm Sun. **Credit** AmEx, MC, V. **Map** p401 R5 ⑤② **Pub**

The inspired chaos of retro-eccentric decor and warm, inclusive atmosphere make this landmark flat-iron corner pub very likeable. It seems to have escaped the attentions of the necking-it-after-work masses, perhaps because of the absence of wall-to-wall lager pumps in favour of some proper real ale. The bar is made up of colourful art deco tiles, and there's a distinct decorative playfulness throughout; it's a great example of how a historic pub can be lit up with new life.

▶ *Just down the street, the fabulous, every-busy Golden Heart (no.110, E1 6LZ, 7247 2158) is a famous nursery for East End artists.*

Grapes

76 Narrow Street, Limehouse, E14 8BP (7987 4396, www.thegrapes.co.uk). Westferry DLR. **Open** noon-3pm, 5.30-11pm Mon-Wed; noon-11pm Thur-Sat; noon-10.30pm Sun. *Food served* noon-2.30pm, 7-9.30pm Mon-Sat; noon-3.30pm Sun. **Credit** AmEx, MC, V. **Pub**

If you're trying to evoke the feel of the Thames docks before their Disneyfication into Docklands, these narrow, ivy-covered and etched-glass 1720 riverside premises are a good place to start: the downstairs is all wood panels and nautical jetsam; the upstairs plainer, but it's easier to find seats for Sunday lunch. It's a fairly blokey pub: expect good ales and a half-dozen wines of each colour by glass and bottle, plus jugs of kir royale or strawberry fizz for summer and port for winter. There's a tiny terrace too.

▶ Nearby, Gordon Ramsay's gastropub, the Narrow (44 Narrow Street, E14 8DQ, 7592 7950, www.gordonramsay.com), serves great bar snacks.

Happiness Forgets

8-9 Hoxton Square, Shoreditch, N1 6NU (7613 0325, www.happinessforgets.com). Old Street tube/rail or Shoreditch High Street rail. **Open** 5.30-11pm Mon-Sat. **Credit** MC, V. **Map** p401 R3 ⊕
Cocktail bar
This tiny basement has such low light that torches ought to be provided to aid with reading the drinks list. But low light makes the room – dark walls and dark wooden floorboards – just that much more appealing. What's more, the cocktails are fabulous: innovative but with impeccable taste and a sure grasp of fundamentals. Two gin-based drinks, the French Pearl (shaken with fresh mint, lime and a dash of absinthe) and MarTeaNi both possessed flawless balance. Served in icy, frosted coupes, they stayed cold for 30 minutes. Minor complaint: the sound system was turned up to full whack. Apart from that, we remember Happiness Forgets with unalloyed pleasure.

Nightjar

129 City Road, Shoreditch, EC1V 1JB (7253 4101, www.barnightjar.com). Old Street tube/rail.
Open 6pm-1am Mon-Wed, Sun; 6pm-3am Thur-Sat. **Credit** AmEx, MC, V. **Map** p401 Q4 ⊕
Cocktail bar
This glam basement hangout has almost everything going for it. Service is wonderful. It doesn't get over-crowded because, being table-service only, there's no standing. And it does fabulous things with alcohol. A beautifully garnished singapore sling aged in wood was well balanced and complex, and a gin fizz (ordered off-menu) was textbook stuff. But Nightjar's huge drinks list can intimidate even seasoned cocktail-hounds: it's organised by era, and ingredients lists are not just lengthy but often baffling. Yet the advice is good and the talent undeniable. Make sure you book, and don't be afraid to order something classic.

★ Mason & Taylor

51 Bethnal Green Road, Shoreditch, E1 6LA (7749 9670, www.masonandtaylor.co.uk). Liverpool Street tube/rail or Shoreditch High Street rail. **Open** 5pm-midnight Mon-Thur; 5pm-2am Fri; noon-2am Sat; noon-midnight Sun. *Food served* 5-10pm Mon-Thur; 5-10.30pm Fri; noon-10.30pm Sat; noon-9pm Sun. **Credit** AmEx, MC, V. **Map** p401 S4 ⊕ **Beer bar**
This two-floor, somewhat urban/industrial space in Shoreditch showcases boutique beers. Behind a concrete bar, a dozen draught taps draw both the obscure and the accessible: Brooklyn Lager, De Koninck and a milk stout from Colorado. The friendly staff are happy to advise on putting together a taster flight. Tapas-style small plates have a British bent and on Sunday it's all about the roasts. It can get pretty busy.

CONSUME

Nightjar.

CONSUME

SOUTH-EAST LONDON

Gipsy Moth

60 Greenwich Church Street, Greenwich,
SE10 9BL (8858 0786, www.thegipsymoth
greenwich.co.uk). Cutty Sark DLR. **Open** 10am-
11pm Mon-Thur; 10am-midnight Fri, Sat; 10am-
10.30pm Sun. *Food served* 10am-10pm Mon-Thur;
10am-11pm Fri, Sat; noon-9pm Sun. **Credit**
AmEx, MC, V. **Map** p405 W2 ⑤⑥ **Pub**
The split-level garden and roomy interior at this moderately funky pub are ideal for a sit-down after roaming around Greenwich. The pub offers an impressive
number of beers (Früli, Budvar, Paulaner and at least
six others), well-priced wines and pretty decent food,
from full breakfasts through bar snacks (olives, pis-
tachios, pork crackling) to solid mains.
▶ *In good weather, the riverside seats of Cutty*
Sark Tavern (4-6 Ballast Quay, SE10 9PD, 8858
3146, www.cuttysarktavern.co.uk) are popular.

Greenwich Union

56 Royal Hill, Greenwich, SE10 8RT (8692 6258,
www.greenwichunion.com). Greenwich rail/DLR.
Open noon-11pm Mon-Fri; 11am-11pm Sat;
11.30am-10.30pm Sun. *Food served* noon-4pm,
5.30-10pm Mon-Fri; 11am-10pm Sat; noon-9pm
Sun. **Credit** MC, V. **Map** p405 W3 ⑤⑦ **Beer bar**
Decorated with framed covers of the *Picture Post*,
this tidy operation is the spiritual home of Alistair
Hook's mission to bring his Meantime Brewery's
German-style beers to the British public. Six tap
options complement a couple of dozen bottled international beers, and food runs from a humble bacon
butty to chargrilled steaks. Coffee, tea and a small
front terrace make it a decent option for non-drink-
ing visitors to Greenwich's many attractions.
▶ *Near the Thames – and on the premises of the*
Old Royal Naval College – the Old Brewery (see
p182) is Meantime's flagship bar-restaurant.

SOUTH-WEST LONDON

Crown & Anchor

246 Brixton Road, Brixton, SW9 6AQ (7737
0060, www.crownandanchorbrixton.co.uk).
Stockwell tube or Brixton tube/rail. **Open** 4.30pm-
midnight Mon-Thur; 4.30pm-1am Fri; noon-1am
Sat; noon-11pm Sun. **No credit cards**. **Beer bar**
See p199 **Here for the Beer**.

Draft House

94 Northcote Road, Battersea, SW11 6QW
(7924 1814, www.drafthouse.co.uk). Clapham
South tube or Clapham Junction rail. **Open** noon-
11pm Mon-Fri; 10am-11pm Sat, Sun. *Food served*
1-10pm Mon-Thur; noon-10.30pm Fri; 10am-
10.30pm Sat; 10am-9.30pm Sun. **Credit** AmEx,
MC, V. **Beer bar**
This attractive beer bistro is clad in wood, warmed
by candlelight and brightened with pop art and green

furniture. The curved bar sports 17 shiny draught
fonts and there are three-dozen bottles in the fridge.
Served in third, half and full pints, the beers range
across Europe and as far as the craft breweries of the
United States, while ale-friendly tucker includes ham
hock salad and a succulent roquefort burger.
Other locations throughout the city.
▶ *The bar also offers tours of the Sambrook's*
Brewery in nearby Battersea.

Effra

38A Kellet Road, Brixton, SW2 1EB (7274 4180).
Brixton tube/rail. **Open** noon-11pm Mon-Thur;
noon-midnight Fri; 10am-midnight Sat; 10am-
10.30pm Sun. *Food served* noon-10pm Mon-Fri;
11am-10pm Sat; 11am-9.30pm Sun. **No credit
cards**. **Pub**
This old-school pub has more of an Afro-Caribbean
community feel than many Brixton watering holes.
The daily changing menu offers the likes of sea-
weed callaloo and jerk pork, and palm fronds tower
over drinkers in the cosy patio garden. One look at
the fading Victorian splendour of the gold-corniced
ceiling and pretty domed glass lamps, and it's no
wonder locals pack the place out each night.

★ White Horse

1-3 Parsons Green, Parsons Green, SW6 4UL
(7736 2115, www.whitehorsesw6.com). Parsons
Green tube. **Open** 9.30am-11.30pm Mon-Wed,
Sun; 9.30am-midnight Thur-Sat. *Food served*
10am-10.30pm daily. **Credit** AmEx, MC, V. **Pub**
Only a lack of ceiling fans stops the main bar of this
renowned hostelry from feeling like something from
the days of the Raj. The Victorian ceilings are airily
high, and wide windows with wooden venetian
blinds let in plenty of light. Chesterfield-style sofas
surround huge tables, though the umbrella-covered
pavement tables are most coveted. Expect plenty of
turned-up collars, rugby shirts and pashminas,
although the mix of customers is wider than you
might imagine. There are usually six to eight hand-
pumped ales alongside the 135 bottled beers.

WEST LONDON

Botanist on the Green

3-5 Kew Green, Kew, Surrey TW9 3AA (8948
4838, www.thebotanistkew.com). Kew Gardens
tube/rail or bus 65, 391. **Open** noon-11pm Mon-
Thur; noon-midnight Fri, Sat; noon-10.30pm Sun.
Food served noon-3pm, 5-9.30pm Mon-Thur;
noon-10pm Fri, Sat; noon-9pm Sun. **Credit** AmEx,
MC, V. **Pub**
The name is a nod to its floral neighbour, the Royal
Botanic Gardens; certainly, this pub's position on
the corner of Kew Green makes it a perfect place
for a relaxing pint after a mooch around the gardens. The space has little nooks – one with a fabulous double-sided fireplace – and raised areas that
give it a more intimate feel.

Shops & Services

Big stores and small independents make for great shopping

In its celebration of both tradition and cutting-edge style, London's signature department store, **Liberty** (*see p204*), revamped in 2009, captures everything that's great about the capital's shopping scene. The opening of a second Oxford Street branch of mega-cheap **Primark** (*see p216*) in October 2012 proved... well, that Londoners like cheap clothes in a recession. Meanwhile, over in Stratford, the £1.45 billion retail monster that is **Westfield Stratford City** (*see p209*), which opened in autumn 2011 at the entrance to the Olympic Park, continues to do business with its 300 retail units, 70 restaurants, bars and cafés, and 17-screen cinema.

But while department stores and malls are part of London's shopping story, they're not the whole story. Independents continue to flourish, with fashion-forward new openings and pop-up stores – east London's **Redchurch Street** (*see p226*) has been particularly lively over the past couple of years. There are also classic independents still going strong after centuries in operation (take a bow, umbrella specialists **James Smith & Sons**, *see p224*).

Between those extremes lies a changing kaleidoscope of places in which to part with your cash: multicultural street markets, deluxe department stores, design-led homewares stores, flashy food shops and, of course, chain-store flagships. You'll also find some of the best places in Europe to buy books, records and second-hand clothes. Despite credit crunches, London is still one of the world's most exciting, exhaustive and exhausting retail centres.

SHOPPING IN LONDON

The listings in this chapter concentrate on British brands and shops that are not only unique to the city, but also relatively centrally located. For the key shopping areas around London, *see p205* **Where to Shop**.

Most goods – with the notable exceptions of books, food and children's clothes – are subject to value added tax (VAT), which is almost always included in the prices advertised by shops. VAT is currently levied at 20 per cent. Some shops, particularly larger stores, operate a scheme allowing visitors from outside the European Union to claim back VAT when leaving the country.

Central London shops stay open late (until 7pm or 8pm) one night a week – it's Thursday in the West End, and Wednesday in Chelsea and Knightsbridge.

General

DEPARTMENT STORES

High-street favourite for undies, sandwiches and ready meals, **Marks & Spencer** (www.marksandspencer.co.uk) also offers several reliable fashion ranges. **John Lewis** (www.johnlewis.com) is a popular department store, known for reliablity, with a flagship branch on at 300 Oxford Street.

Fortnum & Mason
181 Piccadilly, St James's, W1A 1ER (7734 8040, www.fortnumandmason.co.uk). Green Park or Piccadilly Circus tube. **Open** 10am-8pm Mon-Sat; noon-6pm Sun. **Credit** AmEx, DC, MC, V. **Map** p416 V4.
Fortnum & Mason is one of London's most inspiring department stores, and, in business for over 300

CONSUME

Selfridges. *See p207.*

years, it's as historic as it is inspiring. A sweeping spiral staircase soars through the four-storey building, while light floods down from a central glass dome. The iconic eau de nil blue and gold colour scheme with flashes of rose pink abound on both the store design and the packaging of the fabulous ground-floor treats, such as chocolates, biscuits, teas and preserves. The five restaurants are equally impressive, with a new ice-cream parlour a welcome addition. A food hall in the basement has a good range of fresh produce; and beehives installed on top of the building mean that Fortnum's Bees honey is as local as it gets. The shop is redolent of a time when luxury meant the highest degree of comfort rather than ostentation, but that's not to say it's beyond the means of a modest budget. The famous hampers start from £40 – though they rise to a whopping £5,000 for the most luxurious. The Diamond Jubilee hamper, at £200, draws on F&M's beguiling commemorative range, which comes in highly collectable packaging.

Harrods
87-135 Brompton Road, Knightsbridge, SW1X 7XL (7730 1234, www.harrods.com). Knightsbridge tube. **Open** 10am-8pm Mon-Sat; noon-6pm Sun (browsing from 11.30am). **Credit** AmEx, DC, MC, V. **Map** p395 F9.
All the glitz and marble can be a bit much, but in the store that boasts of selling everything, it's hard not to leave with at least one thing. In fact, it even sold itself in 2010: former owner Mohammed Al Fayed received a reported £1.5bn from Qatar Holdings for the place. It's on the fashion floors that Harrods really comes into its own, with a 10,000sq ft Designer Studio on the first floor, featuring well-edited collections from the heavyweights, including a revamped Chanel boutique. There's also an excellent lingerie section, a luxury pet department and a top-notch sport section. The legendary food halls and restaurants range from a branch of 18th-century Venetian coffee bar Caffè Florian to a Xin Dim Sum bar.

▶ *Nearby Harvey Nichols (109-125 Knightsbridge, SW1X 7RJ, 7235 5000, www.harveynichols.com) is coasting a little these days, but you'll still find a worthy clutch of unique fashion brands, plus a belle époque-style champagne bar.*

★ Liberty
Regent Street, Soho, W1B 5AH (7734 1234, www.liberty.co.uk). Oxford Circus tube. **Open** 10am-8pm Mon-Sat; noon-6pm Sun. **Credit** AmEx, DC, MC, V. **Map** p416 U2.
Charmingly idiosyncratic, Liberty is housed in a 1920s mock Tudor structure. The store was given a major revamp in early 2009, with new lines and the creation of a dedicated scarf room. The expanded beauty hall on the ground floor goes from strength to strength, with a perfumerie selling scents from cult brands such as Le Labo and Byredo, skincare from the much-celebrated Egyptian Magic, and a new Margaret Dabbs Sole Spa, for pedicures, polishing and shaping. At the main entrance to the store is Wild at Heart's exuberant floral concession, and just off from here you'll find yourself in a room devoted to the store's own label. Fashion brands focus on high-end British designers, such as Vivienne Westwood and Christopher Kane. But despite being up with the latest fashions, Liberty still respects its dressmaking heritage with an extensive range of cottons in the third-floor haberdashery department. Stationery also pays homage to the traditional, with beautiful Liberty of London notebooks, address books and diaries embossed with the art nouveau 'Ianthe' print, while the interiors departments showcase

Where to Shop

London's shopping neighbourhoods.

COVENT GARDEN & SOHO

The famous former flower market is choked with chains and crowds, but **Neal Street** and the streets radiating off **Seven Dials** rule for streetwear, while new shopping enclave **St Martin's Courtyard** (www.stmartinscourtyard.co.uk), between Long Acre and Upper St Martin's Lane, is good for quality brands such as Jaeger and Twenty8Twelve. Another urbanwear centre is Soho's pedestrianised **Carnaby Street**, as well as **Newburgh Street** and **Kingly Street**, which run parallel on either side of Carnaby Street. **Berwick Street** is the new central London hotspot for vintage clothing shops, as well as a few surviving record shops, while **Charing Cross Road** and **Cecil Court** are prime browsing territory for bookish types.

OXFORD STREET & AROUND

London's commercial backbone, **Oxford Street** is positively heaving with department stores and big chains, which spill over on to elegant **Regent Street**. At its eastern end is **Tottenham Court Road**, known for its electronics shops. **Marylebone**, north-west of Oxford Street, has a villagey atmosphere and small shops that sell everything from designer jewellery to artisan cheeses. Venture further north to **Church Street** for antiques.

NOTTING HILL

Best known for its antiques market on **Portobello Road**, Notting Hill also has an impressive cache of posh boutiques around the intersection of **Westbourne Grove** and **Ledbury Road** – a laid-back alternative to the West End and Chelsea. The area is also good for rare vinyl and vintage clothes.

MAYFAIR & ST JAMES'S

The traditional home of tailors (**Savile Row**) and shirtmakers (**Jermyn Street**), this patch also retains venerable specialist hatters, cobblers and perfumers. **Bond Street** glitters with jewellers and designer stores, while the reinvigorated **Mount Street** is the place for niche upmarket labels.

CHELSEA & KNIGHTSBRIDGE

King's Road made famous in the Swinging Sixties, is pretty bland these days, but punctuated with some interesting shops. An up-and-coming nearby sidestreet is **Pavilion Road**, now home to a clutch of ultra-feminine boutiques. Designer salons line **Sloane Street** and mix with chains on **Knightsbridge**, which is anchored by deluxe department stores.

KENSINGTON

Once a hub of hip fashion, **Kensington High Street** has surrendered to the chains, but it's still worth exploring the backstreets leading up to Notting Hill Gate. Rarefied antiques shops gather on **Kensington Church Street**. In South Kensington, **Brompton Cross** has glossy contemporary furniture showrooms and designer boutiques.

EAST LONDON

East London is great for quirkier shops and some of the city's best markets; go there on a Sunday for **Columbia Road** and Spitalfields markets. Head to **Brick Lane** and its offshoots, especially **Redchurch Street**, for clothing, accessories and home goods that have been made or adapted by idiosyncratic young designers, and heaps of vintage fashion. **Shoreditch** and **Hoxton** have hip boutiques, furniture stores and bookshops, while Hackney's **Broadway Market** hosts a Saturday farmers' market as well as a clutch of cool indie stores.

Portobello Road.

NORTH LONDON

The grungy markets of **Camden** are best left to the under-25s, but nearby **Primrose Hill** has an exquisite selection of small shops selling, among other things, quirky lingerie and vintage clothes. Antiques dealers are thinning out on Islington's **Camden Passage**, but there's a growing number of other indies, including gourmet chocolatier Paul A Young and lifestyle boutique Smug.

CONSUME

DISAFFECTED

URBAN OUTFITTERS

COVENT GARDEN - HIGH ST KENSINGTON - OXFORD STREET - SPITALFIELDS - STRATFORD - WHITE CITY

   UO BLOG WWW.URBANOUTFITTERS.CO.UK WWW.FACEBOOK.CO.UK/UOEUROPE

new furniture designs alongside a dazzling collection of 20th-century classics. Artful and arresting window displays, exciting new collections and luxe labels make it an experience to savour.

★ Selfridges
400 Oxford Street, Marylebone, W1A 1AB (0800 123 400, www.selfridges.com). Bond Street or Marble Arch tube. **Open** 9.30am-9pm Mon-Sat; noon-6pm Sun (browsing from 11.30am). **Credit** AmEx, DC, MC, V. **Map** p396 G6.

With its plethora of concession boutiques, store-wide themed events and collections from all the hottest brands, Selfridges is as dynamic as a department store could be. Although the store changes regularly, the useful floor plans make navigating the place easy-peasy. While the basement is chock-full of hip home accessories and stylish kitchen equipment, it's Selfridges' fashion floors that really get hearts racing. With a winning combination of new talent, hip and edgy labels, high-street brands and luxury high-end designers, the store stays ahead of the pack. Highlights include the huge denim section, and the extensive Shoe Galleries, the world's biggest women's footwear department, while Selfridges' 3rd Central initiative is where you'll find the hippest brands of the day. Level 4 hosts the new Toy Shop. Regularly changing pop-up and special events keep customers on their toes, with recent highlights including the Tracey Emin Concept Store and the Mimi Holliday lingerie pop-up. There are plenty of new draws in the food hall, too, with great deli produce from London-based Baker & Spice. *Photo p204.*

SHOPPING CENTRES & ARCADES

The **Royal Arcades** in the vicinity of Piccadilly are a throwback to shopping past – the Burlington Arcade (*see p207*) is both the largest and grandest, but the Piccadilly Arcade, opposite it, and the Royal Arcade, at 28 Old Bond Street, are also worth a visit.

★ Brixton Village
Corner of Coldharbour Lane & Brixton Station Road, SW9 8PR (7274 2990, http://spacemakers.org.uk/brixton). Brixton tube/rail. **Open** 6am-6.30pm Mon, Tue; 6am-10pm Wed; 6am-midnight Thur-Sat; 8am-6pm Sun; check website for opening hours of individual shops. **Credit** AmEx, MC, V.

Once almost forgotten, Granville Arcade has found a new lease of life. It originally opened in 1937, when it was proclaimed 'London's Largest Emporium', and later became a Caribbean market in the 1960s. But by the 1990s, many of the arcade's units were unoccupied and its old art deco avenues were falling into a dilapidated state. In 2009, Lambeth Council called in urban regeneration agency Space Makers, which launched a competition whereby local entrepreneurs could apply for a unit. It then awarded the best initiatives a place on site, and renamed the space Brixton Village, in line with its eclectic, locally minded new contents – from bijoux bakeries and vintage boutiques to international eateries and fledgling fashion labels. Highlights from the shops here include Margot Waggoner's Leftovers (unit 71), with its Marseille lace and vintage sailor dresses, and Binkie and Tabitha's Circus (unit 70), which juxtaposes retro glassware with an assortment of socialist literature. *See p208* **The World in a Village**.

★ Burlington Arcade
Piccadilly, St James's, W1 (7355 8317, www.burlington-arcade.co.uk). Green Park tube. **Open** 8am-8pm Mon-Fri; 9am-7pm Sat; 11am-6pm Sun. **No credit cards.** **Map** p408 U4.

In 1819, Lord Cavendish commissioned Britain's very first shopping arcade. Nearly two centuries later, the Burlington is still one of London's most prestigious shopping 'streets', patrolled by 'beadles' decked out in top hats and tailcoats. Highlights include collections of classic watches at David Duggan, established British fragrance house Penhaligon's, the British luxury luggage brand Globe-Trotter (*see p220*) and Sermoneta, selling Italian leather gloves in a range of bright colours. High-end food shops come in the form of Luponde Tea and Ladurée; head to the latter for exquisite Parisian macaroons. Burlington also houses a proper shoe-shine boy working with waxes and creams for just £4.

One New Change
New Change Road, the City, EC4M 9AF (7002 8900, www.onenewchange.com). Mansion House or St Paul's tube or Bank tube/DLR. **Open** varies; check website for opening hours of individual shops. **Credit** AmEx, MC, V. **Map** p402 P6.

Burlington Arcade.

CONSUME

The World in a Village

There's a cornucopia of flavours to be tried at Brixton Village.

It feels like fiesta time. A Brazilian band is belting out bossa nova in the alley; a mixed crowd is laughing, chatting and browsing; the narrow passageways are lined with diners spilling out of tiny cafés. African fabric shops sit cheek-by-jowl with butchers' displays. The holiday mood is hard to place – it's not immediately clear which country you're in. But this is Brixton Village.

In the 1980s, the market here was kept going by a few resilient African and Caribbean stores; by the late noughties most units were empty. Granville Arcade, as it was known then, was bought for redevelopment in 2008 – the plan being to knock down the original 1930s building with its high, glass-ceilinged 'arcades'. But, in 2010, it was declared a listed building. This prompted the new owners to think laterally.

One of the first shops was Cornercopia, a café and corner shop selling local produce. Space Makers, a non-profit organisation, asked for locals – business people, entrepeneurs and artists – to come up with ideas for transforming the empty units into

places that could be environmentally and economically sustainable, and sociable.

Another new arrival was Bellantoni's, an Italian trattoria, run by chef proprietor Dario Bellantoni, from Genoa. 'My staff are all Italian. We do a lot of vegetarian dishes, we make our own pasta here, we do a lot of Ligurian and Neapolitan dishes.'

Adding to the international flavour is Elephant, a tiny Pakistani café, containing barely half a dozen small tables. Chef proprietor Imran Bashir's story is not uncommon for many of the newer traders. 'A Colombian friend brought me here [Brixton Village] for dinner, and it was just amazing – lots of new restaurants, lots of things going on, and units to let. So I put my name down on the waiting list, and got Elephant. Ever since then, I've just been really busy.'

Thursday night has become the big night at Brixton Village, in part because of the live music. But any day of the week, the market offers flavours from around the world, to eat in or take home and cook.

For listings and review, *see p207*.

This new development, a short stroll from St Paul's Cathedral, is a sprawling shopping mall designed by Jean Nouvel, and featuring a warren of high-street retailers, office buildings and restaurants (Jamie Oliver's Barbecoa and Gordon Ramsay's Bread Street Kitchen among the latter). Nicknamed the 'stealth building' due to the structure's resemblance to a stealth bomber, the place is unsurprisingly popular with City workers on their lunchbreaks or on post-work spending sprees. Highlights from the shops include Banana Republic, Topshop and Bea's of Bloomsbury bakery.

Westfield Stratford City

Great Eastern Road, Stratford, E20 (8221 7300, www.westfield.com/stratfordcity). Stratford tube/ rail/DLR. **Open** 10am-9pm Mon-Fri; 9am-9pm Sat; noon-6pm Sun; check website for opening hours of individual shops. **Credit** AmEx, MC, V.

The 'city within a city', Westfield's £1.45bn retail behemoth lies between the station and what will eventually reopen as the Queen Elizabeth Olympic Park (in two phases, starting in 2013). There are 300 retail units – the cornerstones of which are gigantic versions of high-street brands John Lewis, Marks & Spencer and Waitrose – 70 restaurants, bars and cafés, and a 17-screen digital cinema. There's no denying that it's a mega-mall, but Stratford City has at least attempted to reflect the diversity and creative vibe of its neighbourhood, with local artists and creatives creating uniforms, lighting systems, public art and environmental projects. And the food market, the Great Eastern Market, looks set to give opportunities to small, independent producers. Westfield enjoyed a guaranteed customer base during the Olymics: in a stroke of planning genius, the route to the stadium passed right through its centre.
▶ *Westfield London (www.westfield.com/london) sits on the other side of town in Shepherd's Bush. Hailed as Europe's largest city shopping centre when it opened in autumn 2008, it houses some 265 shops and 50 restaurants.*

MARKETS

London's neighbourhood markets are a great place to sample streetlife while picking up bargains. Below is a selection of the best; for tourist mecca **Camden Market**, *see p117*; for food markets, *see p223*. See also *p207* **Brixton Village**.

Bermondsey Square Antiques Market

Corner of Bermondsey Street & Long Lane, Bermondsey, SE1 (7234 0805, www.bermondsey square.co.uk/antiques.html). Borough tube or London Bridge tube/rail. **Open** 5am-1pm Fri. **No credit cards.**

Following the redevelopment of Bermondsey Square, the ancient antiques market – which started in 1855 in north London – continues in an expanded space that now accommodates 200 stalls. Traditionally good for china and silverware, as well as furniture and glassware (with items from Georgian, Victorian and Edwardian eras), there are now also food, fashion and crafts stalls. Browsing here is a bit like going through Fagin's gang's loot, and, indeed, the market is famous for being the spot where, back in the day, thieves could sell their goods with impunity. It's half car boot sale, half chic Parisian fleamarket. Insider tip: get there early – lunchtime arrivals will be disappointed to find grouchy antiques sellers (well, they did start work at 4am) packing up.

★ Columbia Road Market

Columbia Road, Bethnal Green, E2. Hoxton rail or bus 26, 48, 55. **Open** 8am-2pm Sun. **Map** p401 S3.

On Sunday mornings, this unassuming East End street is transformed into a swathe of fabulous plant life and the air is fragrant with blooms and the shouts of old-school Cockney stallholders (most offering deals for 'a fiver'). But a visit here isn't only about flowers and pot plants: alongside the market is a growing number of shops selling everything from pottery, Mexican glassware and arty prints to cupcakes and perfume; don't miss Ryantown's delicate paper cut-outs at no.126 (7613 1510). Get there early for the pick of the crops, or around 2pm for the bargains; refuel at Jones Dairy (23 Ezra Street, 7739 5372, www.jonesdairy.co.uk).

Portobello Road Market

Portobello Road, Notting Hill, W10 (www.portobello road.co.uk). Ladbroke Grove or Notting Hill Gate tube. **Open** *General* 8am-6pm Mon-Wed; 9am-1pm

Westfield Stratford City.

CONSUME

YOUR GUIDE TO ARTS, ENTERTAINMENT AND CULTURE IN THE WORLD'S MOST EXCITING PLACES

www.timeout.com/london

Thur; 7am-7pm Fri, Sat. *Antiques* 6am-4pm Fri, Sat. **No credit cards. Map** p404 Y4.

Best known for antiques and collectibles, this is actually several markets rolled into one: antiques start at the Notting Hill end; further up are food stalls; under the Westway and along the walkway to Ladbroke Grove are emerging designer and vintage clothes on Fridays (usually marginally less busy) and Saturdays (invariably manic).

Specialist

BOOKS & MAGAZINES

Central branches of the big bookselling chains, where any bibliophile could happily waste an hour, include the **Waterstones** flagship (203-206 Piccadilly, SW1Y 6WW, 7851 2400, www.waterstones.co.uk), which has a fine bar-café and an on-site branch of the Trailfinders travel agency, and the academic bookseller **Blackwell** (100 Charing Cross Road, Soho, WC2H 0JG, 7292 5100, www.blackwell.co.uk).

General

★ Daunt Books
83-84 Marylebone High Street, Marylebone, W1U 4QW (7224 2295, www.dauntbooks.co.uk). Baker Street tube. **Open** 9am-7.30pm Mon-Sat; 11am-6pm Sun. **Credit** AmEx, MC, V. **Map** p396 G5.

This beautiful Edwardian shop's elegant three-level back room – complete with oak balconies, viridian-green walls and stained-glass window – houses a much-praised travel section featuring row upon row of guidebooks, maps, language reference, travelogues and related fiction. Travel aside, Daunt is also a first-rate stop for literary fiction, biography, gardening and much more.

Other locations 158-164 Fulham Road, Chelsea, SW10 9PR (7373 4997); 112-114 Holland Park Avenue, Holland Park, W11 4UA (7727 7022); 51 South End Road, Hampstead, NW3 2QB (7794 8206); 193 Haverstock Hill, Belsize Park, NW3 4QL (7794 4006); 61 Cheapside, City, EC2V 6AX (7248 1117).

Foyles
113-119 Charing Cross Road, Soho, WC2H 0EB (7437 5660, www.foyles.co.uk). Tottenham Court Road tube. **Open** 9.30am-9pm Mon-Sat; noon-6pm Sun (browsing from 11.30am). **Credit** AmEx, MC, V. **Map** p416 X2.

Probably the single most impressive independent bookshop in London, Foyles built its reputation on the sheer volume and breadth of its stock: there are 56 specialist subjects covered here, in the flagship store. The music, gay interest, foreign fiction, law and philosophy sections are especially strong. The shop's five storeys accommodate several concessions, too, including Unsworth's antiquarian book-

sellers, the new Grant & Cutler foreign-language bookstore and, on the third floor, Ray's Jazz (see *p229*). The popular first-floor café hosts readings from the likes of Douglas Coupland and Sebastian Faulks, as well as occasional gigs and other events.

Other locations Southbank Centre, SE1 8XX (7440 3212); St Pancras International, Euston Road, N1C 4QL (3206 2650); Westfield, Shepherd's Bush, W12 7GE (3206 2656).

▶ *Foyles is set to get even bigger in 2013, when it's due to move into the huge space that currently houses the Central Saint Martins art school, just down the road from its current site.*

Lutyens & Rubinstein
21 Kensington Park Road, Notting Hill, W11 2EU (7229 1010). Ladbroke Grove tube. **Open** 10am-6pm Mon-Sat; noon-6pm Sun. **Credit** AmEx, DC, MC, V. **Map** p404 X4.

Founded in 2009 by literary agents, Lutyens & Rubinstein sells a beautifully arranged selection of literary fiction and general non-fiction. The core stock of titles was put together by the owners canvassing hundreds of readers on which books they would most like to find in a bookshop; thus every book stocked is sold because somebody has recommended it. The result is an appealing alternative to the homogeneous chain bookshops, with some unusual titles available. As well as books, the shop stocks a small range of stationery, greetings cards, paperweights, local honey and literary-inspired scents from CB I Hate Perfume.

Specialist

Artwords
20-22 Broadway Market, Hackney, E8 4QJ (7923 7507, www.artwords.co.uk). London Fields rail. **Open** 10.30am-6.30pm Mon-Fri; 10am-6pm Sat; noon-6pm Sun. **Credit** AmEx, MC, V.

Artwords has its finger firmly on the pulse when it comes to contemporary visual arts publications. Stock relating to contemporary fine art dominates, but there are also plenty of architecture, photography, graphic design, fashion, advertising and film titles on display, plus an excellent range of industry and creative magazines.

Other locations 69 Rivington Street, Shoreditch, EC2A 3QQ (7729 2000).

Gosh!
1 Berwick Street, Soho, W1F 0DR (7636 1011, www.goshlondon.com). Oxford Circus or Tottenham Court Road tube. **Open** 10.30am-7pm daily. **Credit** MC, V. **Map** p416 V3.

There's nowhere better to bolster your comics collection than at this Soho specialist. There's a huge selection of Manga comics, but it's graphic novels that take centre stage, from early classics such as *Krazy Kat* to Alan Moore's Peter Pan adaptation *Lost Girls*. Classic children's books, of the *This is London* vein, are also a strong point.

CONSUME

Stanfords
*12-14 Long Acre, Covent Garden, WC2E 9LP
(7836 1321, www.stanfords.co.uk). Covent Garden
or Leicester Square tube.* **Open** 9am-8pm Mon-Fri;
10am-8pm Sat; noon-6pm Sun. **Credit** MC, V.
Map p416 Y3.
Three floors of travel guides, travel literature, maps,
language guides, atlases and magazines. The basement houses the full range of British Ordnance
Survey maps; you can plan your next trip over
Fairtrade coffee in the Natural Café.

Used & antiquarian

Bookended by Charing Cross Road and St
Martin's Lane, picturesque **Cecil Court**
(www.cecilcourt.co.uk) is known for its
antiquarian book, map and print dealers.
Notable residents include children's specialist
Marchpane (*see p212*), 40-year veteran
**David Drummond of Pleasures of
Past Times** (no.11, 7836 1142), the 100-
year-old mystical and spiritual specialist
Watkins (nos.19 & 21, 7836 2182) and
weclome newcomer **Natalie Galustian**
(no.22, 7240 6822, www.nataliegalustian.com),
specialising in books about poker, and early
gay literature.

Marchpane
*16 Cecil Court, Covent Garden, WC2N 4HE
(7836 8661, www.marchpane.com). Leicester
Square tube.* **Open** 11am-6pm Mon-Sat. **Credit**
MC, V. **Map** p416 X4.
This specialist in classic children's books is on bookshop passageway Cecil Court (*see above*), and a perfect
fit for its locale. Stock includes titles such as *Winnie-
the-Pooh* and *The Wind in the Willows*, but the shop's
forte is Lewis Carroll, with a collection of illustrated
editions of *Alice's Adventures in Wonderland*. A BBC
Dalek and a Scalextric track in the basement add to
the nostalgia.

Quinto/Francis Edwards
*72 Charing Cross Road, Soho, WC2H 0BB
(7379 7669). Leicester Square tube.* **Open** 9am-
9pm Mon-Sat; noon-8pm Sun. **Credit** AmEx, MC,
V. **Map** p416 X3.
This stalwart among the Charing Cross Road bookshops completely changes its stock of antiquarian,
rare, second-hand and collectable books once a
month, when it brings thousands of titles down from
its base in Hay-on-Wye.

Skoob
*Unit 66, The Brunswick, Bloomsbury, WC1N 1AE
(7278 8760, www.skoob.com). Russell Square tube.*
Open 10.30am-8pm Mon-Sat; 10.30am-6pm Sun.
Credit MC, V. **Map** p397 L4.
A back-to-basics basement beloved of students from
the nearby University of London, Skoob showcases

some 50,000 titles covering virtually every subject,
from philosophy and biography to politics and the
occult. Prices are very reasonable.

CHILDREN
Fashion

In addition, try baby superstore **Mamas &
Papas** (256-258 Regent Street, W1B 3AF,
0845 268 2000, www.mamasandpapas.co.uk).

Aravore Babies
*31 Park Road, Crouch End, N8 8TE (8347
5752, www.aravore-babies.com). Archway tube
then bus 41 or Finsbury Park tube/rail then bus
W7.* **Open** 10am-5.30pm Mon-Sat; noon-4.30pm
Sun. **Credit** AmEx, MC, V.
Distinctive fashions for babies from Aravore aren't
cheap, but they'll be much appreciated as gifts for
new parents. The crocheted and knitted organic
clothes go up to age five, and offer much to coo over,
including beautiful merino wool mittens and booties.

Sasti
*6 Portobello Green Arcade, 281 Portobello
Road, Notting Hill, W10 5TZ (8960 1125,
www.sasti.co.uk). Ladbroke Grove tube.* **Open**
10am-6pm Mon-Sat; noon-5pm Sun. **Credit**
AmEx, MC, V. **Map** p404 Y4.
This affordable children's boutique sells delightfully
fun clothes for little girls and boys. Perennial best-
sellers include the bunny dresses, flower-covered
skirts, bus pyjamas, nursery rhyme blouses and kit-
ten scarves. Apart from its own-label clothes, Sasti
also stocks items from Ubang and Pixie Dixie.

Toys

Selfridges (*see p207*) and **Harrods** (*see p204*)
have dedicated toy departments. **Hamley's**
(188-196 Regent Street, W1B 5BT, 0871 704 1977,
www.hamleys.com) has all the must-have toys
but is a noisy experience.

Benjamin Pollock's Toy Shop
*44 The Market, Covent Garden, WC2E 8RF (7379
7866, www.pollocks-coventgarden.co.uk). Covent
Garden tube.* **Open** 10.30am-6pm Mon-Sat; 11am-
4pm Sun. **Credit** AmEx, MC, V. **Map** p416 Z3.
Best known for its toy theatres, Pollock's is also
superb for traditional toys, such as knitted animals,
china tea sets, masks, glove puppets, cards, spinning
tops and fortune-telling fish.

Three Potato Four
*Alliance House, 44-45 Newington Green,
Newington Green, N16 9QH (7704 2228,
www.threepotatofour.co.uk). Canonbury rail.*
Open 10am-5pm Mon-Fri; 9.30am-6pm Sat;
11am-5pm Sun. **Credit** MC, V. **Map** p404 Y4.

This unique children's boutique manages to appeal to both children and adults, blending a child-focused fun factor with a pleasing dose of nostalgia. Among the new and vintage toys for sale are Olive & Moss soft toys, Schleich plastic animals and dinosaurs, and old Fisher Price items. Stylish children's clothes and books are also stocked in the retro-inspired interior.

Playlounge
19 Beak Street, Soho, W1F 9RP (7287 7073, www.playlounge.co.uk). Oxford Circus or Piccadilly Circus tube. **Open** 11am-7pm Mon-Sat; noon-5pm Sun. **Credit** AmEx, MC, V. **Map** p416 V3.
Compact but full of fun, this groovy little shop has action figures, gadgets, books and comics, e-boy posters, T-shirts and clothes that appeal to kids and adults alike. Those nostalgic for illustrated children's literature shouldn't miss the Dr Seuss PopUps and *Where the Wild Things Are* books.

ELECTRONICS & PHOTOGRAPHY
General

Ask
248 Tottenham Court Road, Fitzrovia, W1T 7QZ (7637 0353, www.askdirect.co.uk). Tottenham Court Road tube. **Open** 10am-7pm Mon-Wed, Fri, Sat; 10am-8pm Thur; noon-6pm Sun. **Credit** AmEx, DC, MC, V. **Map** p397 K5.
Ask has four capacious, well-organised floors that give you plenty of space to browse. Stock, spanning digital cameras, MP3 players, laptops, hi-fis and TVs , concentrates on the major consumer brands. Prices are competitive.

Specialist

Behind its grand façade, the **Apple Store** (235 Regent Street, W1B 2 EL, 7153 9000, www.apple. com) offers all the services you'd expect, including the trademark 'Genius Bar' for technical support. Another branch opened in Covent Garden (1-7 The Piazza, 7447 1400) in August 2010. There are lots of electronics shops on **Tottenham Court Road**, with several offering laptop repairs. **Adam Phones** (2-3 Dolphin Square, Edensor Road, Chiswick, W4 2ST, 8742 0101, www.adam phones.com) offers mobile phone handsets for hire at reasonable rates. For film processing, try **Snappy Snaps** (www.snappysnaps.co.uk) and **Jessops** (www.jessops.com); the latter also has a wide range of photography equipment for sale.

Aperture Photographic
44 Museum Street, Bloomsbury, WC1A 1LY (7242 8681, www.apertureuk.com). Holborn or Tottenham Court Road tube. **Open** 11am-7pm Mon-Fri; noon-7pm Sat. **Credit** AmEx, MC, V. **Map** p397 L5.

This camera shop-cum-café has a great atmosphere. The photographic side centres on an excellent selection of new and vintage, manual and autofocus Nikons, Leicas, Canons and Hasselblads, along with a sprinkling of other makes, at reasonable prices. The café is frequented by paparazzi and camera enthusiasts. Staff are happy to answer questions.
Other location 27 Rathbone Place, Bloomsbury (7436 1015).

FASHION
Multi-label boutiques

These shops sell both mens- and womenswear.

Browns
23-27 South Molton Street, Mayfair, W1K 5RD (7514 0000, www.brownsfashion.com). Bond Street tube. **Open** 10am-6.30pm Mon-Wed, Fri, Sat; 10am-7pm Thur. **Credit** AmEx, MC, V. **Map** p396 H6.
Among the 100-odd designers jostling for attention in Joan Burstein's five interconnecting shops (menswear is at no.23) are Chloé, Christopher Kane, Marc Jacobs, Balenciaga and Todd Lynn, with plenty of fashion exclusives. No.24 now also houses Shop 24, selling 'staple items you can't live without'. Browns Focus is younger and more casual; Labels for Less is loaded with last season's leftovers. Browns celebrated its 40th anniversary in 2010.
Other locations Browns Focus, 38-39 South Molton Street, W1K 5RL (7514 0000); Browns Labels for Less, 50 South Molton Street, W1K 5RD (7514 0000); Browns Bride, 11-12 Hinde Street, W1U 3BE (7514 0056); 6C Sloane Street, SW1X 9LE (7514 0040); Vera Wang at Browns, 59 Brook Street, W1K 4HS (7514 0000).

Folk
53 Lamb's Conduit Street, Bloomsbury, WC1N 3NG (8616 4191, www.folkclothing.com). Holborn tube. **Open** 11am-7pm Mon-Sat; noon-5pm Sun. **Credit** AmEx, MC, V. **Map** p397 M4
While the menswear store at no.49 (7404 6458) concentrates on the stylish own-label (albeit with additional pieces from Scandinavian brands Our Legacy and Han Kjøbenhavn), this branch of Folk is a godsend for women, with Scandinavian labels such as Won Hundred and Acne, as well as boutique faves Sessùn and Humanoid. Bags from Ally Capellino provide some tasty icing on a fashion-forward cake.
Other locations 12-14 Shepherd Street, Mayfair, W1J 7JS (7499 8598); 11 Dray Walk, Spitalfields, E1 6QL (7375 2844).

Goodhood
41 Coronet Street, Hoxton, N1 6HD (7729 3600, www.goodhood.co.uk). Old Street tube/rail. **Open** 11am-7pm Mon-Fri; 11am-6.30pm Sat. **Credit** AmEx, MC, V. **Map** p401 R3.

A first stop for East End trendies, Goodhood is owned by streetwear obsessives Kyle and Jo. Japanese independent labels are well represented, while other covetable brands include Pendleton, Norse Projects and Wood Wood.

OTHER/shop
21 Kingly Street, W1B 5QA (7734 6846, www.other-shop.com). Oxford Circus tube. **Open** 10.30am-6.30pm Mon-Fri; noon-5pm Sat. **Credit** AmEx, MC, V. **Map** p416 U3.
The Other shop opened in the summer of 2012, but founders Matthew Murphy and Kirk Beattie have more than a decade's experience in running another successful indie boutique – b Store. Other occupies the same site as its (now defunct) predecessor, sells similar stock, even a continuation of the excellent b Clothing brand – now called Other – that the store had become famous for. A sun-lit basement stocks Other's edit of brands such as Peter Jensen, Our Legacy, Sophie Hulme, Opening Ceremony, and MM6 by Maison Martin Margiela. The store often houses installations and exhibitions by artists, and also stocks a range of mags and coffee-table books.

Single-label boutiques

Margaret Howell
34 Wigmore Street, Marylebone, W1U 2RS (7009 9009, www.margarethowell.co.uk). Bond Street tube. **Open** 10am-6pm Mon-Wed, Fri, Sat; 10am-7pm Thur; noon-5pm Sun. **Credit** AmEx, DC, MC, V. **Map** p396 H5.
Margaret Howell's wearable clothes are made in Britain with an old-fashioned attitude to quality. These principles combine with her elegant designs to make for the best 'simple' clothes for sale in London. Her pared-down approach means prices seem steep, but these are clothes that last and seem only to get better with time.
Other locations 111 Fulham Road, Chelsea, SW3 6RL (7591 2255); 7-8 Duke Street, Mayfair, 8948 5005); **MHL Shop** 19 Nichol Street, E2 7HR (7033 9494).

Preen
5 Portobello Green, 281 Portobello Road, Ladbroke Grove, W10 5TZ (8968 1542, www.preen.eu). **Open** 10am-6pm Thur-Sat. **Credit** AmEx, DC, MC, V. **Map** p404 X4.
Preen – the hip British label from Justin Thornton and Thea Bregazzi – brings imaginative takes to traditional silhouettes. Collections are characterised by urban, minimalist shapes and interesting splashes of colour. Look out for a great range of bags and shoes, plus an accessories range.

Supreme
2-3 Peter Street, Soho, W1F 0AA (7437 0493, www.supremenewyork.com). Piccadilly Circus or Oxford Circus tube. **Open** 11am-7.30pm Mon-Sat; noon-6pm Sun. **Credit** AmEx, MC, V. **Map** p416 W3.

Europe's first Supreme store opened in September 2011, to much excitement among the city's skaters and streetwear fans. The standalone Soho store – which feels more like a gallery than a shop – stocks the entire collection of the cool New York brand's clothing, footwear and boards.

Sunspel
7 Redchurch Street, Shoreditch, E2 7DJ (7739 9729, www.sunspel.com). Shoreditch High Street rail. **Open** 11am-7pm Mon-Sat; noon-6pm Sun. **Credit** AmEx, MC, V. **Map** p401 S4.
It may look like a trendy east London newcomer, but Sunspel is actually a classic British label, which has been producing quality menswear for over 150 years. It even claims to have introduced boxer shorts to the UK. This corner space is the brand's first retail outlet, showcasing the range of underwear, T-shirts, merino wool knitwear and polo shirts, as well as the new smaller line of equally pared-down womenswear.
Other location 40 Old Compton Street, Soho, W1D 4TU (7734 4491).

YMC
11 Poland Street, Soho, W1F 8QA (7494 1619, www.youmustcreate.com). Oxford Circus tube. **Open** 11am-7pm Mon-Sat. **Credit** AmEx, MC, V. **Map** p416 V2.
Impeccably designed staples are the forte of this London label, which opened its first store in 2010. It's the place to head to for simple vest tops and T-shirts, stylish macs and duffle coats, tasteful knits and chino-style trousers, for both men and women.
Other locations 23 Hanbury Street, Spitalfieds, E1 6QR (3432 3010).

Lifestyle boutiques & concept stores

Lifestyle boutiques and concept stores are interchangeable terms that signal shops selling a wide range of covetable and exclusive items, covering fashion, accessories, homewares and gift-type items. The underlying idea is to provide a shopping 'experience' rather than just a marketplace.

Anthropologie
158 Regent Street, W1B 5SW (7529 9800, www.anthropologie.co.uk). Piccadilly Circus tube. **Open** 10am-7pm Mon-Wed, Fri, Sat; 10am-8pm Thur; noc-n-6pm Sun. **Credit** AmEx, MC, V. **Map** p416 U3.
Anthropologie, the romantically inclined elder sister to fellow US brand Urban Outfitters, opened the doors of its first European store in autumn 2009. Stock is of a feminine bent, with delicate necklaces and soft-knit cardies, while the store's signature large-scale window displays and 1,500sq ft living

Dover Street Market.

wall of plants are worth the trip alone. A second store opened on the King's Road in spring 2010. **Other locations** 131-141 King's Road, Chelsea, SW3 4PW (7349 3110).

Darkroom
52 Lamb's Conduit Street, Bloomsbury, WC1N 3LL (7831 7244, www.darkroomlondon.com). Holborn or Russell Square tube. **Open** 11am-7pm Mon-Fri; 11am-6pm Sat; noon-5pm Sun. **Credit** AmEx, MC, V. **Map** p397 M5.
This shop is quite literally dark (with black walls and lampshades), creating a striking backdrop for the carefully chosen selection of unisex fashion, accessories and interiors items for sale. Stock includes Fleet Ilya bags, DMK glassware and Solomia ceramics. The space doubles up as a gallery, with art displays intermingling with a range of sculptural jewellery.

★ Dover Street Market
17-18 Dover Street, Mayfair, W1S 4LT (7518 0680, www.doverstreetmarket.com). Green Park tube. **Open** 11am-6.30pm Mon-Wed; 11am-7pm Thur-Sat; noon-5pm Sun. **Credit** AmEx, MC, V. **Map** p398 J7.
Comme des Garçons designer Rei Kawakubo's ground-breaking six-storey space combines the edgy energy of London's indoor markets – concrete floors, tills inside corrugated iron shacks, Portaloo dressing rooms – with a fine range of rarefied labels. All 14 of the Comme des Garçons collections are here, alongside exclusive lines from such designers as Lanvin and Azzedine Alaïa.

Shop at Bluebird
350 King's Road, Chelsea, SW3 5UU (7351 3873, www.theshopatbluebird.com). Sloane Square tube. **Open** 10am-7pm Mon-Sat; noon-6pm Sun. **Credit** AmEx, MC, V. **Map** p395 D12.
Part lifestyle boutique and part design gallery, the Shop at Bluebird offers a shifting showcase of cloth-

ing for men, women and children (Emma Cook, Peter Jensen, Marc Jacobs), accessories, furniture, books and gadgets. The shop has a retro feel, with vintage furniture, reupholstered seating and hand-printed fabrics. The menswear range is particularly strong.

Smug
13 Camden Passage, Islington, N1 8EA (7354 0253, www.ifeelsmug.com). Angel tube. **Open** 11am-6pm Wed, Fri, Sat; noon-7pm Thur; noon-5pm Sun. **Credit** MC, V. **Map** p400 O2.
Graphic designer Lizzie Evans has decked out this lovely lifestyle boutique with all her favourite things. You'll be treated to a well-edited selection of home accessories (owl ceramic candlesticks, say); vintage homewares (Welsh blankets, 1960s Formica furniture); colourful cushions; Pixie make-up; home-made brooches; old-fashioned notebooks; retro Casio watches; and a range of graphic-print men's T-shirts.

High-end designer

Key British designers include **Vivienne Westwood** (44 Conduit Street, W1S 2YL, 7439 1109, www.viviennewestwood.com); **Paul Smith** (Westbourne House, 120 Kensington Park Road, W11 2EP, 7727 3553, www.paulsmith. co.uk), **Stella McCartney** (30 Bruton Street, W1J 6QR, 7518 3100, www.stellamccartney.com) and **Alexander McQueen** (4-5 Old Bond Street, W1S 4PD, 7355 0088, www.alexander mcqueen.com), headed by Sarah Burton since the designer's death. The diffusion line, **McQ** (*see p216*) opened a new store in October 2012. Those after some Parisian style should head to the luxurious **Louis Vuitton Maison** flagship (17-20 New Bond Street, W1S 2UE, 7399 3856, www.louisvuitton.com), or the more pared-down but equally fashion-forward **Vanessa Bruno** boutique (1A Grafton Street, W1S 4EB, 7499 7838, www.vanessabruno.com), the designer's first London store.

Beyond Retro. *See p218.*

Bosideng

28 South Molton Street, W1K 5RF (7290 3170, www.bosidenglondon.com). Bond Street tube. **Open** 10am-8pm Mon-Sat; noon-6pm Sun. **Credit** AmEx, MC, V. **Map** p396 H6.

Set over three floors and converted from the rather less upmarket Hog in the Pound pub on South Molton Street, Bosideng's first overseas flagship store and honorary European headquarters is looking as plush as its 500-piece collection (and with a £10,000 origami sculpture and a £30 million renovation we'd expect no less). This menswear label is Asia's largest manufacturer of down apparel – every feather is a by-product we might add – jetting straight in from China where it has a whopping 10,000 outlets. Pretty remarkable so far. Every item in the collection is sourced from the UK and Europe (apart from the down) and rendered in posh fabrics: pure cashmere cardys, wool-blend tweed blazers and Egyptian-cotton tops all add to the label's rather sophisticated look. The space itself is ultra-glossy and airy.

Burberry Regent Street

121 Regent Street, W1B 4TB (7806 8904, www.burberry.com). Piccadilly Circus tube. **Open** 10am-9pm Mon-Sat; noon-6pm Sun. *See right* **Roboshop.**

McQ

14 Dover Street, W1S 4LW (www.mcq.com). Green Park tube. **Open** 10am-7pm Mon-Fri; 11am-7pm Sat; noon-5pm Sun. *See right* **Roboshop.**

Discount

Browns Labels for Less (*see p213*) also sells discount pieces.

Burberry Factory Shop

29-31 Chatham Place, Hackney, E9 6LP (8328 4287). Hackney Central rail. **Open** 10am-6pm Mon-Thur; 9am-7pm Fri, Sat; 11am-5pm Sun. **Credit** AmEx, MC, V.

This warehouse space showcases seconds and excess stock reduced by 50% or more. Classic men's macs can be had for around £199 or less.

Paul Smith Sale Shop

23 Avery Row, Mayfair, W1X 9HB (7493 1287, www.paulsmith.co.uk). Bond Street tube. **Open** 10.30am-6.30pm Mon-Wed, Fri, Sat; 10.30am-7pm Thur; noon-6pm Sun. **Credit** AmEx, DC, MC, V. **Map** p398 H7.

Samples and previous season's stock at a 30-50% discount at this sale shop. The varied stock includes clothes for men, women and children, as well as a range of accessories.

Primark

14-28 Oxford Street, W1 1BJ (7580 5510, www.primark.co.uk). Tottenham Court Road tube. **Open** 8am-10pm Mon-Fri; 8am-9pm Sat; noon-6pm Sun. **Credit** MC, V. **Map** p416 W1.

With more than 80,000sq ft over flour floors, this spanking new branch of Primark is even bigger than its sister branch near Marble Arch. What the opening of this new premises makes clear is that the brand we love to hate – and hate to love – is thriving; Primark sales were up 16% in 2012. Stock changes rapidly but an early visit unearthed £6 Breton t-shirts, £15 faux leather trousers and an Alexander McQueen-inspired figure-hugging nylon frock for just £10. Many would argue that the concept of throwaway fashion is increasingly wrong and out-moded, but the value of Primark clothing is precisely that – it trades in trend-led pieces that'll get you through a weekend, a party or a summer holiday, all for a few quid. Primark has even flipped a finger at allegations – proven false – about its overseas production by signing up to the Ethical Trading Initiative. The other big London branch is at 499-517 Oxford Street.

Other locations throughout the city.

High street

The best of the high-street chains are designer-look **Reiss** (Kent House, 14-17 Market Place, Fitzrovia, W1H 7AJ, 7637 9112, www.reiss.co.uk); **Banana Republic** (224 Regent Street, W1B 3BR, 7758 3550, www.bananarepublic.eu) – a recent arrival to British shores, which now has several branches in the city; H&M's upmarket sibling **COS** (222 Regent Street, W1B 5BD, 7478 0400, www.cosstores.com); **Whistles** (12-14 St Christopher's Place, Marylebone, W1U 1NH, 7487 4484, www.whistles.co.uk) for high-quality but on-trend womenswear; and **Urban Outfitters** (200 Oxford Street, W1D 1NU, 7907 0815,

Roboshop

Shopping's brave new world.

After two years of restoration, the future-focused flagship of the **Burberry** brand (*see left*) opened on Regent Street in September 2012, melding together the building's near-200 years of history with all the bells and whistles of hyper-modern retailing. The store's designers have dedicated themselves to making a visit to the building an immersive, memorable experience full of clever audio-visual tricks and reactive technology. Alongside the iPad wielding shop assistants is Radio Frequency Identification Technology that Burberry has woven into certain garments, triggering films and sounds relevant to the product – you might try on a trench coat, say, and suddenly mirrors become video screens showing shots of the same product on the runway, or special video content. Digital signage and nearly 500 speakers and 100 screens pump out sudden (digital) rain showers. An emphasis on natural light (via an atrium created from the building's original cinema auditorium), herringbone parquet, inviting lounge areas and a programme of events and acoustic musical performances take the edge off the store's sci-fi pretensions, creating an inviting, world class flagship.

McQ, the fashion brand by Alexander McQueen, has finally opened its first store in Dover Street (*see left*), and once again, it's all about the tech: step into the Georgian townhouse and you'll be greeted by a large white digital dining table rather like a giant tablet. From here you can project catwalk images and videos on to the wall using small viewing boxes. It's weirdly addictive. Downstairs, past the brutalist concrete walls and thick red carpets, there are 'gesture-control' digital mirrors where you can take a photograph – and then email it – of yourself posing in looks from the collection. Interior designer David Collins (of Wolseley and the Connaught fame) has turned the five-storey building into a sort of retail robot HQ. With glossy white walls and polished steel curves, it's like a raunchy episode of *Star Trek*, which makes sense as sex and futurism were two of the late designer's lasting influences.

These high-end designers aren't alone in marketing their products through futuristic tricks. At **Nike + Fuelstation** at Boxpark (2-4 Bethnal Green Road, E1 6GY, www.boxpark. co.uk, 7033 9441), customers can record their movements on LCD screens, ready to email to their friends. And at the other end of the hipness spectrum, even good, reliable old **John Lewis** (*see p203*) is using QR codes and interactive digital displays these days, as a rather sober nod to the future.

CONSUME

McQ.

www.urbanoutfitters.co.uk), with a great range of boutique labels. **Topshop**'s (*see below*) massive, teenager-filled, throbbing flagship continues to push the envelope, while branches of US casualwear brand **American Apparel** (www.americanapparel.net) can now be found across the city.

★ Topshop

214 Oxford Street, W1W 8LG (0844 848 7487, www.topshop.com). Oxford Circus tube. **Open** 9am-9pm Mon-Wed; 9am-10pm Thur, Fri; 9am-9pm Sat; 11.30am-6pm Sun. **Credit** AmEx, DC, MC, V. **Map** p416 U2.

Topshop has been the queen of the British high street for the past decade, and walking into the busy Oxford Street flagship, it's easy to see why. Spanning three huge floors, the place lays claim to being the world's largest fashion shop, and is always buzzing with fashion-forward teens and twentysomethings keen to get their hands on the next big trends. The store covers a huge range of styles and sizes, and includes free personal shoppers, boutique label concessions, capsule collections, a Daniel Hersheson Blow Dry Bar (*see p225*), Nails Inc manicures, a Metalmorphosis tattoo parlour, a café and sweet shop. Topman is as on-the-ball and innovative as its big sister, stocking niche menswear labels such as Garbstore, and housing a trainer boutique, a suit section, and a new personal shopping suite, featuring consultation rooms, Xbox 360s and an exhibition space. Both shops are even more of a hive of activity than normal during London Fashion Week, when a series of special events are held.

Other locations throughout the city.

Tailors

Chris Kerr

31 Berwick Street, Soho, W1F 8RJ (7437 3727, www.eddiekerr.co.uk). Oxford Circus tube. **Open** 9am-5.30pm Mon-Fri; 9am-1pm Sat. **Credit** AmEx, MC, V. **Map** p416 V2.

Chris Kerr, son of legendary 1960s tailor Eddie Kerr, is the man to visit if Savile Row's prices or attitude aren't to your liking. The versatile Kerr has no house style; instead, he makes every suit to each client's exact specifications, and those clients include Johnny Depp and David Walliams. A good place to get started with British tailoring.

Timothy Everest

35 Bruton Place, Mayfair, W1J 6NS (7629 6236, www.timothyeverest.co.uk). Bond Street tube. **Open** 10am-6pm Mon-Fri; 11am-5pm Sat. **Credit** AmEx, MC, V. **Map** p398 H7.

One-time apprentice to the legendary Tommy Nutter, Everest is a star of the latest generation of London tailors. He's well known for his relaxed 21st-century definition of style.

Used & vintage

East London, and particularly the area around Brick Lane, is still an excellent place to find vintage fashion shops. In the past year, however, Soho has upped its game, with a wave of new vintage shop openings on and around **Berwick Street**.

Beyond Retro

112 Cheshire Street, Shoreditch, E2 6EJ (7613 3636, www.beyondretro.com). Shoreditch High Street rail. **Open** 10am-7pm Mon-Wed, Fri, Sat; 10am-8pm Thur; 10am-6pm Sun. **Credit** MC, V. **Map** p403 S4.

This enormous palace of second-hand clothing and accessories is the starting point for many an expert stylist, thrifter or fashion designer on the hunt for bargains and inspiration. The 10,000 items on the warehouse floor include 1950s dresses, cowboy boots and denim hot pants, many under £20. In-store events, such as live bands, add to the lively and supremely east London vibe. An equally massive new branch opened in Dalston in autumn 2011, with a great café. *Photo p216.*

Other locations 58-59 Great Marlborough Street, Soho, W1F 7JY (7434 1406); Simpson House, 92-100 Stoke Newington Road, Dalston, N16 7XB (7613 3636).

★ Lucy in Disguise

48 Lexington Street, Soho, W1F 0LR (7434 4086, www.lucyindisguiselondon.com). Oxford Circus or Piccadilly Circus tube. **Open** 10am-7pm Mon-Sat; noon-6pm Sun. **Credit** AmEx, MC, V. **Map** p416 V3.

The vintage store owned by Lily Allen and half-sister Sarah Owen, made famous through a tv documentary, has really come into its own since moving to this fabulous Lexington Street space. The shiny chequered floor, big 1950s-style TV and vintage chandeliers create a cool and glamorous vibe in which to shop for good-quality vintage, from dresses and tops by Pierre Cardin and Christian Dior, to silk scarves and beautiful leather handbags. The Lucy in Disguise own-label – new dresses inspired by vintage designs – is also a real draw.

Vintage Emporium

14 Bacon Street, Brick Lane, E1 6LF (7739 0799, www.vintageemporiumcafe.com). Shoreditch High Street rail. **Open** 10am-7pm daily. **Credit** AmEx, MC, V. **Map** p401 S4.

With a well-edited range of clothing (in the basement) from the Victorian era to the 1950s, this café-shop's vintage time frame is somewhat tighter than that of its nearby rivals, but maybe all the better for it. Beautiful lace blouses, 1950s dresses, a great selection of hats, and top-notch accessories are all for sale, and, considering the age of most of the items, prices are very reasonable.

CONSUME

Ally Capellino. See p220.

FASHION ACCESSORIES & SERVICES

Clothing hire

Lipman & Sons

22 Charing Cross Road, Soho, WC2H 0HR (7240 2310, www.lipmanandsons.co.uk). Leicester Square tube. **Open** 9am-6pm Mon-Wed, Fri, Sat; 9am-8pm Thur. **Credit** AmEx, DC, MC, V. **Map** p416 X4.
A reliable, long-serving formalwear specialist.

Cleaning & repairs

British Invisible Mending Service

32 Thayer Street, Marylebone, W1U 2QT (7935 2487, www.invisible-mending.co.uk). Bond Street tube. **Open** 8.30am-5.30pm Mon-Fri; 10am-1pm Sat. **No credit cards**. **Map** p396 G5.
A 24-hour service is offered.

Celebrity Cleaners

9 Greens Court, Soho, W1F 0HJ (7437 5324). Piccadilly Circus tube. **Open** 8.30am-6.30pm Mon-Fri. **No credit cards**. **Map** p416 W3.
Dry-cleaner to West End theatres and the ENO. **Other locations** Neville House, 27 Page Street, Pimlico, SW1P 4JJ (7821 1777).

Fifth Avenue Shoe Repairers

41 Goodge Street, Fitzrovia, W1T 2PY (7636 6705). Goodge Street tube. **Open** 8am-6pm Mon-Fri; 10am-6pm Sat. **Credit** AmEx, MC, V. **Map** p396 J5.
High-calibre, speedy shoe repairs.

Hats

For bold hats by the king of couture headgear, head to **Philip Treacy** (69 Elizabeth Street, SW1 9PJ, 7730 3992, www.philiptreacy.co.uk).

Bernstock Speirs

234 Brick Lane, Brick Lane, E2 7EB (7739 7385, www.bernstockspeirs.com). Shoreditch High Street rail. **Open** 11am-6pm Tue-Fri; 11am-5pm Sat, Sun. **Credit** AmEx, MC, V.
Paul Bernstock and Thelma Speirs's unconventional hats for men and women have a loyal following, being both wearable and fashion-forward. Past ranges have included collaborations with Peter Jensen and Emma Cook.

Jewellery

There are also some lovely pieces for sale in **Contemporary Applied Arts** (*see p224*).

Comfort Station

22 Cheshire Street, Shoreditch, E2 6EH (7033 9099, www.comfortstation.co.uk). Liverpool Street tube/rail or Shoreditch High Street rail. **Open** 11am-6pm Tue-Sun. **Credit** AmEx, MC, V.
Fine art graduate and designer Amy Anderson is the creative talent behind this ladylike Cheshire Street boutique. Offbeat touches, such as birds painted on the door and a piano-turned-display cabinet, provide the ideal environment to showcase her handmade accessories. Alongside the beautiful, ethically made bags and bone-china crockery covered in wonderfully weird collaged prints is her jewellery line. The collection changes each season, with classically elegant but original designs in gold, silver, cord, wood and onyx. Favourites include 'Sliced Poetry' range – delicate leaf-shaped 'books' that fan open to reveal pages of Victorian poetry and Anderson's 'Globe' pendants – moveable silver rings that form a clever 3D sphere.

ec one

41 Exmouth Market, Clerkenwell, EC1R 4QL (7713 6185, www.econe.co.uk). Farringdon tube/rail. **Open** 10am-6pm Mon-Wed, Fri; 11am-7pm Thur; 10.30am-6pm Sat. **Credit** MC, V. **Map** p400 N4.
Husband-and-wife team Jos and Alison Skeates have a magpie's eye for good design, which makes for delightfully varied browsing at this stylish Clerkenwell shop. Over 50 designers are showcased: temptingly inexpensive trinkets include colourful lucite bangles and sweet little heart necklaces. Among the slightly pricier standouts are Celestine Soumah's beguilingly simple silver designs.
Other locations 56 Ledbury Road, Notting Hill, W11 2AJ (7243 8811).

Garrard

24 Albemarle Street, Mayfair, W1S 4HT (0870 871 8888, www.garrard.com). Bond Street or

CONSUME

Green Park tube. **Open** 10am-6pm Mon-Fri; 10am-5pm Sat. **Credit** AmEx, MC, V. **Map** p416 U5.
The Crown Jeweller's diamond-studded designs have appealed to a new generation of bling-seekers since the brand was modernised by Jade Jagger. It's now in the hands of London-based jeweller Stephen Webster, who took over as creative director in 2009.

Lingerie & underwear

Agent Provocateur is now a glossy international chain, but the original outpost of the shop that went on to popularise high-class kink around the world is still in Soho (6 Broadwick Street, W1F 8HL, 7439 0229, www.agentprovocateur.com). For a serious bespoke service, royal corsetière **Rigby & Peller** (22A Conduit Street, W1S 2XT, 0845 076 5545, www.rigbyandpeller.com) is in Mayfair. Erotic emporium **Coco de Mer** (*see p224*) also has a small selection of boudoir-esque lingerie.

Myla
Westfield Shopping Centre, Ariel Way, W12 7GF (8749 9756, www.myla.com). **Open** 10am-9pm Mon-Fri; 9am-9pm Sat; noon-6pm Sun. **Credit** AmEx, MC, V.
Since it was founded in 1999, the luxury lingerie brand Myla has acquired a devoted following (its lace and freshwater pearl g-string acquired infamy after being featured in a classic Samantha *Sex and the City* scene). There are now lots of stores and concessions around town, which makes getting one's hands on the label's stylish, high-quality bras, knickers, toys and accessories a breeze. Seasonally updated collections always include fashion-forward colours and designs, though classics such as the signature silk and lace couture range are always in stock. There's a lovely swimwear range, elegant nightwear (like classic silk satin pyjamas) and accessories such as candles, silk-bow nipple tassels and blindfolds.
Branches throughout the city.

Victoria's Secret
123-124 The Arcade, Westfield Stratford City, E20 1EJ (8536 5700, www.victoriassecret.com). Stratford tube/rail. **Open** 10am-9pm Mon-Fri; 9am-9pm Sat; noon-6pm Sun. **Credit** AmEx, MC, V.
With its glossy quartz floors, black walls and leopard-print padded bras, Victoria's Secret is as different from Marks & Spencer's trusty undies department as you can get. The American lingerie giant, founded in 1977 by Roy Raymond, is known for its brash ad campaigns featuring scantily clad 'Angels' and saucy fashion shows. Being a Victoria's Secret Angel has kickstarted the career of many a young model, Miranda Kerr and Rosie Huntington-Whiteley included. With all this pomp and fizz, it makes sense that the brand's first UK store in Westfield Stratford City does not do subtle – with polyester thongs and low-waisted briefs ('cheekies') many of them £10 a pop (or three for £24) in super-bright shades. A huge hit with teen shoppers.
Branch 111 New Bond Street, W1S 1DP.

Luggage & bags

Harrods (*see p204*), **John Lewis** (*see p203*) and **Selfridges** (*see p207*) have excellent selections of luggage and bags.

★ Ally Capellino
9 Calvert Avenue, Shoreditch, E2 7JP (7613 3073, www.allycapellino.co.uk). Shoreditch High Street rail. **Open** 11am-6pm Tue-Sat; 11am-5pm Sun. **Credit** AmEx, MC, V. **Map** p401 R4.
This shop stocks the full range of Ally Capellino's stylishly understated unisex leather and waxed cotton bags, satchels, wallets, purses and laptop cases. Prices start at around £40 for a cute leather coin purse, rising to over £300 for larger, more structured models. *Photo p219.*
Other locations 312 Portobello Road, Notting Hill, W10 5RU (8964 1022).

Globe-Trotter
54-55 Burlington Arcade, Mayfair, W1J 0LB (7529 5950, www.globe-trotterltd.com). Green Park tube. **Open** 10am-6pm Mon-Sat. **Credit** AmEx, MC, V. **Map** p398 J7.
Globe-Trotter's indestructible steamer-trunk luggage, available here in various sizes and colours, accompanied the Queen on honeymoon. Iconic Mackintosh coats share the shop space.

Primrose Bakery. *See p222.*

Postcard Teas. *See p222.*

▶ *Looking for luggage that's a solution rather than an investment? Marks & Spencer (www. marksandspencer.co.uk) does reliable basics.*

Shoes

Among the best footwear chains is **Office** (57 Neal Street, Covent Garden, WC2H 4NP, 7379 1896, www.office.co.uk), which offers funky styles for guys and girls at palatable prices. **Kurt Geiger** (198 Regent Street, W1B 5TP, 3238 0044, www.kurtgeiger.com) and **Russell & Bromley** (24-25 New Bond Street, W1S 2PS, 7629 6903, www.russellandbromley.co.uk) both turn out classy takes on key trends for both sexes; and **Clarks** (476 Oxford Street, W1C 1LD, 0844 499 9302, www.clarks.co.uk) has shed its school-shoe image and gone on to be known as the inventor of Wallabees.

Carnaby Street is a great place for trainers, with branches of **Size?** (nos.33-34, www.size. co.uk), **Puma** (nos.52-55, www.puma.com) and **Vans** (no.47, www.vans.eu) among the options.

Black Truffle

4 Broadway Market, Hackney, E8 4QJ (7923 9450, www.blacktruffle.co.uk). London Fields rail or bus 394. **Open** 11am-6pm Tue-Fri; 10am-6pm Sat; noon-6pm Sun. **Credit** AmEx, MC, V.
This firm Hackney favourite sells quirky, stylish yet wearable footwear for women, men and children from its deceptively large space on the canal end of Broadway Market. Look out in particular for shoes by Melissa, Vialis, F Troupe and Falke, knee-high boots by Alberto Fermani and bags from Ally Capellino and Matt & Nat.
Other locations 52 Warren Street, Fitzrovia, W1T 5NJ (7388 4547).

Camper

34 Shelton Street, WC2H 9HP (7836 7973, www.camper.com). Covent Garden tube.

Open 10am-8pm Mon-Sat; noon-6pm Sun.
Credit AmEx, MC, V. **Map** p416 Y2.
The successful Spanish eco footwear brand – one of Mallorca's best exports – has become more sophisticated in recent seasons, moving away from its funky but sensible image towards a more fashion-oriented aesthetic, particularly for the women's range. Each year, the label seems to flirt more with ankle boots and high heels (albeit rubbery wedgy ones) and girly straps. However, most of its styles are still distinctively recognisable, with the classic, round-toed and clod-heeled models still featuring. And the guys still have their iconic bowling shoes. Definitely worth another look if you've previously dismissed the brand.
Branches throughout London.

Kate Kanzier

67-69 Leather Lane, Holborn, EC1N 7TJ (7242 7232, www.katekanzier.com). Chancery Lane tube or Farringdon tube/rail. **Open** 8.30am-6.30pm Mon-Fri; 11am-4pm Sat. **Credit** AmEx, MC, V. **Map** p400 N5.
Adored for great-value directional footwear for women, Kate Kanzier is the place to visit for brogues (£30), ballerinas (£20), sandles and leather boots in a huge range of colours. Sexy high-heeled pumps in patent, suede, leather and animal prints are characterised by vintage designs. Handbags and clutches are also stocked in the spacious Holborn shop.

FOOD & DRINK

Bakeries

Konditor & Cook

22 Cornwall Road, Waterloo, SE1 8TW (7261 0456, www.konditorandcook.com). Waterloo tube/rail. **Open** 7.30am-6.30pm Mon-Fri; 8.30am-2.30pm Sat. **Credit** AmEx, MC, V. **Map** p402 N10.

Gerhard Jenne caused a stir when he opened this bakery on a South Bank sidestreet in 1993, selling gingerbread people for grown-ups and lavender-flavoured cakes. Success lay in lively ideas such as magic cakes that spell the recipient's name in a series of individually decorated squares. Quality prepacked salads and sandwiches are also sold. The brand is now a mini-chain, with several branches. **Other locations** throughout the city.

Primrose Bakery

69 Gloucester Avenue, Primrose Hill, NW1 8LD (7483 4222, www.primrosebakery.org.uk). Chalk Farm tube. **Open** 8.30am-6pm Mon-Sat; 10am-5.30pm Sun. **Credit** AmEx, MC, V. **Map** p404 X2.
Catch a serious sugar high from Martha Swift's pretty, generously sized cupcakes in vanilla, coffee and lemon flavours. The tiny, retro-styled shop also sells peanut butter cookies and layer cakes. *Photo p220.*
Other locations 42 Tavistock Street, Covent Garden, WC2E 7PB (7836 3638).

Drinks

★ Algerian Coffee Stores

52 Old Compton Street, Soho, W1V 6PB (7437 2480, www.algcoffee.co.uk). **Open** 9am-7pm Mon-Wed; 9am-9pm Thur, Fri; 9am-8pm Sat. **Credit** AmEx, DC, MC, V. **Map** p416 W3.
For over 120 years, this unassuming little shop has been trading over the same wooden counter. The range of coffees is broad, with house blends sold alongside single-origin beans, and some serious teas and brewing hardware are also available.
▶ *Passing? Take away a single or double espresso for £1, or a cappuccino or a latte for £1.20.*

Berry Bros & Rudd

3 St James's Street, Mayfair, SW1A 1EG (7396 9600, www.bbr.com). Green Park tube. **Open** 10am-6pm Mon-Fri; 10am-5pm Sat. **Credit** AmEx, DC, MC, V. **Map** p398 J8.
Britain's oldest wine merchant has been trading on the same premises since 1698, and its heritage is reflected in its panelled sales and tasting rooms. Burgundy- and claret-lovers will drool at the hundreds of wines, but there are also decent selections from elsewhere in Europe and the New World. Prices are generally fair.

Cadenhead's Whisky Shop & Tasting Room

26 Chiltern Street, Marylebone, W1U 7QF (7935 6999, www.whiskytastingroom.com). Baker Street tube. **Open** 10.30am-6.30pm Mon-Fri; 10.30am-6pm Sat. **Credit** DC, MC, V. **Map** p416 Z3.
Cadenhead's is a survivor of a rare breed: the independent whisky bottler. And its shop is one of a kind, at least in London. Cadenhead's selects barrels from distilleries all over Scotland and bottles them without filtration or any other intervention.
▶ *For a wider range of spirits – the widest to be found in London, according to the staff – try Gerry's (74 Old Compton Street, Soho, W1D 4UW, 7734 4215, www.gerrys.uk.com). It's not far from Milroy's (3 Greek Street, Soho, W1D 4NX, 7437 2385, www.milroys.co.uk), another whisky specialist.*

★ Postcard Teas

9 Dering Street, Mayfair, W1S 1AG (7629 3654, www.postcardteas.com). Bond Street or Oxford

James Smith & Sons. *See p224.*

Circus tube. **Open** 10.30am-6.30pm Mon-Sat.
Credit AmEx, MC, V. **Map** p396 H6.
The range in Timothy d'Offay's exquisite little shop is not huge, but it is selected with great care: for instance, some of its Darjeeling teas (£3.50-£9.95/50g) are currently sourced from the Glenburn estate, regarded as one of the best in the region. There's a central table for those who want to try a pot; or book in for one of the tasting sessions held on Saturdays between 10am and 11am. Tea-ware and accessories are also sold. *Photo p221.*

General

You'll find branches of Britain's most popular supermarkets, **Sainsbury's** (www.sainsburys.co.uk) and **Tesco** (www.tesco.com), throughout the city. Superior-quality **Waitrose** (www.waitrose.com) has central branches on Tottenham Court Road, Marylebone High Street, John Lewis in Oxford Street (*see p203*) and in Bloomsbury's Brunswick Centre (www.brunswick.co.uk). For a more ethical type of supermarket shopping, head to Lamb's Conduit Street for the **People's Supermarket** (nos.72-78, WC1N 3LP, 7430 1827, www.peoplessupermarket.org), a co-operative that focuses on locally sourced produce.

Whole Foods Market

63-97 Kensington High Street, South Kensington, W8 5SE (7368 4500, www.wholefoodmarket.com). High Street Kensington tube. **Open** 8am-10pm Mon-Sat; 10am-6pm Sun. **Credit** AmEx, DC, MC, V.
The London flagship of the American health-food supermarket chain occupies the handsome deco department store that was once Barkers. There are several eateries on the premises.
Other locations throughout the city.

Markets

The farmers' markets in the capital reflect Londoners' concern over provenance and green issues. Two central ones are in **Marylebone** (Cramer Street car park, corner of Moxton Street, off Marylebone High Street, 10am-2pm Sun) and **Notting Hill** (behind Waterstones, access via Kensington Place, W8, 9am-1pm Sat). For a fashion show and farmers' market in one, head to Hackney's **Broadway Market** on Saturday. Contact **London Farmers' Markets** (7833 0338, www.lfm.org.uk).

★ Borough Market

Southwark Street, Borough, SE1 (7407 1002, www.boroughmarket.org.uk). London Bridge tube/rail. **Open** 10am-3pm Mon-Wed; 11am-5pm Thur; noon-6pm Fri; 8am-5pm Sat. **No credit cards. Map** p402 P8.

The food hound's favourite market is also London's oldest, dating back to the 13th century. It's the busiest, too, occupying a sprawling site near London Bridge. Gourmet goodies run the gamut, from fresh loaves from Flour Station to chorizo and rocket rolls from Spanish specialist Brindisa, plus rare-breed meats, fish and game, fruit and veg, cakes and all manner of preserves, oils and teas; head out hungry to take advantage of the numerous free samples. The market is now also open during the week, when it tends to be quieter than on always-mobbed Saturdays. A rail viaduct planned for above the space is still going ahead, despite a campaign against it, but a recent plan for the market to expand into the adjacent Jubilee Market area means that the space shouldn't be lost (even if some Grade II-listed structures are).
► *Borough Market's trade has been challenged by former stallholders who have set up camp under the railway arches on nearby Maltby Street in Bermondsey (www.maltbystreet.com); head here on a Saturday morning (9am-2pm) for Monmouth coffees (Arch 34), delicious raclette from Kappacasein (Arch 1), and the city's finest custard doughnuts, courtesy of the St John Bakery (Arch 72).*

Specialist

Daylesford Organic

44B Pimlico Road, Belgravia, SW1W 8LJ (7881 8060, www.daylesfordorganic.com). Sloane Square tube. **Open** 8am-8pm Mon-Sat; 10am-4pm Sun. **Credit** AmEx, MC, V. **Map** p398 G11.
Goods include ready-made dishes, staples such as pulses, pastas, cakes and breads, and cheeses.
Other locations 208-212 Westbourne Grove, Notting Hill, W11 2RH (7313 8050).

Hope & Greenwood

1 Russell Street, Covent Garden, WC2B 5JD (7240 3314, www.hopeandgreenwood.co.uk). Covent Garden tube. **Open** 11am-7.30pm Mon-Fri; 10.30am-7.30pm Sat; noon-6pm Sun. **Credit** MC, V. **Map** p416 Z3.
Saturday queues are almost inevitable at this small vacuum for pocket money. Everything from chocolate gooseberries to sweetheart candies is prettily displayed in plastic beakers, cellophane bags, glass jars, illustrated boxes, porcelain bowls and cake tins. Relive sweet childhood memories by indulging in a bag of sherbert Flying Saucers, gobstoppers or rhubarb and custard 'rations', as well as Double Dips, sugar mice, Curly Wurlys, Love Hearts and lots more. Posher chocolates are also available, including the delicious-sounding lavender and geranium truffles. Gift possibilities include retro gumball machines, and the refills for them. Ice-cream is available in the warmer months.
Other locations 20 Northcross Road, East Dulwich, SE22 9EU (8613 1777).

CONSUME

Lina Stores

18 Brewer Street, Soho, W1F 0SH (7437 6482).
Leicester Square tube. **Open** 8.30am-6.30pm Mon-
Fri; 10am-6.30pm Sat; 11am-5pm Sun. **Credit**
AmEx, MC, V. **Map** p416 W3.
Behind the 1950s green ceramic Soho frontage and
crowded windows is an iconic family-run Italian deli
that's been in business for over half a century. A
recent modernisation has taken away some of the
old-school character, but a new coffee machine goes
some way to making up for it. Besides dried pastas,
there's a deli counter chock-full of cured meats,
hams, salamis, olives, pesto, cheeses, marinated arti-
chokes and fresh pastas. Lina is also one of the best
places to buy truffles when they are in season.

★ Neal's Yard Dairy

17 Shorts Gardens, Covent Garden, WC2H 9AT
(7240 5700, www.nealsyarddairy.co.uk). Covent
Garden tube. **Open** 10am-7pm Mon-Sat. **Credit**
MC, V. **Map** p416 Y2.
Neal's Yard buys from small farms and creameries
and matures the cheeses in its own cellars until
they're ready to sell in peak condition. Names such
as Stinking Bishop and Lincolnshire Poacher are as
evocative as the aromas in the shop. It's best to walk
in and ask what's good today: you'll be given tasters
by the well-trained staff. There's a shop in Borough
Market too (6 Park Street, SE1 9AB, 7367 0799).
► *There are more great cheeses at Marylebone's*
La Fromagerie (see p171), and Paxton &
Whitfield (93 Jermyn Street, SW1Y 6JE, 7930
0259, www.paxtonandwhitfield.co.uk), which has
been on its site near Green Park since 1894.

Paul A Young Fine Chocolates

33 Camden Passage, Islington, N1 8EA (7424
5750, www.paulayoung.co.uk). Angel tube. **Open**
10am-6.30pm Mon-Thur, Sat; 10am-7pm Fri; noon-
5pm Sun. **Credit** AmEx, MC, V. **Map** p400 O2.
A gorgeous boutique with almost everything –
chocolates, cakes, ice-cream – made in the downstairs kitchen and finished in front of customers.
Young is a respected pâtissier as well as a chocolatier and has an astute chef's palate for flavour combinations: the white chocolate with rose masala is
divine, as are the salted caramels.
Other locations 143 Wardour Street, Soho,
W1F 8WA (7437 0011); 20 Royal Exchange,
Threadneedle Street, the City, EC3V 3LP
(7929 7007).
► *England's oldest chocolatier, Prestat (14 Princes*
Arcade, St James's, SW1Y 6DS, 0800 021 3023,
www.prestat.co.uk) offers unusual and traditional
flavours in brightly coloured gift boxes.

GIFTS & SOUVENIRS

★ Coco de Mer

23 Monmouth Street, Covent Garden, WC2H
9DD (7836 8882, www.coco-de-mer.com). Covent
Garden tube. **Open** 11am-7pm Mon-Wed, Fri, Sat;
11am-8pm Thur; noon-6pm Sun. **Credit** AmEx,
MC, V. **Map** p416 Y2.
London's most glamorous erotic emporium sells a
variety of tasteful books, toys and lingerie, from
glass dildos that double as objets d'art to a Marie
Antoinette costume of crotchless culottes and corset.
Trying on items can be fun as well: the peepshow-
style velvet changing rooms allow your lover to peer
through and watch you undress from a 'confession
box' next door.

Contemporary Applied Arts

2 Percy Street, Fitzrovia, W1T 1DD (7436
2344, www.caa.org.uk). Goodge Street or
Tottenham Court Road tube. **Open** 10am-6pm
Mon-Sat. **Credit** AmEx, MC, V. **Map** p397 K5.
This airy gallery, run by a charitable arts organisation, represents more than 300 makers. The work
embraces the functional – jewellery, tableware,
textiles – but also includes unique, purely decorative
pieces. The ground floor hosts exhibitions by individual artists, or themed by craft; in the basement
shop, you'll find pieces for all pockets. Glass is
always exceptional here. Phone before visiting as the
shop is relocating to Southwark in early 2013.

James Smith & Sons

53 New Oxford Street, Holborn, WC1A 1BL
(7836 4731, www.james-smith.co.uk). Holborn
or Tottenham Court Road tube. **Open** 10am-6pm
Mon-Sat. **Credit** AmEx, MC, V. **Map** p416 Y1.
More than 175 years after it was established, this
charming shop, with Victorian fittings still intact,
is holding its own in the niche market of umbrellas
and walking sticks. The stock here isn't the throwaway type of brolly that breaks at the first sign of
a bit of wind along with the rain. Lovingly crafted
'brellas, such as a classic City umbrella with a
Malacca Cane handle at £120, are built to last. A
repair service is also offered. *Photo p222.*

Luna & Curious

24-26 Calvert Avenue, Shoreditch, E2 7JP
(3222 0034, www.lunaandcurious.com). Old
Street tube/rail or Shoreditch High Street rail.
Open 11am-6pm daily. **Credit** AmEx, MC, V.
Map p401 R4.
The stock here is put together by a collective of
young artisans. Look out for the quintessentially
English teacups and ceramics from Polly George
and welovekaoru, as well as the fabulous hand-
stitched creatures by Finch, and jewellery by
Rheanna Lingham, who uses ceramics, feathers and
old embroidery to make necklaces, earrings and
headbands. Also adorning the walls are taxidermy
gulls by Jane Howarth, while the unique Paperself
patterned paper eyelashes, based on Chinese paper-
cut designs, have been selling thick and fast. In a
new space since February 2011, Luna & Curious
now also doubles up as a gallery space.

Miller Harris. *See p227.*

HEALTH & BEAUTY
Complementary medicine

Hale Clinic
7 Park Crescent, Marylebone, W1B 1PF (7631 0156, www.haleclinic.com). Great Portland Street or Regent's Park tube. **Open** 8.30am-8.30pm Mon-Fri; 9am-5pm Sat. **Credit** MC, V. **Map** p396 H4.
Around 100 practitioners are affiliated to the Hale Clinic, which was founded with the aim of integrating complementary and conventional medicine and opened by the Prince of Wales in 1988. The treatment list is an A-Z of alternative therapies, while the shop stocks supplements, skincare products and books.

Hairdressers & barbers

If the options listed below are out of your range, try a branch of **Mr Topper's** (7631 3233; £9 men, £20 women).

Daniel Hersheson
45 Conduit Street, Mayfair, W1F 2YN (7434 1747, www.danielhersheson.com). Oxford Circus tube. **Open** 9am-6pm Mon-Wed, Sat; 9am-8pm Thur, Fri. **Credit** AmEx, MC, V. **Map** p416 U3.
Despite its location in the heart of upmarket Mayfair, this modern two-storey salon isn't at all snooty, with a staff of very talented cutters and colourists. Prices start at £55 (£40 for men), though you'll pay £300 for a cut with Daniel (£150 for men). There's also a menu of therapies; the swish Harvey Nichols (*see p204*) branch has a dedicated spa. Hersheson's Blow Dry

Bars are located at Topshop (*see p218*; 7927 7888 to book), Westfield London (*see p209*; 8743 0868) and One New Change (*see p207*; 7248 6225).

★ F Flittner
86 Moorgate, the City, EC2M 6SE (7606 4750, www.fflittner.com). Moorgate tube/rail. **Open** 8am-6pm Mon-Wed, Fri; 8am-6.30pm Thur. **Credit** AmEx, MC, V. **Map** p403 Q6.
In business since 1904, Flittner seems not to have noticed that the 21st century has begun. Hidden behind beautifully frosted doors (marked 'Saloon') is a simple, handsome room, done out with an array of classic barber's furniture that's older than your gran. Within these hushed confines, up to six black coat-clad barbers deliver straightforward haircuts (dry cuts £16-£20, wet cuts £24-£30) and shaves (£23 with hot towels).
► *For a modern take on the art of the wet shave, try Murdock (340 Old Street, Shoreditch, EC1V 9DS, 7729 2288, www.murdocklondon.com).*

Tommy Guns
65 Beak Street, Soho, W1F 9SN (7439 0777, www.tommyguns.com). Oxford Circus or Piccadilly Circus tube. **Open** 10am-8pm Mon-Fri; 10am-6pm Sat. **Credit** AmEx, MC, V.
Now over a decade old, and with new branches on Brewer Street and all the way over in New York City, Tommy Guns remains a very cool prospect indeed. This original Soho space, complete with retro fittings, is filled with youthful colourists and cutters and there's a friendly, relaxed buzz to the place most days. Men's cuts start from £39.95, and women's cuts can be had from £49.95.
Other locations 49 Charlotte Road, Shoreditch, EC2A 3QT (7739 2244); 65 Brewer Street, Soho, W1F 9TQ (7287 0011).

Opticians

Dollond & Aitchison (www.danda.co.uk) and **Specsavers** (www.specsavers.com) are chains with branches on most high streets.

Cutler & Gross
16 Knightsbridge Green, Knightsbridge, SW1X 7QL (7581 2250, www.cutlerandgross.com). Knightsbridge tube. **Open** 9.30am-7pm Mon-Sat; noon-5pm Sun. **Credit** AmEx, MC, V.
Map p395 F9.
C&G celebrated its 40th anniversary in 2009, and its stock of handmade frames is still at the cutting edge of optical style. Stock runs from Andy Warhol-inspired glasses to naturally light buffalo-horn frames, and recent collaborations have included frames with trend-leaders Comme des Garçons. Vintage eyewear from the likes of Ray-Ban and Courrèges is at the sister shop down the road.
Other locations 7 Knightsbridge Green, Knightsbridge, SW1X 7QL (7590 9995).

CONSUME

Style Street

Redchurch Street is leading the way with its funky independent shops.

London's fashion- and experience-led shopping scene has been thriving over the past couple of years, with exciting new independents, concept stores and pop-up shops appearing all over town. One shabby Shoreditch cut-through has undergone a particularly dramatic transformation, now finding itself at the centre of London cool. Redchurch Street is now a strong contender for the capital's best shopping street.

One of our favourites is **Aesop** (no.5A, 7613 3793, www.aesop-europe.com), the botanical beauty shop from the Aussie luxury skincare brand. The geranium leaf body balm is an exquisitely scented, paraben-free treat. There's also a really lovely new fashion boutique at no.7: **Sunspel** (www.sunspel.com). The first retail outlet of the classic British menswear-makers, it specialises in quality underwear, T-shirts and polo shirts.

For goods that are equally English, but edible rather than sartorial, head to **Albion** (*see p180*), the café-shop that's part of Terence Conran's Boundary Project, on the corner of Redchurch and Boundary streets. You'll find a wealth of home-grown brands in the shop, from HP Sauce to Daylesford Organic via Neal's Yard. The buzz surrounding Redchurch Street was intensified by the hullabaloo that greeted Boundary and nearby members' club Shoreditch House, which houses an open-to-all branch of the Cowshed spa (7749 4531; *see right*). A little further up Boundary Street, new womenswear boutique **11 Boundary** (no.11, 7033 0330, www.11boundary.com) sells floaty bits from Wildfox and tailoring from Twenty8Twelve.

Further up Redchurch Street, there are more exciting new shops. **Hostem** (nos.41-43, 7739 9733, www.hostem.co.uk) is a darkly lit menswear shop with a well-edited selection from the likes of Philip Lim. Decadent **Maison Trois Garçons** (no.45, 7613 1924, www.lestroisgarcons.com) deals in interiors. The **Painted Lady** (no.65, 7729 2154), a cute hair salon and nail bar, specialises in vintage-style up-dos and offers great-value manicures. There's even a grungy thrift shop, **Sick** (no.105, 7033 2961), run by the founders of cult 1980s label Boy, which specialises in 1990s, for want of a better word, vintage.

Two of the highest-profile arrivals are capacious British concept store **Aubin & Wills** (nos.64-66), where you can buy men's, women's and homeware lines in a sort of grown-up collegiate style reminiscent of Abercrombie & Fitch, as well as catching a film in the small luxury cinema or some art in the gallery, and the large premises of the much-loved homeware shop **Labour & Wait** (*see p228*).

After this style overload, you may need some light refreshment. Head to the **Owl & the Pussycat** (no.34, 7613 3628) for a good pint of bitter. Despite a recent revamp, this is still a proper boozer, one of the few reminders of this happening street's former self.

Labour & Wait.

► *For cool vintage frames and sunglasses, check out Covent Garden's Opera Opera (98 Long Acre, WC2E 9NR, 7836 9246, www.operaopera.net), which has operated from the same corner site for over three decades.*

Pharmacies

National chain **Boots** (www.boots.com) has branches across the city, offering dispensing pharmacies and photo processing. The store on Piccadilly Circus (44-46 Regent Street, W1B 5RA, 7734 6126) is open until midnight (except Sunday, when it closes at 6pm).

DR Harris
29 St James's Street, St James's, SW1A 1HB (7930 3915, www.drharris.co.uk). Green Park or Piccadilly Circus tube. **Open** 8.30am-6pm Mon-Fri; 9.30am-6pm Sat. **Credit** AmEx, MC, V. **Map** p398 J8.
Founded in 1790, this venerable chemist has a royal warrant. Wood-and-glass cabinets are filled with bottles, jars and old-fashioned shaving brushes and manicure kits. The smartly packaged own-brand products such as the bright blue Crystal Eye Gel have a cult following.

Shops

Eco pioneer **Neal's Yard Remedies** (15 Neal's Yard, Covent Garden, WC2H 9DP, 7379 7222, www.nealsyardremedies.com) has several central London branches, offering organic products and a herbal dispensary. Beauty chain **Space NK** (8-10 Broadwick Street, Soho, W1F 8HW, 7734 3734, www.space nk.com) has also expanded in recent years, and is a great source of niche skincare and make-up brands.

Liz Earle Naturally Active Skincare
38-39 Duke of York Square, Chelsea, SW3 4LY (7730 9191, http://uk.lizearle.com). Sloane Square tube. **Open** 10am-7pm Mon, Wed-Sat; 10.30am-7pm Tue; 11am-5pm Sun. **Credit** AmEx, MC, V. **Map** p395 F11.
The London flagship of Liz Earle's botanical skincare range is housed in a large, light, fresh space in Chelsea's Duke of York Square, and stocks the full range of pleasingly gimmick-free and affordable products based on a regime of cleansing, toning and moisturising. Highlights among the products include the Instant Boost Skin Tonic and Superskin Moisturiser. 'Minis' and essentials packs are a great introduction (£13 for a starter kit).
► *Niche Aussie skincare brand Aesop (www. aesop-europe.com) now has three standalone London boutiques, on Mayfair's Mount Street, Westbourne Grove and east London's Redchurch Street (see left Style Street).*

Lost in Beauty
117 Regent's Park Road, Primrose Hill, NW1 8UR (7586 4411, www.lostinbeauty.com). Chalk Farm tube. **Open** 10am-6.30pm Mon-Sat; noon-5pm Sun. **Credit** AmEx, MC, V. **Map** p404 W2.
Kitted out with vintage shop fittings, this chic Primrose Hill boutique stocks a well-edited array of cult beauty brands, including Phyto, Becca, Caudalie, Dr Hauschka, Environ, Art of Hair and Skinceuticals. Illuminated theatre mirrors are perfect for sampling products, while the friendly staff are on hand to offer advice. There's also a choice selection of vintage jewellery.

Miller Harris
14 Monmouth Street, Covent Garden, WC2H 9HB (7836 9378). Covent Garden tube. **Open** 10am-6pm Mon-Sat. **Credit** AmEx, MC, V. **Map** p416 X2.
Grasse-trained British perfumer Lyn Harris's scents, in lovely floral packaging, are made with natural extracts and oils. Noix de Tubéreuse, a lighter and more palatable tuberose scent than many on the market, is a perennial favourite, while Fleurs de Bois evokes a traditional English garden. Newcomers to the range include La Fumée and La Pluie, reflecting the characteristics of smoke and rain respectively. Prices aren't cheap but you'll be paying for top-quality ingredients. This flagship branch, which has recently been refurbished, also has a tea room. *Photo p225.*
Other location 14 Needham Road, Notting Hill, W11 2RP (7221 1545);

Spas & salons

Many of London's luxury hotels – including the **Sanderson** (*see p237*) and the **Dorchester** (*see p248*) – make their excellent spa facilities available to the public.

Cowshed
119 Portland Road, Notting Hill, W11 4LN (7078 1944, www.cowshedclarendoncross.com). Holland Park tube. **Open** 9am-8pm Mon-Fri; 9am-7pm Sat; 10am-5pm Sun. **Credit** AmEx, MC, V. **Map** p404 X6.
The London branch of Cowshed (from Somerset's renowned Babington House) does its country cousin proud. The chic, white ground floor is buzzy, with a tiny café area on one side, and a manicure/pedicure section on the other. For facials, massages and waxing, head downstairs.
Other locations 31 Fouberts Place, Soho, W11 7QG (7534 0870); Shoreditch House, Ebor Street, Bethnal Green, E1 6AW (7749 4531); 162 Chiswick High Road, Chiswick, W4 1PR (8987 1607).

Elemis Day Spa
2-3 Lancashire Court, Mayfair, W1S 1EX (7499 4995, www.elemis.com). Bond Street tube.

Open 10.30am-9pm Mon-Fri; 9am-9pm Sat; 10am-6pm Sun. **Credit** AmEx, MC, V. **Map** p396 H6.
This leading British spa brand's exotic, unisex retreat is tucked away down a cobbled lane off Bond Street. The elegantly ethnic treatment rooms are a lovely setting in which to relax and enjoy a spot of pampering, from wraps to facials.

Hula Nails
203-205 Whitecross Street, EC1Y 8QP (07557142055, www.hulanails.com). Old Street tube/rail. **Open** 10.30am-7pm Mon,Tue, Thur, Fri; 10.30am-9pm Wed; 11am-6pm Sat. **Credit** AmEx, MC, V. **Map** p400 P4.
Georgiana Amador worked at Mac for many years, in contrast, Hula's boudoir style beauty rooms are gloriously decked out in Hawaiian wallcoverings, with plush velvet sofas and burlesque flourishes. The salon specialises in luxurious grooming - come for a vintage style pit-stop, with victory rolls and retro make up all on offer. Nail treatments take place in the window of the parlour, so you can sip on a free grated ginger tea and have a gossip as you watch the media types go by (waxes and spray tans are in cosily decked-out backrooms).

HOUSE & HOME
Antiques & second-hand

Although boutiques have encroached on their territory, there are still some quirky dealers on Islington's **Camden Passage** (off Upper Street, 7359 0190, www.camdenpassage antiques.com); try the Pierrepont Arcade. Marylebone's **Church Street** is now a major area for vintage homewares, and host to **Alfie's Antique Market** (*see below*), but **Portobello Road** (*see p209*) and **Bermondsey Square Antiques Market** (*see p209*) remain the best-known markets for antiques.

Alfie's Antique Market
13-25 Church Street, Marylebone, NW8 8DT (7723 6066, www.alfiesantiques.com). Edgware Road tube or Marylebone tube/rail. **Open** 10am-6pm Tue-Sat. **No credit cards. Map** p393 E4.
Alfie's hosts more than 100 dealers in vintage furniture and fashion, art, books, maps and the like. Check out Dodo Posters for 1920s and '30s ads.

Core One
Gas Works, 2 Michael Road, Fulham, SW6 2AD (7731 7171). Sloane Square tube then bus 11, 19, 22, 319, 211. **Open** 10am-6pm Mon-Fri; 11am-4pm Sat. **No credit cards.**
A group of antique and 20th-century dealers has colonised this industrial building in Fulham, including Dean Antiques (7610 6997, www.deanantiques. co.uk) for dramatic pieces, and De Parma (7736 3384, www.deparma.com) for elegant mid-century design.

Grays Antique Market & Grays in the Mews
58 Davies Street, Mayfair, W1K 5LP & 1-7 Davies Mews, Mayfair, W1K 5AB (7629 7034, www.graysantiques.com). Bond Street tube. **Open** 10am-6pm Mon-Fri; 11am-5pm Sat. **Credit** AmEx, MC, V. **Map** p396 H6.
More than 200 dealers in this smart covered market sell everything from antique furniture and rare books to vintage fashion and jewellery.

Two Columbia Road
2 Columbia Road, Shoreditch, E2 7NN (7729 9933, www.twocolumbiaroad.com). Hoxton or Shoreditch High Street rail. **Open** noon-7pm Tue-Fri; noon-6pm Sat; 10am-3pm Sun. **Credit** MC, V. **Map** p401 S3.
Well-selected 20th-century pieces are the order of the day here, whether it's 1970s chrome pendant lights, Danish 1960s rosewood desks, or Charles Eames wooden chairs. The corner site is owned by Tommy Roberts and run by his son Keith. Expect to find well-known names such as Arne Jacobsen and Willy Rizzo among the stock as well as more affordable pieces.

General

Heals (196 Tottenham Court Road, W1T 7LQ, 7636 1666, www.heals.co.uk) is a good source of mid-range modern design.

Conran Shop
Michelin House, 81 Fulham Road, Fulham, SW3 6RD (7589 7401, www.conranshop.co.uk). South Kensington tube. **Open** 10am-6pm Mon, Tue, Fri; 10am-7pm Wed, Thur; 10am-6.30pm Sat; noon-6pm Sun. **Credit** MC, V. **Map** p395 E10.
Sir Terence Conran's flagship store in the Fulham Road's beautiful 1909 Michelin Building showcases furniture and design for every room in the house as well as the garden. As well as design classics, such as the Eames Dar chair, there are plenty of portable accessories, gadgets, books, stationery and toiletries that make great gifts or souvenirs.
Other locations 55 Marylebone High Street, Marylebone, W1U 5HS (7723 2223).

★ Labour & Wait
85 Redchurch Street, Shoreditch, E2 7DJ (7729 6253, www.labourandwait.co.uk). Shoreditch High Street rail. **Open** 11am-6pm Tue-Sun. **Credit** MC, V. **Map** p401 S4.
This retro-stylish store, now on London's ultra-trendy Redchurch Street (*see p226* **Style Street**), sells the sort of things everybody would have had in their kitchen or pantry 60 years ago: functional domestic goods that have a timeless style. Spend any time here and you'll be filled with the joys of spring cleaning. For the kitchen there are some great simple classics such as enamel milk pans in retro pastels, and lovely 1950s-inspired Japanese teapots, and you can garden beautifully with ash-handled trowels.

Rough Trade East.

Vintage Welsh wool blankets, classic toiletries, and some great old-fashioned gifts, such as a pinhole camera kit and a lovely range of handmade notebooks from Portugal, make it hard to leave empty handed. Labour & Wait also has a space at concept store Dover Street Market (*see p215*).

MUSIC & ENTERTAINMENT
CDs, records & DVDs

Oxford Street's last music megastore, **HMV** (www.hmv.co.uk), offers a comprehensive line-up of CDs and DVDs, plus some vinyl. Serious music browsers, however, head south into Soho, where independent record stores are still clinging on around Berwick and D'Arblay streets.

Ray's Jazz, London's least beardy jazz shop, is to be found on the third floor of Foyles bookshop (*see p211*) on Charing Cross Road. The predominantly CD-based stock contains a good selection of blues, avant-garde, gospel, folk and world, but modern jazz is the main draw.

Flashback
50 Essex Road, Islington, N1 8LR (7354 9356, www.flashback.co.uk). Angel tube then bus 38, 56, 73, 341. **Open** 10am-7pm Mon-Sat; 11.30am-6pm Sun. **Credit** AmEx, MC, V. **Map** p400 O1.
Stock is scrupulously organised at this second-hand treasure trove. The ground floor is dedicated to CDs, while the basement is vinyl-only: an ever-expanding jazz collection jostles for space alongside soul, hip hop and a carpal tunnel-compressing selection of library sounds. A range of rarities is pinned in plastic sleeves to the walls. The shop also sells new vinyl.
Branch 114 Crouch Hill, Stroud Green, N8 9DX (8342 9633).

Harold Moores Records
2 Great Marlborough Street, Soho, W1F 7HQ (7437 1576, www.hmrecords.co.uk). Oxford Circus tube. **Open** 10am-6.30pm Mon-Sat. **Credit** AmEx, MC, V. **Map** p416 V2.
Harold Moores is not your stereotypical classical music store: young, open-minded staff and an expansive stock of new and second-hand music bolster its credentials. This collection sees some great stuff from old masters complemented by a range of eclectic contemporary music. There's a suitably studious basement dedicated to second-hand classical vinyl, including an excellent selection of jazz music.

Honest Jon's
278 Portobello Road, Notting Hill, W10 5TE (8969 9822, www.honestjons.com). Ladbroke Grove tube. **Open** 10am-6pm Mon-Sat; 11am-5pm Sun. **Credit** AmEx, MC, V. **Map** p404 X4.
Honest Jon's found its way to Notting Hill in 1979, and the owner helped James Lavelle set up Mo'Wax records. You'll find jazz, hip hop, soul, broken beat, reggae and Brazilian music on the shelves.

★ Rough Trade East
Dray Walk, Old Truman Brewery, 91 Brick Lane, Spitalfields, E1 6QL (7392 7788, www. roughtrade.com). Liverpool Street tube/rail. **Open** 8am-9pm Mon-Thur; 8am-8pm Fri; 10am-8pm Sat; 11am-7pm Sun. **Credit** AmEx, DC, MC, V. **Map** p401 S5.
Celebrating its 35th birthday in 2011, this infamous temple to indie music has never looked more upbeat, its new-found impetus provided by the 2007 opening of Rough Trade East. The 5,000sq ft record store, café and gig space offers a dizzying range of vinyl and CDs, spanning punk, indie, dub, soul,

electronica and more. With 16 listening posts and a stage for live sets, this is close to musical nirvana. **Other locations** 130 Talbot Road, Notting Hill, W11 1JA (7229 8541).

Sounds of the Universe

7 Broadwick Street, Soho, W1F 0DA (7734 3430, www.soundsoftheuniverse.com). Tottenham Court Road tube. **Open** 11am-7.30pm Mon-Sat. **Credit** AmEx, MC, V. **Map** p416 V2.

This stylish sound store has universal appeal. Its affiliation with reissue kings Soul Jazz records means its remit is broad. This is especially true on the ground floor (new vinyl and CDs), where grime and dubstep 12-inches jostle for space alongside new wave cosmic disco, electro-indie re-rubs and Nigerian compilations, while the second-hand vinyl basement is big on soul, jazz, Brazilian and alt-rock.

Musical instruments

Site of the legendary recording studio Regent Sounds in the 1960s, **Denmark Street**, off Charing Cross Road, is now a hub for music shops, especially those selling guitars.

Chappell of Bond Street

152-160 Wardour Street, Soho, W1F 8YA (7432 4400, www.chappellofbondstreet.co.uk). Tottenham Court Road tube. **Open** 9.30am-6pm Mon-Fri; 10am-5.30pm Sat. **Credit** AmEx, MC, V. **Map** p416 V2.

It's retained its old name, but Chappell recently moved from Bond Street (its home for nearly 200 years) to this amazing three-storey musical temple. This is the leading Yamaha stockist in the UK, and the collection of sheet music (classical, pop and jazz) is reputedly the largest in Europe.

SPORTS & FITNESS

Harrods (*see p204*) has a good fitness department. Bike chains **Evans Cycles** (www.evanscycles.com) and **Cycle Surgery** (www.cyclesurgery.com) each have a number of branches across the city. London's skaters now have a home branch of cult New York brand **Supreme** (*see p214*), selling the full range of boards and apparel. For the best places to find fashion trainers, *see p221*.

Decathlon

Canada Water Retail Park, Surrey Quays Road, Rotherhithe, SE16 2XU (7394 2000, www.decathlon.co.uk). Canada Water tube. **Open** 9am-9pm Mon-Fri; 9am-7pm Sat; 11am-5pm Sun. **Credit** MC, V.

The warehouse-sized London branch of this French chain offers London's biggest single collection of sports equipment. You'll find a vast array of reasonably priced equipment and clothing for all mainstream racket and ball sports as well as swimming, running, surfing, fishing, skiing and more.

Ellis Brigham

Tower House, 3-11 Southampton Street, WC2E 7HA (7395 1010, www.ellis-brigham.com). Covent Garden tube. **Open** 10am-8pm Mon-Fri; 9.30am-6.30pm Sat; 11.30am-5.30pm Sun. **Credit** AmEx, MC, V. **Map** 416 Z3.

This is the largest of the mountain sports shops on Southampton Street. It also houses London's only ice-climbing wall, 8m (26ft) high.

Other locations Unit 2003, Westfield Shopping Centre, Shepherd's Bush, W12 7GF (8222 6300); 178 Kensington High Street, Kensington, W8 7RG (7937 6889); 6 Cheapside Passage, the City, EC2V 6AF (3170 8746); Unit 2092, Westfield Stratford City, Stratford, W12 7GF (8740 3790).

Run & Become

42 Palmer Street, Victoria, SW1H 0PH (7222 1314, www.runandbecome.com). St James's Park tube. **Open** 9am-6pm Mon-Wed, Fri, Sat; 9am-8pm Thur. **Credit** MC, V. **Map** p398 J9.

The experienced staff here, most of them enthusiastic runners, will find the right pair of shoes for your physique and running style. The gamut of running kit, from clothing to speed monitors, is available.

TICKETS

It's always worth booking ahead for London performances – surprisingly obscure acts sell out, and high-profile gigs and sporting events can do so in seconds. It's almost always cheaper to bypass ticket agents and go direct to the box office: agents charge booking fees that often top 20 per cent. If you have to use an agent, booking agencies include **Ticketmaster** (0844 844 0444, www.ticketmaster.co.uk), **Stargreen** (7734 8932, www.stargreen.com), **Ticketweb** (0844 477 1000, www.ticketweb.co.uk), **See Tickets** (0871 220 0260, www.seetickets.com) and **Keith Prowse** (3137 7420, www.keithprowse.com). However, there are several ways to save money on tickets. For specific tips on where to get tickets (and how to keep the cost down) for the theatre, *see p305 and p309* **Inside Track**; for gigs and concerts, *see p285 and p298*.

TRAVELLERS' NEEDS

Independent travel specialist **Trailfinders** (European travel 0845 050 5945, worldwide flights 0845 058 5858, www.trailfinders.com) has several branches in the capital, including in the Piccadilly Waterstone's (nos.203-206, SW1Y 6WW, 0843 290 8549, www.waterstones.co.uk).

Excess Baggage Company

4 Hannah Close, Great Central Way, Wembley, Middx NW10 0UX (0800 524 4822, www.excess-baggage.com). **Credit** AmEx, MC, V.

Ships goods to over 300 countries and territories.

Hotels

Among the many new luxury hotels are signs, too, of affordable style.

After the glut of brand-new hotels that opened for the 2012 Games, London now finds itself in a post-Games lull, right? Wrong. A surprising number of hotels either missed their self-imposed 2012 deadline – or were never aiming for one. This increasingly wealth-focused city continues to make the most noise at the top end of the market: the Foster & Partners-designed **ME by Meliá London** (*see p242* **Straight to the Top**) looks set to jump straight to the front of the pack, but things are also lively among the Edwardian grandes dames, with the recently refitted **Savoy** (*see p241*) and **St**

Pancras Renaissance (*see p237*) soon to be joined by the illustrious **Café Royal** (http://hotelcaferoyal.com), when it's reborn as a hotel in 2013.

Below the radar, there have been endless new additions from the obvious chains, with a predictable focus around the Olympic Park in east London – has a **Holiday Inn** (www.holidayinn.com) ever boasted such stellar guests as the one in Westfield Stratford City did in summer 2012? Among the cheap options, it may be third time lucky at Piccadilly Circus, where a 583-room, seven-storey 'pod' hotel at the **Trocadero** has got the planning go-ahead for the third time. Instead of holding your breath, take a good look at the new glut of classy, moderately priced hotels that have finally decided to follow the pioneering **Hoxton** (*see p257*): **Z Soho** (*see p244*) and **citizenM** (*see p233* **Going Dutch**) both did us proud this year.

Room prices remain high. Significantly, **Dean Street Townhouse** (*see p243*), its slightly younger sibling **Shoreditch Rooms** (*see p257*) and **St John Hotel** (*see p244*), offer 'tiny' or 'post-supper' rooms at lower-than-you-might-fear rates. The popularity of hip new B&Bs and no-frills hotel concepts (*see p251* **Inside Track**) speaks to the same need.

OUR LISTINGS

Hotels in this chapter are classified according to the average price of a double room. You can expect to pay more than £300 a night for hotels in the **Deluxe** category, £200-£300 for **Expensive** hotels, £100-£200 for **Moderate** properties and under £100 a night for hotels listed as **Budget**.

The rates we've listed are only for guidance. The variation within these room rates, top to bottom and over the course of the year, can be huge. As a rule, book as far ahead as possible, and always try hotels' own websites first: many offer special online deals throughout the year. If you do arrive in town without a bed booked, staff at **Visit London** (1 Lower Regent Street, 0870 156 6366, www.visitlondon.com) will be happy to help you out. Room rates in this chapter include VAT (20%). Be aware that not all hotels include VAT in the rates they quote. And watch out for added extras. If you're bringing a car (not recommended), always check with the hotel before you arrive: few central hotels offer parking, and those that do charge steeply for it.

> ❶ Red numbers given in this chapter correspond to the location of each hotel as marked on the street maps. *See pp392-416.*

CONSUME

CONSUME

We've tried to indicate which hotels offer rooms adapted for disabled customers, but it's always best to confirm the precise facilities before you travel. Time Out's **Open London** guide makes several detailed recommendations.

THE SOUTH BANK & BANKSIDE

Moderate

Bermondsey Square Hotel

Bermondsey Square, Tower Bridge Road, SE1 3UN (0870 111 2525, www.bespokehotels.com). Borough tube or London Bridge tube/rail. **Rates** £109-£199 double. **Rooms** 80. **Credit** AmEx, MC, V. **Map** p403 Q10 ❶

This is a deliberately kitsch new-build on a newly developed square. Suites are named after the heroines of psychedelic rock classics (Lucy, Lily and so on), there are classic discs on the walls, and you can kick your heels from the suspended Bubble Chair at reception. But, although occupants of the Lucy suite get a multi-person jacuzzi (with a great terrace view), the real draw isn't the gimmicks – it's well-designed rooms for competitive prices. The restaurant-bar, which serves British food, is a bit hit-or-miss, but the hotel's pretty staff are happy and helpful.
Bar/café. Conference facilities. Internet: wireless (free). Restaurant. TV.

★ citizenM London Bankside

20 Lavington Street, SE1 0NZ (020 3519 1680, www.citizenm.com). Southwark tube or Blackfriars tube/rail. **Rates** £99-£157 double. **Rooms** 192. **Credit** AmEx, MC, V . **Map** p402 O8 X ❷

This casual new-build is a superbly well-designed addition to London's affordably chic hotels. *See right* **Going Dutch**.
Bar/café. Business centre. Internet: wireless (free). TV.

Park Plaza County Hall

1 Addington Street, SE1 7RY (7021 1800, www.parkplaza.com). Waterloo tube/rail. **Rates** £120-£250 double. **Rooms** 398. **Credit** AmEx, MC, V. **Map** p399 M9 ❸

Park Plaza County Hall is an enthusiastically – if somewhat haphazardly – run new-build. Each room has its own kitchenette with microwave and sink, and room sizes aren't bad across the price range (the floor-to-ceiling windows help them feel bigger). There's a handsomely vertiginous atrium, enabling you to peer down into the central restaurant and the frustratingly infrequent glass lifts, and the ground-floor bar is buzzy with business types after work. The gargantuan Park Plaza Westminster Bridge (200 Westminster Bridge Road, SE1 7UT) has now opened nearby, at the southern end of Westminster Bridge. It's London's largest new-build hotel for four decades.

Bars/café. Concierge. Conference facilities. Disabled-adapted rooms. Gym. Internet: wireless (free). Parking: £20/day. Restaurant. Room service. Spa facilities. TV: pay movies.

Premier Inn London County Hall

County Hall, Belvedere Road, SE1 7PB (0871 527 8648, www.premierinn.com). Waterloo tube/rail. **Rates** £69-£191 double. **Rooms** 314. **Credit** AmEx, DC, MC, V. **Map** p399 M8 ❹

Its position right by the London Eye, the Thames, Westminster Bridge and Waterloo Station is a gift for out-of-towners on a bargain weekend break. Extra points are garnered for its friendly and efficient staff, making this newly refurbished branch of the Premier Travel chain the acceptable face of budget convenience. Check-in is quick and pleasant; rooms are spacious, clean and warm with comfortable beds and decent bathrooms with very good showers. Breakfast, a buffet-style affair in a comfortable dining room, is extra but provides ballast for a day of sightseeing/shopping, or indeed meetings. But given the daily cost of the Wi-Fi, you're better off leaving the work at home.
Bars/café. Disabled-adapted rooms. Internet: wireless (£3/day). Restaurant. TV.

THE CITY

Deluxe

Andaz Liverpool Street

40 Liverpool Street, EC2M 7QN (7961 1234, www.london.liverpoolstreet.andaz.com). Liverpool Street tube/rail. **Rates** £165-£315 double. **Rooms** 267. **Credit** AmEx, DC, MC, V. **Map** p403 R6 ❺

A faded railway hotel until its £70m Conran overhaul in 2000, the red-brick Great Eastern became in 2007 the first of Hyatt's new Andaz portfolio. The new approach means out with gimmicky menus, closet-sized minibars and even the lobby reception desk, and in with down-to-earth, well-informed service and eco-friendliness. The bedrooms still wear style-magazine uniform – Eames chairs, Frette linens – but free services (local calls, wireless internet, healthy minibar) are an appreciated touch.
Bars/cafés (5). Business centre. Concierge. Disabled-adapted rooms. Gym. Internet: wireless & high-speed (free). Restaurants (5). Room service. Smoking rooms. TV.

Expensive

DoubleTree by Hilton

7 Pepys Street, EC3N 4AF (7709 1000, http://doubletree3.hilton.com). Tower Hill tube. **Rates** £150-£400 double. **Rooms** 583. **Credit** AmEx, MC, V. **Map** p403 R7 ❻

As you turn from the Tower of London and Tower Bridge among anonymous modern buildings to reach the DoubleTree, you might feel your heart

Going Dutch

There's no need to split the bill at London's new cheap-chic import.

Back in the mists of time – you know, before people thought there was anything to revive from the 1980s, let alone the 1990s... 2009 or so – a hip new hotel opened in arty but then still quite down-at-heel Shoreditch. Its owner reckoned he could give guests all mod cons in small but stylish rooms – at competitive prices. We loved the **Hoxton** (*see p257*), weren't at all surprised it was a success – and awaited a splurge of copy-cat hotels.

A mere three years later, we finally have a challenger. Just in time for the 2012 Games, **citizenM London Bankside** (*see left*) arrived from Holland. It's affordable, it's stylish, it has a real buzz about it, and it cleverly set itself right in the thick

of the arty action: on the South Bank, right behind Tate Modern (*see p43*).

The ground floor is both slick and cosy café-bar and reception area: self-check-in, but with brilliant staff on hand to offer help and, when higher-grade rooms are free, upgrades. Guests are invited to use it as their 'living room' and – thanks to the neat but welcoming design – do so.

The rooms themselves are tiny, comfy and well thought out: there are blackout blinds, free Wi-Fi, a drench shower with removable sidehead, storage under the bed, free movies. The rooms are also fun: those blinds are automatic, controlled – like the movies, the air-con and funky coloured lighting – from a touch-sensitive tablet.

CitizenM London Bankside.

CONSUME

South Place Hotel.

sink. Keep your spirits up: the hotel looks a bit dull, but it has unexpectedly brilliant views. Even if you aren't lucky enough to stay in the spacious Thames suite, the 12th-floor SkyLounge bar, with its outside terrace, looks over the rooftops to provide a fine Thames vista. We were sad that Mint sold its mini-chain of hotel, but under Hilton service here remains smooth and smiley, and the room technology and fittings top-class.

Bars/cafés (3). Concierge. Conference rooms. Disabled-adapted rooms. Gym. Internet: wireless (free). Parking: £20-£30/day. Restaurants (2). Room service. TV.

★ South Place Hotel

3 South Place, EC2M 2AF (020 3503 0000, www.southplacehotel.com). Moorgate or Liverpool Street tube/rail. **Rates** *£176-£290 double.* **Rooms** 80. **Credit** AmEx, MC, V. **Map** p401 Q5 X ❼

D&D runs some of the swankiest restaurants in London, so much was expected of its first hotel. South Place delivers. It manages the difficult balance of sufficient formality to keep expense-accounters satisfied their needs are being attended to, with enough levity for you to want to spend the evening indoors. The muted top-floor Angler restaurant is a superbly oiled operation, there's a pretty interior courtyard garden bar, and the ground-floor 3 South Place bar-diner segues neatly from smooth breakfast operation to boisterous bar. The attention to detail impresses: from conversation-piece art (wire high-heels in one cabinet, a light feature of suspended aeroplanes, steampunk drawings) to touch controls in the rooms or the Bond-themed pool room and library, complete with vinyl and turntable.

Bars/cafés (3). Concierge. Conference rooms. Disabled-adapted rooms. Gym. Internet: wireless (free). Restaurants (2). Room service. TV.

Threadneedles

5 Threadneedle Street, EC2R 8AY (7657 8080, www.theetoncollection.com). Bank tube/DLR. **Rates** *£225-£525 double.* **Rooms** 74. **Credit** AmEx, MC, V. **Map** p403 Q6 ❽

Threadneedles boldly slots some contemporary style into a fusty old dame of a building in the heart of the City; it was formerly the grand Victorian HQ of the Midland Bank, bang next to the Bank of England and the Royal Exchange. The etched glass-domed rotunda of the lobby soars on columns over an artful array of designer furniture and shelving that looks like the dreamchild of some powerful graphics software – it's a calm space, but a stunning one. The bedrooms are individual, coherent and soothing examples of City-boy chic, in muted beige and textured tones, with limestone bathrooms and odd views of local landmarks: St Paul's, Tower 42 and the Lloyd's building. It's all well run and well thought out.

Bar/café. Concierge. Disabled-adapted rooms. Internet: wireless (free). Restaurant. Room service. TV: pay movies.

Moderate

Apex London Wall

7-9 Copthall Avenue, EC2R 7NJ (7562 3030, www.apexhotels.co.uk). Bank tube or Moorgate tube/rail. **Rates** *£130-£311 double.* **Rooms** 89. **Credit** AmEx, MC, V. **Map** p403 Q6 ❾

CONSUME

The mini-chain's second London hotel shares the virtues of the first (Apex City of London, 1 Seething Lane, 7702 2020). The service is obliging, the rooms are crisply designed with all mod cons, and there are comforting details – rubber duck in the impressive bathrooms, free jelly beans, free local calls and internet, kettle and iron provided. The City of London branch has the better location for tourists, a short walk from the Tower of London, but this one is handier for business. From the suites, a terrace peers over commercial buildings, but the view from the restaurant – of the flamboyantly sculpted frieze on a business institute – is rather pleasing.
Bar/café. Disabled-adapted rooms. Gym. Internet: wireless (free). Restaurant. Room service. TV.

Montcalm London City
52 Chiswell Street, EC1Y 4SD (7374 2988, www.themontcalmlondoncity.co.uk). Barbican tube or Moorgate tube/rail. **Rates** £118-£216 double. **Rooms** 235. **Credit** AmEx, DC, MC, V. **Map** p400 P5 ⑩
Montcalm London City stands on the former site of the 18th-century Whitbread brewery. The service is welcoming, the decor very much old meets new: brickwork and an original art deco staircase sit with Swarovski crystal chandeliers and spotlight flooring. All rooms have lime green and brown furnishings and are fitted with slick digital doorbell, housekeeping and privacy sensors, but the furniture arrangement is a little cramped, and despite the media-hubs and flatscreen TVs there's a sense the place was designed by committee – too many good ideas, not enough coherence. The hotel's modern restaurant and cocktail bar is a cracker, though.

Bar. Conference rooms. Internet: wireless (free). Parking: £32/day, free for club and suite guests. Restaurant. Room service. TV.

HOLBORN & CLERKENWELL
Expensive

Malmaison
Charterhouse Square, EC1M 6AH (7012 3700, www.malmaison.com). Barbican tube. **Rates** £265 double. **Rooms** 97. **Credit** AmEx, DC, MC, V. **Map** p400 O5 ⑪
Malmaison is deliciously located, looking out on a lovely cobbled square on the edge of the Square Mile, near the bars, clubs and better restaurants of the East End. This being design-conscious Clerkenwell, it's no surprise that the decor throughout makes a cool statement (note the Veuve Cliquot ice buckets built into the love seats at reception). The rooms overlooking the square are the pick of the bunch, with the best of the views and morning sunshine that pours through large sash windows on to big, white firm beds. Gripes? The muted, business-friendly decor in the rooms is a bit of a let-down after the dark and sultry foyer. There's smiley service downstairs in the lovely basement brasserie, and internet usage is free.
Bars/cafés (2). Disabled-adapted rooms. Internet: wireless (free). Parking: £20/day. Restaurant. Room service. TV.

★ Rookery
12 Peter's Lane, Cowcross Street, EC1M 6DS (7336 0931, www.rookeryhotel.com). Farringdon tube/rail. **Rates** £276-£300 double. **Rooms** 33. **Credit** AmEx, DC, MC, V. **Map** p400 O5 ⑫
Sister hotel to Hazlitt's (*see p243*), the Rookery has long been something of a celebrity hideaway deep in Clerkenwell. Its front door is satisfyingly hard to find, especially when the streets around are teeming with Fabric (*see p281*) devotees; the front rooms can be noisy on these nights, but the place is otherwise as creakily calm as a country manor house. Once inside, guests enjoy an atmospheric warren of rooms, each individually decorated in the style of a Georgian townhouse: huge clawfoot baths, elegant four-posters, brass shower fittings. There's an honesty bar in the bright and airy drawing room at the back, which opens on to a sweet little patio. The ground-floor suite has its own hallway, a cosy boudoir and a subterranean bathroom. Topping it all is the huge split-level Rook's Nest suite, which has views of St Paul's Cathedral.
Bar/café. Concierge. Internet: wireless (free). Room service. TV: DVD.

★ Zetter
86-88 Clerkenwell Road, EC1M 5RJ (7324 4444, www.thezetter.com). Farringdon tube/rail. **Rates** £185-£438 double. **Rooms** 59. **Credit** AmEx, MC, V. **Map** p400 O4 ⑬

CONSUME

Zetter is a fun, laid-back, modern hotel with some interesting design notes. There's a refreshing lack of attitude and a forward-looking approach, with friendly staff and firm eco-credentials (such as free Brompton bikes for guests' use). The rooms, stacked up on five galleried storeys around an impressive atrium, look into an intimate and recently refreshed bar area. They are smoothly functional, but cosied up with choice home comforts such as hot-water bottles and old Penguin paperbacks, as well as having walk-in showers with REN smellies. The superlative Bistrot Bruno Loubet (*see p159*) downstairs, and the fabulous Zetter Townhouse in a historic building just across the square – with its excellent cocktail bar – have only served to widen the place's already considerable appeal.
Bar/café. Concierge. Conference facilities. Disabled-adapted rooms. Internet: wireless (free). Restaurant. Room service. TV: DVD.

Moderate

★ Fox & Anchor
115 Charterhouse Street, EC1M 6AA (0845 347 0100, www.foxandanchor.com). Barbican tube or Farringdon tube/rail. **Rates** £150-£294 double. **Rooms** 6. **Credit** AmEx, MC, V. **Map** p400 O5 ⑭
Check in at the handsome attached boozer (*see p190*) and you'll be pointed to the separate front entrance, with its lovely floor mosaic, and a handful of well-appointed, atmospheric and surprisingly luxurious rooms. All are different, but the high-spec facilities (big flatscreen TV, clawfoot bath and drench shower) and quirky attention to detail (bottles of ale in the minibar, the 'Nursing hangover' privacy signs) are common throughout. Expect some clanking noise in the early mornings, but proximity to the historic Smithfield meat market also means you get a feisty fry-up in the morning in the pub.
Bar/café. Internet: wireless (free). Restaurant. TV: DVD.

BLOOMSBURY & FITZROVIA
Deluxe

Charlotte Street Hotel
15-17 Charlotte Street, W1T 1RJ (7806 2000, www.firmdale.com). Goodge Street or Tottenham Court Road tube. **Rates** £250-£340 double. **Rooms** 52. **Credit** AmEx, MC, V. **Map** p397 K5 ⑮
Now a fine exponent of Kit Kemp's much imitated fusion of flowery English and avant-garde, this gorgeous hotel was once a dental hospital. Public rooms have Bloomsbury Set paintings, by the likes of Duncan Grant and Vanessa Bell, while bedrooms mix English understatement with bold flourishes. The huge, comfortable beds and trademark polished granite and oak bathrooms are suitably indulgent, and some rooms have unbelievably high ceilings.

INSIDE TRACK BUYER BEWARE

Many high-end hotels charge extra for services that some travellers assume will be free, most commonly internet access and breakfast. Always check in advance if you're blowing the budget for a treat.

The Oscar restaurant and bar are classy and busy with a smart crowd of media and ad people. At 5pm on Sundays the mini-cinema holds screenings.
Bar/café. Concierge. Disabled-adapted rooms. Gym. Internet: wireless (free). Restaurant. Room service. Smoking rooms. TV: DVD.

★ St Pancras Renaissance
Euston Road, King's Cross, NW1 2AR (7841 3540, www.marriott.com). King's Cross tube/rail. **Rates** £245-£540. **Rooms** 245. **Credit** AmEx, DC, MC, V. **Map** p397 L3 ⑯
A landmark hotel in every sense of the word, the St Pancras Renaissance is the born-again Midland Grand, the pioneering railway hotel designed into the station's imposing Gothic Revival frontage. It opened in 1873 but fell into disuse in the 20th century (except for appearances as a Harry Potter backdrop and in the Spice Girls' Wannabe video, among other screen roles). The Renaissance group (fittingly) has done a beautiful and painstaking job of restoring it to its breathtaking, Grade I listed best while adding modern comforts. The 120 rooms and suites in the historic hotel (there's a new wing, too) have high ceilings, original features and awesome views over the station concourse or forecourt. Facilities are high-spec – Bose stereo, Nespresso machines, REN toiletries, marble baths – furniture modern classic and design sensitive to the context, re-using motifs from the original decor in the carpets, for example. Public areas, including both restaurants (for the Ticket Office, *see p191*) and the gorgeous grand staircase, are similarly splendid. London loves it.
Bars/cafés (2). Concierge. Conference facilities. Disabled-adapted room. Gym. Internet: wireless (free & £15/day, depending on room). Pool (indoor). Restaurant (2). Room service. Spa facilities. TV.

Sanderson
50 Berners Street, W1T 3NG (7300 1400, www.morganshotelgroup.com). Oxford Circus tube. **Rates** £306-£654 double. **Rooms** 150. **Credit** AmEx, DC, MC, V. **Map** p416 V1 ⑰
No designer flash in the pan, the Sanderson remains a statement hotel, a Schrager/Starck creation that takes clinical chic in the bedrooms to new heights. Colour is generally conspicuous by its absence. The design throughout is all flowing white net drapes, gleaming glass cabinets and retractable screens. The residents-only Purple Bar sports a button-backed

CONSUME

purple leather ceiling and fabulous cocktails; in particular, try the Vesper. The 'billiard room' has a purple-topped pool table, surrounded by strange tribal adaptations of classic dining room furniture.
Bars/cafés (2). Business centre. Concierge. Disabled-adapted rooms. Gym. Internet: wireless (£10/day). Parking: £45/day. Restaurant. Room service. Spa facilities. TV: DVD.

Expensive

Myhotel Bloomsbury (11-13 Bayley Street, WC1B 3HD, 7667 6000, www.myhotels.co.uk) is a grown-up, urban brother to Myhotel Chelsea (*see p251*), giving the trademark Asian touches a masculine, minimalist twist.

Academy Hotel
21 Gower Street, WC1E 6HG (7631 4115, www.theetoncollection.com). Goodge Street tube. **Rates** £230-£345 double. **Rooms** 49. **Credit** AmEx, MC, V. **Map** p397 K5 ⓲
The Academy goes for the country intellectual look to suit Bloomsbury's studious yet decadent history. It's made up of five Georgian townhouses, and provides in all its rooms a tranquil generosity of space that's echoed in the Georgian squares sitting serenely between the arterial traffic rush of Gower Street and Tottenham Court Road. There's a restrained country-house style in the summery florals and checks and a breath of sophistication in the handsome, more plainly furnished suites. The library and conservatory open on to fragrant walled gardens where drinks and breakfast are served in summer.
Bar/café. Internet: wireless (free). Restaurant. Room service. TV.

Moderate

Harlingford Hotel
61-63 Cartwright Gardens, WC1H 9EL (7387 1551, www.harlingfordhotel.com). Russell Square tube or Euston tube/rail. **Rates** £120 double. **Rooms** 40. **Credit** MC, V. **Map** p397 L4 ⓳
An affordable hotel with bundles of charm in the heart of Bloomsbury, the perkily styled Harlingford has light airy rooms with evident boutique aspirations. The decor is lifted from understated sleek to quirky with the help of vibrant colour splashes from coloured glass bathroom fittings and mosaic tiles – overall, the hotel has something of a Scandinavian feel. The crescent it's set in has a lovely and leafy private garden where you can lob a tennis ball about or just dream under the trees on a summer's night.
Internet: wireless (free). TV.

Morgan
24 Bloomsbury Street, WC1B 3QJ (7636 3735, www.morganhotel.co.uk). Tottenham Court Road tube. **Rates** £130 double. **Rooms** 21. **Credit** MC, V. **Map** p397 K5 ⓴

This brilliantly located, comfortable budget hotel in Bloomsbury is tastefully done out in neutral shades. The rooms are well equipped and all are geared up for the electronic age with wireless, voicemail, flatscreen tellies with freeview and air-conditioning. A good, slap-up English breakfast is served in a good-looking room with wood panelling, London prints and blue and white china plates. The spacious flats are excellent value.
Internet: wireless (free). TV.

Rough Luxe
1 Birkenhead Street, WC1H 8BA (7837 5338, www.roughluxe.co.uk). King's Cross tube/rail. **Rates** £199-£289 double. **Rooms** 9. **Credit** AmEx, MC, V. **Map** p397 L3 ㉑
The latest thing in hotel design chic is – at least, according to the owners of this hotel – Rough Luxe. In a bit of King's Cross that's choked with ratty B&Bs and cheap chains, this Grade II-listed property has walls artfully distressed, torn wallpaper, signature works of art, old-fashioned TVs that barely work and even retains the sign for the hotel that preceded Rough Luxe: 'Number One Hotel'. Each room has free wireless internet, but otherwise have totally different characters: there's the one with the free-standing copper tub, the one with the rose motif and so on. The set-up is flexible too: rooms with shared bathrooms can be combined for group bookings, and the owners are more than happy to chat with guests over a bottle of wine in the back courtyard where a great breakfast is served. A place to stay if you're looking for somewhere different from the norm.
Internet: wireless (free).

Budget

Clink78
78 King's Cross Road, WC1X 9QG (7183 9400, www.clinkhostels.com). King's Cross tube/rail. **Rates** £40-£70 double; £17-£32 bed. **Beds** 717. **Credit** MC, V. **Map** p397 M3 ㉒
Located in a listed courthouse, the Clink set the bar high for party-style hosteldom when it opened a few years back. There was the setting: the hostel retains the superb original wood-panelled lobby and courtroom where the Clash once stood before the beak. Then there's the urban chic ethos that permeates the whole enterprise, from the streamlined red reception counter to the Japanese-style 'pod' beds. By the time this guide hits the shelves, a thorough redesign of the public areas and licensed bar downstairs should give things a new rock 'n' roll fillip, with street-art decor and more comfortable furniture to enhance the place's good-time vibe. Clink261 – a rebrand of the nearby Ashlee House, which had its public areas pepped up in 2010 – might be a better choice for older and calmer hostellers.
Bar/café. Internet: shared terminal (£2/hr). TV.
Other locations Clink261, 261-265 Gray's Inn Road, Bloomsbury, WC1X 8QT (7833 9400).

Corinthia.

Jenkins Hotel

45 Cartwright Gardens, WC1H 9EH (7387 2067, www.jenkinshotel.demon.co.uk). Russell Square tube or Euston tube/rail. **Rates** £69-£150 double. **Rooms** 12. **Credit** MC, V. **Map** p397 K3 ㉓

This well-to-do Georgian beauty has been a hotel since the 1920s. It still has an atmospheric, antique air, although the rooms have mod cons enough – TVs, mini-fridges, tea and coffee. Its looks have earned it a role in *Agatha Christie's Poirot*, but it's not chintzy, just floral. The breakfast room is handsome, with snowy cotton tablecloths and Windsor chairs. *Internet: wireless (free). TV.*

YHA London Central

104 Bolsover Street, W1W 5NU (0845 371 9154, www.yha.org.uk). Great Portland Street tube. **Rates** from £19 adult. **Beds** 302. **Credit** MC, V. **Map** p396 J5 ㉔

The Youth Hostel Association's newest hostel is one of its best – as well as being one of the best hostels in London. The friendly and well-informed receptionists are stationed at a counter to the left of the entrance, in a substantial café-bar area. The basement contains a well-equipped kitchen and washing areas; above it, five floors of clean, neatly designed rooms, many en suite. Residents have 24hr access and the location is quiet but an easy walk from most of central London. *Bar/café. Internet: wireless (£5/day). TV.* **Other locations** throughout the city.

COVENT GARDEN & THE STRAND

Deluxe

★ Corinthia

Whitehall Place, SW1A 2BD (7930 8181, www.corinthia.com). Embankment tube or Charing Cross tube/rail. **Rates** £310-£700 double. **Rooms** 294. **Credit** AmEx, MC, V. **Map** p399 L8 ㉕

Firmly in the grand hotel tradition, the Corinthia became a hotel after years as government offices. The colossal, modish chandelier (with 1,000 clear crystal globes, plus one in red) in the expansive lobby complete with central dome; the dark wood and silk-covered walls in the high-spec rooms; the luxurious bathrooms with pool-like oval baths: everything is as you would expect for a hotel in this price range, and it's done well and with a light, modern touch that avoids self-importance or stuffiness. The Espa spa and subterranean pools (with jacuzzi, steam room, sauna and hot seats) form a complex over two floors. Espa products are in bathrooms too. Afternoon tea is a stylish affair, served in the lobby. The Bassoon bar is an intimate, after-dark space, while the Northall restaurant serves British food in a dramatic round space with floor to ceiling windows. The hotel's policy of not setting a check-out or check-in time is a real boon.

Your City Break doesn't have to cost the earth

Trees for Cities

Reduce the impact of your flight by donating to Trees for Cities

To donate, text 'TREE37' to 70070 or visit www.treesforcities.org

Trees for Cities, Prince Consort Lodge, Kennington Park, Kennington Park Place, London SE11 4AS
Tel. +44 (0)20 7587 1320; Charity registration 1032154

*Bars (2). Business centre. Concierge. Gym.
Internet: wireless (free). Pool. Restaurants
(2). Room service. Spa. TV: pay movies.*

★ Covent Garden Hotel

*10 Monmouth Street, WC2H 9LF (7806 1000,
www.firmdale.com). Covent Garden, Leicester
Square or Tottenham Court Road tube.* **Rates**
£310-£355 double. **Rooms** 58. **Credit** AmEx,
MC, V. **Map** p416 X2 ㉖

The excellent location in the heart of London's theatre district and tucked-away screening room of this
Firmdale hotel ensure it continues to attract starry
customers, with anyone needing a bit of privacy
able to retreat upstairs to the lovely panelled private
library and drawing room. In the guest-rooms, Kit
Kemp's distinctive style mixes pinstriped wallpaper, pristine white quilts and floral upholstery with
bold, contemporary elements; each room is unique,
but each has the Kemp trademark upholstered man-
nequin and granite and oak bathroom. On the
ground floor, the 1920s Paris-style Brasserie Max
and its retro zinc bar retain their buzz – outdoor
tables give a perfect viewpoint on Covent Garden
boutique life in summer.

*Bar/café. Concierge. Disabled-adapted rooms.
Gym. Internet: wireless (£20/day). Parking:
£37/day. Restaurant. Room service. Smoking
rooms. TV: DVD.*

★ ME by Meliá London

*336-337 Strand, WC2R 1HA (8234 1953,
www.melondonuk.com). Covent Garden or Temple
tube, or Charing Cross tube/rail.* **Rates** from £340
double. **Rooms** 157. **Credit** AmEx, MC, V. **Map**
p399 M7 X ㉗

With wealthy Londoners and non-doms seeming
immune to recession, top-end hotels have been having a bit of a renaissance. This one might be the best
of the lot. *See p242* **Straight to the Top.**

*Bars/cafés (2). Business centre. Concierge. Gym.
Internet: wireless (free). Parking. Restaurant.
Room service. TV: DVD.*

One Aldwych

*1 Aldwych, WC2B 4RH (7300 1000,
www.onealdwych.com). Covent Garden or Temple
tube, or Charing Cross tube/rail.* **Rates** £282-£474
double. **Rooms** 105. **Credit** AmEx, DC, MC, V.
Map p416 Z3 ㉘

You only have to push through the front door and
enter the breathtaking Lobby Bar to know that you're
in for a treat. Despite the building's weighty history
– the 1907 building was once the offices of the
Morning Post – One Aldwych is a thoroughly modern establishment, with Frette linen, bathroom mini-
TVs and an environmentally friendly loo-flushing
system. Flowers and fruit are replenished daily and
a card with the next day's weather forecast appears
at turndown. The location is perfect for the West End
theatres and has become popular with attendees of

London Fashion Week, particularly since many of
the events are now held nearby in Somerset House.
The three round corner suites are very romantic, and
a cosy screening room, excellent spa and a downstairs swimming pool where soothing music is
played may dissuade you from ever stepping outside.
*Bar/café. Concierge. Disabled-adapted rooms.
Gym. Internet: wireless, high-speed (free). Parking:
£47/day. Pool: indoor. Restaurants (2). Room
service. Spa facilities. TV: DVD & pay movies.*

St Martins Lane Hotel

*45 St Martin's Lane, WC2N 4HX (7300 5500,
www.morganshotelgroup.com). Leicester Square
tube or Charing Cross tube/rail.* **Rates** £282-£564
double. **Rooms** 204. **Credit** AmEx, DC, MC, V.
Map p416 X4 ㉙

When it opened over a decade ago, the St Martins
was the toast of the town. The flamboyant, theatrical
lobby was constantly buzzing, and guests giggled
like schoolgirls at Philippe Starck's playful decor.
The Starck objects – such as the giant chess pieces
and gold tooth stools in the lobby – remain, but the
space, part of the Morgans Hotel Group, lacks the
impact of its heyday. There's still much to be
impressed by: the all-white bedrooms have comfortable minimalism down to a T, with floor-to-ceiling
windows, gadgetry secreted in sculptural cabinets
and sleek limestone bathrooms with toiletries from
the spa at sister property Sanderson (*see p237*).
*Bar/café. Business centre. Concierge. Disabled-
adapted rooms. Gym. Internet: wireless (£10/day).
Parking: £40/day. Restaurant. Room service.
TV: pay movies.*

★ Savoy

*Strand, WC2R 0EU (7836 4343, www.
fairmont.com). Covent Garden or Embankment
tube, or Charing Cross tube/rail.* **Rates** £354-£642
double. **Rooms** 268. **Credit** AmEx, DC, MC, V.
Map p416 Z4 ㉚

The superluxe, Grade II-listed Savoy reopened after
more than £100m of renovations in October 2010 –
the numerous delays testimony to the difficulty of
bringing a listed building, loved by generations of
visitors for its discreet mix of Edwardian neoclassical and art deco, up to scratch as a modern luxury
hotel. Built in 1889 to put up theatregoers from
Richard D'Oyly Carte's Gilbert & Sullivan shows,
the Savoy is the hotel from which Monet painted
the Thames, where Vivien Leigh met Laurence
Olivier, where Londoners learned to love the martini. The famous cul-de-sac at the front entrance
now has a garden of new topiary and centrepiece
Lalique crystal fountain, but the welcome begins
before you arrive with a phone call to ascertain your
particular requirements. There's a new tearoom
with glass-roofed conservatory; the leather counter
of the new Beaufort champagne bar is set on a
stage that once hosted big bands for dinner dances;
and the Savoy Grill is again under the control

CONSUME

Straight to the Top

Just as the grand old palaces get spruced up – here's a hot young newcomer.

ME by Meliá.

If the 2010s were shaping up to be the decade of the grandes dames, with the St Pancras Renaissance (*see p237*) and Savoy (*see p241*) reappearing from under dust sheets after lengthy renovations, 2013 may see a change in direction. London's first **ME by Meliá** (for listing, *see p241*) – its predecessors are in Madrid, Barcelona, Cancún, Cabo San Lucas and Vienna – will be in a less traditionalist mode.

Unusually, ME by Meliá has decided to build its flagship hotel, er, sixth. But, by god, it's a beauty. Designed by Foster + Partners, the finishes are expensive and carefully modelled on what was there before – respecting the lines of Marconi House, the first BBC radio broadcaster. But it now contains a genuinely breathtaking internal atrium, a pyramid nine floors tall, coolly minimal in style – and starting not at ground floor, but from the first. Here guests will sit to calmly sip champagne as they're checked in by personal 'Aura managers'.

In the rooms, the tech and textile details are all taken care of, naturally, but idiosyncratic design touches include triangular windows you can't resist stepping into to peer up and down the Aldwych.

The social spaces have different moods neatly covered: from a bling American steakhouse and a basement events space into which cars can be driven, via a more relaxed Italian restaurant, up to Radio, the rather elegant tenth-floor roof terrace bar, where Thames-side seats and exceptional views will be hugely in demand.

of Gordon Ramsay's company. Traditionalists can relax: the American Bar remains unchanged. *Bars (2). Concierge. Disabled-adapted rooms. Gym. Internet: wireless (£9.95/day). Pool (indoor). Restaurants (4). Room service. Spa facilities. TV: DVD & pay movies.*

SOHO & LEICESTER SQUARE

Deluxe

Soho Hotel
4 Richmond Mews, W1D 3DH (7559 3000, www. firmdale.com). Piccadilly Circus or Tottenham Court Road tube. **Rates** *£335-£490 double.* **Rooms** 91. **Credit** AmEx, DC, MC, V. **Map** p416 W2 ❸
You'd hardly know you were in the heart of Soho once you're inside Firmdale's edgiest hotel: the place is wonderfully quiet, with what was once a car park now feeling like a converted loft building. The big bedrooms exhibit a contemporary edge, with modern furniture, industrial-style windows and nicely planned mod cons (digital radios as well as flatscreen TVs), although they're also classically Kit Kemp with bold stripes, traditional florals, plump sofas, oversized bedheads and upholstered tailor's dummies. The quiet drawing room and other public spaces feature groovy colours while Refuel, the loungey bar and restaurant, has an open kitchen and, yes, a car-themed mural. *Bar/café. Concierge. Disabled-adapted rooms. Gym. Internet: wireless & high-speed (£20/day). Restaurant. Room service. Spa facilities. TV: DVD.*

W London Leicester Square
10 Wardour Street, Leicester Square, W1D 6QF (7758 1000, www.wlondon.co.uk). Leicester Square tube. **Rates** *£300-£350 double.* **Rooms** 192. **Credit** AmEx, DC, MC, V. **Map** p416 W4 ❷

The old Swiss Centre building on the edge of Leicester Square has been demolished and in its place is the UK's first W Hotel. The W brand has made its name with a series of hip hotels around the world that offer glamorous bars, classy food and functional but spacious rooms. The London W is no exception: Spice Market gets its first UK site within the hotel; Wyld is a large nightclub/bar space aiming to become the Met Bar for a new decade, and the W lounge aims to bring New York's cocktail lounge ethos to London. The rooms – 192 of them, across ten storeys – are well equipped and decent-sized, and SWEAT (the hotel's state-of-the-art fitness facility) offers fine views over Soho. Also of note is the W's gob-smacking exterior: the entire hotel is veiled in translucent glass, which is lit in different colours through the day.

Bars/cafés (2). Business centre. Concierge. Disabled-adapted rooms. Gym. Internet: wireless (£15.95/day). Parking: (£49/day). Restaurant. Room service. Smoking rooms. Spa facilities. TV.

Expensive

★ Dean Street Townhouse & Dining Room

69-71 Dean Street, W1D 3SE (7434 1775, www.sohohouse.com). Leicester Square or Piccadilly Circus tube. **Rates** *£90-£410 double.* **Rooms** 39. **Credit** AmEx, MC, V. **Map** p416 W3 ❸❸

This Grade II-listed, 1730s townhouse has been converted into another winning enterprise from the people behind Soho House members' club, Shoreditch Rooms (*see p257*) and High Road House (*see p258*). To one side of a buzzy ground-floor restaurant are four floors of bedrooms that run from full-size rooms with early Georgian panelling and reclaimed oak floors to half-panelled 'Tiny' rooms that are barely bigger than their double beds – but can be had from the website for as little as £90. The atmosphere is gentleman's club cosy (there are cookies in a cute silver Treats container in each room), but modern types also get rainforest showers, 24hr room service, Roberts DAB radios, free wireless internet and big flatscreen TVs. Even the calm little library room behind reception manages to be both low-key and luxurious.

Bar/café. Disabled-adapted rooms. Internet: wireless (free). Restaurant. Room service. TV: DVD.

★ Hazlitt's

6 Frith Street, W1D 3JA (7434 1771, www. hazlittshotel.com). Tottenham Court Road tube. **Rates** £203-£311 double. **Rooms** 30. **Credit** AmEx, DC, MC, V. **Map** p416 W2 ❸❹

Four Georgian townhouses comprise this absolutely charming place, named after William Hazlitt, the spirited 18th-century essayist who died here in abject poverty. With flamboyance and staggering attention to detail the rooms evoke the Georgian era, all heavy fabrics, fireplaces, free-standing tubs and exquisitely carved half-testers, yet modern luxuries

Z Soho. *See p244.*

– air-conditioning, TVs in antique cupboards and double-glazed windows – have been subtly attended to as well. It gets creakier and more crooked the higher you go, culminating in enchanting garret single rooms with rooftop views. Of seven new bedrooms, the main suite is a real knock-out: split-level, with a huge eagle spouting water into the raised bedroom bath and a rooftop terrace with sliding roof, it's a joyous extravaganza. Entertainingly, from the back alley outside, the extension has been made to look like 1700s shopfronts.

Bar/café. Concierge. Conference facilities. Internet: wireless & high-speed (free). Room service. TV: DVD.

★ St John Hotel

1 Leicester Street, off Leicester Square, WC2H 7BL (7251 0848, www.stjohnhotellondon.com). Leicester Square or Piccadilly Circus tube. **Rates** (not incl breakfast) £230-£320 double. **Rooms** 15. **Credit** AmEx, DC, MC, V. **Map** p416 W4 ❸
When one of London's finest restaurants decides to move into the hotel trade, it's well worth taking notice. Co-owner Trevor Gulliver described the hotel as 'that rare thing – a hotel where people would actually want to eat'. To which end, the first floor, ground floor and basement are given over to a bar and restaurant; above them are 15 rooms and a three-bedroom rooftop suite – the bathroom's round window looks west to Big Ben. The decor is in keeping with the white, masculine, minimalist style of the Smithfield original.

Bar. Concierge. Disabled-adapted rooms. Internet: wireless (free). Restaurant. Room service. TV.

Budget

Z Soho

17 Moor Street, W1D 5AP (020 3551 3700, www.thezhotels.com). Leicester Square or Tottenham Court Road tube. **Rates** £85-£110 double. **Rooms** 85. **Credit** MC, V. **Map** p416 X2 ❸
For the money, the Z is a cast-iron bargain. First, the location is superb: it really means Soho, not a short bus-ride away – the breakfast room/bar exits on to Old Compton Street. Then there's the hotel itself, which is surprisingly chic – especially the unexpected interior courtyard, with open 'corridors' stacked above it, and room to sit and drink or smoke at the bottom – and very cheerfully run, down to free wine and nibbles of an evening. The rooms are quite handsome, and have everything you need, from a little desk to free Wi-Fi, but not much more. Including space: expect beds (perhaps a little short for anyone over 6ft tall) to take up most of the room, a feeble shower, and no wardrobes or phones in the rooms. A great little hotel – in both senses. *Photo p243.*

Bar/café. Disabled-adapted rooms. Internet: wireless (free). TV.
Other locations Z Victoria, 5 Lower Belgrave Street, Victoria, SW1W 0NR.

OXFORD STREET & MARYLEBONE

Expensive

Cumberland

Great Cumberland Place, off Oxford Street, W1H 7DL (0871 376 9014, www.guoman.com). Marble Arch tube. **Rates** £100-£400 double. **Rooms** 1,019. **Credit** AmEx, DC, MC, V. **Map** p393 F6 ❸
Perfectly located by Marble Arch tube, the Cumberland is a bit of a monster: in addition to the 900 rooms in the main block, there are another 119 in an annexe down the road. The echoing, rather chaotic lobby has some dramatic modern art and sculptures, as well as an impressive but somewhat severe waterfall. The rooms are minimalist, with acid-etched headboards, neatly modern bathrooms and plasma TVs – nicely designed, but rather small. The hotel's excellent dining room is the exclusive Rhodes W1, but there are also a bar-brasserie and boisterous, trash-industrial style, late-night DJ bar. Weekend breakfasts can feel like feeding the 5,000.

Bars/cafés (3). Concierge. Gym. Internet: wireless (£10/day), high-speed (£15/day). Restaurants (3). Room service. TV: pay movies.

Dorset Square

39-40 Dorset Square, NW1 6QN (7723 7874, www.dorsetsquarehotel.co.uk). Marylebone tube/rail. **Rates** £195-£300 double. **Rooms** 16. **Credit** AmEx, MC, V. **Map** p393 F4 ❸
Grown-up greys are a backdrop for splashes of orange-red and midnight blue, with bold patterns completing a sophisticated modish meets traditional look – the hallmark of owners Firmdale. The Regency townhouse has comfortable, spacious bedrooms, many looking on to the leafy private square; bathrooms are in granite and glass, with Miller Harris products. Downstairs is a comfortable lounge with a fireplace and the Potting Shed restaurant and bar. This property was actually Firmdale's first hotel. Sold in 2002, the company bought it again and refurbished it, before opening in June 2012.

Bar/café. Internet: wireless (£20/day). Restaurant. Rooms service. TV: DVD.

Montagu Place

2 Montagu Place, W1H 2ER (7467 2777, www.montagu-place.co.uk). Baker Street tube. **Rates** £150-£240 double. **Rooms** 16. **Credit** AmEx, DC, MC, V. **Map** p396 G5 ❸
A small, fashionable townhouse hotel, Montagu Place fills a couple of Grade II-listed Georgian residences with sharply appointed rooms graded according to size. The big ones are entitled Swanky, and have king-size beds and big bathrooms – some have narrow front terraces. More modest in size, the Comfy category has queen-size beds and, being at the back of the building, no street views. All rooms have a cool and trendy look, with cafetières and

ground coffee instead of Nescafé sachets, as well as flatscreen TVs. The decision to combine bar and reception desk (situated at the back of the house) means you can get a drink at any time and retire to the graciously modern lounge. Service is at once sharp and very obliging.

Bar/café. Internet: wireless & high-speed (free). Room service. TV: DVD.

Moderate

Sumner
54 Upper Berkeley Street, W1H 7QR (7723 2244, www.thesumner.com). Marble Arch tube. **Rates** (incl breakfast) £160-£280 double. **Rooms** 19. **Credit** AmEx, MC, V. **Map** p393 F6 ⑩
The Sumner's cool, deluxe looks have earned it many fans, not least in the hospitality industry, where it has won a number of awards. You won't be at all surprised when you get here: from the soft dove and slatey greys of the lounge and halls you move up to glossily spacious accommodation with brilliant walk-in showers. The breakfast room feels soft and sunny, with a lovely, delicate buttercup motif and vibrant Arne Jacobsen chairs to cheer you on your way to the museums, but the stylishly moody front sitting room is also a cosy gem.
Concierge. Internet: wireless (free). TV.

22 York Street
22 York Street, W1U 6PX (7224 2990, www.22yorkstreet.co.uk). Baker Street tube. **Rates** £129 double. **Rooms** 10. **Credit** AmEx, MC, V. **Map** p396 G5 ⑪
Bohemian French chic – white furniture, palest pink lime-washed walls, mellow wooden floors, subtly faded textiles and arresting *objets d'époque* – makes this delightfully unpretentious bed and breakfast in the heart of Marylebone a sight to behold. It doesn't announce itself from the outside, so you feel as if you've been invited to stay in someone's arty home, especially when you're drinking good coffee at the gorgeous curved table that dominates the breakfast room-cum-kitchen. Guests are also given free rein with the hot beverages in a lounge full of knick-knacks upstairs, while a cluttered smaller room downstairs has an internet station for those without wireless. All rooms are a decent size and have en suite baths, a rarity at this price and in this part of town.
Internet: wireless (free). TV.

PADDINGTON, BAYSWATER & NOTTING HILL

Deluxe

Hempel
31-35 Craven Hill Gardens, W2 3EA (7298 9000, www.the-hempel.co.uk). Lancaster Gate or Queensway tube or Paddington tube/rail. **Rates** £215-£719 double. **Rooms** 50. **Credit** AmEx, DC, MC, V. **Map** p392 C6 ⑫
Since the mid 1990s, the serried white stucco façades of Craven Hill Gardens, a quiet backwater square in Bayswater, have concealed a dramatic alternative universe dreamed up by Anouska Hempel. The vision still works. Though no longer under her ownership, this boutique hotel started a minimalist

CONSUME

Dorset Square.

La Suite West.

design revolution. H is the logo and clinical the look: the coffee tables sunk into the polished stone floor of the lobby; the empty expanses of magnolia paint on the walls; the green plastic turf in the 'Zen-like' garden. The rooms are all different, but defiantly minimal to the point of barely furnished. The upstairs restaurant serves a menu of European and Japanese fish dishes.

Bar/café. Concierge. Internet: wireless (free). Restaurant. Room service. TV: DVD & pay movies.

Expensive

Portobello Hotel

22 Stanley Gardens, W11 2NG (7727 2777, www.portobellohotel.com). Holland Park or Notting Hill Gate tube. **Rates** (incl breakfast) £234-£384 double. **Rooms** 21. **Credit** AmEx, MC, V. **Map** p404 Y5 ❹

The Portobello is a hotel with approaching half a century of celebrity status, having hosted the likes of Johnny Depp, Kate Moss and Alice Cooper, who used his tub to house a boa constrictor. It remains a pleasingly unpretentious place, with a more civilised demeanour than its legend might suggest. There is now a lift to help rockers who are feeling their age up the five floors, but there's still a 24hr guest-only bar downstairs for those who don't yet feel past it. The rooms are themed – the superb basement Japanese Water Garden, for example, has an elaborate spa bath, its own private grotto and a small private garden – but all are stylishly equipped with a large fan, tall house plants and round-the-clock room service.

Bar/café. Internet: wireless (free). Room service. TV.

Moderate

Hotel Indigo London Paddington

16 London Street, W2 1HL (7706 4444, www.ichotelsgroup.com). Paddington tube/rail. **Rates** £203-£300 double. **Rooms** 64. **Credit** AmEx, DC, MC, V. **Map** p393 D6 ❹

A boutique property from the people behind Crowne Plaza and Holiday Inn has a relaxed all-day bar-restaurant, sharp-witted and friendly staff, and rooms with all mod cons (excellent walk-in showers rather than baths) – the smaller and cheaper attic rooms have most character. The decor is a bit try-hard: a clinical white foyer gives on to acid-bright striped carpets and wardrobe interiors that are an assault by psychedelic swirl. Photographs of Paddington past and ingenious ceiling strips of sky show how less could have been more. A second Hotel Indigo (142 Minories, EC3N 1LS, 7265 1014) opened in 2010, with a third opening in December 2012 in Earl's Court (33-34 Barkston Gardens, SW5 0EW).

Bar/café. Disabled-adapted rooms. Internet: wireless (free). Restaurant. Room service. TV: pay movies.

★ La Suite West

41-51 Inverness Terrace, W2 3JN (7313 8484, www.lasuitewest.com). Bayswater or Queensway tube. **Rates** £155-£295 double. **Rooms** 80. **Credit** AmEx, MC, V. **Map** p392 C6 ❹

A typical row of west London townhouses on the outside, La Suite has been transformed on the inside by designer Anouska Hempel, with sleek lines and a black and white palette – the antithesis of her maximalist Blakes (*see p252*). A discreet side entrance leads into a long minimalist reception area with open

fire and a zen-like feel. An Asian influence persists in the rooms, with slatted sliding screens for windows, wardrobe and bathrooms helping to make good use of space (which is limited in the cheaper rooms). Thoughtfully designed white marble bathrooms, with rainforest shower and bath, give a feeling of luxury despite not being huge. The large terrace running along the front of the building, with trees planted for an arbour-like effect, is a big summer asset. All in all, clever design, a friendly vibe and – importantly – keen pricing make for a great hotel for this price range. Highly recommended.
Restaurant. Internet: wireless (free). Room service. TV: pay movies.

New Linden

59 Leinster Square, W2 4PS (7221 4321, www.newlinden.co.uk). Bayswater tube. **Rates** £95-£149 double. **Credit** AmEx, MC, V. **Map** p392 B6 ㊼

Modern, modish and moderately priced – that's the Mayflower Group for you. This is its Bayswater baby; it chooses to call the area 'trendy Notting Hill' on the website, but that's stretching the bounds of London geography a little far. It looks very cool, however, and it is a fantastically comfortable place to stay. The lobby and lounge are slick and glamorous – there's a beautiful teak arch in the lounge and the rooms are low key with some vibrant, twirly eastern influences. Some of the larger family rooms retain their elaborate period pillars and cornicing. The bathrooms are a symphony in marble; the walk-in showers have deluge heads. There's a pleasant little patio, upstairs at the back, for morning coffee and evening drinks.
Concierge. Internet: wireless (free). TV.

Vancouver Studios

30 Prince's Square, W2 4NJ (7243 1270, www.vancouverstudios.co.uk). Bayswater or Queensway tube. **Rates** £120-£155 double. **Rooms** 51. **Credit** AmEx, DC, MC, V. **Map** p392 B6 ㊾

Step into the hall or comfortably furnished sitting room of this imposing townhouse and it feels like the gracious home of a slightly dotty uncle, with decor in the public spaces comprising colonial swords and historic prints. The studio or apartment accommodation is more modern in tone. Each room has its own style – from cool contemporary lines to a softer, more homely feel – and all are well equipped with kitchen appliances so that guests can do a bit of self-catering, should they wish. Zeus the cat lords it over the building and can show you into the pretty garden with its fountain and heady scent of jasmine – a shady stunner.
Internet: wireless (free). TV: DVD.

Budget

Garden Court Hotel

30-31 Kensington Gardens Square, W2 4BG (7229 2553, www.gardencourthotel.co.uk).

Bayswater or Queensway tube. **Rates** (incl breakfast) £79-£125 double. **Rooms** 32. **Credit** MC, V. **Map** p392 B6 ㊽

Once people have discovered the Garden Court, they tend to keep coming back, says Edward Connolly, owner-manager of this long-established hotel, with quiet pride. There aren't many places this close to Hyde Park and Portobello Market that give such excellent value for money and impeccable service. The rooms in this grand Victorian terrace have a bright, modern look and plenty of space, and the lounge, with its wood floor, leather-covered furniture, sprightly floral wallpaper and elegant mantelpiece is a lovely place to linger. As the name suggests, there's a small walled garden, lushly planted, and laden guests might be cheered by the presence of a lift.
Internet: wireless (£2/day). TV.

Pavilion

34-36 Sussex Gardens, W2 1UL (7262 0905, www.pavilionhoteluk.com). Edgware Road tube, or Marylebone or Paddington tube/rail. **Rates** £85-£100 double. **Rooms** 29. **Credit** MC, V. **Map** p393 E5 ㊾

A hotel that describes itself as 'fashion rock 'n' roll' is never going to be staid, but Danny and Noshi Karne's Pavilion is quite mind-bogglingly excessive. The rooms have attention-grabbing names, such as 'Enter the Dragon' (Chinese themed), 'Flower Power' (blooming flowery) and 'Cosmic Girl' (way out there, man) and are frequently used for fashion shoots: the website has an impressive list of celebrities who have rocked up here over the years. Bizarre and voluptuous choice of decor notwithstanding, this crazy hotel represents excellent value and has the usual amenities. You might be disappointed if you want cool contemporary elegance and poncey toiletries – the Pavilion's much more fun than that.
Internet: wireless (free). Parking: £10/day. TV.

★ Stylotel

160-162 Sussex Gardens, W2 1UD (7723 1026, www.stylotel.com). Edgware Road tube, or Marylebone or Paddington tube/rail. **Rates** £95 double. **Rooms** 39. **Credit** AmEx, MC, V. **Map** p393 E6 ㊿

Partly due to the young manager's enthusiasm, it's hard not to like this place. It's a retro-futurist dream: metal floors and panelling, lots of royal blue (the hall walls, the padded headboards) and pod bathrooms. But the real deal at Stylotel is its bargain studio and apartment (respectively, £120-£150 and £150-£200, breakfast £8 extra), around the corner above a pub. Designed – like the rest of the hotel – by the owner's son, they suggest he's calmed down with age. Here's real minimalist chic: sleek brushed steel or white glass wall panels, simply styled contemporary furniture upholstered in black or white.
Concierge. Internet: wireless (£2/hr). Parking: £15/day. TV.

26 Hillgate Place

26 Hillgate Place, W8 7ST (7727 7717,
www.26hillgateplace.co.uk). Notting Hill Gate tube.
Rates £80-£115 double. **Rooms** 2. **No credit**
cards. Map p404 Y6 ⑤

Artist Hilary Dunne has furnished her B&B with
paintings of glossy-skinned, doe-eyed women inspired
by her travels in the West Indies, as well as the spoils
from her former life as a textiles importer. The ground-
floor room with its large en suite bathroom contains
some of the Caribbean collection; the smaller, more
colourful second room, with shared bathroom, is bright
with wall hangings and cushions from India. The overall effect is of a much-loved, warm and lived-in family
home. Breakfast is taken in a busy little space next to
the galley kitchen, with French windows opening on
to a tiny, ivy-clad courtyard. A slightly larger patio
upstairs, home to Hilary's extensive plant collection,
looks out over the gardens of Hillgate Place.
Internet: wireless (free). TV.

PICCADILLY CIRCUS & MAYFAIR

Deluxe

Brown's

Albemarle Street, W1S 4BP (7493 6020,
www.roccofortecollection.com). Green Park tube.
Rates £393-£705 double. **Rooms** 117. **Credit**
AmEx, DC, MC, V. **Map** p416 U4 ⑥

Brown's was opened in 1837 by James Brown, butler
to Romantic poet, hedonist and freedom-fighter Lord
Byron. The first British telephone call was made
from here in 1876, five years after Napoleon III and
Empress Eugenie took refuge in one of the considerable suites after fleeing the Third Republic.
Ethiopian Emperor Haile Selassie and Rudyard
Kipling were also guests. The bedrooms are all large
and extremely comfortable, furnished with original
art, collections of books and, in the suites, fireplaces;
the elegant, classic British hotel restaurant, Hix at
the Albemarle, gives a nod to modernity with a
series of contemporary British artworks, including
pieces by the likes of Tracey Emin, but the public
spaces of the hotel thrum with history. Non-residents
can visit: try the £37.50 afternoon tea in the English
Tea Room or sip a cocktail in the classily masculine
Donovan Bar.
Bar/café. Business centre. Concierge. Disabled-
adapted rooms. Gym. Internet: wireless & high-
speed (£15/day). Restaurant. Room service. Spa
facilities. TV: pay movies.

★ Claridge's

55 Brook Street, W1K 4HR (7629 8860,
www.claridges.co.uk). Bond Street tube. **Rates**
£359-£828 double. **Rooms** 203. **Credit** AmEx,
DC, MC, V. **Map** p396 H6 ⑥

Claridge's is sheer class and pure atmosphere, with
its signature art deco redesign still simply dazzling.

Photographs of Churchill and sundry royals grace
the grand foyer, as does an absurdly over-the-top
Dale Chihuly chandelier. Without departing too far
from the traditional, Claridge's bars and restaurant
are actively fashionable – Gordon Ramsay is the in-
house restaurateur, and the A-listers can gather for
champers and sashimi in the bar. The rooms divide
evenly between deco and Victorian style, with period
touches such as deco toilet flushes in the swanky
marble bathrooms. Bedside panels control the mod-
con facilities at the touch of a button. If money's no
object, opt for a David Linley suite, done out in gorgeous duck-egg blue and white, or lilac and silver.
Bars/cafés (2). Business centre. Concierge.
Disabled-adapted rooms. Gym. Internet: wireless
(free). Restaurants (2). Room service. Smoking
rooms. Spa facilities. TV: DVD & pay movies.

★ Connaught

Carlos Place, W1K 2AL (7499 7070, www.the-
connaught.co.uk). Bond Street tube. **Rates** £490-
£650 double. **Rooms** 121. **Credit** AmEx, DC,
MC, V. **Map** p398 H7 ⑥

This isn't the only hotel in London to provide butlers, but there can't be many that offer 'a secured gun
cabinet room' for the hunting season. This is traditional British hospitality for those who love 23-carat
gold leaf trimmings and stern portraits in the halls,
but all mod cons in their room, down to flatscreens
in the en suite. Too lazy to polish your own shoes?
The butlers are trained in shoe care by the expert
cobblers at John Lobb. Both of the bars – gentleman's club cosy Coburg (*see p196*) and cruiseship
deco Connaught – are very impressive. In the new wing, which doubled
the number of guestrooms, there's a swanky spa and
60sq m swimming pool.
Bars/cafés (2). Concierge. Disabled-adapted
rooms. Gym. Internet: wireless (free). Pool: indoor.
Restaurants (2). Room service. Smoking rooms.
Spa facilities. TV: DVD.

★ Dorchester

53 Park Lane, W1K 1QA (7629 8888,
www.thedorchester.com). Hyde Park Corner tube.
Rates £354-£720 double. **Rooms** 250. **Credit**
AmEx, DC, MC, V. **Map** p398 G7 ⑥

A Park Lane fixture since 1931, the Dorchester's interior may be thoroughly, opulently classical, but the
hotel is cutting edge in attitude, providing an unri-
valled level of personal service. With the grandest
lobby in town, amazing views of Hyde Park, state-
of-the-art mod cons and a magnificent spa, it's small
wonder the hotel continues to welcome movie stars
(the lineage stretches from Elizabeth Taylor to Tom
Cruise) and political leaders (Eisenhower planned the
D-Day landings here). You're not likely to be eating
out, either: the Dorchester employs 90 full-time chefs
at the Grill Room, Alain Ducasse and the wonderfully
atmospheric China Tang. There's even an angelic tearoom in the new spa: the Spatisserie. The Dorchester

opened an entirely new hotel, 45 Park Lane (*see p249*), early in 2011 in the former Playboy club premises, almost opposite the entrance to its predecessor. *Bar/café. Concierge. Disabled-adapted rooms. Gym. Internet: wireless & high-speed (£19.50). Parking: £50/day. Restaurants (5). Room service. Smoking rooms. Spa facilities. TV: DVD & pay movies.*

★ 45 Park Lane

45 Park Lane, W1K 1PN (7493 4545, www.45parklane.com). Hyde Park Corner tube. **Rates** from £510 double. **Rooms** 46. **Credit** AmEx, MC, V. **Map** p398 G8 **⑤⑥**

Offspring of the Dorchester, which it faces across a twinkly-treed forecourt, 45 Park Lane opened in late 2011 to immediate acclaim in the style and travel press. It had succeeded resoundingly in the task it had set itself: to translate the famously high standards of the Dorchester into a buzzier, boutiquier, even blingier form. Where the Dorchester offers liveried concierges, 45 Park Lane allocates guests a personal host sharply suited in grey; where the Dorchester can arrange a limo, so can 45 – or lend you a folding bike. Wolfgang Puck brings informal glamour and high-end steaks to the Cut restaurant. Rooms are standard rectangles given character by well-chosen art, quality furnishings, great views (ask for an upper floor) and considered touches such as a yoga mat, designer glassware and in-safe electrical outlet. Technology is state of the art; enormous flatscreens swing out from the walls; a TV is embedded in the bathroom mirror (to watch from the giant marble bath); and touchscreens control room functions electronically. Breakfasts are awesome.
Bar. Concierge. Disabled-adapted rooms. Gym. Internet: wireless (free). Restaurant. Room service. TV: DVD.

Haymarket Hotel

1 Suffolk Place, SW1Y 4BP (7470 4000, www.firmdale.com). Piccadilly Circus tube. **Rates** £265-£500 double. **Rooms** 50. **Credit** AmEx, DC, MC, V. **Map** p416 W5 **⑤⑦**

A terrific addition to Kit Kemp's Firmdale portfolio, this block-size building was designed by John Nash, the architect of Regency London. The public spaces are a delight, with Kemp's trademark combination of contemporary arty surprises and plump, floral sofas. Wow-factors include the bling basement swimming pool and bar (shiny sofas, twinkly roof) and the central location. Rooms are generously sized (as are bathrooms), individually decorated and discreetly stuffed with facilities, and there's plenty of attention from the switched-on staff. The street-side bar and restaurant are top-notch, the breakfast exquisite.
Bar/café. Concierge. Disabled-adapted rooms. Gym. Internet: wireless (£20/day). Pool: indoor. Restaurant. Room service. Smoking rooms. Spa facilities. TV: DVD.

Metropolitan

19 Old Park Lane, W1K 1LB (7447 1000, www.metropolitan.como.bz). Hyde Park Corner tube. **Rates** £275-£510 double. **Rooms** 144. **Credit** AmEx, DC, MC, V. **Map** p398 H8 **⑤⑧**

The flashier little sister of the Halkin (*see p252*), the Metropolitan may have had its fashion heyday in the 1990s, but it still retains a buzzy, relaxed sense of cool. The Met bar and Nobu restaurant continue to attract celebrities and models, bands such as Kings of Leon still rock up, and many mere mortals drop by to rubberneck. The hotel itself is bright and uncluttered. The rooms are a little clinical and appear ever-so-slightly dated, but pear-wood furnishings, super-soft mattresses and suede throws keep things very comfortable, and the toiletries in the bathrooms are a cut above the usual chuck-away fodder. The hotel's greatest asset, however, is the prime location, overlooking a corner of Hyde Park.
Bar/café. Business centre. Concierge. Disabled-adapted rooms. Gym. Internet: wireless, high-speed & shared terminal (free). Parking: £45/day. Restaurant. Room service. Smoking rooms. Spa facilities. TV: DVD & pay movies.

Ritz

150 Piccadilly, W1J 9BR (7493 8181, www.theritzlondon.com). Green Park tube. **Rates** £300-£495 double. **Rooms** 134. **Credit** AmEx, DC, MC, V. **Map** p398 J8 **⑤⑨**

If you like the idea of a world where jeans and trainers are banned and jackets must be worn by gentlemen when dining (the requirement is waived for breakfast), the Ritz is the place for you. Founded by hotelier extraordinaire César Ritz, the hotel is deluxe *in excelsis*. The show-stopper is the ridiculously ornate, vaulted Long Gallery, an orgy of chandeliers, rococo mirrors and marble columns, but all the high-ceilinged, Louis XVI-style bedrooms have been painstakingly renovated to their former glory in restrained pastel colours. But amid the old-world luxury, there are plenty of mod cons including free wireless in most rooms, large TVs and a gym. An elegant afternoon tea in the Palm Court (book ahead) is the way in for interlopers.
Bar/café. Concierge. Gym. Internet: high-speed (£26/day); wireless (£26/day). Restaurant. Room service. Smoking rooms. Spa facilities. TV: DVD.

Expensive

No.5 Maddox Street

5 Maddox Street, W1S 2QD (7647 0200, www.living-rooms.co.uk). Oxford Circus tube. **Rates** £300-£350 double. **Rooms** 12. **Credit** AmEx, MC, V. **Map** p416 U2 **⑥⓪**

This bolthole just off Regent Street is perfect for visiting film directors looking to be accommodated in a chic apartment at a reasonable long-term rate. Here they can shut the discreet brown front door, climb the stairs and flop into a home from home with

all contemporary cons, including new flatscreen TVs. The East-meets-West decor is classic 1990s minimalist, but very bright and clean after a gentle refurbishment. Each apartment has a fully equipped kitchen, but room service will shop for you as well as providing usual hotel amenities. There's no bar, but breakfasts and snacks are served, and there's a Thai restaurant (Patara) on the ground floor.
Concierge. Internet: wireless & high-speed (£10/day, £50/wk). Room service. TV: DVD.

WESTMINSTER & ST JAMES'S

Deluxe

Royal Horseguards
2 Whitehall Court, SW1A 2EJ (0871 376 9033, www.guoman.com). Embankment tube or Charing Cross tube/rail. **Rates** £200-£300 double. **Rooms** 280. **Credit** AmEx, MC, V. **Map** p399 L8 ⑥
The Royal Horseguards occupies a French château that is discreetly located off Whitehall. The building was designed by Alfred 'Natural History Museum' Waterhouse for the National Liberal Club in 1887, and the club's founder, William Gladstone, the great reformer that he was, probably would have approved of the recent refurbishment of the interior by the Guoman group. It's immaculately clean, 'classic but modern' in style, with welcoming staff. The bedrooms have useful dressing tables, iPod docks and wonderfully comfortable Hypnos beds, and bathrooms come with flatscreen TV and Guoman toiletries. The buffet-style breakfasts are ordinary, but from the upper floors the river views of County Hall and the London Eye – whisper it – rival those of the Savoy (*see p241*).
Bars/cafés (2). Business centre. Concierge. Disabled-adapted rooms. Gym. Internet: wireless (free). Restaurant. Room service. TV.

Expensive

Eccleston Square Hotel
37 Eccleston Square, SW1V 1PB (3489 1000, www.ecclestonsquarehotel.com). Pimlico tube or Victoria tube/rail. **Rates** £250-£450 double. **Rooms** 39. **Credit** AmEx, MC, V. **Map** p398 H11 ⑫
This Grade II-listed Georgian house has been transformed into a smart, urbane and rather masculine boutique hotel, in a palette of grey, black and white, with high-quality fittings such as Italian marble chevron flooring throughout the ground floor and black Murano glass chandeliers. Upstairs, the monochrome continues, with leather headboards, silk wallpaper and curtains, all in shades of grey. It's in the rooms that the hotel's USP becomes apparent: it's all about the tech. Whether it's the underfloor heating in the bathroom, the lighting or the curtains, it's all operated by finger-tip control pads. The most snazzy is the one that turns the 'smart glass' of the

white marble bathroom walls opaque for privacy. (Bath-lovers note that these are eschewed here in favour of rainfall showers.) In addition, every room comes equipped with an iPad2. It's all super convenient and comfortable.
Bar/café. Concierge. Conference facilities. Internet: wireless (free). Restaurant. Room service. TV: DVD.

Trafalgar
2 Spring Gardens, Trafalgar Square, SW1A 2TS (7870 2900, www.thetrafalgar.com). Charing Cross tube/rail. **Rates** £300-£450 double. **Rooms** 129. **Credit** AmEx, DC, MC, V. **Map** p416 X5 ⑥
The Trafalgar is part of the Hilton chain of hotels, but you'd hardly notice. The mood is young and dynamic at the chain's first 'concept' hotel, for all that it's housed in the imposing edifice that was once the headquarters of Cunard (this was where the *Titanic* was conceived). To the right of the open reception is the Rockwell Bar, boisterous at night, although thick walls should prevent sound leaking up to the rooms; breakfast downstairs is accompanied by gentler music, sometimes played live. It's the none-more-central location, however, that's the hotel's biggest draw – the handful of corner suites look directly into the square (prices reflect location). Those without their own view can always avail themselves of the little rooftop bar, which is now open to the public.
Bars/cafés (2). Business centre. Concierge. Disabled-adapted rooms. Gym. Internet: wireless & high-speed (£15/day). Restaurant. Room service. TV: DVD & pay movies.

Moderate

B+B Belgravia
64-66 Ebury Street, SW1W 9QD (7259 8570, www.bb-belgravia.com). Victoria tube/rail. **Rates** (incl breakfast) £135 double. **Rooms** 17. **Credit** AmEx, MC, V. **Map** p398 H10 ⑭
How do you make a lounge full of white and black contemporary furnishings seem cosy and welcoming? Hard to achieve, but the owners have succeeded at B+B Belgravia, which takes the B&B experience to a new level. It's fresh and sophisticated without being hard-edged: there's nothing here that will make the fastidiously design-conscious wince (leather sofa, arty felt cushions, modern fireplace), but nor is it overly precious. A gleaming espresso machine provides 24/7 caffeine, and there's a large but somewhat dark garden to sit out in at the rear.
Disabled-adapted rooms. Internet: wireless (free). TV.

Windermere Hotel
142-144 Warwick Way, SW1V 4JE (7834 5163, www.windermere-hotel.co.uk). Victoria tube/rail. **Rates** (incl breakfast) £145-£175 double. **Rooms** 19. **Credit** AmEx, MC, V. **Map** p398 H11 ⑮

Heading the procession of small hotels that are strung out along Warwick Way, the Windermere is a comfortable, traditionally decked-out London hotel with, thankfully, no aspirations to boutique status. The decor may be showing its age a bit in the hall, but you'll receive a warm welcome and excellent service – there are over a dozen staff for just 19 rooms. There's a cosy basement restaurant-bar, where the breakfasts are top-notch.

Bar/café. Internet: wireless (free). Restaurant. Room service. TV.

Budget

Morgan House
120 Ebury Street, SW1W 9QQ (7730 2384, www.morganhouse.co.uk). Pimlico tube or Victoria tube/rail. **Rates** (incl breakfast) £84-£108 double. **Rooms** 11. **Credit** MC, V. **Map** p398 G10 ⑥⑤

The Morgan has the understated charm of the old family home of a posh but unpretentious English friend: a pleasing mix of nice old wooden or traditional iron beds, with pretty floral curtains and coverlets in subtle hues, the odd chandelier or big gilt

---

INSIDE TRACK NO FRILLS

Chain hotels aren't covered in this chapter, unless they're new, especially well located (**Premier Inn London County Hall**; see p232) or otherwise unusually praiseworthy. This is simply because the internal logic of chain hotels is that one should be as similar as possible to another, with reliability one major virtue – and price the other. You can find double rooms for around £100 at **Holiday Inn** and **Holiday Inn Express** (www.ichotelsgroup.com), **Ibis** (www.ibishotel.com) and **Travelodge** (www.travelodge.co.uk).

A relatively new development has been the 'no-frills' approach – very low rates, with nothing inessential included. Airline-offshoot **EasyHotel** (www.easyhotel.com) was the first, but it now has a challenger: the first British hotel from **Tune** (www.tune hotels.com) is located not far inland from the South Bank, across the river from the Houses of Parliament. Rooms are usually around £50 a night.

If you've got an awkward departure time from Gatwick or Heathrow, consider the neat 'pod' rooms at a **Yotel** (www.yotel.com); a four-hour stay will cost £45. And due to arrive at Gatwick in summer 2013 is London's first **Bloc** hotel (www.blochotels.com) – a high-tech, no-frills enterprise.

---

mirror over original mantelpieces, and padded wicker chairs and sinks in every bedroom. Though there's no guest lounge, guests can sit in the little patio garden in better weather and, for Belgravia, the prices are a steal.

Internet: wireless (free). TV.

CHELSEA

Expensive

Myhotel Chelsea
35 Ixworth Place, SW3 3QX (7225 7500, www.myhotels.com). South Kensington tube. **Rates** £190-£348 double. **Rooms** 46. **Credit** AmEx, DC, MC, V. **Map** p395 E11 ⑥⑦

The Chelsea Myhotel feels a world away from its sleekly modern Bloomsbury sister (*see p238*). The Sloane Square branch has an aesthetic that is softer and decidedly more English – with a floral sofa and plate of scones in the lobby, and white wicker headboards, velvet cushions and Bee Kind toiletries in the guestrooms. These feminine touches contrast nicely with the mini-chain's feng shui touches, its Eastern-inspired treatment room, and its sleek aquarium. The modernised country farmhouse feel of the bar-restaurant works better for breakfast than it does for a boozy cocktail, but the central library, which is done out conservatory style, is simply wonderful. Just pick up a book, sink into one of the ample comfy chairs and listen to the tinkling water feature.

Bar/café. Business centre. Concierge. Internet: wireless & high-speed (free). Restaurant. Room service. TV: DVD. **Other locations** 11-13 Bayley Street, Bloomsbury, WC1B 3HD (7667 6000).

San Domenico House
29-31 Draycott Place, SW3 2SH (7581 5757, www.sandomenicohouse.com). Sloane Square tube. **Rates** £240-£300 double. **Rooms** 16. **Credit** AmEx, MC, V. **Map** p395 F11 ⑥⑧

Along a quiet terrace of late 19th-century red-stone buildings just off Sloane Square, San Domenico owes much of its tasteful, historic look to previous owner Sue Rogers, the interior designer who transformed this former private residence into a boutique hotel masterpiece. All the categories of guestroom, including the split-level gallery suites and a new junior suite, feature original furnishings or antiques. Royal portraits, Victorian mirrors and Empire-era travelling cases are complemented by fabrics of similar style and taste, offset by contemporary touches to bathrooms. The spacious bedrooms enjoy wide-angle views of London, some from little balconies. Breakfasts are taken up to guests or laid out in the room downstairs, while main meals may be taken in the sumptuous coffee room by the lobby.

Internet: wireless (free). Room service. TV.

KNIGHTSBRIDGE & SOUTH KENSINGTON

Deluxe

Blakes

*33 Roland Gardens, SW7 3PF (7370 6701,
www.blakeshotels.com). South Kensington tube.*
Rates £318-£450 double. **Rooms** 46. **Credit**
AmEx, MC, V. **Map** p395 D11

As original as when Anouska Hempel opened it in
1983 – the scent of oranges and the twittering of a
pair of lovebirds fill the dark, oriental lobby – Blakes
and its maximalist decor have stood the test of time,
a living casebook for interior design students. Each
room is in a different style, with influences from
Italy, India, Turkey and China. Exotic antiques
picked up on the designer's travels – intricately
carved beds, Chinese birdcages, ancient trunks – are
set off by sweeping drapery and piles of plump cushions. Downstairs, the Eastern-influenced restaurant
caters for a celebrity clientele enticed by the hotel's
discreet, residential location.
*Bar/café. Concierge. Internet: wireless & high-
speed (free). Parking: £50/day. Restaurant. Room
service. TV: DVD & pay movies.*

Gore

*190 Queen's Gate, SW7 5EX (7584 6601,
www.gorehotel.com). South Kensington tube.* **Rates**
£140-£240 double. **Rooms** 50. **Credit** AmEx, MC,
V. **Map** p395 D9 ⑩

This fin-de-siècle period piece was founded by
descendants of Captain Cook in two grand Victorian
townhouses. The lobby and staircase are close hung
with old paintings, and the bedrooms all have fan-
tastic 19th-century carved oak beds, sumptuous
drapes and shelves of old books. The suites are spectacular: the Tudor Room has a huge stone-faced fireplace and a minstrels' gallery, while tragedy queens
should plump for the Venus room and Judy
Garland's old bed (and replica ruby slippers). Bistrot
190 provides a casually elegant setting for great
breakfasts, while the warm, wood-panelled 190 bar
is a charming setting for cocktails.
*Bar/café. Concierge. Internet: wireless & high-
speed (£20/day). Restaurant. Room service. TV.*

Halkin

*Halkin Street, SW1X 7DJ (7333 1000,
www.halkin.como.bz). Hyde Park Corner tube.*
Rates £565 double. **Rooms** 41. **Credit** AmEx,
DC, MC, V. **Map** p398 G9 ⑪

Set up by Singaporean fashion mogul Christina Ong
(who also owns the Metropolitan; *see p249*), the
Halkin marries Eastern charm, style and food with
a central and quiet location in Knightsbridge. The
rooms, all located off black curved, almost trompe
l'oeil wooden corridors, are comfortable and full of
Asian artefacts and clever gadgetry (a touch-screen
bedside panel controls everything from the air-con

to the 'do not disturb' sign on the door). Bathrooms
are well equipped and heavy on the marble, and
come stocked with a range of products from Ong's
Shambhala spa. The Michelin-starred Thai restau-
rant Nahm (*see p175*), a gastronomic sensation, is
on the ground floor.
*Bar/café. Concierge. Disabled-adapted rooms.
Gym. Internet: wireless & high-speed (free).
Parking: £45/day. Restaurant. Room service.
TV: DVD & pay movies.*

★ Lanesborough

*1 Lanesborough Place, SW1X 7TA (7259 5599,
www.lanesborough.com). Hyde Park Corner tube.*
Rates £475-£675 double. **Rooms** 93. **Credit**
AmEx, DC, MC, V. **Map** p398 G8 ⑫

Generally considered one of London's more historic
luxury hotels, the Lanesborough was in fact redeveloped – impressively – only in 1991. Occupying
an 1820s Greek Revival building that was designed
as a hospital by William Wilkins (the man behind
the National Gallery; *see p98*), its luxurious guestrooms are traditionally decorated with thick fabrics, antique furniture and lavish Carrera-marble
bathrooms. Electronic keypads control everything
from the air-conditioning to the superb 24hr room
service at the touch of a button. As luxury hotels
go, the Lanesborough's rates are unusually inclusive: high-speed internet access, movies and calls
within the EU and to the USA are complimentary,
as are personalised business cards stating your residence. The Library Bar and the cigar and cognac
lounge are excellent.
*Bar/café. Business centre. Concierge. Disabled-
adapted rooms. Gym. Internet: wireless & high-
speed (free). Parking: £8/hr. Restaurant. Room
service. Spa facilities. TV: DVD & pay movies.*

Milestone Hotel & Apartments

*1-2 Kensington Court, W8 5DL (7917 1000,
www.milestonehotel.com). High Street Kensington
tube.* **Rates** £300-£432 double. **Rooms** 56.
Credit AmEx, DC, MC, V. **Map** p392 C8 ⑬

Wealthy American visitors make annual pilgrim-
ages here, their arrival greeted by the comforting,
gravel tones of their regular concierge, as English
as roast beef, and the glass of sherry in the room.
Yet amid the old-school luxury (butlers on 24-hour
call) thrives inventive modernity (the resistance
pool in the spa). Rooms overlooking Kensington
Gardens feature the inspired decor of South
African owner Beatrice Tillman: the Safari suite
contains tent-like draperies and leopard-print
upholstery; the Tudor Suite has an elaborate
inglenook fireplace, minstrels' gallery and a pouffe
concealing a pop-up TV.
*Bar/café. Business centre. Concierge. Disabled-
adapted rooms. Gym. Internet: wireless & high-
speed (free). Pool: indoor. Restaurant. Room
service. Smoking rooms. Spa facilities. TV:
DVD & pay movies.*

CONSUME

Expensive

★ Number Sixteen

*16 Sumner Place, SW7 3EG (7589 5232,
www.firmdale.com). South Kensington tube.*
Rates £225-£300 double. **Rooms** 41. **Credit**
AmEx, DC, MC, V. **Map** p395 D10 ⑦

This may be Kit Kemp's most affordable hotel but
there's no slacking in the style stakes – witness
the fresh flowers and origami-ed birdbook decora-
tions in the comfortable drawing room. Bedrooms
are generously sized, bright and very light, and
carry the Kit Kemp trademark mix of bold and
traditional. The whole place has an appealing
freshness about it, enhanced by a delicious, large
back garden complete with a central water feature.
By the time you finish breakfast in the sweet conservatory, you'll have forgotten you're in the middle of the city.
*Concierge. Internet: wireless & high-speed
(£20/day). Parking: £45/day. Room service.
TV: DVD.*

Moderate

Ampersand

*10 Harrington Road, SW7 3ER (7589 5895,
www.ampersandhotel.com). South Kensington
tube.* **Rates** £120-£270. **Rooms** 111. **Credit**
AmEx, MC, V. **Map** p395 D10 ⑦

A new hotel for South Kensington, the Ampersand
has a strong design ethos, with dove greys and
duck egg blues enlivened by splashes of purples,
yellows and reds, creating a striking and distinctive look. A whimsical twist on the classic comes
from the likes of tall purple padded headboards
reaching nearly to the ceiling and dove drawings
on the dove-grey walls in the ornithologically
inspired deluxe rooms. In the corridors, botanical
drawings and representations of scientific instruments reference the museums nearby, while the
colourful lounge area – where afternoon tea is
served – has deep sofas and studded armchairs
in scarlet velvets and kingfisher blues and a muti-
coloured teapot collection in a wall cabinet.

CONSUME

Ampersand.

Breakfast and dining is downstairs in the white-tiled Mediterranean-oriented, Apero restaurant.
Gym. Internet: wireless (free). Restaurant. Room service. TV: pay movies.

Aster House

3 Sumner Place, SW7 3EE (7581 5888, www.asterhouse.com). South Kensington tube. **Rates** (incl breakfast) £180-£300 double. **Rooms** 13. **Credit** MC, V. **Map** p395 D11 ⑩
This swish, thoroughly archetypal white-terraced South Kensington street is a great setting for a hotel. But Aster House has not just relied on location; it's become an award-winner through attention to detail (such as impeccable housekeeping, the mobile phone guests can borrow, and the introduction of wireless internet and flatscreen TVs) and the warmth of its managers, Leona and Simon Tan. It's all low-key, comfortably soothing creams with touches of dusty rose and muted green. Star of the show is the plant-filled conservatory that serves as a breakfast room and guest lounge – star, that is, after Ollie and Cordelia, the resident ducks.
Internet: wireless (free). TV.

Vicarage Hotel

10 Vicarage Gate, W8 4AG (7229 4030, www.londonvicaragehotel.com). High Street Kensington or Notting Hill Gate tube. **Rates** (incl breakfast) £107-£136 double. **Rooms** 17. **Credit** AmEx, MC, V. **Map** p392 B8 ⑰
Scores of devotees return regularly to this tall Victorian townhouse, which has a great location, tucked in a quiet leafy square just off High Street Ken, hard by Kensington Gardens. It's a comfortable, resolutely old-fashioned establishment – and that's what the punters come for. The refurbished entrance hall is wonderfully grand, with red and gold striped wallpaper, a huge gilt mirror and chandelier. A sweeping staircase ascends from there to an assortment of good-sized rooms, furnished in pale florals and nice old pieces of furniture.
Internet: wireless (free). TV.

NORTH LONDON

Expensive

York & Albany

127-129 Parkway, Camden, NW1 7PS (7387 5700, www.gordonramsay.com). Camden Town tube. **Rates** £156-£348 double. **Rooms** 9. **Credit** AmEx, DC, MC, V. **Map** p404 X3 ⑱
Overcommitment to TV and transatlantic enterprises might have knocked a little gloss off Gordon Ramsay's restaurants, but his only hotel is still going strong. Housed in a grand John Nash building that was designed as a coaching house but spent the recent past as a pub, it consists of a restaurant (split over two levels), bar and delicatessen downstairs; above them a selection of nine rooms, handsomely

designed by Russell Sage in mellow shades. The decor is an effective mix of ancient and modern, sturdy and quietly charismatic furniture married to modern technology; if you're lucky, you'll have views of Regent's Park from your bedroom window.
Bar/café. Disabled-adapted rooms. Internet: wireless (free). Restaurant. Room service. TV: DVD.

Moderate

Colonnade

2 Warrington Crescent, Little Venice, W9 1ER (7286 1052, www.theetoncollection.com). Warwick Avenue tube. **Rates** £168-£258 double. **Rooms** 43. **Credit** AmEx, MC, V. **Map** p392 C4 ⑲
Housed in an imposingly sited white mansion, the Colonnade has been lushly done up in interior-designer traditional – lots of swagged curtains, deep opulent colours, luxurious fabrics and careful arrangements of smoothly upholstered furniture. Some of the larger high-ceilinged rooms have had mezzanine floors added. Note that the hotel no longer has a restaurant or bar, although it still serves breakfast to guests in the old restaurant space.
Internet: wireless (free). Parking: £20/day. Room service. TV.

Rose & Crown

199 Stoke Newington Church Street, Stoke Newington, N16 9ES (7923 3337, www.roseandcrownn16.co.uk). Bus 73. **Rates** (incl breakfast) £132-£197 double. **Rooms** 6. **Credit** MC, V.
The Rose has always been popular as a pub, but now a separate entrance leads to a contemporary B&B. Landscape gardener Will, who with Diane runs the place, transformed three floors to create individually and tastefully styled guestrooms (drench showers, quality smellies and furnishings), a breakfast room and a sun-catching roof terrace with a large table, a couple of loungers, a patio heater and a view across to central London from the illuminated glow of 13th-century St Mary's Church alongside. Pricier rooms feature a stand-alone bathtub, and the suite by the breakfast room is vast. Truman Brewery touches from yesteryear remain: the pub sign lettering, a finely carved pre-war stair rail and the Mystery Arrow games machine.
Internet: wireless (free). TV.

Budget

Hampstead Village Guesthouse

2 Kemplay Road, Hampstead, NW3 1SY (7435 8679, www.hampsteadguesthouse.com). Hampstead tube or Hampstead Heath rail. **Rates** £80-£125 double. **Rooms** 9. **Credit** AmEx, MC, V.
Owner Annemarie van der Meer loves to point out all the quirky space-saving surprises as she shows you round her wonderful and idiosyncratic bed and breakfast: here's the folding sink, there's the bed that pops out of an antique wardrobe… The special

Aloft. *See p256.*

atmosphere at this double-fronted Victorian house, set on a quiet Hampstead street, means that guests return year after year. Each room is uniquely decorated with eclectic furnishings – such as the French steel bathtub in one room – and there's a self-contained studio with its own kitchen. All guests may make use of a range of home comforts, from hot-water bottles to mobile phones, as well as a laptop to borrow. Breakfast (£7) may be taken in the garden that surrounds this lovely property on all four sides.
Internet: wireless (free). Parking: £15/day. TV.

66 Camden Square
66 Camden Square, Camden, NW1 9XD (7485 4622, rodgerdavis@btinternet.com). Camden Town tube or Camden Road rail. **Rates** (incl continental breakfast) £100 double. **Rooms** 2. **No credit cards. Map** p404 Z1 ⑧
A world away from the Eurobustle of Camden Market, lovely 66 Camden Square isn't actually on Camden Square – it's on Murray Street, behind 1 Camden Square, an easy no.29 bus hop to town. A radical design by co-owner/architect Rodger Davis allows natural light to flood through the open-plan interior. Breakfast, taken in the expansive living room

or on the terrace, is overseen by Rodger's hospitable other half Sue and a colourful parrot by the name of Peckham. The two guestrooms (one double, one single) are upstairs, convivial and comfortable. Neither is en suite, and the owners are keen to point out that they wouldn't have strangers sharing the bathroom. The double room costs £100 per night, the single is £60, there's a £5 supplement for one-nighters and a maximum stay of one week. A foot path will get you to St Pancras International in 15 minutes.
Internet: wireless (free). TV.

EAST LONDON
Expensive

Boundary
2-4 Boundary Street, Shoreditch, E2 7DD (7729 1051, www.theboundary.co.uk). Liverpool Street tube/rail or Shoreditch High Street rail. **Rates** £220-£264 double. **Rooms** 17. **Credit** AmEx, DC, MC, V. **Map** p401 R4 ⑧
Design mogul Sir Terence Conran's Boundary Project warehouse conversion was a labour of love. Its restaurants – which include Albion (*see p180*), a

Hoxton Hotel.

downstairs fine-dining establishment and a rooftop bar – are high quality but relaxed, and all 17 bedrooms are beautifully designed. Each has a wet room and handmade bed, but are otherwise individually furnished with classic furniture and original art. The five split-level suites range in style from the bright and sea-salt fresh Beach to a new take on Victoriana by Polly Dickens, while the remaining rooms (the slightly larger corner rooms have windows along both external walls) are themed by design style: Mies van der Rohe, Eames, Shaker. There's also a charming Heath Robinson room, decorated with the cartoonist's sketches of hilariously complex machines.
Bar/café. Concierge. Disabled-adapted rooms. Internet: wireless (free). Restaurant. Room service. TV: DVD.

Town Hall Hotel

Patriot Square, Bethnal Green, E2 9NF (7871 0460, www.townhallhotel.com). Bethnal Green tube. **Rates** £174-£348 double. **Rooms** 98. **Credit** AmEx, MC, V.

In 2010, a grand, Grade II-listed, early 20th-century town hall was transformed into a classy modern aparthotel – despite its location between a council estate and a scruffy row of shops. The decor is minimal, retaining many features (walnut panelling and marble for the interior, Portland stone outside, stained glass and fire hoses on old brass reels scattered about) that would be familiar to the bureaucrats who used to toil here, but jazzed up with contemporary art and a patterned aluminium 'veil' that covers the new floor at the top of the building. The pale-toned, spacious apartments are well equipped for self-catering, but hotel luxuries such as free wireless internet and TV/DVD players are also in place. The De Montfort suite is the size of most houses, stretching over three floors, with a living room as big as a council chamber, and Viajante restaurant (*see p182*), is one of the hottest

in town. Under a conservatory roof, there's a narrow basement swimming pool with sparkly tiles.
Bar/café. Business centre. Concierge. Disabled-adapted rooms. Gym. Internet: wireless (free). Pool (indoor). Restaurant. Room service. TV: DVD.

Moderate

Aloft

One Eastern Gateway, Royal Victoria Dock, E16 1FR (3203 0700, www.aloftlondonexcel.com). Custom House or Prince Regent DLR. **Rates** £120-£260 double. **Rooms** 252. **Credit** AmEx, MC, V.

In the (Dock)land where chain mediocrity or bland corporate efficiency prevails, Aloft – from the swanky W chain (*see p242*) – is refreshing. Outside, the design is rather cool, a swoop of shiny surfaces with charming coloured lighting; inside, service is winningly off-hand. Shove your credit card into the self-check-in and your key card is dispensed, giving you access to the upper floors by lift, where further funky lighting guides you to your room (nicely finished, masculine decor; remote keyboard to operate the telly; decently appointed wet room). Your card also gets you into the pool and gym, while careless packers have a coin-op mobile phone charger in the lobby. Aloft is right at the exit from the ExCeL conference centre, so Friday night in the bar-diner is lively with post-conference hair being let down. *Photo p255.*
Bar/café. Business centre. Concierge. Disabled-adapted rooms. Gym. Internet: wireless & high-speed (free). Pool (indoor). Restaurant. Room service. TV.

★ 40 Winks

109 Mile End Road, Stepney, E1 4UJ (7790 0259, 07973 653944, www.40winks.org). Stepney Green tube. **Rates** (incl breakfast) £175 double. **Rooms** 2. **No credit cards.**

Opposite a housing estate and cheap Somali diners, the family home of an interior designer has become the B&B of choice for movie stars and fashion movers. The 'micro-boutique hotel' looks extraordinary (kitchen frescoes, a music room with Beatles drumkit, a lion's head tap in the bath), but each stay is made individual by owner David Carter's commitment to his guests, making them feel they're staying with a fabulous friend rather than just renting a room. Too late to book? Intriguing soirées such as Bedtime Stories (for which everyone must wear pyjamas) open the house to a wider audience. It's flamboyant, fashionable and very cool.
Internet: wireless (free). Parking: free.

Hoxton Hotel

81 Great Eastern Street, Shoreditch, EC2A 3HU (7550 1000, www.hoxtonhotels.com). Old Street tube/rail. **Rates** (incl breakfast) £49-£249 double. **Rooms** 208. **Credit** AmEx, MC, V. **Map** p401 Q4 ⊕

Famous for its low rates (including some publicity-garnering £1-a-night rooms), the Hoxton deserves credit for many other things. First, there's the hip Shoreditch location – hip enough for Soho House to have taken over the downstairs bar-brasserie a few years ago. Then there are the great design values (the foyer is a sort of postmodern country lodge, complete with stag's head). Finally, the rooms are well thought out, if mostly rather small, with lots of nice touches – free milk in the fridges, a cold snack for breakfast, free wireless internet. Nowadays, there are even three individually designed suites. The downside? The hotel's popularity. If you don't book well in advance and plan to visit during the week rather than at the weekend, you could pay as much as at one of the big chains.
Bar/café. Business centre. Disabled-adapted rooms. Internet: wireless (free). Restaurant. Room service. TV: pay movies.

★ Shoreditch Rooms

Ebor Street, Shoreditch, E1 6AW (7739 5040, www.shoreditchhouse.com). Shoreditch High Street rail. **Rates** £75-£225 double. **Rooms** 26. **Credit** AmEx, MC, V. **Map** p401 S4 ⊕

The most recent hotel opening from Soho House members' club (*see also p243* Dean Street Townhouse; *p258* High Road House) might even be the best, perfectly catching the local atmosphere with its unfussy, slightly retro design. The rooms feel a bit like urban beach huts, with pastel-coloured tongue-and-groove, shutters and swing doors to the en suite showers. They feel fresh, bright and comfortable, even though they're furnished with little more than a bed, an old-fashioned phone and DAB radio, and a big, solid dresser (minibar, hairdryer and treats within, flatscreen TV on top). Guests get access to the fine eating, drinking and fitness facilities (yes, a gym, but more importantly an excellent rooftop pool) in the members' club next door. Everything's put together with a light touch, from

the 'Borrow Me' bookshelf by the lifts (jelly beans, umbrellas and boardgames) to the room nomenclature: Tiny (from just £75), Small and Small+ (with little rooftop balconies and loungers from which to survey the grey horizon).
Bar/café. Disabled-adapted room. Gym. Internet: wireless (free). Pool: outdoor. Restaurants (2). TV.

SOUTH-EAST LONDON
Moderate

Church Street Hotel

29-33 Camberwell Church Street, Camberwell, SE5 8TR (7703 5984, www.churchstreet hotel.com). Denmark Hill rail or bus 36, 436. **Rates** (incl breakfast) £90-£155 double. **Rooms** 27. **Credit** AmEx, MC, V.

Craftsman José Raido is behind this attractive and original family-run hotel, near Camberwell Green. Funky bathroom tiles in the bright, high-ceilinged bedrooms, for example, come from Guadalajara, and are thus a perfect match for Mexicana such as imported film posters, while the bed frames were forged by José himself. The colours are as vivid as a Mexican sunset. Bathroom products are organic, as are the pastries and cereals served for breakfast in an icon-filled dining room that also operates as a 24hr honesty bar. You pay only £90 for a double with shared bathroom, which is a real bargain, and the hotel tapas restaurant, Angels & Gypsies, is a big hit locally.
Bar/café. Internet: wireless (free). Restaurant. TV.

SOUTH-WEST LONDON
Expensive

★ Bingham

61-63 Petersham Road, Richmond, Surrey TW10 6UT (8940 0902, www.thebingham.co.uk). Richmond tube/rail. **Rates** £195-£295 double. **Rooms** 15. **Credit** AmEx, DC, MC, V.

Quality boutique hotel, destination restaurant (under Shay Cooper's award-winning supervision) and sun-filled cocktail bar in one, the Bingham makes excellent use of its superb riverside location by Richmond Bridge. Six of its individually styled and high-ceilinged rooms overlook the Thames; all of them are named after a poet, in honour of the Bingham's artistic past (lesbian aunt-and-niece couple Katherine Harris Bradley and Edith Emma Cooper lived here in the 1890s, regularly hosting members of the Aesthetic Movement while they were in residence). Each room accommodates an ample bathtub and shower, art deco touches to the furnishings and irresistibly fluffy duck-and-goose feather duvets. Run by the Trinder family for the last 25 years, the Bingham manages to feel both grand and boutique. A treat.
Bar/café. Internet: wireless (free). Parking: £10/day. Restaurant. Room service. TV: DVD.

CONSUME

WEST LONDON

Moderate

Base2Stay

25 Courtfield Gardens, Earl's Court, SW5 0PG (7244 2255, www.base2stay.com). Earl's Court tube. **Rates** £119-£191 double. **Rooms** 65. **Credit** AmEx, MC, V. **Map** p394 B10 84

Base2Stay looks good, with its modernist limestone and taupe tones, and keeps prices low by removing inessentials: no bar, no restaurant. Instead, there's the increasingly popular solution of a 'kitchenette' (microwave, sink, silent mini-fridge, kettle), but here with all details carefully attended to (not just token cutlery, but sufficient kitchenware with corkscrew and can opener, and guidance about where to shop). The rooms, en suite (with power showers) and air-conditioned, are as carefully thought out, with desks, modem points and flatscreens, but the single/bunk bed rooms are small. Discount vouchers for nearby chain eateries are supplied by the friendly duo on 24hr reception duty.

Disabled-adapted rooms. Internet: wireless (free). Parking: £30/day. TV: pay movies.

★ Garret

Troubadour, 263-267 Old Brompton Road, Earl's Court, SW5 9JA (7370 1434, www.troubadour.co.uk). West Brompton tube/rail. **Rates** £175 double. **Rooms** 1. **Credit** AmEx, MC, V. **Map** p394 B11 85

This idiosyncratic attic apartment is an absolute treat. High above the Troubadour, a 1960s counter-culture café that still hosts poetry and music events, it's unjustly named: yes, the rooms are in the attic and have charming pitched roofs, but there are acres of space for two – and even enough for a small family, if the kids sleep on the pull-out sofa in the lounge-kitchen. The huge, high main bed lies under a skylight and there's a writing desk, but any thought of poetic torment is banished by the well-executed Arts & Crafts decor and fully equipped kitchen area, right down to the cafetière and wines.

Bar/café. Internet: wireless (free). Room service. TV: DVD.

High Road House

162 Chiswick High Road, Chiswick, W4 1PR (8742 1717, www.highroadhouse.co.uk). Turnham Green tube. **Rates** £145-£205 double. **Rooms** 14. **Credit** AmEx, MC, V.

This west London outpost of Nick Jones's ever-fashionable Soho House stable (*see also p243* Dean Street Townhouse; *p257* Shoreditch Rooms) features guestrooms designed by Ilse Crawford, and a members' bar and restaurant above the buzzing ground-floor brasserie. Serving a modern British menu, this has a retro sophisticated-Parisian-bistro-meets-Bloomsbury feel and, as you might expect, the food and service are excellent. Guestrooms are soothing, unadorned, white Shaker Modern with little fizzes of colour (and little hidden treats), the bathrooms well stocked with Cowshed products.

Bars/cafés (2). Disabled-adapted rooms. Internet: wireless (free). Restaurants (2). Room service. TV: DVD & pay movies.

★ Mayflower Hotel

26-28 Trebovir Road, Earl's Court, SW5 9NJ (7370 0991, www.mayflower-group.co.uk). Earl's Court tube. **Rates** (incl continental breakfast) £109-£150 double. **Rooms** 46. **Credit** AmEx, MC, V. **Map** p394 B11 86

After fighting on the frontlines of the Earl's Court budget-hotel style revolution, the Mayflower's taken the struggle to other parts of London (New Linden; *see p247*). But this is where the lushly contemporary house style evolved, proving affordability can be opulently chic. The recent complete refurbishment of the hotel, involving public areas and all the guestrooms, shows that it's not resting on its laurels. Hand-carved Asian artefacts complement the richly coloured fabrics. The facilities, too, are well up to scratch, featuring marble bathrooms, Egyptian cotton sheets and CD players in the rooms.

Internet: wireless (free). Parking: £30/day. TV.

Rockwell

181-183 Cromwell Road, Earl's Court, SW5 0SF (7244 2000, www.therockwell.com). Earl's Court tube. **Rates** £160-£200 double. **Rooms** 40. **Credit** AmEx, MC, V. **Map** p394 B10 87

The Rockwell aims for relaxed contemporary elegance – and succeeds magnificently. The listed premises mean there are no identikit rooms here: they're all different sizes and individually designed, but share gleaming woods and muted glowing colours alongside more sober creams and neutrals. Among the rooms, pleasing eccentricities include a pair of central single rooms with skylights, and basement garden rooms that have tiny patios, complete with garden furniture, looking up at the ground-level bridge that leads on to the garden terrace proper from the handsome bar-restaurant. Each room has a power shower, Starck fittings and bespoke cabinets in the bathrooms, and triple-glazing ensures you never notice the noisy road just outside.

Bar/café. Internet: wireless (free). Restaurant. TV: pay movies.

Twenty Nevern Square

20 Nevern Square, Earl's Court, SW5 9PD (7565 9555, www.twentynevernsquare.co.uk). Earl's Court tube. **Rates** (incl breakfast) £90-£150 double. **Rooms** 25. **Credit** AmEx, MC, V. **Map** p394 A11 88

Only the less-than-posh location of this immaculate boutique hotel keeps the rates reasonable. Tucked away in a private garden square, it feels far from its locale. The modern-colonial style was created by its well-travelled owner, who personally sourced many

CONSUME

of the exotic and antique furnishings (as well as those in sister hotel the Mayflower; *see p258*). In the sleek marble bathrooms, toiletries are tidied away in decorative caskets, but the beds are the real stars: from elaborately carved four-posters to Egyptian sleigh styles, all with luxurious mattresses. The vaguely Far Eastern feel extends into the lounge and the airy conservatory, with its dark wicker furniture. *Bar/café. Internet: wireless & high-speed (free). Parking: £30/day. Room service. TV: DVD.*

APARTMENT RENTAL

Holiday Serviced Apartments (0845 060 4477, www.holidayapartments.co.uk) and **Palace Court Holiday Apartments** (7727 3467, www.palacecourt.co.uk) specialise in holiday lets. **London Holiday Accommodation** (7265 0882, www.london holiday.co.uk) offers half a dozen decent-priced self-catering options in the West End and on the South Bank. For serviced apartments, try the South Bank or Earl's Court 'campuses' run by **Think Apartments** (3465 9100, www.think-apartments.com). **Accommodation Outlet** (www.outlet4holidays.com) is a recommended lesbian and gay agency that has some excellent properties across London in general and in Soho in particular.

CAMPING & CARAVANNING

If putting yourself at the mercy of English weather in a far-flung suburban field doesn't put you off, the difficult transport links into central London might do the job instead. Still, you can't really beat the prices.

Crystal Palace Caravan Club *Crystal Palace Parade, Crystal Palace, SE19 1UF (8778 7155). Crystal Palace rail or bus 3.* **Open** *Mar-Sept* 9am-6pm daily. *Oct-Jan* 9.30am-5.30pm daily.

STAYING WITH THE LOCALS

Several agencies can arrange for individuals and families to stay in Londoners' homes. They include **At Home in London** (8748 1943, www.athomeinlondon.co.uk), **Host & Guest Service** (7385 9922, www.host-guest.co.uk), **London Bed & Breakfast Agency** (7586 2768, www.londonbb.com) and **London Homestead Services** (7286 5115, www.lhslondon.co.uk). There is usually a minimum length of stay.

UNIVERSITY RESIDENCES

During vacations, much of London's dedicated student accommodation is available to visitors. Central locations can make these a bargain.

International Students House *229 Great Portland Street, Marylebone, W1W 5PN (7631 8300, www.ish.org.uk). Great Portland Street tube.* **Open** *Reception* 7.45am-10.30pm Mon-Fri; 8am-10.30pm Sat, Sun. **Rates** £21 (per person) dormitory; £43 single; £33 twin. **No credit cards. Map** p396 H4 ❸❾

King's College Conference & Vacation Bureau *Strand Bridge House, 138-142 Strand, Covent Garden, WC2R 1HH (7848 1700, www.kcl.ac.uk/kcvb). Temple tube.* **Rates** from £25 single; £50 double. **No credit cards. Map** p416 Z3 ❾⓪

LSE *Bankside House, 24 Sumner Street, Bankside, SE1 9JA (7107 5750, www.lsevacations.co.uk). London Bridge tube.* **Rates** £45-£62 single; £59-£81 twin. **Credit** MC, V. **Map** p402 O8 ❾❶ The LSE has vacation rentals across town, but Bankside House is the best located.

YOUTH HOSTELS

For Youth Hostel Assocation venues, you can get extra reductions on the rates detailed below if you're a member of the IYHF (International Youth Hostel Federation): you'll pay £3 less a night. Joining costs only £15.95 (£9.95 for under-25s), and can be done on arrival or through www.yha.org.uk prior to departure. All under-18s receive a 25 per cent discount, in any case. YHA hostel beds are arranged either in dormitories or in twin rooms. Our favourite hostels are reviewed (**YHA London Central**, *see p239*; **Clink78**, *see p238*), but those listed below are all handily located across town.

Earl's Court *38 Bolton Gardens, Earl's Court, SW5 0AQ (7373 7083, www.yha.org.uk). Earl's Court tube.* **Open** 24hrs daily. **Rates** £16-£67. **No credit cards. Map** p394 B11 ❾❷

Holland Park *Holland Walk, South Kensington, W8 7QU (7937 0748, www.yha.org.uk). High Street Kensington tube.* **Open** 24hrs daily. **Rates** £13-£26. **Credit** MC, V. **Map** p392 A8 ❾❸

Meininger *Baden-Powell House, 65-67 Queen's Gate, South Kensington, SW7 5JS (7590 6910, www.meininger-hostels.com). Gloucester Road or South Kensington tube.* **Rates** £15-£40. **Credit** AmEx, MC, V. **Map** p395 D10 ❾❹

Oxford Street *14 Noel Street, Soho, W1F 8GJ (7734 1618, www.yha.org.uk). Oxford Circus tube.* **Open** 24hrs daily. *Reception* 7am-11pm daily. **Rates** £17-£70. **Credit** MC, V. **Map** p416 V2 ❾❺

St Pancras *79-81 Euston Road, King's Cross, NW1 2QE (7388 9998, www.yha.org.uk). King's Cross tube/rail.* **Open** 24hrs daily. **Rates** £19-£69. **Credit** MC, V. **Map** p397 L3 ❾❻

St Paul's *36 Carter Lane, the City, EC4V 5AB (7236 4965, www.yha.org.uk). St Paul's tube or Blackfriars rail.* **Open** 24hrs daily. **Rates** £15-£72. **Credit** MC, V. **Map** p402 O6 ❾❼

CONSUME

Arts & Entertainment

Children

Strongholds, family-friendly museums and great playgrounds.

London has a lot to offer young visitors. Its museums go out of their way to engage the minds of children, there are gorgeous parks and playgrounds, brilliant theatres with child-oriented productions and world-famous attractions. Many of these, such as the **Natural History Museum** and the **Science Museum** (for both, *see p112*), are free; many of those that aren't, such as the **Tower of London** (*see p64*), give you a lot of fun for your entry fee.

Plan carefully, but don't try to cram too much in one day. Sometimes, the most fun happens in the gaps between the official itinerary.

For children's festivals, *see pp24-33* **London Diary**. For weekly event listings, check the 'Things to Do' pages in *Time Out* magazine. For useful tips, visit the Mayor's site at www.london.gov.uk/young-london.

WHERE TO GO

South Bank & Bankside (pp36-46)

This is one of the all-time favourite spots for a family day out in London. Just strolling along the wide riverside promenade will lead you past skateboarders, installations, street artists, book stalls and, often, free performances. The expensive end is around **London Eye** (*see p37*), **London Aquarium** (*see p38*) and **London Film Museum** (*see p37*). Moving east, visit the **Southbank Centre** (*see p38 and p301*), where free shows and workshops take place in holidays and weekends in the Clore Ballroom. Don't miss Jeppe Hein's 'Appearing Rooms' play fountains in summer. Next, the **National Theatre** (*see p305*) offers free entertainment in summer at its Inside Out festival.

Keep going along the riverbank, past Gabriel's Wharf, a riverside cluster of restaurants and shops, to reach **Tate Modern** (*see p43*). Tate Modern is a day out in itself, with its dramatic Turbine Hall, free family trails and a Bloomberg Learning Zone on Level 5. At weekends and in school holidays, age-appropriate activity packs are available from Level 3. (There's a boat service from here to **Tate Britain**; *see p104*.)

Once you've emerged, pick up the Bankside Walk, ducking under the southern end of Southwark Bridge. Walk down cobbly Clink Street towards the **Golden Hinde** (*see p41*)

and **Southwark Cathedral** (*see p44*), having passed the **Clink Prison Museum** (*see p41*), a cheaper alternative to the **London Dungeon** (*see p38*), moving in 2013 to share a building with the Aquarium and Film Museum. From Tooley Street, march through Hays Galleria to regain the riverside path, which takes you to the warship museum **HMS Belfast** (*see p46*) and on, past the dancing fountains, to **City Hall** and **Tower Bridge** (*see p64*).

The City (pp47-64)

It seems pricey, but the **Tower of London** (*see p64*) is a top day out for all ages. If it is free stuff you're after, though, the **Museum of London** (*see p55*) is superb. Its new Galleries of Modern London put interactivity and drama at the heart of exciting exhibits, and there are lots of regular child-friendly storytelling sessions and workshops. Nearby, the **Bank of England Museum** (*see p59*) kids can try to lift a gold bar.

Bloomsbury (pp69-72)

Children are captivated by the mummies at the **British Museum** (*see p70*). However, the size of the collection can make it overwhelming. The beautifully produced and well-conceived free trails for different ages take a theme and lead families around an edited selection (available in the Paul Hamlyn Library). Alternatively, there are regular events and workshops or free backpacks for kids, filled with puzzles and games. For weekends and school holidays, the Ford Centre for Young Visitors provides a picnic-style eating area.

Central London's best playground, **Coram's Fields** (*see p267*), is close, and the **Foundling Museum** (*see p71*) is well worth a visit.

Covent Garden & the Strand (pp75-79)

At the lively **London Transport Museum** (*see p76*), children can make believe they are driving a bus or riding in a horse-drawn carriage. They love the numbered stamp trail too. The museum also has a programme of school-holiday events. Across the Piazza, the acts pulling in crowds in front of **St Paul's Covent Garden** (*see p76*) are worth watching. On the south side of the Strand, **Somerset House** (*see p79*) allows kids to play outside among the fountains in summer and skate on the winter ice rink. There are also regular art workshops.

Trafalgar Square (pp97-99)

London's central square (www.london.gov.uk/trafalgarsquare) has been a free playground for children since time immemorial – those lions beg to be clambered on. Festivals take place most weekends. Even if all is quiet in the square, the **National Gallery** has paper trails and audio tours, as well as regular kids' and teens' workshops and storytelling sessions for under-fives. For three- to 12-year-olds, the **National Portrait Gallery** runs Family Art Workshops at weekends and during the school holidays. For both venues, *see p98*.

Just nearby, **St Martin-in-the-Fields** (*see p98*) has London's only brass-rubbing centre (kids are transfixed by this absorbing activity)

**INSIDE TRACK
EMIRATES AIR LINE**

A thrilling ride on the **Emirates Air Line** (*see p130*), London's first urban cable car, is a surefire hit with children. Running from the Greenwich Peninsula to Royal Victoria Dock and ascending to nearly 300 feet above the Thames, with London's landmarks jostling for attention below – this is no mere expensive attraction, but part of London's transport system, with its own special line marked on the tube map. Adult trips using Oyster pay-as-you-go cost £3.20; for 5- to 15-year-olds with Oyster card, it costs £1.60; under-5s travel free.

Frizzante@Hackney City Farm. See p294.

as well as a fine café that does plenty of the type of food that goes down well with children.

South Kensington (pp111-114)

Top of any Grand Day Out itinerary is this cultural goldmine. The **Science Museum** (*see p112*) offers heaps of excitement, with six play zones for all ages, from the Garden in the basement for under-sixes to the new Atmosphere gallery upstairs, where children can use touchscreens to learn about climate change. Dinosaur fans won't rest until they've visited the **Natural History Museum** (*see p112*), and seen the animatronic beasties in action. A butterfly tunnel in summer and ice rink in winter also draw the crowds. The **Victoria & Albert Museum** (*see p113*) marks interactive displays on its floorplan. Its free weekend and school holiday drop-in family events (featuring trails, activity-based backpacks, and interactive workshops) provide great ways of focusing on the collection. Educational resources are available in the Sackler Centre studios and the Theatre & Performance Galleries. (Its sister gallery, Bethnal Green's **V&A Museum of Childhood**, *see p128*, has an excellent programme of events for children.)

Greenwich (pp138-141)

Magical Greenwich provides a lovely day out away from the mayhem of the West End. Arrive by boat to appreciate its riverside charms, then take time to check out the newly restored **Cutty Sark** (*see p136* **A Ship that Floats on Air**) and excellent **Discover Greenwich** (*see p139*). Then head to the very child-friendly **National Maritime Museum** (*see p140*) and visit the new Sammy Ofer Wing. From here it's a pleasant leg-stretch in the Royal Park for views

Gracelands

Trot around the pigs, poultry and sheep outside, then settle down to eat their relatives (or stick to vegetarian options). The oilcloth-covered tables always heave with families tucking into healthy nosh, including big farm breakfasts. *Photo p293.*

Gracelands
118 College Road, NW10 5HD (8964 9161, www.gracelandscafe.com). Kensal Green tube/rail. **Open** 8.30am-4.30pm Mon-Fri; 9am-4.30pm Sat; 9.30am-2.30pm Sun. **Main courses** £7-£13. **Credit** AmEx, MC, V.
While many places claim to be child-friendly, this café really means it, with its toy-filled play area, a healthy tots-own menu (£3.70 for the likes of pasta bolognese or sausage and mash), and chefs cooing at high-chair diners from the open-plan kitchen. For grown-ups, the burger, made from 21-day matured beef, has proper foodie pedigree and the salads are unfailingly excellent.

Mudchute Kitchen
Mudchute Park & Farm, Pier Street, Isle of Dogs, Docklands, E14 3HP (3069 9290, www.mudchute.org). Mudchute DLR. **Open** 9.30am-3.30pm Tue-Fri; 9.30am-4.30pm Sat, Sun. **Main courses** £2.50-£9. **Credit** MC, V.
A farm fenced in by skyscrapers is an amusing place for anyone to eat lunch, but Mudchute is ideal for families. You can eat at farmhouse kitchen tables in the courtyard, while your babies roll around on a big futon or in the toy corner, or in the spacious interior. Frizzante (*see above*) took over in 2011, which means the food is excellent.

Rainforest Café
20 Shaftesbury Avenue, Piccadilly, W1D 7EU (7434 3111, www.therainforestcafe.co.uk). Piccadilly Circus tube. **Open** noon-10pm Mon-Fri; 11.30am-8pm Sat; 11.30am-10pm Sun. During the school holidays the restaurant is open at 11.30am every day. **Main courses** £12.95-£18.90. **Credit** AmEx, MC, V. **Map** p416 W4.
This themed restaurant is designed to thrill children with animatronic wildlife, cascading waterfalls and jungle sound-effects. The menu has lots of family-friendly fare, from 'paradise pizza' and 'Bamba's bangers' to amusing dishes for grown-ups. The children's menu costs £12.50 for two courses.

★ Tate Modern Café: Level 2
Tate Modern, Sumner Street, Bankside, SE1 9TG (7401 5014, www.tate.org.uk). Southwark tube or London Bridge tube/rail. **Open** 10am-5.30pm Mon-Thur; 10am-8.30pm Fri; 9am-6.30pm Sat; (am-5.30pm Sun. **Main courses** £9.95-£11.50. **Credit** AmEx, MC, V. **Map** p402 O7.
In addition to views from the windows framing the busy River Thames, there are literacy and art activities on the junior menu, handed out with a pot of crayons. Children can choose haddock fingers with

from the top of the hill, crowned by the **Royal Observatory & Planetarium** (*see p141*). When the stars come out, keep an eye out for the luminous green Meridian Line that cuts across the sky towards the city.

Further north, the new **Emirates Air Line** cable car is an exciting way to cross the river. It runs from North Greenwich tube to the Royal Victoria Dock DLR (*see p293* **Inside Track**).

EATING & DRINKING

Of the venues in 'Restaurants & Cafés', **Inn the Park** (*see p172*) and **Masala Zone** (*see p185*) are particularly suitable for children.

Big Red Bus
30 Deptford Church Street, SE8 4RZ (3490 8346, www.thebigredpizza.com). Deptford Bridge DLR. **Open** 5-11pm Tue-Fri; 11am-1am Sat; noon-6pm Sun. **Main courses** £6-£10. **Credit** MC, V.
Kids love this pizzeria – inside an old double-decker bus. You can either sit inside, or on the pretty decked terrace. It's beside the DLR, so travel is easy, and the nearby Creekside Centre (*see p266*) makes a good excursion.

Frizzante@Hackney City Farm
1A Goldsmith's Row, Hackney, E2 8QA (7739 2266, www.frizzanteltd.co.uk). Hoxton rail. **Open** 10am-4.30pm Tue, Sat and Sun; 10am-10pm Wed and Fri; 10am-4pm, 7-11pm Thur. **Main courses** £5-£17. **Credit** MC, V.

chips, pasta bolognese with parmesan or a ham and cheese bake with focaccia, finished off with ice-cream or a fruit salad; a free children's main is offered when an adult orders a regular main. There is also a 'teen menu' of reduced-price dishes from the adult menu.

That Place on the Corner

1-3 Green Lanes, Stoke Newington, N16 9BS (7704 0079, www.thatplaceonthecorner.co.uk). Canonbury rail then bus 73, 141, 341. **Open** 9.15am-6pm Mon-Fri; 9.30am-3pm Sat. Closes Sat for functions; phone ahead. **Main courses** £4-£8.25. **Credit** MC, V.

London's only child-friendly café that won't allow unaccompanied grown-ups to enter. Even better, children's needs are provided for by a library, a puppet theatre, two play areas and a dressing-up corner, as well as classes in baking, dance and music. The menu sticks to the trusted formula of pasta, panini and big breakfasts, but also offers some brasserie staples such as fish cakes.

Meet the Animals

Helping children to get even closer to their furry favourites.

A trip to any zoo is a brilliant family day out. **London Zoo** (*see p89*) continues its transformation year on year, with its animals rehoused in imaginative enclosures and inter-active elements introduced across the site. Perhaps the most exciting addition for younger visitors has been Gorilla Kingdom, where you can get to within a foot of the gorillas – albeit separated from them by reinforced glass. The lovely beasts also have a big area of landscaped greenery to explore.

To meet animals without reinforced glass, head to the Children's Zoo. Here, kids can groom goats and sheep, meet the llamas, climb with coatis, expore tunnels in the Roots Zone or listen to a story in the tipi. Children also love Animals in Action, an event held every weekend (and weekdays during the school holidays) at 12.30pm in the Amphitheatre. It's a chance to come virtually face to face with parrots, owls, rats, meerkats and more, demonstrating their natural behaviour – flying (low, you may have to duck), leaping, climbing, and walking along a rope in the case of a demonstration of just how easily rats found their way on to ships.

Older children (11-16s) with a well-developed interest in animals might enjoy being a junior keeper for a day. The programme, run during school holidays, has groups of up to five youngsters mucking out, grooming, feeding, and helping with life enrichment programmes for animals such as giraffes, meerkats and llamas. In addition, on Mondays and Fridays juniors get to meet the zoo's Galapagos tortoises; on Tuesdays and Thursdays they go behind the scene at BUGS, and on Wednesdays they feed the tamarins in the rainforest biome. The website (www.zsl.org) has more details of all the zoo's animals and events.

ARTS & ENTERTAINMENT

ZSL London Zoo.

Unicorn Theatre.

ENTERTAINMENT
City farms & zoos

There's always something new at **ZSL London Zoo** (*see p89*); Sumatran Tigers will be the next big addition. The admission charge seems high, but it's a guaranteed winner (*see also p295* **Meet the Animals**). Easier on the budget is the adorable **Battersea Park Children's Zoo** (www.batterseaparkzoo.co.uk), where ring-tailed lemurs, giant rabbits, inquisitive meerkats, playful otters and kune kune pigs are among the inhabitants.

City farms all over London charge nothing to get in. Try **Freightliners City Farm** (www.freightlinersfarm.org.uk) and **Kentish Town City Farm** (www.aapi.co.uk/cityfarm) or, in the east, **Mudchute City Farm** (www.mudchute.org) and **Hackney City Farm** (www.hackneycityfarm.co.uk), both of which have terrific cafés (for both, *see opposite*).

Puppets

★ Little Angel Theatre
14 Dagmar Passage, off Cross Street, Islington, N1 2DN (7226 1787, www.littleangeltheatre.com). Angel tube or Highbury & Islington tube/rail. **Box Office** 10am-6pm Mon-Fri; 9am-4pm Sat, Sun. **Tickets** £5-£14. **Credit** MC, V. **Map** p400 O1.
London's only permanent puppet theatre is set in a charming old Victorian temperance hall and stages diverse productions. All aspects of puppetry are covered, with themes, styles and stories drawn from a broad array of traditions. There's a Saturday Puppet Club and a youth puppet theatre. Shows are often for fives and above.

Puppet Theatre Barge
Opposite 35 Blomfield Road, Little Venice, W9 2PF (07836 202745 summer, 7249 6876 winter, www.puppetbarge.com). *Warwick Avenue tube.* **Box Office** 10am-6pm daily. **Tickets** £10; £8.50 reductions. **Credit** AmEx, MC, V.
This intimate waterborne stage is the setting for quality puppet shows that put a modern twist on traditional tales, such as *Mr Rabbit meets Brer Santa* and *The Flight of Babuscha Baboon*. The barge is moored here between October and July; shows themselves are held at 3pm on Saturday and Sunday, and daily during school holidays, plus some matinées. During the summer, the barge also holds performances in Richmond.

Science & nature

Creekside Centre
14 Creekside, Greenwich, SE8 4SA (8692 9922, www.creeksidecentre.org.uk). Deptford Bridge or Greenwich DLR, or bus 53, 177, 188. **Open** phone for details. **Admission** normally free, although activities vary; check for details.
Deptford Creek is a tributary of the Thames and this centre allows visitors to explore its surprisingly diverse wildlife and rich heritage. Low tide walks take place on selected weekend days for accompanied eight-year-olds and above and there's also a programme of puppet theatre. Events vary, so it's best to phone ahead and find out what's going on.

★ WWT Wetland Centre
Queen Elizabeth's Walk, Barnes, SW13 9WT (8409 4400, www.wwt.org.uk/london). Hammersmith tube then bus 33, 72, 209 (alight at Red Lion pub). **Open** *Summer* 9.30am-6pm daily. *Winter* 9.30am-5pm daily. **Admission** £10.99; £8.20 reductions; £6.10 4-16s; free under-4s; £30.60 family (2+2). *Tours* free. **Credit** MC, V.
This wetland reserve is one of London's best-kept secrets. If you can get children past the giant snakes and ladders game (with giant dice), there are 104 acres for them to stretch their legs in, along paths that take them past the main lake, reed beds, ponds and wetland meadows, as well as one of the best

playgrounds in London. A series of interactive exhibits exploring the environment was added in 2010.

Theatre

Polka Theatre

240 Broadway, Merton, SW19 1SB (8543 4888, www.polkatheatre.com). South Wimbledon tube or Wimbledon tube/rail, then bus 57, 93, 219, 493. **Box Office** (by phone and in person) 9.30am-4.30pm Mon-Fri; 10am-4.30pm Sat. **Tickets** £9-£16. **Credit** MC, V.

This children's theatre pioneer has been up and running since 1979. Daily shows are staged by touring companies in the main auditorium, while shorter works for babies and toddlers take over at the Adventure Theatre once a week.

Unicorn Theatre

147 Tooley Street, Bankside, SE1 2HZ (7645 0560, www.unicorntheatre.com). London Bridge tube/rail. **Box Office** 9.30am-6pm Mon-Fri; 10am-6pm Sat; noon-5pm Sun. **Tickets** £9-£22; £7-£13 reductions. **Credit** MC, V. **Map** p403 Q8.

This light, bright building near Tower Bridge, with its huge white unicorn in the foyer, has two performance spaces. Its small ensemble company of actors performs in all Unicorn shows and focuses on an outreach programme for local children.

Theme parks

There are several theme parks within easy reach of London. Heading out west, **Legoland** (Winkfield Road, Windsor, Berks SL4 4AY,0871 2222 001, www.legoland.co.uk) is always a hit with youngsters, with rides including the wet 'n' wild Viking's River Splash, and the extraordinary Miniland London, made of 13 million Lego bricks. **Thorpe Park** (Staines Road, Chertsey, Surrey KT16 8PN, 0871 663 1673, www.thorpepark.com) has the fastest rollercoaster in Europe, called Stealth, and the terrifying horror-movie ride, Saw; it's best for older kids and teens. And **Chessington World of Adventures** (Leatherhead Road, Chessington, Surrey KT9 2NE, 0871 663 4477, www.chessington.com) is a gentler option. This theme park, open since the 1930s, is partly a zoo, and children can pay to be zoo keeper for a day.

Likely to be on any child's visiting wishlist is the new Harry Potter studio tour near Watford, a short journey north of town; *see p324* **Warner Bros Studio Tour London**.

For a day with less of an adrenaline rush, try **Bekonscot Model Village** (Warwick Road, Beaconsfield, Bucks HP9 2PL, 01494 672919, www.bekonscot.com), a haven of vintage miniature villages with a ride-on train that takes you around the site. To the north, the fast-developing **Butterfly World** (Miriam Lane,

Chiswell Green, Herts AL2 3NY, 01727 869203, www.butterflyworldproject.com) is designed to look like an enormous butterfly head from the air with a 330-foot diameter walk-through biome (the butterfly's eye) opening in autumn 2012. There's plenty to see before then with a large walk-through butterfly tunnel and the butterfly breeding house showing kids all the incredible stages of a butterfly's life cycle.

SPACES TO PLAY

London's parks are lovely. **Hyde Park** (*see pp114-5*) and **St James's Park** (*see p105*) are very central, but it isn't much further to **Regent's Park** (*see p89*), and **Greenwich Park** (*see p138*) is easily reached by river.

FREE Coram's Fields

93 Guilford Street, Bloomsbury, WC1N 1DN (7837 6138, www.coramsfields.org). Russell Square tube. **Open** *Apr-Sept* 9am-7pm daily. *Oct-Mar* 9am-dusk daily. **Admission** free (adults only admitted if accompanied by child under 16). **No credit cards. Map** p397 L4.

No adult can enter the amazing Coram's Fields without a child. The historic site dates to 1747, when Thomas Coram established the Foundling Hospital, but only opened as a park in 1936. It has sandpits, a small petting zoo, ride-on toys and playgrounds for different age groups.

▶ *For the Foundling Hospital's museum, see p71.*

★ FREE Diana, Princess of Wales Memorial Playground

Near Black Lion Gate, Broad Walk, Kensington Gardens, South Kensington, W8 2UH (7298 2141, www.royalparks.gov.uk). Bayswater or Queensway tube. **Open** *Summer* 10am-6.45pm daily. *Winter* 10am-dusk daily. **Admission** free; adults only admitted if accompanied by under-12s. **No credit cards. Map** p393 E8.

Bring buckets and spades, if you can, to this superb playground: the huge, central pirate ship is moored in a sea of sand. Other attractions include a tepee camp and a treehouse encampment, and excellent provision is made for children with special needs.

Discover Children's Story Centre

383-387 High Street, Stratford, E15 4QZ (8536 5555, www.discover.org.uk). Stratford tube/rail/DLR. **Open** 10am-5pm Tue-Fri; 11am-5pm Sat, Sun. *School holidays* 10am-5pm Mon-Fri; 11am-5pm Sat, Sun. **Admission** £4.50; £16 family of 4; free under-2s. **Credit** MC, V.

The UK's first creative learning centre for children is committed to promoting diversity and providing learning opportunities for socially and economically disadvantaged children. The main floor offers all sorts of imaginative exploration, while downstairs houses temporary interactive exhibitions. The garden is fun.

ARTS & ENTERTAINMENT

Film

Independents give the multiplexes a run for their money.

Londoners still seem to have a feel for the romance of film that suburban multiplexes just can't satisfy. Perhaps that's why there's such a lively and varied range of screenings in the capital. Giant picture palaces hosting red-carpet premières attended by A-list actors? Check out the **Odeon Leicester Square**. Cheap-as-chips repertory cinema? The **Prince Charles** is right around the corner. Refurbished art deco gems? Try the gorgeous, historic **Phoenix** or the **Rio** in Dalston. A world-class film festival? Happens every autumn. Outdoor screenings in remarkable settings, ciné clubs, film seasons devoted to every genre and national cinema under the sun? Yes, yes and yes. And the opening of a whole new cinema to add to the screening space at the **Barbican** in late 2012 means there's now even more choice. So get some popcorn and sit yourself down.

WHERE TO GO

Leicester Square underwent a major and much-needed facelift in 2011 and has the biggest first-run cinemas and stages most of the big-budget premières – but it also has the biggest prices. By contrast, the independents provide a cheaper and often more enjoyable night out, and they often show films that wouldn't come within a million miles of a red carpet.

Among the rep cinemas, the British Film Institute's flagship venue gets top billing. **BFI Southbank** (*see p272*) screens seasons exploring and celebrating various genres of cinema and TV. It also has a brilliant bar. After the BFI, London's best repertory cinema is found at the **Riverside Studios** (*see p272*), where

you'll find special seasons and film events. Despite the loss of two of the three screens at the **Barbican** (*see p269*), it's always worth checking out the self-explanatory Directorspective strand.

Unexpected venues for film-viewing include the big museums and galleries. The **British Museum** (*see p70*), **National Gallery** (*see p98*), **Imperial War Museum** (*see p133*) and **Tate Modern** (*see p43*) all have regular screenings themed to their temporary exhibitions, and the **Museum of London Docklands** (*see p130*) screens a classic London film on the second Friday of every month. Several luxury hotels open their screening rooms to the public; those at the **Soho Hotel** (*see p242*), **Charlotte Street Hotel** (*see p237*), **Covent Garden Hotel** (*see p241*) and **One Aldwych** (*see p241*) are favourites. Films in these luxe surroundings usually include drinks, lunch, dinner or tea, for an all-inclusive price.

Outdoor summertime screens have popped up across the capital. The most glamorous is the **Somerset House Summer Screen** (www.somersethouse.org.uk/film), for which recent blockbusters and old classics are run in a magnificent Georgian courtyard, and Park Nights at the **Serpentine Gallery** (*see p115*), where film screenings are among the arts events taking place in the annual temporary, starchitect-built pavilion. Fans of memorabilia can check out the enjoyable **London Film Museum** (*see p37*), but the latest trend is to

INSIDE TRACK
SECRET CINEMA

Go on the website (www.secretcinema.org) and book yourself a couple of tickets for a rollercoaster ride of a film experience. Venue and a theme for costumes are announced just 24 hours before curtain-up. It's an immersive experience, in a setting transformed to fit in with your film. This may give you a clue, but you won't know for sure until the film starts rolling.

Festivals Film

What not to miss this year.

There's a film festival in the capital on pretty much any given week during the year, but the **London Film Festival** (www.bfi.org.uk/lff, Oct) is far and away the most prestigious. Nearly 200 new British and international features are screened, mainly at the BFI Southbank and Leicester Square's Vue West End. It's preceded by the leftfield **Raindance Festival** (www.raindance.co.uk), with a terrific shorts programme. New for 2012, and in the big league, is a London off-shoot of Robert Redford's Sundance Festival (www.sundance-london.com), in April.

Highlighting the importance of the city's LGBT communities, the **London Lesbian & Gay Film Festival** (7928 3232, www.bfi.org.uk/llgff, late Mar) is the UK's third largest film festival. Also taking place in spring are **Human Rights Watch International Film Festival** (7713 1995, www.hrw.org/iff, mid-late Mar) and the **East End Film Festival** (www.eastendfilmfestival.com, late Apr), which explores cinema's potential to cross cultural boundaries, with a special place for films starring London.

Several festivals screen the output of a particular foreign territory. Among them are the Polish Cultural Institute's **Kinoteka** (www.kinoteka.org.uk, Mar); the **London Turkish Film Festival** (www.ltff.co.uk, Nov-Dec), the wonderful **Mosaïques** festival (Ciné Lumière, www.institut-francais.org.uk/mosaiques, June); and the **French Film Festival** (www.frenchfilmfestival.org.uk, Ciné Lumière, Nov), which shows off the best of new French cinema.

Short films hog the limelight at the **London Short Film Festival** (www.shortfilms.org.uk, Jan), while September's **London International Animation Festival** (www.liaf.org.uk) screens 300 or more animated shorts from around the globe. The **Portobello Film Festival** (www.portobellofilmfestival.com, early Sept) offers an eclectic programme of free screenings, while a noble addition to the schedule since June 2011 is the **Open City London Documentary Festival** (www.opencitylondon.com, June), which is organised by and takes place mainly at UCL.

ARTS & ENTERTAINMENT

mix cinema with other forms of entertainment, and to screen the films in a range of unusual locations (*see p268* **Inside Track**).

The lowdown

Consult *Time Out* magazine's weekly listings or visit www.timeout.com/film for full details of what's on and performance times; note that the programmes change on a Friday. Films released in the UK are classified as follows: U – suitable for all ages; **PG** – open to all, parental guidance is advised; **12A** – under-12s only admitted with an over-18; **15** – no one under 15 is admitted; **18** – no one under 18 is admitted.

FIRST-RUN CINEMAS

Central London

Barbican
Silk Street, the City, EC2Y 8DS (7638 8891, www.barbican.org.uk). Barbican tube or Moorgate tube/rail. **Tickets** £10.50; £7.50-£8.50 reductions; £5 Mon. **Screens** 1. **Credit** AmEx, MC, V. **Map** p400 P5.
A single screen has been showing the Barbican's well-curated film programme since the closure of tiny screens 2 and 3 in 2010. But new screens, accessible

from the street, were set to open at the corner of Beech Street and Whitecross Street in late 2012. Cinema 1 will remain open. Expect new releases of quality world and independent films, and surveys of the likes of Werner Herzog and Ingmar Bergman in the Directorspective strand.

Curzon Cinemas
Chelsea *206 King's Road, SW3 5XP (0871 703 3990). Sloane Square tube then bus 11, 19, 22, 319.* **Screens** 1. **Map** p395 E12.
Mayfair *38 Curzon Street, W1J 7TY (0871 703 3989). Green Park or Hyde Park Corner tube.* **Screens** 2. **Map** p398 H8.
Soho *99 Shaftesbury Avenue, W1D 5DY (0871 703 3988). Leicester Square tube.* **Screens** 3. **Map** p416 X3.
All *www.curzoncinemas.com.* **Tickets** £9.50-£12.50; £6-£8.50 reductions. **Credit** MC, V.
Expect a superb range of shorts, rarities, double-bills and seasons alongside new international releases across the small Curzon chain. There's 1970s splendour in Mayfair (it's sometimes used for premières) and comfort in Chelsea, which is perfect for a Sunday screening after a King's Road brunch. But the coolest of the bunch is the Soho outpost, which has a buzzing café, a decent basement bar and sometimes themes its eating and drinking spaces to tie in with event releases.

Phoenix.

★ ICA Cinema

Nash House, the Mall, SW1Y 5AH (7930 0493, 7930 3647 tickets, www.ica.org.uk). Charing Cross tube/rail. **Tickets** £7-£10; £8 reductions. **Screens** 2. **Credit** MC, V. **Map** p399 K8.
London's small contemporary arts centre (*see p107*) has met its brief not only by screening an eclectic range of cinema, but by distributing some of the most noteworthy films of recent years. After an uninspiring few years, there are signs of a renaissance under new leadership. Serious types can often be seen discussing the evening's programme afterwards in the ICA Café.

Odeon Leicester Square

Leicester Square, WC2H 7LQ (0871 224 4007, www.odeon.co.uk). Leicester Square tube. **Tickets** vary; check website for details. **Screens** 6. **Credit** AmEx, MC, V. **Map** p416 X4.
You'll often find the red carpets and crush barriers up outside this art deco gem – it's the city's leading site for star-studded premières and hosts the opening and closing nights of the London Film Festival. If you're lucky, you might catch one of the silent film screenings, with accompaniment on a 1937 Compton organ. Otherwise, it's big-volume mainstream hits.

Neighbourhood London

Electric Cinema

191 Portobello Road, Notting Hill, W11 2ED (7908 9696, www.electriccinema.co.uk). Ladbroke Grove or Notting Hill Gate tube. **Tickets** £12.50-£14.50; £8-£10.50 Mon. **Screens** 1. **Credit** AmEx, MC, V. **Map** p404 X4.
The Electric had gone from past-it fleapit to luscious luxury destination with leather seats and sofas, footstools and a bar inside the auditorium when it was hit by a kitchen fire in the Electric Brasserie next

door in June 2012. It's been closed since then, but was set to reopen in November 2012 with a host of new developments: a restored interior, upgraded sound system and digital projection, and new seats.

Everyman & Screen Cinemas

Everyman *5 Hollybush Vale, Hampstead, NW3 6TX. Hampstead tube.* **Tickets** £13-£16; £7.50 reductions. **Screens** 2.
Screen on the Green *83 Upper Street, Islington, N1 0NP. Angel tube.* **Tickets** £11-£13.50; £7.50 reductions. **Screens** 2. **Map** p400 O2.
Both *0871 906 9060, www.everymancinema.com.* **Credit** MC, V.
London's most elegant cinema, the Everyman has a glamorous bar and two-seaters (£30) in its 'screening lounges', complete with foot stools and wine coolers. Everyman now also owns three former Screen cinemas, of which the Islington's Screen on the Green is the best – carefully refurbished in late 2009, it lost seats to make space for the more comfortable kind, gained an auditorium bar and a stage for live events, but kept its lovely exterior neon sign.

Hackney Picturehouse

270 Mare Street, Hackney, E8 1HE (0871 902 5734, www.picturehouses.co.uk). Hackney Central or London Fields rail. **Tickets** check website for details. **Screens** 4. **Credit** AmEx, MC, V.
Opened in autumn 2011, the four-screen Hackney Picturehouse is the newest of the Picturehouse chain, and has become the flagship cinema for a borough woefully served for film. As well as showing the more interesting new releases and hosting festivals and seasons geared towards the diverse local community, the Picturehouse has an excellent café.

★ Phoenix

52 High Road, East Finchley, N2 9PJ (8444 6789, www.phoenixcinema.co.uk). East Finchley tube. **Tickets** £6-£9.50; £6 reductions. **Screens** 1. **Credit** MC, V.
Built in 1910 and revamped in the 1930s, the Grade II-listed Phoenix has recently been restored to its copper and gold, art deco glory. It has real old-fashioned glamour, and is London's oldest cinema to have remained in continuous operation. Owned by a charitable trust enjoying strong community support, it runs a varied programme including live theatre and opera transmissions, and now has a café-bar on the premises. The best cinema in north London.

Rio Cinema

107 Kingsland High Street, Dalston, E8 2PB (7241 9410, www.riocinema.org.uk). Dalston Kingsland rail. **Tickets** £9; £7 reductions. **Screens** 1. **Credit** AmEx, MC, V.
Another great deco survivor, restored to its original sleek lines, the Rio is east London's finest independent. Alongside mainstream releases, the Rio is well known for its Turkish and Kurdish film festivals.

Essential London Films

We pick out six of the capital's star turns.

BLOWUP
dir Michelangelo Antonioni, 1966
It's Swinging London, and a fashion photographer (David Hemmings) is at a loose end, having ditched his jobs for the day. He wanders into Maryon Park and when he develops the pictures he takes there, they appear to show a murder. Music from the Yardbirds.

FRENZY
dir Alfred Hitchcock, 1972
Covent Garden was still a fruit and veg market when this was made, and a serial killer is loose in the area, raping women and strangling them. Fruit merchant Robert Rusk is revealed to viewers as the murderer, but suspicion falls on his friend, Richard Blaney. Will the real culprit be uncovered?

PASSPORT TO PIMLICO
dir Henry Cornelius, 1949
An antidote to the grimness of post-war austerity, cosy Ealing comedy *Passport to Pimlico* sees the citizens of that area of London discover that they are really Burgundians and declare independence. So it's out with the ration books and in with free-for-all shopping, boozing and jollity.

CROUPIER
dir Mike Hodges, 1998
Thriller set in the nocturnal world of London's casinos and after-hours drinking clubs. Jack Manfred is an aspiring writer going nowhere fast. To make some cash he falls back on his old skills as a croupier. Soon, the job plunges him into a dangerous world where the rules are waiting to be broken.

LONDON
dir Patrick Keiller, 1994
Lying at the point where documentary meets fiction, the film follows the travels of an unseen narrator around London with his friend/ex-lover to research English Romanticism. But events soon distract the pair from their planned focus. A fascinating study of 1990s London in the era of the Major government.

PERFORMANCE
dir Nicolas Roeg, 1970
Roeg's complex visual kaleidoscope sees an enforcer for a protection racket (James Fox) involved in murder and forced to hide from retribution in a Notting Hill basement. There, as he waits to escape abroad, he gets involved with a fading pop star (Mick Jagger) brooding over the loss of his powers of incantation.

ARTS & ENTERTAINMENT

Vue Westfield London

Westfield London, Shepherd's Bush, W12 7GF
(0871 224 0240, www.myvue.com). White City
or Wood Lane tube, or Shepherd's Bush tube/rail.
Tickets check website for details. **Screens** 14.
Credit MC, V.
This Vue multiplex was a great addition to the vast
shopping centre (*see p209*). All the screens are
digital, with five 3D-ready and two 18m by 10m
whoppers. The main rooms are functional black
boxes with good sightlines, but you can also fork out
for over-18s 'Scene' screens: you get reclining chairs
and access to a private bar and a cloakroom. There's
a branch at the new Westfield centre in Stratford.
Other locations throughout the city.

REPERTORY CINEMAS

Several first-run cinemas also offer rep-style fare
– check www.timeout.com for locations.

★ BFI Southbank

South Bank, SE1 8XT (7928 3535, 7928 3232
tickets, www.bfi.org.uk). Embankment tube or
Waterloo tube/rail. **Tickets** £9.50; £6.75
reductions; £6.50 Tue. **Screens** 4. **Credit**
AmEx, MC, V. **Map** p399 M8.
For many years this was the NFT (National Film
Theatre). Five years ago it gained a new name, a des-
tination bar-restaurant and the superb Mediatheque.
But the BFI's success is still built on its core function:
providing thought-provoking seasons that give film-
hungry locals the chance to enjoy rare and significant
British and foreign films.
▶ *Mediatheque gives you free access to the BFI's*
huge film and documentary archive.

Ciné Lumière

Institut Français, 17 Queensberry Place,
South Kensington, SW7 2DT (7073 1350,
www.institut-francais.org.uk). South Kensington
tube. **Tickets** £8-£10; £6-£8 reductions; £8 Mon.
Screens 1. **Credit** MC, V. **Map** p395 D10.
Ciné Lumière reopened in early 2009 with better
seating and a refreshed art deco interior. No longer
screening French films only (there are still, however,
regular French previews and classics), the Lumière
is a standard-bearer for world cinema in the capital.

Prince Charles

7 Leicester Place, off Leicester Square, WC2H
7BY (0870 811 2559, www.princecharles
cinema.com). Leicester Square tube. **Tickets**
£6.50-£10; £4-£6 reductions. **Screens** 2.
Credit MC, V. **Map** p416 X3.
Central and cheap, the Prince Charles is just up
an alley from the pricey Leicester Square monsters,
but even films on the new screen are a bargain.
Perfect for catching up on still-fresh films you
missed first time round, it is renowned for riotous
singalong screenings and cult programming such as

The Room, billed as 'the worst film ever made' and
shown to a packed house once a month.

★ Riverside Studios

Crisp Road, Hammersmith, W6 9RL (8237 1111,
www.riversidestudios.co.uk). Hammersmith tube.
Tickets £8.50; £7.50 reductions. **Screens** 1.
Credit MC, V.
The Riverside offers a superb programme of films
and has become well known for inventive double-
bills. The café-bar and riverside terrace are usually
packed with a voluble mix of film- and theatregoers.

IMAX

BFI IMAX

1 Charlie Chaplin Walk, South Bank, SE1
8XR (0870 787 2525, www.bfi.org.uk/imax).
Waterloo tube/rail. **Tickets** £10-£18.50; £8.50-
£15 reductions. **Screens** 1. **Credit** AmEx, MC, V.
Map p399 M8.
London's biggest screen mixes made-for-IMAX fare
and scenery-heavy documentaries with mainstream
blockbusters, such as *Harry Potter*, shown either
very big – or very big and in disorienting 3D.

OUTDOOR SCREENINGS

There's nothing like gathering on a summer
evening for a film in the open air. Best known
are those at **Somerset House**, but you can find
plenty more – some in unusual locations. **Free
Film Festivals** (www.freefilmfestivals.org)
puts on free outdoor screenings in interesting
public spces in south-east London: *Battleship
Potemkin* on the roof of a Peckham multistorey
car park, say. The Scoop (*see p46*), a sunken
outdoor amphitheatre beside City Hall, is the
location for summer screenings as part of **More
London Free Festival** (www.morelondon.
com), while **Pop Up Screens** (www.popup
screens.co.uk) shows popular films like *Top Gun*
throughout the summer in parks like west London.

Rooftop Film Club

Queen of Hoxton, 1-5 Curtain Road, Hoxton,
EC2A 3JX (7422 0958, www.rooftopfilmclub.com).
Tickets £8.50-£12. **Credit** AmEx, MC, V.
In summer, the rooftop garden at this bar/club/arts
collective screens around five films a week. You're
issued with wireless headphones, and you can sip a
beer or order some food while you watch. Tickets
are only available online; see the website for details.

Somerset House

The Strand, WC2R 1LA (7845 4600,
www.somersethouse.org.uk/film). **Tickets** vary.
Credit AmEx, MC, V. **Map** p399 M7.
This summer season takes place in the lovely neoclassical courtyard of Somerset House; tickets sell
out way in advance. Bring a picnic and cushions.

Gay & Lesbian

Where the out go out.

While Pride 2012 may have been a minor disaster, with a funding shortfall meaning no floats and no Soho party, London's smaller, more DIY homo goings-on seem to be positively thriving in the recession. Whatever your taste in music, from thunderous indie to thumping disco, you'll find somewhere that specialises in it, on a nightlife scene that runs around the clock and throughout the week, from bars to superclubs to festivals. And away from the dancefloors, the scene is more varied still, with an array of cabaret nights and literary salons and plays, a handful of cafés and restaurants, a major gay and lesbian film festival and – as far as we know at this point – annual Pride celebrations.

THE GAY SCENE IN LONDON

Roughly speaking, London's gay scene is split into three distinct zones: **Soho**, **Vauxhall** and **east London**. Each of these three districts has its own character: in a nutshell, Soho is the most mainstream, Vauxhall is the most decadent and east London is the most outré.

Centred on Old Compton Street, the Soho scene continues to attract the crowds. Luvvies take in a singalong at the **Green Carnation**, fit freaks work out at **Sweatbox** and everyone else mills around the plethora of gay-slanted bars and cafés. And just down the road, close to Charing Cross Station, sits the legendary **Heaven**, home to **G-A-Y**. If your dream has always been to see Madonna or Kylie in a club, here's your chance – the list of singers who've done live PAs here reads like a *Who's Who* of squeal-tastic gay pop icons.

Down south, Vauxhall is more hedonistic. You could arrive in London on a Friday evening and dance non-stop here for an entire weekend before flying out of town again, with venues such as the **RVT** and the Eagle (home to the superb **Horse Meat Disco**) and now **Popstarz** providing great alternatives to the standard Vauxhall offerings of throngs of shirtless, sweaty chaps.

The most alternative and creative of the capital's queer scenes is in east London. In the likes of the **George & Dragon** and **Dalston Superstore**, you'll be rubbing shoulders with fashion and music's movers and shakers (plus assorted straight folk), to

soundtracks built by ferociously underground DJs. With so much coolness going on, it can get a little snooty, but a lot of the bars and clubs round Shoreditch and Dalston are also properly mixed, which makes the area ideal for a night out with straight mates.

Keen to cut to the chase? **Chariots** is the sauna chain of choice, although **Vault 139** and **Pleasuredrome** (Arch 124, Cornwall Road, Waterloo, SE1 8XE, 7633 9194, www.pleasure drome.com) also have their followers. Most regular bars don't have backrooms, but some club nights in Vauxhall can get raunchy. The monthly **Hard On** (www.hardonclub.co.uk) is the top pick on the calendar for lovers of fetish and leather.

For lesbians, clubby **Candy Bar** is the key venue. For bars, Monday or Wednesday at **Retro** are good choices and the women-only **Glass Bar**

INSIDE TRACK CAB LORE

'**Vauxhall** has a big one-way system,' says taxi driver Angela. 'After a club, make your way to the bridge, on the south side of the railway, to go north of the river. You'll catch cabs that have come south and are turning back.' If you're in **Soho**, says Peter, another cabbie, 'try and get on to Shaftesbury Avenue, Charing Cross Road or Oxford Street. The Soho sidestreets become very congested at night so not many drivers go there.'

Balans.

For thirtysomething lesbians, there are fun cocktail evenings amid the mom-and-pop Italian vintage decor of **Star at Night** (22 Great Chapel Street, Soho, W1F 8FR, 7494 2488, www.the staratnight.com, open 6-11.30pm Tue-Sat) – by day, it's just an old greasy spoon.

Balans

60 Old Compton Street, Soho, W1D 4UG (7439 2183, www.balans.co.uk). Leicester Square or Piccadilly Circus tube. **Open** 7.30am-5am Mon-Thur, Sun; 7am-6am Fri, Sat; 7.30am-2am Sun. **Admission** £2.50 after midnight Mon-Sat. **Credit** AmEx, MC, V. **Map** p416 W3.

The gay café-restaurant of choice for many years, Balans is all about location, location, location (plus hot waiters, decent food and ridiculous opening hours). Situated across from Compton's bar and next door to Clone Zone, it's the beating heart of the Soho scene. The nearby Balans Café (no.34) serves a shorter version of the menu. Both are open almost all night and are good for a post-club bite. **Other locations** throughout the city.

NIGHTCLUBS

London's club scene is particularly subject to change: venues close, nights end and new soirées start. Check *Time Out* magazine or www.time out.com for details on what's on when you're here.

If you want to stay up all night and next day as well, head to **Vauxhall**. At **Fire** (South Lambeth Road, SW8 1UQ, www.fireclub.co.uk), popular nights include midweek urban music stalwart Work!, and popular funky house parties Beyond and Orange, which keep dancers going from Friday morning through until Tuesday. Still in Vauxhall, on the Albert Embankment, try **Union** (no.66, www.club union.co.uk) and **Area** (nos.67-68, www.area clublondon.com). **East Bloc** (217 City Road,

(www.theglassbar.org.uk), having lost its own premises a few years ago, now runs events such as **Pout** (third Saturday of the month at Drift Bar, 110 Bishopsgate, the City, EC2N 4AY). New stand-alone nights for clubbing, cabaret and entertainment of all kinds pop up all the time, but Bird Club at the **Bethnal Green Working Men's Club** (*see p295*), exclusive Code at **Green Carnation** (*see p277*) and Ruby Tuesdays at **Ku** (*see p278*) are recommended. Over the last decade, **100% Babe** at the Roxy (3-5 Rathbone Place, Fitzrovia, W1P 1DA, 7636 1598, www.theroxy.co.uk) has become an institution. Happening every Sunday night before a bank holiday, expect house music, feel-good floorfillers and a party mood. And queer performance nights Duckie (hosted by Amy Lamé) and Bar Wotever at **RVT** (*see p276*) are popular with both the girls and the boys.

Lastly, special mention should go to the **NYC Downlow**, a travelling homo disco straight out of 1970s New York that you can catch at festivals across the country (http://thedownlowradio.com/the-downlow/) including **Lovebox** (*see p275* **Festivals**), the Sunday of which competes with **Summer Rites** (http://summer-rites.com) in Shoreditch Park for the title of London's gayest festival.

RESTAURANTS & CAFÉS

More or less every café and restaurant in London welcomes gay custom. Certainly nowhere in or around Soho will so much as bat an eyelid at you and your other half having a romantic dinner.

Candy Bar.

Festivals Gay & Lesbian

Key dates in the queer year.

July 2012's **Pride London** (www.pride london.org), or World Pride as it was supposed to be, turned from being an international celebration set to attract an extra million visitors into a bit of a damp squib after budgets were cut and floats and street parties cancelled. **Black Pride** (www.ukblackpride.org.uk) continues to grow every year; the 2012 celebration was held at the Ministry of Sound. And out east, the Sunday of Victoria Park's **Lovebox** festival has turned into a huge homo knees-up (www.lovebox.net), while **Summer Rites** (www.summer-rites.com) sees a lot of gay clubs gang together for a festival day out. In spring, there's the annual **London Lesbian & Gay Film Festival** (*see p269* **Festivals**), with an emphasis on cooler, more indie fare in the wake of indie romantic gem *Weekend*. Also worth checking out is July's **London Literature Festival** (*see p29*), which often hosts gay-oriented readings and talks.

Pride London.

EC1V 1JN, www.eastbloc.co.uk), near Old Street, is also worth keeping an eye on.

★ Candy Bar

4 Carlisle Street, Soho, W1D 3BJ (7287 5041, www.candybarsoho.com). Tottenham Court Road tube. **Open** 3pm-3am Mon-Thur; 1pm-3am Fri, Sat; 1pm-12.30am Sun. **Credit** MC, V.
Map p416 W2.

Opened in 1996, the Candy Bar was London's first full-time drinking den for lesbians. It made a splash with its location – in Soho, right at the heart of boys-town – and entertainment: female strippers and lap-dances for lesbians, and it has since gone on to become the location for a reality TV show, *Candy Bar Girls*. DJs spin everything from house and R&B to electro and old school. The crowd varies from lip-stick lesbian to butch, from student to professional, and men must be accompanied by at least two women. Saturdays are a highlight: Monster sees resident DJs Lady Bex and Sandra D playing chart hits from classic to current, plus the odd surprise. On Wednesday there's karaoke with Girls-A-Loud.

Club Kali

Dome, 1 Dartmouth Park Hill, Tufnell Park, N19 5QQ (7272 8153, www.clubkali.com). Tufnell Park tube. **Open** 10pm-3am 3rd Fri of mth. **Admission** £8; £5 reductions. **No credit cards.**

The world's largest LGBT Asian dance club offers Bollywood, bhangra, Arabic tunes, R&B and dance classics spun by DJs Ritu, Riz & Qurra.

Exilio Latin Dance Club

Guy's Bar, Boland House, St Thomas Street, Bankside, SE1 9RT (07931 374391, www.exilio. co.uk). London Bridge tube/rail. **Open** 9.30pm-2.30am every other Sat. **Admission** £6-£12. **No credit cards. Map** p399 M6.

This is London's principal queer Latino spot, with girls and guys getting together for merengue, salsa, cumbia and reggaeton.

Heaven

Underneath the Arches, Villiers Street, Covent Garden, WC2N 6NG (7930 2020, www.heaven nightclublondon.com). Embankment tube or Charing Cross tube/rail. **Open** hrs vary. **Admission** prices vary. **No credit cards.**
Map p416 Y5.

London's most famous gay club is a bit like *Les Misérables* – it's camp, it's full of history, and tourists love it. Popcorn (Mon) has long been a good bet, but it's really all about G-A-Y (Thur-Sat). For years, divas with an album to flog (Madonna, Kylie, Girls Aloud) have turned up to play here at the weekend.

★ Horse Meat Disco

Eagle London, 349 Kennington Lane, Vauxhall, SE11 5QY (7793 0903, www.eaglelondon.com). Vauxhall tube/rail. **Open** 8pm-3am Sun. **Admission** £6. **No credit cards.**

Not your average gay club. Skinny Soho boys and fashionistas rub shoulders with scally lads and bears in a traditional old boozer. The hip soundtrack

Horse Meat Disco.

is an inspired mix of Studio 54, New York punk and new wave. As one *Time Out* critic put it: 'If you ever wished you could hang out in a club like the one in *Beyond the Valley of the Dolls* or *Scarface*, you'll love Horse Meat Disco.' A must.

▶ *When Horse Meat isn't in residence, the Eagle is a hub for those wishing to try a bit of leather without a strict dress code.*

Popstarz
Hidden, 100 Tinworth Street, Vauxhall, SE11 5EQ (7820 6613, www.popstarz.org). Holborn or Tottenham Court Road tube. **Open** 10pm-4am Fri. **Admission** free before 11pm, then £5-£8. **Credit** MC, V. **Map** p416 Y1.
What G-A-Y is to cheese, Popstarz is to indie. It's studenty, drunken, attitude-free and popular – so popular, in fact, that the club has spawned imitators from New York to Paris. There are also occasional PAs from in-demand acts.

★ RVT
Royal Vauxhall Tavern, 372 Kennington Lane, Vauxhall, SE11 5HY (7820 1222, www.rvt.org. uk). Vauxhall tube/rail. **Open** 7pm-midnight Mon, Wed, Thur; 6pm-midnight Tue; 7pm-2am Fri; 9pm-2am Sat; 2pm-midnight Sun. **Admission** £5-£7. **Credit** MC, V.
This pub-turned-legendary-gay-cabaret-venue, a much-loved stalwart on the scene for years, operates an anything-goes booking policy. The most famous fixture is Saturday's queer performance night Duckie (www.duckie.co.uk), with Amy Lamé hosting performances at midnight that range from strip cabaret to porn puppets. On Sundays there's S.L.A.G.S chillout, with live song and witty banter from the D.E. Experience at 5.30pm, followed by house and party anthems spun by DJs Simon Le Vans, Andy Almighty and Sean Sirrs. The aim is always to please the crowd of regulars, reliably vocal with their feedback. Punters verge on the bear, but the main dress code is 'no attitude'.

Vogue Fabrics
66 Stoke Newington Road, Dalston, N16 7XB (http://voguefabricsdalston.com/club). Dalston Junction or Dalston Kingsland rail. **Open** 10pm-3am Fri, Sat. **Admission** £3-£5 Fri, Sat. **No credit cards**.
Small, sweaty and seemingly illegal (but in fact perfectly legitimate), Vogue Fabrics is the place to come if you like your nights messy and your men of the bear and otter variety. While the regular parties come and go, the electro-, disco-, Italo-pumpin' Dirtbox remains a favourite.

▶ *A little boy heavy? The guys behind Dirtbox run Dick and Fanny (see p278* **One-off Parties***).*

XXL
The Arches, 51-53 Southwark Street, Borough, SE1 1RU (7403 4001, www.xxl-london.com).

London Bridge tube/rail. **Open** 10pm-3am Wed; 10pm-6am Sat. **Admission** £3-£15. **No credit cards**. **Map** p402 P8.
The world's biggest club – naturally! – for bears and their friends, XXL is nirvana for chubbier, hairier and blokier gay men and their twinky admirers. True to its name, the venue is bigger than average, with two dancefloors, two bars and even an outdoor beer garden.

PUBS & BARS

Unless otherwise stated, the pubs and bars listed here are open to both gay men and lesbians. The bar at **Ku** (*see p278*) is another good option if you're in the West End.

Barcode Vauxhall
Arch 69, Goding Street, Vauxhall, SE11 4AD (7582 4180, www.bar-code.co.uk). Vauxhall tube. **Open** 4pm-1am Mon-Wed; 4pm-2am Thur; 4pm-5am Fri; 4pm-7am Sat; 5pm-1am Sun. **Admission** £4 after 10pm Fri; £5 after 10pm Sat. **Credit** MC, V.
Prior to the arrival of Barcode Vauxhall, Vauxhall was mostly for clubbing, with those oh-so-necessary pre-dance drinks to be enjoyed anywhere-else-but here. Now those pre-dancing punters are joined by folks just after a drink at this massive, lavish venue, which generally attracts a blokey-ish crowd despite its shiny, sparkly surfaces.

★ Dalston Superstore
117 Kingland High Street, Dalston, E8 2PB (7254 2273, http://dalstonsuperstore.com). Dalston Kingsland rail. **Open** noon-2am Mon; 10am-2am Tue-Thur; 10am-3am Fri, Sat; 10am-2am Sun. **Credit** MC, V.
The opening of this gay arts space-cum-bar a few years back cemented Dalston's status as the final frontier of the East End's gay scene. Come during

the day for the café grub (food's good and breakfast is quite a trendy scene), Wi-Fi and art exhibitions on the walls; at night, you can expect queues for an impressive roster of guest DJs spinning anything from garage to pop. Regular dates such as Tutti Frutti (Sunday soul, disco and house) and Let's Get Quizzical, London's only pop culture quiz that transforms into a disco, every first Tuesday of the month, are well worth putting in the diary. *Photos p279.*

Freedom Bar

66 Wardour Street, Soho, W1F 0TA (7734 0071, www.freedombarsoho.com). Leicester Square or Piccadilly Circus tube. **Open** 4pm-3am Mon-Thur; 2pm-3am Fri, Sat; 2-11.30pm Sun. **Admission** £5 after 10pm Fri, Sat. **Credit** MC, V. **Map** p416 W3.
A glitzy cocktail lounge and DJ bar, spread over two floors. The glam ground-floor bar attracts a fashion-conscious crowd, who sip cocktails among chandeliers, zebra-print banquettes and Venetian mirrors. A few 'strays' and dolled-up gal pals add colour. The large basement club and performance space hosts weekday cabaret and gets busy with the gay party crowd over the weekend.
▶ *In winter, the cosy alcoves of nearby retro-styled basement bar Friendly Society (no.79, 7434 3804) are great for cocktails and first dates.*

G-A-Y Bar

30 Old Compton Street, Soho, W1D 4UR (7494 2756, www.g-a-y.co.uk). Leicester Square or Tottenham Court Road tube. **Open** noon-midnight daily. **Credit** MC, V. **Map** p416 W3.
The G-A-Y night at Heaven (*see p275*) gets the celebrity cameos, but this popular bar is still a shrine to queer pop idols, with nightly drinks promos every time they play a video from the current diva du jour. There's also a women's bar in the basement, called

RVT.

(delightfully) Girls Go Down – popular with flirty, studenty lesbians, loathed by most older women.
▶ *G-A-Y bar's plush late-night sibling, G-A-Y Late, is round the corner on 5 Goslett Yard.*

George & Dragon

2 Hackney Road, Bethnal Green, E2 7NS (7012 1100). Old Street tube/rail or Hoxton rail. **Open** 6pm-midnight daily. **Credit** MC, V. **Map** p401 S3.
The trendy location of this mini-pub ensures a stylish and up-for-it clientele, while the decor (a wall-mounted horse's head, creepy puppets, random garbage) keeps the vibe fun. The music here – pop, indie and accessible electronica – is often delivered with a healthy sense of humour. Gay pub or not, this is one of London's best boozers.
▶ *Wondering where everyone went at closing time? To the Joiners Arms, of course (see below).*

Green Carnation

4-5 Greek Street, Soho, W1D 4DB (8123 4267, www.greencarnationsoho.co.uk). Tottenham Court Road tube. **Open** 4pm-2am Mon-Sat; 4pm-12.30am Sun. **Admission** £5 after 11pm Mon-Sat. **Credit** AmEx, MC, V. **Map** p416 W2.
The Green Carnation had a major refit a few years back, to spectacular effect. Head upstairs for cocktails in posh surroundings, with chandeliers and piano music to heighten the senses and raise the tone. There's a bar and a dancefloor downstairs. It's a haven for West End Wendies, always on hand to belt out a minor Sondheim in the wee hours.

Hoist

Arches 47B & 47C, South Lambeth Road, Vauxhall, SW8 1RH (7735 9972, www.the hoist.co.uk). Vauxhall tube/rail. **Open** 9pm-1am Wed; 10pm-3am Fri; 10pm-4am Sat; 2pm-2am Sun. **Admission** £6 Fri, Sun; £2-£10 Sat. **No credit cards.**
One of two genuine leather bars in town, this club sits under the arches and makes the most of its underground and industrial setting. The Saturday night event SBN (Stark Bollock Naked) gives you the tone; leather, uniforms, rubber, skinhead or boots are the usual dress code. Strictly no trainers.

Joiners Arms

116-118 Hackney Road, Bethnal Green, E2 7QL (www.joinershoreditch.com). Old Street tube/rail or Hoxton rail. **Open** 5pm-2am Mon-Wed; 5pm-3am Thur; 5pm-4am Fri, Sat; 2pm-2am Sun. **Credit** MC, V. **Map** p401 S3.
Love it or loathe it, come midnight this is where all the gays in Shoreditch end up. At least, they've returned since the management abandoned its attempt to charge a £10 entry fee. A mix of fashion types, queer East End geezers and tourists cabbing it from Soho get down to pop, house and electro. The queue for the loos is obscene and the vibe can be obnoxiously trendy but on the whole it's

friendly, drunken and fun. Word to the wise: Sunday nights are often where it's at.

KW4

77 Hampstead High Street, Hampstead, NW3 1RE (7435 5747, www.kingwilliamhampstead. co.uk). Hampstead tube or Hampstead Heath rail. **Open** 11am-11pm Mon-Thur; 11am-midnight Fri-Sun. **Credit** AmEx, MC, V.

The perfect evening ending (or beginning) to time spent on the heath, this fabulous old local – the King William IV, or King Willy to those with longer memories – attracts a very Hampstead crowd (read: well-off and ready for fun). On summer weekends, the cute little beer garden tends to fill up with a mix of gay and straight punters keen to put down their shopping bags. The pub is more popular with lesbians in summer, too, as a stop-off after a dip in the heath's women's bathing pond.

★ Ku

30 Lisle Street, Chinatown, WC2H 7BA (7437 4303, www.ku-bar.co.uk). Leicester Square tube. **Open** noon-3am Mon-Sat; noon-midnight Sun. **Credit** MC, V. **Map** p416 X3.

With a string of awards to its name, Ku must be doing something right. Formerly known as West Central, it has morphed from a mediocre space into a popular bar and club that offers everything from film nights to comedy. The sheer variety of club nights (held in the basement) is impressive, from Sandra D's Ruby Tuesdays for lesbians to kitsch-fest Shinky Shonky on Wednesdays and the Ku DJ Quest Winners – Doug Silva and Athanas Sak – on Saturday nights.

▶ *Ku has recently opened a three-floor bar-club in the heart of the local scene, on the corner of Frith and Old Compton streets. Serious competition for G-A-Y, then (see p277).*

One-off Parties

Where it's at, out east.

The east London gay scene has gone from strength to strength over the last few years, but many of its best queer club nights are hard-to-track-down, irregular parties that advertise little and change location a lot. To navigate the scene successfully, you'll need some pointers.

Cheap entry (rarely exceeding a fiver) and armies of Facebook fans can often mean mammoth queues, so get there super-early or super-late – and download discount fliers in advance or, if necessary, click 'join' on the Facebook link. It's a scene that runs the gamut from the almost menacingly trendy to the lighthearted and silly.

Trailer Trash (www.clubtrailertrash.com) is a roaming club night run by the guys behind Dalston Superstore (*see p276*), and pulls in an equally fashion-forward pack of partiers for local up-and-coming DJ talent and internationally renowned stars such as Green Velvet and Switch – though the DJs' limelight is regularly stolen by a hilarious crew of trannies. **TheMenWhoFell2Earth** (www.themenwhofell2earth.co.uk) and **Dick and Fanny** (www.dickandfanny.tumblr.com) also tend to get occasional big-name DJ guests such as Kim Ann Foxman of Hercules and Love Affair, with D&F a particular hit with boys of the vest-wearing, hairy-chested variety. Meanwhile, **Hot Boy Dancing Spot** (www.hotboydancingspot.com) is popular with everyone from art school undergrads to beary professionals who pack its warehouse bashes and dive bar parties for superlative

Trailer Trash.

DJing from residents the Lovely Jonjo and Hello Mozart! The vibe is deeply trendy – don't bother turning up if you're on a hen do.

A little more indie – and good for girls (gay and straight) – is **Unskinny Bop** (www. unskinnybop.co.uk) at the Bethnal Green Working Men's Club (*see p295*). Here you can expect to hear music from Mariah to bubblegum pop to Riot Grrrl. At **Club Lesley** at the Dalston Superstore girls get down to pop, hip hop, R&B, disco, house and electro, while monthly-ish girlie party **Holla** (http://hollablog.tumblr.com) plays hip hop and R&B of the more crunky, gangsta lean variety. Finally, **Club Motherfu*ker** (www. clubmotherfucker.com) at the Shacklewell Arms in Dalston pulls in a clued-up crowd for acts such as Bloc Party, Simian Mobile Disco and Friendly Fires – years before anyone else has heard of them.

ARTS & ENTERTAINMENT

Retro Bar

2 George Court, off the Strand, Covent Garden,
WC2N 6HH (7839 8760, www.retrobarlondon.
co.uk). Charing Cross tube/rail. **Open** noon-11pm
Mon-Fri; 2-11pm Sat; 2-10.30pm Sun. **Credit** MC, V.
Map p416 Y4.

Iggy Pop and Kate Bush are on the walls of this bar
of the Popstarz ilk (*see p276*), where nights are dedicated to indie rock and 1980s hits (Echo Beach on
Thursdays). The crowd here is mixed in every
sense: gay/straight, gay/lesbian and scene
queen/true eccentric. Quiz nights (Tue) are popular,
too, and the bar on occasions even relinquishes control of the music and lets punters be the DJ – bring
your iPod.

Shadow Lounge

5 Brewer Street, Soho, W1F 0RF (7287 7988,
www.theshadowlounge.co.uk). Leicester Square
or Piccadilly Circus tube. **Open** 10pm-3am Mon-
Sat. **Admission** £5 Tue-Thur; £10 Fri, Sat.
Credit AmEx, MC, V. **Map** p416 W3.

For celebrity sightings, suits, cutes and fancy boots,
this is your West End venue. Expect a hefty cover
charge and a queue on the weekends, but there's
often a sublime atmosphere inside.

Yard

57 Rupert Street, Soho, W1V 7BJ (7437 2652,
www.yardbar.co.uk). Piccadilly Circus tube. **Open**
4-11.30pm Mon-Thur; 4pm-midnight Fri; 2pm-
midnight Sat; 2-10.30pm Sun. **Credit** AmEx, MC, V.
Map p416 W3.

Possibly the most reliable gay bar in Soho. Come for
the courtyard in summer, stay for the Loft Bar in
winter. This unpretentious bar offers a great open-
air courtyard in a central location, attracting pretty
boys, blokes and lesbians in equal measure.

ADULT CLUBS & SAUNAS

Chariots

1 Fairchild Street, Shoreditch, EC2A 3NS
(7247 5333, www.gaysauna.co.uk). Liverpool
Street tube/rail or Shoreditch High Street rail.
Open noon-9am daily. **Admission** £16;
£14 reductions. **Credit** AmEx, MC, V.
Map p401 R4.

Chariots is a sauna chain with outlets all over town.
The original is this one in Shoreditch, the biggest
and busiest, although not necessarily the best. That
accolade probably goes to the one on the Albert
Embankment at Vauxhall (nos.63-64, 7247 5333).
The Waterloo branch (101 Lower Marsh, 7401 8484)
has the biggest sauna in the UK.
Other locations throughout the city.

★ Sweatbox

Ramillies House, 1-2 Ramillies Street, Soho,
W1F 7LN (3214 6014, www.sweatboxsoho.com).
Oxford Circus tube. **Open** noon-2am Mon-Thur,

Dalston Superstore. *See p276.*

Sun; noon-7am Fri, Sat. **Admission** £16 day;
£10 under-25s. **Credit** MC, V. **Map** p416 U2.

Sweatbox Soho looks more like a nightclub than a
typical gym, with the sleek design offset by friendly
staff. Though small, the space is well laid out, with
a multigym and a free weights room. Qualified
masseurs offer treatments. If that doesn't do the
trick, there's a sauna downstairs.

Vault 139

139B-143 Whitfield Street, Fitzrovia, W1T 5EN
(7388 5500, www.vault139.com). Warren Street
tube. **Open** 4pm-1am Mon-Sat; 1pm-1am Sun.
No credit cards. Map p396 J4.

Hidden away on a quiet backstreet, Vault 139 is
London's most central cruise bar – and it's classy,
too, with plush sofas, TV screens and a DJ booth.

Nightlife

When the sun goes down, Londoners come out to play.

To say that London has a brilliant and diverse nightlife is an understatement. Whether it's clubbing, cabaret, live music or comedy, there's a spectrum of entertainment that takes you from the mainstream (big gigs, West End clubs) to the left left field (a club night that just plays re-edited Fleetwood Mac songs, say).

These days, though, big is rarely best. London is home to one of the largest, best-run and most influential nightclubs in the world, **Fabric** (*see p281*), but as a credible superclub, it stands alone in London. It's in smaller venues in the further reaches of the capital that things are really buzzing. In particular, good clubbing is easy to come by along the many venues of the Kingsland Road strip in Dalston, where the **Nest** (*see p282*), **Dalston Superstore** (*see p312*) and a range of party bars have bedded in. There's more new music from the edge at places such as **XOYO** (*see p283*), which – like many venues – doubles as a club and live space, and the **Shacklewell Arms** (*see p283*). The latter, in particular, is proof that the London cliché of indie bands in sticky dives happily endures.

There are 250 comedy gigs a week in London, ranging from open-mic nights in pubs to arena tour performances; the **Comedy Store** (*see p296*) is a good place to start. Meanwhile, the cabaret juggernaut rolls on, smashing through into mainstream clubland in places like **Bethnal Green Working Men's Club** (*see p295*).

The free *Time Out* magazine has salient highlights of London's nightlife. For much, much more, check out the website: www.timeout.com.

Clubs

In this era of boutique clubbing, London has all the bases covered – you don't even always have to go to a club to have the club experience. Try bowling and boogieing at **Bloomsbury Bowling Lanes** (*see p289*), for example, or dress up for one of the city's burgeoning number of 'vintage'-themed parties. And these days, some of the best events happen in secret warehouse locations, usually in east or south London. For more on events with a twist, *see p284* **All Dressed Up**.

CITY SOUNDS AND TOP NIGHTS

What's hot? Big, beefy, speakerstack-destroying bass. Always. Dubstep is huge – and heavy – its reverberating beats sending dancefloors wild across the capital as it continues to morph through urban genres such as funky, future house, bassline, dancehall and 2step – all characterised as UK bass, and popularised by labels such as Hyperdub, Night Slugs. R&S and Rinse. The popularity of disco may be tailing off, but you can still find its progeny at the latest wave of parties influenced by labels Wolf + Lamb, Crosstown Rebels, Hot Natured and their crisp, deep disco-tech sound, such as Kubicle (www.myspace.com/kubicle) and Krankbrother (www.krankbrother.com) and often in room three at Fabric (*see right*) on a Saturday night. There is also a growing number of specialist, backward-looking nights: **Fleet Macwood** (www.facebook.com/FleetmacWood) plays only re-edited Fleetwood Mac songs , and **Ultimate Power** (www.ultimatepowerclub.com), devoted to power ballads, remains enormously popular. Meanwhile, Berlin-influenced deep and glitchy sounds still work a treat at either seminal

seasonal nights such as **Secretsundaze**
(www.secretsundaze.net) and bank holiday
mini-festivals such as **Eastern Electrics**
(www.easternelectricsfestival.com). And last
but certainly not least, **Boiler Room** runs
some of the most popular and forward-thinking
nights around; these are also streamed live on
the internet at http://boilerroom.tv.

VENUES

Shoreditch was the hub of the capital's
nightlife scene for a long time. It has, however,
become increasingly commercialised in recent
years (witness the trails of hen and office parties
between Old Street and Spitalfields) and there's
more action elsewhere. However, its latest live
space and club **XOYO** (*see p283*) is a welcome
addition. Big in Japan at **Book Club** (*see p282*)
is recommended for non-threatening clubbing
with a disco edge, and **Plastic People** (*see
p282*) is still great, particularly the hugely
influential dubstep and bass night, FWD>>.

The city's cool kids now take the bus north
up the Kingsland Road from Shoreditch into
Dalston and further on into Stoke Newington.
The former has much-improved transport
connections to the rest of the city since the
London Overground arrived at Dalston Junction
station, but it can be difficult to find the clubs –
even more so what's happening in them. Spend
a few moments checking *Time Out* magazine,
www.timeout.com/clubs or hunting on Facebook
and you'll unearth fabulous happenings at the
likes of **Dalston Superstore** (*see p312*),
hipster-magnet **Alibi** (91 Kingsland High Street,
E8 2PB, 7249 2733, www.thealibilondon.co.uk)
next door and the **Visions Video Bar** (588
Kingland Road, E84 AH, 07848 999151 and on
Facebook) – its House of Trax vogueing night
(on Facebook) is one of Dalston's hippest events.

The appeal of clubbing in the **West End** has
steeply declined; with the exception of **Madame
JoJo's** (*see p295*), there's little here beside bars,
pubs and a bustling gay scene.

To the north, up in **King's Cross, Egg**
(200 York Way, N7 9AP, 7871 7111, www.egg
london.net) and the **Big Chill House** (257-259
Pentonville Road, N1 9NL, 020 7427 2540, www.
bigchill.net/house) are all that remain of a former
clubbing nexus lost to redevelopment. But the
Star of Kings pub-club (126 York Way, N1
0AX, 7278 9708, www.starofkings.co.uk), with
its late licence and killer sound system, signifies
that the area has still got hedonistic potential.
And the **Lexington** (*see p291*) is known for its
rough and ready nights with a studenty feel in
its upstairs room – Paris is Burning is a decent
electro-house night.

Further north, **Camden** is still very popular –
especially with tourists. Indie student hangout
Proud (*see p282*), teeny pub-rave spot the **Lock**

Cable.

Tavern (*see p282*) and new bourbon-soaked gig
haunt the **Blues Kitchen** (*see p289*) offer credible
nights for London party people too. And **Koko**
(*see p286*) runs some of the biggest student nights
around – Club NME and Annie Mac Presents.

There's more of interest to the south. The
gay village in **Vauxhall** is just as welcoming
to open-minded, straight-rolling types, with club
promoters looking towards south-of-the-river
venues such as **Fire** (South Lambeth Road,
SW8 1UQ, www.firelondon.net), which has some
big line-ups, and **Hidden** (100 Tinworth Street,
SE11 5EQ, 7820 6613, www.hiddenclub.co.uk)
as occasional homes for their (largely drum 'n'
bass and electronic) parties. The calendar is
even fuller at **Cable** (*see below*) and **Corsica
Studios** (*see p283*).

CENTRAL

Cable

*33A Bermondsey Street, Borough, SE1 2EG
(7403 7730, www.cable-london.com). London
Bridge tube/rail.* **Open** 10pm-6am Fri; 10pm Sat-
1pm Sun. **Admission** £5-£15. **Credit** MC, V.
All old-style brickwork and industrial air-con ducts,
this new spot has a similar feel to Fabric. The venue
has two dance arenas, a bar with a spot-and-be-spot-
ted mezzanine, plenty of seating and a great covered
smoking area out the back. It has swiftly become a
home for the capital's bass-hungry kids as nights with
names like Ergh, DNB Noize and Licked Beatz take
over the weekends and shake the speaker stacks.

Fabric

*77A Charterhouse Street, Clerkenwell, EC1M 3HN
(7336 8898, www.fabriclondon.com). Farringdon*

tube/rail. **Open** 10pm-6am Fri; 11pm-8am Sat; 11pm-6am Sun. **Admission** £8-£24. **Credit** AmEx, MC, V. **Map** p400 O5.

Fabric is the club that most party people come to see in London, with good reason. Located in a former meatpacking warehouse, it has a well-deserved reputation as the capital's biggest and best club. The line-ups are legendary. Fridays belong to the bass: guaranteed highlights include DJ Hype, with his drum 'n' bass and dubstep night Playaz, plus Andy C's Ram Records takeover and Caspa's Dub Police label nights. Saturdays descend into techy, minimal, deep house territory, with the world's most famous DJs regularly making appearances. Be warned: the queues are also legendary. Blag on to the guestlist or buy tickets in advance to avoid a three-hour wait.

NORTH LONDON

Better known as gig venues, **Koko** (*see p286*) and **Barfly** (*see p288*) have good reputations for feisty club nights, and the live music at the **Blues Kitchen** (*see p282*) can really rock.

Lock Tavern
35 Chalk Farm Road, Chalk Farm, NW1 8AJ (7482 7163, www.lock-tavern.com). Chalk Farm tube. **Open** noon-midnight Mon-Thur; noon-1am Fri, Sat; noon-11pm Sun. **Admission** free. **Credit** AmEx, MC, V. **Map** p404 X1.

A favourite of artfully distressed rock urchins, it teems with aesthetic niceties inside (cosy black couches and warm wood panels downstairs; open-air terrace on the first floor), but it's the unpredictable after-party vibe that packs in the punters, with big-name DJs regularly providing the tunes.

Old Queen's Head
44 Essex Road, Islington, N1 8LN (7354 9993, www.theoldqueenshead.com). Angel tube. **Open** noon-midnight Mon-Wed, Sun; noon-1am Thur; noon-2am Fri, Sat. **Admission** £4 after 8pm Fri, Sat. **Credit** AmEx, MC, V. **Map** p400 O1.

Pulling in fun-seekers since its relaunch way back in 2006, the Old Queen's Head is another place with long queues at the weekends. There are two floors and outside seating front and back, and during the week you can lounge on the battered sofas. Weekends are for dancing, minor league celeb-spotting and chatting up the bar staff, or trying out the all-new private karaoke room.

Proud
Horse Hospital, Stables Market, Camden, NW1 8AH (7482 3867, www.proudcamden.com). Chalk Farm tube. **Open** 11am-1.30am Mon-Wed; 11am-2.30am Thur-Sat; 11am-12.30pm Sun. **Admission** free-£10. **Credit** AmEx, MC, V. **Map** p404 W2.

The north London guitar-slingers have given way to dubstep, rock 'n' rave and drum 'n' bass, but the action at this former equine hospital is still rock 'n'

roll. Drape yourself – cocktail in hand – over the luxurious textiles in the individual stable-style booths (you must book in advance), sink into deckchairs on the outdoor terrace, or spin around in the main band room at its naughtily themed nights.

EAST LONDON

In addition to the venues below, check out gay hangout the **Dalston Superstore** (*see p312*).

Book Club
100-106 Leonard Street, Shoreditch, EC2A 4RH (7684 8618, www.wearetbc.com). Old Street tube/rail. **Open** 8am-midnight Mon-Wed; 8am-2am Thur, Fri; 10am-2am Sat; noon-midnight Sun. **Admission** free-£5. **Credit** AmEx, MC, V. **Map** p401 Q4.

The Book Club aims to fuse lively creative events, table tennis (there's a ping pong table upstairs and regular tournaments) and late-night drinking seven nights a week. Events range from Electro-Swing, the night that started a huge trend in mashing up vintage sounds with electro beats, to arty think-and-drink workshops that give the nerds a good night out.

East Village
89 Great Eastern Street, Shoreditch, EC2A 3HX (7739 5173, www.eastvillageclub.co.uk). Old Street tube/rail. **Open** times vary Thur-Sun; check website for details. **Admission** free-£10. **Credit** AmEx, MC, V. **Map** p401 Q4.

Stuart Patterson, one of the Faith crew who've been behind all-day house music parties across London for more than a decade (they started in 1999), has transformed what was once the Medicine Bar into this 'real house' bar-club that punches above its weight. The top-notch DJs should suit any sophisticated clubber – it's had everyone from Juan Atkins to David Rodigan on its basement decks in the past year. Meanwhile, upstairs, the newly transformed Villain Bar boasts more laid-back beats.

Nest
36-44 Stoke Newington Road, Dalston, N16 7XJ (7354 9993, www.ilovethenest.com). Dalston Junction rail. **Open** 9pm-3am Thur; 9pm-4am Fri, Sat. **Admission** free-£7. **Credit** MC, V.

We love the Nest, one of Dalston's finest. It's kind of like a corridor, but in a good way, with an industrial chic look. Line-ups are usually great, with music on the dancefloor-focused disco, electro and house end of the spectrum.

Plastic People
147-149 Curtain Road, Shoreditch, EC2A 3QE (7739 6471, www.plasticpeople.co.uk). Old Street tube/rail. **Open** 9.30pm-2am Thur; 10pm-3am Fri; 10am-4pm Sat; 7-11pm 2nd Sun of mth. **Admission** free-£15. **Credit** MC, V. **Map** p403 R4.

The long-established and ever-popular Plastic People subscribes to the old-school line that all you need for a kicking party is a dark basement and a sound system. The programming remains true to form: deep techno to house, all-girl DJ line-ups and many a star DJ (Thom Yorke, anyone?) squeezing through the doors for a secret gig. Hugely influential bass night FWD>> takes place every Thursday.

Shacklewell Arms

71 Shacklewell Lane, Dalston, E8 2EB (7249 0810, www.shacklewellarms.com). Dalston Junction rail. **Open** 5pm-midnight Mon-Wed; 5pm-1am Thur; 5pm-3am Fri; noon-3am Sat; noon-midnight Sun. **Admission** free-£8. **Credit** MC, V.

The latest contender on the Dalston club scene is a magnet for leftfield music. Live bands and DJs come from the electronic, lo-fi, chillwave and post-dubstep arenas, contrasting brilliantly with the shabby interior of this former Afro-Caribbean hotspot.

XOYO

32-37 Cowper Street, Shoreditch, EC2A 4AP (7729 5959, www.xoyo.co.uk). Old Street tube/rail. **Open/admission** varies; check website for details. **Credit** AmEx, MC, V. **Map** p401 Q4.

Relaunched in September 2012 under the management of Andy Peyton, 800-capacity XOYO is first and foremost a nightclub. This former printworks is a bare concrete cell, defiantly taking the 'chic' out of 'shabby chic'. The open space means the atmosphere is always buzzing, as the only place to escape total immersion in the music is the small smoking courtyard outside. The Victorian loft-style space provides the sort of effortlessly cool programming you might expect from a club with such credentials, with big names like Jacques le Conte and Larry Tee among the DJs. There's live music during the week (*see p286*).

SOUTH LONDON

Corsica Studios

4-5 Elephant Road, Elephant & Castle, SE17 1LB (7703 4760, www.corsicastudios.com). Elephant & Castle tube/rail. **Open** 8pm-2am Mon-Thur; 10pm-6am Fri, Sat; 8pm-midnight Sun. **Admission** free-£15. **Credit** MC, V.

An independent warehouse-styled complex, Corsica aims to breed creativity and culture in areas of regeneration. It's certainly rough around the edges with its makeshift bars and toilets but its club nights are second to none: flagship night Trouble Vision boasts the best of bass and, up until recently, a silent disco room, while cult online radio platform the Boiler Room hosts invite-only shows on Tuesdays.

Electric Brixton

Town Hall Parade, Brixton, SW2 1RJ (7274 2290, www.electricbrixton.com). Brixton tube/rail. **Open** times vary Thur-Sun; check website for details. **Admission** £10-£35. **Credit** MC, V.

The Fridge in Brixton was a rave paradise in the early '90s, a stomping ground for the rare groove scene, funky jazz-house and, later, hard dance and psy-trance beats. In 2011, however, it underwent a £1m refit, with new management, and was reborn as Electric Brixton, with a mix of club nights – the likes of Skreamizm with Skream, featuring dubstep with forays into jungle, drum and bass and disco – and live music.

Ministry of Sound

103 Gaunt Street, off Newington Causeway, Elephant & Castle, SE1 6DP (7740 8600, www.ministryofsound.com). Elephant & Castle tube/rail. **Open** 10.30pm-6am Fri; 11pm-7am Sat. **Admission** £10-£20. **Credit** AmEx, MC, V. **Map** p402 O10.

ARTS & ENTERTAINMENT

East Village.

All Dressed Up?

Here's where to go.

Blitz Party
Don 1940s thriftstore threads, period glam or Home Front uniform to swing at these World War II-themed parties (www.theblitzparty.com). Expect big band tunes, performers and DJs.

Candlelight Club
A dazzling, clandestine pop-up cocktail bar – at a secret location, naturally – with a 1920s speakeasy flavour, lit by flickering candles (www.thecandlelightclub.com). There's live music, period shellac spun by DJs, guest cabaret acts and monthly themes. Dress for the Jazz Age: think flappers, good grooming, LBDs and DJs.

Die Freche Muse
Promising decadent cabaret in the grand European tradition, host Baron Von Sanderson invites you to this soirée in a Dalston venue (www.diefreche muse.co.uk). The dress code is 1920s to '40s, jeans and trainers are strictly verboten.

Gangbusters
Tim's Jumpin' Jive hosts this great club at the Lexington on the first Sunday of the month (www.hellzapoppin.co.uk). There's a lindy hop dance class before DJs spin 1920s to 1950s swing, early jazz, jump blues and more.

Last Tuesday Society
'The future belongs to the dandy,' say these party organisers par excellence, whose one-off soirées are masked, decadent and not a little kinky (www.thelasttuesdaysociety.org).

Magic Theatre
Forget a theme: you can dress up any which way you want at Magic Theatre (www.magic-theatre.co.uk) – so long as you make an effort. The evening is based around a live band, with blues and retro dance DJs to follow. It's held at the Rivoli, London's only intact '50s ballroom.

Prohibition
It's back to the 1920s for these Prohibition-era themed parties (www.prohibition1920s. com), boasting jazz bands, tap and Charleston dancers, gambling tables and silent movie screenings. The dress code is stylish '20s (think flapper dresses, feathered headbands, tuxedos, top hats and spats), and the location secret.

Shore Leave
Sailor boys and girls wring the last drop of rum from their remaining hours on dry land at this itinerant evening (www.shore leave.co.uk). There are bawdy bands and burlesque, DJs spinning sounds from far-flung ports and a tattoo shack. Wear vintage nautical attire.

Volupté's Vintage Ball
Every third Saturday of the month at Volupté (www.volupte-lounge.com), 'The Most Decadent Little Supper Club in Town', the Black Cotton Club (www.myspace.com/blackcottonclub) hosts the Vintage Ball. Book a table for the early evening burlesque dinner show, or arrive from 9pm for dancing until late. Dress for Prohibition.

White Blackbird
The country house party is alive and highkicking at the White Blackbird (www.thewhiteblackbird.com). It's held at Stoke Place, a 17th-century mansion-turned-hotel near Stoke Poges: stay overnight, or join the coach party from central London. Take your costume seriously, and dress to theme; previous soirées include a 'Tainted Love' Valentine's ball.

White Mischief
If White Mischief (www.whitemischief.info) is behind it, you can count on a cabaret extravaganza, with a Victorian/steampunk ethos infusing everything from poster design, decor and dress to theme.

Last Tuesday Society.

Ministry of Sound was once the epitome of warehouse cool and is still possibly the UK's best-known clubbing venue. Laid out across four bars, five rooms and three dancefloors, there's lots to explore. Trance night the Gallery has made its home at Ministry of Sound on Fridays, while Saturday nights boast big-name DJ takeovers from the likes of Afrojack, Laidback Luke, Roger Sanchez and Erick Morillo.

Plan B

418 Brixton Road, Brixton, SW9 7AY (7733 0926, www.plan-brixton.co.uk). Brixton tube/rail. **Open** times vary Fri-Sun; check website for details. **Admission** £5-£12.50. **Credit** AmEx, MC, V.
It may be small, but Plan B is very cool. Having been refurbished after a fire, it reopened in late 2009 and the flow of great nights resumed, now with weekly block party Bump and irregular '90s R&B and hip hop night Supa Dupa Fly.

WEST LONDON

Notting Hill Arts Club

21 Notting Hill Gate, Notting Hill, W11 3JQ (7460 4459, www.nottinghillartsclub.com). Notting Hill Gate tube. **Open** hours vary, but around 7pm-2am Tue-Sat; 6pm-1am Sun. **Admission** free-£8. **Credit** MC, V. **Map** p404 Y4.
Notting Hill Arts Club almost single-handedly keeps this side of town on the radar thanks to its mid-weeker Death2Disco, plus nights such as Cheapdate, with house, disco and acid soul.

Paradise

19 Kilburn Lane, Kensal Green, W10 4AE (8969 0098, www.theparadise.co.uk). Kensal Green tube or Kensal Rise rail. **Open** 4pm-midnight Mon-Wed, Sun; 4pm-1am Thur; 4pm-2am Fri; noon-2am Sat. **Admission** £4 after 10pm Fri; £5 after 9pm Sat. **Credit** MC, V.
This is a star among the legion of pub-clubs, thanks to its alternative programme of art auctions, burlesque life drawing and late-night club nights, making it more than just a good local spot.

Music

ROCK, POP & ROOTS

The capital's rock and pop scene is far from predictable. Consult the listings on www.timeout.com and you might find yourself watching an American country star in a tiny basement, an African group under a railway arch or a torch singer in an ancient church.

While corporations – HMV and O2 – have invested in venues, resulting in positives, such as improved facilities and sound systems, and negatives, such as overpriced bars and uniformity, there's still rough and ready

individuality – as well as the newest sounds – to be found in venues like the **Shacklewell Arms** (*see p291*) and **XOYO** (*see p283*) .

TICKETS & INFORMATION

Your first stop should be www.timeout.com, which lists hundreds of gigs every week. Most venues' websites detail future shows. Check ticket availability before setting out: venues large and small can sell out weeks in advance. The main exceptions are pub venues, which sell tickets only on the day. Many venues offer tickets online via their websites, but beware: most online box offices are operated by ticket agencies, which add booking fees that can raise the ticket price by as much as 30 per cent. Try to pay cash in person if possible; for details of London's ticket agencies, *see p230*.

There's often a huge disparity between door times and stage times; doors may open at 7pm, for instance, but the gigs often don't start until after 9pm. Some venues run club nights after the gigs, which means the show has to be wrapped up by 10.30pm; but at other venues, the main act won't even start until 11pm. If in doubt, call ahead.

MAJOR VENUES

In addition to the venues listed below, the **Barbican Centre** (*see p299*), the **Southbank Centre** (*see p301*) and the **Royal Albert Hall** (*see p300*) also stage regular gigs.

Notting Hill Arts Club.

Koko.

Alexandra Palace

Alexandra Palace Way, N22 7AY (8365 2121, www.alexandrapalace.com). Alexandra Palace rail or W3 bus. **Tickets** vary; venue doesn't sell tickets itself. **Credit** AmEx, MC, V.

This hilltop landmark venue, adorned with scuptures and frescoes, opened in 1873 as the People's Palace and was devastated by fire twice – once only 16 days after opening, and the second time in 1980. Bar and toilet provision for some of the big shows remains patchy thanks to the layout, but the sound system is beloved of audiophiles – the Pixies chose it for the first London shows when they reformed, and James Murphy for the last UK appearances of LCD Soundsystem.

HMV Forum

9-17 Highgate Road, Kentish Town, NW5 1JY (7428 4099 information, 0844 847 2405 tickets, www.hmvforum.com). Kentish Town tube/rail. **Box office** *In person* 5-9.30pm performance days. *By phone* 24hrs daily. **Tickets** £5-£30. **Credit** MC, V. **Map** p400 N2.

Originally constructed as part of a chain of art deco cinemas with a spurious Roman theme (hence the name, the incongruous bas relief battle scenes and imperial eagles flanking the stage), the 2,000-capacity Forum became a music venue back in the early 1980s. Since then, it's been vital to generations of gig-goers, whether they cut their teeth on the Velvet Underground, Ian Dury & the Blockheads, Duran Duran, Killing Joke, the Pixies or the Wu-Tang Clan, all of whom have played memorable shows here.

► *The time-honoured choice for a pre-gig pint is the nearby Bull & Gate, which also stages gigs.*

HMV Hammersmith Apollo

45 Queen Caroline Street, Hammersmith, W6 9QH (8563 3800 information, 0844 844 4748 tickets, www.hmvhammersmithapollo.com). Hammersmith tube. **Box office** *In person* 4-8pm performance days. *By phone* 24hrs daily. **Tickets** £10-£35. **Credit** MC, V.

This 1930s cinema doubles as a 3,600-capacity all-seater theatre (popular with big comedy acts and children's shows) and a 5,000-capacity standing-room-only gig space, hosting shows by major rock bands and others not quite ready for the O2.

IndigO2

For listings, see right **O2 Arena***.*

The little brother of the vast O2 Arena (*see right*) is really only little in comparison with the huge expanses of its elder sibling; with a capacity of 2,350 (part-standing room, part-amphitheatre seating, sometimes part-table seating), IndigO2 is impressive in its own right. Its niche roster of MOR acts is dominated by soul, funk, pop-jazz and wearied old pop acts, though it also hosts after-show parties for those headlining at the O2.

★ Koko

1A Camden High Street, Camden, NW1 7JE (0870 432 5527 information, 0844 847 2258 tickets, www.koko.uk.com). Mornington Crescent tube. **Box office** *In person* noon-5pm Mon-Fri (performance days only). *By phone* 24hrs daily. **Tickets** £3-£25. **Credit** AmEx, MC, V. **Map** p404 Z3.

Koko is akin to the London music scene's Forrest Gump, having had a hand in the gestation of numerous styles over the decades. As the Music Machine it hosted a four-night residency with the Clash in 1978; the venue changed its name to Camden Palace in the '80s, whereupon it became home to the emergent new romantic movement and saw Madonna's UK debut. Later it was one of the first 'official' venues to host acid house events. Since a spruce-up in the early noughties, it has hosted acts as diametrically opposed as Joss Stone and Queens of the Stone Age. But the 1,500-capacity hall majors on weekend club nights – Annie Mac Presents and Club NME – and gigs by indie rockers, from the small and cultish to those on the up.

★ O2 Academy Brixton

211 Stockwell Road, Brixton, SW9 9SL (7771 3000 information, 0844 477 2000 tickets, www.o2academybrixton.co.uk). Brixton tube/rail. **Box office** *In person* 2hrs before doors on performance days. *By phone* 24hrs daily. **Tickets** £10-£40. **Credit** AmEx, MC, V.

Brixton is still the preferred venue for metal, indie and alt rock bands looking to play their triumphant 'Look, ma, we've made it!' headline show. Built in the 1920s, this ex-cinema is the city's most atmospheric big venue. The 5,000-capacity art deco gem straddles the chasm between the pomp and volume of a stadium show and the intimate (read: sweaty) atmosphere of a club. Since becoming a full-time music venue in the '80s, it's hosted names from James Brown to the Stones to Springsteen, Dylan, Prince and Madonna, via the Chili Peppers. And with its raked dancefloor, everyone's guaranteed a decent view.

O2 Academy Islington

N1 Centre, 16 Parkfield Street, Islington, N1 0PS (7288 4400 information, 0844 477 2000 tickets, www.o2academyislington.co.uk). Angel tube. **Box office** *In person* noon-4pm Mon-Sat. *By phone* 24hrs daily. **Tickets** £10-£25. **Credit** AmEx, MC, V. **Map** p400 N2.

Located in the heart of a shopping mall, this 800-capacity room was never likely to be London's edgiest venue. Still, as a stepping stone between the pubs of Camden and the city's larger venues, it's a good place to catch fast-rising indie acts and reformed '80s bands, not least because of the great sound system. The adjacent Bar Academy plays host to smaller bands.

★ O2 Arena

Millennium Way, North Greenwich, SE10 0BB (8463 2000 information, 0844 856 0202 tickets, www.theo2.co.uk). North Greenwich tube. **Box office** *In person* noon-7pm daily. *By phone* 24hrs daily. **Tickets** £10-£100. **Credit** AmEx, MC, V.

Symbolic of the turn of the 20th century's cash-rich, commonsense-poor mentality, the Millennium Dome was a national embarrassment that took years to sell off. Even once it was off the public's hands, doubts remained about its viability as a venue, what with its relatively remote location. But the plucky 20,000 seater proved the doubters wrong and established itself as the city's de facto home of the megagig. With outstanding sound, unobstructed sightlines and the potential for artists to perform 'in the round', shows from even the world's biggest acts (Britney, Led Zep) don't feel very far away. IndigO2 (*see p286*) is on the same site.

O2 Shepherd's Bush Empire

Shepherd's Bush Green, Shepherd's Bush, W12 8TT (8354 3300 information, 0844 477 2000 tickets, www.o2shepherdsbushempire.co.uk). Shepherd's Bush Market tube or Shepherd's Bush tube/rail. **Box office** *In person* 4-8pm performance days. *By phone* 24hrs daily. **Tickets** £8-£40. **Credit** AmEx, MC, V.

Once a BBC television theatre, the Empire's baroque interior exudes a grown-up glamour few venues can match. The environment lends a gravitas to the chirpiest performance, as Lily Allen ably demonstrated in the flush of her fame. So you can imagine the sensation of seeing the likes

ARTS & ENTERTAINMENT

Festivals Rock, Pop & Roots

What not to miss this year.

Both Camden and Shoreditch are home to a handful of rock and pop 'microfestivals', which are a cross between a pub crawl and a music festival. Buy a ticket (usually a coloured wristband) and you get access to a multitude of gigs in proximate venues over a couple of days. May's two-day **Camden Crawl** (www.thecamdencrawl. com) is the original, presenting a mix of hip indie acts.

As the weather improves, outdoor events take over for the summer. As well as one-off mega gigs, Hyde Park hosts heritage-rock weekender **Hard Rock Calling** (www.hard rockcalling.co.uk) and the poppier, more contemporary **Wireless Festival** (www. wirelessfestival.co.uk) in late June. In June, Victoria Park is home to the leftfield **Field Day** (www.fielddayfestivals.com), family-friendly Apple Cart Festival (www.the applecartfestival.com) and Groove Armada's **Lovebox Weekender** (www.lovebox.net) and Clapham Common lords it over the August Bank Holiday with its **SW4** rave-up (www.southwestfour.com).

There's more mainstream fare for the **Radio One Hackney Weekend** (June 2013), a six-stage showcase for international pop acts. If you're after something more salubrious, there's **Somerset House Summer Series**, during which Somerset House (*see p79*) welcomes an array of big and generally pretty mainstream acts for roughly ten days of open-air shows. And in summer, the Southbank Centre (*see p301*) invites a guest artist to curate **Meltdown**, a fortnight of gigs, films and other events. David Bowie, Ornette Coleman, Patti Smith and Richard Thompson are among the previous curators.

Other events are limited to a single genre. The best of them include the Southbank Centre's **London African Music Festival** (7328 9613, www.joyful noise.co.uk, Sept); **La Linea** (8693 1042, www.comono.co.uk, early Apr), a fortnight of contemporary Latin American music; and the terrific, ever-changing series of thematic folk and world events at the **Barbican** (*see p299*).

of David Bowie or Bob Dylan here. It holds 2,000 standing or 1,300 seated, sightlines are good, the sound is decent (with the exception of the alcove behind the stalls bar and the scarily vertiginous top floor) and the roster of shows is quite varied, with acts at the poppier end of the scale joined by everyone from folkies to grizzled '70s rockers.

★ Roundhouse

Chalk Farm Road, Camden, NW1 8EH (7424 9991 information, 0844 482 8008 tickets, www.roundhouse.org.uk). Chalk Farm tube. **Box office** *In person* 11am-6pm Mon-Sat. *By phone* 9am-7pm Mon-Fri; 9am-4pm Sat; 9.30am-4pm Sun. **Tickets** £5-£50. **Credit** MC, V. **Map** p404 W1.

The main auditorium's supporting pillars mean there are some poor sightlines at the Roundhouse, but this one-time railway turntable shed (hence the name), which was used for hippie happenings in the 1960s before becoming a famous rock (and punk) venue in the '70s, has been a fine addition to London's music venues since its reopening in 2006. Expect a mix of arty rock gigs (the re-formed Led Zeppelin played here), dance performances, theatre and multimedia events.

Scala

275 Pentonville Road, King's Cross, N1 9NL (7833 2022, www.scala-london.co.uk). King's Cross tube/rail. **Box office** 10am-6pm Mon-Fri. **Tickets** £8-£15. **Credit** MC, V. **Map** p397 L3.

Although the venue has vacillated between use as a picturehouse and concert hall, the Scala's one consistent trait has been its lack of respect for authority: its stint as a cinema was ended after Stanley Kubrick sued it into bankrupcy for showing *A Clockwork Orange*. Nowadays, it's one of the most rewarding venues to push your way to the front of for those cusp-of-greatness shows by big names in waiting – names as varied as the Chemical Brothers and Joss Stone.

Wembley Arena

Arena Square, Engineers Way, Wembley, Middx, HA9 0DH (8782 5566 information, 0844 815 0815 tickets, www.livenation.co.uk/wembley). Wembley Park tube. **Box office** *In person* 10.30am-4.30pm Mon-Fri; noon-4.30pm Sat (performance days only); 1hr before performance start Sun (performance days only). *By phone* 24hrs daily. **Tickets** £5-£100. **Credit** AmEx, MC, V.

Wembley Arena may have seen its commercial heyday end with the arrival of the O2 Arena (*see p287*). It's hardly anyone's favourite venue, not least because the food and drink could be cheaper and better, but most Londoners have warm memories of at least one Arena megagig, and a £30 million refurbishment has done a lot to improve this 12,500-capacity venue.

Club & pub venues

In addition to the venues listed below, a handful of London nightclubs also stage gigs. Try the **Notting Hill Arts Club** (*see p285*), **Madame JoJo's** (*see p295*), **Proud** (*see p282*), **XOYO** (*see p283*) and the **ICA** (*see p107*).

12 Bar Club

22-23 Denmark Place, Soho, WC2H 8NL (7240 2622, www.12barclub.com). Tottenham Court Road tube. **Open** *Café* 8am-7pm Mon-Sat; noon-7pm Sun. *Bar* 7pm-3am Mon-Sat; 7-12.30am Sun. *Shows* from 7.30pm; nights vary. **Admission** £3-£13. **Credit** MC, V. **Map** p416 X2.

A London treasure, this easy-to-miss hole-in-the-wall venue set among the guitar shops of Denmark Street books a grab-bag of low-key stuff, though its tiny size (it has an audience capacity of 100 and a minuscule stage) dictates a predominance of singer-songwriters.

93 Feet East

150 Brick Lane, Spitalfields, E1 6QL (7770 6006, www.93feeteast.co.uk). Aldgate East tube. **Open** 5-11pm Mon-Thur; 5pm-1am Fri; 5pm-1am Sat; 3-10.30pm Sun. *Shows* vary. **Admission** free-£10. **Credit** MC, V. **Map** p401 S5.

With three rooms, a balcony and a wraparound courtyard that's great for barbecues, 93 Feet East manages by its breadth of programme to overcome its not very late licence. You can expect tech-house DJs, a mix of indie-dance bands and various art-rockers, plus short films and arty happenings.

★ 100 Club

100 Oxford Street, Soho, W1D 1LL (7636 0933, www.the100club.co.uk). Oxford Circus tube. **Open** *Shows* vary; check website for details. **Tickets** £6-£20. **Credit** MC, V. **Map** p416 V1.

The 100 Club is synonymous with punk, hosting shows by the Sex Pistols, the Clash, Siouxsie and the Banshees and the Buzzcocks. One historic show, in September 1976, featured the Sex Pistols, the Clash and the Damned. These days, though, the famous, 350-capacity basement room is more of a hub for blues rockers, pub rockers and trad jazzers, coming into its own for the odd secret gig by A-list bands such as Primal Scream and Oasis.

► *The 100 Club also hosts the monthly Limelight (http://londonlimelight.co.uk) – concert hall-quality classical music in a relaxed environment.*

Barfly

49 Chalk Farm Road, Chalk Farm, NW1 8AN (7688 8994 information, 0870 907 0999 tickets, www.barflyclub.com). Chalk Farm tube. **Open** 3pm-2am Mon, Thur; 3pm-1am Tue, Wed; 3pm-3am Fri, Sat; 3pm-midnight Sun. *Shows* from 7pm daily. **Admission** £5-£20. **Credit** MC, V. **Map** p404 X1.

Roundhouse.

As other similarly sized venues open with smarter decor and less conventional booking policies, this 200-capacity venue's star was beginning to fade until the kicking London Sessions moved in. The venue is part of London's indie-rock fabric, a key player in the fusion of indie guitars and electro into an unholy, danceable row.

Bloomsbury Bowling Lanes

Basement, Tavistock Hotel, Bedford Way, Bloomsbury, WC1H 9EU (7183 1979, www.bloomsburybowling.com). Russell Square tube. **Open** noon-2am Mon-Thur; noon-3am Fri; 11am-3am Sat; noon-midnight Sun. **Credit** varies. **Map** p397 K4.
Offering a late-night drink away from Soho, BBL has been putting on live bands and DJs for a while now – and the range of activities make it like a playground for grown-ups. As well as the eight lanes for bowling, there's pool by the hour, table football, karaoke booths and, beside the entrance, a small cinema. Music includes regular funk party Funk and Soul Club, with appearances by the likes of Hackney Colliery Band and DJ Craig Charles.

★ Borderline

Orange Yard, off Manette Street, Soho, W1D 4JB (0844 847 2465, www.theborderline.co.uk). Tottenham Court Road tube. **Open** hrs vary. **Admission** £3-£20. **Credit** AmEx, MC, V. **Map** p416 W2.
A small, sweaty dive bar and juke joint right in the heart of Soho, the Borderline has long been a favoured stop-off for touring American bands of the country and blues varieties, though you'll also find a range of indie acts and singer-songwriters going through their repertoire here. Be warned, though, that it can get very, very cramped.

Blues Kitchen

111 Camden High Street, Camden, NW1 7JN (7387 5277, www.theblueskitchen.com). Camden Town or Mornington Crescent tube. **Open** noon-midnight Mon, Tue; noon-1am Wed, Thur; noon-3am Fri; 11am-3am Sat; 11am-1am Sun. **Admission** free; £4 after 9pm Fri; £5 after 9pm Sat. **Map** p404 Y3.
The Blues Kitchen combines credible live music (roots blues, rockabilly and so on) with a rather high-end interior. The food is spicy New Orleans fare and there's a huge range of American bourbon for sippin'. All in all, it makes for a pleasant Sunday afternoon hangout as well as a late-opening gig venue.

★ Bush Hall

310 Uxbridge Road, Shepherd's Bush, W12 7LJ (8222 6955, www.bushhallmusic.co.uk). Shepherd's Bush Market tube. **Open** hrs vary. *Shows* from 7.30pm. **Tickets** £6-£20. **Credit** MC, V.
This handsome room has been a dance hall, soup kitchen and snooker club. Now, with original fittings intact, it plays host to big bands performing stripped-down shows, top folk outfits and rising indie rockers.

Cecil Sharp House

2 Regent's Park Road, Camden, NW1 7AY (7485 2206, www.efdss.org). Camden Town tube. **Open** hrs vary. **Tickets** vary. **Credit** AmEx, MC, V.
Headquarters of the British Folk Dance and Song Society, Cecil Sharp House is a great place to visit, even when there isn't any music playing – there's a fascinating folk arts education centre and archive open during the day. But the Kennedy Hall performance space boasts a comfortably sprung floor and, most importantly, a well-informed and enthusiastic team of bookers ensuring all angles of trad music are well represented without being preserved in aspic. Live music events range from regular Scottish ceilidhs to more contemporary alt folk.

Corsica Studios

Elephant Road, Elephant & Castle, SE17 1LB (7703 4760, www.corsicastudios.com). Elephant & Castle tube/rail. **Open** hrs vary. **Tickets** £5-£15. **No credit cards. Map** p402 O10.
Corsica Studios is an independent, not-for-profit arts complex whose ethos is to breed creativity and culture. The flexible performance space is increasingly

being used as one of London's most adventurous live music venues and clubs, supplementing bands with sundry poets, live painters and lunatic projectionists. Main nights here include Trouble Vision, a mashing of different genres of dance music.

Garage

20-22 Highbury Corner, Highbury, N5 1RD (7619 6720 information, 0844 847 1678 tickets, http://venues.meanfiddler.com). Highbury & Islington tube/rail. **Box office** *By phone* 24hrs daily. **Tickets** £3-£20. **Credit** AmEx, MC, V.

This 650-capacity alt-rock venue reopened in 2009 after three years of impressive refurbishment. It now books an exciting and surprisingly wide-ranging calendar of indie and art rock gigs, from ancient punk survivors such as the Pop Group and Sham 69 to the poppier end of the indie singer-songwriter scale (Fran Healy in the smaller Upstairs, for example).

Green Note

106 Parkway, Camden, NW1 7AN (7485 9899, www.greennote.co.uk). Camden Town tube. **Open** 7-11pm Mon-Thur, Sun; 7pm-midnight Fri; 6.30pm-midnight Sat. *Shows* 9pm daily. **Tickets** £4-£15. **Credit** MC, V. **Map** p404 X3.

A stone's throw from Regent's Park, this cosy little venue and vegetarian café-bar was a welcome addition to the city's roots circuit back in 2005. Singer-songwriters, folkies and blues musicians make up the majority of the gig roster, with a handful of big names in among the listings.

Hoxton Square Bar & Kitchen

2-4 Hoxton Square, Shoreditch, N1 6NU (7613 0709, www.hoxtonsquarebar.com). Old Street tube/rail or Shoreditch High Street rail. **Open** 11am-midnight Mon; 11am-1am Tue-Thur; 11am-2am Fri, Sat; 11am-12.30am Sun. **Tickets** £5-£12. **Credit** AmEx, MC, V. **Map** p401 R3.

This 450-capacity venue is more than just a place to be seen: the venue's finger-on-the-pulse line-ups are always cutting edge and fun, with the venue often hosting a band's first London outing. Get there early or be prepared for a long queue.

Jazz Café

5 Parkway, Camden, NW1 7PG (7688 8899 information, 0844 847 2514 tickets, http://venues.meanfiddler.com). Camden Town tube. **Box office** *In person* 10.30am-5.30pm Mon-Sat. *By phone* 24hrs daily. **Tickets** £10-£30. **Credit** MC, V. **Map** p404 Y2.

Given its sterling reputation, you wouldn't think that the jazz café was such a newbie on the London music map, converted from a branch of Barclays in 1990. In those days, the support pillars famously boasted the command of 'STFU' – this was a venue that took music seriously. These days, though, the interpretation of jazz is pretty loose, stretching to intimate shows by US hip hop legends (such as De La Soul)

and racing certainties (such as Aloe Blacc's incredible UK debut), as well as funk, soul and R&B legends such as Marlena Shaw and Mary J Blige.

★ Lexington

96-98 Pentonville Road, Islington, N1 9JB (7837 5371, www.thelexington.co.uk). Angel tube. **Open** noon-2am Mon-Wed, Sun; noon-3am Thur; noon-4am Fri, Sat. **Tickets** free-£10. **Credit** AmEx, MC, V. **Map** p400 N2.

Effectively the common room for the music industry's perennial sixth form, this 200-capacity venue has a superb sound system in place for the leftfield indie bands that dominate the programme. It's where the hottest US exports often make their London debut: indie greats such as the Drums and Sleigh Bells have cut their teeth here in front of London's most receptive crowds. Downstairs, there's a lounge bar with a vast array of US beers and bourbons, above-par bar food and a Rough Trade music quiz (every Monday).

★ Nest

36-44 Stoke Newington Road, Dalston, N16 7XJ (7354 9993, www.ilovethenest.com). Dalston Kingsland rail. **Open** hrs vary. **Tickets** free-£10. **Credit** AmEx, MC, V.

Formerly the site of the beloved Dalston hipster institution Bardens Boudoir, the Nest retains much of its predecessor's eclectic, forward-looking booking policy, with the benefit of a big money 'distressed industrial' refurbishment and, crucially, much improved toilets.

★ Shacklewell Arms

71 Shacklewell Lane, Dalston, E8 2EB (7249 0810, www.shacklewellarms.com). Dalston Kingsland or Dalston Junction rail. **Open** 5pm-midnight Mon-Thur; 5pm-3am Fri; noon-3am Sat; noon-11pm Sun. *Shows* 8pm. **Admission** £3-£8. **Credit** AmEx, MC, V.

A Dalston location and a roster of the sharpest acts on the edge make the Shacklewell Arms the venue de jour in fashionable hearts. This quirkily decorated gaff hosted a triumphant secret gig by the Horrors to launch their great-leap-forward album *Skying* in 2011 and in 2012 it saw a residency from next big things Toy.

Underworld

174 Camden High Street, Camden, NW1 0NE (7734 1932, www.theunderworldcamden.co.uk). Camden Town tube. **Box office** *In person* 11am-11pm Mon-Sat; noon-10.30pm Sun. *By phone* 24hrs daily. **Shows** hrs vary. **Admission** £5-£20. **No credit cards.** **Map** p404 Y2.

A dingy maze of pillars and bars below Camden, this subterranean oddity is an essential for metal and hardcore fans who want their ears bludgeoned by bands with names such as the Atomic Bitchwax, Skeletonwitch and Decrepit Birth. Tickets are purchased from the World's End pub upstairs.

ARTS & ENTERTAINMENT

★ Union Chapel
Compton Terrace, Islington, N1 2XD (7226 1686, www.unionchapel.org.uk). Highbury & Islington tube/rail. **Open** hrs vary. **Tickets** free-£40. **No credit cards.**
In 2012, readers of *Time Out* magazine voted Union Chapel their top music venue. The Grade I-listed Victorian Gothic church still holds services and runs a homeless centre, while doubling as an atmospheric gig venue. It made its name hosting acoustic events and occasional jazz shows, becoming a magnet for thinking bands and their fans, particularly as part of the rightly lauded Little Noise Sessions for Mencap. These days, you'll also find classy intimate shows from bigger artists such as Paloma Faith. Look out for its free Daylight gigs on Sundays.

★ Windmill
22 Blenheim Gardens, Brixton, SW2 5BZ (8671 0700, www.windmillbrixton.co.uk). Brixton tube/rail. **Open** *Shows* 8-11pm Mon-Thur; 8pm-1am Fri, Sat; 2-11pm Sun. **Admission** free-£10. **Credit** MC, V.
There's a free barbecue every Sunday afternoon in summer; a somewhat scary dog lives on the roof, frightening unsuspecting smokers; and an actual windmill stands in the adjacent park. The Windmill is certainly not your average music venue, but it's been revelling in its rough-around-the-edges eccentricity for years, its unprepossessing exterior a cloak for its dedication to new leftfield music. The programming is biased towards alt country, alt folk, alt punk, but even if alt none of these is your bag, it's worth a visit just to pick up an 'I Believe in Roof Dog' T-shirt. Admission is cheap, too.

Union Chapel.

JAZZ

The international big hitters keep on visiting London, but these are exciting times, too, for the city's homespun jazz scene. Inspired by freewheeling attractions at the **Vortex** (*see p294*) and the sporadic, unhinged **Boat-Ting Club** nights (www.boat-ting.co.uk), acts such as Portico Quartet, Led Bib and Kit Downes Trio have won Mercury Prize nominations with recent albums, and the F-IRE and Loop Collectives are busy nurturing future stars.

In addition to the venues below, the **100 Club** (*see p288*) hosts trad groups, while the **Spice of Life** at Cambridge Circus (6 Moor Street, W1D 5NA, 7437 7013, www.spiceoflife soho.com) has solid mainstream jazz. The **Jazz Café** (*see p291*) lives up to its name from time to time; there's a lot of very good jazz at the excellent **Kings Place** (*see p300*); and both the **Barbican** (*see p299*) and the **Southbank Centre** (*see p301*) host dozens of big names. For the increasingly excellent **London Jazz Festival**, *see p294* **Festivals**.

606 Club
90 Lots Road, Chelsea, SW10 0QD (7352 5953, www.606club.co.uk). Imperial Wharf rail or bus 11, 211. **Shows** 8.30pm Mon, Thur, Sun; 7.30pm Tue, Wed; 9.30pm Fri, Sat. **Admission** (non-members) £8-£12. **Credit** AmEx, MC, V.
Since 1976, Steve Rubie has run this spot, which relocated to this 150-capacity club in 1987. Alongside its Brit-dominated bills, expect informal jams featuring musos who've come from gigs elsewhere. There's no entrance fee as such; bands are funded from a music charge added to bills at the end of the night.

Bull's Head
373 Lonsdale Road, Barnes, SW13 9PY (8876 5241, www.thebullshead.com). Barnes Bridge rail. **Open** noon-11.30pm daily. *Shows* 8.30pm Mon-Sat; 1-3.30pm, 8.30-11pm Sun. **Admission** £5-£12. **Credit** MC, V.
This venerable, ancient Thames-side pub won a reputation for hosting modern jazz in the 1960s but today specialises in mainstream British jazz and swing, with guests such as the Humphrey Lyttelton band.

★ Café Oto
18-22 Ashwin Street, Dalston, E8 3DL (7923 1231, www.cafeoto.co.uk). Dalston Junction or Dalston Kingsland rail. **Open** 9.30am-1am Mon-Fri; 10.30am-midnight Sat, Sun. *Shows* from 8pm; days vary. **Admission** £3-£10. **No credit cards.**
Opened in 2008, this 150-capacity café and music venue can't easily be categorised, though its website offers the tidy definition that it specialises in 'creative new music that exists outside of the mainstream'. That means Japanese noise rockers ('Oto' is Japanese for 'sound'), electronica pioneers,

Essential London Albums

Quintessential city music.

LONDON CALLING
THE CLASH (1979)

Era-defining punk classic, with cover artwork that pays homage to Elvis Presley's first album. The rocking title track now gets all the airplay (from British Airways ads to Olympic Stadium shout-outs), but the West London art school rapscallions put their guitars into a varied set of songs, among them 'The Guns of Brixton'.

NEW BOOTS
AND PANTIES!!
IAN DURY (1977)

The title refers to the only clothes a thrifty Dury wouldn't buy from charity shops, and the cover shows him with his son, Baxter. Classic tracks like 'Wake Up and Make Love to Me', 'Billericay Dickie' and 'Clever Trevor' make this some of the finest work by the Essex pub-rock maestro.

PARKLIFE
BLUR (1994)

Launched at the defunct Walthamstow Dog Track, *Parklife* was a hymn to the East End, with the laddish Britpoppers on cheekily good form. 'Girls and Boys', 'End of a Century' and 'To the End' join the iconic 'Parklife' on an album that came to epitomise the emerging 1990s Britpop scene.

TONGUE N' CHEEK
DIZZEE RASCAL (2009)

The east London rapper makes a serious bid for pop superstardom, taking rhymes rough enough for the toughest estates up the charts with him. As well as the lubricious 'Dirtee Disco' and 'Holiday', 'Bonkers' made violent mental derangement seem enough fun to merit an Olympic Opening Ceremony slot.

SOMETHING ELSE
THE KINKS (1967)

Early evidence of Ray Davies' melancholy romanticism lies in the most enduring track on the album that propelled a million moony couples to watch their very own 'Waterloo Sunset'. Listen too for the careful blend of self-deception, veiled homoeroticism and waspish irony on 'David Watts'.

ORIGINAL PIRATE
MATERIAL
THE STREETS (2002)

Mike Skinner almost singlehandedly invented geezer rap with his debut album. The keynotes of his later style are already present – wearily lovelorn entreaties and sordid tales of dope-smoking and brandy-toting – often revolving around late late nights at the Dogstar in Brixton.

improvising noiseniks and artists from the stranger ends of the rock, folk and classical spectrums.

★ Charlie Wright's International Bar

45 Pitfield Street, Hoxton, N1 6DA (7490 8345, www.charliewrights.com). Old Street tube/rail. **Open** noon-1am Mon-Wed; noon-4am Thur, Fri; 5pm-4am Sat; 5pm-2am Sun. *Shows* from 8.30pm daily. **Admission** free-£10. **Credit** MC, V. **Map** p401 Q3.

When Zhenya Strigalev and Patsy Craig began programming the line-up here in 2006, London's jazz fans were given a reason to visit what had previously been merely a rather good after-hours boozer. Now this agreeably scruffy venue stages a fine jazz programme every night of the week except Saturday. Gigs don't usually start until 10pm, and run late on Thursdays and Fridays.

Forge & Caponata

3-7 Delancey Street, Camden, NW1 7NL (7383 7808, www.forgevenue.org). Camden Town or Mornington Crescent tube. **Open** hrs vary. **Admission** free-£15. **Credit** AmEx, MC, V. **Map** p404 Y3.

Run by a non-profit community organisation, this innovative music/restaurant space incorporates a stunning atrium, and hosts concerts of various sizes and formalities thanks to the flexible nature of its layout. The booking policy is skewed heavily to jazz, but the programme also features a carefully curated selection of roots and classical shows. There's a worthwhile on-site Italian restaurant, Caponata: you can dine while you listen at some performances, and there's an interesting Sunday brunch programme.

Pizza Express Jazz Club

10 Dean Street, Soho, W1D 3RW (0845 602 7017, www.pizzaexpresslive.com). Tottenham Court Road tube. **Shows** 8.30-10.30pm Mon-Thur; 9-11pm Fri, Sat; 8-10pm Sun. **Admission** £15-£25. **Credit** AmEx, DC, MC, V. **Map** p416 W2.

The upstairs restaurant (7437 9595) is jazz-free, but the 120-capacity basement is one of the best mainstream jazz venues in town. Singers such as Kurt Elling and Lea DeLaria join instrumentalists from home and abroad on the nightly bills.

★ Ronnie Scott's

47 Frith Street, Soho, W1D 4HT (7439 0747, www.ronniescotts.co.uk). Leicester Square or Tottenham Court Road tube. **Shows** 7.15pm-1am Mon-Sat; 8pm-late Sun. **Admission** (non-members) £20-£40. **Credit** AmEx, MC, V. **Map** p416 W2.

Opened (on a different site) by the British saxophonist Ronnie Scott in 1959, this jazz institution – the setting for Jimi Hendrix's last ever UK performance among many other distinctions – was completely refurbished in 2006. The capacity was expanded to 250, the food got better and the bookings became drearier. Happily,

though, Ronnie's has got back on track, with jazz heavyweights dominating once more – from trad talents such as Chick Corea to hotly tipped purists such as Kurt Elling to futuristic mavericks such as Robert Glasper. Perch by the rear bar or get table service at the crammed side-seating or more spacious (but noisier) central tables in front of the stage.

★ Vortex Jazz Club

Dalston Culture House, 11 Gillet Street, Dalston, N16 8JN (7254 4097, www.vortexjazz.co.uk). Dalston Kingsland rail. **Shows** 8pm daily. **Admission** £8-£15. **Credit** MC, V.

There are few venues in the city you could visit on spec and be guaranteed to hear something interesting. With the possible exception (depending on your tolerance for Japanese no-wave) of the nearby Café Oto *(see p292)*, the Vortex is one of London's most lovingly curated venues. Jazz is the order of the day, but the Vortex serves it up in kaleidoscopic variety. For the less daring, there's a regular calendar of big band, piano trio, vocal, free improv, world music, gypsy/east European and folk-oriented sounds each month. The Vortex hosts its own strand of the London Jazz Festival *(see below* **Festivals***)* and various other forward-thinking events. The bar stays open late.

Cabaret

To see the best cabaret, head to **Volupté**, which hosts opulent burlesque nights; the always interesting **Bethnal Green Working Men's Club** (for both, *see right*); and the even more alternative **RVT** *(see p312)*. A recent trend has been for cabaret in posh venues. The **Savoy**

Festivals Jazz

What not to miss this year.

Showcasing London's thriving jazz scene while simultaneously welcoming an array of big names from abroad, November's excellent **London Jazz Festival** (7324 1880, www.londonjazzfestival.org.uk) covers most bases, from trad to free improv. It's comfortably the biggest jazz festival of the year, though you may also find some interesting events at the all-free, open-air **Ealing Jazz Festival** (8825 6064, www.ealing.gov.uk, July). For something edgier, look out for occasional showcases organised by the **Loop Collective** (www.loopcollective.org) and the **F-IRE Collective** (www.f-ire.com), which feature some of the best young talents in the country.

(see p241) has hosted evenings in the Beaufort Bar mixing burlesque, variety and song; **Brasserie Zédel** (see p196) puts on shows at its Crazy Coqs venue; comedy chanteuse Miss Hope Springs is currently in residence on Sunday nights; and the **Hippodrome** (see p83), now primarily a casino, also hosts music and cabaret. Again, many of the best cabaret nights are one-off parties in a range of formal and informal venues – wherever you party, bring an open mind. For more cabaret events, see p284 **All Dressed Up**.

★ Bethnal Green Working Men's Club

42-44 Pollard Row, Bethnal Green, E2 6NB (7739 7170, www.workersplaytime.net). Bethnal Green tube. **Open** hrs vary; check website for details. **Admission** free-£8. **Credit** AmEx, MC, V.
Sticky red carpet and broken lampshades perfectly suit the programme of quirky lounge, retro rock 'n' roll and fancy-dress burlesque parties here. You might get to watch a spandex-lovin' dance duo or get hip with burlesque starlets on a 1960s dancefloor. The mood is friendly, the playlist upbeat and the air full of artful, playful mischief.

CellarDoor

Zero Aldwych, Covent Garden, WC2E 7D (7240 8848, www.cellardoor.biz). Covent Garden Tube. **Open** hrs vary; check website for details. **Admission** varies. **Credit** AmEx, MC, V. **Map** p399 L7.
Some staggeringly clever design means that although there's room for just 60 in this subterranean converted Victorian loo, CellarDoor never feels claustrophobic. Musical-theatre cabaret crooners, drag queens and snuff parties (as in taking snuff) are the order of the day, giving this sleek establishment a vintage feel. Nearly all shows are free and often great fun – EastEnd Cabaret regularly appear and Champagne Charlie's Tuesday open-mic night is an institution.

Madame JoJo's

8-10 Brewer Street, Soho, W1F 0SD (7734 3040, www.madamejojos.com). Leicester Square or Piccadilly Circus tube. **Open** 8pm-3am Tue, Wed; 10pm-3am Fri, Sat; 10pm-2.30am Sun. **Admission** £3-£10. **Credit** AmEx, MC, V. **Map** p416 W3.
The red and slightly shabby basement space at JoJo's is a beacon for those seeking to escape the West End's post-work chain pubs. The most treasured nights tend towards variety – Kitsch Cabaret is every Saturday night – but its long-running Tuesday nighter, White Heat, still books up-and-coming bands and DJs for a largely indie and student crowd.

Pheasantry

152-154 King's Road, Chelsea, SW3 4UT (0845 6027 017, www.pizzaexpresslive.com/popList.aspx). Sloane Square tube. **Open** performance times vary; check website for details. **Admission** varies. **Credit** AmEx, MC, V. **Map** p395 F11.

The successor to the institution that was Pizza on the Park, this jazz and cabaret venue is also part of the Pizza Express stable. The bright, spacious basement space has something of a cruise-ship feel (where does that staircase actually go?) and sightlines aren't always great but it's the city's premier platform for New York-style jazz singing and musical-theatre-influenced cabaret work, often attracting big names from the West End and across the pond.

Proud Cabaret

1 Mark Lane, corner of Dunster Court & Mark Lane, the City, EC3R 7AH (020 7283 1940, www.proudcabaret.com). Tower Hill or Monument tube. **Open** hrs vary. Check website for details. **Admission** varies. **Credit** AmEx, MC, V. **Map** p403 R7.
Tucked away in a corner of the City, this cabaret outpost from the Proud stable is one of the lushest dinner-cabaret spaces in town, with a well-positioned thrust stage nestling below plush, cosy booths. The modern British menu is good, too, particularly at special-offer rates, though the shows aim for spectacle rather than substance: often high on technical skills, they tend to be low on character or provocation. A popular choice for hen parties.

★ Volupté

7-9 Norwich Street, Holborn, EC4A 1EJ (7831 1622, www.volupte-lounge.com). Chancery Lane tube. **Open** 4.30pm-1am Tue, Wed; 5pm-3am Thur, Fri; 1pm-3am Sat. **Admission** £15-£25. **Credit** MC, V. **Map** p416 N5.
Expect to suffer wallpaper envy as you enter the ground-floor bar and then descend to the club. Punters enjoy some of the best cabaret talent and retro nights in town, from tables set beneath absinthe-inspired vines. Its daytime soirée, Afternoon Tease, coupled with scones and cream teas, is near legendary.

Comedy

Explore dingy pubs and clubs where skills are honed, arenas and theatres for the finished acts. London's comedy scene gets a bit quieter during the exodus to Edinburgh every August. For weekly line-ups, check *Time Out* magazine and www.timeout.com.

Amused Moose Soho

Moonlighting, 17 Greek Street, Soho, W1D 4DR (7287 3727, www.amusedmoose.com). Leicester Square or Tottenham Court Road tube. **Shows** Sept-June 7.30pm Sat. **Admission** £10-£14. **Credit** MC, V. **Map** p416 W2.
Hils Jago's rosters are always strong, with names such as Bill Bailey and Eddie Izzard continuing to justify the club's multi-award-winning status. Jago

has a lot of special guests who can't be named – in other words, really top names trying out new material – and runs the Amused Moose Laugh Offs; finalists have included Jimmy Carr and Simon Amstell.

Boat Show

Tattershall Castle, Kings Reach, Victoria Embankment, SW1A 2HR (07932 658895, www.boatshowcomedy.co.uk). Embankment tube. **Shows** 8.30pm 1st Mon of mth; 8pm Fri, Sat. **Admission** £10, £8 reductions Mon; £13.50, £11 reductions Fri, Sat. **No credit cards.** **Map** p399 L8.

The line-ups aboard this floating comedy club situated opposite the London Eye are consistently strong. Ticket prices are reasonable, and for those wishing to party into the small hours, a nightclub follows the comedy every Friday and Saturday at no extra charge.

Canal Café Theatre

Delamere Terrace, Little Venice, W2 6ND (7289 6054, www.canalcafetheatre.com). Royal Oak or Warwick Avenue tube. **Shows** 9.30pm Thur-Sat; 9pm Sun. **Admission** £10-£11.50. **Credit** MC, V. **Map** p392 C4.

This charming little theatre, perched on the edge of a canal in Little Venice, offers a number of shows a week. Past performers include Stewart Lee and Pete Firman, and it's a good place to catch young comics and sketch acts, as well as NewsRevue, who have a residency performing their topical sketches and songs every Thursday to Sunday.

Comedy Café

66-68 Rivington Street, Shoreditch, EC2A 3AY (7739 5706, www.comedycafe.co.uk). Liverpool Street or Old Street tube/rail. **Shows** 9pm Wed-Sat. **Admission** £10-£16; free Wed. **Credit** MC, V. **Map** p401 R4.

The Comedy Café is another purpose-built club set up by a comedian. Noel Faulkner, who worked on trawlers and was wanted by the FBI in his time, now mainly keeps to the back room but, with the emphasis on inviting bills and satisfied punters, his influence can still be felt. The atmosphere is fun and food is an integral part of the experience.

★ Comedy Store

1A Oxendon Street, Soho, SW1Y 4EE (0844 871 7699, www.thecomedystore.co.uk). Leicester Square or Piccadilly Circus tube. **Shows** phone for details Mon; 8-10.30pm Tue-Thur, Sun; 8pm & midnight Fri, Sat. **Admission** £15-£22.50. **Credit** AmEx, MC, V. **Map** p416 W4.

Alternative line-ups at this, the daddy of British comedy clubs, helped launch jokers such as Alexei Sayle, Dawn French and Paul Merton. The legendary gong show, in which would-be stand-ups are given only as much time on stage as the audience will allow, is on the last Monday of the month.

Downstairs at the King's Head

2 Crouch End Hill, Crouch End, N8 8AA (8340 1028, www.downstairsatthekingshead.com). Finsbury Park tube/rail then bus W7. **Shows** 8pm Thur, Sat, Sun. **Admission** £3-£10. **No credit cards.**

Founded in what seems like the comedic pre-history of 1981, this venue is still run with huge enthusiasm by its immensely knowledgeable promoter Pete Grahame. It's an easygoing, comfortable place where comedians can experiment and play around with new material and routines in complete freedom. It's popular with comics wanting to do warm-up shows for TV and tours.

Etcetera Theatre

The Oxford Arms, 256 Camden High Street, Camden, NW1 7BU (7482 4857, www.etcetera theatre.com). Camden Town tube. **Shows** vary; check website for details. **Admission** £5-£10. **No credit cards.** **Map** p404 Y2.

This intimate black box theatre above the Oxford Arms pub on bustling Camden High Street is a great place to catch Edinburgh previews, comedy in August's Camden Fringe, and occasionally big names warming up for tours, which in the past have included Russell Brand and We Are Klang.

Fat Tuesdays

Compass, 58 Penton Street, Islington, N1 9PZ (www.fattuesdaycomedy.co.uk). Angel tube. **Shows** 8pm alternate Tue. **Admission** £7-£8. **No credit cards.** **Map** p440 N2.

Charming compere Tiernan Douieb previously ran this intimate Islington gig, establishing it as one of the most welcoming comedy clubs in London. It's now in the hands of comedian Nish Kumar, and this tiny room above the Compass pub still hosts consistently brilliant line-ups, with wonderfully varied bills and headliners at the top of their game.

Feature Spot

The 100 Club, 100 Oxford Street, Soho, W1D 1LL (07956 834135, www.featurespot.co.uk). Oxford Circus or Tottenham Court Road tube. **Shows** vary; check website for details. **Admission** £10-£15. **Credit** AmEx, MC, V. **Map** p416 V1.

Feature Spot's comedy nights often feature in critics' choices lists. Previous acts include Russell Howard, Stephen Merchant, Adam Buxton and Tim Minchin. But whoever's on the bill, you're guaranteed an excellent show. Check the website for upcoming shows.

Funny Side of Covent Garden

The George, 213 the Strand, Covent Garden, WC2R 1AP (0844 478 0404, www.thefunny side.info). Covent Garden tube or Leicester Square tube. **Shows** 8pm Fri, Sat. **Admission** £12.50. **Credit** MC, V. **Map** p399 M6.

This is an enjoyable club upstairs in a mock Tudor pub, but calling it 'Covent Garden' is a bit of a stretch, geographically speaking – it's on the fringes of the City near the Royal Courts of Justice. Well-known comedians such as Felix Dexter, Josie Long, Tom Wrigglesworth and Phil Kay have all performed here. **Other locations** Spectator (downstairs), 6 Little Britain, the City, EC1A 7BX; Café Koha, 11 St Martin's Court, the City, WC2N 4AJ; Tara Arts Studio, 356 Garrett Lane, Earlsfield, SW18 4ES; The Alexandra (upstairs), 14 Clapham Common South Side, Clapham, SW4 7AA.

Hen & Chickens
109 St Paul's Road, Highbury Corner, Islington, N1 2NA (7704 2001, www.henandchickens.com). Highbury & Islington tube/rail. **Shows** times vary. **Admission** £4-£12.50. **No credit cards.**
This dinky, black-box theatre above a cosy Victorian corner pub is well known as the place to see great solo shows, especially those warming up for a tour. Acts have included Jenny Eclair, Frankie Boyle, Rhona Cameron and Jimmy Carr.

Leicester Square Theatre
Leicester Square Theatre, 6 Leicester Place, Leicester Square, Soho, WC2H 7BX (0844 873 3433, www.leicestersquaretheatre.com). Leicester Square tube. **Shows** vary; check website for details. **Admission** £6-£10. **Credit** MC, V. **Map** p416 X4.

With a mixture of mixed-bill shows and solo offerings, the theatre programmes comedy names in the main house, and rising stars in the basement. A favourite of many big-name American comics, the list of names who play here is getting better and better.

Soho Theatre
For listings, *see p311*.
The Soho Theatre is one of the best places to see comics break out of their normal club sets to perform more substantial solo shows. There's always a good mix of home-grown and international talent.

Up the Creek
302 Creek Road, Greenwich, SE10 9SW (8858 4581, www.up-the-creek.com). Greenwich DLR/rail. **Shows** 8.15pm Thur; 8.45pm Fri, Sat; 7.30pm Sun. **Admission** £4 Thur; £11, £7 reductions Fri; £15, £12 reductions Sat; £6, £4 reductions Sun. **Credit** AmEx, MC, V. **Map** p405 W2.
Set up by the late and legendary Malcolm Hardee ('To say that he has no shame is to drastically exaggerate the amount of shame he has,' quipped one critic), this purpose-built club has been around since the 1990s, and it remains to this day one of the best places to see live comedy. It's renowned for its lively, not to say bearpit atmosphere, but there's a more chilled-out feel to the 'Sunday Special Club' (www.sundayspecial.co.uk).

Laughter Costs Nothing...
... At London's free comedy nights.

The quality can be a little hit and miss, but who knows, you might be seeing a future star taking their first comedy steps at one of London's free comedy gigs, or a well-known headliner trying out new material. Bear in mind that although there's no entry fee, many clubs invite donations at the end of the night. Don't feel bad if you can't contribute, but if you've had a good night, why not pay what you can?

Top of our list is the **Absolutely Free Comedy Night**, MCed by the very funny Henry Ginsberg on Mondays and Thursdays at the Blue Posts (28 Rupert Street, Soho, W1D 6DJ, 8.30pm). You'll see the best new talent here, alongside circuit headliners and the occasional big TV name – in an intimate room with a super-friendly atmosphere. Also on Monday is **Set Up... Punchline Comedy Night** (Archangel, 11-13 Kensington High Street, W8 5NP, 8pm), with line-ups showcasing mostly new material from established comics, plus new comics working up their first few minutes of material. There's Saturday night comedy from the best of the

Comedy Café.

open-mic circuit, plus an experienced headliner, at the **Angel Comedy** (Camden Head, 2 Camden Walk, Islington, N1 8DY, 8pm); and the free comedy continues with **Free and Funny on Thursday** and **Free and Funny on Sunday** at the same venue. Over in Shoreditch, Wednesday night is the legendary open-mic night **Comedy Café New Act Night** (Comedy Café, *left*), where many of today's biggest names first took to the stage. The crowd can be rowdy, making it a challenging gig, but many leave the stage as heroes.

Performing Arts

Let London entertain and inspire you.

The current crop of London-based classical musicians seems unusually open-minded. There are classical nights in pubs (*see right* **Beer, Bars and Bach**) and jazz strands programmed at august classical auditoriums. Street-wise dubstep producers rub shoulders with high-minded young orchestras. But as well as this mix-and-match aesthetic, passionate purists remain – **Barbican** (*see p299*) and **Royal Festival Hall** (*see p301*) still deliver a big orchestral punch with the traditional repertoire, in addition to serving more outré interests. Even such highfalutin venues as the **Royal Opera House** (*see p302*) and **ENO** (*see p302*) have realised the value of – younger – bums on seats, and are following initiatives to bring in a new crowd.

Music, of a different stripe, dominates the West End theatre scene too: the biggest attractions remain the indomitable musicals. However, some of the old-timers have finally fallen off the perch, just as drama has been making a real comeback. A couple of these successes began life in the **National Theatre** (*see p305*), London's flagship publicly funded theatre; it celebrates its 50th anniversary in 2013. Other centres of cutting-edge excellence include the **Royal Court** (*see p306*) and the **Barbican**.

London is a hub for dance in a way few other cities can match. Stylistically, it lies somewhere between the experimental, cerebral European scene and the eye-pleasing pure dance stylings of the US, with a truly international roster of choreographers and dancers. Even the 80-year-old **Royal Ballet** (*see p311*) is now producing groundbreaking new work, thanks to resident choreographer Wayne McGregor.

Check the free *Time Out* magazine for the performing arts highlights of the week, or check out www.timeout.com for comprehensive cultural listings.

Classical Music & Opera

London's classical scene has never looked or sounded more current, with the **Southbank Centre**, the **Barbican Centre**) and **Kings Place** (*see p300*) all working with strong programmes, and youthful music directors such as Edward Gardner at the **English National Opera** keen to retain a spirit of adventure. Even the once-stuffy **Royal Opera House** now leavens its programme with occasional commissions such as Mark-Anthony Turnage's 2011 opera *Anna Nicole*, the tragic tale of a Playboy model and her ancient sugar-daddy.

Tickets & information

Tickets for most classical and opera events are available direct from the venues, online or by phone. It's advisable always to book ahead. Several venues, such as the Barbican and the Southbank Centre, operate standby schemes, offering unsold tickets at cut-rate prices just before the show.

CLASSICAL VENUES

In addition to the major venues below, you can hear what tomorrow's classical music might sound like at the city's music schools, which stage regular concerts by pupils and visiting professionals. Check the websites of the **Royal**

Beer, Bars and Bach

Classical music but without the frosty penguin suits.

The vibrancy of London's classical music scene can hardly be doubted, but when you find yourself among reverent octagenarians at some London venues, you might feel you have to be on your best behaviour. Not so at a recent Purcell concert, in the unlikely setting of an east London boozer, where a far younger audience were cajoled into drunkenly singing some of the British maestro's pub ditties – with lyrics not fit for publication in a family guidebook.

This was one of the Orchestra of the Age of Enlightenment's ongoing **Night Shift** series (www.oae.co.uk/thenightshift), where a small group of string players from the orchestra gather in the back rooms of various pubs (notably the Old Queen's Head; *see p282*) to perform such stellar composers as Mozart, Haydn and Handel. There's no attempt to shy away from difficult pieces: the professional and seriously talented performers trust to the combination of their skill and enthusiasm with the relaxed settings to win new audiences to the baroque music they love.

Night Shift isn't alone. For 'classical music in a rock 'n' roll setting', head to the 100 Club (*see p288*) where **Limelight** (www.londonlimelight.co.uk) hosts regular gigs – a mix of classical genres and eras,

performed by a mix of young up-and-comers and stars such as Danielle De Niese.

Arguably, the pioneer of this thriving informal classical scene, is one Gabriel Prokofiev, grandson of the famous Russian composer. He founded **Nonclassical** (www. nonclassical.co.uk), which has now been mixing new classical music and DJs for nearly a decade. Its main home is currently at the Macbeth (70 Hoxton Street, Hackney, N1 6LP, 7749 0600, www.themacbeth. co.uk), but check their website for events across London.

Night Shift.

Academy of Music (7873 7373, www.ram. ac.uk), the **Royal College of Music** (7591 4314, www.rcm.ac.uk), the **Guildhall School of Music & Drama** (7628 2571, www.gsmd.ac.uk) and **Trinity College of Music** (8305 4444, www.tcm.ac.uk). There's also an engaging trend for top-class classical and contemporary classical music in relaxed – for which read 'alcohol-friendly' – settings (*see above* **Beers, Bars and Bach**).

★ Barbican Centre
Silk Street, the City, EC2Y 8DS (7638 4141 information, 7638 8891 tickets, www.barbican. org.uk). Barbican tube or Moorgate tube/rail. **Box office** 10am-8pm Mon-Sat; 11am-8pm Sun. **Tickets** £7-£36. **Credit** AmEx, MC, V. **Map** p400 P5.

Europe's largest multi-arts centre is easier to navigate than ever after a renovation – although 'easier' still isn't quite the same as 'with ease', so allow a little extra time to get to your seat. The programming remains as rich as ever: the Los Angeles Philharmonic and Jazz

at Lincoln Center Orchestra returned as International Associates for the 2012/13 season, while the London Symphony Orchestra, guided by principal conductor Valery Gergiev, remains in residence. The BBC Symphony Orchestra also performs an annual series of concerts, and there's a laudable amount of contemporary classical music. Beyond classical, programming falls into a wide range of genres: from Sufi music to New York rock legends. Great free concerts too.

Cadogan Hall
5 Sloane Terrace, off Sloane Street, Chelsea, SW1X 9DQ (7730 4500, www.cadoganhall.com). Sloane Square tube. **Box office** *Non-performance days* 10am-6pm Mon-Sat. *Performance days* 10am-8pm Mon-Sat; 3-8pm Sun. **Tickets** £8-£50. **Credit** MC, V. **Map** p398 G10.

Jazz groups and rock bands have been attracted by the acoustics in this renovated former Christian Science church, but the programming at the austere yet comfortable 900-seat hall is dominated by classical. The Royal Philharmonic are resident; other orchestras also perform, and there's regular chamber music.

★ Kings Place

90 York Way, King's Cross, N1 9AG (0844 264 0321, www.kingsplace.co.uk). King's Cross tube/rail. **Box office** 10am-6pm Mon; noon-8pm Tue-Sat; noon-7pm Sun (performance days only). **Tickets** £6.50-£34.50. **Credit** MC, V. **Map** p397 L2.

Once a lone pioneer in the revival of King's Cross, Kings Place suddenly finds itself part of the King's Cross Central cultural hub. Beneath seven office floors and a ground-floor restaurant-bar (with prized seats on the canal basin outside, the 400-seat main hall is a beauty, dominated by wood carved from a single, 500-year-old oak tree and ringed by invisible rubber pads that kill unwanted noise that might interfere with the immaculate acoustic. There's also a versatile second hall and a number of smaller rooms for workshops and lectures. The programming is tremendous. It consists of mini-series on diverse, classical-dominated but hugely wide-ranging themes, among them the year-long concerts by a single composer: watch out for Bach Unwrapped in 70 instalments through 2013. Other strands include chamber music and experimental classical, as well as the prodigious Kings Place Festival each September: 100 events in three days.

LSO St Luke's

161 Old Street, the City, EC1V 9NG (7588 1116 information, 7638 8891 tickets, www.lso.co.uk/lsostlukes). Old Street tube/rail. **Box office** 10am-8pm Mon-Sat; 11am-8pm Sun. **Tickets** free-£32. **Credit** AmEx, MC, V. **Map** p400 P4.

This Grade I-listed church, built by Nicholas Hawksmoor in the 18th century, was beautifully converted into a performance and rehearsal space by the LSO several years ago. The orchestra occasionally welcomes the public for open rehearsals (book ahead); the more formal side of the programme takes in global sounds and some pop alongside classical music, including lunchtime concerts every Thursday that are broadcast on BBC Radio 3.

▶ *Intrigued by St Luke's obelisk spire? Hawksmoor also designed the brutal spike of Christ Church Spitalfields (see p124) and the mini-ziggurat atop St George's Bloomsbury (see p72).*

Royal Albert Hall

Kensington Gore, South Kensington, SW7 2AP (7589 3203 information, 0845 401 5045 tickets, www.royalalberthall.com). South Kensington tube or bus 9, 10, 52, 452. **Box office** 9am-9pm daily. **Tickets** £5-£275. **Credit** AmEx, MC, V. **Map** p395 D9.

In constant use since opening in 1871, with boxing matches, motorshows and Allen Ginsberg's 1965 International Poetry Incarnation among the headline events, the Royal Albert Hall continues to host a very broad programme. The classical side is dominated by the superb BBC Proms (*see below*), which runs every night for two months in summer and sees

Kings Place

a huge array of orchestras and other ensembles battling the difficult acoustics. It's well worth catching a concert that features the thunderous Grand Organ.

St James's Piccadilly

197 Piccadilly, Piccadilly, W1J 9LL (7381 0441, www.st-james-piccadilly.org). Piccadilly Circus tube. **Box office** 10am-6pm Mon-Sat. **Tickets** free; donations appreciated. **No credit cards. Map** p416 V4.

This community-spirited Wren church holds free lunchtime recitals (Mon, Wed, Fri at 1.10pm) and offers regular evening concerts in a variety of fields.

St John's, Smith Square

Smith Square, Westminster, SW1P 3HA (7222 1061, www.sjss.org.uk). Westminster tube. **Box office** 10am-5pm Mon-Fri. **Tickets** £5-£50. **Credit** MC, V. **Map** p399 K10.

This curiously shaped 18th-century church – it is said the four-turret design was the result of Queen Anne's demand that architect Thomas Archer make it look like a footstool that she had kicked over – hosts concerts more or less nightly, with everything from symphony orchestras to solo recitals making the most of good acoustics. Down in the crypt are two bars for interval drinks and the Smith Square Bar & Restaurant.

St Martin-in-the-Fields

Trafalgar Square, Westminster, WC2N 4JJ (7766 1100, www.stmartin-in-the-fields.org). Charing Cross tube/rail. **Box office** *In person* 10am-5pm Mon, Tue; 10am-9pm Wed; 10am-8.30pm Thur-Sat. *By phone* 10am-5pm Mon-Sat. **Tickets** free-£28. **Credit** MC, V. **Map** p416 X4.

This church is one of the capital's most amiable and populist venues, hosting performances of the likes of Bach, Mozart and Vivaldi by candlelight, jazz in the crypt's improved café and lunchtime recitals (Mon, Wed, Fri) from young musicians. There's a fine atmosphere in the beautifully restored interior.
▶ *For more on the church, see p98.*

★ Southbank Centre

Belvedere Road, South Bank, SE1 8XX (7960 4200 information, 0844 875 0073 tickets, www.southbankcentre.co.uk). Embankment tube or Waterloo tube/rail. **Box office** *In person* 10am-8pm daily. *By phone* 9am-8pm daily. **Tickets** £7-£75. **Credit** AmEx, MC, V. **Map** p399 M8.

The centrepiece of the cluster of cultural venues collectively known as the Southbank Centre is the 3,000-seater Royal Festival Hall, which was renovated acoustically and externally to the tune of £90m back in 2007; now the neighbouring 900-seat Queen Elizabeth Hall and attached 365-seat Purcell Room are due a little TLC – the Arts Council has promised £3.3m towards refurbishment. All three programme a wide variety of events – spoken word, jazz, rock and pop gigs – but classical is very well represented. The RFH has four resident orchestras (the London Philharmonic and Philharmonia Orchestras, the London Sinfonietta and the Orchestra of the Age of Enlightenment), and hosts music from medieval motets to Messiaen via Beethoven and Elgar. Beneath this main hall, facing the main bar, the foyer stage puts on hundreds of free concerts each year.
▶ *For the Hayward Gallery, third leg of the Southbank Centre's tripod, see p39.*

★ Wigmore Hall

36 Wigmore Street, Marylebone, W1U 2BP (7935 2141, www.wigmore-hall.org.uk). Bond Street tube. **Box office** *In person* 10am-8.30pm daily. *By phone* 10am-7pm daily. **Tickets** £10-£75. **Credit** AmEx, DC, MC, V. **Map** p396 G6.

Built in 1901 as the display hall for Bechstein pianos, this world-renowned, 550-seat concert venue has perfect acoustics for the 400 concerts that take place each year. Music from the classical and romantic periods are mainstays, usually performed by major classical stars to an intense audience, but under artistic director John Gilhooly there has been a broadening in the remit: more baroque and increased jazz (Joshua Redman is curating the Jazz Series), including late-night gigs. Monday lunchtime recitals are broadcast live on BBC Radio 3.

OPERA VENUES

In addition to the two big venues below, look out for performances at the **Linbury Studio**, downstairs at the Royal Opera House, **Cadogan Hall** (*see p299*), summer's **Opera Holland Park** (*see p300* **Festivals**), sporadic

ARTS & ENTERTAINMENT

appearances by **English Touring Opera** (www.englishtouringopera.org.uk) and much promising work, often directed by big names, at the city's music schools. A small but lively fringe opera scene has sprung up with the annual **Tête-à-Tête Opera Festival** (*see p300* **Festivals**), **OperaUpClose** branching out from its King's Head Theatre base in Islington (www.kingsheadtheatre.com) to play up west at the Soho and Charing Cross Theatres; and the **Charles Court Opera** company doing fine operetta at its Rosemary Branch home on Shepperton Road (www.charlescourtopera.com).

English National Opera, Coliseum

St Martin's Lane, Covent Garden, WC2N 4ES (0871 911 0200 tickets, www.eno.org). Leicester Square tube or Charing Cross tube/rail. **Box office** *In person* 10am-6pm Mon-Sat. *By phone* 24hrs daily. **Tickets** £19-£99. **Credit** AmEx, MC, V. **Map** p416 X4.

Built as a music hall in 1904, the home of the English National Opera (ENO) is in fine condition following a renovation in 2004. And after a shaky period several years ago, ENO itself is in solid shape under the youthful stewardship of music director Edward Gardner, with the last few years having offered some fascinating collaborations (such as with physical theatre troupe Complicité and Blur's Damon Albarn on *Doctor Dee*) and rare contemporary works (a flamboyant version of Ligeti's *Le Grand Macabre*), but his 'Undress for the Opera', encouraging new, younger audience members to attend some classic operas in their everyday clothes, may be the boldest initiative yet. All works are in English, and prices are cheaper than at the Royal Opera.

★ Royal Opera, Royal Opera House

Covent Garden, WC2E 9DD (7304 4000, www.roh.org.uk). Covent Garden tube. **Box office** 10am-8pm Mon-Sat. **Tickets** £10-£210. **Credit** AmEx, MC, V. **Map** p416 Z3.

Thanks to a refurbishment at the start of the century, the Royal Opera House has once again taken its place among the ranks of the world's great opera houses. Critics sometimes suggest that the programming can be a little spotty, especially so given the famously elevated ticket prices, but we applaud chief executive Tony Hall's attempts to win a new audiences (*Anna Nicole* by Mark-Anthony Turnage is not alone in this regard – although new works by the likes of Thomas Adès were more widely welcomed by the serious-minded). The spine of the programme is, of course, fine productions of the classics, often taking place under the baton of Antonio Pappano. Productions take in favourite composers (Donizetti, Mozart, Verdi) and some modern (Benjamin Britten, Harrison Birtwistle).

▶ *It's not just music at the Opera House. The Royal Ballet is also based here; see p312.*

Theatre

The West End has managed to ride out the recession on a tide of song – in other words, those big-production musicals, the most ancient of which had been hoofing it on the London stage since the late 1980s. But a hint of change is afoot: *Blood Brothers* – the aforementioned old-timer – closed in October 2012, after 24 years; *Chicago*'s gone; *Shrek* is closing in February 2013; *Ghost* has gone too. That's not to say there's no more musical fun to be had. In fact, a bunch of lively, thoroughly modern new musicals is arriving on the London stage; *see p303* **Mormons, Chocolate & Computer Geeks**.

The good news is that as some of the musicals sing their last, drama is making a very real comeback. In 2011 a record 3,784,975 play tickets were sold in the West End, with the way led by the colossal success of National Theatre transfers *War Horse* and *One Man Two Guvnors* and the Royal Court's titanic *Jerusalem*.

The **Donmar Warehouse** (*see p310*) traditionally lures high-profile film stars to perform at its tiny Earlham Street home, while appearances by Kevin Spacey and his stellar chums at the **Old Vic** (*see p305*) have put bums on seats there.

On a smaller scale, Off-West End houses such as the **Young Vic** (*see p312*) and the **BAC** (*see p311*) continue to produce some of London's most exciting, best-value theatre. The **Haymarket** continues its unique practice of operating as a producing house: Trevor Nunn's season was remarkable for top-notch revivals of plays by Tom Stoppard and Terence Rattigan. The **Barbican Centre** (*see p306*), continues to programme visually exciting and physically expressive work from around the world.

THEATRE DISTRICTS

In strictly geographical terms, the **West End** refers to London's traditional theatre district, a busy area bounded by Shaftesbury Avenue, Drury Lane, the Strand and the Haymarket. Most major musicals and big-money dramas run here, alongside transfers of successful smaller-scale shows. However, the 'West End' appellation is now also applied to other major theatres elsewhere in town, including subsidised venues such as the Barbican Centre (in the City), the National Theatre (on the South Bank) and the Old Vic (near Waterloo).

Off-West End denotes theatres with smaller budgets and smaller capacities. These venues, many of them sponsored or subsidised, push the creative envelope with new writing, often brought to life by the best young acting and directing talent. The Bush is good for up-and-coming writers, while the Almeida and Donmar Warehouse offer elegantly produced shows with the occasional big star.

THE FRINGE

The best places to catch next-generation talent include Battersea's **Theatre 503**, above the Latchmere pub (503 Battersea Park Road, SW11 3BW, 7978 7040, www.theatre503.com), which recently won a Peter Brook Empty Space award for its work with new writers. The theatre above the **Finborough** (118 Finborough Road, SW10 9ED, 7244 7439, www.finboroughtheatre.co.uk), a pub in Earl's Court, attracts national critics with its small but perfectly formed revivals of forgotten classics.

Other venues that are worth investigating include the excellent **Arcola Theatre** (24 Ashwin Street, Dalston, E8 3DL, 7503 1646, www.arcolatheatre.com), a former paint factory with bags of bohemian appeal; the **Southwark Playhouse** (Shipwright Yard, corner of Tooley

Mormons, Chocolate & Computer Geeks

Sharp new musicals, and a revival of a classic, are hitting the West End.

While some of London's dinosaur musicals are finally singing their last (*Blood Brothers*, the granddaddy of them all, has closed after 24 years), there's a refreshing new crop of luscious, thoroughly modern musicals setting the agenda in the West End.

Sam Mendes' new musical adaptation of *Charlie and the Chocolate Factory* is taking the place of *Shrek* at the Theatre Royal Drury Lane (Catherine Street, WC2B 5JF, 020 7492 9930). Another Roald Dahl adaptation, it follows the lead of award-winning *Matilda the Musical* (*see p308*). Meanwhile, computer nerds make their West End debut over at the Garrick (2 Charing Cross Road, WC2H 0HH, 0844 482 9673) with *Loserville*, a geek-tastic new British musical by Elliot Davis and James Bourne. And the long-mooted Spice Girls' musical, *Viva Forever!*, written by Jennifer Saunders, finally makes its debut at the Piccadilly Theatre (4 Denman Street, W1D 7DY, 0844 871 7618) at the end of November 2012.

Very different in tone is the return of Kander and Ebb's unsettling *Cabaret*, revived in 2006 and recast for 2012, with Will Young as the enigmatic MC of the Kit Kat Club in the last days of the Weimar Republic. It's playing at the Savoy (Savoy Court, the Strand, WC2R 0ET, 0844 871 7627).

Perhaps the most heralded arrival of, though, is the Broadway smash *The Book of Mormon*, by South Park creators Trey Parker and Matt Stone, opening at the Prince of Wales (Coventry Street, W1D 6AS, 0844 482 5115) on 25 February 2013. It tells the story of mismatched but equally clueless Mormon missionaries – one a narcissistic overachiever and one a misfit – posted to Uganda. They discover that the country is nothing like the Africa of their imaginations. 'Africa is nothing like *The Lion King*! I think that movie took a lot of artistic licence!', complains one on arrival. Part buddy story, part tale of how trying to fix things in other countries doesn't always work, this whip-smart show has won nine Tony awards in the US, so tickets for the London production will be pretty hot.

Bags packed, milk cancelled, house raised on stilts.

You've packed the suntan lotion, the snorkel set, the stay-pressed shirts. Just one more thing left to do – your bit for climate change. In some of the world's poorest countries, changing weather patterns are destroying lives.

You can help people to deal with the extreme effects of climate change. Raising houses in flood-prone regions is just one life-saving solution.

**Climate change costs lives.
Give £5 and let's sort it *Here & Now***

www.oxfam.org.uk/climate-change

Be Humankind Oxfam

Street & Bermondsey Street, Southwark, SE1 2TF, 7407 0234, www.southwark playhouse.co.uk), housed in refurbished railway arches at London Bridge; and the nearby **Menier Chocolate Factory** (53 Southwark Street, Southwark, SE1 1RU, 7378 1713, www.menierchocolatefactory.com), which, like the **Union Theatre** (204 Union Street, Southwark, SE1 0LX, 7261 9876, www.uniontheatre.biz) has a knack for musicals up-close.

BUYING TICKETS

If there's a specific show you want to see, aim to book ahead. And, if possible, always try to do so at the theatre's box office, at which booking fees are generally smaller than they are with agents such as Ticketmaster (*see p230*). Shop around: different agencies offer different ticket prices and discounts.

If you're more flexible about your choice of show, consider buying from one of the **Tkts** booths or taking your chances with standby seats (for both, *see p309* **Inside Track**).

THE WEST END
Major theatres

Barbican Centre

For listings, *see p299.*

The annual BITE (Barbican International Theatre Events) season continues to cherry-pick exciting and eclectic theatre companies from around the globe. Programme highlights in 2012 included new works by Ninagawa Company and You Me Bum Bum Train. Following a sold-out season of Complicite's latest production, Mikhail Bulgakov's *The Master and Margarita*, the play returns for a limited run from 14 December 2012 to 19 January 2013. Watch out, too, for imaginatively leftfield family-friendly theatre and installations during school holidays.

★ National Theatre

South Bank, SE1 9PX (information 7452 3400, tickets 7452 3000, www.nationaltheatre.org.uk). Embankment or Southwark tube, or Waterloo tube/rail. **Box office** 9.30am-8pm Mon-Sat. **Tickets** *Olivier & Lyttelton* £12-£47. *Cottesloe* £12-£32. **Credit** AmEx, MC, V. **Map** p399 M8.

This concrete monster is the flagship venue of British theatre, and no theatrical tour of London is complete without a visit. Three auditoriums allow for different kinds of performance: in-the-round, promenade, even classic proscenium arch. Nicholas Hytner's artistic directorship, with landmark successes such as Alan Bennett's *The History Boys,* has shown that the state-subsidised home of British theatre can turn out quality drama at a profit. Among the 2013 productions are Maxim Gorky's *Children*

Festivals Theatre
What not to miss this year.

The **Greenwich+Docklands International Festival** (www.festival.org) combines acrobatics, dance and theatre, with aerial performances and fireworks over the Queen's House and in Woolwich. Expect eye-catching stunts at this year's free street art and outdoor theatre spectacular, held over ten days from late June. At around the same time of year, **LIFT** (the **London International Festival of Theatre**; www.liftfest.org.uk) gathers an extraordinary number of performances (last year, nearly 90 in under a month) under the directorship of Mark Ball.

In July and August, the National Theatre (*see p305*) rolls out a large square of astroturf by the river for **Watch This Space** (www.nationaltheatre.org.uk), a programme of alfresco theatre, dance and circus. Also during the month of August, an eclectic bunch of new, experimental and short shows sprint through the **Camden Fringe** (www.camdenfringe.org). Finally, more outré and challenging work can be seen at January's **London International Mime Festival** (www.mimefest.co.uk), from haunting visual theatre to puppetry for adults.

---

of the Sun (running Jan-Apr), directed by Howard Davies, and *Othello*, directed by Nicholas Hytner, with Adrian Lester as Othello and Rory Kinnear as Iago (Apr-June). The Travelex season ensures a widening audience by offering tickets for £12, £20 and £30, as does the free outdoor performing arts stage, Watch This Space, every summer. The National celebrates its 50th birthday in 2013; *see p306* **Inside Track**.

★ Old Vic

The Cut, Waterloo, SE1 8NB (0844 871 7628, www.oldvictheatre.com). Southwark tube or Waterloo tube/rail. **Box office** *In person* 10am-7pm Mon-Sat. *By phone* 9am-10pm Mon-Sat; 10am-8pm Sun. **Tickets** £10-£49.50. **Credit** AmEx, MC, V. **Map** p402 N9.

Oscar-winner Kevin Spacey has been the artistic director here since 2003, and the theatre continues to have commercial success; plays are sometimes a critical hit as well, especially when Spacey himself or one of his stellar Hollywood chums takes to the stage. The Old Vic is a beautiful venue, where programming runs from grown-up Christmas pantomimes to serious drama: *Hedda Gabler* won rave reviews in 2012. Broadway classic *Kiss Me Kate*,

Open Air Theatre.

directed by Trevor Nunn, runs from September 2012 until 2 March 2013.

▶ *From early 2010, the theatre has been operating an informal space in the arches beneath Waterloo Station. The Old Vic Tunnels has hosted everything from immersive theatre to an 'audio project' by genius graphic novelist Alan Moore.*

Open Air Theatre

Regent's Park, Inner Circle, Marylebone, NW1 4NR (0844 826 4242, www.openairtheatre.org). Baker Street tube. **Tickets** £22-£42.50. **Credit** AmEx, MC, V. **Map** p396 G3.

The verdant setting of this alfresco theatre lends itself perfectly to summery Shakespeare romps – A *Midsummer Night's Dream* is a regular here. In the pipeline for summer 2013 are *The Sound of Music* (25 July-7 Sept) and *To Kill a Mockingbird* (16 May-15 June).

▶ *If you don't want to bring a picnic, good-value, tasty food can be bought at the Garden Café; or plump for traditional tea or Pimm's on the lawn.*

★ Royal Court Theatre

Sloane Square, Chelsea, SW1W 8AS (7565 5000, www.royalcourttheatre.com). Sloane Square tube. **Box office** 10am-6pm Mon-Sat. **Tickets** £10-£28. **Credit** AmEx, MC, V. **Map** p398 G11.

From John Osborne's *Look Back in Anger*, staged in the theatre's opening year of 1956, to the numerous discoveries of the past decade, among them Sarah Kane, Joe Penhall and Conor McPherson, the emphasis at the Royal Court has always been on new voices in British theatre. Artistic director Dominic Cooke has injected plenty of politics into the programme, and successfully lowered the age of his audiences in the process. Expect to find rude, lyrical new work by first-time playwrights, as well as better established American and European writers with a message. Look out for quality shorts and more of the usual vividly produced British and international work by young writers.

Royal Shakespeare Company

Information 01789 403444, tickets 0844 800 1110, www.rsc.org.uk. **Box office** By phone 10am-6pm Mon-Sat. **Tickets** £5-£60. **Credit** AmEx, MC, V.

Britain's flagship company hasn't had a London base since it quit the Barbican in 2002, although it is turning its mind towards finding one now the £100m redevelopment of its home theatres in

---

INSIDE TRACK
NATIONAL THEATRE AT 50

The National – Britain's most prominent publicly funded theatre – celebrates its 50th anniversary in 2013. Since the 1970s it has occupied a purpose-built, once-controversial, Brutalist building that's part of the South Bank complex. An ambitious refurbishment project is now in the pipeline. Costing £70m, the work should result in what National Theatre director Nicholas Hytner describes as 'a dramatic opening up and renewal of Denys Lasdun's 1970s building'. The changes should make the theatre more visible, with a new main entrance. New dedicated learning spaces and a backstage viewing gallery are also planned.

Stratford-upon-Avon has reached completion. In the meantime, it continues its itinerant existence, now usually appearing for three months from December in the Roundhouse (*see p288*), as well as popping up in smaller venues to stage new plays. In 2012, *Much Ado About Nothing* was staged at the Nöel Coward theatre, in an Indian setting.

Shakespeare's Globe

21 New Globe Walk, Bankside, SE1 9DT (7401 9919, www.shakespeares-globe.org). Southwark tube or London Bridge tube/rail. **Box office** *In person* 10am-8pm Mon-Sat; 10am-7pm Sun. *By phone* 10am-5pm Mon-Sat; 10am-4pm Sun. **Tickets** £5-£35. **Credit** AmEx, MC, V. **Map** p402 O7.

Sam Wanamaker's dream to recreate the theatre where Shakespeare first staged many of his plays has become a successful reality, perhaps reaching its peak with the 2012 Globe to Globe Festival: 85,000 tickets were sold for an ambitious six-week marathon of Shakespeare plays by international casts. Comedy is usually what the Globe does best, but the venue's been on great form for a while under Dominic Dromgoole, with the Shakespeare classics paralleled by new plays on similar themes. The open-air, standing-room Pit tickets are excellent value, if a little marred by low-flying aircraft. Watch out for the Globe's new 320-seater Indoor Jacobean Theatre, due to open in late 2013. For tours, *see p42*.

Long-runners & musicals

For more on new and revival musicals coming to the London stage, *see p303* **Mormons, Chocolate & Computer Geeks**.

★ Billy Elliot the Musical

Victoria Palace Theatre, Victoria Street, Victoria, SW1E 5EA (0844 248 5000, 7834 1317, www. billyelliotthemusical.com). Victoria tube/rail. **Box office** 10am-8.30pm Mon-Sat. **Tickets** £19.50-£95. **Credit** AmEx, MC, V. **Map** p398 H10.

The combination of Elton John's music and a heart-melting yarn about a northern working-class lad with an unlikely talent for ballet has scooped more awards internationally than any other British musical and launched the careers of dozens of young Billies. It's an uplifting, humane night at the theatre.

Jersey Boys

Prince Edward Theatre, 28 Old Compton Street, Soho, W1D 4HS (0844 482 5151, www.jerseyboyslondon.com). Leicester Square tube. **Box office** *In person* 10am-7.45pm Tue-Sun. *By phone* 24hrs daily. **Tickets** £20-£95. **Credit** AmEx, MC, V. **Map** p416 W2.

This Broadway import had the critics singing the praises of Ryan Molloy, who hits the high notes in Frankie Valli & the Four Seasons' doo-wop standards. The well-trodden storyline of early struggle, success and break-up is elevated by pacy direction.

ARTS & ENTERTAINMENT

Shakespeare's Globe.

Wilton's Music Hall. See p311.

Les Misérables
Queen's Theatre, 51 Shaftesbury Avenue, Soho, W1D 6BA (0844 482 5160, www.lesmis.com). Leicester Square or Piccadilly Circus tube. **Box office** *In person* 9am-8pm Mon-Sat. *By phone* 10am-8pm Mon-Sat. **Tickets** £20-£85. **Credit** AmEx, MC, V. **Map** p416 W3.
The RSC's version of Boublil and Schönberg's musical first came to the London stage in 1985 – and no fewer than three celebratory versions ran simultaneously on one October night in 2010. The version currently at the Queen's should manage a few more anniversaries, which has good and bad consequences. When actors have been singing these songs since their first audition, it's easy to take it that half-inch too far. Still, the voices remain lush, the revolutionary sets are film-fabulous, and the lyrics and score (based on Victor Hugo's novel) will be considerably less trivial than whatever's on next door.

★ Matilda the Musical
Cambridge Theatre, 32-34 Earlham Street, Covent Garden, WC2H 9HU (0844 800 1110, www.matildathemusical.com). Covent Garden tube or Charing Cross tube/rail. **Box office** *In person* 10am-8pm daily. *By phone* 10am-6pm Mon-Sat. **Tickets** £20-£62.50. **Credit** AmEx, MC, V. **Map** p397 L6.
Adapted from Roald Dahl's riotous children's novel, with songs by superstar Aussie comedian Tim Minchin, this RSC transfer received rapturous reviews on its first outing in Stratford-upon-Avon and has been going strong ever since, winning multiple Olivier awards.

Mousetrap
St Martin's Theatre, West Street, Cambridge Circus, Covent Garden, WC2H 9NZ (0844 499 1515, www.the-mousetrap.co.uk). Leicester Square tube. **Box office** 10am-8pm Mon-Sat. **Tickets** £16-£60. **Credit** AmEx, MC, V. **Map** p416 X3.
Running in the West End since 1952, Agatha Christie's drawing-room whodunnit is a murder mystery Methuselah, and will probably still be booking when the last trump sounds.

★ One Man Two Guvnors
Theatre Royal Haymarket, 18 Suffolk Street, Covent Garden, SW1Y 4HT (0845 481 1870, www.onemantwoguvnors.com). Charing Cross tube/rail. **Box office** *In person* 10am-7pm Mon-Sat. *By phone* 24hrs daily. **Tickets** £15-£55. **Credit** AmEx, MC, V. **Map** p426 W5.
A new cast has moved into Richard Bean's uproarious update of *A Servant to Two Masters* without loss. As hapless hero Francis Henshall, James Corden's proudly Welsh former understudy Owain Arthur is a proper old-school star, with shades of Oliver Hardy and George Formby.

ARTS & ENTERTAINMENT

Young Vic. *See p311.*

Singin' in the Rain
Palace Theatre, Shaftesbury Avenue, Soho, W1D 5AY (0844 412 4656, ww.singinintherain.co.uk). Leicester Square or Piccadilly Circus tube. **Box office** *In person* 10am-8pm Mon-Sat. **By phone** 24hrs daily. **Tickets** £15-£65. **Credit** AmEx, MC, V. **Map** p416 X3.

Jonathan Church's exuberant production looks back to the 1952 film, which itself looks back to 1927, when flappers, film stars and aviators were partying like there was no tomorrow. Katherine Kingsley revels in her role as obsolete silent film actress Lina Lamont. As Don Lockwood, her reluctant on-screen lover, dance star Adam Cooper manages to steer the right course between smooth and narcissistically slimy.

★ War Horse
New London Theatre, Drury Lane, Covent Garden, WC2B 5PW (0844 412 4654, www.nationaltheatre.org.uk/warhorse). Covent Garden tube. **Box office** *In person* 10am-8pm Mon-Sat. *By phone* 24hrs daily. **Tickets** £15-£55. **Credit** AmEx, MC, V. **Map** p416 Z2.

Transferred from the National Theatre, *War Horse* is an incredibly moving piece of theatre (and a massive critical and popular hit). The play is based on Michael Morpurgo's children's novel about a horse separated from his young master and spirited off to World War I. Bereft Albert duly signs up, to seek Joey in the mud and carnage of the Flanders front. The real stars are the extraordinary puppet horses. Each visibly manipulated by three actors, who make them gallop, pant and emote as clearly as any human actor, these plywood and leather frames become astonishingly expressive beasts.

OFF-WEST END THEATRES

Almeida
Almeida Street, Islington, N1 1TA (7359 4404, www.almeida.co.uk). Angel tube. **Box office** *In person* 10am-6pm Mon-Sat. *By phone* 10am-7.30pm Mon-Sat. **Tickets** £8-£32. **Credit** AmEx, MC, V. **Map** p400 O1.

Well groomed and with a rather funky bar, the Almeida turns out thoughtfully crafted theatre for grown-ups. In October 2012, artistic director Michael Attenborough announced he was stepping down after 11 years in the job. He has drawn top directors such as Thea Sharrock and Rupert Goold, and premières from Neil LaBute. Notable shows in recent years have included *Hedda Gabler*, David Eldridge's 2004 adaptation of *Festen* and 2011's staging of Edward Albee's *A Delicate Balance*. Nick Dear's new play, *The Dark Earth and the Light Sky*, about the life of poet Edward Thomas, runs 8 November 2012 to 12 January 2013.

ARTS & ENTERTAINMENT

Royal Ballet.

★ Battersea Arts Centre (BAC)

Lavender Hill, Battersea, SW11 5TN (7223 2223, www.bac.org.uk). Clapham Common tube, Clapham Junction rail or bus 77, 77A, 345. **Box office** *In person & by phone 10am-6pm Mon-Fri; 3-6pm Sat.* **Tickets** £3-£10; pay what you can Thur-Sat (phone ahead). **Credit** MC, V.

Housed in the old Battersea Town Hall, the forward-thinking BAC hosts young theatre troupes; expect quirky, fun and physical theatre from the likes of cult companies Kneehigh and 1927. In December 2012, International innovators Forced Entertainment brought their successful show *The Coming Storm*, with tangled multiple stories creating an unsettling whole, to the theatre.

★ Bush

Shepherd's Bush Green, 7 Uxbridge Road, Shepherd's Bush, W12 8LJ (8743 5050, www.bushtheatre.co.uk). Shepherd's Bush Market tube. **Box office** *In person & by phone noon-7.30pm Mon-Sat (performance days); noon-8pm Mon-Fri (non-performance days).* **Tickets** £10-£19.50. **Credit** AmEx, MC, V.

This diminutive venue punches well above its weight, with well-designed productions and an impressive record of West End transfers. It's famous for its new writers; among the alumni are Stephen Poliakoff and David Edgar.

★ Donmar Warehouse

41 Earlham Street, Covent Garden, WC2H 9LX (0844 871 7624, www.donmarwarehouse.com). Covent Garden or Leicester Square tube. **Box office** *In person 10am-6pm Mon-Sat. By phone 9am-10pm Mon-Sat; 10am-8pm Sun.* **Tickets** £12-£30. **Credit** AmEx, MC, V. **Map** p416 Y2.

The Donmar is less a warehouse than a boutique chamber. Multi-award-winning artistic director Michael Grandage kept the venue on the fresh, intelligent path established by Sam Mendes, and his successor, Josie Rourke, is continuing the good work. The Donmar's combination of artistic integrity and intimate size, with audience right alongside the stage, has proved hard to resist, with many high-profile film actors appearing: among them Nicole Kidman, Gwyneth Paltrow and Ewan McGregor.

Gate Theatre

Prince Albert, 11 Pembridge Road, Notting Hill, W11 3HQ (7229 0706, www.gatetheatre.co.uk). Notting Hill Gate tube. **Box office** *By phone 10am-6pm Mon-Fri. In person 6.30-7.30pm Mon-Fri; 2-3pm, 6.30-7.30pm Sat.* **Tickets** £20; £15 reductions. **Credit** MC, V. **Map** p404 Z6.

A doll's house of a theatre, with rickety wooden chairs as seats, the Gate is the only producing theatre in London dedicated to international work.

★ Lyric Hammersmith

Lyric Square, King Street, Hammersmith, W6 0QL (8741 6850, www.lyric.co.uk). Hammersmith tube. **Box office** *By phone 10am-5.30pm Mon-Sat. In person 9.30am-7.30pm on performance days.* **Tickets** £12.50-£35. **Credit** MC, V.

Artistic director Sean Holmes launched his tenure in 2009 with a pledge to bring writers back into the building, making space for neglected modern classics and new plays alongside the cutting-edge physical and devised work for which the Lyric is known.

Soho Theatre

21 Dean Street, Soho, W1D 3NE (7478 0100, www.sohotheatre.com). Tottenham Court Road tube. **Box office** *In person* 10am-6pm Mon-Sat; 10am-7.30pm performance nights. *By phone* 10am-10pm Mon-Sat. **Tickets** £5-£37.50. **Credit** MC, V. **Map** p395 K6.

Its cool blue neon lights and front-of-house café help it blend it into the Soho landscape, but this theatre has made a name for itself since opening in 2000. It attracts a young, hip crowd and plays very effectively to the theatre/comedy/cabaret crossover scene.

▶ *For comedy at the Soho, see p297.*

Theatre Royal Stratford East
Gerry Raffles Square, Stratford, E15 1BN (8534 0310, www.stratfordeast.com). Stratford tube/rail/DLR. **Box office** *In person & by phone* 10am-6pm Mon-Sat. **Tickets** £5-£24. **Credit** MC, V.

The Theatre Royal Stratford East is a community theatre, with many shows written, directed and performed by black or Asian artists. Musicals are big here – *The Harder They Come* went on to West End success – but there is also a Christmas pantomime and harder-hitting fare.

★ Tricycle
269 Kilburn High Road, Kilburn, NW6 7JR (information 7372 6611, tickets 7328 1000, www.tricycle.co.uk). Kilburn tube. **Box office** *In person & by phone* 10am-9pm Mon-Sat; 2-8pm Sun. **Tickets** £5-£28. **Credit** MC, V.

Passionate and political, the Tricycle consistently finds original ways into difficult subjects. It has pioneered its own genre of 'tribunal' docu-dramas.

★ Wilton's Music Hall
Graces Alley, off Ensign Street, Whitechapel, E1 8JB (7702 2789, www.wiltons.org.uk). Aldgate East or Tower Hill tube. **Box office** 10am-6pm Mon-Fri. **Tickets** £10-£25. **Credit** MC, V. **Map** p403 S7.

London's last surviving example of the giant pub halls that flourished in the mid 19th century, Wilton's Music Hall once entertained the masses with acts ranging from Chinese performing monkeys to acrobats, contortionists to opera singers. It was here that Victorian music hall star George Leybourne made his name in character as Champagne Charlie, and that the can-can first scandalised London. Roughly 150 years after opening, Wilton's still serves as a theatre, offering an atmospheric stage for everything from situation-specific Bach to immersive theatre to magic. *Photo p208.*

★ Young Vic
66 The Cut, Waterloo, SE1 8LZ (7922 2922, www.youngvic.org). Waterloo tube/rail. **Box office** 10am-6pm Mon-Sat. **Tickets** £10-£32.50. **Credit** MC, V. **Map** p402 N8.

As the name suggests, this Vic (actually now in its forties) has more youthful bravura than its older sis-

Festivals Dance
What to see, when.

London's three general dance festivals are the well-established **Dance Umbrella** (Oct, www.danceumbrella.co.uk, multiple venues) and the Place's **Resolution!** festival (Jan-Feb, www.theplace.org.uk), staging the work of young choreographers, and the **Place Prize** (biennial in even years, Sept, www.theplaceprize.com) choreography competition. Niche festivals include the four-day, Thames-side **London International Tango Festival** (Nov, www.tangoinlondon.com), the **Flamenco Festival** (Feb, www.sadlerswells.com) and hip hop weekend **Breakin' Convention** (May, www.breakinconvention.com).

ter up the road, and draws a younger crowd, who pack out the open-air balcony at its popular restaurant and bar on the weekends. They come to see European classics with a modern edge, new writing with an international flavour and collaborations with leading companies. *Photo p309.*

Dance

There are two long-established classical dance companies. The **Royal Ballet**, founded in 1931 and resident at the Royal Opera House (*see p302*), is a company of global stature, whose 100 or so dancers include such global guest stars as Carlos Acosta. The only slightly less prestigious **English National Ballet** is a touring company, founded in 1950, that performs most often at the Coliseum (*see below*) and, for the regular *Swan Lake* 'in the round', at the **Royal Albert Hall** (*see p300*). Its principals include Londoner Begoña Cao.

MAJOR VENUES

Barbican Centre
For listings, see p299.
Conceived in the 1960s and completed in 1982, the Barbican attracts and nurtures experimental dance, especially in the perfectly intimate Pit Theatre. The year-round Barbican International Theatre Events series (BITE; www.barbican.org.uk/theatre) offers plenty of noteworthy dance performances.

Coliseum
For listings, see p302.
Once a music hall, the Coliseum is in fine condition following a renovation in 2004. The English National

ARTS & ENTERTAINMENT

Ballet performs here when it's in town, along with the likes of the Peter Schaufuss Ballet.

★ The Place
17 Duke's Road, Bloomsbury, WC1H 9PY (7121 1100, www.theplace.org.uk). Euston tube/rail. **Box office** *In person & by phone* 10am-6pm Mon-Sat; 10am-8pm on performance days. **Tickets** £9-£20. **Credit** MC, V. **Map** p399 K3.
For genuinely emerging dance, look to the Place. The theatre is behind the biennial Place Prize for choreography, which rewards the best in British contemporary dance as well as regular seasons of new work such as Resolution! (short works; Jan/Feb) and Spring Loaded (Apr/May).

★ Royal Opera House
For listings, see p302.
For the full ballet experience, nothing beats the Royal Opera House, home of the Royal Ballet. The current incarnation of the building is an appropriately grand space in which to see dreamy ballerinas including Alina Cojocaru and Tamara Rojo. There's edgier fare in the Linbury Studio Theatre and the Clore Studio Upstairs. Royal Ballet in Rehearsal sessions offer a rare – and thrillingly close-up – glimpse behind the scenes. The 90-minute sessions are held in the Linbury Studio Theatre or the Clore Studio Upstairs, with capacities of 400 and 170 respectively. This is ballet at its most stripped down: no sets, no exquisite costumes and no grand stage. Instead, there's just the piano, the squeak of shoes on the scuffed grey floor, and the intense concentration of the dancers. The casting is generally only revealed on the night, and the old hands eagerly scan the programme to find out who will be rehearsing.

★ Sadler's Wells
Rosebery Avenue, Finsbury, EC1R 4TN (0844 412 4300, www.sadlerswells.com). Angel tube. **Box office** *In person & by phone* 10am-8pm Mon-Sat. **Tickets** £10-£60. **Credit** AmEx, MC, V. **Map** p402 N3.
Purpose-built in 1998 on the site of a 17th-century theatre of the same name, this dazzling complex is home to impressive local and international performances. The Lilian Baylis Studio offers smaller-scale new works and works-in-progress, and the Peacock Theatre (on Portugal Street in Holborn) operates as a satellite venue.

Siobhan Davies Dance Studios
85 St George's Road, Southwark, SE1 6ER (7091 9650, www.siobhandavies.com). Elephant & Castle tube/rail. **Box office** 10am-6pm Mon-Fri; 10am-5pm Sat, Sun (varies). **Tickets** £3-£10. **Credit** MC, V. **Map** p402 N10.
This award-winning studio was designed in consultation with dancers, ensuring it met their needs. As well as being home to Davies's own company,

the studio hosts talks and performances at the more experimental end of the scale. The performance programme is sporadic: it's best to check details before setting out.

Southbank Centre
For listings, see p301.
From international contemporary dance to hip hop to physical theatre to South Asian dance, there's an eclectic programme at the cluster venues collectively known as the Southbank Centre: the mammoth RFH, the medium-sized Queen Elizabeth Hall, the intimate Purcell Room and the riverside terrace.

OTHER VENUES

Blue Elephant
59A Bethwin Road, Camberwell, SE5 0XT (7701 0100, 0844 477 1000 tickets, www.blue elephanttheatre.co.uk). Oval tube. **Box office** *In person* 1hr before performance. *By phone* 24hrs. **Tickets** free-£16.50. **No credit cards.**
Hidden away in south London, the Blue Elephant Theatre is a little off the beaten path but it hosts occasional contemporary dance performances alongside its programme of theatre and other performance.

Greenwich Dance
Borough Hall, Royal Hill, Greenwich, SE10 8RE (8293 9741, www.greenwichdance.org.uk). Greenwich DLR/rail. **Box Office** 9.30am-9pm Mon-Thur; 9.30am-5.30pm Fri; 10am-3pm Sat. **Tickets** free-£15. **Credit** MC, V. **Map** p405 X2.
This art deco venue in Greenwich hosts classes and workshops and a regular tea dance, as well as unique cabaret nights, which deliver entertaining dance performances in short bursts.

Laban Centre
Creekside, Deptford, SE8 3DZ (8691 8600, 8469 9500 tickets, www.trinitylaban.ac.uk). Deptford DLR or Greenwich DLR/rail. **Open** 10am-8pm Mon-Sat. **Tickets** £6-£15 for the centre's own events. **Credit** MC, V.
Originally founded (in Manchester) by the innovative and influential movement theoretician Rudolf Laban (1879-1958), in 2005 the Laban Centre joined forces with Trinity College of Music to create the first ever UK conservatoire for music and dance. The centre was designed by Herzog & de Meuron of Tate Modern fame and features a curving, multicoloured glass frontage. The stunning premises include a 300-seat auditorium and are home to Transitions Dance Company. The company has a new initiative in the pipeline, by which a ticket price will be suggested but ticket buyers can pay what they can afford.
▶ *Also in Deptford, the Albany (Douglas Way, SE8 4AG, 8692 4446, www.thealbany.org.uk) specialises in hip hop theatre.*

Sport & Fitness

Lap up London's Olympic legacy.

As the last specks of Olympic stardust drifted to the ground after a glorious feel-good summer of sport, the word on everyone's lips – in sporting circles and beyond – was 'legacy'. Would elite sports maintain the edge that led to a formidable medals haul? And would there really be a take-up of sport among the general populace, leading to a fitter Britain?

Even London in 'normal' mode has a busy sporting life, with week-in week-out matches featuring professional teams and a calendar dotted with major one-off events. It also offers the UK's best facilities for participating in sport and fitness activities.

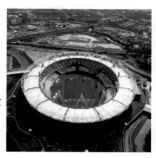

Spectator Sports

THE SPORTING YEAR

Below is a list of major sporting events from spring 2013. For all events held in enclosed spaces (basically, everything except the Boat Race, the London Marathon and the cycling events), you'll have to book tickets in advance.

Spring

Rugby Union: Six Nations
Twickenham (see p316). **Dates** 2 Feb, 10 Mar.
England take on Scotland (2 Feb) and Italy (10 Mar) at Twickenham in this tournament, which also features France, Wales and Ireland.

Football: Capital One Cup Final
Wembley Stadium (see p314). **Date** 24 Feb.
The League Cup is less prestigious than the FA Cup, but the winners play in the UEFA Europa League.

★ **Athletics: Virgin London Marathon**
Around London. **Date** 21 Apr.
One of the world's elite long-distance races – and a huge participation event, with 35,000 starters. If you haven't applied to run, you're too late, but it costs nothing to watch the spectacle.

★ **Rowing: The Boat Race**
River Thames. **Date** 31 Apr.
Blue-clad Oxbridge students race each other in a pair of rowing eights, watched by tens of millions worldwide and around 250,000 people on the riverbank. This historic race was first held in 1829.

Summer

★ **Cricket: Internationals**
Kia Oval (see p315). **Dates** *Ashes 5th Test* (England v Australia) 21-25 Aug. *T20s* (England v New Zealand) 25, 27 June.
Lord's (see p315). **Dates** *Test* (England v New Zealand) 16-20 May. *Ashes 2nd Test* (England v Australia) 18-22 July. *One-Day Internationals* (England v New Zealand) 31 May.
England play a series of Test matches (the classic five-day format – most spectators only attend one day's play) and One-Day Internationals (50 overs per side.) In 2013, the Australians fly in for the most famous contest in cricket: the five-test Ashes series. Dating back to 1882, the Ashes takes place every two years, played alternately in England and Australia.

Football: 131st FA Cup Final
Wembley Stadium (see p314). **Date** 11 May.
The world's oldest domestic knockout tournament.

Rugby Union: Heineken Cup Final
Twickenham (see p316). **Date** 18 May.
The climax to the European Club season.

★ **Horse Racing: Epsom Derby**
Epsom Racecourse (see p316).
Date 31 May-1 June.
The world's most famous flat race, which is run over a distance of one and a half miles.

Tennis: Aegon Championships
Queens Club, Palliser Road, West Kensington, W14 9EQ (7386 3400, www.queensclub.co.uk). Barons Court tube. **Date** 10-16 June.

The pros tend to treat this grass-court tournament as a summer warm-up session for world-famous Wimbledon (*see p314*).

Horse Racing: Royal Ascot

Ascot Racecourse (see p316). **Date** 18-22 June.
Major races include the Ascot Gold Cup on the Thursday, which is Ladies' Day. Expect sartorial extravagance and fancy hats.

★ Tennis: The Championships at Wimbledon

All England Lawn Tennis Club, Church Road, Wimbledon, SW19 5AE (8971 2700, www.wimbledon.org). Southfields tube.
Date 24 June-7 July.
Getting into Wimbledon requires considerable forethought. Seats on the show courts are distributed by a ballot, which closes the previous year; enthusiasts who queue on the day may gain entry to the outer courts. You can also turn up later in the day and pay reduced rates for seats vacated by spectators who've left the ground early.

Rowing: Henley Royal Regatta

Henley Reach, Henley-on-Thames, Oxon RG9 2LY (01491 572153, www.hrr.co.uk). Henley-on-Thames rail. **Date** 3-7 July.
First held in 1839, and under royal patronage since 1851, Henley is a posh, five-day affair.

Athletics: Aviva London Grand Prix

Crystal Palace National Sports Centre (see right). **Date** 2-3 August.
Many of athletics' biggest names gather for this major championship.

Rugby League: Carnegie Challenge Cup Final

Wembley Stadium (see right). **Date** 26 Aug.
Rugby league is mainly played in the north of the country, but for the Challenge Cup Final the north heads south, bringing boisterous, convivial crowds to Wembley Stadium.

Autumn

Cycling: Tour of Britain

Around London. **Date** mid Sept.
Join thousands of spectators on the streets of the capital for a stage of British cycling's biggest outdoor event. See the rising stars of arguably Britain's fastest growing sport.

American Football: NFL

Wembley Stadium (see right). **Date** Oct.
The NFL took a regular-season fixture out of North America for the first time in 2007. In 2012, the Jacksonville Jaguars announced they had agreed to play a home game in London for four seasons from 2013 through to 2016.

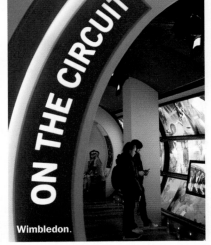

Wimbledon.

Winter

★ Darts: PDC World Championship

Alexandra Palace (www.pdcworldchampionship. co.uk). **Date** Dec-Jan.
The raucous, good-humoured PDC Championships are widely regarded as being of greater stature than the rival BDO tournament in January at Frimley Green (www.bdodarts.com).

Horse Racing: William Hill Winter Festival

Kempton Park (see p316). **Date** 26-27 Dec.
The King George VI three-mile chase on Boxing Day is the highlight of this festival, a Christmas staple for racing fans.

MAJOR STADIUMS

The most important new venue in London is the **Olympic Stadium**, but it won't reopen for another year. For more on the Olympic venues after the Games, *see p316* **Inside Track**.

Crystal Palace National Sports Centre

Ledrington Road, Crystal Palace, SE19 2BB (8778 0131, www.better.org.uk). Crystal Palace rail.
This Grade II-listed building and leisure centre was the major athletics venue in the country until the building of the Olympic Stadium, and hosts popular summer Grand Prix events.

★ Wembley Stadium

Stadium Way, Wembley, Middx HA9 0WS (0844 980 8001, www.wembleystadium.com). Wembley Park tube or Wembley Stadium rail.
The new incarnation of Britain's most famous sports venue opened in 2007 after a famously expensive redevelopment. Designed by Lord Norman Foster, the 90,000-capacity stadium is some sight,

its futuristic steel arch now an imposing feature of the skyline (though less so from within). England football internationals and cup finals are played here, as are a number of one-off sporting events. Guided tours offer alternative access. A small aside: shame there's so little cycle parking.

INDIVIDUAL SPORTS

Cricket

Typically, the English national team hosts Test and one-day series against two international sides each summer. (Test matches are the classic five-day format; one-day internationals last 50 overs a side.) For this summer's international fixtures, *see p313*. It should be an interesting season, as England captain Andrew Strauss quit in 2012. Seats are easier to come by for county games, both four-day and one-day matches. The season runs from April through to September. Surrey play at the Kia Oval and Middlesex at Lord's.

Kia Oval *Kennington Oval, Kennington, SE11 5SS (0871 246 1100, www.kiaoval.com). Oval tube.* **Tickets** *International* £55-£110. *County* £5-£20.
★ **Lord's** *St John's Wood Road, St John's Wood, NW8 8QN (7432 1000, www.lords.org). St John's Wood tube.* **Tickets** *International* call for details. *County* £5-£15.

Football

Playing in the lucrative Barclays Premier League, **Arsenal**, **Tottenham** and **Chelsea** are the city's major players. Arsenal, who play a slick-moving, quick-passing game but have won few trophies of late, are based in the 60,000-capacity Emirates Stadium. The team is under considerable pressure to deliver a trophy this year. **Chelsea**, with young Portuguese manager Andre Villas-Boas, are once again looking like title contenders. Their main London challenge will be from Tottenham Hotspur if they can produce a little more consistency. Other London-based Premier League sides are popular **Fulham** and the financially gifted **Queens Park Rangers**. For football stadium tours, *see right* **Inside Track**.

Tickets for Premier League games can be hard to obtain, but a visit to Fulham is a treat: a superb setting by the river, a historic ground, a life-size statue of Michael Jackson and seats in the 'neutral' section often available on the day. For clubs in the lower leagues (the Championship, Football Leagues 1 and 2), tickets are cheaper and easier to obtain. Prices given are for adult non-members.

The English national team plays its home fixtures at **Wembley Stadium** (*see p314*). Tickets can be hard to come by.

Arsenal *Emirates Stadium, Ashburton Grove, Highbury, N7 7AF (0844 277 3625, www.arsenal.com). Arsenal tube.* **Tickets** £25.50-£123.50. Premier League.
Brentford *Griffin Park, Braemar Road, Brentford, Middx TW8 0NT (0845 345 6442, www.brentfordfc.co.uk). Brentford rail.* **Tickets** £19-£23. League 1.
Charlton Athletic *The Valley, Floyd Road, Charlton, SE7 8BL (0871 226 1905, www.cafc.co.uk). Charlton rail.* **Tickets** £20-£25. Championship.
Chelsea *Stamford Bridge, Fulham Road, Chelsea, SW6 1HS (0871 984 1905, www.chelseafc.com). Fulham Broadway tube.* **Tickets** £36-£87. Premier League.
Crystal Palace *Selhurst Park, Whitehorse Lane, South Norwood, SE25 6PU (0871 200 0071, www.cpfc.co.uk). Norwood Junction or Selhurst rail or bus 468.* **Tickets** £22-£30. Championship.
Dagenham & Redbridge *Victoria Road, Dagenham, Essex RM10 7XL (8592 1549, www.daggers.co.uk). Dagenham East tube.* **Tickets** £15-£22. League 2.
Fulham *Craven Cottage, Stevenage Road, Fulham, SW6 6HH (0870 442 1234, www.fulhamfc.com). Putney Bridge tube.* **Tickets** £20-£60. Premier League.
Leyton Orient *Matchroom Stadium, Brisbane Road, Leyton, E10 5NF (8926 1111, www.leytonorient.com). Leyton tube.* **Tickets** £21-£40. League 1.
Millwall *The Den, Zampa Road, Bermondsey, SE16 3LN (7232 1222, www.millwallfc.co.uk). South Bermondsey rail.* **Tickets** £25-£30. Championship.

INSIDE TRACK FOOTBALL FUN

If you fail to get tickets for a Premiership game, you can still see the inside of a football stadium by going on a tour. However, you'll need to decide who to support: **Chelsea** (0871 984 1955, www.chelseafc.com), **West Ham United** (0871 222 2700, www.whufc.com), **Tottenham Hotspur** (0844 844 0102, www.tottenhamhotspur.com) and **Arsenal** (7619 5000, www.arsenal.com) all offer tours of their stadiums. But perhaps you'd do best instead to tour **Wembley Stadium** (0844 800 2755, www.wembley stadium.com; *see also p314*), the home of English football.

Queens Park Rangers *Loftus Road Stadium, South Africa Road, Shepherd's Bush, W12 7PA (0844 477 7007, www.qpr.co.uk). White City or Wood Lane tube.* **Tickets** £25-£70. Premier League.

Tottenham Hotspur *White Hart Lane Stadium, 748 High Road, Tottenham, N17 0AP (0844 844 0102, www.tottenhamhotspur.com). White Hart Lane rail.* **Tickets** £32-£81. Premier League.

West Ham United *Upton Park, Green Street, West Ham, E13 9AZ (0871 222 2700, www.whufc.com). Upton Park tube.* **Tickets** £45-£64. Premier League.

Horse racing

The racing year is roughly divided into the flat-racing season, from April to September, and the National Hunt season over jumps, from October to April. Racing is currently experiencing major changes in an effort to attract more followers. For more information about the 'sport of kings', visit www.british horseracing.com.

The Home Counties around London are liberally sprinkled with a fine variety of courses, each of which offers an enjoyable day out from the city. Impressive **Epsom** hosts the Derby in June, while **Royal Ascot** offers the famous Royal Meeting in June and the King George Day in July; book well ahead for all of them. **Sandown Park** hosts the Whitbread Gold Cup in April and the Coral Eclipse Stakes in July. There's also high-quality racing at popular **Kempton Park** and delightful **Windsor**.

Epsom *Epsom Downs, Epsom, Surrey KT18 5LQ (01372 726311 information, 0844 579 3004 tickets, www.epsomdowns.co.uk). Epsom Downs or Tattenham Corner rail.* **Admission** £15-£50.
Kempton Park *Staines Road East, Sunbury-on-Thames, Middx TW16 5AQ (01932 782292, www.kempton.co.uk). Kempton Park rail.* **Admission** from £15.
★ **Royal Ascot** *Ascot Racecourse, Ascot, Berks SL5 7JX (0844 346 3000, www.ascot.co.uk). Ascot rail.* **Admission** phone for details.
Sandown Park *Portsmouth Road, Esher, Surrey KT10 9AJ (01372 464348, www.sandown.co.uk). Esher rail.* **Admission** £18-£30.
Windsor *Maidenhead Road, Windsor, Berks SL4 5JJ (01753 498400, www.windsor-racecourse. co.uk). Windsor & Eton Riverside rail.* **Admission** £13-£23.

Rugby

For more than a century, there have been two rival rugby 'codes', each with their own rules and traditions: rugby union and rugby league.

Rugby union dominates the south of England. The Guinness Premiership runs from early September to May; most games are played on Saturday and Sunday afternoons. Look out, too, for matches in the Heineken Cup, a pan-European competition. The local Premiership teams are listed below. Many more teams in the lower leagues are based close to central London; for a full list of clubs, contact the Rugby Football Union (0871 222 2120, www.rfu.com).

The English national team's home games in the Six Nations Championship (Jan-Mar; *see p313*) are held at **Twickenham** (Rugby Road, Twickenham, Middx, TW1 1DZ, 8892 2000, www.rfu.com), the home of English rugby union. Tickets are difficult to get hold of, but other matches are more accessible. There are also internationals in October and November.

Rugby league's heartland is in the north of England: London's sole Super League club is **London Broncos**. In late summer, the sport moves south as Wembley hosts the Challenge Cup final; *see p314*.

Harlequins *Stoop Memorial Ground, Langhorn Drive, Twickenham, Middx TW2 7SX (8410 6000 information, 0871 527 1315 tickets,*

INSIDE TRACK
AFTER THE GAMES

The post-Games Olympic Park – renamed the Queen Elizabeth Olympic Park – has two distinct areas: North and South Park.

It's the South Park that has the key sporting destinations. Dominating the park, the **Olympic Stadium** will be the venue for the 2017 World Athletics Championships, and shortlisted as a venue for the 2015 Rugby World Cup. Next door, Zaha Hadid's sinuous **Aquatics Centre**, with seating stripped down to a more manageable 2,500, will be a public swimming pool.

In the North Park, the Velodrome and BMX track, with new mountain bike and road circuits added, will become the **Lee Valley VeloPark**, for both community and elite use. while Eton Manor, used for aquatics training and wheelchair tennis during the Games, becomes the **Lee Valley Hockey and Tennis Centre**. But the first to reopen (in July 2013) will be the Copper Box, now the 7,500-capacity **Multi-Use Arena**.

For more details on the immediate future of the Olympic Park, *see pp21-23*.

Herne Hill Velodrome.

www.quins.co.uk). Twickenham rail. **Tickets** £22-£45.

London Broncos *Stoop Memorial Ground, Langhorn Drive, Twickenham, Middx TW2 7SX (8410 6000 information, 0871 527 1315 tickets, www.quinsrl.co.uk). Twickenham rail.* **Tickets** £10-£15.

London Irish *Madejski Stadium, Shooters Way, Reading, Berks RG2 0FL (0844 249 1871, www.london-irish.com). Reading rail then £2 shuttle bus.* **Tickets** £20-£40.

London Wasps *Adams Park, Hillbottom Road, High Wycombe, Bucks HP12 4HJ (0844 225 2990, www.wasps.co.uk). High Wycombe rail.* **Tickets** £15-£45.

Saracens *Vicarage Road Stadium, Watford, Herts WD18 0EP (0844 847 1876, www.saracens.com). Watford High Street rail.* **Tickets** £20-£65.

Tennis

For **Wimbledon**, *see p314*; for the **Aegon Championships**, *see p313*.

Participation & Fitness

CYCLING

Cycling in London is more popular than ever, especially with the introduction of the City Hall-sponsored bike rental scheme (www.tfl. gov.uk). Those in need of longer-term rental should try the South Bank-located **London Bicycle Tour Company**.

Sports riders currently have two options (pending the redevelopment of the Olympic Park's cycling venues into the much-anticipated Velopark). Track cyclists can try the outdoor track at the beautiful **Herne Hill Velodrome** (Burbage Road, Herne Hill, SE24 9HE,

www.hernehillvelodrome.com), the world's oldest cycling circuit and the only single-sport venue to have survived from the 1948 Games. For road riders, there's the **Redbridge Cycle Centre** (Forest Road, Hainault, Essex IG6 3HP, 8500 9359, www.vision-rcl.org.uk), which has a road circuit, a mountain bike track and seven different circuit combinations.

Time Out's *Cycle London* book contains lots of advice and information plus 32 specially commissioned rides around town.

London Bicycle Tour Company *1A Gabriel's Wharf, 56 Upper Ground, South Bank, SE1 9PP (3318 3088, www.londonbicycle.com). Southwark tube.* **Open** 10am-6pm daily. **Hire** £3.50/hr; £20/1st day, then £5-£10/day. *Deposit* with credit card, or £180 cash. **Credit** AmEx, MC, V. **Map** p402 N7.

GOLF

You don't have to be a member to play at public courses in the London area, but you will need to book. Clubs are listed at www. englishgolfunion.org; two beauties are the lovely **Dulwich & Sydenham Hill Golf Club** in Dulwich (8693 8491, www.dulwich golf.co.uk, £35-£45, members only Sat & Sun) and the testing **North Middlesex Golf Club** near Arnos Grove (8445 1604, www.northmiddlesexgc.co.uk, £18-£34, members only before 1pm Sat & Sun).

GYMS & SPORTS CENTRES

A lot of London hotels have gym facilities, some of very high quality. But if you're looking for something more serious than your hotel can offer, many health clubs and sports centres admit non-members and allow them to join classes. Some of the best are listed below; for a list of all venues in Westminster, call 7641 1846, or for Camden, call 7974 1542. Note that last entry is normally 45-60 minutes before the listed closing times. For more independent spirits, **Hyde Park/Kensington Gardens** (*see p114*) and **Battersea Park** (*see p143*) have good jogging trails.

Boom! Cycle

2 Scrutton Street, Shoreditch, EC2A 4RT (7426 0702, www.boommybody.com). Old Street tube/rail. **Open** noon-8.30pm Mon; 7.15am-8.45pm Tue, Wed; 10am-8.45pm Thur; 7am-8pm Fri; 10.15am-2.45pm Sat; 10.30am-1pm Sun. **Map** p401 Q4.

As one of the first purpose-built indoor cycling gyms to open in London, the loud music and flashing lights make this 2,500sq ft studio feel more like a nightclub than a gym. With workouts available for all skill levels, instructors aim to create a highly energised, fun and motivational class environment.

Frame

29 New Inn Yard, Shoreditch, EC2A 3EY (7033 1855, www.moveyourframe.com). Shoreditch High Street rail. **Open** 6.30am-10pm Mon-Fri; 8am-6.30pm Sat, Sun. **Map** p401 R4.

This dance, fitness, yoga and Pilates studio has adopted the refreshing ethos that exercise doesn't have to be a chore.

Jubilee Hall Leisure Centre

30 The Piazza, Covent Garden, WC2E 8BE (7836 4007, www.jubileehallclubs.co.uk). Covent Garden tube. **Open** 6.45am-10pm Mon-Fri; 9am-9pm Sat; 10am-5pm Sun. **Map** p416 Z3.

This venue provides calm surroundings for workouts, Jubilee Hall also offers a selection of therapies and treatments. There are other centres available in Southwark, Westminster and Hampstead.

Westway Sports Centre

1 Crowthorne Road, Ladbroke Grove, W10 6RP (8969 0992, www.westwaysportscentre.org). Ladbroke Grove or Latimer Road tube. **Open** 7am-10pm Mon-Fri; 7am-8pm Sat; 8am-9pm Sun.

A smart sports centre: all-weather pitches, tennis courts, a swim centre and gym, plus the largest indoor climbing facility in the country are on offer.

ICE SKATING

There's a permanent indoor rink in Bayswater: **Queens Ice & Bowl** (17 Queensway, Bayswater, W2 4QP, 7229 0172, www.queens iceandbowl.co.uk). But at Christmas, a variety of temporary rinks spring up all over town. **Somerset House** (*see p79*) set the trend; it's since been followed by **Hampton Court Palace** (*see p147*), the **Tower of London** (*see p64*) and the **Natural History Museum** (*see p112*) among others. Check www.timeout.com for a full list.

RIDING

There are various stables in and around the city; for a list, see www.bhs.org.uk. Those below run classes for all ages and abilities.

Hyde Park & Kensington Stables *63 Bathurst Mews, Paddington, W2 2SB (7723 2813, www.hydeparkstables.com). Lancaster Gate tube.* **Map** p393 D6.

Mudchute Equestrian Centre *Mudchute Park & Farm, Pier Street, Isle of Dogs, E14 3HP (7515 0749, www.mudchute.org). Crossharbour or Mudchute DLR.*

STREET SPORTS

Under the Westway in Acklam Road, W10, **Baysixty6 Skate Park** (www.baysixty6. com) has a large street course and four halfpipes, all wooden and covered. **Stockwell Skate Park** (Stockwell Park Road, SW9) is one of the city's most popular outdoor parks; it's rivalled by **Cantelowes Skatepark** (Cantelowes Gardens, Camden Road, Camden, NW1, www.cantelowesskatepark.co.uk) and **Mile End Skatepark** (corner of Burdett Road and St Pauls Way, E3), which opened in May 2009. Many skateboarders and BMXers prefer unofficial street spots such as the **South Bank** under the Royal Festival Hall. The unofficial centre of inline skating is Hyde Park, where you can find rides and lessons (see, for example, www.citiskate.co.uk). For rental nearby, try **London Skate Centre** (27 Leinster Terrace, W2, 7706 8769, www.lonskate.com).

SWIMMING

There are indoor pools scattered all over London. The **Oasis Sports Centre**'s indoor and outdoor pools are both worth a visit, but the historic **Marshall Street** baths, reopened in 2010, are certainly the best located and most beautiful – the impressively restored building

Cantelowes Skatepark.

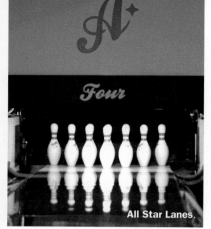

All Star Lanes

in the public area (plus three in private rooms). Although only members can book tables, anyone can come along, enjoy something to eat or drink, and wait for a table to become free.

TENNIS

Many parks around the city have council-run courts that cost little or nothing to use; keener players should try the indoor and outdoor courts at the **Islington Tennis Centre**, though non-members may only book up to five days ahead. If you fancy a couple of sets on a grass court, phone the Lawn Tennis Association's Information Department (8487 7000, www.lta.org.uk).

Islington Tennis Centre *Market Road, Islington, N7 9PL (7700 1370, www.aquaterra.org). Caledonian Road tube.* **Open** 7am-11pm Mon-Thur; 7am-10pm Fri; 8am-10pm Sat, Sun. **Court rental** £10.50-£24/hr.

TEN-PIN BOWLING

For a classier take on bowling, dine and drink cocktails while you strike at the branches of **All Star Lanes** (*see p191*).

Queens Ice & Bowl *17 Queensway, Bayswater, W2 4QP (7229 0172, www.queensiceandbowl. co.uk). Bayswater or Queensway tube.* **Open** 10am-11pm daily. **Bowling** £6.50/game. **Lanes** 12. **Map** p392 C7.
Rowans Bowl *10 Stroud Green Road, Finsbury Park, N4 2DF (8800 1950, www.rowans.co.uk). Finsbury Park tube/rail.* **Open** 10.30am-12.30am Mon-Thur, Sun; 10.30am-2.30am Fri, Sat. **Bowling** £3.70-£4.90. **Lanes** 24.

WHITE WATER RAFTING

Lee Valley White Water Centre (Station Road, Waltham Cross, Herts EN9 1AB, 0845 677 0600, www.gowhitewater.co.uk), site of the London 2012 Canoe Slalom, can be reached in 25 minutes by train from Liverpool Street. The centre offers exhilarating half-day sessions of rafting for £49. Booking ahead is essential. The course used for the Games is 300 metres from start to finish, with a 5.5-metre drop. Five powerful machines pump up to 15,000 litres of water per second, so there's plenty of white froth. The rapids are equivalent to a grade three or four river, but because the course isn't as long as a river, public rafting sessions involve four or five runs that take about an hour and a half. And there's no hauling the boat up a steep bank – one of the best bits is the giant conveyer that takes you and your canoe or raft to the starting pool.

dates back to 1931. To find your nearest pool, see www.activeplaces.co.uk. For pools suited to children, check www.swimming.org/britishswimming.

If alfresco swimming is more your thing, there are open-air lidos at **Parliament Hill Fields**, the **Serpentine**, **Tooting Bec**, **Brockwell Park** and **London Fields** (heated, and of Olympic proportions at 50 metres long). All are rammed in summer.

Marshall Street Leisure Centre *15 Marshall Street, Soho, W1F 7EL (7871 7222, www. better.org.uk). Oxford Circus or Piccadilly Circus tube.* **Open** 6.30am-10pm Mon-Fri; 8am-8pm Sat, Sun. **Map** p416 V2.
Oasis Sports Centre *32 Endell Street, Covent Garden, WC2H 9AG (7831 1804, www.better.org.uk). Holborn tube.* **Open** *Indoor and Outdoor* 6.30am-10pm Mon-Fri; 9.30am-6pm Sat, Sun. **Map** p416 Y2.

TABLE TENNIS

The **Ping** initiative saw table tennis tables appear in outdoor spots all over the country, for free use. Some tables remain, though, including ones in Cavendish Square and Soho Square. The Ping website, http://pingengland. co.uk, has details of clubs and other places to play in its 'play on' section.

Bounce London

121 Holborn, EC1N 2TD (020 3657 6525, www.bouncelondon.com). Chancery Lane tube. **Open** 5pm-midnight Mon-Wed; 5pm-1am Thur; noon-1.30am Fri, Sat; noon-11pm Sun. *Table hire* £10/30mins; £18/hr. *Membership* £400/yr. **Credit** AmEx, MC, V. **Map** p400 N5.
Drinks, pizza and… ping pong. This is the unique formula of Bounce London, a restaurant, bar and members' club equipped with 14 table tennis tables

Escapes & Excursions

Escapes & Excursions

Historic towns and the coast are just an hour or two away by train.

You'll never run out of things to do in London. But everyone who lives here feels an irresistible urge to leave occasionally, so why would visitors be any different? And with good train services out of London, it's easy to reach some interesting destinations in under two hours. In this chapter, there are four suggested excursions that should refresh and reinvigorate you, as well as introducing you to the UK's south-east corner. Two are by the sea, but could otherwise hardly be more different: **Brighton** offers traditional seaside kitsch and a full-on nightlife scene, while **Dungeness**, **Rye** and **Romney** come with cranky charm and an other-

worldly atmosphere. Inland and nestling happily in the lee of the North Downs, **Canterbury** is a lively medieval city, its cathedral and ruined abbey of such historical significance that they're listed as a UNESCO World Heritage Site. And **Cambridge**, as flat as the fenlands it sits upon, is perfect for those who like to peek into cloistered courts and college chapels.

GETTING AROUND

All of the destinations included in this chapter are within easy reach of London, which makes them perfect either for a day trip or a more leisurely overnight stay. **Brighton** and **Cambridge** are the easiest of the four to reach by train; they're both within an hour of London, with rail services running from early in the morning until relatively late at night; **Canterbury** is also a direct rail journey from London, and now with its new high-speed rail link from St Pancras International, it too takes under an hour to get to. It's more of an effort to reach **Dungeness**, **Romney** and **Rye**, but the journey is well worth the effort. If you don't fancy negotiating the train network, and are happy to hire a car, it's a relatively easy journey by road.

For the main attractions, we've included details of opening times, admission prices and transport details, but be aware that these can change without notice: always phone to check. Major sights are open all through the year, but many of the minor ones close out of season, often from November to March.

Before setting out, drop in on the **Britain & London Visitor Centre** (*see p374*) for additional information.

By train

Notwithstanding the occasional strike or weather-related line closure, Britain's rail network is generally reliable. However, ticket prices on some services are insultingly high, and with different rail companies sharing some routes, it's easy to inadvertently pay too much or buy a ticket that limits your options. Factor in varying definitions of peak and off-peak travel and you'll usually be better off discussing your needs at a ticket office window, than buying blind at a machine. If more than two of you are travelling, ask about family and group tickets, which offer excellent value.

The website **www.nationalrail.co.uk** has a good journey planner and gives live advice on engineering works and other delays, which are a regular occurence, particularly at weekends. You can buy tickets on the website, too, but there's generally no advantage, unless your journey takes you outside the south-eastern network (in which case, the further ahead you purchase, the lower the price). National Rail's phone number is 0845 748 4950.

If you need extra help, there are rail travel centres in London's mainline stations, as well as at Heathrow and Gatwick airports. Staff can give you guidance on timetables and booking.

Escapes & Excursions

© Copyright Time Out Group 2013

40 km
20 miles

pp.390-391

GREATER LONDON

ESSEX
Thaxted
Stansted
Bishop's Stortford
Harlow
Chelmsford
Maldon
Burnham-on-Crouch
Southend
Colchester
Clacton-on-Sea

HERTFORDSHIRE
Stevenage
Hertford
Hatfield
St Albans
Watford
Luton

BEDS
Buckingham
Bicester
Aylesbury
Thame

BUCKINGHAMSHIRE
Amersham
High Wycombe
Beaconsfield
Marlow
Cookham
Maidenhead
Slough

OXFORDSHIRE
Stow-on-the-Wold
Woodstock
Oxford
Wantage
Henley-on-Thames
Reading
Newbury

BERKSHIRE

WILTSHIRE
Andover

HAMPSHIRE
Basingstoke
Winchester
Alton
Petersfield
Southampton
Fareham
Gosport
Portsmouth

NEW FOREST
To Weymouth

SURREY
Staines
Heathrow
Kingston-upon-Thames
Leatherhead
Dorking
Guildford
Woking
Aldershot
Farnham

WEST SUSSEX
Horsham
Crawley
Gatwick
Reigate
Redhill
Midhurst
Chichester
Bognor Regis
Littlehampton
Arundel
Worthing

THE SOUTH DOWNS

EAST SUSSEX
East Grinstead
Royal Tunbridge Wells
Lewes
Newhaven
Eastbourne
Hastings
Battle

KENT
Sevenoaks
Maidstone
Rochester
Chatham
Tilbury
Dartford
Swanley
Bexleyheath
Erith
Rainham
Chislehurst
Croydon
Sutton
Ashford
Canterbury
Whitstable
Reculver
Sheerness
Margate
Broadstairs
Ramsgate
Sandwich
Deal
Dover
Folkestone
New Romney
Old Romney
Camber Sands
Winchelsea
Rye
Dungeness

THE NORTH DOWNS

THE WEALD

THE COTSWOLDS

THE CHILTERNS

River Thames

A1(M)
M1
M11
M25
M40
M4
M3
M20
M2
M23
M27

Time Out London **323**

Profile Warner Bros Studio Tour London

Accio! Apprentice wizards summoned to Harry Potter tour.

Wannabe-wizards can stop mourning the end of their favourite film franchise: Warner Bros Studios in Leavesden – where all eight Harry Potter blockbusters were created is now open.

Studio tours are commonplace in Hollywood, but this will be the first of its kind in Britain, and for followers of the bespectacled child-wizard, the Harry Potter

Studio Tour offers a rare opportunity to learn just how JK Rowling's magical world was brought to life in the highest-grossing film series of all time.

The Leavesden Studios, a former aircraft hangar 20 miles from London, are spread over 150,000 square feet. The three-hour walking tour will take in such iconic sets as Hagrid's hut and the Gryffindor common room, plus it offers the chance to check out the special effects, animatronics, props and costumes used in the films.

One of the highlights for many fans will be the set of the Great Hall. It was first seen in *Harry Potter and the Philosopher's Stone* and was designed by BAFTA-winning production designer Stuart Craig – it's 120 feet long and 40 feet wide with a solid stone floor and has the original tables and benches where Daniel Radcliffe, Emma Watson et al once sat. Another highlight will be Dumbledore's office, which was built for *Harry Potter and the Chamber of Secrets* and is home to the Sorting Hat, the Sword of Gryffindor and Albus Dumbledore's desk.

TICKETS
Tickets must be booked in advance at www.wbstudio tour.co.uk or through approved tour operators; £29 adults, £21.50 children.

GETTING THERE
The Leavesden Studios are just off the A405, less than 3 miles from Watford town centre. Fast trains go direct from London Euston in less than 20 minutes; a shuttle bus to the studios runs from Watford Junction station.

We specify departure stations in the 'Getting there' section for each destination; the journey times cited are the fastest available.

By coach

Coaches operated by **National Express** (0871 781 8181, www.nationalexpress.com) are scheduled to run throughout the country. Services depart from Victoria Coach Station (*see p362*), which is ten minutes' walk from Victoria rail and tube stations. **Green Line Travel** (0844 801 7261, www.greenline.co.uk) also operates coaches.

Victoria Coach Station
164 Buckingham Palace Road, Victoria, SW1W 9TP (0843 222 1234, www.tfl.gov.uk). Victoria tube/rail. **Map** p400 H11.
Britain's most wide-ranging coach services are run by National Express (*see p362*). They mostly depart from Victoria Coach Station, as do the services run by many other companies to and from Europe; some depart from Marble Arch.

By car

If you're in a group of three or four, it may be cheaper to hire a car (*see p365*), especially if you plan to take in several sights within an area. The road directions in the listings below should be used in conjunction with a proper map.

By bicycle

Capital Sport (01296 631671, www.capital-sport.co.uk) offers gentle cycling tours along the Thames from London. Leisurely itineraries include plenty of time to explore royal palaces, parks and historic attractions; the website contains full details. Alternatively, try **Country Lanes** (01590 622627, www.countrylanes.co.uk), which leads cycling tours all over the beautiful New Forest in Hampshire.

London-on-Sea
BRIGHTON

Britain's youngest city, England's most popular tourist destination after London and host to the nation's biggest annual arts festival outside Edinburgh, Brighton is thriving. It's also a bracingly liberal kind of place: the constituency of Brighton Pavilion elected Britain's first Green Party MP, Caroline Lucas, in the 2010 General Election. However, novelty is nothing new to Brighton, which has been evolving throughout its existence.

Brighton began life as Brighthelmstone, a small fishing village; it remained so until 1783, when the future George IV transformed it into a fashionable retreat. George kept the architect John Nash busy converting a modest abode into a bizarre piece of orientalist kitsch; it's now the **Royal Pavilion** (*see below*), and remains an ostentatious sight. Next door, the **Brighton Museum & Art Gallery** (Royal Pavilion Gardens, 03000 290900, www.brighton-hove-rpml.org.uk) has entertaining displays and a good permanent art collection.

Lacy, delicate **Brighton Pier**, dating from the 1890s, is a clutter of hot-dog stands, karaoke and fairground rides, filled with customers in the summertime. Still, with seven miles of coastline, Brighton retains all the traditional seaside resort trappings. Look out for the free **Brighton Fishing Museum** (201 King's Road Arches, on the lower prom between the piers, 01273 723064, www.brighton fishingmuseum.org.uk) and the **Sea-Life Centre** (*see p327*), the world's oldest functioning aquarium.

Brighton's West Pier has fallen victim to a series of fires and the depredations of the elements; its remains are a skeletal monument to its historic past. A spectacular 490-foot-high viewing tower is planned to open soon at its foot: see www.brightoni360.co.uk for more.

A gay hub, a major student town and a child-friendly spot, Brighton still welcomes weekend gaggles of hen parties, ravers, nudists, discerning vegetarians, surfers, sunseekers and all-round wastrels. Many are satisfied to tumble from station to seafront, calling in at a couple of bars down the hill – and, perhaps, visiting the huge number of independent shops in and around **North Laine**, and in the charming network of narrow cobbled streets known as the **Lanes** – before plunging on to the pier or hobbling over the pebbles.

But to get the best out of Brighton, it's advisable to seek out its unusual little pockets: the busy gay quarter of **Kemp Town**, the savage drinking culture of **Hanover**, the airy terraces of **Montpelier**. Although hilly, the city has an award-winning bus network, with an all-night service on main lines, making all parts easily accessible.

If you're going for something longer than a day trip, Time Out's *Shortlist: Brighton* will prove invaluable.

Royal Pavilion
Brighton, BN1 1EE (03000 290900, www.royal pavilion.org.uk). **Open** *Apr-Sept* 9.30am-5.45pm daily. *Oct-Mar* 10am-5.15pm daily. *Tours* by appointment. Last entry 45mins before closing. **Admission** £10; £8 reductions; £5.70 under-15s; free under-5s. **Credit** MC, V.

Sea-Life Centre

Marine Parade, BN2 1TB (01273 604234, www.visitsealife.com). **Open** 10am-7pm daily. Last entry 1hr before closing. **Admission** £16.20; £11.40-£15 reductions; free under-3s; £48 family. **Credit** MC, V.

Where to eat & drink

Brighton offers a ridiculous number of dining possibilities for a town of its size, a handful of which would hold their head up in any city in the UK. **Gingerman** (21A Norfolk Square, 01273 326688, www.gingermanrestaurants.com) offers top-quality modern British dishes at accessible prices. At **Bill's** (The Depot, North Road, 01273 692894, www.bills-website.co.uk) organic deli and restaurant, diners sit at long communal tables and tuck into buttermilk pancakes, salads and burgers. **Fishy Fishy** (36 East Street, 01273 723750, www.fishyfishy.co.uk) does laid-back seafood dishes. **Terre à Terre** (71 East Street, 01273 729051, www.terreaterre. co.uk) is an inventive vegetarian restaurant. **Jamie's Italian** (11 Black Lion Street, 01273 915480, www.jamieoliver.com) is an affordable Italian eaterie and is everything you'd expect from brand Jamie. And **Riddle & Finns** (12B Meeting House Lane, 01273 323008, www. riddleandfinns.co.uk) is an accomplished champagne and oyster bar.

Of the city's drinking holes, **Brighton Rocks** (6 Rock Place, 01273 600550, www.brightonrocks pub.com) is Kemp Town's most talked-up small bar, with a heated terrace, quality cocktails and inspired bar snacks and tapas. Quite possibly the best pub in Brighton is the **Basketmakers Arms** (12 Gloucester Road, 01273 689006, http://basket-makers-brighton.co.uk), with its comprehensive selection of cask ales and whiskies; another boozer also beloved by ale enthusiasts is the **Hand in Hand** (33 Upper St James Street, 01273 699595). The **Lion & Lobster** (24 Sillwood Street, 01273 327299, www.thelionandlobster.co.uk) is a wonderful little pub with a nice vibe. The **Medicine Chest** (51-55 Brunswick Street East, 01273 770002, www.themedicinechest.co.uk) is a speakeasy-style cocktail bar. Of the gay bars, the most fun is to be had at the **Amsterdam Hotel** (11-12 Marine Parade, 01273 688825, www.amsterdam.uk.com). **Doctor Brighton's** (16-17 King's Road, 01273 208113, www.doctorbrightons.co.uk), on the seafront, is also worth a punt, with regular DJs playing house and techno.

Where to stay

Given Brighton's popularity with tourists, it's unsurprising that hotel prices can be on the high side. **Drakes** (43-44 Marine Parade,

Brighton.

Canterbury.

01273 696934, www.drakesofbrighton.com, doubles £115-£345) is one of Brighton's high-end designer hotels. The in-house restaurant serves food that is as polished as the surrounds. Another worthwhile option is the typically chic **Myhotel Brighton** (17 Jubilee Street, 01273 900300, www.myhotels.com, doubles £69-£419), which has a penthouse suite containing a 400-year-old carousel horse.

Hotel Pelirocco (10 Regency Square, 01273 327055, www.hotelpelirocco.co.uk, doubles £99-£185) describes itself as 'England's most rock 'n' roll hotel'. It's a friendly and much-loved spot, with rooms like the Leigh Bowery Room and Betty's Boudoir stamping a striking note of individuality. The pampering **Nineteen** (19 Broad Street, 01273 675529, www.hotel nineteen.co.uk, doubles £90-£250) has just eight rooms in a stylish townhouse.

A good-quality stop on Ship Street is the classy **Hotel du Vin** (nos.2-6, 01273 718588, www.hotelduvin.com, doubles £129-£280). The **Amherst** (2 Lower Rock Gardens, 01273 670131, www.amhersthotel.co.uk, doubles £100-£130) is one of the best bargains among Brighton's contemporary hotels, while the **George IV** (32-34 Regency Square, 01273 321196, www.georgeivbrighton.co.uk, doubles £72-£155) is surely the best bargain, with many of the rooms offering sea views. Next door, the **Artist Residence** (33 Regency Square, 01273 324302,, http://arthotelbrighton.co.uk, doubles £55-£200) has 15 bold and colourful rooms, each used as a canvas by different artists, among them cartoonist Ben Allen.

Getting there

By train Trains for Brighton leave from Victoria (50mins; map p400 H10) or King's Cross/St Pancras and London Bridge (1hr 15mins; map p397 L3 & p403 Q8).
By coach National Express coaches for Brighton leave from Victoria Coach Station (1hr 50mins).
By car Take the A23, the M23, then the A23 again to Brighton (approx 1hr 20mins).

Tourist information

Tourist Information Centre *Royal Pavilion, Brighton, BN1 1JS (01273 290337, www.visit brighton.com).* **Open** 10am-5pm Mon-Sat.

Ancient History
CANTERBURY

The home of the Church of England since St Augustine was based here in 597, the ancient city of Canterbury is rich in atmosphere. Gaze up at its soaring spires, or around you at the enchanting medieval streets, and you'll soon feel blessed, even if you're not an Anglican.

Sidney Cooper, as well as work by Van Dyck and Sickert, on display. The museum reopened in September 2012 after a refurbishment that included the removal of partitions to reveal the original scale of the rooms and repair of the Italian terrazzo flooring, made of coloured marble fragments and including swirling patterns and the Canterbury coat of arms.

Founded to provide shelter for pilgrims, **Eastbridge Hospital** (25 High Street, 01227 471688, www.eastbridgehospital.org.uk) retains the smell and feel of ages past. Visitors can tour the hospital and admire the undercroft with its Gothic arches, the Chantry Chapel, the Pilgrims' Chapel and the refectory with an enchanting early 13th-century mural showing Christ in Majesty (there's only one other like this, and it's in France).

The **Roman Museum** (*see below*) has the remains of a townhouse and mosaic floor among its treasures, augmented with computer reconstructions and time tunnels. From here, you get a super view of the cathedral tower. After the Romans comes **St Augustine**, or at least the ruins of the abbey he built (Longport, 01227 767345, www.english-heritage.org.uk). English Heritage has attached a small museum and shop to the site.

Everything you want to see, do or buy in Canterbury is within walking distance. And that includes the seaside – at least, it does if you fancy a long (seven-mile) walk or cycle along the Crab & Winkle Way, a disused railway line to pretty Whitstable.

Canterbury Cathedral
The Precincts, CT1 2EH (01227 762862, www.canterbury-cathedral.org). **Open** *Summer* 9am-5.30pm Mon-Sat; 12.30-2.30pm Sun. *Winter* 9am-5pm Mon-Sat; 12.30-2.30pm Sun. Admission is restricted during services and special events. **Admission** £9.50; £6.50-£8.50 reductions; free under-5s. **Credit** MC, V.

Canterbury Tales
St Margaret's Street, CT1 2TG (01227 479227, www.canterburytales.org.uk). **Open** *Summer* 10am-5pm daily. *Winter* 10am-4.30pm daily. **Admission** £8.25; £6.25-£7.25 reductions; free under-4s. **Credit** MC, V.

Roman Museum
Butchery Lane, CT1 2JR (01227 785575, www.canterbury.co.uk). **Open** 10am-5pm daily. Last entry 45mins before closing. **Admission** £6; £5 reductions. **Credit** MC, V.

Where to eat & drink

Chef Michael Caines has added a smart touch to the Canterbury eating scene, with **Michael Caines at ABode** (01227 826684,

The town's busy tourist trade and large university provide a counterweight to the brooding mass of history present in its old buildings. And, of course, to the glorious **Canterbury Cathedral** (*see right*); it's at its most inspirational just before dusk, especially if there's music going on within and the coach parties are long gone. Inside, you'll find superb stained glass, stone vaulting and a vast Norman crypt, which since early 2011 has been home to *Transport*, an Anthony Gormley sculpture made from antique Canterbury Cathedral nails. A plaque near the altar marks what is believed to be the spot where Archbishop Thomas Becket was murdered; the Trinity Chapel contains the site of the original shrine, plus the tombs of Henry IV and the Black Prince.

A pilgrimage to Becket's tomb was the focus of one of the earliest and finest long poems in all English literature: Geoffrey Chaucer's *Canterbury Tales*, written in the 14th century. At the exhibition named after the poem, visitors are given a device that they point at tableaux inspired by Chaucer's tales of a knight, a miller, a wife of Bath, and others, enabling them to hear the rollicking stories that Chaucer brought to astonishingly vivid life.

Just down the road from Christ Church Gate lies the **Beaney House of Art & Knowledge** (High Street, 01227 452747, www.thebeaney.co.uk), a monument to high Victorian values, with a collection of art by cattle painter Thomas

www.michaelcaines.com, main courses £22.50-£26.50). The two-Michelin-starred chef's influence is evident in the ambitious, fine dining menu. There's also his **Old Brewery Tavern** (Stour Street, 01227 826682, www.michael caines.com, mains £9.95-£19), where prints of grizzled coopers rolling barrels hang on the walls.

Another notable restaurant is the **Goods Shed** (Station Road West, 01227 459153, www.thegoodsshed.co.uk, mains £13-£19), which occupies a lofty Victorian building, which was formerly a railway freight store. On a raised wooden platform, diners sit at scrubbed tables and choose from the specials chalked on the board. Only ingredients on sale in the farmers' market below are used in the restaurant. For people who care about their food and its provenance, this is heaven. Vegetarians will love **Hutch** (13 Palace Street, 0127 766700, www.thehutchcanterbury.co.uk), which is a dapper little restaurant and a relatively new addition to the Kent foodie scene.

Pub-wise, most of the better ones are owned by Shepherd Neame, the local brewery based up the road in the town of Faversham. The best for real ales is the **Unicorn** (61 St Dunstan's Street, 01227 463187, www.unicorn inn.com), which also has a great pub garden for summer drinking. Built in 1370, the **Parrot** (1-9 Church Lane, St Radigands, 01227 454170, www.theparrotcanterbury. com) is the oldest pub in Canterbury and also one of the oldest buildings. A good choice of ales and cider is served in a charming setting. Recently refurbished, the **White Hart** (Worthgate Place, 01227 765091, www.whitehartcanterbury.co.uk) is gaining a good reputation locally.

Where to stay

The third in a small chain of smart hotels created by Andrew Brownsword, **ABode** (30-33 High Street, 01227 766266, www.abode hotels.co.uk, doubles £105-£165) has brought a welcome breath of chic into Canterbury's chintzy accommodation options. The 72 rooms are ordered by price and size ranging from 'comfortable', through 'desirable' and 'enviable' to 'fabulous' (a penthouse with superior views and a tennis court-sized bed). The restaurant (*see above*) is superb.

Canterbury Cathedral Lodge (The Precincts, 01227 865350, www.canterbury cathedrallodge.org, doubles £85-£129) is right inside the cathedral precincts. There is bright and comfortable accommodation in a private courtyard and, while the hotel is hardly historic (it's only a decade old), the views certainly are. Nearby, the **Cathedral Gate Hotel** (36

Burgate, 01227 464381, www.cathgate.co.uk, doubles £62-£105) is a splendid old hotel built in 1438. It pre-dates the Christ Church Gate it sits alongside. The 25 rooms, with atmospheric sloping floors and ceilings, are reached via dark narrow corridors and low doorways.

Magnolia House (36 St Dunstan's Terrace, 01227 765121, www.magnoliahousecanter bury.co.uk, doubles £95-£110) is compact but recommended; the breakfast is delicious and well worth lingering over. The walk to and from town takes you through peaceful Westgate Gardens. Opposite St Augustine's Abbey, **Number 7 Longport** (01227 455367, www.7longport.co.uk) is a tiny 15th-century cottage that has been beautifully renovated to become a chic one-bedroom B&B. Further out, the **Ebury Hotel** (65-67 New Dover Road, 01227 768433, www.ebury-hotel.co.uk, doubles £75-£150) is really quite grand-looking, with a sweeping drive and a Gothic exterior. The best bedrooms have views of the garden, but most of them are large, light and comfortable.

Getting there

By train From Victoria to Canterbury East (1hr 20mins; map p398 H10), or from Charing Cross (map p416 Y5) to Canterbury West (1hr 30mins). A new high-speed train service from St Pancras International brings the journey time down to about an hour.
By coach National Express from Victoria Coach Station (1hr 50mins).
By car Take the A2, the M2, then the A2 again (approx 2hrs).

Tourist information

Tourist Information Centre *12-13 Sun Street, Buttermarket, Canterbury, CT1 2HX (01227 378100, www.canterbury.co.uk).* **Open** 9am-5pm Mon-Sat; 10am-5pm Sun.

Wild Horizons
DUNGENESS, ROMNEY & RYE

Perhaps because it's difficult to reach from London (though there are rail links to Rye and Hastings), **Romney Marsh** is other-worldly in a way that conjures up science-fiction scenarios in Tarkovsky movies; you half expect to see Steed and Mrs Peel from *The Avengers* supping ale in the eerily unchanged villages. It's a strange, appealing mix of olde-worlde cobbled streets and ancient inns, sandy beaches, the world's largest expanse of shingle and event-horizoned marshland, criss-crossed by canals and studded with tiny medieval churches and curious concrete defence constructions dating to the period after World War I. So long as the transport links remain as poor as they are, there probably – hopefully – won't be any real changes here for decades to come. **Hastings** is the ideal starting point for a circular tour (by car) that takes in the towns of Winchelsea and Rye, Romney Marsh and Dungeness.

Winchelsea was built on a never-completed medieval grid pattern, first laid out by King Edward I, when the 'old' settlement was swept into the sea in the storms of 1287. The place is proud of its status as England's smallest town, but really it's a sleepy village of 400 residents. It's almost too quaint to be true – like **Rye**, which is a photogenic jumble of Norman, Tudor and Georgian architecture perched on one of the area's few hills. It's worth taking a look at the medieval Landgate gateway and the **Castle Museum** and 13th-century **Ypres Tower** (*see p332*). The **Rye Art Gallery** (107 High Street, 01797 222433, www.ryeartgallery.co.uk) offers a changing series of excellent exhibitions, mostly by local artists.

Dungeness.

East from Rye lies **Romney Marsh**, flat as a pancake and laced with cycle paths. Bikes can be hired from **Rye Hire** (1 Cyprus Place, Rye, 01797 223033, www.ryehire.co.uk); it's an ideal way to explore the lonely medieval churches that dot the level marsh. Heading out of Rye along the coast road takes you to **Camber Sands**, a vast sandy beach that's a great spot for kite-flying, riding, sand-yachting and invigorating walking.

Beyond is **Dungeness Point**, a huge beach of flint shingle stretching miles out into the sea. Clustered on this strange promontory are a lighthouse that offers wonderful views and a good café. The light on this remote, gloriously bleak patch of land is odd, reflected from the sea on both sides. The oddness of the landscape is enhanced by the presence of the massive Dungeness nuclear power station that dominates the horizon; such man-made wonders are set against a magnificent natural backdrop.

When the miniature **Romney, Hythe & Dymchurch Railway** train (01797 362353, www.rhdr.org.uk) barrels by, you know you're in an episode of *The Prisoner*. Proudly proclaiming to be the 'world's smallest public railway', it's fully functioning but one-third of the standard size. The diminutive train, built by millionaire racing driver Captain Howey in 1927, even includes a buffet car. Sitting in one of the tiny carriages is a surreal experience, as you meander from the wide-open shingle of the Point behind back gardens and caravan parks, through woodland and fields to arrive at **Hythe** (roughly 13 miles away).

Rye Castle Museum & Ypres Tower

3 East Street, TN31 7JY (01797 226728, www.ryemuseum.co.uk). Open Museum Apr-Oct 10.30am-5pm Sat, Sun. Tower Apr-Oct 10.30am-5pm daily. Nov-Mar 10.30am-3.30pm daily. **Admission** *Museum* £1.50; £1 reductions. *Tower* £3; £2.50 reductions. *Both* £4; £3 reductions. **No credit cards.**

Where to eat & drink

You'll find some of the finest food on the south-east coast here. In Rye, the **Landgate Bistro** (5-6 Landgate, Rye, 01797 222829, www.land gatebistro.co.uk, mains £13.20-£19.20) places its emphasis firmly on local produce such as potted wild rabbit or Romney Marsh lamb with gratin potatoes. One of the best seafood restaurants in the area is **Webbe's at the Fish Café** (17 Tower Street, 01797 222226, www.webbes restaurants.co.uk, mains £11-£23). If you're looking for lovingly prepared food with an emphasis on locally sourced ingredients, there are few better places to eat on the peninsula than the **Romney Bay House Hotel** (*see right*).

If fancy isn't your thing, Rye has plenty of simpler eateries: pasta at **Simply Italian** (The Strand, 01797 226024, www.simplyitalian.co.uk, mains £5.95-£14.95) or sound pub food at any number of lovely boozers in town.

The finest option on the seaside is the **Gallivant** (New Lydd Road, 01797 225057, http://thegallivanthotel.com, mains £13.50-£22) at Camber Sands, which prides itself on its use of locally sourced and eco-friendly produce. Further east, Lydd's **Pilot** (Battery Road, 01797 320314, www.thepilot.uk.com, mains £8.25-£13.50) has a jovial pub atmosphere and the food is decent enough.

Of the many pubs, the **Mermaid Inn** in Rye (Mermaid Street, 01797 223065, www.mermaid inn.com) is one of the best; with cellars dating from 1156 and the main building from 1420, the place oozes history. It's also a hotel and has an accomplished restaurant. The tiny, multi-award-winning **Red Lion** (Snargate, 01797 344648) is something of a Romney Marsh institution, famed for the fact that its interior hasn't been touched since World War II. It doesn't offer food, but you're welcome to bring your own.

Where to stay

Luxury guesthouses reign supreme in Rye, and visitors will find plenty of well-run establishments in fascinating buildings. If you want somewhere with character and some individuality, the **Hope Anchor Hotel** (Watchbell Street, 01797 222216, www.thehopeanchor.co.uk, doubles £110-£170) is set in a lovely location at the end of a pretty, cobbled street. The seven guestrooms at the **White Vine House** (24 High Street, 01797 224748, www.whitevinehouse.co.uk, doubles £130-£170) are beautifully appointed and are perfect for romantic weekends away.

Wonderfully located on Rye's quaintest cobbled street, the atmospheric 17th-century **Jeake's House** (Mermaid Street, 01797 222828, www.jeakeshouse.com, doubles £45-£80) has nearly a dozen individually decorated rooms, each taking their name from literary and artistic figures who have visited the area, Radclyffe Hall and Malcolm Lowry among them. The **George** (98 High Street, 01797 222114, www.thegeorge inrye.com. doubles £135-£195) is possibly Rye's premier hotel. It's a handsome coaching inn, dating from 1575, with 24 bedrooms, a Georgian ballroom and an excellent restaurant and bar.

In Winchelsea, **Strand House** (Tanyard's Lane, 01797 226276, www.thestrandhouse. co.uk, doubles £70-£155) dates to the 15th century, and there's a delightful garden. The **Romney Bay House Hotel** (Coast Road, Littlestone-on-Sea, New Romney, 01797 364747, www.romneybayhousehotel.co.uk, doubles

£95-£164) is a ten-bedroom mansion designed for Hollywood gossip columnist Hedda Hopper by Sir Clough Williams-Ellis of Portmeirion fame. In Hastings, the **Zanzibar International Hotel** (9 Eversfield Place, 01424 460109, www.zanzibarhotel.co.uk, doubles £115-£165) is a tall, thin seafront house that feels like a private house rather than a boutique hotel.

Getting there

By train From London Bridge or Cannon Street to Rye via Ashford International (approx 1hr 45mins; map p403 Q8 & p402 P7). From Charing Cross, Waterloo East or London Bridge to Hastings (approx 1hr 30mins; map p416 Y5, p399 M8 & p403 Q8).
By car Take the A20, the M20, then the A259 (approx 2hrs 30mins).

Tourist information

Hastings Tourist Information *Queen Square, Hastings, TN34 1TL (01424 451111, www.visit1066country.com).* **Open** 8.30am-6.15pm Mon-Fri; 9am-5pm Sat; 10.30am-4pm Sun.
Rye Tourist Information *4-5 Lion Street, Rye, TN31 7LB (01797 229049, www.visitrye.co.uk).* **Open** *Apr-Sept* 10am-5pm daily. *Oct-Mar* 10am-4pm daily.

Colleges & Culture

CAMBRIDGE

Gorgeous, intimidating Cambridge has the feel of an enclosed city. With the narrow streets and tall old buildings of the town centre, it has a way of conveying disapproval to visitors architecturally – and that's before you even reach the 'Keep off the Grass' signs. But pluck up the courage to pass through those imposing gates with their stern porters: within and behind the colleges are pretty green meadows and the idle River Cam, a place where time seems to have stopped back in the 18th century.

Cambridge first became an academic centre when a fracas at Oxford – involving a dead woman, an arrow and a scholar holding a bow – led to some of the learned monks bidding a hasty farewell to Oxford and a hearty hello to Cambridge. Once the dust settled, the monks needed somewhere to peddle their knowledge: the first college, **Peterhouse** (01223 338200, www.pet.cam.ac.uk), was established in 1284. The original hall survives, though most of the present buildings are from the 19th century. Up the road is **Corpus Christi** (01223 338000, www.corpus.cam.ac.uk), founded in 1352. Its Old Court dates from that time and is linked by a

gallery to the 11th-century **St Bene't's Church** (Bene't Street, www.stbenetschurch.org), the oldest surviving building in town.

Past Corpus Christi, grand **King's College** (01223 331100, www.kings.cam.ac.uk) was founded by Henry VI in 1441. Its chapel (01223 331315), built between 1446 and 1515 on a scale that would humble many cathedrals, has breathtaking interior fan vaulting and the original stained glass. Attend a service in term-time to hear its wonderful choirboys.

Continue north to find pretty **Trinity** (01223 338400, www.trin.cam.ac.uk), a college founded in 1336 by Edward III and then refounded by Henry VIII in 1546. A fine crowd of Tudor buildings surrounds the Great Court where, legend has it, Lord Byron would bathe naked in the fountain with his pet bear. Wittgenstein studied and taught here, and the library (a cool and airy design by Wren) is open to visitors at certain times. Within, covered cases contain such treasures as a lock of Newton's hair, a Shakespeare first folio and Otto Robert Frisch's crisp and moving account of the first atomic bomb test. From behind the library, you can see the neo-Gothic Bridge of Sighs that connects the major courts of **St John's** (01223 338600, www.joh.cam.ac.uk) across the Cam.

Each of the 31 Cambridge colleges is an independent entity, so entry times (and, for the more famous ones, prices) vary considerably: www.cam.ac.uk/colleges has the details. But Cambridge isn't only about the colleges. Behind its impressive neoclassical façade, the **Fitzwilliam Museum** (*see p334*) has a superb collection of paintings and sculpture (by Titian, Modigliani and Picasso), as well as ancient artefacts from Egypt, Greece and Rome. A short walk south, the 40 relaxing acres of the **Botanic Gardens** (*see p334*) have 8,000 plants; at the entrance is a descendant of Sir Isaac Newton's apple tree.

Fans of eccentric and ghoulish museums should head to Downing Street. On the south side are both the towering totem poles and toucan-shaped 'lime scoop' of the **Museum of Archaeology & Anthropology** (01223 333516, www.maa-cambridge.org) and the fossils and scintillating gemstones of the **Sedgwick Museum of Earth Sciences** (01223 333456, www.sedgwickmuseum.org). On the north side,

---

INSIDE TRACK FOUR MORE

Other surefire winning trips for children around the London area include **Butterfly World, Thorpe Park** (home of Europe's fastest rollercoaster), **Legoland, Chessington World of Adventures** (with zoo) and **Butterfly World**. For all, *see p263*.

you'll find the strange scientific devices and grand orreries of the **Whipple Museum of the History of Science** (01223 330906, www.hps. cam.ac.uk/whipple) and, beneath a suspended whale skeleton, the animal skeletons and stuffed birds of the **Museum of Zoology** (01223 336650, www.museum.zoo.cam.ac.uk).

One of the real treats during a visit to Cambridge is **Kettle's Yard** (*see right*), once Tate curator Jim Ede's home and now a magnificently atmospheric collection of early 20th-century artists – Miró, Brancusi, Hepworth – arranged just as he left it. Settle in one of Ede's chairs and read a book from his shelves.

Behind the main colleges, the beautiful meadows bordering the willow-shaded Cam are known as the **Backs**. Carpeted with crocuses in spring, the Backs are idyllic for summer strolling and 'punting' (pushing flat boats with long poles). Punts can be hired; **Scudamore's Boatyard** (01223 359750, www.scudamores.com) is the largest operator. If you get handy at the difficult skill of punting, you can boat down to the **Orchard Tea Rooms** (45-47 Mill Way, 01223 551125, www.orchard-grantchester.com), where Ted Hughes and Sylvia Plath courted and Rupert Brooke lodged as a student.

Cambridge University Botanic Gardens

1 Brookside, CB2 1JE (01223 336265, www.botanic.cam.ac.uk). **Open** *Apr-Sept* 10am-6pm daily. *Oct, Feb, Mar* 10am-5pm daily. *Nov-Jan* 10am-4pm daily. **Admission** £4.50; £3.95 reductions.

Fitzwilliam Museum

Trumpington Street, CB2 1RB (01223 332900, www.fitzmuseum.cam.ac.uk). **Open** 10am-5pm Tue-Sat; noon-5pm Sun. **Admission** free.

Kettle's Yard

Castle Street, CB3 0AQ (01223 748100, www.kettlesyard.co.uk). **Open** *House* 2-4pm Tue-Sun. *Gallery & bookshop* 11.30am-5pm Tue-Sun & bank hol Mon. **Admission** free.

Where to eat & drink

Occupying an enviable riverside spot, **Midsummer House** (Midsummer Common, 01223 369299, www.midsummerhouse.co.uk, £40 3 courses) produces Michelin-starred French food that rises to the occasion. Service is as fussy as you'd expect, but the food is perfectly presented and meticulously prepared in flavour combinations that are never less than intriguing.

The **Cambridge Chop House** (1 King's Parade, 01223 359506, www.chophouses.co.uk, mains £11.50-£26) is a great come-one-come-all bistro opposite King's College, where you can tuck into British comfort food and draught ales. Nearby, the busy subterranean **Rainbow Café** (9A King's Parade, 01223 321551, www.rainbow cafe.co.uk, mains £8.95-£10.95) serves cheap, hearty vegetarian food. A branch of **Jamie's Italian** (Old Library, Wheeler Street, 01223 654094, www.jamieoliver.com/italian) opened in 2010 in the historic Guildhall, which is just off the central market square. Reopened and

Cambridge.

refurbished in 2011, the legendary **Fitzbillies** (52 Trumpington Street, 01223 352500, www.fitz-billies.com), loved by generations of students, is still the place to go to tuck into a Chelsea bun or teatime treat.

Cambridge has many creaky old inns in which to settle down and enjoy one of the city's decent local ales. The **Eagle** on Bene't Street (01223 505020) is the most famous – Crick and Watson drank here after fathoming the mysteries of DNA – but there are many others, including the **Pickerel Inn** (30 Magdalene Street, 01223 355068) and, down a back alley a little off the beaten track, the sweet little **Free Press** (Prospect Row, 01223 368337, www.freepresspub.com).

Where to stay

Because of the university's prominence in the city, there are plenty of guesthouses, with a cluster of B&Bs nicely located just across the Cam from the centre of town to the north of Midsummer Common. **Harry's** (39 Milton Road, 01223 503866, www.welcometoharrys.co.uk, doubles £75), **Worth House** (152 Chesterton Road, 01223 316074, www.worth-house.co.uk, doubles £69-£95) and **Victoria Guest House** (57 Arbury Road, 01223 350086, www.victoria-guesthouse.co.uk, doubles £65-£95) are all good value.

The pick of the luxury hotels is the **Hotel du Vin** (15-19 Trumpington Street, 01223 227330, www.hotelduvin.com, doubles £185-£335), a cheerfully but carefully run operation, painstakingly converted from listed terraced houses. A basement bar (with wine cellar) extends the whole length of the hotel, the busy all-day restaurant occupies one end of the ground floor and there's a heated and covered cigar 'room' outside.

DoubleTree by Hilton (Granta Place, Mill Lane, 01223 259988, www.doubletree cambridge.com, doubles £139-£264) is located right on the Cam behind Peterhouse, and has an indoor swimming pool. Finally, the **Hotel Felix** (Whitehouse Lane, Huntingdon Road, 01223 277977, www.hotelfelix.co.uk, doubles £120-£200), a modern hotel centred on a characterful 1852 Victorian mansion, is a little remote for walkers, but it has loads of parking space and a good decked area outside its twinkly bar-restaurant.

Getting there

By train Trains to Cambridge leave from King's Cross (50mins; map p397 L3) or Liverpool Street (map p401 R5; 1hr 15mins).
By coach National Express coaches to Cambridge leave from Victoria Coach Station (1hr 50mins).
By car Take Junction 11 or Junction 12 off the M11.

Tourist information

Cambridge Tourist Information Centre
Peas Hill, CB2 3AD (0871 226 8006, www.visit cambridge.org). **Open** *Apr-Sept* 10am-5pm Mon-Sat; 11am-3pm Sun. *Oct-Mar* 10am-5pm Mon-Sat.

In Context

History

The making of modern London.

Over the 2,000 years since London began life as a small trading station by a broad and marshy river, the city has faced plagues and invasions, fires and wars, religious turbulence and financial turmoil. There have been natural disasters and acts of terrorism, all borne by Londoners with a characteristic upbeat pessimism until the moment arrives when the frenzy of commerce can begin again. More than anything, this city's past is a tale of resilience.

In the City, Wren churches – built from the ruins of the Great Fire – have walls still blackened by the German incendiary bombs dropped during the Blitz, and shrapnel scars around Cleopatra's Needle beside the Thames remain from a World War I biplane raid. A fragment of glass, deeply embedded in a wall at the Old Bailey, tells of an IRA terrorist attack back in 1973, while 52 austere steel columns in Hyde Park commemorate those killed by suicide bombers in the summer of 2005.

Evidence of strife is everywhere in this city and the true Londoner will cheerfully insist there's more and worse to come. Just don't bet against them handling their portion of strife with aplomb.

LATIN LESSONS

The city's origins are hardly grand. Celtic tribes lived in scattered communities along the banks of the Thames before the Romans arrived in Britain, but there's no evidence of a settlement on the site of the future metropolis before the invasion of the Emperor Claudius in AD 43. During the Roman conquest, they forded the Thames at its shallowest point (probably near today's London Bridge) and, later, built a timber bridge there. A settlement developed on the north side of this crossing.

Over the next two centuries, the Romans built roads, towns and forts in the area. Progress was halted in AD 61 when Boudicca, the widow of an East Anglian chieftain, rebelled against the imperial forces who had seized her land, flogged her and raped her daughters. She led the Iceni in a revolt, destroying the Roman colony at Colchester before marching on London. The Romans were massacred and their settlement razed.

After order was restored, the town was rebuilt; around AD 200, a two-mile, 18-foot wall was put up around it. Chunks of the wall survive today; the early names of the original gates – Ludgate, Newgate, Bishopsgate and Aldgate – are preserved on the map of the modern city, with the street known as London Wall tracing part of its original course. But through to the fourth century, racked by invasions and internal strife, the Roman Empire was clearly in decline (see below **Time Machine**). In 410, the last troops were withdrawn, and London became a ghost town.

INTO THE DARK

During the fifth and sixth centuries, history gives way to legend. The Saxons crossed the North Sea; apparently avoiding the ruins of London, they built farmsteads and trading posts outside the city walls. Pope Gregory sent Augustine to convert the English to Christianity in 596; Mellitus, one of his missionaries, was appointed the first Bishop of London, founding a cathedral dedicated to St Paul inside the old city walls in 604.

From this period, the history of London is one of expansion. Writing in 731, the Venerable Bede described 'Lundenwic' as 'the mart of many nations resorting to it by land and sea'. Yet the city faced a new danger during the ninth century: the Vikings. The city was ransacked in 841 and again in 851, when Danish raiders returned with 350 ships. It was not until 886 that King Alfred of Wessex, Alfred the Great, regained the city, re-establishing London as a major trading centre.

Throughout the tenth century the city prospered. Churches were built, parishes established and markets set up. However, the 11th century brought more harassment from the Vikings, and the English were

IN CONTEXT

Time Machine AD 290s

By Jenny Hall, Roman curator at the Museum of London.

Who's in control? Carausius declares Home Rule for Britain in AD 293 and makes London his base; Constantius Chlorus, junior emperor of the Roman Empire, is charged with returning Britain to Roman control.
Average wage Unskilled labourer, 25 to 50 silver denarii a day.
Life expectancy 26 to 45.
Key concerns How long could this unofficial empire last? What would happen to Londoners who sided with Carausius and Allectus if the Roman Empire won back Britain?
Local legislation Coins are minted in London for the first time after a period of rampant inflation.
Flash point Allectus assassinates Carausius, giving Constantius the opportunity to make a two-pronged attack from the sea and save London from Allectus's rebel army in AD 296. Constantius's son was Constantine.

Time Machine 1210s

By Jackie Keily, medieval curator at the Museum of London.

Who's in control? Nominally, King John.
Average wage Unskilled labourer, 2d a day; skilled craftsman, 3d to 5d a day.
Key concerns Fire, fighting, Frenchmen.
Local legislation After a Southwark fire in 1212, straw roofs are banned.
Flash point In 1215, the inhabitants of London side with the barons against

King John; and in 1216, they support Prince Louis of France when he arrives in the city. Never crowned king, Louis is defeated at the Battle of Lincoln in 1217.

IN CONTEXT

forced to accept a Danish king, Cnut (Canute, 1016-35), during whose reign London replaced Winchester as the capital of England.

After a brief spell under Danish rule, the country reverted to English control in 1042 under Edward the Confessor, who devoted himself to building England's grandest church two miles west of the City on an island in the river marshes at Thorney: 'the West Minster' (Westminster Abbey; *see p103*). Just a week after the consecration, he died. London now had two hubs: Westminster, centre of the royal court, government and law; and the City of London, centre of commerce.

On Edward's death, foreigners took over. Duke William of Normandy was crowned king on Christmas Day 1066, having defeated Edward's brother-in-law Harold at the Battle of Hastings. The pragmatic Norman resolved to win over the City merchants by negotiation rather than force, and in 1067 granted the burgesses and the Bishop of London a charter – still available to researchers in the London Metropolitan Archives – that acknowledged their rights and independence in return for taxes. He also ordered strongholds to be built at the city wall 'against the fickleness of the vast and fierce population', including the White Tower (the tallest building in the Tower of London; *see p64*) and the now-lost Baynard's Castle that stood at Blackfriars.

PARLIAMENT AND RIGHTS

In 1295, the Model Parliament, held at Westminster Hall by Edward I and attended by barons, clergy and representatives of

knights and burgesses, agreed the principles of English government. The first step towards establishing personal rights and political liberty, not to mention curbing the power of the king, had already been taken in 1215 with the signing of the Magna Carta by King John (*see above* **Time Machine**). Then, in the 14th century, subsequent assemblies gave rise to the House of Lords and the House of Commons. During the 12th and 13th centuries, the king and his court travelled the kingdom, but the Palace of Westminster was now the permanent seat of law and government; noblemen and bishops began to build palatial houses along the Strand from the City to Westminster, with gardens stretching down to the river.

Relations between the monarch and the City were never easy. Londoners guarded their privileges, and resisted attempts by kings to squeeze money out of them to finance wars and construction projects. Subsequent kings were forced to turn to Jewish and Lombard moneylenders, but the City merchants were intolerant of foreigners too.

The self-regulation privileges granted to the City merchants under Norman kings were extended by the monarchs who followed – in return for finance. In 1191, the City of London was recognised by Richard I as a self-governing community; six years later, it won control of the Thames. King John had in 1215 confirmed the city's right 'to elect every year a mayor', a position of authority with power over the sheriff and the Bishop of London. A month later, the mayor joined the rebel barons in signing the Magna Carta.

Over the next two centuries, the power and influence of the trade and craft guilds (later known as the City Livery Companies) increased as dealings with Europe grew. The City's markets drew produce from miles around: livestock at Smithfield, fish at Billingsgate, poultry at Leadenhall. The street markets ('cheaps') around Westcheap (now Cheapside) and Eastcheap were crammed with a variety of goods. The population within the city walls grew from about 18,000 in 1100 to well over 50,000 in the 1340s.

> 'The street of Houndsditch was so named because Londoners threw their dead animals into the furrow there.'

WAKE UP AND SMELL THE ISSUE

Lack of hygiene became a serious problem. Water was provided in cisterns, but the supply, more or less direct from the Thames, was limited and polluted. The street of Houndsditch was so named because Londoners threw their dead animals into the furrow there; in the streets around Smithfield (the Shambles), butchers dumped entrails into the gutters. These conditions helped foster the greatest catastrophe of the Middle Ages: the Black Death of 1348 and 1349, which killed about 30 per cent of England's population. The plague came to London from Europe, carried by rats on ships, and was to recur in London several times during the next three centuries.

Disease left the harvest short-handed, causing unrest among the peasants whose labour was in such demand. Then a poll tax of a shilling a head was imposed. It was all too much: the Peasants' Revolt began in 1381. Thousands marched on London,

led by Jack Straw from Essex and Wat Tyler from Kent; the Archbishop of Canterbury was murdered and hundreds of prisoners were set free. After meeting the Essexmen near Mile End, the 14-year-old Richard II rode out to the rioters at Smithfield and spoke with Tyler. During their discussion, Tyler was fatally stabbed by the Lord Mayor; the revolt collapsed and the ringleaders were hanged. But no more poll taxes were imposed.

ROSES, WIVES AND THE ROYAL DOCKS

Its growth spurred by the discovery of America and the opening of ocean routes to Africa and the Orient, London became one of Europe's largest cities under the Tudors (1485-1603). The first Tudor monarch, Henry VII, had ended the Wars of the Roses by might, defeating Richard III at the Battle of Bosworth, and policy, marrying Elizabeth of York, a daughter of his rivals (*see p342* **Time Machine**). By the time his son took the throne, the Tudor dynasty was firmly established. But progress under Henry VIII was not without its hiccups. His first marriage to Catherine of Aragon failed to produce an heir, so in 1527 he determined the union should be annulled. When the Pope refused to co-operate, Henry defied the Catholic Church, demanding to be recognised as Supreme Head of the Church in England and ordering the execution of anyone who opposed the plan (including Sir Thomas More, his otherwise loyal chancellor). The subsequent dissolution of the monasteries transformed the face of the medieval city.

When not transforming the politico-religious landscape, Henry found time to develop a professional navy, founding the Royal Dockyards at Woolwich in 1512. He also established palaces at Hampton Court (*see p147*) and Whitehall, and built a residence at St James's Palace. Much of the land he annexed for hunting became today's Royal Parks, among them Greenwich Park, Hyde Park and Regent's Park.

RENAISSANCE MEANS REBIRTH

Elizabeth I's reign (1558-1603) saw the founding of the Royal Exchange in 1566, which enabled London to emerge as

IN CONTEXT

Europe's commercial hub. Merchant venturers and the first joint-stock companies established new trading enterprises, as pioneering seafarers Francis Drake, Walter Raleigh and Richard Hawkins sailed to the New World. As trade grew, so did London: it was home to some 200,000 people in 1600, many living in dirty, overcrowded conditions. The most complete picture of Tudor London is given in John Stow's *Survey of London* (1598), a fascinating first-hand account by a diligent Londoner whose monument stands in the church of St Andrew Undershaft.

These were the glory days of English drama. The Rose (1587) and the Globe (1599, now recreated; *see p42*) were erected at Bankside, providing homes for the works of popular playwrights Christopher Marlowe and William Shakespeare. Deemed officially 'a naughty place' by royal proclamation, 16th-century Bankside was a vibrant mix of entertainment and 'sport' (bear-baiting, cock-fighting), drinking and whoring – and all within easy reach of the City, which had outlawed theatres in 1575.

In 1605, two years after the Tudor dynasty ended with Elizabeth's death, her Stuart successor, James I, escaped assassination on 5 November, when Guy Fawkes was found underneath the Palace of Westminster. Commemorated with fireworks each year as Bonfire Night, the Gunpowder Plot was hatched in protest at the failure to improve conditions for the persecuted Catholics, but only resulted in an intensification of anti-papist sentiment. James I is more positively remembered for hiring Inigo Jones to design court masques (musical dramas) and London's first influential examples of the classical Renaissance architectural style: the Queen's House (1616; *see p140*), the Banqueting House (1619; *see p101*) and St Paul's Covent Garden (1631; *see p76*).

ROYALISTS AND ROUNDHEADS

Charles I succeeded his father in 1625, but gradually fell out of favour with the City of London and an increasingly independent-minded Parliament over taxation. The country slid into civil war (1642-49), the supporters of Parliament (the Roundheads, led by Puritan Oliver Cromwell) opposing the supporters of the King (the Royalists).

Both sides knew that control of the country's major city and port was vital for victory, and London's sympathies were with the Parliamentarians. In 1642, 24,000 citizens assembled at Turnham

Time Machine 1480s

By Jackie Keily, medieval curator at the Museum of London.

Who's in control? Complicated! Four kings in three years: Edward IV and his son, Edward V, both die in 1483 and are succeeded by Edward IV's brother Richard III, who is defeated and killed at Bosworth Field in 1485 by Henry Tudor, the future Henry VII.
Average wage Unskilled labourer, 4d a day.
Unusual imports In 1480-81, Portuguese ships bring 300,000 oranges; a single Venetian galley brings a mixed cargo including coral beads, pepper, sponges, ginger, satin, silk, Corinth raisins and two apes.

Key concerns Avoiding major unrest.
Local legislation In 1484, statutes are passed to stop the importation of certain foreign manufactured goods, so as to protect local jobs.
Flash point In June 1483, London supports Richard III as king instead of the 12-year-old Edward V, who is in prison. The young prince never leaves the Tower (*see p64*) – he and his brother, Richard of Shrewsbury, are later known as the 'Princes in the Tower'.

The plague

Green to face Charles's army, but the King withdrew. The move proved fatal: Charles never threatened the capital again, and was eventually found guilty of treason. Taken to the Banqueting House in Whitehall on 30 January 1649, he declared himself a 'martyr of the people' and was beheaded. A commemorative wreath is still laid at the site of the execution on the last Sunday in January each year.

For the next decade, the country was ruled as a Commonwealth by Cromwell. But his son Richard's subsequent rule was brief: due to the Puritans closing theatres and banning Christmas (a Catholic superstition), the Restoration of the exiled Charles II in 1660 was greeted with great rejoicing. The Stuart king had Cromwell exhumed from Westminster Abbey, and his body was hung in chains at Tyburn (near modern-day Marble Arch). His severed head was displayed on a pole outside the abbey until 1685.

PLAGUE, FIRE AND REVOLUTION

The year 1665 saw the most serious outbreak of bubonic plague since the Black Death, killing nearly 100,000. Then, on 2 September 1666, a second disaster struck. The fire that spread from a carelessly tended oven in Thomas Farriner's baking shop on Pudding Lane raged for three days and consumed four-fifths of the City.

The Great Fire at least allowed planners the chance to rebuild London as a modern city. Many blueprints were considered, but Londoners were so impatient to get on with business that the City was reconstructed largely on its medieval street plan (albeit in brick and stone rather than wood). The prolific Sir Christopher Wren oversaw work on 51 of the 54 rebuilt churches. Among them was his masterpiece: the new St Paul's (see p53), completed in 1710 and effectively the world's first Protestant cathedral.

In the wake of the Great Fire, many well-to-do City dwellers moved to new residential developments west of the old quarters, an area subsequently known as the West End. In the City, the Royal Exchange was rebuilt, but merchants increasingly used the new coffeehouses to exchange news. With the expansion of the joint-stock companies and the chance to invest capital, the City emerged as a centre not of manufacturing but of finance. Even at this early stage, economic instability was common: the 1720 financial disaster known as the South Sea Bubble ruined even Sir Isaac Newton.

Anti-Catholic feeling still ran high. The accession in 1685 of Catholic James II aroused such fears of a return to papistry that a Dutch Protestant, William of Orange, was invited to take the throne with his wife, Mary Stuart (James's daughter). James fled to France in 1688 in what became known (by its beneficiaries) as the 'Glorious Revolution'. It was during William's reign that the Bank of England was founded, initially to finance the King's religious wars with France.

CREATION OF THE PRIME MINISTER

In 1714, the throne passed to George, the Hanover-born great-grandson of James I. The German-speaking king (he never learned English) became the first of four Georges in the Hanoverian line.

During George I's reign (1714-27), and for several years after, Sir Robert Walpole's Whig party monopolised Parliament. Their opponents, the Tories, supported the Stuarts and had opposed the exclusion of the Catholic James II. On the king's behalf, Walpole chaired a group of ministers (the forerunner of today's Cabinet), becoming, in effect, Britain's first prime minister. Walpole was presented with 10 Downing Street (built by Sir George Downing) as a residence; it remains the official prime ministerial home.

During the 18th century, London grew with astonishing speed. New squares and terraced streets spread across Soho, Bloomsbury, Mayfair and Marylebone, as wealthy landowners and speculative developers cashed in on the new demand for leasehold properties. South London also became more accessible with the opening of the first new bridges for centuries: Westminster Bridge (opened 1750) and Blackfriars Bridge (completed 1769) joined London Bridge, previously the only Thames crossing.

GIN-SOAKED POOR, NASTY RICH

In London's older districts, people were living in terrible squalor. Some of the most notorious slums were located around Fleet Street and St Giles's (north of Covent Garden), only a short distance from fashionable residences. To make matters worse, gin ('mother's ruin') was readily available at low prices; many poor Londoners drank excessive amounts in an attempt to escape the horrors of daily life. The well-off seemed complacent, amusing themselves at the popular Ranelagh and Vauxhall Pleasure Gardens or with trips to mock the patients at the Bedlam lunatic asylum. Public executions at Tyburn were popular events in the social calendar; it's said that 200,000 people gathered to see the execution (after he had escaped from prison four times) of the folk-hero thief Jack Sheppard in 1724.

The outrageous imbalance in the distribution of wealth encouraged crime, and there were daring daytime robberies in the West End. Reformers were few, though there were exceptions. Henry Fielding, author of the picaresque novel *Tom Jones*, was also an enlightened magistrate at Bow Street Court. In 1751, he and his blind half-brother John set up a volunteer force of 'thief-takers' to back up the often ineffective efforts of the parish constables and watchmen who were, until then, the city's only law-keepers. This crime-busting group of proto-cops, known as the Bow Street Runners, were the earliest incarnation of today's Metropolitan Police (established in 1829).

Meanwhile, five major new hospitals were founded by private philanthropists. St Thomas's and St Bartholomew's were long-established monastic institutions for the care of the sick, but Westminster (1720), Guy's (1725), St George's (1734), London (1740) and the Middlesex (1745) went on to become world-famous teaching hospitals. Thomas Coram's Foundling Hospital (*see p108*) was another remarkable achievement.

INDUSTRY AND CAPITAL GROWTH

It wasn't just the indigenous population of London that was on the rise. Country folk, whose common land had been

Another London

The city seen from the outside.

London has always attracted people from around the world. Its portrayal by foreign photographers is the theme of a major photographic collection donated to Tate Britain by Eric and Louise Franck. An exhibition of works from the collection took place in 2012, and an accompanying book, *Another London* (£16.99), with 100 photographs, is available from the gallery.

Artists represented include some of the greatest names of the 20th century, from Henri Cartier-Bresson to Bruce Davidson. Each brings their own artistic perspective and aim, their era and personal experience, and their technical style. Some seek to perpetuate stereotypes, others to undermine them; some portray people, others buildings.

The human subjects in the earlier photographs – like the *Pearly King Collecting Money for the Empire Day* (Dora Maar, 1935), or *Charwomen, London* (Iriving Penn, 1950) – can seem as exotic and 'other' to a 21st-century viewer as they must have appeared to the foreign photographers. *Housewife, Bethnal Green* (Bill Brandt, 1937) shows a young woman scrubbing her front step – a practice Londoners abandoned long ago, along with much of the culture and class structure that the image reflects. Toffs inhabit a different, lost world, too, as in Henri Cartier-Bresson's *Queen Charlotte's Ball* (1959) – an ethereal image of dancing couples and long, floaty dresses.

Buildings and structures, though, are often enduringly recognisable, like Tower Bridge from a smoky Pool of London (Edouard Boubat, 1958) or Tower Bridge from a boat with a boatman (Wolfgang Suschitzky, 1934). A blitzed City of London in *View From St Paul's Cathedral* (Wolfgang Suschitzky, 1942), has a still-standing Tower Bridge in the background.

As we draw nearer to the present, the people depicted become – on the whole – more like people we know. *Mike Eghan at Piccadilly Circus, London* (James Barnor, 1967; *pictured*), shows a smartly dressed young man running down the steps at Eros, arms outstretched. He's an individual with a name, not a type, and he seems exhilarated by life in the city at that moment.

replaced by sheep enclosures, were faced with a choice between starvation wages or unemployment, and so drifted into the towns. Just outside the old city walls, the East End drew many poor immigrant labourers to build the docks towards the end of the 18th century. London's total population had grown to one million by 1801, the largest of any city in Europe. By 1837, when Queen Victoria came to the throne (see p22 **Time Machine**), five more bridges and the capital's first passenger railway (from Greenwich to London Bridge) gave hints of huge expansion.

As well as being the administrative and financial capital of the British Empire, London was its chief port and the world's largest manufacturing centre. On one hand, it had splendid buildings, fine shops, theatres and museums; on the other, it was a city of poverty, pollution and disease. Residential areas were polarised into districts of fine terraces maintained by squads of servants and overcrowded, insanitary slums.

The growth of the metropolis in the century before Victoria came to the throne had been spectacular, but during her reign (1837-1901), thousands more acres were covered with roads, houses and railway lines. If you visit a street within five miles of central London, its houses will be mostly Victorian. By the end of the 19th century, the city's population had swelled to more than six million, an incredible growth of five million in just 100 years.

Despite social problems of the Victorian era, memorably depicted in the writings of Charles Dickens, steps were being taken to improve conditions for the majority of Londoners by the turn of the century. The Metropolitan Board of Works installed an efficient sewerage system, street lighting and better roads. The worst slums were replaced by low-cost building schemes funded by philanthropists such as the American George Peabody, whose Peabody Donation Fund continues to provide subsidised housing to the working classes. The London County Council (created in 1888) also helped to house the poor.

The Victorian expansion would not have been possible without an efficient public transport network with which to speed workers into and out of the city from the new suburbs. The horse-drawn bus appeared on London's streets in 1829, but it was the opening of the first passenger railway seven years later that heralded the commuters of the future. The first underground line, which ran between Paddington and Farringdon Road, opened in 1863 and proved an instant success, attracting 30,000 travellers on the first day. The world's first electric track in a deep tunnel – the 'tube' – opened in 1890 between the City and Stockwell, later becoming part of the Northern line.

THE CRYSTAL PALACE

If any single event symbolised this period of industry, science, discovery and invention, it

Time Machine 1830s

By Alex Werner, head of history at the Museum of London.

Who's in control? In 1837, 18-year-old Queen Victoria arrives on the throne. Prime Minister Lord Melbourne holds together a divided cabinet and mentors the young Queen, who turns a blind eye to past indiscretions (and his wife's affair with Lord Byron).
Population About two million.
Average wage Tailor, 5s a day;

about half of the total female labour force are servants.
Key concerns Stopping cholera: many die in epidemics during the 1830s.
Local legislation The London to Birmingham Railway opens in 1837, but the line is not yet ready; early riders can only get as far as Hemel Hempstead.

Time Machine 1910s

By Jenny Hall, curator of social history at the Museum of London.

Who's in control? In 1910, the London County Council assumes greater responsibility for governing London, particularly in areas such as education, health and housing.

Life expectancy Men, 52; women, 55.

Average wage 31s 6d.

Prices The maximum retail price of a 4lb loaf in 1912 is 6d.

Key concerns The death of a whole generation of young men during World War I: about 60,000 Londoners will die in the trenches.

Local legislation In 1918, the Representation of the People Act gives eight million women over 30 the right to vote in parliamentary elections for the first time, and also enfranchises all adult males over the age of 21 who are resident householders.

Flash point In May 1914, police stop suffragettes entering Buckingham Palace (*see p106*) in a bid to present a 'Votes for Women' petition to the King; 66 women are arrested, among them Emmeline Pankhurst.

was the Great Exhibition of 1851. Prince Albert, the Queen's Consort, helped organise the triumphant showcase, for which the Crystal Palace, a vast building of iron and glass, was erected in Hyde Park. It looked like a giant greenhouse; hardly surprising as it was designed not by a professional architect but by the Duke of Devonshire's gardener, Joseph Paxton. Condemned by art critic John Ruskin as the model of dehumanisation in design, the Palace came to be presented as the prototype of modern architecture. During the five months it was open, the Exhibition drew six million visitors. The profits were used by the Prince Consort to establish a permanent centre for the study of the applied arts and sciences; the enterprise survives today in the South Kensington museums of natural history, science, and decorative and applied arts (*see pp112-114*), and in three colleges (of art, music and science. After the Exhibition closed, the Crystal Palace was moved to Sydenham and used as an exhibition centre until it burned down in 1936.

ZEPPELINS ATTACK FROM THE SKIES

London entered the 20th century as the capital of the largest empire in history.

Its wealth and power were there for all to see in grandstanding monuments such as Tower Bridge (*see p101*) and the Midland Grand Hotel at St Pancras Station (*see p192*), both of which married the retro stylings of High Gothic with modern iron and steel technology. During the brief reign of Edward VII (1901-10), London regained some of the gaiety and glamour it had lacked in the later years of Victoria's reign. Parisian chic came to London with the opening of the Ritz; Regent Street's Café Royal hit the heights as a meeting place for artists and writers; gentlemen's clubs proliferated; and 'luxury catering for the little man' was provided at the new Lyons Corner Houses (the Coventry Street branch held 4,500 people).

Road transport, too, was revolutionised in this period. By 1911, horse-drawn buses were abandoned, replaced by motor cars, which put-putted around the city's streets, and the motor bus, introduced in 1904. Disruption came in the form of devastating air raids during World War I (1914-18). Around 650 people lost their lives in Zeppelin raids, but the greater impact was psychological – the mighty city and its populace had experienced helplessness.

IN CONTEXT

'Raids on London continued for 57 consecutive nights, then intermittently for a further six months.'

CHANGE, CRISIS AND SHEER ENTERTAINMENT

Political change happened quickly after the war. At Buckingham Palace (*see p106*), the suffragettes had fiercely pressed the case for women's rights before hostilities began (*see below* **Time Machine**) and David Lloyd George's government averted revolution in 1918-19 by promising 'homes for heroes' (the returning soldiers). It didn't deliver, and in 1924 the Labour Party, led by Ramsay MacDonald, formed its first government.

A live-for-today attitude prevailed in the Roaring '20s among the young upper classes, who flitted from parties in Mayfair to dances at the Ritz. But this meant little to the mass of Londoners, who were suffering in the post-war slump. Civil disturbances, brought on by the high cost of living and rising unemployment, resulted in the nationwide General Strike of 1926, when the working classes downed tools en masse in support of striking miners. Prime Minister Baldwin encouraged volunteers to take over the public services, and the streets teemed with army-escorted food convoys, aristocrats running soup kitchens and students driving buses. After nine days of chaos, the strike was finally called off.

The economic situation only worsened in the early 1930s following the New York Stock Exchange crash of 1929. By 1931, more than three million Britons were jobless. During these years, the London County Council (LCC) began to have a greater impact on the city, clearing slums and building new houses, creating parks and taking control of public services. All the while, London's population increased, peaking at nearly 8.7 million in 1939. To accommodate the influx, the suburbs expanded, particularly to the north-west with the extension of the Metropolitan line to an area that became known as 'Metroland'. Identical gabled houses sprang up in their thousands.

At least Londoners were able to entertain themselves with film and radio. Not long after London's first radio broadcast was beamed from the roof of Marconi House in the Strand in 1922, families were gathering around huge Bakelite wireless sets to hear the BBC (the British Broadcasting Company; from 1927 the British Broadcasting Corporation). TV broadcasts started on 26 August 1936, when the first telecast went out from Alexandra Palace, but few Londoners could afford televisions until the 1950s.

BLITZKRIEG

Abroad, events had taken on a frightening impetus. Neville Chamberlain's policy of appeasement towards Hitler's Germany collapsed when the Germans invaded Poland. Britain duly declared war on 3 September 1939. The government implemented precautionary measures against air raids, including the evacuation of 600,000 children and pregnant mothers, but the expected bombing raids didn't happen during the autumn and winter of 1939-40 (the so-called 'Phoney War'). Then, in September 1940, hundreds of German bombers dumped explosives on east London and the docks, destroying entire streets and killing or injuring more than 2,000 in what was merely an opening salvo. The Blitz had begun. Raids on London continued for 57 consecutive nights, then intermittently for a further six months. Londoners reacted with stoicism, famously asserting 'business as usual'. After a final raid on 10 May 1941, the Nazis had left a third of the City and the East End in ruins.

From 1942 onwards, the tide began to turn, but Londoners had a new terror to face: the V1 or 'doodlebug'. Dozens of these deadly, explosive-packed, pilotless planes descended on the city in 1944, causing widespread destruction. Later in the year, the more powerful V2 rocket was launched. The last fell on 27 March 1945 in Orpington, Kent, around six weeks before Victory in Europe (VE Day) was declared on 8 May 1945.

'NEVER HAD IT SO GOOD'

World War II left Britain almost as shattered as Germany. Soon after VE Day, a general election was held and Winston Churchill was defeated by the Labour Party under Clement Attlee. The new government established the National Health Service in 1948, and began a massive nationalisation programme that included public transport, electricity, gas, postal and telephone services. For most people, however, life remained regimented and austere. In war-ravaged London, local authorities struggled with a critical shortage of housing. Prefabricated bungalows provided a temporary solution for some (60 years later, six prefabs on the Excalibur estate in Catford, south-east London, were given protection as buildings of historic interest), but the

huge new high-rise housing estates that the planners devised proved unpopular with their residents.

There were bright spots. London hosted the Olympic Games in 1948; three years later came the Festival of Britain, resulting in the first full redevelopment of the riverside site into the South Bank (now Southbank) Centre. As the 1950s progressed, life and prosperity returned, leading Prime Minister Harold Macmillan in 1957 to proclaim that 'most of our people have never had it so good'. However, Londoners were leaving. The population dropped by half a million in the late 1950s, causing a labour shortage that prompted huge recruitment drives in Britain's former colonies. London Transport and the National Health Service were both particularly active in encouraging West Indians to emigrate to Britain. Unfortunately, as the Notting Hill race riots of 1958 illustrated, the welcome these new immigrants received was rarely friendly. Still, there were several areas of tolerance:

King George VI and Queen Elizabeth survey bomb damage, 1940.

Soho, for instance, which became famous for its mix of cultures and the café and club life they brought with them.

THE SWINGING '60S

By the mid 1960s, London had started to swing. The innovative fashions of Mary Quant and others broke the stranglehold Paris had on couture: boutiques blossomed along the King's Road, while Biba set the pace in Kensington. Carnaby Street became a byword for hipness as the city basked in its new-found reputation as music and fashion capital of the world – made official, it seemed, when *Time* magazine devoted its front cover to 'swinging London' in 1966. The year of student unrest in Europe, 1968, saw the first issue of *Time Out* hit the streets in August; it was a fold-up sheet, sold for 5d. The decade ended with the Rolling Stones playing a free gig in Hyde Park that drew around 500,000 people.

Then the bubble burst. Many Londoners remember the 1970s as a decade of economic strife, the decade in which the IRA began its bombing campaign on mainland Britain. After the Conservatives won the general election in 1979, Margaret Thatcher instituted an economic policy that cut public services and widened the gap between rich and poor. Riots in Brixton (1981) and Tottenham (1985) were linked to unemployment and heavy-handed policing, keenly felt in London's black communities. The Greater London Council (GLC), led by Ken Livingstone, mounted vigorous opposition to the government with a series of populist measures, but it was abolished in 1986. The replacement of Margaret Thatcher by John Major in October 1990 signalled a short-lived upsurge of hope among Londoners.

THINGS CAN ONLY GET BETTER?

In May 1997, the British electorate ousted the Tories and gave Tony Blair's Labour Party the first of three election victories. Blair left London with two significant legacies. First, the government commissioned the Millennium Dome, whose turn-of-the-century celebrations it hoped would be a 21st-century rival to the Great Exhibition of 1851. Instead,

the Dome ate £1 billion and became a national joke. However, even as Labour's fortunes declined, the Dome's saw an upturn. In its guise as the O2 Arena (*see p287*), it has hosted concerts by the likes of Prince and Lady Gaga; as the North Greenwich Arena, it was a key venue in the London 2012 Olympic and Paralympic Games. Second, following a referendum, Labour instituted the Greater London Assembly (GLA) and London mayoralty. Thus 2000 saw Ken Livingstone return to power as London's first directly elected mayor. He was re-elected in 2004, a thumbs-up for policies that included a traffic congestion charge. Summer 2005 brought elation, as London won the bid to host the 2012 Games, and devastation the very next day, as bombs on tube trains and a bus killed 52 people and injured 700.

Aided by support from the suburbs that Livingstone had neglected, thatch-haired Tory Boris Johnson became mayor in 2008 with a healthy majority. Publicity-friendly early policies, such as the introduction of a bike rental scheme and the development of an updated Routemaster bus, more recently took a back seat to the sober realities of working with the new national government, a Conservative–Liberal Democrat coalition – whose policies and spending cuts don't always favour city life – and ensuring a smooth run-up to the Games. The disturbing riots and looting of August 2011, whose flashpoint was again in Tottenham, brought issues of youth unemployment and alienation to the fore, and a new gravity to the task of governing the city. In May 2012, Boris Johnson won another term as mayor by a slim margin.

It was all eyes on London for the 2012 Games, and from Danny Boyle's glorious and original opening ceremony to the extinguishing of the flame at the end of the Paralympic closing ceremony, the Games flashed by in a haze of all-round success, acknowledged even by pre-Games cynics as a triumph of organisation, volunteerism and community spirit. Plans for a post-Games 'legacy' played a big part in the success of London's hosting bid; the question now is how much long-term impact the Games will actually have on the lives of Londoners and on their city.

IN CONTEXT

Key Events

London in brief.

43 The Romans invade; the settlement of Londinium is founded.
61 Boudicca burns Londinium; the city is rebuilt and made provincial capital.
200 A city wall is built.
410 Roman troops evacuate Britain.
c600 Saxon London is built to the west.
841 The Norse raid for the first time.
c871 The Danes occupy London.
886 Alfred the Great takes London.
1042 Edward the Confessor builds a palace and 'West Minster' upstream.
1066 William I is crowned in Westminster Abbey.
1078 The Tower of London is begun.
1123 St Bart's Hospital is founded.
1197 Henry Fitzalwin is the first mayor.
1215 The mayor signs the Magna Carta.
1240 First Parliament at Westminster.
1290 Jews are expelled from London.
1348 The Black Death arrives.
1381 The Peasants' Revolt.
1397 Richard Whittington is Lord Mayor.
1476 William Caxton sets up the first printing press at Westminster.
1534 Henry VIII cuts England off from the Catholic Church.
1555 Martyrs burned at Smithfield.
1565 Sir Thomas Gresham proposes the Royal Exchange.
1572 First known map of London.
1599 The Globe Theatre opens.
1605 Guy Fawkes's plot to blow up James I fails.
1642 The start of the Civil War.
1649 Charles I is executed; Cromwell establishes Commonwealth.
1664 Beginning of the Great Plague.
1666 The Great Fire.
1675 Building starts on the new St Paul's Cathedral.
1694 The Bank of England is set up.
1766 The city wall is demolished.
1773 The Stock Exchange is founded.
1824 The National Gallery is founded.
1836 The first passenger railway opens; Charles Dickens publishes *The Pickwick Papers*, his first novel.

1851 The Great Exhibition takes place.
1858 The Great Stink: pollution in the Thames reaches hideous levels.
1863 The Metropolitan line opens as the world's first underground railway.
1866 London's last major cholera outbreak; the Sanitation Act is passed.
1868 The last public execution is held at Newgate prison (now the Old Bailey).
1884 Greenwich Mean Time is established as a global standard.
1888 Jack the Ripper prowls the East End; London County Council is created.
1890 The Housing Act enables the LCC to clear the slums; the first electric underground railway opens.
1897 Motorised buses are introduced.
1908 London hosts the Olympic Games for the first time.
1915 Zeppelins begin three years of bombing raids on London.
1940 The Blitz begins.
1948 London again hosts the Olympic Games; forerunner of the Paralympics, the Stoke Mandeville Games are organised in Buckinghamshire by neurologist Sir Ludwig Guttman.
1951 The Festival of Britain is held.
1952 The last 'pea-souper' smog.
1953 Queen Elizabeth II is crowned.
1981 Riots in Brixton.
1982 The last London docks close.
1986 The Greater London Council is abolished.
1992 One Canada Square tower opens on Canary Wharf.
2000 Ken Livingstone becomes London's first directly elected mayor; Tate Modern and the London Eye open.
2005 The city wins its bid to host the 2012 Games; suicide bombers kill 52 on public transport.
2008 Boris Johnson becomes mayor.
2010 Hung parliament leads to new Conservative–Lib Dem coalition.
2011 Riots and looting around the city.
2012 London 2012 Olympic Games and Paralympic Games take place.

IN CONTEXT

Architecture

A wonderful jumble of architectural highlights.

Long before Britain emerged from its double-dip recession, London's financial powerhouse, the City, had dusted down its cranes and started to build. In a basket of scaffolding, the concrete of Rafael Viñoly's 'Walkie Talkie', a curvaceous 38-storey building at 20 Fenchurch Street, was fast emerging to join the 'Cluster' of City skyscrapers: the Gherkin, Tower 42 and the recently completed Heron Tower on Bishopsgate. Yet even this last, the City's new tallest building, is a mere foot maiden to Renzo Piano's 1,016ft-tall Shard, the huge spike that opened on the opposite bank of the Thames in 2012.

For all the annual top ten lists of loathed new buildings, the best modern architecture is taken to the city's heart. Some is swiftly loved (the Gherkin), other buildings become favourites over time: the BT Tower and the Barbican are once-hated structures that find themselves dearly loved. None of which is new: in the 17th century, the authorities objected to Wren's magnificent St Paul's Cathedral because it looked too Roman Catholic for their Anglican sensibilities.

Beneath its lofty post-modern blocks, London has Baroque churches, discreet Georgian squares, grand colonnades, even lumps of Roman wall. In fact, this city's defining characteristic is its aesthetically unhappy mix of buildings. London is a mess of historic bits and modern bobs, which give the city its unique capacity to surprise and delight.

ANCIENT STREETS, NEW CITY

Modern London sprang into being after the Great Fire of 1666, which destroyed four-fifths of the City of London, burning 13,200 houses and 89 churches. The devastation was explicitly commemorated by Sir Christopher Wren's 202-foot **Monument** (*see p63*), but many of the finest buildings in the City stand testament to his talent as the architect of the great remodelling, and to the work of his successors.

London had been a densely populated place built largely of wood, and fire control was primitive. It was only after the three-day inferno that the authorities insisted on a few basic regulations. Brick and stone became the construction materials of choice, and key streets were widened to act as firebreaks. Yet, despite grand, classical proposals from several architects (Wren among them), London reshaped itself around its old street pattern, and some structures that survived the Fire still stand as reminders of earlier building styles. Chief of these are the City's fragments of Roman wall (Tower Hill tube station and the grounds of the Museum of London, *see p55*, have good examples)

and the central Norman keep at the **Tower of London** (*see p64*), begun soon after William's 1066 conquest and extended over the next 300 years; the Navy saved the Tower from the flames by blowing up surrounding houses before the inferno could reach it.

Another longstanding building, **Westminster Abbey** (*see p103*) was begun in 1245 when the site lay far outside London's walls; it was completed in 1745 by Nicholas Hawksmoor's distinctive west towers. The abbey is the most French of England's Gothic churches, but the chapel – begun by Henry VII – is pure Tudor. Centuries later, Washington Irving gushed: 'Stone seems, by the winning labour of the chisel, to have been robbed of its weight and density, suspended aloft, as if by magic.'

A LATE FLOWERING

The European Renaissance came late to Britain, making its London debut with Inigo Jones's 1622 **Banqueting House** (*see p101*). The sumptuously decorated ceiling, added in 1635 by Rubens, celebrated the Stuart monarchy's Divine Right to rule, although 14 years later King

IN CONTEXT

Tower of London Gundulf of Rochester, 1078.

Charles I provided a greater spectacle as he was led from the room and beheaded on a stage outside. Tourists also have Jones to thank for **St Paul's Covent Garden** (*see p76*) and the precise little **Queen's House** (*see p140*) in Greenwich, but they're not his only legacies. He mastered the art of piazzas (notably at Covent Garden), porticos and pilasters, changing British architecture forever. His work influenced the careers of succeeding generations of architects and introduced a habit of venerating the past that it would take 300 years to kick.

Nothing cheers a builder like a natural disaster, and one can only guess at the relish with which Wren and co began rebuilding after the Fire. They brandished classicism like a new broom: the pointed arches of English Gothic were rounded off, Corinthian columns made an appearance and church spires became as complex, frothy and multi-layered as a wedding cake.

Wren blazed the trail with his daring plans for **St Paul's Cathedral** (*see p53*), spending an enormous (for the time) £500 on just the oak model of his proposal. But the scheme, incorporating a Catholic dome rather than a Protestant steeple, was too Roman for the establishment and the design was rejected. Wren quickly produced a redesign and gained planning permission by incorporating a spire, only to set about a series of mischievous U-turns to give us the building, domed and heavily suggestive of an ancient temple, that survives to this day.

Wren's baton was picked up by Nicholas Hawksmoor and James Gibbs, who benefited from a 1711 decree that 50 extra churches should be built using the money raised by a tax on coal. Gibbs became busy around Trafalgar Square with the steepled Roman temple of **St Martin-in-the-Fields** (*see p98*), as well as the Baroque **St Mary-le-Strand** and the tower of **St Clement Danes** (for both, *see p79*). His work was well received, but the more experimental Hawksmoor had a rougher ride. For one thing, not everyone admired his stylistic innovations; for another, even fewer approved of his

financial planning, or lack of it: **St George's Bloomsbury** (*see p72*) cost three times its £10,000 budget and took 15 years to build. Nonetheless, Hawksmoor designed, in whole or part, eight new places of worship. Like Wren, Hawksmoor loved the classical temple, a style at odds with the Act's insistence on spires. **St George-in-the-East**, **St Anne Limehouse** and **St Mary Woolnoth** (*see p59*) are all unorthodox resolutions of this contradiction, but the 'spire' of St George's Bloomsbury is the barmiest. Apeing the Mausoleum of Halicarnassus, Hawksmoor created a peculiar stepped pyramid design, plopped a giant statue of George I in a toga on top and then added unicorns and lions. Hawksmoor's ruinous overspends were one reason why just a dozen of the proposed 50 churches were built.

After action, reaction: one of a large family of Scottish architects, Robert Adam found himself at the forefront of a movement that came to see Italian Baroque as a corruption of the real thing, with architectural exuberance dropped in favour of a simpler interpretation of ancient forms. The best surviving work of Robert and his brothers James, John and William can be found in London's great suburban houses **Syon House** (*see p152*) and **Kenwood House** (*see p120*), but the project for which they're most famous no longer stands: the cripplingly expensive Adelphi housing estate. Almost all of the complex was pulled down in the 1930s and replaced by an office block, apart from the **Royal Society of Arts** building, just off the Strand on John Adam Street.

SOANE AND NASH

Just as the first residents were moving into the Adelphi, a young unknown called John Soane was embarking on a domestic commission in Ireland. It was never completed, but Soane eventually returned to London and went on to build the **Bank of England** (*see p56*) and **Dulwich Picture Gallery** (*see p135*). The Bank was demolished between the wars, leaving only the perimeter walls of Soane's masterpiece, but his gracious Stock Office

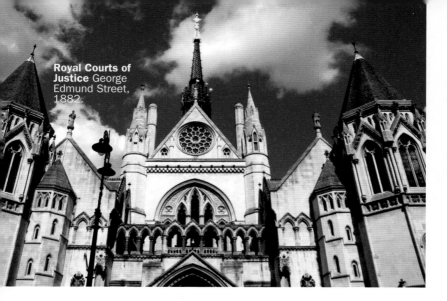

Royal Courts of Justice George Edmund Street, 1882.

has been reconstructed in the Bank's museum (*see p59*). A further glimpse of what the bankers might have enjoyed can be gleaned from his house, the quirkily marvellous **Sir John Soane's Museum** (*see p67* **Happy Birthday, Sir John's House!**), an exquisite architectural experiment.

A near-contemporary of Soane's, John Nash was a less talented architect, but his contributions – among them the inner courtyard of **Buckingham Palace** (*see p106*), the **Theatre Royal Haymarket** and **Regent Street** (*see p92*) – have comparable influence in the look of contemporary London to those of Wren. Regent Street began as a proposal to link the West End to the planned park further north, as well as a device to separate the toffs of Mayfair from the riff-raff of Soho; in Nash's own words, a 'complete separation between the Streets occupied by the Nobility and Gentry, and the narrow Streets and meaner houses occupied by mechanics and the trading part of the community'.

By the 1830s, the classical form of building had been established in England for some 200 years, but this didn't prevent a handful of upstarts from pressing for change. In 1834, the **Houses of Parliament** (*see p101*) burned down, leading to the construction of Sir Charles Barry's Gothic masterpiece. Barry sought out Augustus Welby Northmore Pugin. Working alongside Barry, if not always in agreement with him (of Barry's symmetrical layout, he famously remarked, 'All Grecian, sir. Tudor details on a classic body'), Pugin created a Victorian fantasy that would later be condemned as the Disneyfication of history.

GETTING GOTHIC

This was the beginning of the Gothic Revival, a move to replace what was considered foreign and pagan with something that was native and Christian. Architects would often decide that buildings weren't Gothic enough; as with the 15th-century Great Hall at the **Guildhall** (*see p59*), which gained its corner turrets and central spire only in 1862. The argument between Classicists and Goths erupted in 1857, when the government hired Sir George Gilbert Scott, a leading light of the Gothic movement, to design a new home for the Foreign Office. Scott's design incensed anti-Goth Lord Palmerston, then prime minister, whose diktats prevailed. But Scott exacted his revenge by building an office in which everyone hated working, and by going on to construct wonderful Gothic edifices all over town, among them the **Albert Memorial** (*see p112*) and what is now the **Renaissance St Pancras** hotel (*see p237*), forming the front of St Pancras International train station (*see p73*).

St Pancras was completed in 1873, after the Midland Railway commissioned Scott to build a London terminus that would dwarf that of its rivals next door at King's Cross. Using the project as an opportunity to show his mastery of the Gothic form, Scott built an asymmetrical castle that obliterated views of the train shed behind, itself an engineering marvel completed earlier by William Barlow. Other charming, imposing neo-Gothic buildings around the city include the **Royal Courts of Justice** (*see p49*), the **Natural History Museum** (*see p112*) and **Tower Bridge** (*see p64*). Under the influence of the Arts and Crafts movement, medievalism morphed into such mock Tudor buildings as the wonderful half-timbered **Liberty** department store (*see p204*).

BEING MODERN
World War I and the coming of modernism led to a spirit of renewal and a starker aesthetic. **Freemasons' Hall** (*see p77*) and the BBC's **Broadcasting House** (*see p86*) are good examples of the pared-down style of the 1920s and '30s, but perhaps the finest example of between-the-wars modernism can be found at **London Zoo** (*see p89*). Built by Russian émigré Bertold Lubetkin and the Tecton group, the spiral ramps of the former Penguin Pool were a showcase for the possibilities of concrete. The material was also put to good use on the London Underground, enabling the quick, cheap building of cavernous spaces with sleek lines and curves: the collaboration between London Underground supremo Frank Pick and architect Charles Holden created design masterpieces such as **Southgate** and **Arnos Grove stations** on the Piccadilly line, and **Chiswick Park station** on the District line, as well as the transport headquarters at **55 Broadway** – which featured sculptures by modern masters Jacob Epstein, Eric Gill and Henry Moore. Further innovations were employed on the gorgeous **Daily Express** building (121-128 Fleet Street), built in 1931 using the pioneering 'curtain wall' construction, its radical black vitrolite and glass façade hung on an internal frame.

The bombs of World War II left large areas of London ruined, providing another opportunity for builders to cash in. Lamentably, the city was little improved

City Hall Norman Foster, 2002.

The **Shard** Renzo Piano, 2012.

HERE COME THE STARCHITECTS

The 1970s and '80s offered up a pair of alternatives to concrete: postmodernism and high-tech. The former is represented by César Pelli's blandly monumental **One Canada Square** (*see p129*) in Docklands, an oversized obelisk that's perhaps the archetypal expression of late '80s architecture – and whose impact is hard to imagine now it stands in a copse of inferior office blocks. Richard Rogers' high-tech **Lloyd's of London** building (*see p61*) is much more widely admired. A clever combination of commercial and industrial aesthetics that adds up to one of the most significant British buildings since the war, it was mocked on completion in 1986; opposite, Rogers' 48-storey **122 Leadenhall Street** ('the Cheese Grater') is now under way again, while nearby Bishopsgate has both the City's current tallest building, the 755ft, 46-storey **Heron Tower**, and the footings of the building that will soon exceed it: the **Pinnacle** ('the Helter Skelter'), planned to reach 945 feet.

Apart from Rogers, the city's most visible contemporary architect has been Norman Foster, whose **City Hall** and **30 St Mary Axe** (aka 'the Gherkin'; *see p61*) caught up with Big Ben and black taxis as movie shorthand for 'Welcome to London!' – only to be overtaken in 2012 by the giant glass spike of Renzo Piano's **Shard** (*see p46* **The Shard of Glass**), on the opposite bank of the Thames. Foster's prolific practice set new standards in sports design with the soaring arch of the new **Wembley Stadium** (*see p314*); the exercise in complexity that is the £100 million Great Court at the **British Museum** (*see p70*) did the same for London's cultural gem. The Great Court is the largest covered square in Europe, but each of the 3,300 triangular glass panels that make up its roof is unique.

Much new architecture is to be found cunningly inserted into old buildings. Herzog & de Meuron's fabulous transformation of a Bankside power station into **Tate Modern** (*see p43*) is the most famous example – the firm aims to repeat its success with an ambitious new

by the rebuild; in many cases, it was left worse off. The destruction left the capital with a dire housing shortage, so architects were given a chance to demonstrate the grim efficiency with which they could house large numbers of families in tower blocks. There were post-war successes, however, including the **Royal Festival Hall** (*see p38*) on the South Bank. The sole survivor of the 1951 Festival of Britain, the RFH was built to celebrate the end of the war and the centenary of the Great Exhibition, held in 1851 and responsible for the foundation in South Kensington of the Natural History Museum, the Science Museum and the V&A. Next door to the RFH, the **Hayward** gallery (*see p39*) is an exemplar of the 1960s vogue for Brutalist architecture, a style more thoroughly explored at the **Barbican** (*see p54*), loved by many but never fully rehabilitated from the vilification it received in the years after it opened in 1982.

extension, the bottom of which opened in 2012 as The Tanks. We must wait until, perhaps, 2016 to see the pyramid folded out of origami that will loom above. Equally ground-breaking was Future Systems' NatWest Media Centre at **Lord's Cricket Ground** (*see p119*). Built from aluminium in a boatyard and perched high above the pitch, it's one of London's most daring constructions to date, especially given the traditional setting.

LOCAL COLOUR AND OPEN ARTS

Architecture hasn't all been about headline projects and eye-troubling commercial developments. Will Alsop's multicoloured **Peckham Library** (122 Peckham Hill Street) helped redefine community architecture in 2000, but architects have continued to play a major role in redefining public libraries: David Adjaye subsequently designed the **Idea Stores** (www.ideastore.co.uk) in Poplar (1 Vesey Path, East India Dock Road) and Whitechapel (321 Whitechapel Road), with a crisp, softened industrial aesthetic that is a world away from the familiar Victorian versions, and at the end of 2011 Piers Gough's **Canada Water Library** (21 Surrey Quays Road), an upside-down pyramid that provides a focus for a rather incoherent district in south-east London. The subtle Robbrecht en Daem expansion of **Whitechapel Gallery** (*see p125*) into the stylistically very different former library next door reversed this process, giving a new democratic openness to a pair of landmark Victorian buildings.

THE END – OR BEGINNING? – OF THE MEGABUILDS

In the north of the London, the transformation of King's Cross is approaching its conclusion. Here you'll find the reopened St Pancras International Station, a refurbished **King's Cross station** with a spectacular new roof, a new-build office/concert venue **Kings Place** (*see p300*) and **Central St Martins** art college, in a redeveloped Victorian granary on a fine new square with geometric, choreographed fountains and terracing down to the canal. This 67-acre brownfield redevelopment, King's Cross Central (*see p71* **Hip to Be a Square**), will eventually also comprise 1,900 new homes, serviced by 20 new streets and another four squares, in a part of London that has its very own new postcode: N1C.

Even more impressive – and also with its own postcode, E20, cannily borrowed from the fictional London borough in long-running BBC TV soap opera *EastEnders* – is the **Olympic Park** (*see pp21-23*). Having admirably fulfilled its function as the major venue for the 2012 Olympics

IN CONTEXT

Looking at London

Get the inside view on the city's architecture.

Both the **Architectural Association** (36 Bedford Square, WC1B 3ES, 7887 4000, www.aaschool.net; closed Sun) and **Royal Institute of British Architects** (66 Portland Place, WC1E 7BT, 7580 5533, www.architecture.com; closed Sun) have terrific exhibitions on different aspects of architecture, but for a focused look at London's architectural future, get off the tube at Goodge Street and visit **New London Architecture** (26 Store Street, WC1E 7BT, 7636 4044, www.newlondonarchitecture.org; closed Sun). NLA's centrepiece is a 39-foot-long scale model of the city, with all major developments with planning permission marked in white. Around the model, boards have copious information on key new buildings, providing real insight into the city's recent and future architecture and plans. In addition, Open-City's **Open House London** festival (*see p31*) is the key date in the architecture calendar each year. It does a terrific job of getting locals engaged with their city by giving public access to amazing buildings of all ages that are normally inaccessible.

ArcelorMittal Orbit Anish Kapoor and Cecil Balmond, 2012.

and Paralympics, it is now being made fit for public ('legacy' in the jargon) use – and the taxpayer may expect rather a lot from a project for which the original budget of £2.4bn had to be increased to an eye-watering 9.3bn, apparently due to a failure to include VAT and security costs. In the short term, the Park's temporary venues are being stripped out, leaving the Olympic Stadium, the beautiful wood-clad Velodrome (to be centrepiece of a VeloPark that will add a cycle trail to the Olympic BMX track), Zaha Hadid's stunning Aquatics Centre (finally without its disfiguring temporary seating stands), the Copper Box, the ugly media centre, the water-based hockey pitches (migrating north to Eton Manor), the Athletes' Village (renamed 'East Village') and, presiding over it all, the cordially loathed red spirals of the Anish Kapoor-designed **ArcelorMittal Orbit** – which, we suspect, will gradually turn out to be rather popular when the southern section reopens to the public in 2014 as the 500-acre Queen Elizabeth Olympic Park.

While the value of the Olympic 'legacy' will be fought over for a long time, changes have been seen around other 2012 Games venues: new 'town centres' at Stratford, on the eastern flank of the Olympic Park, where the **Westfield Stratford City** mall (*see p209*) has been doing serious business, and in Woolwich; the £30m Siemens sustainability centre on the Royal Docks, linked across the Thames by Mayor Boris Johnson's latest vanity project – the **Emirates Air Line** cable car (*see p130*) – to the **O2 Arena** (*see p138*), with its own cluster of new buildings, including a university campus. Planners have pointed to this bit of London, start of the 'Thames Gateway', as the city's future for many years now – that possibility is now underpinned by the beginning of the colossally ambitious **Crossrail** project. Not due for completion until 2018, this railway is already worming its way under key areas of the city, including Oxford Street, to connect suburbs to the east and west with the centre of London. It is an extraordinary feat of civil engineering.

Are we on the way to a better future city? The arguments on both sides are fierce. But one thing is clear: heading up, out and under, we are well on our way to a bigger future London.

Essential Information

Getting Around

ARRIVING & LEAVING

By air

Gatwick Airport *0844 892 0322, www.gatwickairport.com. About 30 miles south of central London, off the M23.*
Of the three rail services that link Gatwick to London, the quickest is the **Gatwick Express** (0845 850 1530, www.gatwickexpress.com) to Victoria; it takes 30mins and runs 3.30am-12.30am daily. Tickets cost £18.90 single or £33.20 for an open return (valid for 30 days). Under-15s pay £9.45 for a single and £16.60 for returns; under-5s go free.
  Southern (0845 127 2920, www.southernrailway.com) also runs a rail service between Gatwick and Victoria, with trains every 5-10mins (every 30mins between 1am and 4am). It takes about 35mins, and costs £12.50 for a single, £13 for a day return (after 9.30am) and £30.80 for an open period return (valid for one month). Under-16s get half-price tickets; under-5s go free.
  If you're staying in King's Cross or Bloomsbury, consider trains run by **First Capital Connect** (0845 748 4950, www.firstcapital connect.co.uk) to St Pancras. Tickets are £9.90 single, £10 day return (after 9.32am); £18 for a 30-day open return.
  A **taxi** to the centre costs about £100 and takes a bit over an hour.

Heathrow Airport *0844 335 1801, www.heathrowairport.com. About 15 miles west of central London, off the M4.*
The **Heathrow Express** train (0845 600 1515, www.heathrow express.co.uk) runs to Paddington every 15mins (5.10am-11.25pm daily), and takes 15-20mins. The train can be boarded at the tube station that serves Terminals 1, 2 and 3 (aka Heathrow Central; Terminal 2 is currently closed for rebuilding), or the separate station serving the new Terminal 5; for passengers travelling to or from Terminal 4, a shuttle train connects with Heathrow Central. Tickets cost £18 single (£1 less online, £5 more if you buy on board) or £34 return (£5 more if you buy on board);

under-16s go half-price. Many airlines have check-in desks at Paddington Station.
  The journey by tube into central London is longer but cheaper. The 50-60min **Piccadilly line** ride into central London costs £5.30 one way (£2.60 under-16s). Trains run every few minutes from about 5am to 11.42pm daily (5.45am-11.30pm Sun).
  The **Heathrow Connect** (0845 678 6975, www.heathrow connect.com) rail service offers direct access to Hayes, Southall, Hanwell, West Ealing, Ealing Broadway and Paddington stations in west and north-west London. The trains run every half-hour, terminating at Heathrow Central (Terminals 1 and 3). From there to Terminal 4 get the free shuttle; between Central and Terminal 5, there's free use of the Heathrow Express. A single from Paddington is £9.10; an open return is £17.80.
  National Express (0871 781 8181, www.nationalexpress.com) runs daily coach services to London Victoria (90mins, 5am-9.35pm daily), leaving Heathrow Central bus terminal every 20-30mins. It's £8.50 for a single (£3 under-16s) or £11 (£5.50 under-16s) for a return. A taxi into town will cost £45-£65 and take 30-60mins.

London City Airport *7646 0088, www.londoncityairport.com. About 9 miles east of central London.*
The Docklands Light Railway (DLR) now includes a stop for London City Airport. The journey to Bank station in the City takes around 20mins, and trains run 5.35am-12.17am Mon-Sat or 7.07am-11.17pm Sun. By road, a taxi costs around £30 to central London; less to the City or to Canary Wharf.

Luton Airport *01582 405100, www.london-luton.com. About 30 miles north of central London, J10 off the M1.*
It's a short bus ride from the airport to Luton Airport Parkway station. From here, the **First Capital Connect** rail service *(see left)* calls at many stations (St Pancras International and City among them); journey time is 35-45mins. Trains leave every 15mins or so and cost £14.50 single one-

way and £25 return, or £15 for a cheap day return (after 9.16am Mon-Fri, all day weekends). Trains between Luton and St Pancras run at least hourly all night.
  By coach, the Luton to Victoria journey takes 60-90mins. **Green Line** (0844 801 7261, www.green line.co.uk) runs a 24hr service. A single is £15 and returns cost £22; under-16s £12 single, £17 return. A taxi to London costs £70-£80.

Stansted Airport *0844 335 1803, www.stanstedairport.com. About 35 miles north-east of central London, J8 off the M11.*
The **Stansted Express** train (0845 748 4950, www.stansted express.com) runs to and from Liverpool Street Station; the journey time is 40-45mins. Trains leave every 15mins, and tickets cost £22.50 single, £31.50 return; under-16s travel half-price, under-5s free.
  Several companies run coaches to central London. The **Airbus** (0871 781 8181, www.national express.com) coach service from Stansted to Victoria takes at least 80mins. Coaches run roughly every 30mins (24hrs daily), more at peak times. A single is £10 (£5 for under-16s), return is £17 (£8.50 for under-16s).
  A **taxi** into the centre of London costs around £100.

By coach

Coaches run by **National Express** (0871 781 8181, www.nationalexpress.com), the biggest coach company in the UK, arrive at **Victoria Coach Station** (164 Buckingham Palace Road, SW1W 9TP, 0843 222 1234, www.tfl.gov.uk), a good 10min walk from Victoria tube station. This is where companies such as Eurolines (01582 404511, www.eurolines.com) dock their European services.

By rail

Trains from mainland Europe run by Eurostar (0843 218 6186, www.eurostar.com) arrive at **St Pancras International** (Pancras Road, King's Cross, NW1 2QP, 7843 7688, www.stpancras.com).

PUBLIC TRANSPORT

Getting around London on public transport is straightforward but it's certainly not cheap.

Information

Details on timetables and other travel information are provided by **Transport for London** (0843 222 1234, www.tfl.gov.uk/journey planner). Complaints or comments on most forms of public transport can also be taken up with **London TravelWatch** (7505 9000, www. londontravelwatch.org.uk).

Travel Information Centres

TfL's Travel Information Centres provide help with the tube, buses and Docklands Light Railway (DLR; *see p364*). You can find them in **King's Cross tube station**, (7.15am-8.15pm Mon-Sat; 8.15am-7.15pm Sun) and in the stations below. Call 0843 222 1234 for more information.

Euston Station 7.15am-7pm Mon-Thur, Sat; 7.15am-8pm Fri; 8.15am-7pm Sun.
Heathrow Terminals 1, 2 & 3 tube station 7.15am-7.30pm daily.
Liverpool Street tube station 7.15am-7pm Mon-Thur, Sat; 7.15am-8pm Fri; 8.15am-7pm Sun.
Piccadilly Circus tube station 7.45am-7pm Mon-Fri; 9.15am-7pm Sat; 9.15am-6pm Sun.
Victoria Station 7.15am-8pm Mon-Sat; 8.15am-7pm Sun.

Fares & tickets

Tube and DLR fares are based on a system of six zones, stretching 12 miles out from the centre of London. A flat cash fare of £4.30 per journey applies across zones 1-4 on the tube, and £5.30 for zones 1-6; customers save up to £2.60 per journey with a pre-pay Oyster card (*see below*). Anyone caught without a ticket or Oyster card is subject to a £50 on-the-spot fine (reduced to £25 if you pay within three weeks).

Oyster cards A pre-paid smart-card, Oyster is the cheapest way of getting around on public transport. You can charge up standard Oyster cards at tube stations, Travel Information Centres (*see above*), some rail stations and newsagents. There is a £5 refundable deposit payable on each card; to collect your deposit, call 0845 330 9876.
Visitor Oyster cards are available from Gatwick Express

outlets, National Express coaches, Superbreak, visitlondon.com, visit britaindirect.com, Oxford Tube coach service and on Eurostar services. The only difference between Visitor Oysters and 'normal' Oysters is that they come pre-loaded with money.

A tube journey in zone 1 using Oyster pay-as-you-go costs £2 (75p for under-16s), compared to the cash fare of £4.30. A single tube ride within zones 2, 3, 4, 5 or 6 costs £1.50 (75p for under-16s); single journeys from zones 1 through to 6 using Oyster are £4.80 (6.30-9.30am, 4-7pm Mon-Fri) or £2.90 (all other times), or 75p for children. Up to four children pay just £1 each for their fares when accompanied by an adult with a Travelcard.

If you make a number of different journeys using an Oyster pay-as-you-go card on a particular day, the total fare deducted will always be capped at the price of an equivalent Day Travelcard. However, if you only make one journey using Oyster pay-as-you-go, you will only be charged a single Oyster fare.

Day Travelcards If you're only using the tube, DLR, buses and trams, using Oyster to pay as you go will always be capped at the same price as an equivalent Day Travelcard. However, if you're also using National Rail services, Oyster may not be accepted: opt, instead, for a Day Travelcard, a standard ticket with a coded stripe that allows travel across all networks.

Anytime Day Travelcards can be used all day. They cost from £8.40 for zones 1-2 (£4.20 child), up to £15.80 for zones 1-6 (£7.90 child). Tickets are valid for journeys begun by 4.30am the next day. The cheaper **Off-Peak Day Travelcard** allows travel after 9.30am Mon-Fri and all day at weekends and public holidays. It costs from £7 for zones 1-2 up to £8.50 for zones 1-6.

Children Under-5s travel free on buses and trams without the need to provide any proof of identity. Five- and 10-year-olds can also travel free, but need to obtain a 5-10 Zip Oyster photocard. For details, visit www.tfl.gov.uk/fares or call 0845 330 9876.

An 11-15 Zip Oyster photocard is needed by 11- to 15-year-olds to pay as they go on the tube/DLR and to buy 7-Day, monthly or longer period Travelcards, and by 11- to 15-year-olds to use the tram to/from Wimbledon for free.

Photocards Photocards are not required for 7-Day Travelcards or Bus Passes, adult-rate Travelcards or Bus Passes charged on an Oyster card. For details of how to obtain 5-10, 11-15 or 16+ Oyster photocards, see www.tfl.gov.uk/fares or call 0845 330 9876.

London Underground

Delays are fairly common, with lines closing at weekends for engineering works. Trains are hot and crowded in rush hour (8-9.30am and 4-7.30pm Mon-Fri). Even so, the 12 colour-coded lines that together comprise the underground rail system – also known as 'the tube' – remain the quickest way to get around London (for a map of the Underground, *see pp414-415*), carrying some 3.5 million passengers every weekday. Comments or complaints are dealt with by **LU Customer Services** on 0845 330 9880 (8am-8pm daily); for lost property, *see p370*.

Using the system You can get Oyster cards from www.tfl.gov.uk/oyster, by calling 0845 330 9876, at tube stations, Travel Information Centres, some rail stations and newsagents. Single or day tickets can be bought from ticket offices or machines. You can buy most tickets and top up Oyster cards at self-service machines. Some ticket offices close early (around 7.30pm); carry a charged-up Oyster card to avoid being stranded.

To enter and exit the tube using an Oyster card, simply touch it to the yellow reader, which will open the gates. Make sure you also touch the card to the reader when you exit the tube, or you'll be charged a higher fare when you next use your card to enter a station. On certain lines, you'll see a pink 'validator' –touch this reader in addition to the yellow entry/exit readers and on some routes it will reduce your fare.

To enter using a paper ticket, place it in the slot with the black magnetic strip facing down, then pull it out of the top to open the gates. Exiting is done in much the same way; however, if you have a single journey ticket, it will be retained by the gate as you leave.

Timetables Tube trains run daily from around 5am (except Sunday, when they start an hour or so later, and Christmas Day, when there's no service). You shouldn't have to wait more than 10mins for a train; during peak times, services should run every 2-3mins. Times of last trains vary; they're usually around 12.30am daily (11.30pm on Sun). The tubes run all night only on New Year's Eve; otherwise, you're limited to night buses (*see right*).

Fares The single fare for adults across the network is £4.30. Using Oyster pay-as-you-go, the fare varies by zone: zone 1 costs £2; zones 1-2 costs £2 or £2.70, depending on the time of day; zones 1-6 is £2.90 or £4.80. The single fare for children aged 5-15 is 70p or 75p for any journey depending on the time of day. Under-5s travel for free. .

National Rail & London Overground services

Independently run commuter services co-ordinated by **National Rail** (0845 748 4950, www.national rail.co.uk) leave from the city's main rail stations. Visitors heading to south London, or to more remote destinations such as Hampton Court Palace, will need to use these overground services. Travelcards are valid on these services within the right zones, but not all routes accept Oyster pay-as-you-go; check before you travel.

Operated by Transport for London, meaning it does accept Oyster, the **London Overground** is a fabulously useful new service. Originally the rail line ran through north London from Stratford in the east to Richmond in the south-west, with spurs connecting Willesden Junction in the north-west to Clapham Junction in the south-west, and Gospel Oak in the north to Barking in the east, as well as heading north-west from Euston. Then, in 2010, the reopened East London line was incorporated into the Overground network, connecting trains south of the river to trains to the north: effectively, Crystal Palace, West Croydon and New Cross are now connected (via useful, brand-new intermediate stations such as Shoreditch High Street) to Highbury & Islington and the northerly extent of the Overground. Trains run about every 20mins (every half an hour on Sunday).

For lost property, *see p370*.

Docklands Light Railway (DLR)

DLR trains (7363 9700, www.tfl. gov.uk/dlr) run from Bank station (where they connect with the tube

system's Central and Waterloo & City lines) or Tower Gateway, close to Tower Hill tube (Circle and District lines). At Westferry station, the line splits east and south via Island Gardens to Greenwich and Lewisham; a change at Poplar can take you north to Stratford. The easterly branch forks after Canning Town to either Beckton or Woolwich Arsenal. Trains run 5.30am-12.30am daily. For lost property, *see p370*.

Fares Adult single fares on the DLR are the same as for the tube (*see p263*) except for DLR-only journeys in zones 2-3, which cost £4.30 (£1.40-£1.50 with Oyster pay-as-you-go) or £2.10 for 11-15s (70p-75p with Oyster pay-as-you-go).

The DLR also offers a one-day Rail River Rover Pass, combining one day's travel on DLR with hop-on, hop-off travel on City Cruises riverboats between Westminster, London Eye, Tower and Greenwich piers (*see p266*).

Trains leave Tower Gateway hourly from 10am for a special tour, with a guide adding commentary. It costs £15 for adults or £8 for kids.

Buses

You must have a ticket or valid pass before boarding any bus in zone 1, and before boarding any articulated, single-decker bus ('bendy buses', which are in the process of being phased out) anywhere in the city. You can buy a ticket (or a 1-Day Bus Pass) from machines at bus stops, although they're often not working; better to travel with an Oyster card or some other pass (*see p263*). Inspectors patrol buses at random; if you don't have a ticket or pass, you may be fined £50.

All buses are now low-floor vehicles that are accessible to wheelchair-users and passengers with buggies. The only exceptions are Heritage routes 9 and 15, which are served by the world-famous open-platform Routemaster buses.

For lost property, *see p370*.

Fares Using Oyster pay-as-you-go costs £1.35 a trip; your total daily payment, regardless of how many journeys you take, will be capped at £4.20. Paying with cash at the time of travel costs £2.30 for a single trip. Under-16s travel for free (using an Under-11 or 11-15 Oyster photocard as appropriate; *see p263*). A 1-Day Bus Pass gives unlimited

bus and tram travel for £4.20.

Night buses Many bus routes operate 24hrs a day, seven days a week. There are also some special night buses with an 'N' prefix, which run from about 11pm to 6am. Most night services run every 15-30mins, but busier routes run a service around every 10mins. Fares are the same as for daytime buses; Bus Passes and Travelcards can be used at no extra fare until 4.30am of the morning after they expire.

Green Line buses Green Line buses (0844 801 7261, www.green line.co.uk) serve the suburbs within 40 miles of London. Its office is opposite **Victoria Coach Station** (*see p262*); services run 24hrs.

Tramlink

In south London, trams run between Beckenham, Croydon, Addington and Wimbledon. Travelcards that cover zones 3, 4, 5 or 6 are valid, as are Bus Passes. Cash fares are £2.30 (£1.35 with Oyster pay-as-you-go).

For lost property, *see p370*.

Water transport

Most river services operate every 20-60mins between 10.30am and 5pm, and may run more often and later in summer. From commuters, **Thames Clippers** (0870 781 5049, www.thamesclippers.com) runs a service between Embankment Pier and Royal Arsenal Woolwich Pier; stops include Blackfriars, Bankside, London Bridge, Canary Wharf and Greenwich. A standard day roamer ticket (valid 9am-9pm) costs £13.60, while a single from Embankment to Greenwich is £6, or £5.40 for Oyster cardholders. **Thames Executive Charters** (www. thamesexecutivecharters.com) also offers Travelcard discounts on its River Taxi between Putney and Blackfriars, calling at Wandsworth, Chelsea Harbour, Cadogan Pier and Embankment, meaning a £4.50 standard single becomes £3.

Westminster Passenger Service Assocation (7930 2062, www.wpsa.co.uk) runs a daily service from Westminster Pier to Kew, Richmond and Hampton Court from April to October. At around £12 for a single, it's not cheap, but it is a lovely way to see the city, and there are discounts of 33%-50% for Travelcard holders.

Thames River Services (www.westminsterpier.co.uk) operates from the same pier, offering trips to Greenwich, Tower Pier and the Thames Barrier. A trip to Greenwich costs £10, though £13.50 buys you a Rivercard, which allows you to hop on and off at will. Travelcard holders get a third off.

For commuter service timetables, plus a full list of leisure operators and services, see www.tfl.gov.uk.

For lost property, *see p370.*

TAXIS

Black cabs

The licensed London taxi, aka 'black cab' (although, since on-car advertising, they've come in many colours), is a much-loved feature of London life. Drivers must pass a test called 'the Knowledge' to prove they know every street in central London, and the shortest route to it.

If a taxi's orange 'For Hire' sign is lit, it can be hailed. If a taxi stops, the cabbie must take you to your destination if it's within seven miles. It can be hard to find an empty cab, especially just after the pubs close. Fares rise after 8pm on weekdays and at weekends.

You can book black cabs from the 24hr **Taxi One-Number** (0871 871 8710, a £2 booking fee applies, plus 12.5% if you pay by credit card), **Radio Taxis** (7272 0272) and **Dial-a-Cab** (7253 5000); credit cards only, with a booking fee of £2 plus a 12.5% handling charge). Complaints about black cabs should be made to the **Public Carriage Office** (0845 602 7000, www.tfl.gov.uk/pco). Note the cab's badge number, which should be displayed in the rear of the cab and on its back bumper.

Minicabs

Minicabs (saloon cars) are generally cheaper than black cabs, but can be less reliable. Only use licensed firms (look for a plate in the front and rear windows), and avoid those that illegally tout for business in the street: drivers may be unlicensed, uninsured and dangerous.

Trustworthy and fully licensed firms include **Addison Lee** (0844 800 6677), which will text you when the car arrives, and **Lady Cabs** (7272 3300), **Ladybirds** (8295 0101) and **Ladycars** (8558 9511), which employ only women drivers. Otherwise, text HOME to 60835 ('60tfl'). Transport for London will then text you the numbers of the two nearest licensed minicab operators and the number for Taxi One-Number, which provides

licensed black taxis in London. The service costs 35p plus standard call rate. Always ask the price when you book and confirm it with the driver.

Motorbike taxis

Passenger Bikes (0844 561 6147, www.passengerbikes.com) and **Taxybikes** (7255 4269, www.addisonlee.com/passengers/taxybikes) have a minimum £30 charge, and offer fixed airport rates; the bikes are equipped with panniers, and can carry a small to medium suitcase. Central London to Gatwick currently costs £120-£130.

DRIVING

London's roads are often clogged with traffic and roadworks, and parking (*see right*) is a nightmare. Walking or using public transport are better options. If you hire a car, you can use any valid licence from outside the EU for up to a year after arrival. Speed limits in the city are generally 20 or 30mph on most roads. Don't use a mobile phone (unless it's hands-free) while driving or you risk a £1,000 fine.

Car hire

All firms below have branches at the airport; several also have offices in the city centre. Shop around for the best rate; always check the level of insurance included in the price.

Alamo *UK: 0871 384 1086, www.alamo.co.uk. US: 1-877 222 9075, www.alamo.com.*
Avis *UK: 0844 581 0147, www.avis.co.uk. US: 1-800 331 1212, www.avis.com.*
Budget *UK: 0844 544 3439, www.budget.co.uk. US: 1-800 472 3325, www.budget.com.*
Enterprise *UK: 0800 800 227, www.enterprise.co.uk. US: 1-800 261 7331, www.enterprise.com.*
Europcar *UK: 0871 384 1087, www.europcar.co.uk. US: 1-877 940 6900, www.europcar.com.*
Hertz *UK: 0843 309 3099, www.hertz.co.uk. US: 1-800 654 3001, www.hertz.com.*
National *UK: 0870 400 4552, www.nationalcar.co.uk. US: 1-800 222 9058, www.nationalcar.com.*
Thrifty *UK: 01494 751500, www.thrifty.co.uk. US: 1-800 847 4389, www.thrifty.com.*

Congestion charge

Drivers coming into central London between 7am and 6pm Monday to

Friday have to pay £10, a fee known as the congestion charge. The congestion charge zone is bordered by Marylebone, Euston and King's Cross (N), Old Street roundabout (NE), Aldgate (E), Tower Bridge Road (SE), Elephant & Castle (S), Vauxhall, Victoria (SW), Park Lane and Edgware Road (W). You'll know when you're about to drive into the charging zone from the red 'C' signs on the road. You can also enter the postcode of your destination at www.tfl.gov.uk/roadusers/congestioncharging to discover if it's within the charging zone.

There are no tollbooths – the scheme is enforced by numberplate recognition from CCTV cameras. Passes can be bought from some newsagents, garages and NCP car parks; you can also pay online at www.tfl.gov.uk/roadusers/congestioncharging, by phone on 0845 900 1234 or by SMS (you'll need to pre-register at the website for the latter option). You can pay any time during the day; payments are also accepted until midnight on the next charging day, although the fee is £12 if you pay then. Expect a fine of £60 if you fail to pay, rising to £120 if you delay payment.

Breakdown services

AA (Automobile Association)
0870 550 0600 information, 0845 788 7766 breakdown, www.theaa.com.
ETA (Environmental Transport Association) *0845 389 1010, www.eta.co.uk.*
RAC (Royal Automobile Club) *0870 572 2722 information, 0800 828282 breakdown, www.rac.co.uk.*

Parking

Central London is scattered with parking meters, but finding an unoccupied one is usually difficult. Meters cost upwards of £1 for 15mins, and in some areas they are limited to 2hrs. Parking on a single or double yellow line, a red line or in residents' parking areas during the day is illegal, and you may be fined, clamped or towed.

However, in the evening (from 6pm or 7pm in much of central London) and at various times at weekends, parking on single yellow lines is legal and free. If you find a clear spot on a single yellow line during the evening, look for a sign giving the local regulations. Meters also become free at certain times during evenings and weekends.

Parking on double yellow lines and red routes is illegal at all times.

NCP 24hr car parks (0845 050 7080, www.ncp.co.uk) are numerous but pricey. Central ones include Carrington Street, Mayfair, W1 (£12/2hrs); Snowsfields, Southwark, SE1 (£8/2hrs); and Brewer Street, Soho, W1 (£14/2hrs).

Clamping & vehicle removal

The immobilising of illegally parked vehicles with a clamp is common in London. There will be a label on the car telling you which payment centre to phone or visit. You'll have to stump up an £80 release fee and show a valid licence. The payment centre will de-clamp your car within four hours. If you don't remove your car at once, it may get clamped again, so wait by your vehicle.

If your car has disappeared, it's either been stolen or, if it was parked illegally, towed to a car pound by the local authorities. A release fee of £200 is levied for removal, plus upwards of £21 per day from the first midnight after removal. You'll also probably get a parking ticket of £60-£100 when you collect the car (reduced by 50% if paid within 14 days). To retrieve your car, call the **Trace Service** hotline (0845 206 8602).

CYCLING

The **Transport for London** (0843 222 1234, www.tfl.gov.uk) cycle hire scheme has been a great success, allowing when-you-want-it access to a string of bicycle stations across central London. The scheme has expanded further east, and is due to expand westwards to Olympia and eastwards to the Olympic Park.

To hire a bike, go to a docking station, touch the 'Hire a cycle' icon and insert a credit or debit card. The machine will print out a five-digit access code, which you then tap into the docking point of a bike, releasing the cycle, and away you go. £1 buys 24-hour access to the bike and the first 30 minutes are free. Serious cyclists should contact the **London Cycle Network** (www.londoncyclenetwork.org.uk) and **London Cycling Campaign** (7234 9310, www.lcc.org.uk). For details of other London cycle hire companies, see p339.

WALKING

The best way to see London is on foot, but the city's street layout is complicated. We've included street maps of central London in the back of this book; the standard Geographers' *London A-Z* and Collins' *London Street Atlas* are useful supplements. There's also route advice at www.tfl.gov.uk/gettingaround.

GUIDED TOURS

By bicycle

The **London Bicycle Tour Company** (*see p317*) runs a range of tours in central London.

By boat

City Cruises: Rail River Rover 7740 0400, www.citycruises.com. **Rates** £14.50; £7.25 reductions. Combines hop-on, hop-off travel on any regular City Cruise route (pick-ups at Westminster, Waterloo, Tower and Greenwich Piers) with free travel on the DLR.
Jason's Trip Canal Boats www.jasons.co.uk. **Rates** £9 return; £8 reductions. Popular 90min narrowboat tours between Little Venice and Camden.
London Kayak Tours 0845 453 2002, www.londonkayaktours.co.uk. **Tours** from £19.99.
Want to investigate Tower Bridge, Hampton Court Palace or Regent's Canal under your own steam? Guided kayak tours run from March to October.
Thames RIB Experience 7930 5746, www.thamesribexperience.com. **Rates** £34-£48; £20-£29 reductions.
Our favourite of the growing number of Thames RIB tours (a RIB is a powerful speedboat) zooms you from the Embankment, either to Canary Wharf (50mins) or the Thames Barrier (80mins), and back. You'll need to book in advance.

By bus

Big Bus Company 7233 9533, www.bigbustours.com. **Rates** £29; £12 reductions; free under-5s. These open-top buses (8.30am-6pm, or 4.30pm in winter) ply over 70 stops covering all the central areas of interest. There's live commentary in English, and a recorded version in eight other languages; you can hop on and off at any stop. Tickets include a river cruise.
Original London Sightseeing Tour 8877 1722, www.theoriginal tour.com. **Rates** £26; £13 reductions; family £91; free under-5s. OLS's hop-on, hop-off bus tours cover 90 stops in central London,

including Marble Arch and Trafalgar Square. Commentary comes in seven languages. Tickets include a river cruise.
London Duck 7928 3132, www.londonducktours.co.uk. **Rates** £21; £14-£17 reductions; £62 family. Tours of Westminster in an amphibious vehicle. The 75min road/river trip starts on Chicheley Street (behind the London Eye) and enters the Thames at Vauxhall.

By air

Adventure Balloons 01252 844222, www.adventure balloons.co.uk. **Rates** from £185. Balloon flights operate from a number of take-off sites and glide over many of the capital's iconic sights. They run at dawn on weekdays between late April and the middle of August.
The London Helicopter Tour 7887 2626, www.thelondon helicopter.com. **Rates** from £144.50 each for two seats. 30min flights depart from the heliport in Redhill, Surrey – check the website for details.

By car

Black Taxi Tours of London 7935 9363, www.blacktaxi tours.co.uk. **Rates** £130-£145. Tailored 2hr tours for up to five.
Small Car Big City 7585 0399, www.smallcarbigcity.com. **Rates** £54-£239. Feeling a little retro? Tour town in a classic Mini Cooper.

On foot

Head to www.walklondon. org.uk for free walks and events. Good choices for paid group tours include **And Did Those Feet** (8806 4325, www.chr.org.uk), **Performing London** (01234 404774, www.performinglondon. co.uk), **Silver Cane Tours** (07720 715295, www.silver canetours.com) and **Urban Gentry** (8149 6253, www.urban gentry.com). **Original London Walks** (7624 3978, www.walks. com) provides an astonishing 140 different walks on a variety of themes. Idiosyncratic outings follow old London maps (www. londontrails.wordpress.com) or the new London art scene (www.foxandsquirrel.com and streetartlondon.co.uk/tours). **The Guardian** (www.guardian.co.uk/travel/series/london-walks) offers a great set of themed audio walks.

Resources A-Z

TRAVEL ADVICE

For up-to-date information on travel to a specific country – including the latest on safety and security, health issues, local laws and customs – contact your home country government's department of foreign affairs. Most have websites with useful advice for would-be travellers. For information on travelling to the United Kingdom from within the European Union, including details of visa regulations and healthcare provision, see http://europa.eu/travel.

AUSTRALIA
www.smartraveller.gov.au

CANADA
www.voyage.gc.ca

NEW ZEALAND
www.safetravel.govt.nz

REPUBLIC OF IRELAND
http://foreignaffairs.gov.ie

UK
www.fco.gov.uk/travel

USA
www.state.gov/travel

ADDRESSES

London postcodes are rather less helpful than they could be for locating addresses. The first element starts with a compass point – N, E, SE, SW, W and NW, plus the smaller EC (East Central) and WC (West Central). However, the number that follows relates not to geography (unless it's a 1, which indicates central) but to alphabetical order. So N2 is way out in the boondocks (East Finchley), while W2 covers the very central Bayswater.

AGE RESTRICTIONS

Buying/drinking alcohol 18.
Driving 17.
Sex 16.
Smoking 18.

ATTITUDE & ETIQUETTE

Don't mistake reserve for rudeness or indifference: strangers striking up a conversation are likely to be foreign, drunk or mad. The weather is a safe subject on which to broach a conversation. Avoid personal questions or excessive personal contact beyond a handshake.

If you want to really rile people in the Underground, stand blocking the escalator during rush hour (stand on the right, walk on the left).

BUSINESS

As the financial centre of Europe, London is well equipped to meet the needs of business travellers. The financial action is increasingly centred on Canary Wharf. Marketing, advertising and entertainment companies have a strong presence in the West End.

Conventions & conferences

Visit London *0870 156 6366, www.visitlondon.com.* Enquiries.
Queen Elizabeth II Conference Centre *Broad Sanctuary, Westminster, SW1P 3EE (7222 5000, www.qeiicc.co.uk).* Westminster tube. **Open** 8am-6pm Mon-Fri. *Conference facilities* 24hrs daily. **Map** p399 K9.
Excellent conference facilities.

Couriers & shippers

DHL *0844 248 0999, www.dhl.co.uk.*
UPS *0845 787 7877, www.ups.com.*

Office services

British Monomarks *27 Old Gloucester Street, Holborn, WC1N 3AX (7419 5000, www.britishmonomarks.co.uk).* Holborn tube. **Open** 9am-5.30pm Mon-Fri. **Credit** AmEx, MC, V. **Map** p397 L5.

CONSUMER

Consumer Direct *0845 404 0506, www.consumerdirect.gov.uk.* Funded by the government's Office of Fair Trading, this is a good place to start for consumer advice on all goods and services.

CUSTOMS

Citizens entering the UK from outside the EU must adhere to duty-free import limits:

- 200 cigarettes or 100 cigarillos or 50 cigars or 250g of tobacco
- 4 litres still table wine plus either 1 litre spirits or strong liqueurs (above 22% abv) or 2 litres fortified wine (under 22% abv), sparkling wine or other liqueurs
- 60cc/ml perfume
- 250cc/ml toilet water
- other goods to the value of no more than £390

The import of meat, poultry, fruit, plants, flowers and protected animals is restricted or forbidden; there are no restrictions on the import or export of currency if travelling from another EU country. If you are travelling from outside the EU, amounts over €10,000 must be declared.

People over the age of 17 arriving from an EU country are able to import unlimited goods for their own personal use, if bought tax-paid (so not duty-free). For more details, see www.hmrc.gov.uk.

DISABLED

As a city that evolved long before the needs of disabled people were considered, London is difficult for wheelchair users, though access and facilities are slowly improving. The capital's bus fleet is now low-floor for easier wheelchair access; there are no steps for any of the city's trams; and all DLR stations have either lifts or ramp access. However, steps and escalators to the tube and overland trains mean they are often of only limited use to wheelchair users. A blue symbol on the tube map (*see pp414-415*) indicates stations with step-free access. The *Step-free Tube Guide*

ESSENTIAL INFORMATION

map is free; call 0843 222 1234 for more details. For London Overground, call 0845 601 4867.

Most major attractions and hotels offer good accessibility, though provisions for the hearing- and sight-disabled are patchier. Enquire about facilities in advance. *Access in London* is an invaluable reference book for disabled traveller. It's available for a £10 donation (sterling cheque, cash US dollars or via PayPal to gordon.couch@yahoo.com) from **Access Project** (39 Bradley Gardens, W13 8HE, www.accessinlondon.org). Or there's Time Out's *Open London* guide to the capital for disabled people.

Artsline *www.artsline.org.uk.* Information on disabled access to arts and culture.
Can Be Done *Congress House, 14 Lyon Road, Harrow, Middx HA1 2EN (8907 2400, www.canbe done.co.uk). Harrow on the Hill tube/rail.* **Open** 9.30am-5pm Mon-Fri. Disabled-adapted holidays and tours in London, around the UK and worldwide.
Royal Association for Disability & Rehabilitation *250 City Road, EC1V 8AF (7250 3222, 7250 4119 textphone, www.radar.org.uk). Old Street tube/rail.* **Open** 9am-5pm Mon-Fri. **Map** p400 P3.
A national organisation for disabled voluntary groups publishing books and the bimonthly magazine *New Bulletin* (£35/yr).
Tourism for All *0845 124 9971, www.tourismforall.org.uk.* **Open** *Helpline* 9am-5pm Mon-Fri. Information for older people and people with disabilities in relation to accessible accommodation and other tourism services.
Wheelchair Travel & Access Mini Buses *1 Johnston Green, Guildford, Surrey GU2 9XS (01483 233640, www.wheelchair-travel.co.uk).* **Open** 9am-6pm Mon-Fri; 9am-noon Sat. Hires out converted vehicles (driver optional), plus cars with hand controls and wheelchair-adapted vehicles.

DRUGS

Illegal drug use remains higher in London than the UK as a whole, though it's becoming less visible on the streets and in clubs. Despite fierce debate, cannabis has been reclassified from Class C to Class B (where it rejoins amphetamine), but possession of a small amount might attract no more than a

warning for a first offence. More serious Class B and A drugs (ecstasy, LSD, heroin, cocaine and the like) carry stiffer penalties, with a maximum of seven years in prison for possession.

ELECTRICITY

The UK uses the European 220-240V, 50-cycle AC voltage. British plugs use three pins, so travellers with two-pin European appliances should bring an adaptor, as should anyone using US appliances, which run off 110-120V, 60-cycle.

EMBASSIES & CONSULATES

American Embassy *24 Grosvenor Square, Mayfair, W1A 2LQ (7499 9000, http://london.usembassy.gov). Bond Street or Marble Arch tube.* **Open** 8.30am-5.30pm Mon-Fri. **Map** p398 G7.
Australian High Commission *Australia House, Strand, Holborn, WC2B 4LA (7379 4334, www. uk.embassy.gov.au). Holborn or Temple tube.* **Open** 9am-5pm Mon-Fri. **Map** p399 M6.
Canadian High Commission *38 Grosvenor Street, Mayfair, W1K 4AA (7258 6600, www.canada. org.uk). Bond Street or Oxford Circus tube.* **Open** 9.30am-4pm Mon-Fri. **Map** p398 H7.
Embassy of Ireland *17 Grosvenor Place, Belgravia, SW1X 7HR (7235 2171, 7225 7700 passports & visas, www.embassyofireland.co.uk). Hyde Park Corner tube.* **Open** 9.30am-5pm Mon-Fri. **Map** p398 G9.
New Zealand High Commission *New Zealand House, 80 Haymarket, St James's, SW1Y 4TQ (7930 8422, www.nzembassy.com). Piccadilly Circus tube.* **Open** 9am-5pm Mon-Fri. **Map** p416 W4.

EMERGENCIES

In the event of a serious accident, fire or other incident, call 999 – free from any phone, including payphones – and ask for an ambulance, the fire service or police. For hospital Accident & Emergency departments, *see p369*; for helplines, *see p369*; for police stations, *see p372*.

GAY & LESBIAN

Time Out Gay & Lesbian London (£12.99) is the ultimate handbook to the capital. The phonelines below offer help and information; for HIV and AIDS, *see p369*.

London Friend *7837 3337, www.londonfriend.org.uk.* **Open** 7.30-9.30pm Mon-Wed, Fri.
London Lesbian & Gay Switchboard *0300 330 0630, www.llgs.org.uk.* **Open** 10am-11pm daily.

HEALTH

British citizens or those working in the UK can go to any general practitioner (GP). People ordinarily resident in the UK, including overseas students, are also permitted to register with a National Health Service (NHS) doctor. If you fall outside these categories, you will have to pay to see a GP. Your hotel concierge should be able to recommend one.

A pharmacist may dispense medicines on receipt of a prescription from a GP. NHS prescriptions cost £7.65; under-16s and over-60s are exempt from charges. Contraception is free for all. If you're not eligible to see an NHS doctor, you'll be charged cost price for any medicines prescribed.

Free emergency medical treatment under the NHS is available to:
● EU nationals and those of Iceland, Norway and Liechtenstein; all may also be entitled to state-provided treatment for non-emergency conditions with an EHIC (European Health Insurance Card)
● nationals of New Zealand, Russia, most former USSR states and the former Yugoslavia
● residents (irrespective of nationality) of Anguilla, Australia, Barbados, the British Virgin Islands, the Falkland Islands, the Isle of Man, Montserrat, Poland, Romania, St Helena and the Turks & Caicos Islands
● anyone who has been in the UK for the previous 12 months, or who has come to the UK to take up permanent residence
● students and trainees whose courses require more than 12 weeks in employment in the first year
● refugees and others who have sought refuge in the UK
● people with HIV/AIDS at a special STD treatment clinic

There are no NHS charges for:
● treatment in A&E wards
● emergency ambulance transport to a hospital
● diagnosis and treatment of certain communicable diseases
● family planning services
● compulsory psychiatric treatment

Accident & emergency

Listed below are most of the central London hospitals that have 24-hour Accident & Emergency (A&E) departments.
Charing Cross Hospital *Fulham Palace Road, Hammersmith, W6 8RF (3311 1234, www.imperial. nhs.uk). Barons Court or Hammersmith tube.*
Chelsea & Westminster Hospital *369 Fulham Road, Chelsea, SW10 9NH (8746 8000, www.chelwest.nhs.uk). South Kensington tube.* **Map** p394 C12.
Royal Free Hospital *Pond Street, Hampstead, NW3 2QG (7794 0500, www.royalfree.nhs.uk). Belsize Park tube or Hampstead Heath rail.*
Royal London Hospital *Whitechapel Road, Whitechapel, E1 1BB (7377 7000, www.bartsandthe london.nhs.uk). Whitechapel tube.*
St Mary's Hospital *Praed Street, Paddington, W2 1NY (3312 6666, www.imperial.nhs.uk). Paddington tube/rail.* **Map** p393 D5.
St Thomas' Hospital *Lambeth Palace Road, Lambeth, SE1 7EH (7188 7188, www.guysandstthomas. nhs.uk). Westminster tube or Waterloo tube/rail.* **Map** p399 L9.
University College Hospital *235 Euston Road, NW1 2BU (0845 155 5000, www.uclh.nhs.uk). Euston Square or Warren Street tube.* **Map** p396 J4.

Complementary medicine

British Homeopathic Association *01582 408675, www.trust homeopathy.org.* **Open** *Enquiries* 9am-5pm Mon-Fri. Referrals.

Contraception & abortion

Family planning advice, contraceptive supplies and abortions are free to British citizens on the NHS, and to EU residents and foreign nationals living in Britain. Phone 0845 122 8690 or visit www.fpa.org.uk for your local Family Planning Association. The 'morning after' pill (around £25), effective up to 72 hours after intercourse, is available over the counter at pharmacies.

British Pregnancy Advisory Service *0845 730 4030, www. bpas.org.* **Open** *Helpline* 8am-9pm Mon-Fri; 8.30am-6pm Sat; 9.30am-2.30pm Sun. Callers are referred to their nearest clinic for treatment.
Brook Advisory Centre *7284 6040, 0808 802 1234 helpline, www.brook.org.uk.* **Open** *Helpline*

9am-7pm Mon-Fri. Information on sexual health, contraception and abortion, plus free pregnancy tests for under-25s.
Marie Stopes House *Family Planning Clinic/Well Woman Centre, 108 Whitfield Street, Fitzrovia, W1T 5BE (0845 300 8090, www.mariestopes.org.uk). Warren Street tube.* **Open** *Clinic* 8.30am-5pm Mon, Wed, Fri; 9.30am-6pm Tue, Thur; 9am-4pm Sat. *Helpline* 24hrs daily. **Map** p396 J4.
Contraceptive advice, emergency contraception, pregnancy testing, an abortion service, cervical and health screening or gynaecological services. Fees may apply.

Dentists

Dental care is free for resident students, under-18s and people on benefits. All others must pay. To find an NHS dentist, contact the local Health Authority or a Citizens' Advice Bureau (*see right*).

Dental Emergency Care Service *Guy's Hospital, St Thomas Street, Borough, SE1 9RT (7188 0511). London Bridge tube/rail.* **Open** 9am-5pm Mon-Fri. **Map** p402 Q8. Queues start forming at 8am; arrive by 10am if you're to be seen at all.

Hospitals

For a list of hospitals with Accident & Emergency departments, *see above*; for other hospitals, see www.yell.com.

Opticians

See p225.

Pharmacies

Also called 'chemists' in the UK. Branches of Boots and larger supermarkets have a pharmacy, and there are independents on the high street (*see p227*). Staff can advise on over-the-counter medicines. Most pharmacies keep shop hours (9am-6pm Mon-Sat).

STDs, HIV & AIDS

NHS Genito-Urinary Clinics (such as the Centre for Sexual Health) are affiliated to major hospitals. They provide free, confidential STD testing and treatment, as well as treating other problems such as thrush and cystitis. They also offer counselling about HIV and other STDs, and can conduct blood tests.

The 24-hour **Sexual Healthline** (0800 567 123, www.nhs.uk/ worthtalkingabout) is free and confidential. See below for your nearest clinic. For other helplines, *see below*; for abortion and contraception, *see left*.
Mortimer Market Centre for Sexual Health *Mortimer Market, off Capper Street, Bloomsbury, WC1E 6JB (3317 5100). Goodge Street or Warren Street tube.* **Open** 9am-6pm Mon, Thur; 9am-7pm Tue; 1-6pm Wed; 8.30am-3pm Fri. **Map** p396 J4.
Terrence Higgins Trust Lighthouse *314-320 Gray's Inn Road, King Cross, WC1X 8DP (0845 122 1200, www.tht.org.uk). King's Cross tube/rail.* **Open** *Helpline* 10am-10pm Mon-Fri; noon-6pm Sat, Sun. **Map** p397 M5.
Advice for those with HIV/AIDS, their relatives, lovers and friends. It also offers free leaflets about AIDS and safer sex.

HELPLINES

Helplines dealing with sexual health issues are listed under STDs, HIV & AIDS (*see above*).

Alcoholics Anonymous *0845 769 7555, www.alcoholics-anonymous.org.uk.* **Open** 10am-10pm daily.
Citizens' Advice Bureaux *www.citizensadvice.org.uk.* The council-run Citizens' Advice Bureax offer free legal, financial and personal advice to all. Check the phone book or see the website for the address of your nearest office.
Missing People *0500 700 700, www.missingpeople.org.uk.* **Open** 24hrs daily. Information on anyone reported missing.
NHS Direct *0845 4647, www.nhsdirect.nhs.uk.* **Open** 24hrs daily.
A free, first-stop service for medical advice on all subjects.
Rape & Sexual Abuse Support Centre *0808 802 9999, www.rapecrisis.org.uk.* **Open** noon-2.30pm, 7-9.30pm daily. Information and support.
Samaritans *0845 790 9090, www.samaritans.org.uk.* **Open** 24hrs daily. General helpline for those under emotional stress.
Victim Support *0845 303 0900, www.victimsupport.org.uk.* **Open** 9am-9pm Mon-Fri; 9am-7pm Sat, Sun. **Map** p396 H5. Emotional and practical support to victims of crime.

ESSENTIAL INFORMATION

ID

Passports and photographic driver's licences are acceptable forms of ID.

INSURANCE

Insuring personal belongings can be difficult to arrange once you have arrived, so do so before you leave home. Medical insurance is usually included in travel insurance packages. Unless your country has an arrangement with the UK (*see p368*), it's important to ensure you have adequate health cover.

INTERNET

Many hotels now have high-speed internet access, whether via a cable or as wireless. Many cafés have wireless access; see below for four central establishments. You'll also find internet terminals in public libraries (*see right*).

Benugo Bar & Kitchen *BFI Southbank, Belvedere Road, South Bank, SE1 8XT (7401 9000, www.benugobarandkitchen.com). Waterloo tube/rail.* **Open** 11am-11pm Mon-Sat; 11am-10.30pm Sun.
5th View *Waterstone's, 203-206 Piccadilly, W1J 9HA (7851 2433, www.5thview.co.uk). Piccadilly Circus tube.* **Open** 9am-10pm Mon-Sat; noon-5pm Sun.
Hummus Brothers *88 Wardour Street, Soho, W1F 0TH (7734 1311, www.hbros.co.uk). Oxford Circus tube.* **Open** noon-10pm Mon-Wed, Sun; noon-11pm Thur-Sat.
Peyton & Byrne *Wellcome Collection, 183 Euston Road, Bloomsbury, NW1 2BE (7611 2138, www.peytonandbyrne.com). Euston tube/rail.* **Open** 10am-6pm Mon-Wed, Fri, Sat; 10am-10pm Thur; 11am-6pm Sun.

LEFT LUGGAGE

Airports

Gatwick Airport *01293 502014 South Terminal, 01293 569900 North Terminal.*
Heathrow Airport *8759 3344.*
London City Airport *7646 0000.*
Stansted Airport *01279 663213.*

Rail & bus stations

Security precautions mean that London stations tend to have left-luggage desks rather than lockers. Call 0845 748 4950 for details.

Charing Cross *7930 5444.* **Open** 7am-11pm daily.
Euston *7387 8699.* **Open** 7am-11pm daily.
King's Cross *7837 4334.* **Open** 7am-11pm daily.
Paddington *7313 1514.* **Open** 7am-11pm daily.
Victoria *7963 0957.* **Open** 7am-midnight daily.

LEGAL HELP

Those in difficulties can visit a Citizens' Advice Bureau (*see p369*) or contact the groups below. Try the **Legal Services Commission** (0845 345 4345, www.legalservices. gov.uk) for information. If you're arrested, your first call should be to your embassy (*see p368*).

Law Centres Federation *7839 2998, www.lawcentres.org.uk.* **Open** 10am-5.30pm Mon-Fri. Free legal help for people who can't afford a lawyer and live or work in the immediate area; this office connects you with the nearest centre.

LIBRARIES

Unless you're a resident, you won't be able to join a lending library. At the British Library (*see p73*), only exhibition areas are open to non-members, but the libraries below can be used for reference by all.

Barbican Library *Barbican Centre, Silk Street, the City, EC2Y 8DS (7638 0569, www.cityof london.gov.uk/barbicanlibrary). Barbican tube.* **Open** 9.30am-5.30pm Mon, Wed; 9.30am-7.30pm Tue, Thur; 9.30am-2pm Fri; 9.30am-4pm Sat. **Map** p400 P5.
Holborn Library *32-38 Theobald's Road, Bloomsbury, WC1X 8PA (7974 6345, www.camden.gov.uk). Chancery Lane tube.* **Open** 10am-7pm Mon-Fri; 10am-5pm Sat. **Map** p397 M5.
Kensington Central Library *12 Philimore Walk, Kensington, W8 7RX (7361 3010, www.rbkc.gov.uk/libraries). High Street Kensington tube.* **Open** 9.30am-8pm Mon, Tue, Thur; 9.30am-5pm Wed, Fri, Sat.
Marylebone Library *109-117 Marylebone Road, Marylebone, NW1 5PS (7641 1300, www. westminster.gov.uk/libraries). Baker Street tube or Marylebone tube/rail.* **Open** 9.30am-8pm Mon, Tue, Thur, Fri; 10am-8pm Wed; 9.30am-5pm Sat; 1.30-5pm Sun. **Map** p393 F4.
Victoria Library *160 Buckingham Palace Road, Belgravia, SW1W 9UD*

(7641 1300, www. westminster.gov.uk/libraries). Victoria tube/rail. **Open** 9.30am-8pm Mon; 9.30am-7pm Tue, Thur, Fri; 10am-7pm Wed; 9.30am-5pm Sat. **Map** p398 H10.
Westminster Reference Library *35 St Martin's Street, Westminster, WC2H 7HP (7641 1300, www. westminster.gov.uk/libraries). Leicester Square tube.* **Open** 10am-8pm Mon-Fri; 10am-5pm Sat. **Map** p416 X4.
Women's Library *25 Old Castle Street, Whitechapel, E1 7NT (7320 2222, www.thewomens library.ac.uk). Aldgate tube or Aldgate East tube.* **Open** Reading room 9.30am-5pm Tue, Wed, Fri; 9.30am-8pm Thur. **Map** p403 S6.

LOST PROPERTY

Always inform the police if you lose anything, if only to validate insurance claims. Only dial 999 if violence has occurred; use 101 for non-emergencies. Report lost passports both to the police and to your embassy (*see p368*).

Airports

For items left on the plane, contact the relevant airline. Otherwise, phone the following:

Gatwick Airport *01253 503162.*
Heathrow Airport *0844 824 3115.*
London City Airport *7646 0000.*
Luton Airport *01582 395219.*
Stansted Airport *01279 663293.*

Public transport

If you've lost property in an overground station or on a train, call 0870 000 5151, and give the operator the details.

Transport for London *Lost Property Office, 200 Baker Street, Marylebone, NW1 5RZ (0845 330 9882, www.tfl.gov.uk). Baker Street tube.* **Open** 8.30am-4pm Mon-Fri. **Map** p396 G4. Allow three working days from the time of loss. If you lose something on a bus, call 0843 222 1234 and ask for the numbers of the depots at either end of the route. For tube losses, pick up a lost property form from any station.

Taxis

The Transport for London office (*see p363*) deals with property found in registered black cabs.

Allow seven days from the time of loss. For items lost in a minicab, contact the relevant company.

MEDIA
Magazines

Time Out remains London's only quality listings magazine. Widely available in central London every Tuesday, it gives listings for the week from Thursday – and since September 2012 it's been available for free. If you want to know what's going on and whether it's any good, this is the place to look.

Nationally, *Loaded*, *FHM* and *Maxim* are big men's titles, while women often buy *Glamour* and *Grazia* alongside *Vogue*, *Marie Claire* and *Elle*. The appetite for gossip rags such as *Heat*, *Closer* and *OK* has abated only slightly.

The *Spectator*, *Prospect*, the *Economist* and the *New Statesman* are at the serious, political end of the market, with the satirical *Private Eye* bringing some levity to the subject. The *London Review of Books* ponders life and letters in considerable depth. The laudable *Big Issue* is sold across the capital by registered homeless vendors.

Newspapers

London's main daily paper is the sensationalist *Evening Standard*, published Monday to Friday. It became a freesheet in 2009, after a major revamp under a new owner failed to bring in enough sales. In the mornings, in tube station dispensers and discarded in the carriages, you'll still find *Metro*, a free *Standard* spin-off that led a deluge of low-quality free dailies – but has outlived most of them.

Quality national dailies include, from right to left of the political spectrum, the *Daily Telegraph* (best for sport), *The Times*, the *Independent* (which launched a cheap daily digest, *i*, in 2010) and the *Guardian* (best for the arts). All go into overdrive on Saturdays and all have bulging Sunday equivalents bar the *Guardian*, which instead has a sister Sunday paper, the *Observer*. The pink *Financial Times* (daily except Sunday) is the best for business.

In the middle market, the leader is the right-leaning *Daily Mail* (and *Mail on Sunday*), but the *Daily Express* (and *Sunday Express*) offers some competition.

The tabloid leader is the *Sun*, with the *Daily Star* and the *Mirror* its main lowbrow contenders.

Radio

The stations below are broadcast on standard wavebands as well as digital, where they are joined by some interesting new channels (mostly from the BBC). The format is not yet widespread, but you may be lucky enough to have digital in your hotel room or hire car.

Absolute *105.8 FM*. Laddish rock.
BBC Radio 1 *98.8 FM*. Youth-oriented pop, indie and dance.
BBC Radio 2 *89.1 FM*. Bland during the day; better after dark.
BBC Radio 3 *91.3 FM*. Classical music dominates, but there's also discussion, world music and arts.
BBC Radio 4 *93.5 FM, 198 LW*. The BBC's main speech station is led by news agenda-setter *Today* (6-9am Mon-Fri, 7-9am Sat).
BBC Radio 5 Live *693, 909 AM*. Rolling news and sport. Avoid the morning phone-ins.
BBC London *94.9 FM*. Danny Baker (3-5pm Mon-Fri) is brilliant.
BBC World Service *648 AM*. Some repeats, some new shows, transmitted globally.
Capital FM *95.8 FM*. Pop and chat.
Classic FM *100.9 FM*. Easy-listening classical.
Heart FM *106.2 FM*. Capital for grown-ups.
Kiss *100 FM*. Dance music.
LBC *97.3 FM*. Phone-ins and talk.
Magic *105.4 FM*. Familiar pop.
Smooth *102.2 FM*. Aural wallpaper.
Resonance *104.4 FM*. Arts radio – an inventively oddball mix.
XFM *104.9 FM*. Alternativish rock.

Television

With a multiplicity of formats, there are plenty of pay-TV options. However, the relative quality of free TV keeps subscriptions from attaining US levels.

The five main free-to-air networks are as follows:

BBC1 The Corporation's mass-market station. Relies too much on soaps, game shows and lifestyle TV, but does have quality offerings. As with all BBC stations, there are no commercials.
BBC2 A reasonably intelligent cultural cross-section, but now upstaged by BBC4.
ITV1 Monotonous weekday mass-appeal shows. ITV2 produces similar shows. .

Channel 4 Extremely successful US imports (the likes of *Ugly Betty* and *ER*), more or less unwatchable home-grown entertainments and the occasional great documentary.
Five From high culture to lowbrow filth. A strange, unholy mix.

Satellite, digital and cable channels include the following:

BBC3 Often appalling home-grown comedy and dismal documentary.
BBC4 Highbrow stuff, including fine documentaries and dramas.
BBC News Rolling news.
BBC Parliament Live debates.
CBBC, CBeebies Children's programmes, the latter is younger.
Discovery Channel Science and nature documentaries.
E4, More4, Film4 Channel 4's entertainment and movie channels.
Fiver US comedy and drama, plus Australian soaps.
ITV2, ITV3, ITV4 US shows on 2, British reruns on 3 and 4.
Sky News Rolling news.
Sky One Sky's version of ITV.
Sky Sports Four channels.

MONEY

Britain's currency is the pound sterling (£). One pound equals 100 pence (p). Coins are copper (1p, 2p), silver (round: 5p, 10p; seven-sided: 20p, 50p), yellowy-gold (£1) or silver in the centre with a yellowy-gold edge (£2). Paper notes are blue (£5), orange (£10), purple (£20) or red (£50). You can exchange foreign currency at banks, bureaux de change and post offices; there's no commission charge at the last of these (for addresses of the most central, *see p373*). Many large stores also accept euros (€).

Western Union 0808 234 9168, *www.westernunion.co.uk*. The old standby. Chequepoint (*see p372*) also offers this service.

Banks & ATMs

ATMs can be found inside and outside banks, in some shops and in larger stations. Machines in many commercial premises levy a charge for each withdrawal, usually £1.85. If you're visiting from outside the UK, your card should work via one of the debit networks, but check charges in advance. ATMs also allow you to make withdrawals on your credit card if you know your PIN; you'll be charged interest plus, usually, a currency exchange fee. Generally, getting cash with a card is the cheapest form of currency exchange but there are hidden charges, so do your research.

Credit cards, especially Visa and MasterCard, are accepted in most shops (except small corner shops) and restaurants (except caffs). However, American Express and Diners Club tend to be accepted only at more expensive outlets. You will usually have to have a PIN number to make a purchase. For more, see www.chipandpin.co.uk.

No commission is charged for cashing sterling travellers' cheques if you go to one of the banks affiliated with the issuing company. You do have to pay to cash travellers' cheques in foreign currencies, and to change cash. You will always need to produce ID to cash travellers' cheques.

Bureaux de change

You'll be charged for cashing travellers' cheques or buying and selling foreign currency at bureaux de change. Major stations have bureaux, and there are many in tourist areas and on major shopping streets. Most open 8am-10pm.

Chequepoint *550 Oxford Street, Marylebone, W1C 1LY (7724 6127, www.chequepoint.com). Marble Arch tube.* **Open** 24hrs. **Map** p396 G6. **Other locations** throughout the city.
Covent Garden FX *30A Jubilee Market Hall, Covent Garden, WC2E 8BE (7240 9921, www.coventgardenfx.com). Covent Garden tube.* **Open** 9am-6pm daily. **Map** p416 Z3.
Thomas Exchange *13 Maddox Street, Mayfair, W1S 2QG (7493 1300, www.thomasexchange.co.uk). Oxford Circus tube.* **Open** 9am-6pm Mon-Fri. **Map** p416 U3.

Lost/stolen credit cards

Report lost or stolen credit cards both to the police and the 24-hour phone lines listed below. Inform your bank by phone and in writing.

American Express *01273 696933, www.americanexpress.com.*
Diners Club *0870 190 0011, www.dinersclub.co.uk.*
MasterCard *0800 964767, www.mastercard.com.*
Visa *0800 891725, www.visa.com.*

Tax

With the exception of food, books, newspapers and a few other items,

purchases in the UK are subject to Value Added Tax (VAT), aka sales tax. The rate is currently set at 20%. VAT is included in all prices quoted by mainstream shops, although it may not be included in hotel rates.

Foreign visitors may be able to claim back the VAT paid on most goods that are taken out of the EC (European Community) as part of a scheme generally called 'Tax Free Shopping'. To be able to claim a refund, you must be a non-EC visitor to the UK, or a UK resident emigrating from the EC. When you buy the goods, the retailer will ask to see your passport, and will then ask you to fill in a simple refund form. You need to have one of these forms to make your claim; till receipts alone will not do. If you're leaving the UK direct for outside the EC, you must show your goods and refund form to UK customs at the airport/port from which you're leaving. If you're leaving the EC via another EC country, you must show your goods and refund form to customs staff of that country.

After customs have certified your form, get your refund by posting the form to the retailer from which you bought the goods, posting the form to a commercial refund company or handing your form at a refund booth to get immediate payment. Customs are not responsible for making the refund: when you buy the goods, ask the retailer how the refund is paid.

OPENING HOURS

Government offices close on bank (public) holidays (see *p376*), but big shops often remain open, with only Christmas Day sacrosanct. Most attractions remain open on the other public holidays.

Banks 9am-4.30pm (some close at 3.30pm, some 5.30pm) Mon-Fri; some also Sat mornings.
Businesses 9am-5pm Mon-Fri.
Post offices 9am-5.30pm Mon-Fri; 9am-noon Sat.
Pubs & bars 11am-11pm Mon-Sat; noon-10.30pm Sun.
Shops 10am-6pm Mon-Sat, some to 8pm. Many also open on Sun, usually 11am-5pm or noon-6pm.

POLICE

London's police are used to helping visitors. If you've been robbed, assaulted or involved in a crime, go to your nearest police station. (We've listed a handful in central London; look under 'Police' in

Directory Enquiries or call 118 118, 118 500 or 118 888 for more.)

If you have a complaint, ensure that you take the offending officer's identifying number (it should be displayed on his or her epaulette). You can then register a complaint with the **Independent Police Complaints Commission** (90 High Holborn, WC1V 6BH, 0845 300 2002, www.ipcc.gov.uk). In non-emergencies, call 101; for emergencies, call 999.

Belgravia Police Station *202-206 Buckingham Palace Road, Pimlico, SW1W 9SX (0300 123 1212). Victoria tube/rail.* **Map** p398 H10.
Camden Police Station *60 Albany Street, Fitzrovia, NW1 4EE (0300 123 1212). Great Portland Street tube.* **Map** p396 H4.
Charing Cross Police Station *Agar Street, Covent Garden, WC2N 4JP (0300 123 1212). Charing Cross tube/rail.* **Map** p416 Y4.
Chelsea Police Station *2 Lucan Place, Chelsea, SW3 3PB (0300 123 1212). South Kensington tube.* **Map** p395 E10.
Islington Police Station *2 Tolpuddle Street, Islington, N1 0YY (0300 123 1212). Angel tube.* **Map** p400 N2.
Kensington Police Station *72 Earl's Court Road, Kensington, W8 6EQ (0300 123 1212). Earl's Court tube.* **Map** p394 B11.
Marylebone Police Station *1-9 Seymour Street, Marylebone, W1H 7BA (0300 123 1212). Marble Arch tube.* **Map** p393 F6.
West End Central Police Station *27 Savile Row, Mayfair, W1S 2EX (0300 123 1212). Piccadilly Circus tube.* **Map** p416 U3.

POSTAL SERVICES

The UK has a fairly reliable postal service. If you have a query, contact Customer Services on 0845 774 0740. For business enquiries, call 0845 795 0950.

Post offices are usually open 9am-5.30pm during the week and 9am-noon on Saturdays, although some post offices shut for lunch and smaller offices may close for one or more afternoons each week. Some central post offices are listed below; for others, call the **Royal Mail** on 0845 722 3344 or check online at www.royalmail.com.

You can buy individual stamps at post offices, and books of four or 12 first- or second-class stamps at newsagents and supermarkets that display the appropriate red sign. A first-class stamp for a regular letter costs 46p; second-class stamps are 36p. It costs 68p to send a postcard abroad. For details of other rates, see www.royalmail.com.

See also p367 **Business: Couriers & shippers**.

Post offices

Post offices are usually open 9am-6pm Mon-Fri and 9am-noon Sat, with the exception of Trafalgar Square Post Office (24-28 William IV Street, WC2N 4DL, 0845 722 3344), which opens 8.30am-6.30pm Mon, Wed-Fri; 9.15am-6.30pm Tue; 9am-5.30pm Sat. Listed below are the other main central London offices. For general enquiries, call 0845 722 3344 or consult www.postoffice.co.uk.

Albemarle Street *nos.43-44, Mayfair, W1S 4DS. Green Park tube.* **Map** p416 U5.
Baker Street *no.111, Marylebone, W1U 6SG. Baker Street tube.* **Map** p396 G5.
Great Portland Street *nos.54-56, Fitzrovia, W1W 7NE. Oxford Circus tube.* **Map** p396 H4.
High Holborn *no.181, Holborn, WC1V 7RL. Holborn tube.* **Map** p416 Y1.

Poste restante

If you want to receive mail while you're away, you can have it sent to Trafalgar Square Post Office (*see above*), where it will be kept for a month. Your name and 'Poste Restante' must be clearly marked on the letter. You'll need ID to collect it.

RELIGION

Times may vary; phone to check.

Anglican & Baptist

Bloomsbury Central Baptist Church *235 Shaftesbury Avenue, Covent Garden, WC2H 8EP (7240 0544, www.bloomsbury.org.uk). Tottenham Court Road tube.* **Services & meetings** 11am, 5.30pm Sun. **Map** p397 Y1.
St Paul's Cathedral *For listings, see p53.* **Services** 7.30am, 8am, 12.30pm, 5pm Mon-Sat; 8am, 10.15am, 11.30am, 3.15pm, 6pm Sun. **Map** p402 O6.
Westminster Abbey *For listings, see p103.* **Services** 7.30am, 8am, 12.30pm, 5pm Mon-Fri; 8am, 9am, 12.30pm, 3pm Sat; 8am,

10am, 11.15am, 3pm, 5.45pm, 6.30pm Sun. **Map** p399 K9.

Buddhist

Buddhapadipa Thai Temple *14 Calonne Road, Wimbledon, SW19 5HJ (8946 1357, www.buddha padipa.org). Wimbledon tube/rail then bus 93.* **Open** *Temple* 9-6pm Sat, Sun. *Meditation retreat* 7-9pm Tue, Thur; 4-6pm Sat, Sun.
London Buddhist Centre *51 Roman Road, Bethnal Green, E2 0HU (0845 458 4716, www.lbc.org.uk). Bethnal Green tube.* **Open** 10am-5pm Mon-Fri.

Catholic

Brompton Oratory *For listings, see p111.* **Services** 7am, 8am (Latin mass), 10am, 12.30am, 6pm Mon-Fri; 7am, 8am, 10am, 6pm Sat; 7am, 8am, 9am (tridentine), 10am, 11am (sung Latin), 12.30pm, 4.30pm, 7pm Sun. **Map** p395 E10.
Westminster Cathedral *For listings, see p104.* **Services** 7am, 8am, 10.30am, 12.30pm, 1.05pm, 5.30pm Mon-Fri; 8am, 9am, 10.30am, 12.30pm, 6pm Sat; 8am, 9am, 10.30am, noon, 5.30pm, 7pm Sun. **Map** p398 J10.

Islamic

East London Mosque *82-92 Whitechapel Road, Whitechapel, E1 1JQ (7650 3000, www.east londonmosque.org.uk). Aldgate East tube.* **Services** *Friday prayer* 1.30pm (1.15pm in winter). **Map** p403 S6.
Islamic Cultural Centre & London Central Mosque *146 Park Road, Marylebone, NW8 7RG (7725 2213, www.iccuk.org). Baker Street tube or bus 13, 113, 274.* **Services** times vary; check website for details.

Jewish

Liberal Jewish Synagogue *28 St John's Wood Road, St John's Wood, NW8 7HA (7286 5181, www.ljs.org). St John's Wood tube.* **Services** 6.45pm Fri; 11am Sat.
West Central Liberal Synagogue *21 Maple Street, Fitzrovia, W1T 4BE (7636 7627, www.wcls.org.uk). Warren Street tube.* **Services** 3pm Sat. **Map** p396 J4.

Methodist & Quaker

Methodist Central Hall *Central Hall, Storey's Gate, Westminster, SW1H 9NH (7222 8010,

www.c-h-w.co.uk). St James's Park tube.* **Services** 12.45pm Wed; 11am, 6.30pm Sun. **Map** p399 K9.
Religious Society of Friends (Quakers) *173-177 Euston Road, Bloomsbury, NW1 2BJ (7663 1000, www.quaker.org.uk). Euston tube/rail.* **Meetings** 6.30pm Thur; 11am Sun. **Map** p397 K3.

SAFETY & SECURITY

Despite the riots during 2011, there are no real 'no-go' areas in London, and you're much more likely to get hurt in a car accident than as a result of criminal activity, but thieves haunt busy shopping areas and transport nodes as they do in all cities.

Use common sense and follow some basic rules. Keep wallets and purses out of sight, and handbags securely closed. Never leave bags or coats unattended, beside, under or on the back of a chair – even if they aren't stolen, they're likely to trigger a bomb alert. Don't put bags on the floor near the door of a public toilet. Don't take short cuts through dark alleys and car parks. Keep your passport, cash and credit cards in separate places. Don't carry a wallet in your back pocket. And always be aware of your surroundings.

SMOKING

July 2007 saw the introduction of a ban on smoking in all enclosed public spaces, including pubs, bars, clubs, restaurants, hotel foyers and shops, as well as on public transport. Smokers now face a penalty fee of £50 or a maximum fee of £200 if they are prosecuted for smoking in a smoke-free area. Many bars and clubs offer smoking gardens or terraces.

TELEPHONES

Dialling & codes

London's dialling code is 020; standard landlines have eight digits after that. You don't need to dial the 020 from within the area, so we have not given it in this book.

If you're calling from outside the UK, dial your international access code, then the UK code, 44, then the full London number, omitting the first 0 from the code. For example, to make a call to 020 7813 3000 from the US, dial 011 44 20 7813 3000. To dial abroad from the UK, first dial 00, then the relevant country code from the list below.

ESSENTIAL INFORMATION

For more international dialling codes, check the phone book or see www.kropla.com/dialcode.htm.
Australia 61
Canada 1
New Zealand 64
Republic of Ireland 353
South Africa 27
USA 1

Mobile phones

Mobile phones in the UK operate on the 900 MHz and 1800 MHz GSM frequencies common throughout most of Europe. If you're travelling to the UK from Europe, your phone should be compatible; if you're travelling from the US, you'll need a tri-band handset. Either way, check your phone is set for international roaming, and that your service provider at home has a reciprocal arrangement with a UK provider.

The simplest option may be to buy a 'pay-as-you-go' phone (about £10-£200); there's no monthly fee, you top up talk time using a card. Check before buying whether it can make and receive international calls. **Phones4u** (www.phones4u.co.uk) and **Carphone Warehouse** (www.carphonewarehouse.com), which both have stores throughout the city, offer options.

Operator services

Call 100 for the operator if you have difficulty in dialling; for an alarm call; to make a credit card call; for information about the cost of a call; and for help with international person-to-person calls. Dial 155 for the international operator if you need to reverse the charges (call collect) or if you can't dial direct; this service is very expensive.

Directory enquiries

This service is now provided by various six-digit 118 numbers. They're pretty pricey to call: dial (free) 0800 953 0720 for a rundown of options and prices. The best known is 118 118, which charges 38p per call, then £1.59 per minute thereafter; 118 888 charges 29p per call, then £1.69 per minute; 118 180 charges 70p per call, then 14p per minute. Online, the www.ukphone book.com offers five free credits a day to UK residents; overseas users get the same credits if they keep a positive balance in their account.

Yellow Pages This 24-hour service lists phone numbers of businesses in the UK. Dial 118 247 (£1.50p

connection charge plus 70p/min) and identify the type of business you require, and where in London.

Public phones

Public payphones take coins or credit cards (sometimes both). The minimum cost is 60p (including a 40p connection charge), local and national calls are charged at 60p for 30mins then 10p for each subsequent 15mins. Some payphones, such as the counter-top ones found in pubs, require more. International calling cards, offering bargain minutes via a freephone number, are widely available.

Telephone directories

There are several telephone directories for London, divided by area, which contain private and commercial numbers. Available at post offices and libraries, these hefty tomes are also issued free to all residents, as is the invaluable *Yellow Pages* directory (also online at www.yell.com), which lists businesses and services.

TIME

London operates on Greenwich Mean Time (GMT), five hours ahead of the US's Eastern Standard time. In spring (31 March 2013) the UK puts its clocks forward by one hour to British Summer Time. In autumn (27 October 2013), the clocks go back to GMT.

TIPPING

In Britain it's accepted that you tip in taxis, minicabs, restaurants (some waiting staff rely heavily on tips), hotels, hairdressers and some bars (not pubs). Around 10% is normal, but some restaurants add as much as 15%. Always check whether service has been included in your bill: some restaurants include an automatic service charge, but also leave space for a gratuity on your credit card slip.

TOILETS

Pubs and restaurants generally reserve the use of their toilets for customers. However, all mainline rail stations and a few tube stations – Piccadilly Circus, for one – have public toilets (you may be charged a small fee). Department stores usually have loos that you can use free of charge, and museums (most of which no longer charge an entry

fee) generally have good facilities. At night, options are worse. The coin-operated toilet booths around the city may be your only option.

TOURIST INFORMATION

In addition to the tourist offices below, there is a brand-new centre by **St Paul's** (*see p53*).
Britain & London Visitor Centre *1 Regent Street, Piccadilly Circus, SW1Y 4XT (7808 3800, www.visitlondon.com). Piccadilly Circus tube.* **Open** 9.30am-5.30pm Mon-Sat; 10am-4pm Sun. **Map** p416 W4.
Greenwich Tourist Information Centre *Discover Greenwich, Pepys House, 2 Cutty Sark Gardens, SE10 9LW (0870 608 2000, www.visitgreenwich.org.uk). Cutty Sark DLR.* **Open** 10am-5pm daily. **Map** p405 X1.
London Information Centre *Leicester Square, Soho, WC2H 7BP (7292 2333, www.london informationcentre.com). Leicester Square tube.* **Open** 8am-midnight daily.
Twickenham Visitor Information Centre *44 York Street, Twickenham, Middx, TW1 3BZ (8734 3363, www.visit richmond.co.uk). Twickenham rail.* **Open** 9am-5.15pm Mon-Thur; 9am-5pm Fri.

VISAS & IMMIGRATION

EU citizens do not require a visa to visit the UK; citizens of the USA, Canada, Australia, South Africa and New Zealand can also enter with only a passport for tourist visits of up to six months as long as they can show they can support themselves during their visit and plan to return. Go online to www.ukvisas.gov.uk to check your visa status well before you travel, or contact the British embassy, consulate or high commission in your own country. You can arrange visas online at www.fco.gov.uk.

Home Office Immigration & Nationality Bureau *Lunar House, 40 Wellesley Road, Croydon, CR9 1AT (0870 606 7766 enquiries, 0870 241 0645 applications, www.homeoffice.gov.uk).*

WEIGHTS & MEASURES

It has taken a considerable amount of time, and some heavy-handed intervention from the European authorities, but the UK is moving towards full metrication. Distances are still measured in miles but all goods are officially sold in metric quantities, with no legal requirement for the imperial equivalent to be given. We've used the still more common imperial measurements in this guide.

Below are listed some useful conversions, first into the metric equivalents from the imperial measurements, then from the metric units back to imperial:

1 inch (in) = 2.54 centimetres (cm)
1 yard (yd) = 0.91 metres (m)
1 mile = 1.6 kilometres (km)
1 ounce (oz) = 28.35 grams (g)
1 pound (lb) = 0.45 kilograms (kg)
1 UK pint = 0.57 litres (l)
1 US pint = 0.8 UK pints
or 0.46 litres

1 centimetre (cm) = 0.39 inches (in)
1 metre (m) = 1.094 yards (yd)
1 kilometre (km) = 0.62 miles
1 gram (g) = 0.035 ounces (oz)
1 kilogram (kg) = 2.2 pounds (lb)
1 litre (l) = 1.76 UK pints or 2.2 US pints

WHEN TO GO

Climate

The British climate is famously unpredictable. The best websites for weather news and features include www.metoffice.gov.uk, www.weather.com and www.bbc.co.uk/london/weather, which all offer good detailed long-term forecasts and are easily searchable.

Spring extends from March to May, though frosts can last into April. March winds and April showers may be a month early or a month late, but May is often very pleasant.

Summer (June, July and August) can be very unpredictable, with searing heat one day followed by sultry greyness and violent thunderstorms the next. There are usually pleasant sunny days, though they vary greatly in number from year to year. High temperatures, humidity and pollution can create problems for those with hay fever or breathing difficulties, and temperatures down in the tube can be uncomfortably hot in rush hour. Do as the locals do and carry a bottle of water.

Autumn starts in September, although the weather can still have a mild, summery feel. Real autumn comes with October, when the leaves start to fall; on sunny days, the red and gold leaves can be breathtaking. When the November cold, grey and wet set in, though, you'll be reminded that London is situated on a northerly latitude.

Winter can have some delightful crisp, cold days, but don't bank on them. The usual scenario is for a disappointingly grey, wet Christmas, followed by a cold snap in January and February, when London may even see a sprinkling of snow, and immediate public transport chaos.

Public holidays

On public holidays (bank holidays), many shops remain open, but public transport services generally run to a Sunday timetable. On Christmas Day, almost everything, including public transport, closes down. All dates below are for 2013.

Good Friday Fri 29 Mar
Easter Monday Mon 1 Apr
May Day Holiday Mon 6 May
Spring Bank Holiday Mon 27 May

Summer Bank Holiday
   Mon 26 Aug
Christmas Day Wed 25 Dec
Boxing Day Thur 26 Dec
New Year's Day Wed 1 Jan 2014

WOMEN

London is home to dozens of women's groups and networks; www.wrc.org.uk provides information and many links. It also has Europe's largest women's studies archive, the Women's Library (see p370).

For helplines, see p369; for health issues, see pp368-369.

WORK

Finding short-term work in London can be a full-time job. Temporary jobs are posted on Gumtree (www.gumtree.com). It's also worth trying recruitment agencies such as Reed (www.reed.co.uk) or Tate (www.tate.co.uk), or the various London markets for work on the stalls.

Work permits

With few exceptions, citizens of non-European Economic Area (EEA) countries have to have a work permit before they can legally work in the United Kingdom. Permits are issued only for high-level jobs. A youth mobility scheme is open to young residents of Australia, Canada, Japan and New Zealand, however. The **UK Border Agency** website (www.ukba.home office.gov.uk) has details.

Useful addresses

BUNAC *16 Bowling Green Lane, Clerkenwell, EC1R 0QH (7251 3472, www.bunac.org). Farringdon tube/rail.* **Open** 9.30am-5.30pm Mon-Thur; 9.30am-5pm Fri. **Map** p400 N4.
Council on International Educational Exchange *300 Fore Street, Portland, ME 04101, USA (+1-207 553 4000, www.ciee.org).* **Open** 9am-5pm (EST) Mon-Fri. BUNAC and CIEE help youngsters to study, work and travel abroad.
Home Office *Border & Immigration Agency, Lunar House, 40 Wellesley Road, Croydon, Surrey CR9 2BY (0870 606 7766, www.ind.home office.gov.uk).* **Open** *Enquiries by phone* 9am-4.45pm Mon-Thur; 9am-4.30pm Fri.
Advice on whether or not a work permit is required. If it is, application forms can be downloaded from the website.

THE LOCAL CLIMATE

Average temperatures and monthly rainfall in London.

	High (°C/°F)	Low (°C/°F)	Rainfall (mm/in)
Jan	6 / 43	2 / 36	54 / 2.1
Feb	7 / 44	2 / 36	40 / 1.6
Mar	10 / 50	3 / 37	37 / 1.5
Apr	13 / 55	6 / 43	37 / 1.5
May	17 / 63	8 / 46	46 / 1.8
June	20 / 68	12 / 54	45 / 1.8
July	22 / 72	14 / 57	57 / 2.2
Aug	21 / 70	13 / 55	59 / 2.3
Sept	19 / 66	11 / 52	49 / 1.9
Oct	14 / 57	8 / 46	57 / 2.2
Nov	10 / 50	5 / 41	64 / 2.5
Dec	7 / 44	4 / 39	48 / 1.9

ESSENTIAL INFORMATION

Further Reference

BOOKS

Fiction & poetry

Peter Ackroyd *Hawksmoor*;
The House of Doctor Dee; *The
Great Fire of London* Intricate
fiction about the arcane city.
Martin Amis *London Fields*
Darts and drinking way out east.
Anthony Burgess
Dead Man in Deptford
A fictionalised life of Marlowe.
Norman Collins
London Belongs to Me
A witty saga of 1930s Kennington.
Sir Arthur Conan Doyle
The Complete Sherlock Holmes
Reassuring sleuthing shenanigans.
Joseph Conrad *The Secret Agent*
Anarchism in seedy Soho.
Charles Dickens *Oliver Twist*;
David Copperfield; *Bleak House*
Three of the Victorian master's
most London-centric novels.
Anthony Frewin *London Blues*
Kubrick assistant explores the
1960s Soho porn movie industry.
Jeremy Gavron *An Acre of
Common Ground* The best of
the glut of Brick Lane fiction.
Graham Greene
The End of the Affair
Adultery, Catholicism and the Blitz.
Patrick Hamilton *Twenty
Thousand Streets Under the Sky*
Dashed dreams at the bar of the
Midnight Bell in Fitzrovia.
Neil Hanson *The Dreadful
Judgement* Embers of the Great Fire.
Alan Hollinghurst *The Swimming
Pool Library*; *The Line of Beauty*
Gay life around Russell Square;
metropolitan debauchery.
BS Johnson *Christie Malry's
Own Double Entry*
A London clerk plots revenge on…
everybody.
Doris Lessing *The Golden
Notebook*; *The Good Terrorist*
Nobel winner's best London books.
Colin MacInnes *City of Spades*;
Absolute Beginners
Coffee 'n' jazz, Soho 'n' Notting Hill.
Gautam Malkani *Londonstani*
A violent tale of South Asian
immigrants in Hounslow.
Michael Moorcock
Mother London
A roomful of psychiatric patients
live a love letter to London.
Alan Moore *From Hell*
Dark graphic novel on the Ripper.

Derek Raymond
I Was Dora Suarez
The blackest London noir.
Nicholas Royle *The Matter of
the Heart*; *The Director's Cut*
Abandoned buildings and secrets.
Iain Sinclair *Downriver*; *White
Chappell/Scarlet Tracings
Heart of Darkness* on the Thames;
the Ripper and book dealers.
Sarah Waters *The Night Watch*
World War II Home Front.
HG Wells *War of the Worlds*
SF classic with Primrose Hill finale.
Virginia Woolf *Mrs Dalloway*
A kind of London *Ulysses.*

Non-fiction

Peter Ackroyd *London: The
Biography*; *Thames: Sacred River*
Loving and obscurantist histories
of the city and its river.
Richard Anderson *Bespoke:
Savile Row Ripped and Smoothed*
Inside story of a Savile Row tailor.
Nicholas Barton
The Lost Rivers of London
Classic studies of old watercourses.
James Boswell *Boswell's
London Journal 1762-1763*
Rich account of a ribald literary life.
Paul Du Noyer *In the City*
London in song.
Ed Glinert *A Literary Guide to
London*; *The London Compendium*
Essential London minutiae.
Sarah Hartley *Mrs P's Journey*
Biography of Phyllis Pearsall, the
woman who created the *A–Z*.
Leo Hollis *The Stones of London*
A superb take on the city's history –
through 12 of its key buildings.
**Edward Jones & Christopher
Woodward** *A Guide to the
Architecture of London*
A brilliant exploration.
Jenny Landreth *The Great Trees
of London* Ancient trees in famous
and unlikely city locations.
Jenny Linford
The London Cookbook
Unsung producers and chefs share
their food secrets.
Jack London
The People of the Abyss
Poverty in the East End.
Anna Minton *Ground Control*
Important questions about Canary
Wharf-style developments –
including the Olympic Park.
HV Morton *In Search of London*
A tour of London from 1951.

George Orwell *Down and Out
in Paris and London*
Waitering, begging and starving.
Samuel Pepys *Diaries*
Plagues, fires and bordellos.
Cathy Phillips (ed) *London
through a Lens*; *Londoners through
a Lens* Captivating photographs of
the city from the Getty archive.
Roy Porter
London: A Social History
An all-encompassing work.
Steen Eller Rasmussen
London: The Unique City
London buildings through a
visitor's eyes.
Sukhdev Sandhu *Night Haunts*
London and Londoners after dark.
Iain Sinclair *Lights Out for
the Territory*; *London Orbital*
Time-warp visionary crosses and
then circles London.
Adrian Tinniswood
His Invention So Fertile
Biography of Sir Christopher Wren.
**Richard Trench & Ellis
Hillman** *London under London:
A Subterranean Guide*
Tunnels, lost rivers, disused tube
stations, military bunkers.
**Ben Weinreb &
Christopher Hibbert (eds)**
The London Encyclopaedia
Indispensable reference guide.
Jerry White *London in the 19th
Century*; *London in the 20th Century*
How London became a global city.

FILMS

Alfie *dir Lewis Gilbert, 1966*
What's it all about, Michael?
Blow-Up *dir Michelangelo
Antonioni, 1966* Unintentionally
hysterical film of Swinging London.
Bourne Ultimatum
dir Paul Greengrass, 2007
Pacy thriller with brilliantly staged
CCTV scene in Waterloo Station.
Death Line
dir Gary Sherman, 1972
The lost Victorian cannibal race is
discovered in Russell Square tube.
Dirty Pretty Things
dir Stephen Frears, 2002
Body organ smuggling.
Fires Were Started
dir Humphrey Jennings, 1943
Drama-doc war propaganda about
the London Fire Brigade.
Fish Tank *dir Andrea Arnold,
2009* Violent, oddly life-affirming
film about a rough Essex estate.

The Krays *dir Peter Medak, 1990*
The life and times of the most
notorious of East End gangsters.
The Ladykillers *dir Alexander
Mackendrick, 1951*
Classic Ealing comedy.
Life is Sweet; **Naked**; **Secrets
& Lies**; **Vera Drake**; **Happy-Go-
Lucky** *dir Mike Leigh, 1990-2008*
Metroland; urban misanthropy;
familial tensions; sympathy for
post-war abortionist; day and night
with a north London optimist.
**Lock, Stock & Two Smoking
Barrels**; **Snatch**; **RocknRolla**
dir Guy Ritchie, 1998-2008
Former Mr Madonna's cheeky
London faux-gangster flicks.
London; **Robinson in Space** *dir
Patrick Keiller, 1994, 1997*
Arthouse documentaries tracing
London's lost stories.
London River *dir Rachid
Bouchareb, 2010* French African
man and Guernsey widow brought
together by 7 July 2005 bombings.
The Long Good Friday
dir John MacKenzie, 1989
Classic London gangster flick.
Oliver! *dir Carol Reed, 1968*
Fun musical Dickens adaptation.
Passport to Pimlico
dir Henry Cornelius, 1949
Another superb Ealing comedy.
Peeping Tom
dir Michael Powell, 1960
Powell's creepy serial killer flick.
Performance *dir Nicolas Roeg
& Donald Cammell, 1970*
Cult movie to end all cult movies.
Sex & Drugs & Rock & Roll
dir Mat Whitecross, 2009 Delirious
biopic of splenetic rocker Ian Drury.
Skyfall *dir Sam Mendes, 2012*
See the SIS building blown up and
Bond nearly run over by a Tube.
28 Days Later
dir Danny Boyle, 2002
Post-apocalyptic London, with
bravura opening sequence.
We Are the Lambeth Boys
dir Karel Reisz, 1959 'Free cinema'
classic doc on Teddy Boy culture.
Withnail & I *dir Bruce Robinson,
1987* Classic Camden lowlife comedy.
Wonderland *dir Michael
Winterbottom, 1999*
Love, loss and deprivation in Soho.

MUSIC

Lily Allen *Alright, Still*
Feisty, urban reggae-pop.
Blur *Parklife*
Modern classic by Essex exiles.
Billy Bragg *Must I Paint You a
Picture? The Essential Billy Bragg*
The bard of Barking's greatest hits.
Burial *Untrue*
Dubstep ode to the brooding city.

Chas & Dave
Don't Give a Monkey's
Cockney singalong revivalists.
The Clash *London Calling*
Era-defining punk classic.
Dizzee Rascal *Boy in Da Corner*
Rough-cut sounds and inventive
lyrics from a Bow council estate.
Ian Dury *New Boots & Panties!!*
Cheekily essential listening from
the Essex pub maestro.
Hot Chip *The Warning*
Wonky electro-pop.
The Jam *This is the Modern World*
Weller at his fiercest and finest.
The Kinks *Something Else*
'Waterloo Sunset' and all.
Linton Kwesi Johnson
*Dread, Beat an' Blood; Forces of
Victory; Bass Culture*
Angry reggae from the man Brixton
calls 'the Poet'.
Madness *The Liberty of
Nolton Folgate* Nutty Boys'
psychogeographical concept album.
Micachu *Jewellery* Weird sounds
make songs on a precocious debut.
Saint Etienne *Tales from
Turnpike House* Kitchen-sink opera
by London-loving indie dance band.
Squeeze *Greatest Hits*
Lovable south London geezer pop.
The Streets *Original Pirate
Material* Pirate radio urban meets
Madness on Mike Skinner's debut.
The xx *Coexist* More shiny, slinky
melancholia from the 2010 Mercury
Prize winners.

WEBSITES

www.bbc.co.uk/london
News, travel, weather, sport.
www.britishpathe.com
Newsreels, from spaghetti-eating
contests to pre-war Soho scenes.
www.classiccafes.co.uk
Fascinating archive of the city's
best 1950s and '60s caffs.
**http://diamondgeezer.
blogspot.com** Superb blogger.
www.filmlondon.org.uk
London's cinema organisation.
**http://greatwenlondon.word
press.com** Fun, engaged, often
thought-provoking blog, by our
'London Today' chapter's author.
www.hidden-london.com
Undiscovered gems.
www.londoneater.com
Passionate food reviews.
www.london-footprints.co.uk
Free walks and event listings.
www.london.gov.uk
The Greater London Assembly's
official website.
http://londonist.com
News, culture and things to do.
**http://london.randomness.
org.uk** Want Finnish food near a

music shop? Review site-cum-wiki
of interesting London places.
**http://londonreconnections.
blogspot.com** Transport projects.
www.londonremembers.com
Plaques and statues.
**http://londonreviewof
breakfasts.blogspot.com**
Start the day in pun-tastic style.
**http://london-underground.
blogspot.com** Annie Mole's fun
and informative daily tube blog.
http://mappinglondon.co.uk
Best maps – and ways of
mapping – the city.
www.nickelinthemachine.com
Terrific blog on history, culture and
music of 20th-century London.
http://onabus.com Enter a bus
number to map its route.
www.timeout.com
A vital source: eating and drinking
reviews, features and events listings.
www.tfl.gov.uk/tfl Information,
journey planners and maps from
Transport for London, the city's
central travel organisation.

APPS

Hackney Hear (free) Hyperlocal –
and totally brilliant – audio guide to
London Fields in Hackney.
Hailo (free) Calls a black cab, tells
you how long it will be, and deducts
the meter fare from your account –
but there's no call-out fee.
iCockneyDialect (free) Talk like a
local – over 800 translations into
London's traditional rhyming slang.
London Cycle: Maps & Routes
(free) Most popular of many apps
showing the nearest Boris Bike.
London Bus Live (free) Tells you
how far away your next bus is.
London Jigsaw (69p) Excellent
mix of puzzle and trivia challenge.
Mission:Explore London (free)
Fun for kids and adults – very silly
challenges around the city.
Street Art London (£2.99) The
city's graffiti artists and their work.
StreetMuseum (free) Brilliant
Museum of London app – archive
shots geolocated to where you're
standing, with informative captions.
StreetMuseum Londinium (free)
StreetMuseum, but for Romans.
Time Out London Magazine
(free) Indispensable guide to the
week's happenings in the capital.
Time Travel Explorer (£1.99)
Overlays your location with any of
four historic maps, the oldest from
1746; a slider blends old and new.
Toiluxe – central London (69p)
Where's the nearest public loo?
Tube Deluxe (69p) There are free
apps, but not with departure boards,
travel news and journey planning.

ESSENTIAL INFORMATION

Index

INDEX

INDEX

INDEX

INDEX

Advertisers' Index

Please refer to the relevant pages for contact details.

Maps

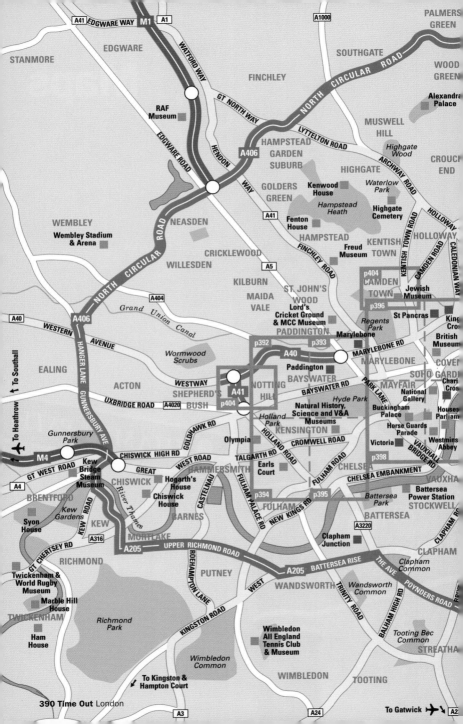

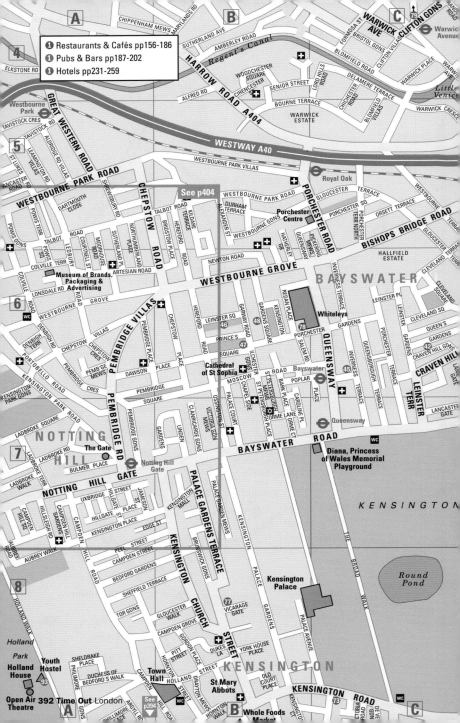

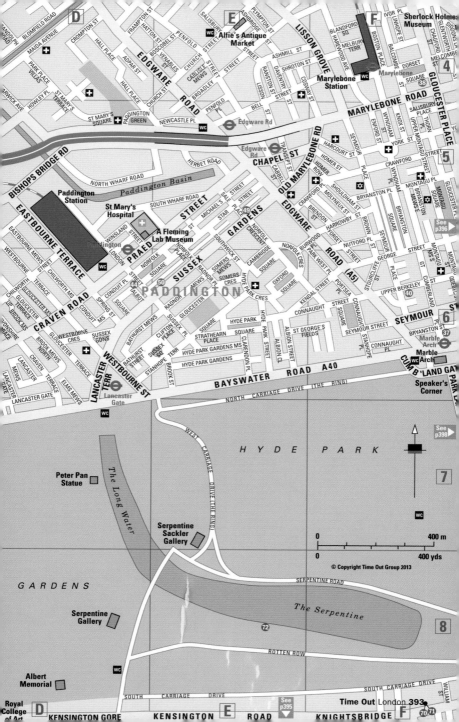

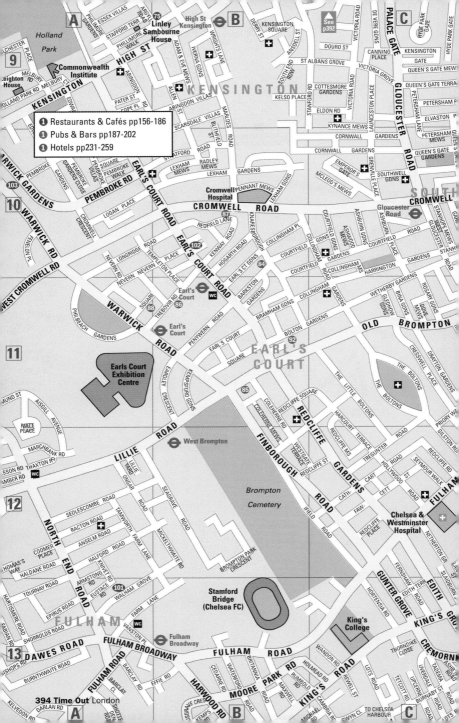

Restaurants & Cafés pp156-186

Pubs & Bars pp187-202

Hotels pp231-259

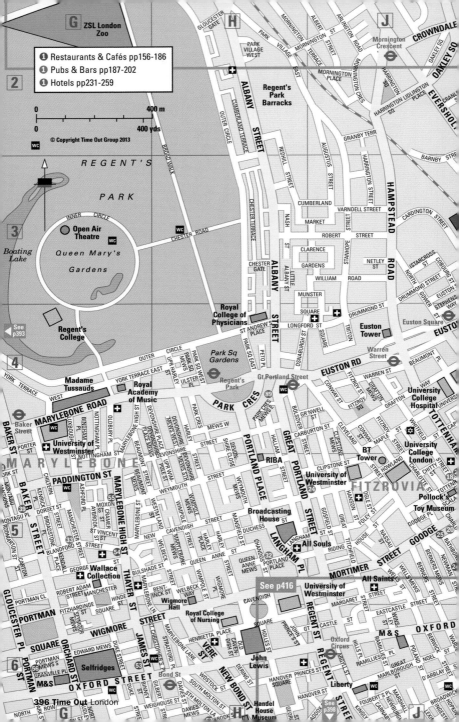

G ZSL London Zoo

❶ Restaurants & Cafés pp156-186
❶ Pubs & Bars pp187-202
❶ Hotels pp231-259

0 ————— 400 m
0 ————— 400 yds
© Copyright Time Out Group 2013

R E G E N T ' S

P A R K

Boating Lake

Open Air Theatre

Queen Mary's Gardens

Regent's College

Madame Tussauds

Royal Academy of Music

Royal College of Physicians

Regent's Park

Park Sq Gardens

Gt Portland Street

EUSTON RD

Euston Tower

Warren Street

University College Hospital

University College London

BT Tower

MARYLEBONE ROAD

University of Westminster

MARYLEBONE

PADDINGTON ST

Baker Street

University of Westminster

FITZROVIA

Pollock's Toy Museum

Broadcasting House

All Souls

Wallace Collection

Wigmore Hall

Royal College of Nursing

All Saints

University of Westminster

Selfridges

OXFORD STREET

John Lewis

Oxford Circus

Liberty

M&S

M&S

Handel House Museum

CROWNDALE

Mornington Crescent

Regent's Park Barracks

HAMPSTEAD ROAD

Euston Square

Warren Street

See p393

See p416

See p398

Time Out London **397**

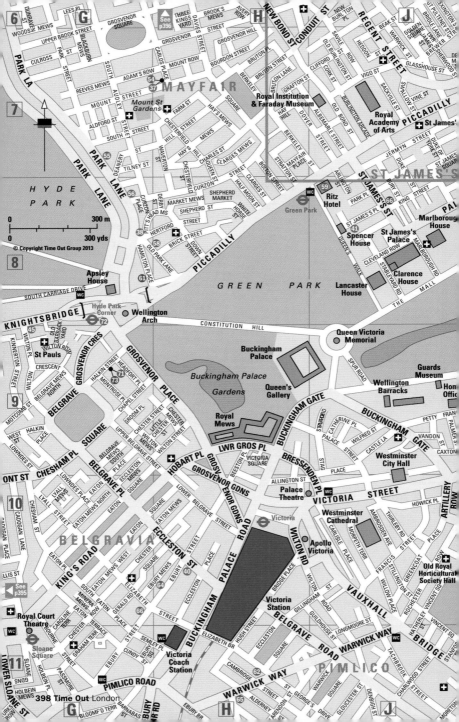

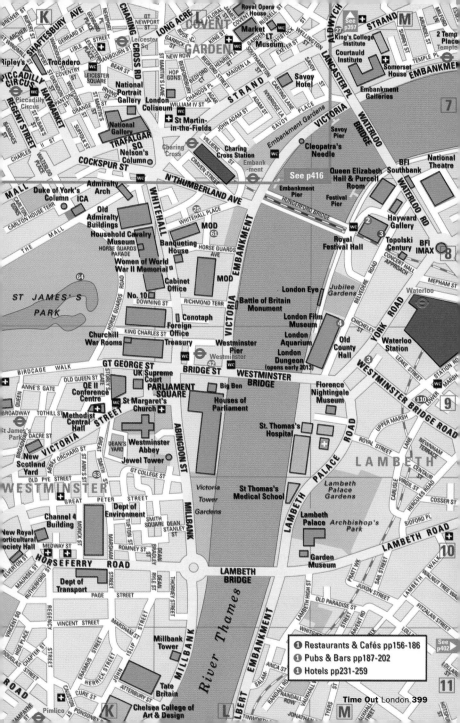

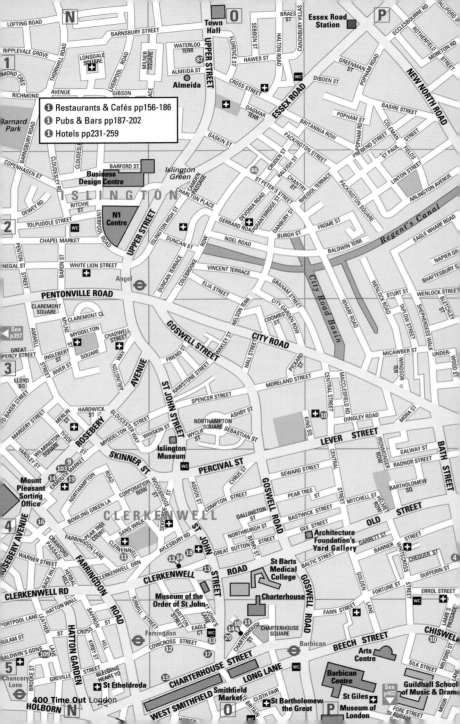

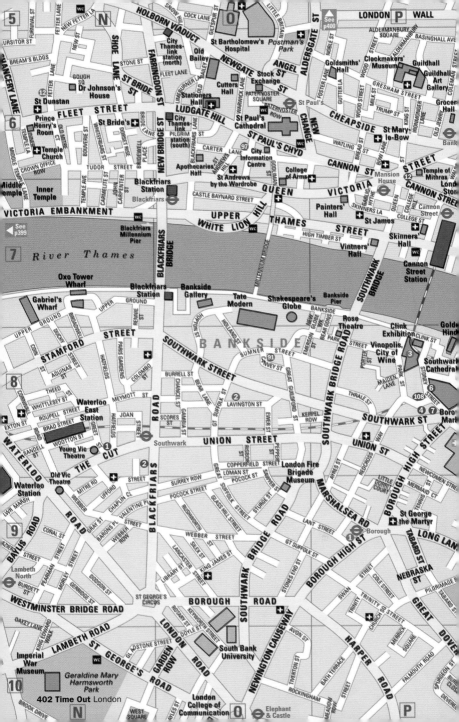

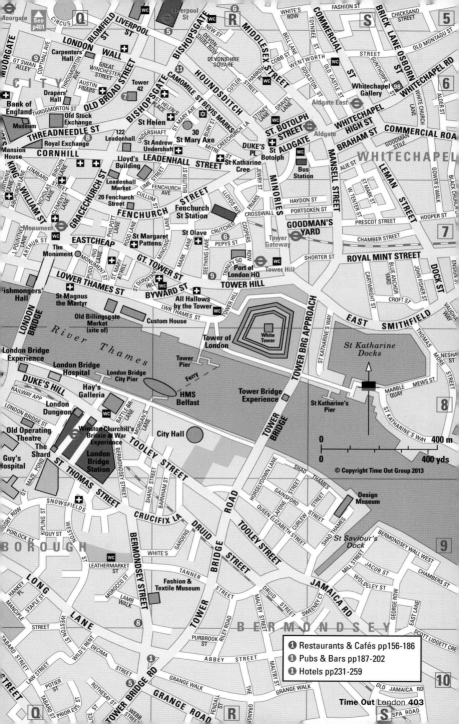

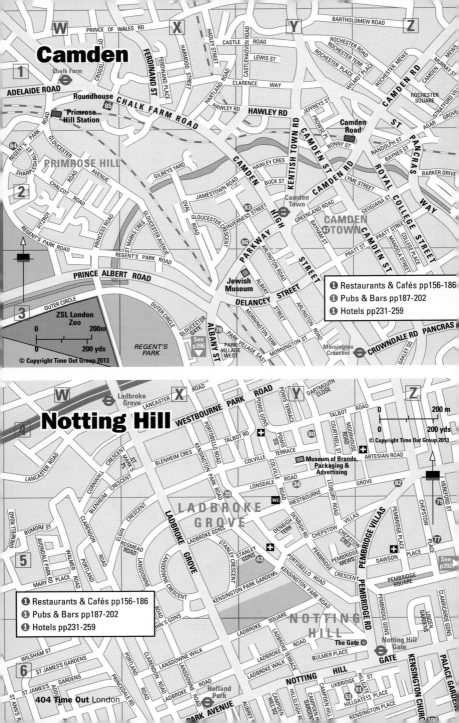

Greenwich

W · Island Gardens
X
Y
Z · PELTON ROAD

1

River Thames

Greenwich Foot Tunnel

TRAFALGAR ROAD

LASSELL ST
HOSKINS ST
OLD WOOLWICH RD
WOODLINE GR
EARLSWOOD ST
COLOMB ST
WOODLANDS PARK RD
TUSKAR ST

VANBURGH HILL

Old Royal Naval College

Discover Greenwich

99

Chapel

Cutty Sark

Maze Hill Station

Painted Hall

ROMNEY ROAD

THAMES ST

Cutty Sark

56

PARK VISTA

Queen's House

2

REEK ROAD

BARDSLEY LANE

Greenwich Market

National Maritime Museum

GREENWICH

MAZE HILL

VANBURGH HILL

FOYLE ROAD

WESTCOMBE PARK RD

ROAN STREET

STRAIGHTSMOUTH

Greenwich Theatre

BURNEY STREET

Prime Meridian Lane

G r e e n w i c h

VANBURGH FIELDS

enwich ation

Greenwich

Fan Museum

CROOM'S HILL

THE AVENUE

Royal Observatory & Planetarium

GREENWICH HIGH ROAD

ROYAL HILL

CIRCUS ST

BRAND ST

GEORGE STREET

P a r k

BLACKHEATH AVENUE

BOWER AVENUE

3

MAZE HILL

GREENWICH SOUTH ST

URNHAM PL

URNHAM ROVE

57

HYDE VALE

CHARLTON WAY

HIRE

BLISSETT ST

WINFORTON ST

POINT HILL

WESTGROVE LANE

DUTTON ST

MAIDENSTONE HILL

CHESTERFIELD WALK

GENERAL WOLFE ROAD

Ranger's House

SHOOTERS HILL

4

SHOOTERS HILL

LONG POND ROAD

PRINCE CHARLES ROAD

LEWISHAM ROAD

DARTMOUTH HILL

DARTMOUTH ROW

DARTMOUTH GR

WATT TYLER ROAD

B l a c k h e a t h

MORDEN HILL

BLACKHEATH RISE

HARE AND BILLET ROAD

GOFFERS ROAD

MOUNTS POND ROAD

THE ORCHARD

THE ELIOT VALE

ELIOT PLACE

CAMDEN ROW

5

Lewisham Station

OAKCROFT ROAD

ELIOT PARK

WALERAND RD

GRANVILLE PARK

HEATH LANE

BAIZDON ROAD

Blackheath Station

STON RD

MPIT VALE

CRESSINGHAM RD

BOYNE ROAD

LOCKMEAD RD

CATERHAM ROAD

LEE PARK

6

0   200 m
0   200 yds

BELMONT HILL

LEE HIGH ROAD

MARISCHAL RD

❶ Restaurants & Cafés pp156-186
❶ Pubs & Bars pp187-202
❶ Hotels pp231-259

Time Out London **405**

© Copyright Time Out Group 2013

Street Index

STREET INDEX

STREET INDEX

Street Index

STREET INDEX

London Underground